Globe Theatre

Boxes

Boxes

Galleries

The Platform

The Entrance

one Penny Groundlings

The Yard

A. + M. PROVENSEN

SHAKESPEARE
TEN GREAT PLAYS

WITH AN INTRODUCTION
AND COMMENTARIES BY
SIR TYRONE GUTHRIE

SHAKESPEARE
TEN GREAT PLAYS

ILLUSTRATED BY ALICE
AND MARTIN PROVENSEN
GOLDEN PRESS NEW YORK

The publishers extend their grateful thanks to Macmillan and Company, Ltd. of London and St. Martin's Press, Inc., New York for permission to use the quotation from *Shakespearian Tragedy* by A. C. Bradley that appears on page 350.

ACT
I
SCENE
I

CONTENTS

INTRODUCTION

THIS BOOK contains ten of Shakespeare's plays. The total number of plays ascribed to his authorship is thirty-seven: the ten here chosen are among the best known and best loved.

It is not possible to say for certain that the plot of any of Shakespeare's plays was the author's own invention. He derived most of his stories either from history or romances or from older plays which he revised and re-worked. This means that Shakespeare's plays are themselves comments on literature, on the originals which he transmogrified, as well as on life and character.

To carry this a bit further, every work of art is inevitably a comment made by its creator as a result of his observations both of his own natural environment and of other works of art. It is possible to say of no work of art that it is wholly original. This is not to say that they are all plagiarisms—far from it; simply that they are influenced, usually far more than their creators realize, by other works of art. And influences can work upon an artist both positively and negatively. While imitating what he admires, he also avoids what he dislikes in the work of others.

Often it is possible to see in a writer's work an ambivalent comment upon that of his illustrious predecessors. Shakespeare, for example, seems to me to write both in conscious mockery and perhaps less conscious admiration of his slightly older fellow-countryman, Christopher Marlowe. Sometimes, as in the dialogue of Ancient Pistol in *Henry the Fifth,* he is deliberately burlesqueing the high-flown Marlovian rhodomontade; at other times, maybe without his being aware, this style creeps into his own verse—and with magnificent effect.

In a similar manner, every contact with a work of art by every member of the public involves comment. No one can look at Leonardo's "Mona Lisa," let us say, and find out exactly what the painter's intention was, what comment he was making in the portrait. Each one of us can only make his own strictly subjective comment or observation.

One person can look at a meadow and see nothing but grass; another can look at the same meadow and see seven different kinds of grass, a dozen different kinds of flowering plants, and be able to name them and make all kinds of observations and deductions about them. Yet the first person's impression, sketchy and unsophisticated as it is, may be the more vivid and memorable. The putting together of a lot of facts is not necessarily productive of wisdom, happiness or of any desirable result.

To apply this to the matter at hand, knowing a great deal about Shakespeare's plays, about his prosody, drama-turgy and imagery, knowing about the style of Elizabethan theatrical productions, about the context of the period, about subsequent changes in theatrical fashion and techniques—all this is necessary equipment for the expert. But without it, a reader or playgoer can still enjoy the plays, just as a person totally innocent of botanical or agricultural knowledge can enjoy the sight of a fresh, green field. The enjoyment will be of a different kind, and the comment which will be made will be of a different kind, than that of the expert, but it will not be inferior. Neither one is "better" than the other.

There is a persistent but, I believe, fallacious notion that an expert does things better than a tyro. He does not do them better; only more expertly. If the object of a game of tennis be enjoyment, then do not you and I with our rabbity service, our short lobs, our mistimed volleys and scoopy backhand have enormously more fun on Saturday afternoons at Aunt Isabel's than do the international champions clenched in a deadly combat on which their "careers" depend?

In connection with Shakespeare there is another widely held fallacy which underlies a great deal of criticism, both theatrical and literary. This is the notion that there exists a "right", an ideal, interpretation of each play, and that a performer—or for that matter, the impression of a reader—is good or bad insofar as his interpretation gets close to or far from this hypothetical ideal.

I do not think that anyone who has worked long and intimately in the professional theatre could possible believe that any dramatist has in his mind such a hypothetical, ideal performance. The mind of a playwright just does not work that way. For great portions of his play, the author has only the dimmest idea where most of his characters are to stand, when and how they are to move, what they are thinking and the like. He will, of course, envisage that, for the great speech of abdication, the king will be on the steps of the cathedral; but whether the archbishop is on the king's left hand or his right, he will not know; nor whether the steps have treads of one foot or eighteen inches. Now the exact position of the archbishop and the exact width of the steps are neither of them of the slightest importance to the imaginative impact or artistic value of the scene. There really is no good reason why the author should bother with them. But someone must bother. For example, if the steps are too narrow the actors cannot move with dignity or ease; if they are too wide, there will not be room for a flight high enough for the king, standing on the top step, to be above the helmets of the Lifeguards.

In other words, the script of a play never does, never can and never should attempt to supply a complete indication of everything that goes on. Shakespeare's plays are notably sketchy in this respect. There is a minimum of stage direction, and the action often has to be inferred from the evidence—often ambiguous—of the lines which the characters speak.

In general (there are, of course, exceptions, notably Barrie), the professionally competent author is, like Shakespeare, very terse in his stage directions. He knows that a good cast is only fretted and inhibited by too much guidance, and that for no-good collaborators, guidance is useless anyway. Consequently, he leaves the details of the performance to others.

If it be granted that this is not merely the normal but the only sensible attitude for a professional author to take towards his work, then I think there can be no possibility of the existence in his mind of an ideal, hypothetical performance.

But if more proof be demanded, there is an even stronger argument. It rests upon the belief that what gives to a work of art its greatest significance and value is not the conscious work of the artist at all, but rather what creeps in "between the lines," is "over and above" his conscious intention. I do not know whether this can be proved or refuted; I only know that from my own observation it seems to be the case.

Certainly the greatest effort does not produce the greatest work of art. The adage "Genius consists in the ability to take infinite pains" is, like many another adage, no more than a half-truth. It is true that most geniuses can and do take infinite pains, but this is because it is pleasant to work hard at something you do well. The "pains" of the adage apply better to the labour of acquiring the skill without which genius cannot express itself. But, alas, all the skill in the world does not necessarily produce works of genius. The novelist Anthony Trollope towards the end of his career had developed such a facility that he could write at the rate of two hundred and fifty words every quarter of an hour, and do so for several hours day after day. The result, as every-

one knows, is extremely readable fiction and an extraordinary tribute to Trollope's capacity for taking pains, but it is not work of the highest genius.

Shakespeare, too, was a monument of industry, a literary Stakhanovite. We know that, in addition to writing his thirty-seven plays in much less than thirty-seven years, he was keenly and successfully engaged in theatrical management. There is also a belief that he appeared from time to time as an actor; however this may be, it is certainly impossible to believe that he developed his extraordinary mastery of theatrical effect in an ivory tower. He obviously spent a great deal of time and energy in the day-to-day routine of theatrical rehearsal.

The phenomenal energy required for all this might, in some sense, be described as taking infinite pains; but the literary result was most certainly not what we are accustomed to describe as "painstaking." Throughout his work appear the stigmata of hasty and slapdash workmanship. It is only reasonable to assume on the evidence of his huge output and what we know of his business activities that he wrote at top speed, with a specific deadline in view, and that the conscious object was not to create works of genius but to make money by catering successfully to popular taste.

Further, had his conscious attempt been to create works of art, can we possibly believe that he would have been so careless about what happened to his work that when, some years after his death, his friends Heminge and Condell decided to publish a collection of his plays they had the utmost difficulty assembling the texts?

The evidence adds up to the fact that he regarded himself as a theatrical man-of-all-work, a highly successful, popular and confident tradesman, but not an important or immortal genius.

When he planned *Hamlet*—I use it as an instance because it is the most familiar of his plays, accepted in every epoch and every part of the civilized world as a masterpiece as lively now as when he wrote it—can we credit that he sat down with the deliberate intention of creating a character so interesting, so enigmatic and so universal as to provoke the mountain of commentary that now exists? Or that he deliberately planned to write his play in language so musical, so apt and so memorable that with the single exception of Holy Writ it is the most quoted work in the world?

Surely it is more reasonable to suppose that he set to work on what he hoped would be a successful "vehicle" for Burbage, his partner in management. A summary of the plot of *Hamlet* shows it rather absurd, over-complicated and implausible, relying heavily on such stagey devices as a majestic spook, poisoned cups, stabbing the

Come, Sweet Audrey:
We must be married, or we
must live in bawdry.
Farewell, Good Master Oliver:
not. O sweet Oliver!
    O brave Oliver!

Leave me not behind thee
but. —
        Wind away,
        Beg.   say
    will . wedding with
                    thee.

Go thou with me, and
    let me counsel thee

Exeunt Jaques
Touchstone and Audrey

wrong person who is hidden behind an arras, a picturesque mad scene for the heroine, a midnight interment, a blood-bolstered finale to compete with the bear-baiting offered in a neighboring and rival place of entertainment.

The central figure became so enormously interesting because into it Shakespeare poured not only his experienced cunning in the contrivance of effective "situations," not merely the conscious observation of a brilliant journalist, not just his rational thoughts about man's predicament in this dangerous and apparently hostile universe, but his own deepest feelings and intuitions. Feeling and intuition are not sought by conscious effort. They occur spontaneously, they creep in "between the lines" while the playwright is engaged at the conscious level with plot-development, the motivation of character, the manipulation of situation, the comings and the goings, the bricks and mortar with which the craftsman builds his dramatic house.

On the altogether less exalted plane of my own professional experience I have noticed that all the finest "strokes" of the authors with whom I have worked have either come into their heads suddenly, while they were apparently thinking of something else—lunch, maybe, or the time the train leaves for Wilmington; or else they were unaware that something which they had written bore the full implication which in performance it turned out to have.

James Bridie, the Scottish dramatist, was also a doctor, with a medical man's particular knowledge of human nature, which comes from constantly encountering people in their defenceless and self-revealing position as patients. He used often to send me the scripts of his new plays. They usually seemed to me original, witty and hard to understand. I would ask "What do you mean? What are you trying to say?" His invariable reply was "How should I know? I only wrote the thing."

At first I thought that this was just an ironic joke. But gradually I came to believe that it was profoundly true. Of course he knew in a limited sense what he had tried to say; but he also knew that if the work were any good, his *conscious* intention was comparatively insignificant. A masterpiece, he used to say, is like an iceberg: ninety

"'Tis no matter: ne'er a fantastical
Knave of   them all shall
flout me   out of
my calling

percent of its meaning lies below the surface of its author's consciousness.

The same principle holds good with acting. The actor, like the author, must consciously and carefully plan his effects. The performance must be as deliberately composed as a picture—light contrasted with shadow, stress balanced by relaxation. But the moments that distinguish great performances from the merely competent are flashes which proceed not from reason but feeling, which are achieved not by the exertion of taking thought but by making oneself passively available, by being ready to hurl oneself into the pool at the moment when the Angel troubles the waters.

I suspect that what most critics, amateur and professional, have in mind when they relate a performance— whether of Shakespeare or someone else—to a hypothetical ideal is no more than a synthesis which exists in each critic's own imagination, which is composed partly of what he has himself particularly enjoyed in previous contacts with the work in question, partly of stereotypes deriving from important or very successful past performances and partly from notions derived from what is loosely called "tradition."

There is no Shakespeare tradition in the sense that there exists a Molière tradition. The *Comédie Française* has an unbroken link with the original performances, acted and directed by Molière himself. Ideas, bits of business, characterisations have been handed on from generation to generation of *sociétaires*. Quite often traditional ideas are discarded and new ones substituted, but the tradition continues to exist.

In England, however, very soon after Shakespeare's death, the Puritan Reformation succeeded in outlawing the professional theatre. For twenty years it was driven underground; and when, after the Restoration of the Monarchy in 1660, performances were again allowed, the Elizabethan and Jacobean tradition had disappeared. The new theatre was an opera house; its architecture, repertory, style of acting and the quality of its audience were all entirely different.

What we of the twentieth century have inherited in the English-speaking theatre is not a Shakespearian tradition at all. It is merely a legacy of how Shakespeare's plays were altered, adapted and "improved" in order to make them conform to the requirements of proscenium theatres and a public which had grown accustomed to "illusion."

There is nonetheless a "tradition" that Hamlet should be a pale, weak, vacillating young person, dressed in black. The black clothes are justified by the text. The rest is not. This conception derives from early nineteenth century criticism. Goethe, Schlegel and Coleridge were all heavyweights, but they were not necessarily right about *Hamlet*. They did, however, exert an immense influence on the minds of their own and the subsequent two or three generations. Nearly all important productions of *Hamlet* in the latter part of the nineteenth and early part of the twentieth centuries expressed their conception of a weak, wavering, Werther-like Hamlet. Irving's performance did so. So did Booth's. So did Gielgud's, the most admired Hamlet of our own day.

A stereotype has been created. And anyone who presents a Hamlet which differs radically from this stereotype may expect short shrift from the critics. They will tell him categorically that he has the Wrong Idea. Alec Guinness once essayed the part in a beard, and presented a rather assertively clever and sceptical Renaissance prince in a production of his own, heavily influenced by De Madariaga. He got the daylights beaten out of him by critics who "knew" that Hamlet is, of course, clean shaven and that the "right" way to speak the verse is in the mellifluous, pathetic but respectfully hopeful tone of a wellbred Anglican bishop pronouncing a eulogy over a royal coffin.

Similarly a stereotype exists in the case of Lady Macbeth. She has to be a big, beefy, booming contralto. The best Lady Macbeth whom I have ever seen is a Welsh actress called Gwen ffrancon-Davies. She presented a desperately, ferociously ambitious spirit in a tiny body. I read no notice of the performance which did not say she was wildly miscast. More recently I have read notices of Jessica Tandy's Lady Macbeth which admitted the talent of the actress "in spite of her being rather small for the part."

I think it probable that the stereotype came into being because the part will have been allotted to the Senior Leading Lady, often the manager's wife, of stock companies; and Senior Leading Ladies, who habitually play dominant heavies, are apt to be persons of considerable stature with a booming, punishing vocal delivery.

For the same reason—stock company casting—Ophelia has to be the Ingenue: blond, sweet, and babyishly innocent. The evidence of the text is that she is a highly intelligent girl who has been brought up in a sophisticated environment by her father, an extremely worldly, cynical, time-serving politician; that under the stress of mental derangement she sings not merely "snatches of old lauds," but snatches of popular song highly spiced with bawdry, which suggest, and are obviously intended to suggest, an experience somewhat beyond the range of Little Miss Babydoll. If, however, I were a young actress who set great store by good notices, I would ignore these indications. I would concentrate on being just as winsome and dainty as ever I could be.

My endeavour in all the foregoing has been to suggest that there is no Right Way of realizing Shakespeare's intention; that every contact with his work involves on the part of a reader or performer or audience an element of comment; and that such comment is entirely subjective, each person making such comment as he can. Naturally the quality of these comments will vary enormously, and it is my opinion that the comment of the learned expert is not better than that of the beginner, only more learned and more expert. The beginner, indeed, may have a fresher, livelier approach.

We are inclined to put rather too much value upon the acquisition of verifiable facts and on their orderly presentation, and rather too little upon our subjective emotional reaction to such facts. I can see very little point in knowing a great deal about Shakespeare's plays if it does not make you more apt to enjoy them, to love them. In fact, knowing more about them *is* apt to make you love them better, but not necessarily.

Shakespeare is generally regarded as being the greatest dramatist in the English language, perhaps the greatest writer in the English language, perhaps even the most important spokesman who has yet appeared to represent the human race. There are excellent reasons for this view. But many people who earnestly profess it have hardly read a line, and never seen a play, of Shakespeare's. They accept the view because in our culture it is the correct view to hold—like taking off your hat in church or allowing a lady to precede you through a doorway. They even expect their children to know something about this Shakespeare, not because they expect that knowledge to be at all enjoyable or even spiritually profitable, but because it is the symbol of culture.

It is my hope that whoever opens this book does so in search of wisdom and happiness, to open the windows of the mind, not just to memorize a heap of facts or to bone up on cultural topics in order to keep up with the Joneses. What I like to believe is that someone will open this book who has never really made contact with Shakespeare before; that, lured by the pictures, he will dip into the text; that having dipped, he plunge; and having plunged, become a lifelong addict.

TYRONE GUTHRIE

ROMEO AND JULIET

Romeo and Juliet is the story of two "star-crossed" lovers, of their "death-marked" love.

It is not a tragedy in the classical sense, in the sense that the tragic figure must be a person of heroic stature whose character contains a tragic flaw that ultimately brings about his downfall. Romeo and Juliet are not personages of tragic stature. They are teenagers, and the "tragedy", if such it must be called—and folios and quartos both so call it—lies in their inexperience, which makes them unable to deal either with the emotional turmoil within themselves or the emotional turmoil within their families and their city. They are fatally advised by Friar Laurence, but in fact the catastrophe is precipitated by a series of accidents. In endeavoring to part Tybalt and Mercutio, Romeo is the accidental cause of Mercutio's death; owing to the accident of pestilence in Mantua, Friar John is unable to deliver Friar Laurence's letter to Romeo. In a realistic play such accidents would be a bar to credibility. In classical tragedy they would seem trivial. In *Romeo and Juliet* they are justified because they make the point that these lovers *are* star-crossed, their love death-marked.

Comic plausibility is not the author's aim, nor is tragic grandeur. Rather it is to suggest the fragility of our life, to contrast this fragility with the power of our emotions and to contrast these eloquent, fragile nightingales—Taine, the French critic, refers to the lovers' scenes as "roulades of nightingales"—with the blind, brute, unconscious forces that destroy them.

It is hard to find young people who can play the parts of Romeo and Juliet, who have the necessary technical command for their technically exacting scenes. Mere feeling and imagination are not enough. It is a sad paradox of the theatre that by the time the needful technique has been learnt, and by the time a Romeo, and still more a Juliet, has the emotional maturity to know what the scenes are about, he or she has lost the youthful freshness and eagerness that are very nearly, but not quite, indispensable. This applies especially to Britain, where youngsters are apt to mature quite late and where social and educational systems deliberately put a premium upon "innocence" and unsophistication.

Occasionally—just now and again—a young actor or actress can be found with both freshness and sufficient accomplishment. However, I have never known a production in which both Romeo and Juliet have had both.

The Nurse is a superb creation and has been many times splendidly performed. It is more rare to find a really good Friar Laurence. Too many actors—too many literary commentators, also—see in him only a moralizing senior. In fact, he is a most endearing fellow who is carried away by his sympathy for the lovers and by the naive enthusiasm of an amateur pharmacist. Like the young people, he is faced with emotions beyond his comprehension to solve. It is an irony most delicately understated that, as their ghostly father, he assumes a position of authority—to do otherwise would have been grossly irresponsible—and, with the very highest intentions, counsels their destruction in this world and perdition in the next.

I am always puzzled by Shakespeare's attitude toward banishment. In this play, Romeo regards banishment as scarcely less terrible and final than death. Yet it is clear that Friar Laurence, at all events, believed that the Duke would relent and let Romeo return home after quite a short term. It is also clear that Mantua is to be imagined, as it in fact is, at no great distance from Verona. Friar John was sent there with a letter; Romeo's page comes and goes several times; Romeo returns thence in short order after buying the poison from the Apothecary. Therefore Shakespeare's view of banishment as a disaster does not arise from the relatively greater distance of one place from another when one had to get there on foot or horseback compared with the fast, easy and frequent transport available nowadays.

It might be that Romeo's reaction to his banishment was that of a hysterical youngster to whom next week is as remote as next century, and to whom ten miles' distance from Juliet made him feel as though upon another planet. But in *Richard the Second,* the banished Bolingbroke regards his banishment in a similar light, as an almost insurmountable disaster. And Bolingbroke, as Shakespeare saw him, was no Romeo, no love-crazed teenager; quite the reverse, he was a hard-headed, long-sighted, close-calculating realist.

Banishment implies the separation from familiar places and faces, from familiar language and ways, and from the protection and privileges of citizenship. It further implies that these hardships are undergone as a grave punishment, to expiate a guilt, which to a sensitive person would be a heavier load than all the external discomforts.

Yet we reflect on the fate of those who, for example, were "transported", often for quite minor offences, from Britain to Australia; or the slaves who were brought from Africa to America; or even the Irish emigrants who, often in conditions of terrible hardship, left homes which they loved no less than Bolingbroke his England, Romeo his Verona, to seek a most uncertain fortune in the uttermost parts of the earth, in places about which, in their ignorance and simplicity, they could form hardly the vaguest conjectures.

Then we turn back to Bolingbroke and Romeo, who had so much more sophistication in addition to the self-confidence that a moneyed upper-class childhood engenders. We are forced to the conclusion that, in rational terms, their reaction to banishment is so full of abject and unmanly self-pity that it ceases not merely to be sympathetic but even becomes implausible. The idea of banishment must have held for Shakespeare some symbolical connections, some overtones, or possibly some relation to emotional experience of his own.

The implausibility, as I find it, of Romeo's reaction to banishment need not interfere with enjoyment of the play. The point is that the young people are separated, and in circumstances in which it is emotionally impossible to make sensible, prudent, long-term plans. Their parents are involved in the Montague/Capulet feud, and anyway, Juliet's parents—Romeo's scarcely appear in the play—are neither very wise nor sympathetic. The nurse is, in many respects, Juliet's substitute-mother. We may infer from Romeo's relation with Laurence, which is very like Juliet's with her nurse, that his parents are no wiser or more sympathetic than hers.

The banishment is no more than the occasion that makes the two young people, in their panic and inexperience, totally dependent upon grown-up advice. The real parents are useless. Of the substitute-parents, the Nurse turns out to be worldly and entirely on the side of "the Establishment". Laurence's advice is disinterested, affectionate, sustained by the weight of his office, and, in the end, utterly disastrous.

In the theatre, apart from the already mentioned difficulty of casting the lovers, the play goes splendidly until the scenes in and around the tomb. I have never seen a production that grappled successfully with the the problem of how to arrange these scenes.

From the mention of lantern, crow, mattock and spade, and from the business of opening the tomb, some realism seems to be indicated. It is important to know who is inside the vault and who outside, and those who are outside must be sufficiently far away from those inside for it to be plausible that their words are not audible within. There cannot, at the stage when this scene occurs, possibly be a break in the continuity of the action; and the tomb, so it seems to me, simply must be placed in an intimate relation to the audience and so that all the actors can get around it.

The problem sums up thus: how to set on something representing the tomb which will justify the use, or indeed even the presence, of mattock, crow and spade, and which can also occupy the main acting area during the two preceding scenes—Mantua and the Friar's Cell.

There is another difficulty at the end of the play: I cannot believe that so experienced a dramatist as the author of *Romeo and Juliet* already was, would hold up the last moments of his play for Friar Laurence's long speech of explanation, in which he recapitulates a number of events unknown to the Duke but which the audience has already seen. If this recapitulation gave any unexpected comment or were even in superbly vivid language there might be some purpose for it. So far as I can see, no such purposes are served.

It is also quite unlike the way in which Shakespeare solves similar problems in other romances. In general, as the denouement becomes clear and before any boring explanations can ensue, the characters are swept off the stage with some high-handed lines, obviously spoken on the move, such as those that conclude the great finale of

Measure for Measure:

> So bring us to our palace, where we'll show
> What's yet behind that's meet you all should know.

Or of *All's Well That Ends Well*:

> Of that and all the progress more and less
> Resolvedly more leisure shall express.
> All yet seems well, and if it end so meet
> The bitter past, more welcome is the sweet.

It is quite evident that the musical shape demanded at the end of *Romeo and Juliet* is a slow, dignified decrescendo, of which the dramatic point is the reconciliation of the warring clans over the symbolically intertwined bodies of the dead lovers. To my way of thinking there is no place in this for the Friar to explain events which the action has already more vividly explained and which have ceased to be relevant. Cutting this speech and the subsequent evidence of the page still enables the Duke and the two fathers to achieve a dignified, monumental and moving reconciliation. Naturally one hesitates to recommend cuts in the text of a masterpiece unless there is reason to suppose that it is corrupt. Editors do believe that the latter half of this play was "worked over" and revised by Shakespeare at a late stage in his career. Is it possible that this tedious and inexpert piece of dramaturgy is a hangover from an earlier version which remained, by mistake, in the text from which the Second Quarto was printed?

Chorus; Three Musicians;
Citizens of Verona;
several Men and Women;
relations to both houses;
Maskers; Guards;
Watchmen and Attendants.

PETER,
servant to
Juliet's
nurse

Nurse to
Juliet

CAPULET
LADY CAPULET, his wife
JULIET, his daughter

ESCALUS, Prince of Verona
Page to Paris, Another Page, An Officer

An old man,
cousin to
Capulet

PARIS, a young nobleman,
Kinsman to the Prince

SAMSON
GREGORY, servants to
Capulet

TYBALT,
nephew
to
Lady Capulet

SCENE: VERONA; MANTUA

BALTHASAR,
servant to
Romeo

ABRAHAM,
servant to
Montague

An apothecary

MONTAGUE
LADY MONTAGUE, his wife
ROMEO, his son
BENVOLIO,
Nephew to Montague,
friend to Romeo
MERCUTIO,
Kinsman to the Prince,
friend to Romeo
FRIAR LAURENCE,
FRIAR JOHN,
Franciscans

ROMEO AND JULIET
DRAMATIS PERSONAE
PROLOGUE

Two households, both alike in dignity,
  In fair Verona, where we lay our scene,
From ancient grudge break to new mutiny,
  Where civil blood makes civil hands unclean.
From forth the fatal loins of these two foes
  A pair of star-crossed lovers take their life;
Whose misadventured piteous overthrows
  Do with their death bury their parents' strife.
The fearful passage of their death-marked love,
  And the continuance of their parents' rage,
Which, but their children's end, nought could remove,
  Is now the two hours' traffic of our stage;
The which if you with patient ears attend,
What here shall miss, our toil shall strive to mend.

ACT I

SCENE I *Verona: a public place*

Enter SAMPSON *and* GREGORY, *of the house of Capulet, armed with swords and bucklers*

SAMPSON. Gregory, o' my word, we'll not carry coals.

GREGORY. No, for then we should be colliers.

SAMPSON. I mean, an we be in choler, we'll draw.

GREGORY. Ay, while you live, draw your neck out o' the collar.

SAMPSON. I strike quickly, being moved.

GREGORY. But thou art not quickly moved to strike.

SAMPSON. A dog of the house of Montague moves me.

GREGORY. To move is to stir; and to be valiant is to stand. Therefore, if thou art moved, thou runn'st away.

SAMPSON. A dog of that house shall move me to stand. I will take the wall of any man or maid of Montague's.

GREGORY. That shows thee a weak slave; for the weakest goes to the wall.

SAMPSON. True; and therefore women, being the weaker

vessels, are ever thrust to the wall. Therefore I will push Montague's men from the wall, and thrust his maids to the wall.

GREGORY. The quarrel is between our masters and us their men.

SAMPSON. 'Tis all one; I will show myself a tyrant. When I have fought with the men, I will be cruel with the maids, and cut off their heads.

GREGORY. The heads of the maids?

SAMPSON. Ay, the heads of the maids, or their maidenheads; take it in what sense thou wilt.

GREGORY. They must take it in sense that feel it.

SAMPSON. Me they shall feel while I am able to stand; and 'tis known I am a pretty piece of flesh.

GREGORY. 'Tis well thou art not fish; if thou hadst, thou hadst been Poor John. Draw thy tool! Here comes two of the house of the Montagues.

SAMPSON. My naked weapon is out. Quarrel, I will back thee.

GREGORY. How! turn thy back and run?

SAMPSON. Fear me not.

GREGORY. No, marry; I fear thee!

SAMPSON. Let us take the law of our sides; let them begin.

GREGORY. I will frown as I pass by, and let them take it as they list.

SAMPSON. Nay, as they dare. I will bite my thumb at them; which is a disgrace to them, if they bear it.

Enter ABRAHAM *and* BALTHASAR

ABRAHAM. Do you bite your thumb at us, sir?

SAMPSON. I do bite my thumb, sir.

ABRAHAM. Do you bite your thumb at us, sir?

SAMPSON. [*Aside to Gregory*] Is the law of our side if I say ay?

GREGORY. No.

SAMPSON. No, sir, I do not bite my thumb at you, sir; but I bite my thumb, sir.

GREGORY. Do you quarrel, sir?

ABRAHAM. Quarrel, sir! No, sir.

SAMPSON. If you do, sir, I am for you. I serve as good a man as you.

ABRAHAM. No better?

SAMPSON. Well, sir.

GREGORY. Say "better." Here comes one of my master's kinsmen.

SAMPSON. Yes, better, sir.

ABRAHAM. You lie.

SAMPSON. Draw, if you be men. Gregory, remember thy swashing blow.   *They fight*

Enter BENVOLIO

BENVOLIO. Part, fools!
Put up your swords; you know not what you do.
                    Beats down their swords

Enter TYBALT

TYBALT. What, art thou drawn among these heartless hinds?
Turn thee, Benvolio, look upon thy death.

BENVOLIO. I do but keep the peace. Put up thy sword,
Or manage it to part these men with me.

TYBALT. What, drawn, and talk of peace! I hate the word,
As I hate hell, all Montagues, and thee.
Have at thee, coward!   *They fight*

17

Enter several of both houses, who join the fray; then enter
Citizens, *with clubs*

FIRST CITIZEN. Clubs, bills, and partisans! Strike! beat
    them down!
  Down with the Capulets! Down with the Montagues!

Enter CAPULET *in his gown, and* LADY CAPULET

CAPULET. What noise is this? Give me my long
    sword, ho!
LADY CAPULET. A crutch, a crutch! Why call you for a
    sword?
CAPULET. My sword, I say! Old Montague is come,
  And flourishes his blade in spite of me.

Enter MONTAGUE *and* LADY MONTAGUE

MONTAGUE. Thou villain Capulet—hold me not, let
  me go.
LADY MONTAGUE. Thou shalt not stir a foot to seek a foe.

Enter PRINCE, *with Attendants*

PRINCE. Rebellious subjects, enemies to peace,
  Profaners of this neighbour-stained steel—
  Will they not hear? What, ho! you men, you beasts,
  That quench the fire of your pernicious rage
  With purple fountains issuing from your veins!
  On pain of torture, from those bloody hands
  Throw your mistempered weapons to the ground,
  And hear the sentence of your moved prince.
  Three civil brawls, bred of an airy word,
  By thee, old Capulet and Montague,
  Have thrice disturbed the quiet of our streets,
  And made Verona's ancient citizens
  Cast by their grave beseeming ornaments,
  To wield old partisans, in hands as old,
  Cankered with peace, to part your cankered hate.
  If ever you disturb our streets again,
  Your lives shall pay the forfeit of the peace.
  For this time, all the rest depart away.
  You, Capulet, shall go along with me;
  And, Montague, come you this afternoon,
  To know our further pleasure in this case,
  To old Free-town, our common judgement place.
  Once more, on pain of death, all men depart.

Exeunt all but MONTAGUE,
LADY MONTAGUE, *and* BENVOLIO

MONTAGUE. Who set this ancient quarrel new abroach?
  Speak, nephew, were you by when it began?
BENVOLIO. Here were the servants of your adversary,
  And yours, close fighting ere I did approach.
  I drew to part them. In the instant came
  The fiery Tybalt, with his sword prepared,
  Which, as he breathed defiance to my ears,
  He swung about his head and cut the winds,
  Who nothing hurt withal hissed him in scorn.
  While we were interchanging thrusts and blows,
  Came more and more and fought on part and part,
  Till the Prince came, who parted either part.
LADY MONTAGUE. O, where is Romeo? Saw you him
    today?
  Right glad I am he was not at this fray.
BENVOLIO. Madam, an hour before the worshipped sun
  Peered forth the golden window of the east,
  A troubled mind drave me to walk abroad;
  Where, underneath the grove of sycamore
  That westward rooteth from the city's side,
  So early walking did I see your son.
  Towards him I made, but he was ware of me
  And stole into the covert of the wood.
  I, measuring his affections by my own,
  That most are busied when they're most alone,
  Pursued my humour not pursuing his,
  And gladly shunned who gladly fled from me.
MONTAGUE. Many a morning hath he there been seen,
  With tears augmenting the fresh morning's dew,
  Adding to clouds more clouds with his deep sighs;
  But all so soon as the all-cheering sun

Should in the furthest east begin to draw
The shady curtains from Aurora's bed,
  Away from light steals home my heavy son,
  And private in his chamber pens himself,
  Shuts up his windows, locks fair daylight out,
  And makes himself an artificial night.
  Black and portentous must this humour prove,
  Unless good counsel may the cause remove.
BENVOLIO. My noble uncle, do you know the cause?
MONTAGUE. I neither know it nor can learn of him.
BENVOLIO. Have you importuned him by any means?
MONTAGUE. Both by myself and many other friends;
  But he, his own affections' counsellor,
  Is to himself—I will not say how true—
  But to himself so secret and so close,
  So far from sounding and discovery,
  As is the bud bit with an envious worm
  Ere he can spread his sweet leaves to the air
  Or dedicate his beauty to the sun.
  Could we but learn from whence his sorrows grow,
  We would as willingly give cure as know.

Enter ROMEO

BENVOLIO. See, where he comes. So please you, step
    aside;
  I'll know his grievance, or be much denied.
MONTAGUE. I would thou wert so happy by thy stay,
  To hear true shrift. Come, madam, let's away.

Exeunt MONTAGUE *and* LADY MONTAGUE

BENVOLIO. Good morrow, cousin.
ROMEO.   Is the day so young?
BENVOLIO. But new struck nine.
ROMEO.   Ay me! Sad hours seem long.
  Was that my father that went hence so fast?
BENVOLIO. It was. What sadness lengthens Romeo's
    hours?
ROMEO. Not having that which having makes them short.
BENVOLIO. In love?
ROMEO. Out—
BENVOLIO. Of love?
ROMEO. Out of her favour, where I am in love.
BENVOLIO. Alas, that love, so gentle in his view,
  Should be so tyrannous and rough in proof!
ROMEO. Alas, that love, whose view is muffled still,
  Should, without eyes, see pathways to his will!
  Where shall we dine? O me! What fray was here?
  Yet tell me not, for I have heard it all.
  Here's much to do with hate, but more with love.
  Why, then, O brawling love! O loving hate!
  O any thing, of nothing first create!
  O heavy lightness, serious vanity!
  Misshapen chaos of well-seeming forms!
  Feather of lead, bright smoke, cold fire, sick health!
  Still-waking sleep, that is not what it is!
  This love feel I, that feel no love in this.
  Dost thou not laugh?

BENVOLIO.   No, coz, I rather weep.
ROMEO. Good heart, at what?
BENVOLIO.   At thy good heart's oppression.
ROMEO. Why, such is love's transgression.
 Griefs of mine own lie heavy in my breast,
 Which thou wilt propagate, to have it prest
 With more of thine. This love that thou hast shown
 Doth add more grief to too much of mine own.
 Love is a smoke raised with the fume of sighs;
 Being purged, a fire sparkling in lovers' eyes;
 Being vexed, a sea nourished with lovers' tears.
 What is it else? a madness most discreet,
 A choking gall and a preserving sweet.
 Farewell, my coz.
BENVOLIO.   Soft! I will go along;
 An if you leave me so, you do me wrong.
ROMEO. Tut, I have lost myself; I am not here;
 This is not Romeo, he's some other where.
BENVOLIO. Tell me in sadness, who is that you love.
ROMEO. What, shall I groan and tell thee?
BENVOLIO.   Groan! Why, no;
 But sadly tell me who.
ROMEO. Bid a sick man in sadness make his will.
 Ah, word ill urged to one that is so ill!
 In sadness, cousin, I do love a woman.
BENVOLIO. I aimed so near, when I supposed you loved.
ROMEO. A right good markman! And she's fair I love.
BENVOLIO. A right fair mark, fair coz, is soonest hit.
ROMEO. Well, in that hit you miss. She'll not be hit
 With Cupid's arrow; she hath Dian's wit;
 And, in strong proof of chastity well armed,

From love's weak childish bow she lives unharmed.
She will not stay the siege of loving terms,
Nor bide the encounter of assailing eyes,
Nor ope her lap to saint-seducing gold.
O, she is rich in beauty, only poor,
That when she dies, with beauty dies her store.
BENVOLIO. Then she hath sworn that she will still live
 chaste?
ROMEO. She hath, and in that sparing makes huge waste,
 For beauty starved with her severity
 Cuts beauty off from all posterity.
 She is too fair, too wise, wisely too fair,
 To merit bliss by making me despair.
 She hath forsworn to love, and in that vow
 Do I live dead that live to tell it now.
BENVOLIO. Be ruled by me, forget to think of her.
ROMEO. O, teach me how I should forget to think.
BENVOLIO. By giving liberty unto thine eyes;
 Examine other beauties.
ROMEO.   'Tis the way
 To call hers exquisite, in question more.
 These happy masks that kiss fair ladies' brows
 Being black put us in mind they hide the fair;
 He that is strucken blind cannot forget
 The precious treasure of his eyesight lost.
 Show me a mistress that is passing fair,
 What doth her beauty serve, but as a note
 Where I may read who passed that passing fair?
 Farewell; thou canst not teach me to forget.
BENVOLIO. I'll pay that doctrine, or else die in debt.

Exeunt

SCENE II *A street*

Enter CAPULET, PARIS, *and* Servant

CAPULET. But Montague is bound as well as I,
 In penalty alike; and 'tis not hard, I think,
 For men so old as we to keep the peace.
PARIS. Of honourable reckoning are you both;
 And pity 'tis you lived at odds so long.
 But now, my lord, what say you to my suit?
CAPULET. But saying o'er what I have said before:
 My child is yet a stranger in the world;
 She hath not seen the change of fourteen years;
 Let two more summers wither in their pride,
 Ere we may think her ripe to be a bride.
PARIS. Younger than she are happy mothers made.
CAPULET. And too soon marred are those so early made.
 The earth hath swallowed all my hopes but she;
 She is the hopeful lady of my earth.
 But woo her, gentle Paris, get her heart,
 My will to her consent is but a part;
 An she agree, within her scope of choice
 Lies my consent and fair according voice.
 This night I hold an old accustomed feast,

Whereto I have invited many a guest,
Such as I love; and you, among the store,
One more, most welcome, makes my number more.
At my poor house look to behold this night
Earth-treading stars that make dark heaven light.
Such comfort as do lusty young men feel
When well-apparelled April on the heel
Of limping winter treads, even such delight
Among fresh female buds shall you this night
Inherit at my house; hear all, all see,
And like her most whose merit most shall be;
Which on more view, of many mine being one
May stand in number, though in reckoning none.
Come, go with me. [*To Servant, giving a paper*]
 Go, sirrah, trudge about
Through fair Verona; find those persons out
Whose names are written there, and to them say,
My house and welcome on their pleasure stay.

Exeunt CAPULET *and* PARIS

SERVANT. Find them out whose names are written here!
It is written, that the shoemaker should meddle with
his yard, and the tailor with his last, the fisher with
his pencil, and the painter with his nets; but I am sent
to find those persons whose names are here writ, and
can never find what names the writing person hath
here writ. I must to the learned—in good time.

Enter BENVOLIO *and* ROMEO

BENVOLIO. Tut, man, one fire burns out another's
    burning,
  One pain is lessened by another's anguish;
  Turn giddy, and be holp by backward turning;
  One desperate grief cures with another's languish.
  Take thou some new infection to thy eye,
  And the rank poison of the old will die.
ROMEO. Your plaintain leaf is excellent for that.
BENVOLIO. For what, I pray thee?
ROMEO.   For your broken shin.
BENVOLIO. Why, Romeo, art thou mad?
ROMEO. Not mad, but bound more than a madman is;
  Shut up in prison, kept without my food,
  Whipped and tormented and—God den, good fellow.
SERVANT. God gi' god den. I pray, sir, can you read?
ROMEO. Ay, mine own fortune in my misery.
SERVANT. Perhaps you have learned it without book;
  but, I pray, can you read any thing you see?
ROMEO. Ay, if I know the letters and the language.
SERVANT. Ye say honestly. Rest you merry!
ROMEO. Stay, fellow; I can read.   *Reads*
  "Signior Martino and his wife and daughters; County
Anselme and his beauteous sisters; the lady widow of
Vitruvio; Signior Placentio and his lovely nieces;
Mercutio and his brother Valentine; mine uncle

Capulet, his wife, and daughters; my fair niece
Rosaline; Livia; Signior Valentio and his cousin
Tybalt; Lucio and the lively Helena."
  A fair assembly. Whither should they come?
SERVANT. Up.
ROMEO. Whither?
SERVANT. To supper; to our house.
ROMEO. Whose house?
SERVANT. My master's.
ROMEO. Indeed, I should have asked you that before.
SERVANT. Now I'll tell you without asking: My master
  is the great rich Capulet; and if you be not of the
  house of Montagues, I pray, come and crush a cup of
  wine. Rest you merry!   *Exit*
BENVOLIO. At this same ancient feast of Capulet's
  Sups the fair Rosaline whom thou so lovest,
  With all the admired beauties of Verona.
  Go thither; and, with unattainted eye,
  Compare her face with some that I shall show,
  And I will make thee think thy swan a crow.
ROMEO. When the devout religion of mine eye
    Maintains such falsehood, then turn tears to fires;
  And these, who often drowned could never die,
    Transparent heretics, be burnt for liars!
  One fairer than my love! The all-seeing sun
  Ne'er saw her match since first the world begun.
BENVOLIO. Tut, you saw her fair, none else being by,
  Herself poised with herself in either eye;
  But in that crystal scales let there be weighed
  Your lady's love against some other maid
  That I will show you shining at this feast,
  And she shall scant show well that now shows best.
ROMEO. I'll go along, no such sight to be shown,
  But to rejoice in splendour of mine own.   *Exeunt*

SCENE III *A room in Capulet's house*

Enter LADY CAPULET *and* Nurse

LADY CAPULET. Nurse, where's my daughter? Call her
  forth to me.
NURSE. Now, by my maidenhead, at twelve year old,
  I bade her come. What, lamb! What, lady-bird!
  God forbid! Where's this girl? What, Juliet!
Enter JULIET
JULIET. How now! Who calls?
NURSE.   Your mother.
JULIET.   Madam, I am here.
  What is your will?
LADY CAPULET. This is the matter—Nurse, give leave
  awhile,
  We must talk in secret. Nurse, come back again;
  I have remembered me, thou's hear our counsel.
  Thou know'st my daughter's of a pretty age.
NURSE. Faith, I can tell her age unto an hour.
LADY CAPULET. She's not fourteen.

NURSE. I'll lay fourteen of my teeth—
  And yet, to my teen be it spoken, I have but four—
  She is not fourteen. How long is it now
  To Lammastide?
LADY CAPULET.   A fortnight and odd days.
NURSE. Even or odd, of all days in the year,
  Come Lammas Eve at night shall she be fourteen.
  Susan and she—God rest all Christian souls!—
  Were of an age: well, Susan is with God;
  She was too good for me. But, as I said,
  On Lammas Eve at night shall she be fourteen;
  That shall she, marry; I remember it well.
  'Tis since the earthquake now eleven years;
  And she was weaned—I never shall forget it—
  Of all the days of the year, upon that day;
  For I had then laid wormwood to my dug,
  Sitting in the sun under the dovehouse wall;

My lord and you were then at Mantua—
Nay, I do bear a brain—but, as I said,
When it did taste the wormwood on the nipple
Of my dug and felt it bitter, pretty fool,
To see it tetchy and fall out with the dug!
"Shake" quoth the dovehouse; 'twas no need, I trow,
To bid me trudge.
And since that time it is eleven years;
For then she could stand alone; nay, by the rood,
She could have run and waddled all about;
For even the day before, she broke her brow;
And then my husband—God be with his soul!
A' was a merry man—took up the child.
"Yea," quoth he, "dost thou fall upon thy face?
Thou wilt fall backward when thou hast more wit,
Wilt thou not, Jule?" and, by my holidame,
The pretty wretch left crying and said "Ay."
To see, now, how a jest shall come about!
I warrant, an I should live a thousand years,
I never should forget it. "Wilt thou not, Jule?"
    quoth he;
And, pretty fool, it stinted and said "Ay."

LADY CAPULET. Enough of this; I pray thee, hold thy
    peace.

NURSE. Yes, madam. Yet I cannot choose but laugh,
To think it should leave crying and say "Ay."
And yet, I warrant, it had upon its brow
A bump as big as a young cockerel's stone;
A perilous knock; and it cried bitterly.
"Yea," quoth my husband, "fall'st upon thy face?
Thou wilt fall backward when thou comest to age,
Wilt thou not, Jule?" It stinted and said "Ay."

JULIET. And stint thou too, I pray thee, nurse, say I.

NURSE. Peace, I have done. God mark thee to his grace!
Thou wast the prettiest babe that e'er I nursed.
An I might live to see thee married once,
I have my wish.

LADY CAPULET. Marry, that "marry" is the very theme
I came to talk of. Tell me, daughter Juliet,
How stands your disposition to be married?

JULIET. It is an honour that I dream not of.

NURSE. An honour! Were not I thine only nurse,
I would say thou hadst sucked wisdom from thy teat.

LADY CAPULET. Well, think of marriage now; younger
    than you,
Here in Verona, ladies of esteem,
Are made already mothers. By my count,
I was your mother much upon these years
That you are now a maid. Thus then in brief:
The valiant Paris seeks you for his love.

NURSE. A man, young lady! Lady, such a man
As all the world—why, he's a man of wax.

LADY CAPULET. Verona's summer hath not such a flower.

NURSE. Nay, he's a flower; in faith, a very flower.

LADY CAPULET. What say you? Can you love the gentle-
    man?
This night you shall behold him at our feast;
Read o'er the volume of young Paris' face
And find delight writ there with beauty's pen;
Examine every married lineament
And see how one another lends content,
And what obscured in this fair volume lies
Find written in the margent of his eyes.
This precious book of love, this unbound lover,
To beautify him, only lacks a cover.
The fish lives in the sea, and 'tis much pride
For fair without the fair within to hide.
That book in many's eyes doth share the glory,
That in gold clasps locks in the golden story;
So shall you share all that he doth possess,
By having him, making yourself no less.

NURSE. No less! Nay, bigger; women grow by men.

LADY CAPULET. Speak briefly, can you like of Paris' love?

JULIET. I'll look to like, if looking liking move;
But no more deep will I endart mine eye
Than your consent gives strength to make it fly.

Enter a Servant

SERVANT. Madam, the guests are come, supper served up,
you called, my young lady asked for, the nurse cursed
in the pantry, and every thing in extremity. I must
hence to wait; I beseech you, follow straight.

LADY CAPULET. We follow thee. [*Exit Servant*] Juliet,
the County stays.

NURSE. Go, girl, seek happy nights to happy days.

                                                    Exeunt

SCENE IV *A street*

Enter ROMEO, MERCUTIO, BENVOLIO, *with five or six* Maskers, Torchbearers, *and others*

ROMEO. What, shall this speech be spoke for our excuse?
Or shall we on without apology?

BENVOLIO. The date is out of such prolixity.
We'll have no Cupid hoodwinked with a scarf,
Bearing a Tartar's painted bow of lath,
Scaring the ladies like a crowkeeper;
Nor no without-book prologue, faintly spoke

After the prompter, for our entrance;
But let them measure us by what they will;
We'll measure them a measure, and be gone.

ROMEO. Give me a torch. I am not for this ambling;
Being but heavy, I will bear the light.

MERCUTIO. Nay, gentle Romeo, we must have you dance.

ROMEO. Not I, believe me. You have dancing shoes

With nimble soles; I have a soul of lead
So stakes me to the ground I cannot move.

MERCUTIO. You are a lover; borrow Cupid's wings,
And soar with them above a common bound.

ROMEO. I am too sore enpierced with his shaft
To soar with his light feathers, and so bound,
I cannot bound a pitch above dull woe.
Under love's heavy burden do I sink.

MERCUTIO. And, to sink in it, should you burden love;
Too great oppression for a tender thing.

ROMEO. Is love a tender thing? It is too rough,
Too rude, too boisterous, and it pricks like thorn.

MERCUTIO. If love be rough with you, be rough with
love;
Prick love for pricking, and you beat love down.
Give me a case to put my visage in:
A visor for a visor! What care I
What curious eye doth quote deformities?
Here are the beetle brows shall blush for me.

BENVOLIO. Come, knock and enter; and no sooner in,
But every man betake him to his legs.

ROMEO. A torch for me—let wantons light of heart
Tickle the senseless rushes with their heels,
For I am proverbed with a grandsire phrase;
I'll be a candle-holder, and look on.
The game was ne'er so fair, and I am done.

MERCUTIO. Tut, dun's the mouse, the constable's own
word:
If thou art dun, we'll draw thee from the mire
Of, save your reverence, love, wherein thou stick'st
Up to the ears. Come, we burn daylight, ho!

ROMEO. Nay, that's not so.

MERCUTIO.   I mean, sir, in delay
We waste our lights in vain, like lamps by day.
Take our good meaning, for our judgement sits
Five times in that ere once in our five wits.

ROMEO. And we mean well in going to this mask;
But 'tis no wit to go.

MERCUTIO.   Why, may one ask?

ROMEO. I dreamed a dream tonight.

MERCUTIO.   And so did I.

ROMEO. Well, what was yours?

MERCUTIO.   That dreamers often lie.

ROMEO. In bed asleep, while they do dream things true.

MERCUTIO. O, then, I see Queen Mab hath been with
you.
She is the fairies' midwife, and she comes
In shape no bigger than an agate stone
On the forefinger of an alderman,
Drawn with a team of little atomies
Athwart men's noses as they lie asleep;
Her waggon spokes made of long spinners' legs,
The cover of the wings of grasshoppers,
The traces of the smallest spider's web,
The collars of the moonshine's watery beams,
Her whip of cricket's bone, the lash of film,

Her waggoner a small grey-coated gnat,
Not half so big as a round little worm
Pricked from the lazy finger of a maid;
Her chariot is an empty hazelnut
Made by the joiner squirrel or old grub,
Time out o' mind the fairies' coachmakers.
And in this state she gallops night by night
Through lovers' brains, and then they dream of love;
O'er courtiers' knees, that dream on courtesies
straight,
O'er lawyers' fingers, who straight dream on fees,
O'er ladies' lips, who straight on kisses dream,
Which oft the angry Mab with blisters plagues,
Because their breaths with sweetmeats tainted are.
Sometime she gallops o'er a courtier's nose,
And then dreams he of smelling out a suit;
And sometime comes she with a tithe-pig's tail
Tickling a parson's nose as a' lies asleep,
Then dreams he of another benefice.
Sometime she driveth o'er a soldier's neck,
And then dreams he of cutting foreign throats,
Of breaches, ambuscadoes, Spanish blades,
Of healths five fathom deep; and then anon
Drums in his ear, at which he starts and wakes,
And being thus frighted swears a prayer or two
And sleeps again. This is that very Mab
That plats the manes of horses in the night,
And bakes the elf-locks in foul sluttish hairs,
Which once untangled much misfortune bodes.
This is the hag, when maids lie on their backs,
That presses them and learns them first to bear,
Making them women of good carriage.
This is she—

ROMEO.   Peace, peace, Mercutio, peace!
Thou talk'st of nothing.

MERCUTIO.   True, I talk of dreams,
Which are the children of an idle brain,
Begot of nothing but vain fantasy,
Which is as thin of substance as the air
And more inconstant than the wind, who wooes
Even now the frozen bosom of the north,
And, being angered, puffs away from thence,
Turning his face to the dew-dropping south.

BENVOLIO. This wind, you talk of, blows us from ourselves;
Supper is done, and we shall come too late.

ROMEO. I fear, too early; for my mind misgives
Some consequence yet hanging in the stars
Shall bitterly begin his fearful date
With this night's revels and expire the term
Of a despised life closed in my breast
By some vile forfeit of untimely death.
But He, that hath the steerage of my course,
Direct my sail! On, lusty gentlemen!

BENVOLIO. Strike, drum.

                                        Exeunt

SCENE V *A hall in Capulet's house*

Musicians *waiting.* Enter Servingmen, *with napkins*

FIRST SERVANT. Where's Potpan, that he helps not to take away? He shift a trencher? He scrape a trencher?

SECOND SERVANT. When good manners shall lie all in one or two men's hands and they unwashed too, 'tis a foul thing.

FIRST SERVANT. Away with the joint-stools, remove the court-cupboard, look to the plate. Good thou, save me a piece of marchpane; and, as thou lovest me, let the porter let in Susan Grindstone and Nell. Antony, and Potpan!

SECOND SERVANT. Ay, boy, ready.

FIRST SERVANT. You are looked for and called for, asked for and sought for, in the great chamber.

SECOND SERVANT. We cannot be here and there too. Cheerly, boys; be brisk awhile, and the longer liver take all.

Enter CAPULET, *with* JULIET *and others of his house, meeting*
the Guests *and* Maskers

CAPULET. Welcome, gentlemen! Ladies that have their
    toes
  Unplagued with corns will have a bout with you.
  Ah ha, my mistresses! Which of you all
  Will now deny to dance? She that makes dainty,
  She, I'll swear, hath corns; am I come near ye now?
  Welcome, gentlemen! I have seen the day
  That I have worn a visor and could tell
  A whispering tale in a fair lady's ear,
  Such as would please. 'Tis gone, 'tis gone, 'tis gone!
  You are welcome, gentlemen! Come, musicians, play.
  A hall, a hall! Give room! and foot it, girls.
                      Music plays, and they dance

25

More light, you knaves; and turn the tables up,
And quench the fire, the room is grown too hot.
Ah, sirrah, this unlooked-for sport comes well.
Nay, sit, nay, sit, good cousin Capulet;
For you and I are past our dancing days.
How long is't now since last yourself and I
Were in a mask?
SECOND CAPULET. By'r Lady, thirty years.
CAPULET. What, man! 'Tis not so much, 'tis not so
   much.
   'Tis since the nuptial of Lucentio,
   Come Pentecost as quickly as it will,
   Some five and twenty years; and then we masked.

SECOND CAPULET. 'Tis more, 'tis more! His son is elder,
   sir;
   His son is thirty.
CAPULET.   Will you tell me that?
   His son was but a ward two years ago.
ROMEO. [*To a Servingman*] What lady is that, which doth
   enrich the hand
   Of yonder knight?
SERVANT. I know not, sir.
ROMEO. O, she doth teach the torches to burn bright!
   It seems she hangs upon the cheek of night
   Like a rich jewel in an Ethiope's ear;
   Beauty too rich for use, for earth too dear!

So shows a snowy dove trooping with crows,
As yonder lady o'er her fellows shows.
The measure done, I'll watch her place of stand,
And, touching hers, make blessed my rude hand.
Did my heart love till now? Forswear it, sight!
For I ne'er saw true beauty till this night.

TYBALT. This, by his voice, should be a Montague.
Fetch me my rapier, boy. What dares the slave
Come hither, covered with an antic face,
To fleer and scorn at our solemnity?
Now, by the stock and honour of my kin,
To strike him dead I hold it not a sin.

CAPULET. Why, how now, kinsman! Wherefore storm
you so?

TYBALT. Uncle, this is a Montague, our foe,
A villain that is hither come in spite,
To scorn at our solemnity this night.

CAPULET. Young Romeo is it?

TYBALT.   'Tis he, that villain Romeo.

CAPULET. Content thee, gentle coz, let him alone;
He bears him like a portly gentleman;
And, to say truth, Verona brags of him
To be a virtuous and well-governed youth.
I would not for the wealth of all the town
Here in my house do him disparagement.
Therefore be patient, take no note of him.
It is my will, the which if thou respect,
Show a fair presence and put off these frowns,
An ill-beseeming semblance for a feast.

TYBALT. It fits, when such a villain is a guest.
I'll not endure him.

CAPULET.   He shall be endured;
What, goodman boy! I say, he shall. Go to;
Am I the master here, or you? Go to.
You'll not endure him! God shall mend my soul!
You'll make a mutiny among my guests!
You will set cock-a-hoop! You'll be the man!

TYBALT. Why, uncle, 'tis a shame.

CAPULET.   Go to, go to;
You are a saucy boy. Is't so, indeed?
This trick may chance to scathe you, I know what.
You must contrary me! Marry, 'tis time.
Well said, my hearts! You are a princox, go.
Be quiet, or—more light, more light! For shame!
I'll make you quiet. What, cheerly, my hearts!

TYBALT. Patience perforce with wilful choler meeting
Makes my flesh tremble in their different greeting.
I will withdraw; but this intrusion shall
Now seeming sweet convert to bitter gall.   *Exit*

ROMEO. [*To Juliet*] If I profane with my unworthiest
hand
This holy shrine, the gentle fine is this:
My lips, two blushing pilgrims, ready stand
To smooth that rough touch with a tender kiss.

JULIET. Good pilgrim, you do wrong your hand too
much,

Which mannerly devotion shows in this;
For saints have hands that pilgrims' hands do touch,
And palm to palm is holy palmers' kiss.

ROMEO. Have not saints lips, and holy palmers too?

JULIET. Ay, pilgrim, lips that they must use in prayer.

ROMEO. O, then, dear saint, let lips do what hands do;
They pray, grant thou, lest faith turn to despair.

JULIET. Saints do not move, though grant for prayers'
sake.

ROMEO. Then move not, while my prayer's effect I take.
Thus from my lips, by yours, my sin is purged.
                                                They Kiss

JULIET. Then have my lips the sin that they have took.

ROMEO. Sin from my lips? O trespass sweetly urged!
Give me my sin again.   *They Kiss*

JULIET.   You kiss by the book.

NURSE. Madam, your mother craves a word with you.

ROMEO. What is her mother?

NURSE.   Marry, bachelor,
Her mother is the lady of the house,
And a good lady, and a wise and virtuous.
I nursed her daughter, that you talked withal;
I tell you, he that can lay hold of her
Shall have the chinks.

ROMEO.   Is she a Capulet?
O dear account! My life is my foe's debt.

BENVOLIO. Away, be gone; the sport is at the best.

ROMEO. Ay, so I fear; the more is my unrest.

CAPULET. Nay, gentlemen, prepare not to be gone;
We have a trifling foolish banquet towards.
Is it e'en so? Why, then, I thank you all;
I thank you, honest gentlemen; good night.
More torches here! Come on then, let's to bed.
Ah, sirrah, by my fay, it waxes late;
I'll to my rest.   *Exeunt all but* JULIET *and* Nurse

JULIET. Come hither, nurse. What is yond gentleman?

NURSE. The son and heir of old Tiberio.

JULIET. What's he that now is going out of door?

NURSE. Marry, that, I think, be young Petrucio.

JULIET. What's he that follows there, that would not
dance?

NURSE. I know not.

JULIET. Go, ask his name. If he be married,
My grave is like to be my wedding bed.

NURSE. His name is Romeo, and a Montague;
The only son of your great enemy.

JULIET. My only love sprung from my only hate!
Too early seen unknown, and known too late!
Prodigious birth of love it is to me,
That I must love a loathed enemy.

NURSE. What's this? What's this?

JULIET.   A rhyme I learned even now
Of one I danced withal.
                          One calls within, "Juliet"

NURSE. Anon, anon!
Come, let's away; the strangers all are gone.   *Exeunt*

ACT II

PROLOGUE

Enter Chorus

CHORUS. Now old desire doth in his deathbed lie,
　And young affection gapes to be his heir;
That fair for which love groaned for and would die,
　With tender Juliet matched, is now not fair.
Now Romeo is beloved and loves again,
　Alike bewitched by the charm of looks,
But to his foe supposed he must complain,
　And she steal love's sweet bait from fearful hooks.
Being held a foe, he may not have access
　To breathe such vows as lovers use to swear;
And she as much in love, her means much less
　To meet her new beloved any where;
But passion lends them power, time means, to meet,
Tempering extremities with extreme sweet.　　*Exit*

SCENE I *A lane by the wall of Capulet's orchard*

Enter ROMEO

ROMEO. Can I go forward when my heart is here?
  Turn back, dull earth, and find thy centre out.
        He climbs the wall, and leaps down within it

Enter BENVOLIO *and* MERCUTIO

BENVOLIO. Romeo! My cousin Romeo!
MERCUTIO.   He is wise;
  And, on my life, hath stol'n him home to bed.
BENVOLIO. He ran this way, and leaped this orchard wall.
  Call, good Mercutio.
MERCUTIO.   Nay, I'll conjure too.
  Romeo! Humours! Madman! Passion! Lover!
  Appear thou in the likeness of a sigh.
  Speak but one rhyme, and I am satisfied;
  Cry but "Ay me!" pronounce but "love" and
    "dove";
  Speak to my gossip Venus one fair word,
  One nickname for her purblind son and heir,
  Young Adam Cupid, he that shot so trim,
  When King Cophetua loved the beggar maid!
  He heareth not, he stirreth not, he moveth not;
  The ape is dead, and I must conjure him.
  I conjure thee by Rosaline's bright eyes,
  By her high forehead and her scarlet lip,
  By her fine foot, straight leg and quivering thigh

And the demesnes that there adjacent lie,
  That in thy likeness thou appear to us!
BENVOLIO. An if he hear thee thou wilt anger him.
MERCUTIO. This cannot anger him. 'Twould anger him
  To raise a spirit in his mistress' circle
  Of some strange nature, letting it there stand
  Till she had laid it and conjured it down;
  That were some spite. My invocation
  Is fair and honest, and in his mistress' name
  I conjure only but to raise up him.
BENVOLIO. Come, he hath hid himself among these trees,
  To be consorted with the humorous night.
  Blind is his love and best befits the dark.
MERCUTIO. If love be blind, love cannot hit the mark.
  Now will he sit under a medlar tree,
  And wish his mistress were that kind of fruit
  As maids call medlars, when they laugh alone.
  O, Romeo, that she were, O, that she were
  An open et cetera, thou a poperin pear!
  Romeo, good night. I'll to my truckle bed;
  This field bed is too cold for me to sleep.
  Come, shall we go?
BENVOLIO.   Go, then; for 'tis in vain
  To seek him here that means not to be found.
                                        Exeunt

SCENE II *Capulet's orchard*

Enter ROMEO

ROMEO. He jests at scars that never felt a wound.
              JULIET *appears above at a window*
  But, soft! What light through yonder window breaks?
  It is the east, and Juliet is the sun.
  Arise, fair sun, and kill the envious moon,
  Who is already sick and pale with grief,
  That thou her maid art far more fair than she.
  Be not her maid, since she is envious;
  Her vestal livery is but sick and green
  And none but fools do wear it; cast it off.
  It is my lady, O, it is my love!
  O, that she knew she were!
  She speaks, yet she says nothing. What of that?
  Her eye discourses; I will answer it.
  I am too bold, 'tis not to me she speaks.
  Two of the fairest stars in all the heaven,
  Having some business, do entreat her eyes
  To twinkle in their spheres till they return.
  What if her eyes were there, they in her head?
  The brightness of her cheek would shame those stars,
  As daylight doth a lamp; her eyes in heaven
  Would through the airy region stream so bright
  That birds would sing and think it were not night.

See, how she leans her cheek upon her hand!
  O, that I were a glove upon that hand,
  That I might touch that cheek!
JULIET.   Ay me!
ROMEO.   She speaks.
  O, speak again, bright angel! For thou art
  As glorious to this night, being o'er my head,
  As is a winged messenger of heaven
  Unto the white-upturned wondering eyes
  Of mortals that fall back to gaze on him
  When he bestrides the lazy pacing clouds
  And sails upon the bosom of the air.
JULIET. O Romeo, Romeo! wherefore art thou Romeo?
  Deny thy father and refuse thy name;
  Or, if thou wilt not, be but sworn my love,
  And I'll no longer be a Capulet.
ROMEO. [*Aside*] Shall I hear more, or shall I speak at this?
JULIET. 'Tis but thy name that is my enemy;
  Thou art thyself, though not a Montague.
  What's Montague? It is nor hand, nor foot,
  Nor arm, nor face, nor any other part
  Belonging to a man. O, be some other name!
  What's in a name? That which we call a rose

By any other name would smell as sweet;
So Romeo would, were he not Romeo called,
Retain that dear perfection which he owes
Without that title. Romeo, doff thy name,
And for that name which is no part of thee
Take all myself.

ROMEO.   I take thee at thy word.
Call me but love, and I'll be new baptized;
Henceforth I never will be Romeo.

JULIET. What man art thou that thus bescreened in night
So stumblest on my counsel?

ROMEO.   By a name
I know not how to tell thee who I am:
My name, dear saint, is hateful to myself,
Because it is an enemy to thee;
Had I it written, I would tear the word.

JULIET. My ears have not yet drunk a hundred words
Of that tongue's utterance, yet I know the sound.
Art thou not Romeo and a Montague?

ROMEO. Neither, fair saint, if either thee dislike.

JULIET. How camest thou hither, tell me, and wherefore?
The orchard walls are high and hard to climb,
And the place death, considering who thou art,
If any of my kinsmen find thee here.

ROMEO. With love's light wings did I o'erperch these
    walls;
For stony limits cannot hold love out,
And what love can do that dares love attempt;
Therefore thy kinsmen are no let to me.

JULIET. If they do see thee, they will murder thee.

ROMEO. Alack, there lies more peril in thine eye
Than twenty of their swords. Look thou but sweet,
And I am proof against their enmity.

JULIET. I would not for the world they saw thee here.

ROMEO. I have night's cloak to hide me from their sight;
And but thou love me, let them find me here.
My life were better ended by their hate,
Than death prorogued, wanting of thy love.

JULIET. By whose direction found'st thou out this place?

ROMEO. By love, who first did prompt me to inquire;
He lent me counsel and I lent him eyes.
I am no pilot; yet, wert thou as far
As that vast shore washed with the farthest sea,
I would adventure for such merchandise.

JULIET. Thou know'st the mask of night is on my face,
Else would a maiden blush bepaint my cheek
For that which thou hast heard me speak tonight.
Fain would I dwell on form, fain, fain deny
What I have spoke; but farewell compliment!
Dost thou love me? I know thou wilt say "Ay,"
And I will take thy word. Yet, if thou swear'st,
Thou mayst prove false; at lovers' perjuries,
They say, Jove laughs. O gentle Romeo.
If thou dost love, pronounce it faithfully.
Or if thou think'st I am too quickly won,
I'll frown and be perverse and say thee nay,

So thou wilt woo; but else, not for the world.
In truth, fair Montague, I am too fond,
And therefore thou mayst think my 'haviour light.
But trust me, gentleman, I'll prove more true
Than those that have more cunning to be strange.
I should have been more strange, I must confess,
But that thou overheard'st, ere I was ware,
My true love's passion. Therefore pardon me,
And not impute this yielding to light love,
Which the dark night hath so discovered.
ROMEO. Lady, by yonder blessed moon I swear
That tips with silver all these fruit-tree tops—
JULIET. O, swear not by the moon, the inconstant moon,
That monthly changes in her circled orb,
Lest that thy love prove likewise variable.
ROMEO. What shall I swear by?
JULIET.   Do not swear at all;
Or, if thou wilt, swear by thy gracious self,
Which is the god of my idolatry,
And I'll believe thee.
ROMEO.   If my heart's dear love—
JULIET. Well, do not swear. Although I joy in thee,
I have no joy of this contract tonight:
It is too rash, too unadvised, too sudden;
Too like the lightning, which doth cease to be
Ere one can say "It lightens." Sweet, good night!
This bud of love, by summer's ripening breath,
May prove a beauteous flower when next we meet.
Good night, good night! as sweet repose and rest
Come to thy heart as that within my breast!
ROMEO. O, wilt thou leave me so unsatisfied?
JULIET. What satisfaction canst thou have tonight?
ROMEO. The exchange of thy love's faithful vow for
mine.
JULIET. I gave thee mine before thou didst request it;
And yet I would it were to give again.
ROMEO. Wouldst thou withdraw it? For what purpose,
love?
JULIET. But to be frank, and give it thee again.
And yet I wish but for the thing I have.
My bounty is as boundless as the sea,
My love as deep; the more I give to thee,
The more I have, for both are infinite.
                                    Nurse calls within
I hear some noise within; dear love, adieu!
Anon, good Nurse! Sweet Montague, be true.
Stay but a little, I will come again.   Exit, above
ROMEO. O blessed, blessed night! I am afeard,
Being in night, all this is but a dream,
Too flattering-sweet to be substantial.

Re-enter JULIET, *above*

JULIET. Three words, dear Romeo, and good night in-
deed.
If that thy bent of love be honourable,
Thy purpose marriage, send me word tomorrow,

By one that I'll procure to come to thee,
Where and what time thou wilt perform the rite;
And all my fortunes at thy foot I'll lay
And follow thee my lord throughout the world.
NURSE. [*Within*] Madam!
JULIET. I come, anon—but if thou mean'st not well,
I do beseech thee—
NURSE. [*Within*] Madam!
JULIET.   By and by, I come—
To cease thy suit, and leave me to my grief;
Tomorrow will I send.
ROMEO.   So thrive my soul—
JULIET. A thousand times good night!   *Exit, above*
ROMEO. A thousand times the worse, to want thy light.
Love goes toward love, as schoolboys from their books,
But love from love, toward school with heavy looks.
                                            Retiring

Re-enter JULIET, *above*

JULIET. Hist! Romeo, hist! O, for a falconer's voice,
To lure this tassel-gentle back again!
Bondage is hoarse, and may not speak aloud;
Else would I tear the cave where Echo lies,
And make her airy tongue more hoarse than mine,
With repetition of my Romeo's name.
ROMEO. It is my soul that calls upon my name.
How silver-sweet sound lovers' tongues by night,
Like softest music to attending ears!
JULIET. Romeo!
ROMEO.   My dear?
JULIET.   At what o'clock tomorrow
Shall I send to thee?
ROMEO.   At the hour of nine.
JULIET. I will not fail: 'tis twenty years till then.
I have forgot why I did call thee back.
ROMEO. Let me stand here till thou remember it.
JULIET. I shall forget, to have thee still stand there,
Remembering how I love thy company.
ROMEO. And I'll still stay, to have thee still forget,
Forgetting any other home but this.
JULIET. 'Tis almost morning; I would have thee gone:
And yet no further than a wanton's bird,
Who lets it hop a little from her hand,
Like a poor prisoner in his twisted gyves,
And with a silk thread plucks it back again,
So loving-jealous of his liberty.
ROMEO. I would I were thy bird.
JULIET.   Sweet, so would I.
Yet I should kill thee with much cherishing.
Good night, good night! parting is such sweet sorrow,
That I shall say good night till it be morrow.
                                            Exit, above
ROMEO. Sleep dwell upon thine eyes, peace in thy breast!
Would I were sleep and peace, so sweet to rest!
Hence will I to my ghostly father's cell,
His help to crave, and my dear hap to tell.   *Exit*

31

SCENE III *Friar Laurence's cell*

Enter FRIAR LAURENCE, *with a basket*

FRIAR LAURENCE. The grey-eyed morn smiles on the
    frowning night,
Chequering the eastern clouds with streaks of light,
And flecked darkness like a drunkard reels
From forth day's path and Titan's fiery wheels.
Now, ere the sun advance his burning eye,
The day to cheer and night's dank dew to dry,
I must up-fill this osier cage of ours
With baleful weeds and precious-juiced flowers.
The earth that's nature's mother is her tomb;
What is her burying grave that is her womb,
And from her womb children of divers kind
We sucking on her natural bosom find,
Many for many virtues excellent,
None but for some and yet all different.
O, mickle is the powerful grace that lies
In herbs, plants, stones, and their true qualities;
For nought so vile that on the earth doth live
But to the earth some special good doth give,
Nor aught so good but strained from that fair use
Revolts from true birth, stumbling on abuse.
Virtue itself turns vice, being misapplied;
And vice sometimes by action dignified.
Within the infant rind of this small flower
Poison hath residence and medicine power.
For this, being smelt, with that part cheers each part;
Being tasted, slays all senses with the heart.
Two such opposed kings encamp them still
In man as well as herbs, grace and rude will;
And where the worser is predominant,
Full soon the canker death eats up that plant.

Enter ROMEO

ROMEO. Good morrow, father.
FRIAR LAURENCE.   Benedicite!
    What early tongue so sweet saluteth me?
    Young son, it argues a distempered head
    So soon to bid good morrow to thy bed.
    Care keeps his watch in every old man's eye,
    And where care lodges, sleep will never lie;
    But where unbruised youth with unstuffed brain
    Doth couch his limbs, there golden sleep doth reign.
    Therefore thy earliness doth me assure
    Thou art uproused by some distemperature;
    Or if not so, then here I hit it right,
    Our Romeo hath not been in bed tonight.
ROMEO. That last is true; the sweeter rest was mine.
FRIAR LAURENCE. God pardon sin! Wast thou with
    Rosaline?
ROMEO. With Rosaline, my ghostly father? No,
    I have forgot that name, and that name's woe.
FRIAR LAURENCE. That's my good son, but where hast
    thou been, then?

ROMEO. I'll tell thee, ere thou ask it me again.
    I have been feasting with mine enemy,
    Where on a sudden one hath wounded me,
    That's by me wounded. Both our remedies
    Within thy help and holy physic lies.
    I bear no hatred, blessed man, for, lo,
    My intercession likewise steads my foe.
FRIAR LAURENCE. Be plain, good son, and homely in
    thy drift;
    Riddling confession finds but riddling shrift.
ROMEO. Then plainly know my heart's dear love is set
    On the fair daughter of rich Capulet:
    As mine on hers, so hers is set on mine;
    And all combined, save what thou must combine
    By holy marriage. When and where and how
    We met, we wooed and made exchange of vow,
    I'll tell thee as we pass; but this I pray,
    That thou consent to marry us today.
FRIAR LAURENCE. Holy Saint Francis, what a change is
    here!
    Is Rosaline, whom thou didst love so dear,
    So soon forsaken? Young men's love then lies
    Not truly in their hearts, but in their eyes.
    Jesu Maria, what a deal of brine
    Hath washed thy sallow cheeks for Rosaline!
    How much salt water thrown away in waste,
    To season love, that of it doth not taste!
    The sun not yet thy sighs from heaven clears,
    Thy old groans ring yet in my ancient ears;
    Lo, here upon thy cheek the stain doth sit
    Of an old tear that is not washed off yet.
    If e'er thou wast thyself and these woes thine,
    Thou and these woes were all for Rosaline.
    And art thou changed? Pronounce this sentence then,
    Women may fall, when there's no strength in men.
ROMEO. Thou chid'st me oft for loving Rosaline.
FRIAR LAURENCE. For doting, not for loving, pupil mine.
ROMEO. And bad'st me bury love.
FRIAR LAURENCE.   Not in a grave,
    To lay one in, another out to have.
ROMEO. I pray thee, chide not. She whom I love now
    Doth grace for grace and love for love allow;
    The other did not so.
FRIAR LAURENCE.   O, she knew well
    Thy love did read by rote and could not spell.
    But come, young waverer, come, go with me,
    In one respect I'll thy assistant be;
    For this alliance may so happy prove,
    To turn your households' rancour to pure love.
ROMEO. O, let us hence; I stand on sudden haste.
FRIAR LAURENCE. Wisely and slow; they stumble that
    run fast.
                                        Exeunt

SCENE IV *A street*

Enter BENVOLIO *and* MERCUTIO

MERCUTIO. Where the devil should this Romeo be?
  Came he not home tonight?

BENVOLIO. Not to his father's; I spoke with his man.

MERCUTIO. Ah, that same pale hard-hearted wench,
    that Rosaline,
  Torments him so, that he will sure run mad.

BENVOLIO. Tybalt, the kinsman of old Capulet,
  Hath sent a letter to his father's house.

MERCUTIO. A challenge, on my life.

BENVOLIO. Romeo will answer it.

MERCUTIO. Any man that can write may answer a letter.

BENVOLIO. Nay, he will answer the letter's master, how
  he dares, being dared.

MERCUTIO. Alas, poor Romeo! He is already dead;
  stabbed with a white wench's black eye; shot through
  the ear with a love song; the very pin of his heart
  cleft with the blind bow-boy's butt-shaft; and is he a
  man to encounter Tybalt?

BENVOLIO. Why, what is Tybalt?

MERCUTIO. More than prince of cats, I can tell you.
  O, he is the courageous captain of compliments. He
  fights as you sing prick-song, keeps time, distance, and
  proportion; rests me his minim rest, one, two, and
  the third in your bosom; the very butcher of a silk
  button, a duellist, a duellist; a gentleman of the very
  first house, of the first and second cause. Ah, the
  immortal passado! The punto reverso! The hai!

BENVOLIO. The what?

MERCUTIO. The pox of such antic, lisping, affecting
  fantasticoes; these new tuners of accents! "By Jesu,
  a very good blade! A very tall man! A very good
  whore!" Why, is not this a lamentable thing, grandsire, that we should be thus afflicted with these
  strange flies, these fashionmongers, these perdona-
  mi's, who stand so much on the new form, that they
  cannot sit at ease on the old bench? O, their bones,
  their bones!

Enter ROMEO

BENVOLIO. Here comes Romeo, here comes Romeo.

MERCUTIO. Without his roe, like a dried herring. O
  flesh, flesh, how art thou fishified! Now is he for the
  numbers that Petrarch flowed in: Laura to his lady
  was but a kitchen wench; marry, she had a better
  love to berhyme her; Dido a dowdy; Cleopatra a
  gipsy; Helen and Hero hildings and harlots; Thisbe a
  grey eye or so, but not to the purpose. Signior Romeo,
  bon jour! There's a French salutation to your French
  slop. You gave us the counterfeit fairly last night.

ROMEO. Good morrow to you both. What counterfeit
  did I give you?

MERCUTIO. The slip, sir, the slip; can you not conceive?

ROMEO. Pardon, good Mercutio, my business was great;
  and in such a case as mine a man may strain courtesy.

MERCUTIO. That's as much as to say, such a case as
  yours constrains a man to bow in the hams.

ROMEO. Meaning, to curtsy.

MERCUTIO. Thou hast most kindly hit it.

ROMEO. A most courteous exposition.

MERCUTIO. Nay, I am the very pink of courtesy.

ROMEO. Pink for flower.

MERCUTIO. Right.

ROMEO. Why, then is my pump well flowered.

MERCUTIO. Well said. Follow me this jest now till thou
  hast worn out thy pump, that when the single sole of
  it is worn, the jest may remain after the wearing
  sole singular.

ROMEO. O single-soled jest, solely singular for the
  singleness!

MERCUTIO. Come between us, good Benvolio; my wits
  faint.

ROMEO. Switch and spurs, switch and spurs; or I'll cry
  a match.

MERCUTIO. Nay, if thy wits run the wild goose chase,
  I have done, for thou hast more of the wild goose in
  one of thy wits than, I am sure, I have in my whole
  five. Was I with you there for the goose?

ROMEO. Thou wast never with me for any thing when
  thou wast not there for the goose.

MERCUTIO. I will bite thee by the ear for that jest.

ROMEO. Nay, good goose, bite not.

MERCUTIO. Thy wit is a very bitter sweeting; it is a
  most sharp sauce.

ROMEO. And is it not well served in to a sweet goose?

MERCUTIO. O, here's a wit of cheveril, that stretches
  from an inch narrow to an ell broad!

ROMEO. I stretch it out for that word "broad"; which
  added to the goose, proves thee far and wide a broad
  goose.

MERCUTIO. Why, is not this better now than groaning
  for love? Now art thou sociable, now art thou Romeo;
  now art thou what thou art, by art as well as by
  nature. For this drivelling love is like a great natural,
  that runs lolling up and down to hide his bauble in
  a hole.

BENVOLIO. Stop there, stop there.

MERCUTIO. Thou desirest me to stop in my tale against
  the hair.

BENVOLIO. Thou wouldst else have made thy tale large.

MERCUTIO. O, thou art deceived; I would have made
  it short; for I was come to the whole depth of my tale;
  and meant, indeed, to occupy the argument no longer.

ROMEO. Here's goodly gear!

Enter Nurse *and* PETER

MERCUTIO. A sail, a sail!

BENVOLIO. Two, two; a shirt and a smock.

MERCUTIO. God ye good den, fair gentlewoman.

NURSE. Is it good den?

MERCUTIO. 'Tis no less, I tell you, for the bawdy hand of the dial is now upon the prick of noon.

NURSE. Out upon you! What a man are you!

ROMEO. One, gentlewoman, that God hath made for himself to mar.

NURSE. By my troth, it is well said; "for himself to mar," quoth a'? Gentlemen, can any of you tell me where I may find the young Romeo?

ROMEO. I can tell you; but young Romeo will be older when you have found him than he was when you sought him. I am the youngest of that name, for fault of a worse.

NURSE. You say well.

MERCUTIO. Yea, is the worst well? Very well took, i' faith; wisely, wisely.

NURSE. If you be he, sir, I desire some confidence with you.

BENVOLIO. She will indite him to some supper.

MERCUTIO. A bawd, a bawd, a bawd! So ho!

ROMEO. What hast thou found?

MERCUTIO. No hare, sir; unless a hare, sir, in a lenten pie, that is something stale and hoar ere it be spent.

> [Sings] An old hare hoar,
> And an old hare hoar,
> Is very good meat in lent;
> But a hare that is hoar
> Is too much for a score,
> When it hoars ere it be spent.

Romeo, will you come to your father's? We'll to dinner, thither.

ROMEO. I will follow you.

MERCUTIO. Farewell, ancient lady; farewell, [singing] "lady, lady, lady." *Exeunt* MERCUTIO *and* BENVOLIO

NURSE. Marry, farewell! I pray you, sir, what saucy merchant was this, that was so full of his ropery?

ROMEO. A gentleman, nurse, that loves to hear himself talk, and will speak more in a minute than he will stand to in a month.

NURSE. An a' speak any thing against me, I'll take him down, an a' were lustier than he is, and twenty such Jacks; and if I cannot, I'll find those that shall. Scurvy knave! I am none of his flirt-gills; I am none of his skainsmates. And thou must stand by too, and suffer every knave to use me at his pleasure?

PETER. I saw no man use you at his pleasure; if I had, my weapon should quickly have been out, I warrant you. I dare draw as soon as another man, if I see occasion in a good quarrel, and the law on my side.

NURSE. Now, afore God, I am so vexed, that every part about me quivers. Scurvy knave! Pray you, sir, a word: and as I told you, my young lady bade me inquire you out; what she bade me say, I will keep to myself. But first let me tell ye, if ye should lead her into a

NURSE. Peter!

PETER. Anon!

NURSE. My fan, Peter.

MERCUTIO. Good Peter, to hide her face; for her fan's the fairer face.

NURSE. God ye good morrow, gentlemen.

fool's paradise, as they say, it were a very gross kind
of behaviour, as they say, for the gentlewoman is
young; and, therefore, if you should deal double with
her, truly it were an ill thing to be offered to any
gentlewoman, and very weak dealing.

ROMEO. Nurse, commend me to thy lady and mistress.
I protest unto thee—

NURSE. Good heart, and, i' faith, I will tell her as much.
Lord, Lord, she will be a joyful woman.

ROMEO. What wilt thou tell her, nurse? Thou dost not
mark me.

NURSE. I will tell her, sir, that you do protest; which,
as I take it, is a gentlemanlike offer.

ROMEO. Bid her devise
Some means to come to shrift this afternoon;
And there she shall at Friar Laurence' cell
Be shrived and married. Here is for thy pains.

NURSE. No, truly, sir; not a penny.

ROMEO. Go to; I say you shall.

NURSE. This afternoon, sir? Well, she shall be there.

ROMEO. And stay, good nurse, behind the abbey wall.
Within this hour my man shall be with thee,
And bring thee cords made like a tackled stair;
Which to the high topgallant of my joy
Must be my convoy in the secret night.
Farewell; be trusty, and I'll quit thy pains.
Farewell; commend me to thy mistress.

NURSE. Now God in heaven bless thee! Hark you, sir.

ROMEO. What say'st thou, my dear nurse?

NURSE. Is your man secret? Did you ne'er hear say,
Two may keep counsel, putting one away?

ROMEO. I warrant thee, my man's as true as steel.

NURSE. Well, sir; my mistress is the sweetest lady—
Lord, Lord! when 'twas a little prating thing—O,
there is a nobleman in town, one Paris, that would
fain lay knife aboard; but she, good soul, had as lief
see a toad, a very toad, as see him. I anger her sometimes and tell her that Paris is the properer man; but,
I'll warrant you, when I say so, she looks as pale as
any clout in the versal world. Doth not rosemary and
Romeo begin both with a letter?

ROMEO. Ay, nurse; what of that? Both with an R.

NURSE. Ah, mocker! That's the dog's name; R is for
the—no; I know it begins with some other letter—
and she hath the prettiest sententious of it, of you and
rosemary, that it would do you good to hear it.

ROMEO. Commend me to thy lady.

NURSE. Ay, a thousand times. [Exit Romeo] Peter!

PETER. Anon!

NURSE. Peter, take my fan, and go before, and apace.

                                                        Exeunt

SCENE V Capulet's orchard

Enter JULIET

JULIET. The clock struck nine when I did send the nurse;
In half an hour she promised to return.
Perchance she cannot meet him—that's not so.
O, she is lame! Love's heralds should be thoughts,
Which ten times faster glide than the sun's beams,
Driving back shadows over louring hills.
Therefore do nimble-pinioned doves draw love,
And therefore hath the wind-swift Cupid wings.
Now is the sun upon the highmost hill
Of this day's journey, and from nine till twelve
Is three long hours, yet she is not come.
Had she affections and warm youthful blood,
She would be as swift in motion as a ball;

My words would bandy her to my sweet love,
And his to me.
But old folks, many feign as they were dead;
Unwieldy, slow, heavy and pale as lead.
O God, she comes!

Enter Nurse and PETER

              O honey nurse, what news?
Hast thou met with him? Send thy man away.

NURSE. Peter, stay at the gate.   Exit PETER

JULIET. Now, good sweet nurse—O Lord, why look'st
thou sad?
Though news be sad, yet tell them merrily;

If good, thou shamest the music of sweet news
By playing it to me with so sour a face.

NURSE. I am aweary, give me leave awhile.
Fie, how my bones ache! What a jaunt have I had!

JULIET. I would thou hadst my bones, and I thy news.
Nay, come, I pray thee, speak; good, good nurse,
speak.

NURSE. Jesu, what haste? Can you not stay awhile?
Do you not see that I am out of breath?

JULIET. How art thou out of breath, when thou hast
breath
To say to me that thou art out of breath?
The excuse that thou dost make in this delay
Is longer than the tale thou dost excuse.
Is thy news good, or bad? Answer to that;
Say either, and I'll stay the circumstance.
Let me be satisfied, is't good or bad?

NURSE. Well, you have made a simple choice; you
know not how to choose a man. Romeo! No, not he;
though his face be better than any man's, yet his leg
excels all men's; and for a hand, and a foot, and a
body, though they be not to be talked on, yet they are
past compare. He is not the flower of courtesy, but,
I'll warrant him, as gentle as a lamb. Go thy ways,
wench; serve God. What, have you dined at home?

JULIET. No, no, but all this did I know before.
What says he of our marriage? What of that?

NURSE. Lord, how my head aches! What a head have I!
It beats as it would fall in twenty pieces.
My back o' t' other side—O, my back, my back!

Beshrew your heart for sending me about,
To catch my death with jaunting up and down!

JULIET. I' faith, I am sorry that thou art not well.
Sweet, sweet, sweet nurse, tell me, what says my love?

NURSE. Your love says, like an honest gentleman, and a
courteous, and a kind, and a handsome, and, I warrant, a virtuous—Where is your mother?

JULIET. Where is my mother! Why, she is within;
Where should she be? How oddly thou repliest!
"Your love says, like an honest gentleman,
'Where is your mother?' "

NURSE.   O God's Lady dear!
Are you so hot? Marry, come up, I trow;
Is this the poultice for my aching bones?
Henceforward do your messages yourself.

JULIET. Here's such a coil! Come, what says Romeo?

NURSE. Have you got leave to go to shrift today?

JULIET. I have.

NURSE. Then hie you hence to Friar Laurence' cell;
There stays a husband to make you a wife.
Now comes the wanton blood up in your cheeks,
They'll be in scarlet straight at any news.
Hie you to church; I must another way,
To fetch a ladder, by the which your love
Must climb a bird's nest soon when it is dark.
I am the drudge and toil in your delight,
But you shall bear the burden soon at night.
Go; I'll to dinner; hie you to the cell.

JULIET. Hie to high fortune! Honest nurse, farewell.

Exeunt

SCENE VI *Friar Laurence's cell*

Enter FRIAR LAURENCE and ROMEO

FRIAR LAURENCE. So smile the heavens upon this holy
act,
That after hours with sorrow chide us not!

ROMEO. Amen, amen! But come what sorrow can,
It cannot countervail the exchange of joy
That one short minute gives me in her sight.
Do thou but close our hands with holy words,
Then love-devouring death do what he dare;
It is enough I may but call her mine.

FRIAR LAURENCE. These violent delights have violent
ends
And in their triumph die, like fire and powder,
Which as they kiss consume. The sweetest honey
Is loathsome in his own deliciousness
And in the taste confounds the appetite.
Therefore love moderately; long love doth so;
Too swift arrives as tardy as too slow.

Enter JULIET

Here comes the lady. O, so light a foot
Will ne'er wear out the everlasting flint
A lover may bestride the gossamer

That idles in the wanton summer air,
And yet not fall; so light is vanity.

JULIET. Good even to my ghostly confessor.

FRIAR LAURENCE. Romeo shall thank thee, daughter,
for us both.

JULIET. As much to him, else is his thanks too much.

ROMEO. Ah, Juliet, if the measure of thy joy
Be heaped like mine and that thy skill be more
To blazon it, then sweeten with thy breath
This neighbour air, and let rich music's tongue
Unfold the imagined happiness that both
Receive in either by this dear encounter.

JULIET. Conceit, more rich in matter than in words,
Brags of his substance, not of ornament.
They are but beggars that can count their worth;
But my true love is grown to such excess
I cannot sum up sum of half my wealth.

FRIAR LAURENCE. Come, come with me, and we will
make short work;
For, by your leaves, you shall not stay alone
Till holy church incorporate two in one.   *Exeunt*

ACT III

SCENE I *A public place*

Enter MERCUTIO, BENVOLIO, Page, *and* Servants

BENVOLIO. I pray thee, good Mercutio, let's retire.
The day is hot, the Capulets abroad,
And, if we meet, we shall not scape a brawl;
For now, these hot days, is the mad blood stirring.

MERCUTIO. Thou art like one of those fellows that when
he enters the confines of a tavern claps me his sword
upon the table and says "God send me no need of
thee!" and by the operation of the second cup draws
it on the drawer, when indeed there is no need.

BENVOLIO. Am I like such a fellow?

MERCUTIO. Come, come, thou art as hot a Jack in thy
mood as any in Italy, and as soon moved to be moody,
and as soon moody to be moved.

BENVOLIO. And what to?

MERCUTIO. Nay, an there were two such, we should
have none shortly, for one would kill the other. Thou!
Why, thou wilt quarrel with a man that hath a hair
more, or a hair less, in his beard, than thou hast;
thou wilt quarrel with a man for cracking nuts, having
no other reason but because thou hast hazel eyes;
what eye but such an eye would spy out such a quarrel?
Thy head is as full of quarrels as an egg is full of meat,
and yet thy head hath been beaten as addle as an egg
for quarrelling; thou hast quarrelled with a man for
coughing in the street, because he hath wakened thy
dog that hath lain asleep in the sun. Didst thou not fall
out with a tailor for wearing his new doublet before
Easter? With another, for tying his new shoes with
old ribbon? And yet thou wilt tutor me from quarrelling!

BENVOLIO. An I were so apt to quarrel as thou art, any
man should buy the fee-simple of my life for an hour
and a quarter.

MERCUTIO. The fee-simple! O simple!

BENVOLIO. By my head, here come the Capulets.

MERCUTIO. By my heel, I care not.

Enter TYBALT *and others*

TYBALT. Follow me close, for I will speak to them.
Gentlemen, good den: a word with one of you.

MERCUTIO. And but one word with one of us? Couple
it with something; make it a word and a blow.

TYBALT. You shall find me apt enough to that, sir, an
you will give me occasion.

MERCUTIO. Could you not take some occasion without
giving?

TYBALT. Mercutio, thou consort'st with Romeo—

MERCUTIO. Consort! What, dost thou make us minstrels? An thou make minstrels of us, look to hear
nothing but discords. Here's my fiddlestick; here's
that shall make you dance. 'Zounds, consort!

BENVOLIO. We talk here in the public haunt of men.
Either withdraw unto some private place,
And reason coldly of your grievances,
Or else depart; here all eyes gaze on us.

MERCUTIO. Men's eyes were made to look, and let
them gaze;
I will not budge for no man's pleasure, I.

Enter ROMEO

TYBALT. Well, peace be with you, sir. Here comes my
man.

MERCUTIO. But I'll be hanged, sir, if he wear your livery.
Marry, go before to field, he'll be your follower;
Your worship in that sense may call him "man."

TYBALT. Romeo, the hate I bear thee can afford
No better term than this—thou art a villain.

ROMEO. Tybalt, the reason that I have to love thee
Doth much excuse the appertaining rage
To such a greeting. Villain am I none;
Therefore farewell; I see thou know'st me not.

TYBALT. Boy, this shall not excuse the injuries
That thou hast done me; therefore turn and draw.

ROMEO. I do protest, I never injured thee,
But love thee better than thou canst devise,
Till thou shalt know the reason of my love;
And so, good Capulet—which name I tender
As dearly as my own—be satisfied.

MERCUTIO. O calm, dishonourable, vile submission!
Alla stoccata carries it away.   *Draws*
Tybalt, you ratcatcher, will you walk?

TYBALT. What wouldst thou have with me?

MERCUTIO. Good king of cats, nothing but one of your
nine lives; that I mean to make bold withal, and, as you
shall use me hereafter, dry-beat the rest of the eight.
Will you pluck your sword out of his pilcher by the
ears? Make haste, lest mine be about your ears ere
it be out.

TYBALT. I am for you.   *Drawing*

ROMEO. Gentle Mercutio, put thy rapier up.

MERCUTIO. Come, sir, your passado.   *They fight*

ROMEO. Draw, Benvolio; beat down their weapons.
Gentlemen, for shame, forbear this outrage!
Tybalt, Mercutio, the prince expressly hath
Forbidden bandying in Verona streets.
Hold, Tybalt! Good Mercutio!

TYBALT *under* ROMEO's *arm stabs* MERCUTIO,
and flies with his followers

MERCUTIO.   I am hurt.
A plague o' both your houses! I am sped.
Is he gone, and hath nothing?

BENVOLIO.   What, art thou hurt?

MERCUTIO. Ay, ay, a scratch, a scratch; marry, 'tis
enough.
Where is my page? Go, villain, fetch a surgeon.

Exit Page

ROMEO. Courage, man; the hurt cannot be much.

MERCUTIO. No, 'tis not so deep as a well, nor so wide
as a church door; but 'tis enough, 'twill serve. Ask
for me tomorrow, and you shall find me a grave man.
I am peppered, I warrant, for this world. A plague o'
both your houses! 'Zounds, a dog, a rat, a mouse, a
cat, to scratch a man to death! A braggart, a rogue,
a villain, that fights by the book of arithmetic! Why
the devil came you between us? I was hurt under
your arm.

ROMEO. I thought all for the best.

MERCUTIO. Help me into some house, Benvolio,
Or I shall faint. A plague o' both your houses!
They have made worms' meat of me; I have it,
And soundly too. Your houses!

Exeunt MERCUTIO and BENVOLIO

ROMEO. This gentleman, the Prince's near ally,
My very friend, hath got his mortal hurt
In my behalf; my reputation stained
With Tybalt's slander—Tybalt, that an hour
Hath been my kinsman! O sweet Juliet,
Thy beauty hath made me effeminate
And in my temper softened valour's steel!

Re-enter BENVOLIO

BENVOLIO. O Romeo, Romeo, brave Mercutio's dead!
That gallant spirit hath aspired the clouds,
Which too untimely here did scorn the earth.

ROMEO. This day's black fate on more days doth depend;
This but begins the woe others must end.

BENVOLIO. Here comes the furious Tybalt back again.

ROMEO. Alive, in triumph! And Mercutio slain!
Away to heaven, respective lenity,
And fire-eyed fury be my conduct now!

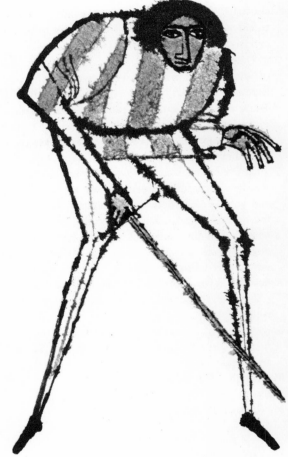

Re-enter TYBALT

Now, Tybalt, take the "villain" back again,
That late thou gavest me; for Mercutio's soul
Is but a little way above our heads,
Staying for thine to keep him company.
Either thou, or I, or both, must go with him.

TYBALT. Thou, wretched boy, that didst consort him
here,
Shalt with him hence.

ROMEO.   This shall determine that.

They fight; TYBALT falls

BENVOLIO. Romeo, away, be gone!
  The citizens are up, and Tybalt slain.
  Stand not amazed. The Prince will doom thee death,
  If thou art taken. Hence, be gone, away!
ROMEO. O, I am fortune's fool!
BENVOLIO.   Why dost thou stay?
                          Exit ROMEO

          Enter Citizens, &c.

FIRST CITIZEN. Which way ran he that killed Mercutio?
  Tybalt, that murderer, which way ran he?
BENVOLIO. There lies that Tybalt.
FIRST CITIZEN.   Up, sir, go with me;
  I charge thee in the Prince's name, obey.

Enter Prince, *attended;* MONTAGUE, CAPULET, *their* Wives,
             and others

PRINCE. Where are the vile beginners of this fray?
BENVOLIO. O noble prince, I can discover all
  The unlucky manage of this fatal brawl.
  There lies the man, slain by young Romeo,
  That slew thy kinsman, brave Mercutio.
LADY CAPULET. Tybalt, my cousin! O my brother's
    child!
  O Prince! O cousin! Husband! O, the blood is split
  Of my dear kinsman! Prince, as thou art true,
  For blood of ours, shed blood of Montague.
  O cousin, cousin!
PRINCE. Benvolio, who began this bloody fray?
BENVOLIO. Tybalt, here slain, whom Romeo's hand did
    slay;
  Romeo that spoke him fair, bade him bethink
  How nice the quarrel was, and urged withal
  Your high displeasure. All this uttered
  With gentle breath, calm look, knees humbly bowed,
  Could not take truce with the unruly spleen
  Of Tybalt deaf to peace, but that he tilts
  With piercing steel at bold Mercutio's breast,
  Who, all as hot, turns deadly point to point,
  And, with a martial scorn, with one hand beats
  Cold death aside, and with the other sends
  It back to Tybalt, whose dexterity
  Retorts it. Romeo he cries aloud,
  "Hold, friends! Friends, part!" and, swifter than his
    tongue,
  His agile arm beats down their fatal points,
  And 'twixt them rushes; underneath whose arm
  An envious thrust from Tybalt hit the life
  Of stout Mercutio, and then Tybalt fled;
  But by and by comes back to Romeo,
  Who had but newly entertained revenge,
  And to 't they go like lightning, for, ere I
  Could draw to part them, was stout Tybalt slain,
  And, as he fell, did Romeo turn and fly.
  This is the truth, or let Benvolio die.
LADY CAPULET. He is a kinsman to the Montague;

Affection makes him false; he speaks not true.
Some twenty of them fought in this black strife,
And all those twenty could but kill one life.
I beg for justice, which thou, Prince, must give;
Romeo slew Tybalt, Romeo must not live.
PRINCE. Romeo slew him, he slew Mercutio;
  Who now the price of his dear blood doth owe?
MONTAGUE. Not Romeo, Prince, he was Mercutio's
    friend;
  His fault concludes but what the law should end,
  The life of Tybalt.
PRINCE.   And for that offence

Immediately we do exile him hence.
I have an interest in your hate's proceeding,
My blood for your rude brawls doth lie a-bleeding;
But I'll amerce you with so strong a fine
That you shall all repent the loss of mine.
I will be deaf to pleading and excuses;
Nor tears nor prayers shall purchase out abuses.
Therefore use none. Let Romeo hence in haste,
Else, when he's found, that hour is his last.
Bear hence this body and attend our will;
Mercy but murders, pardoning those that kill.

                                                                    Exeunt

SCENE II *Capulet's orchard*

Enter JULIET

JULIET. Gallop apace, you fiery-footed steeds,
  Towards Phœbus' lodging; such a waggoner
  As Phæthon would whip you to the west,
  And bring in cloudy night immediately.
  Spread thy close curtain, love-performing night,
  That runaways' eyes may wink, and Romeo
  Leap to these arms, untalked of and unseen.
  Lovers can see to do their amorous rites
  By their own beauties; or, if love be blind,
  It best agrees with night. Come, civil night,
  Thou sober-suited matron, all in black,
  And learn me how to lose a winning match,
  Played for a pair of stainless maidenhoods.
  Hood my unmanned blood, bating in my cheeks,
  With thy black mantle; till strange love, grown bold,
  Think true love acted simple modesty.
  Come, night; come, Romeo; come, thou day in night;
  For thou wilt lie upon the wings of night
  Whiter than new snow on a raven's back.
  Come, gentle night, come, loving, black-browed
    night,
  Give me my Romeo; and, when he shall die,
  Take him and cut him out in little stars,
  And he will make the face of heaven so fine
  That all the world will be in love with night
  And pay no worship to the garish sun.
  O, I have bought the mansion of a love,
  But not possessed it, and, though I am sold,
  Not yet enjoyed. So tedious is this day
  As is the night before some festival
  To an impatient child that hath new robes
  And may not wear them. O, here comes my nurse,
  And she brings news; and every tongue that speaks
  But Romeo's name speaks heavenly eloquence.

Enter Nurse, *with cords*

  Now, nurse, what news? What hast thou there?
    The cords
  That Romeo bid thee fetch?

NURSE.   Ay, ay, the cords.
                                Throws them down
JULIET. Ay me! What news? Why dost thou wring thy
    hands?
NURSE. Ah, well-a-day! He's dead, he's dead, he's
    dead!
  We are undone, lady, we are undone!
  Alack the day! He's gone, he's killed, he's dead!
JULIET. Can heaven be so envious?
NURSE.   Romeo can,
  Though heaven cannot. O Romeo, Romeo!
  Who ever would have thought it? Romeo!
JULIET. What devil art thou, that dost torment me thus?
  This torture should be roared in dismal hell.
  Hath Romeo slain himself? Say thou but "ay,"
  And that bare vowel "I" shall poison more
  Than the death-darting eye of cockatrice.
  I am not I, if there be such an I;
  Or those eyes shut, that make thee answer "ay."
  If he be slain, say "ay"; or if not, "no."
  Brief sounds determine of my weal or woe.
NURSE. I saw the wound, I saw it with mine eyes—
  God save the mark!—here on his manly breast.
  A piteous corpse, a bloody piteous corpse;
  Pale, pale as ashes, all bedaubed in blood,
  All in gore-blood; I swounded at the sight.
JULIET. O, break, my heart! Poor bankrupt, break at
    once!
  To prison, eyes, ne'er look on liberty!
  Vile earth, to earth resign; end motion here;
  And thou and Romeo press one heavy bier!
NURSE. O Tybalt, Tybalt, the best friend I had!
  O courteous Tybalt! Honest gentleman!
  That ever I should live to see thee dead!
JULIET. What storm is this that blows so contrary?
  Is Romeo slaughtered, and is Tybalt dead?
  My dear-loved cousin, and my dearer lord?
  Then, dreadful trumpet, sound the general doom!
  For who is living, if those two are gone?

NURSE. Tybalt is gone, and Romeo banished;
  Romeo that killed him, he is banished.
JULIET. O God! Did Romeo's hand shed Tybalt's blood?
NURSE. It did, it did; alas the day, it did!
JULIET. O serpent heart, hid with a flowering face!
  Did ever dragon keep so fair a cave?
  Beautiful tyrant! Fiend angelical!
  Dove-feathered raven! Wolvish-ravening lamb!
  Despised substance of divinest show!
  Just opposite to what thou justly seem'st,
  A damned saint, an honourable villain!
  O nature, what hadst thou to do in hell,
  When thou didst bower the spirit of a fiend
  In mortal paradise of such sweet flesh?
  Was ever book containing such vile matter
  So fairly bound? O, that deceit should dwell
  In such a gorgeous palace!
NURSE.   There's no trust,
  No faith, no honesty in men; all perjured,
  All forsworn, all naught, all dissemblers.
  Ah, where's my man? Give me some aqua vitæ.
  These griefs, these woes, these sorrows make me old.
  Shame come to Romeo!
JULIET.   Blistered be thy tongue
  For such a wish! He was not born to shame.
  Upon his brow shame is ashamed to sit;
  For 'tis a throne where honour may be crowned
  Sole monarch of the universal earth.
  O, what a beast was I to chide at him!
NURSE. Will you speak well of him that killed your
    cousin?
JULIET. Shall I speak ill of him that is my husband?
  Ah, poor my lord, what tongue shall smooth thy name,
  When I, thy three-hours wife, have mangled it?
  But, wherefore, villain, didst thou kill my cousin?
  That villain cousin would have killed my husband.
  Back, foolish tears, back to your native spring;
  Your tributary drops belong to woe,
  Which you, mistaking, offer up to joy.
  My husband lives, that Tybalt would have slain;

And Tybalt's dead, that would have slain my husband.
All this is comfort; wherefore weep I then?
Some word there was, worser than Tybalt's death,
That murdered me. I would forget it fain;
But, O, it presses to my memory,
Like damned guilty deeds to sinners' minds.
"Tybalt is dead, and Romeo—banished";
That "banished," that one word "banished,"
Hath slain ten thousand Tybalts. Tybalt's death
Was woe enough, if it had ended there;
Or, if sour woe delights in fellowship
And needly will be ranked with other griefs,
Why followed not, when she said "Tybalt's dead,"
Thy father, or thy mother, nay, or both,
Which modern lamentation might have moved?
But with a rearward following Tybalt's death,
"Romeo is banished," to speak that word,
Is father, mother, Tybalt, Romeo, Juliet,
All slain, all dead. "Romeo is banished!"
There is no end, no limit, measure, bound,
In that word's death; no words can that woe sound.
Where is my father, and my mother, nurse?
NURSE. Weeping and wailing over Tybalt's corpse.
  Will you go to them? I will bring you thither.
JULIET. Wash they his wounds with tears; mine shall be
    spent,
  When theirs are dry, for Romeo's banishment.
  Take up those cords. Poor ropes, you are beguiled,
  Both you and I; for Romeo is exiled.
  He made you for a highway to my bed;
  But I, a maid, die maiden-widowed.
  Come, cords, come, nurse; I'll to my wedding-bed;
  And death, not Romeo, take my maidenhead!
NURSE. Hie to your chamber: I'll find Romeo
  To comfort you. I wot well where he is.
  Hark ye, your Romeo will be here at night.
  I'll to him; he is hid at Laurence' cell.
JULIET. O, find him! Give this ring to my true knight,
  And bid him come to take his last farewell.

Exeunt

SCENE III *Friar Laurence's cell*

Enter FRIAR LAURENCE

FRIAR LAURENCE. Romeo, come forth; come forth,
    thou fearful man.
  Affliction is enamoured of thy parts,
  And thou art wedded to calamity.

Enter ROMEO

ROMEO. Father, what news? What is the Prince's doom?
  What sorrow craves acquaintance at my hand,
    That I yet know not?
FRIAR LAURENCE.   Too familiar
  Is my dear son with such sour company;

I bring thee tidings of the Prince's doom.
ROMEO. What less than doomsday is the Prince's doom?
FRIAR LAURENCE. A gentler judgement vanished from
    his lips,
  Not body's death, but body's banishment.
ROMEO. Ha, banishment! Be merciful, say "death";
  For exile hath more terror in his look,
  Much more than death. Do not say "banishment."
FRIAR LAURENCE. Hence from Verona art thou banished.
  Be patient, for the world is broad and wide.
ROMEO. There is no world without Verona walls

But purgatory, torture, hell itself.
Hence-banished is banished from the world,
And world's exile is death; then banished,
Is death mistermed; calling death banishment,
Thou cutt'st my head off with a golden axe,
And smilest upon the stroke that murders me.

FRIAR LAURENCE. O deadly sin! O rude unthankfulness!
Thy fault our law calls death; but the kind prince,
Taking thy part, hath rushed aside the law,
And turned that black word death to banishment.
This is dear mercy, and thou seest it not.

ROMEO. 'Tis torture, and not mercy. Heaven is here,
Where Juliet lives; and every cat and dog
And little mouse, every unworthy thing,
Live here in heaven and may look on her;
But Romeo may not. More validity,
More honourable state, more courtship lives
In carrion flies than Romeo. They may seize
On the white wonder of dear Juliet's hand
And steal immortal blessing from her lips,
Who, even in pure and vestal modesty,
Still blush, as thinking their own kisses sin;
But Romeo may not; he is banished.
Flies may do this, but I from this must fly.
They are free men, but I am banished
And say'st thou yet that exile is not death?
Hadst thou no poison mixed, no sharp-ground knife,
No sudden mean of death, though ne'er so mean,
But "banished" to kill me?—"banished"?
O friar, the damned use that word in hell;
Howlings attend it. How hast thou the heart,
Being a divine, a ghostly confessor,
A sin-absolver, and my friend professed,
To mangle me with that word "banished"?

FRIAR LAURENCE. Thou fond mad man, hear me but
speak a word.

ROMEO. O, thou wilt speak again of banishment.

FRIAR LAURENCE. I'll give thee armour to keep off that
word;
Adversity's sweet milk, philosophy,
To comfort thee, though thou art banished.

ROMEO. Yet "banished"? Hang up philosophy!
Unless philosophy can make a Juliet,
Displant a town, reverse a prince's doom,
It helps not, it prevails not. Talk no more.

FRIAR LAURENCE. O, then I see that madmen have no
ears.

ROMEO. How should they, when that wise men have
no eyes?

FRIAR LAURENCE. Let me dispute with thee of thy estate.

ROMEO. Thou canst not speak of that thou dost not feel.
Wert thou as young as I, Juliet thy love,
An hour but married, Tybalt murdered,
Doting like me and like me banished,
Then mightst thou speak, then mightst thou tear they
hair,
And fall upon the ground, as I do now,
Taking the measure of an unmade grave.

Knocking within

FRIAR LAURENCE. Arise; one knocks; good Romeo,
hide thyself.

ROMEO. Not I; unless the breath of heartsick groans,
Mistlike, infold me from the search of eyes.

Knocking within

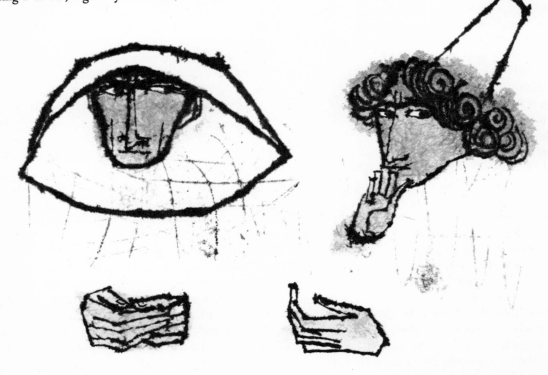

FRIAR LAURENCE. Hark, how they knock! Who's there?
  Romeo, arise;
  Thou wilt be taken. Stay awhile! Stand up;   *Knocking*
  Run to my study. By and by! God's will,
  What simpleness is this! I come, I come!   *Knocking*
  Who knocks so hard? Whence come you? What's
  your will?
NURSE. [*Within*] Let me come in, and you shall know
  my errand;
  I come from Lady Juliet.
FRIAR LAURENCE.   Welcome, then.

Enter Nurse

NURSE. O holy friar, O, tell me, holy friar,
  Where is my lady's lord, where's Romeo?
FRIAR LAURENCE. There on the ground, with his own
  tears made drunk.
NURSE. O, he is even in my mistress' case,
  Just in her case! O woeful sympathy!
  Piteous predicament! Even so lies she,
  Blubbering and weeping, weeping and blubbering.
  Stand up, stand up; stand, an you be a man.
  For Juliet's sake, for her sake, rise and stand;
  Why should you fall into so deep an O?
ROMEO. Nurse!
NURSE. Ah sir! Ah sir! Well, death's the end of all.
ROMEO. Spakest thou of Juliet? How is it with her?
  Doth she not think me an old murderer,
  Now I have stained the childhood of our joy
  With blood removed but little from her own?
  Where is she? And how doth she? And what says
  My concealed lady to our cancelled love?
NURSE. O, she says nothing, sir, but weeps and weeps;
  And now falls on her bed; and then starts up,
  And Tybalt calls; and then on Romeo cries,
  And then down falls again.
ROMEO.   As if that name,
  Shot from the deadly level of a gun,
  Did murder her; as that name's cursed hand
  Murdered her kinsman. O, tell me, friar, tell me,
  In what vile part of this anatomy
  Doth my name lodge? Tell me, that I may sack
  The hateful mansion.   *Drawing his sword*
FRIAR LAURENCE.   Hold thy desperate hand.
  Art thou a man? Thy form cries out thou art.
  Thy tears are womanish; thy wild acts denote
  The unreasonable fury of a beast.
  Unseemly woman in a seeming man!
  Or ill-beseeming beast in seeming both!
  Thou hast amazed me. By my holy order,
  I thought thy disposition better tempered.
  Hast thou slain Tybalt? Wilt thou slay thyself?
  And slay thy lady too that lives in thee,
  By doing damned hate upon thyself?
  Why rail'st thou on thy birth, the heaven, and earth?
  Since birth, and heaven, and earth, all three do meet

In thee at once; which thou at once wouldst lose.
Fie, fie, thou shamest thy shape, thy love, thy wit;
Which, like a usurer, abound'st in all,
And usest none in that true use indeed
Which should bedeck thy shape, thy love, thy wit.
Thy noble shape is but a form of wax,
Digressing from the valour of a man;
Thy dear love sworn but hollow perjury,
Killing that love which thou hast vowed to cherish;
Thy wit, that ornament to shape and love,
Misshapen in the conduct of them both,
Like powder in a skill-less soldier's flask,
Is set afire by thine own ignorance,
And thou dismembered with thine own defence.
What, rouse thee, man! Thy Juliet is alive,
For whose dear sake thou wast but lately dead;
There art thou happy. Tybalt would kill thee,
But thou slew'st Tybalt; there art thou happy too.
The law that threatened death becomes thy friend
And turns it to exile; there art thou happy.
A pack of blessings lights upon thy back;
Happiness courts thee in her best array;
But, like a misbehaved and sullen wench,
Thou pout'st upon thy fortune and thy love.
Take heed, take heed, for such die miserable.
Go, get thee to thy love, as was decreed,
Ascend her chamber, hence and comfort her.
But look thou stay not till the watch be set,
For then thou canst not pass to Mantua;
Where thou shalt live, till we can find a time
To blaze your marriage, reconcile your friends,
Beg pardon of the prince, and call thee back
With twenty hundred thousand times more joy
Than thou went'st forth in lamentation.
Go before, nurse. Commend me to thy lady;
And bid her hasten all the house to bed,
Which heavy sorrow makes them apt unto.
Romeo is coming.
NURSE. O Lord, I could have stayed here all the night
  To hear good counsel. O, what learning is!
  My lord, I'll tell my lady you will come.
ROMEO. Do so, and bid my sweet prepare to chide.
NURSE. Here, sir, a ring she bid me give you, sir.
  Hie you, make haste, for it grows very late.   *Exit*
ROMEO. How well my comfort is revived by this!
FRIAR LAURENCE. Go hence; good night; and here
  stands all your state.
  Either be gone before the watch be set,
  Or by the break of day disguised from hence.
  Sojourn in Mantua; I'll find out your man,
  And he shall signify from time to time
  Every good hap to you that chances here.
  Give me thy hand; 'tis late; farewell; good night.
ROMEO. But that a joy past joy calls out on me,
  It were a grief, so brief to part with thee. Farewell.
                                    Exeunt

SCENE IV *A room in Capulet's house*

Enter CAPULET, LADY CAPULET, *and* PARIS

CAPULET. Things have fall'n out, sir, so unluckily,
That we have had no time to move our daughter.
Look you, she loved her kinsman Tybalt dearly,
And so did I—well, we were born to die.
'Tis very late, she'll not come down tonight.
I promise you, but for your company,
I would have been abed an hour ago.
PARIS. These times of woe afford no time to woo.
Madam, good night; commend me to your
daughter.
LADY CAPULET. I will, and know her mind early
tomorrow;
Tonight she is mewed up to her heaviness.
CAPULET. Sir Paris, I will make a desperate tender
Of my child's love. I think she will be ruled
In all respects by me; nay, more, I doubt it not.
Wife, go you to her ere you go to bed;
Acquaint her here of my son Paris' love;
And bid her, mark you me, on Wednesday next—
But, soft! What day is this?

PARIS. Monday, my lord.
CAPULET. Monday! Ha, ha! Well, Wednesday is too
soon,
O' Thursday let it be—o' Thursday, tell her,
She shall be married to this noble earl.
Will you be ready? Do you like this haste?
We'll keep no great ado—a friend or two;
For, hark you, Tybalt being slain so late,
It may be thought we held him carelessly,
Being our kinsman, if we revel much.
Therefore we'll have some half a dozen friends,
And there an end. But what say you to Thursday?
PARIS. My lord, I would that Thursday were tomorrow.
CAPULET. Well, get you gone. O' Thursday be it, then.
Go you to Juliet ere you go to bed,
Prepare her, wife, against this wedding day.
Farewell, my lord. Light to my chamber, ho!
Afore me! It is so very very late,
That we may call it early by and by.
Good night. *Exeunt*

SCENE V *Capulet's orchard*

Enter ROMEO *and* JULIET *above, at the window*

JULIET. Wilt thou be gone? It is not yet near day.
It was the nightingale, and not the lark,
That pierced the fearful hollow of thine ear;
Nightly she sings on yond pomegranate tree.
Believe me, love, it was the nightingale.
ROMEO. It was the lark, the herald of the morn,
No nightingale. Look, love, what envious streaks
Do lace the severing clouds in yonder east.
Night's candles are burnt out, and jocund day
Stands tiptoe on the misty mountain tops.
I must be gone and live, or stay and die.
JULIET. Yond light is not daylight, I know it, I.
It is some meteor that the sun exhales,
To be to thee this night a torchbearer,
And light thee on thy way to Mantua.
Therefore stay yet; thou need'st not to be gone.
ROMEO. Let me be ta'en, let me be put to death;
I am content, so thou wilt have it so.
I'll say yon grey is not the morning's eye,
'Tis but the pale reflex of Cynthia's brow;
Nor that is not the lark, whose notes do beat
The vaulty heaven so high above our heads.
I have more care to stay than will to go.
Come, death, and welcome! Juliet wills it so.
How is't, my soul? let's talk; it is not day.
JULIET. It is, it is; hie hence, be gone, away!
It is the lark that sings so out of tune,
Straining harsh discords and unpleasing sharps.

Some say the lark makes sweet division;
This doth not so, for she divideth us.
Some say the lark and loathed toad change eyes;
O, now I would they had changed voices too!
Since arm from arm that voice doth us affray,
Hunting thee hence with hunt's-up to the day.
O, now be gone; more light and light it grows.
ROMEO. More light and light; more dark and dark our
woes!

Enter Nurse, *to the chamber*

NURSE. Madam!
JULIET. Nurse?
NURSE. Your lady mother is coming to your chamber.
The day is broke; be wary, look about. *Exit*
JULIET. Then, window, let day in, and let life out.
ROMEO. Farewell, farewell! One kiss, and I'll descend.
He goes down
JULIET. Art thou gone so? Love, lord, ay, husband,
friend!
I must hear from thee every day in the hour,
For in a minute there are many days.
O, by this count I shall be much in years
Ere I again behold my Romeo!
ROMEO. Farewell!
I will omit no opportunity
That may convey my greetings, love, to thee.
JULIET. O, think'st thou we shall ever meet again?

ROMEO. I doubt it not; and all these woes shall serve
  For sweet discourses in our time to come.
JULIET. O God, I have an ill-divining soul!
  Methinks I see thee, now thou art below,
  As one dead in the bottom of a tomb.
  Either my eyesight fails, or thou look'st pale.
ROMEO. And trust me, love, in my eye so do you.
  Dry sorrow drinks our blood. Adieu, adieu!   *Exit*
JULIET. O fortune, fortune! All men call thee fickle.
  If thou art fickle, what dost thou with him
  That is renowned for faith? Be fickle, fortune;
  For then, I hope, thou wilt not keep him long,
  But send him back.
LADY CAPULET. [*Within*] Ho, daughter! Are you up?
JULIET. Who is 't that calls? Is it my lady mother?
  Is she not down so late, or up so early?
  What unaccustomed cause procures her hither?

Enter LADY CAPULET

LADY CAPULET. Why, how now, Juliet!
JULIET.   Madam, I am not well.
LADY CAPULET. Evermore weeping for your cousin's
    death?
  What, wilt thou wash him from his grave with tears?
  An if thou couldst, thou couldst not make him live;
  Therefore, have done. Some grief shows much of love;
  But much of grief shows still some want of wit.
JULIET. Yet let me weep for such a feeling loss.
LADY CAPULET. So shall you feel the loss, but not the
    friend
  Which you weep for.

JULIET.   Feeling so the loss,
  I cannot choose but ever weep the friend.
LADY CAPULET. Well, girl, thou weep'st not so much
    for his death,
  As that the villain lives which slaughtered him.
JULIET. What villain, madam?
LADY CAPULET.   That same villain, Romeo.
JULIET. [*Aside*] Villain and he be many miles asunder—
  God pardon him! I do, with all my heart;
  And yet no man like he doth grieve my heart.
LADY CAPULET. That is, because the traitor murderer
    lives.
JULIET. Ay, madam, from the reach of these my hands.
  Would none but I might venge my cousin's death!
LADY CAPULET. We will have vengeance for it, fear thou
    not.
  Then weep no more. I'll send to one in Mantua,
  Where that same banished runagate doth live,
  Shall give him such an unaccustomed dram,
  That he shall soon keep Tybalt company.
  And then, I hope, thou wilt be satisfied.
JULIET. Indeed, I never shall be satisfied
  With Romeo, till I behold him—dead—
  Is my poor heart so for a kinsman vexed.
  Madam, if you could find out but a man
  To bear a poison, I would temper it;
  That Romeo should, upon receipt thereof,
  Soon sleep in quiet. O, how my heart abhors
  To hear him named, and cannot come to him,
  To wreak the love I bore my cousin
  Upon his body that hath slaughtered him!

LADY CAPULET. Find thou the means, and I'll find such
  a man.
  But now I'll tell thee joyful tidings, girl.
JULIET. And joy comes well in such a needy time.
  What are they, I beseech your ladyship?
LADY CAPULET. Well, well, thou hast a careful father,
  child;
  One who, to put thee from thy heaviness,
  Hath sorted out a sudden day of joy,
  That thou expect'st not nor I looked not for.
JULIET. Madam, in happy time, what day is that?
LADY CAPULET. Marry, my child, early next Thursday
  morn,
  The gallant, young and noble gentleman,
  The County Paris, at Saint Peter's Church,
  Shall happily make thee there a joyful bride.
JULIET. Now, by Saint Peter's Church and Peter, too
  He shall not make me there a joyful bride.
  I wonder at this haste; that I must wed
  Ere he, that should be husband, comes to woo.
  I pray you, tell my lord and father, madam,
  I will not marry yet; and, when I do, I swear,
  It shall be Romeo, whom you know I hate,
  Rather than Paris. These are news indeed!
LADY CAPULET. Here comes your father; tell him so
  yourself,
  And see how he will take it at your hands.

Enter CAPULET *and* Nurse

CAPULET. When the sun sets, the air doth drizzle dew;
  But for the sunset of my brother's son
  It rains downright.
  How now! A conduit, girl? What, still in tears?
  Evermore showering? In one little body
  Thou counterfeit'st a bark, a sea, a wind;
  For still thy eyes, which I may call the sea,
  Do ebb and flow with tears; the bark thy body is,
  Sailing in this salt flood; the winds, thy sighs;
  Who, raging with thy tears, and they with them,
  Without a sudden calm, will overset
  Thy tempest-tossed body. How now, wife!
  Have you delivered to her our decree?
LADY CAPULET. Ay, sir; but she will none, she gives
  you thanks.
  I would the fool were married to her grave!
CAPULET. Soft! Take me with you, take me with you,
  wife.
  How! Will she none? Doth she not give us thanks?
  Is she not proud? Doth she not count her blest,
  Unworthy as she is, that we have wrought
  So worthy a gentleman to be her bridegroom?
JULIET. Not proud, you have; but thankful, that you have.
  Proud can I never be of what I hate;
  But thankful even for hate, that is meant love.
CAPULET. How now, how now, chop-logic! What is
  this?

"Proud," and "I thank you," and "I thank you not";
  And yet "not proud." Mistress minion, you,
  Thank me no thankings, nor proud me no prouds,
  But fettle your fine joints 'gainst Thursday next,
  To go with Paris to Saint Peter's Church,
  Or I will drag thee on a hurdle thither.
  Out, you green-sickness carrion! Out, you baggage!
  You tallow-face!
LADY CAPULET.   Fie, fie! What, are you mad?
JULIET. Good father, I beseech you on my knees,
  Hear me with patience but to speak a word.
CAPULET. Hang thee, young baggage! Disobedient
  wretch!
  I tell thee what: Get thee to church o' Thursday,
  Or never after look me in the face.
  Speak not, reply not, do not answer me;
  My fingers itch. Wife, we scarce thought us blest
  That God had lent us but this only child;
  But now I see this one is one too much,
  And that we have a curse in having her.
  Out on her, hilding!
NURSE.   God in heaven bless her!
  You are to blame, my lord, to rate her so.
CAPULET. And why, my lady wisdom? Hold your tongue,
  Good prudence; smatter with your gossips, go.
NURSE. I speak no treason.
CAPULET.   O, God ye god den.
NURSE. May not one speak?
CAPULET.   Peace, you mumbling fool!
  Utter your gravity o'er a gossip's bowl;
  For here we need it not.
LADY CAPULET.   You are too hot.
CAPULET. God's bread! It makes me mad.
  Day, night, hour, tide, time, work, play,
  Alone, in company, still my care hath been
  To have her matched; and having now provided
  A gentleman of noble parentage,
  Of fair demesnes, youthful, and nobly trained,
  Stuffed, as they say, with honourable parts,
  Proportioned as one's thought would wish a man;
  And then to have a wretched puling fool,
  A whining mammet, in her fortune's tender,
  To answer "I'll not wed; I cannot love,
  I am too young; I pray you, pardon me."
  But, an you will not wed, I'll pardon you.
  Graze where you will, you shall not house with me.
  Look to 't, think on 't, I do not use to jest.
  Thursday is near; lay hand on heart, advise.
  An you be mine, I'll give you to my friend;
  An you be not, hang, beg, starve, die in the streets,
  For, by my soul, I'll ne'er acknowledge thee,
  Nor what is mine shall never do thee good.
  Trust to 't, bethink you; I'll not be forsworn.   *Exit*
JULIET. Is there no pity sitting in the clouds,
  That sees into the bottom of my grief?
  O, sweet my mother, cast me not away!

Delay this marriage for a month, a week;
Or, if you do not, make the bridal bed
In that dim monument where Tybalt lies.
LADY CAPULET. Talk not to me, for I'll not speak a word.
  Do as thou wilt, for I have done with thee.   *Exit*
JULIET. O God!—O nurse, how shall this be prevented?
  My husband is on earth, my faith in heaven;
  How shall that faith return again to earth,
  Unless that husband send it me from heaven
  By leaving earth? Comfort me, counsel me.
  Alack, alack, that heaven should practise stratagems
  Upon so soft a subject as myself!
  What say'st thou? Hast thou not a word of joy?
  Some comfort, nurse.
NURSE.   Faith, here it is.
  Romeo is banished; and all the world to nothing,
  That he dares ne'er come back to challenge you;
  Or, if he do, it needs must be by stealth.
  Then, since the case so stands as now it doth,
  I think it best you married with the County.
  O, he's a lovely gentleman!
  Romeo's a dishclout to him; an eagle, madam,
  Hath not so green, so quick, so fair an eye

As Paris hath. Beshrew my very heart,
I think you are happy in this second match,
For it excels your first; or if it did not,
Your first is dead; or 'twere as good he were,
As living here and you no use of him.
JULIET. Speakest thou from thy heart?
NURSE.   And from my soul too;
  Or else beshrew them both.
JULIET.   Amen!
NURSE.   What?
JULIET. Well, thou hast comforted me marvelous much.
  Go in; and tell my lady I am gone,
  Having displeased my father, to Laurence' cell,
  To make confession and to be absolved.
NURSE. Marry, I will; and this is wisely done.   *Exit*
JULIET. Ancient damnation! O most wicked fiend!
  Is it more sin to wish me thus forsworn,
  Or to dispraise my lord with that same tongue
  Which she hath praised him with above compare
  So many thousand times? Go, counsellor;
  Thou and my bosom henceforth shall be twain.
  I'll to the friar, to know his remedy.
  If all else fail, myself have power to die.   *Exit*

ACT IV

SCENE I *Friar Laurence's cell*

Enter FRIAR LAURENCE *and* PARIS

FRIAR LAURENCE. On Thursday, sir? The time is very
   short.
PARIS. My father Capulet will have it so;
   And I am nothing slow to slack his haste.
FRIAR LAURENCE. You say you do not know the lady's
   mind.
   Uneven is the course, I like it not.
PARIS. Immoderately she weeps for Tybalt's death,
   And therefore have I little talked of love;
   For Venus smiles not in a house of tears.
   Now, sir, her father counts it dangerous
   That she doth give her sorrow so much sway,
   And in his wisdom hastes our marriage,
   To stop the inundation of her tears;
   Which, too much minded by herself alone,
   May be put from her by society.
   Now do you know the reason of this haste.
FRIAR LAURENCE. [*Aside*] I would I knew not why it
   should be slowed.
   Look, sir, here comes the lady towards my cell.

Enter JULIET

PARIS. Happily met, my lady and my wife!
JULIET. That may be, sir, when I may be a wife.
PARIS. That may be must be, love, on Thursday next.
JULIET. What must be shall be.
FRIAR LAURENCE.   That's a certain text.
PARIS. Come you to make confession to this father?
JULIET. To answer that, I should confess to you.
PARIS. Do not deny to him that you love me.
JULIET. I will confess to you that I love him.
PARIS. So will ye, I am sure, that you love me.
JULIET. If I do so, it will be of more price,
   Being spoke behind your back, than to your face.

PARIS. Poor soul, thy face is much abused with tears.
JULIET. The tears have got small victory by that;
   For it was bad enough before their spite.
PARIS. Thou wrong'st it, more than tears, with that
   report.
JULIET. That is no slander, sir, which is a truth;
   And what I spake, I spake it to my face.
PARIS. Thy face is mine, and thou hast slandered it.
JULIET. It may be so, for it is not mine own.
   Are you at leisure, holy father, now;
   Or shall I come to you at evening mass?
FRIAR LAURENCE. My leisure serves me, pensive daugh-
   ter, now.
   My lord, we must entreat the time alone.
PARIS. God shield I should disturb devotion!
   Juliet, on Thursday early will I rouse ye.
   Till then, adieu; and keep this holy kiss.   *Exit*
JULIET. O, shut the door! And when thou hast done so,
   Come weep with me; past hope, past cure, past help!
FRIAR LAURENCE. Ah, Juliet, I already know thy grief;
   It strains me past the compass of my wits.
   I hear thou must, and nothing may prorogue it,
   On Thursday next be married to this County.
JULIET. Tell me not, friar, that thou hear'st of this,
   Unless thou tell me how I may prevent it.
   If, in thy wisdom, thou canst give no help,
   Do thou but call my resolution wise,
   And with this knife I'll help it presently.
   God joined my heart and Romeo's, thou our hands;
   And ere this hand, by thee to Romeo sealed,
   Shall be the label to another deed,
   Or my true heart with treacherous revolt
   Turn to another, this shall slay them both.
   Therefore, out of thy long-experienced time,
   Give me some present counsel, or, behold,
   'Twixt my extremes and me this bloody knife
   Shall play the umpire, arbitrating that
   Which the commission of thy years and art
   Could to no issue of true honour bring.
   Be not so long to speak; I long to die,
   If what thou speak'st speak not of remedy.
FRIAR LAURENCE. Hold, daughter. I do spy a kind of
   hope,
   Which craves as desperate an execution
   As that is desperate which we would prevent.
   If, rather than to marry County Paris,
   Thou hast the strength of will to slay thyself,
   Then is it likely thou wilt undertake
   A thing like death to chide away this shame,
   That copest with death himself to scape from it;
   And, if thou darest, I'll give thee remedy.
JULIET. O, bid me leap, rather than marry Paris,
   From off the battlements of yonder tower;
   Or walk in thievish ways; or bid me lurk
   Where serpents are; chain me with roaring bears;
   Or shut me nightly in a charnel house,

O'er-covered quite with dead men's rattling bones,
With reeky shanks and yellow chapless skulls;
Or bid me go into a new-made grave
And hide me with a dead man in his shroud;
Things that, to hear them told, have made me tremble;
And I will do it without fear or doubt,
To live an unstained wife to my sweet love.

FRIAR LAURENCE. Hold, then; go home, be merry, give
 consent
To marry Paris. Wednesday is tomorrow.
Tomorrow night look that thou lie alone;
Let not thy nurse lie with thee in thy chamber.
Take thou this vial, being then in bed,
And this distilled liquor drink thou off;
When presently through all thy veins shall run
A cold and drowsy humour, for no pulse
Shall keep his native progress, but surcease;
No warmth, no breath, shall testify thou livest;
The roses in thy lips and cheeks shall fade
To paly ashes, thy eyes' windows fall,
Like death, when he shuts up the day of life;
Each part, deprived of supple government,
Shall, stiff and stark and cold, appear like death;
And in this borrowed likeness of shrunk death

Thou shalt continue two and forty hours,
And then awake as from a pleasant sleep.
Now, when the bridegroom in the morning comes
To rouse thee from thy bed, there art thou dead.
Then, as the manner of our country is,
In thy best robes uncovered on the bier
Thou shalt be borne to that same ancient vault
Where all the kindred of the Capulets lie.
In the mean time, against thou shalt awake,
Shall Romeo by my letters know our drift,
And hither shall he come; and he and I
Will watch thy waking, and that very night
Shall Romeo bear thee hence to Mantua.
And this shall free thee from this present shame;
If no inconstant toy, nor womanish fear,
Abate thy valour in the acting it.

JULIET. Give me, give me! O, tell not me of fear!

FRIAR LAURENCE. Hold; get you gone, be strong and
 prosperous
In this resolve. I'll send a friar with speed
To Mantua, with my letters to thy lord.

JULIET. Love give me strength! And strength shall help
 afford.
Farewell, dear father!   *Exeunt*

SCENE II *Hall in Capulet's house*

Enter CAPULET, LADY CAPULET, Nurse, *and two* Servingmen

CAPULET. So many guests invite as here are writ.
          Exit first Servant
Sirrah, go hire me twenty cunning cooks.

SECOND SERVANT. You shall have none ill, sir; for I'll
try if they can lick their fingers.

CAPULET. How canst thou try them so?

SECOND SERVANT. Marry, sir, 'tis an ill cook that cannot lick his own fingers. Therefore he that cannot lick
his fingers goes not with me.

CAPULET. Go, be gone.   *Exit second* Servant
We shall be much unfurnished for this time.
What, is my daughter gone to Friar Laurence?

NURSE. Ay, forsooth.

CAPULET. Well, he may chance to do some good on her.
A peevish self-willed harlotry it is.

NURSE. See where she comes from shrift with merry
look.

Enter JULIET

CAPULET. How now, my headstrong! Where have you
been gadding?

JULIET. Where I have learned me to repent the sin
Of disobedient opposition
To you and your behests, and am enjoined
By holy Laurence to fall prostrate here,
And beg your pardon. Pardon, I beseech you!
Henceforward I am ever ruled by you.

CAPULET. Send for the County; go tell him of this.

I'll have this knot knit up tomorrow morning.

JULIET. I met the youthful lord at Laurence' cell;
And gave him what becomed love I might,
Not stepping o'er the bounds of modesty.

CAPULET. Why, I am glad on 't; this is well; stand up.
This is as 't should be. Let me see the County;
Ay, marry, go, I say, and fetch him hither.
Now, afore God! This reverend holy friar,
All our whole city is much bound to him.

JULIET. Nurse, will you go with me into my closet,
To help me sort such needful ornaments
As you think fit to furnish me tomorrow?

LADY CAPULET. No, not till Thursday; there is time
enough.

CAPULET. Go, nurse, go with her. We'll to church
tomorrow.   *Exeunt* JULIET *and* Nurse

LADY CAPULET. We shall be short in our provision.
'Tis now near night.

CAPULET.   Tush, I will stir about,
And all things shall be well, I warrant thee, wife.
Go thou to Juliet, help to deck up her;
I'll not to bed tonight; let me alone;
I'll play the housewife for this once. What, ho!
They are all forth. Well, I will walk myself
To County Paris, to prepare him up
Against tomorrow. My heart is wondrous light,
Since this same wayward girl is so reclaimed. *Exeunt*

SCENE III *Juliet's chamber*

Enter JULIET *and* Nurse

JULIET. Ay, those attires are best; but, gentle nurse,
I pray thee, leave me to myself tonight;
For I have need of many orisons
To move the heavens to smile upon my state,
Which, well thou know'st, is cross and full of sin.

Enter LADY CAPULET

LADY CAPULET. What, are you busy, ho? Need you my
help?
JULIET. No, madam; we have culled such necessaries
As are behoveful for our state tomorrow:
So please you, let me now be left alone,
And let the nurse this night sit up with you;
For, I am sure, you have your hands full all,
In this so sudden business.
LADY CAPULET.   Good night.
Get thee to bed, and rest; for thou hast need.

Exeunt LADY CAPULET *and* Nurse

JULIET. Farewell! God knows when we shall meet again.
I have a faint cold fear thrills through my veins,
That almost freezes up the heat of life.
I'll call them back again to comfort me.
Nurse! What should she do here?
My dismal scene I needs must act alone.
Come, vial.
What if this mixture do not work at all?
Shall I be married then tomorrow morning?
No, no; this shall forbid it; lie thou there.

Laying down her dagger

What if it be a poison, which the friar
Subtly hath ministered to have me dead,
Lest in this marriage he should be dishonoured,
Because he married me before to Romeo?

I fear it is; and yet, methinks, it should not,
For he hath still been tried a holy man.
How if, when I am laid into the tomb,
I wake before the time that Romeo
Come to redeem me? There's a fearful point!
Shall I not, then, be stifled in the vault,
To whose foul mouth no healthsome air breathes in,
And there die strangled ere my Romeo comes?
Or, if I live, is it not very like,
The horrible conceit of death and night,
Together with the terror of the place—
As in a vault, an ancient receptacle,
Where, for these many hundred years, the bones
Of all my buried ancestors are packed.
Where bloody Tybalt, yet but green in earth,
Lies festering in his shroud; where, as they say,
At some hours in the night spirits resort—
Alack, alack, is it not like that I,
So early waking, what with loathsome smells,
And shrieks like mandrakes' torn out of the earth,
That living mortals, hearing them, run mad—
O, if I wake, shall I not be distraught,
Environed with all these hideous fears?
And madly play with my forefathers' joints?
And pluck the mangled Tybalt from his shroud?
And, in this rage, with some great kinsman's bone,
As with a club, dash out my desperate brains?
O, look! Methinks I see my cousin's ghost
Seeking out Romeo, that did spit his body
Upon a rapier's point. Stay, Tybalt, stay!
Romeo, I come! This do I drink to thee.

She falls upon her bed, within the curtains

SCENE IV *Hall in Capulet's house*

Enter LADY CAPULET *and* Nurse

LADY CAPULET. Hold, take these keys, and fetch more
spices, nurse.
NURSE. They call for dates and quinces in the pastry.

Enter CAPULET

CAPULET. Come, stir, stir, stir! The second cock hath
crowed,
The curfew bell hath rung, 'tis three o'clock.
Look to the baked meats, good Angelica.
Spare not for cost.
NURSE.   Go, you cotquean, go,
Get you to bed; faith, you'll be sick tomorrow
For this night's watching.

CAPULET. No, not a whit. What! I have watched ere
now
All night for lesser cause, and ne'er been sick.
LADY CAPULET. Ay, you have been a mouse-hunt in your
time;
But I will watch you from such watching now.

Exeunt LADY CAPULET *and* Nurse

CAPULET. A jealous-hood, a jealous-hood!

Enter three or four Servingmen,
with spits, logs, and baskets

Now, fellow.
What's there?

First Servant. Things for the cook, sir, but I know
not what.
Capulet. Make haste, make haste. [*Exist first* Servant]
Sirrah, fetch drier logs.
Call Peter, he will show thee where they are.
Second Servant. I have a head, sir, that will find out
logs,
And never trouble Peter for the matter.   *Exit*
Capulet. Mass, and well said; a merry whoreson, ha!
Thou shalt be loggerhead. Good faith, 'tis day:
The County will be here with music straight,
For so he said he would. I hear him near.

                                                  Music within
Nurse! Wife! What, ho! What, nurse, I say!

                    Re-enter Nurse

Go waken Juliet, go and trim her up;
I'll go and chat with Paris. Hie, make haste,
Make haste; the bridegroom he is come already;
Make haste, I say.   *Exeunt*

SCENE V *Juliet's chamber*

Enter Nurse

NURSE. Mistress! What, mistress! Juliet! Fast, I war-
 rant her, she—
Why, lamb! Why, lady! Fie, you slug-a-bed!
Why, love, I say! Madam! Sweetheart! Why, bride!
What, not a word? You take your pennyworths now;
Sleep for a week; for the next night, I warrant,
The County Paris hath set up his rest,
That you shall rest but little. God forgive me,
Marry, and amen, how sound is she asleep!
I must needs wake her. Madam, madam, madam!
Ay, let the County take you in your bed;
He'll fright you up, i' faith. Will it not be?
          Undraws the curtains
What, dressed! And in your clothes! And down again!
I must needs wake you: Lady! lady! lady!
Alas, alas! Help, help! my lady's dead!
O, well-a-day, that ever I was born!
Some aqua vitæ, ho! My lord! My lady!

Enter LADY CAPULET

LADY CAPULET. What noise is here?
NURSE.   O lamentable day!
LADY CAPULET. What is the matter?
NURSE.   Look, look! O heavy day!
LADY CAPULET. O me, O me! My child, my only life,
Revive, look up, or I will die with thee!
Help, help! Call help.

Enter CAPULET

CAPULET. For shame, bring Juliet forth; her lord is
 come.
NURSE. She's dead, deceased, she's dead; alack the day!
LADY CAPULET. Alack the day, she's dead, she's dead,
 she's dead!
CAPULET. Ha! Let me see her. Out, alas! She's cold;
Her blood is settled, and her joints are stiff;
Life and these lips have long been separated.
Death lies on her like an untimely frost
Upon the sweetest flower of all the field.
NURSE. O lamentable day!
LADY CAPULET.   O woeful time!
CAPULET. Death, that hath ta'en her hence to make
 me wail,
Ties up my tongue, and will not let me speak.

Enter FRIAR LAURENCE *and* PARIS,
with Musicians

FRIAR LAURENCE. Come, is the bride ready to go to
 church?
CAPULET. Ready to go, but never to return.
O son! The night before thy wedding day
Hath Death lain with thy wife. There she lies,
Flower as she was, deflowered by him.

Death is my son-in-law, Death is my heir;
My daughter he hath wedded. I will die,
And leave him all; life, living, all is Death's.
PARIS. Have I thought long to see this morning's face,
And doth it give me such a sight as this?
LADY CAPULET. Accursed, unhappy, wretched, hateful
 day!
Most miserable hour that e'er time saw
In lasting labour of his pilgrimage!
But one, poor one, one poor and loving child,
But one thing to rejoice and solace in,
And cruel death hath catched it from my sight!
NURSE. O woe! O woeful, woeful, woeful day!
Most lamentable day, most woeful day,
That ever, ever, I did yet behold!
O day! O day! O day! O hateful day!
Never was seen so black a day as this.
O woeful day, O woeful day!
PARIS. Beguiled, divorced, wronged, spited, slain!
Most detestable Death, by thee beguiled,
By cruel cruel thee quite overthrown!
O love! O life! not life, but love in death!
CAPULET. Despised, distressed, hated, martyred, killed!
Uncomfortable time, why camest thou now
To murder, murder our solemnity?
O child! O child! My soul, and not my child!
Dead art thou! Alack! my child is dead;
And with my child my joys are buried.
FRIAR LAURENCE. Peace, ho, for shame! Confusion's
 cure lives not
In these confusions. Heaven and yourself
Had part in this fair maid; now heaven hath all,
And all the better is it for the maid.
Your part in her you could not keep from death,
But heaven keeps his part in eternal life.
The most you sought was her promotion;
For 'twas your heaven she should be advanced;
And weep ye now, seeing she is advanced
Above the clouds, as high as heaven itself?
O, in this love, you love your child so ill,
That you run mad, seeing that she is well.
She's not well married that lives married long;
But she's best married that dies married young.
Dry up your tears, and stick your rosemary
On this fair corpse; and, as the custom is,
In all her best array bear her to church;
For though fond nature bids us all lament,
Yet nature's tears are reason's merriment.
CAPULET. All things that we ordained festival,
Turn from their office to black funeral;
Our instruments to melancholy bells,
Our wedding cheer to a sad burial feast,
Our solemn hymns to sullen dirges change,

Our bridal flowers serve for a buried corpse,
And all things change them to the contrary.
FRIAR LAURENCE. Sir, go you in; and, madam, go with
  him;
And go, Sir Paris; every one prepare
To follow this fair corpse unto her grave.
The heavens do lour upon you for some ill;
Move them no more by crossing their high will.

  Exeunt CAPULET, LADY CAPULET, PARIS, *and* FRIAR
FIRST MUSICIAN. Faith, we may put up our pipes, and
  be gone.
NURSE. Honest good fellows, ah, put up, put up;
  For, well you know, this is a pitiful case.   *Exit*
FIRST MUSICIAN. Ay, by my troth, the case may be
  amended.

Enter PETER

PETER. Musicians, O, musicians, "Heart's Ease," "Heart's
  Ease": O, an you will have me live, play "Heart's
  Ease."
FIRST MUSICIAN. Why "Heart's Ease"?
PETER. O, musicians, because my heart itself plays
  "My heart is full of woe." O, play me some merry
  dump, to comfort me.
FIRST MUSICIAN. Not a dump we; 'tis no time to play
  now.
PETER. You will not, then?
FIRST MUSICIAN. No.
PETER. I will then give it you soundly.
FIRST MUSICIAN. What will you give us?
PETER. No money, on my faith, but the gleek; I will
  give you the minstrel.

FIRST MUSICIAN. Then will I give you the serving-
  creature.
PETER. Then will I lay the serving-creature's dagger on
  your pate. I will carry no crotchets. I'll re you, I'll fa
  you; do you note me?
FIRST MUSICIAN. An you re us and fa us, you note us.
SECOND MUSICIAN. Pray you, put up your dagger, and
  put out your wit.
PETER. Then have at you with my wit! I will dry-beat
  you with an iron wit, and put up my iron dagger.
  Answer me like men:
    "When griping grief the heart doth wound,
      And doleful dumps the mind oppress,
    Then music with her silver sound—"
  Why "silver sound"? Why "music with her silver
  sound"? What say you, Simon Catling?
FIRST MUSICIAN. Marry, sir, because silver hath a sweet
  sound.
PETER. Pretty! What say you, Hugh Rebeck?
SECOND MUSICIAN. I say "silver sound," because musi-
  cians sound for silver.
PETER. Pretty too! What say you, James Soundpost?
THIRD MUSICIAN. Faith, I know not what to say.
PETER. O, I cry you mercy; you are the singer.
  I will say for you. It is "music with her silver sound,"
  because musicians have no gold for sounding.
    "Then music with her silver sound
      With speedy help doth lend redress."   *Exit*
FIRST MUSICIAN. What a pestilent knave is this same!
SECOND MUSICIAN. Hang him, Jack! Come, we'll in
  here; tarry for the mourners, and stay dinner.
                                              Exeunt

ACT V

SCENE I *Mantua. A street*

Enter ROMEO

ROMEO. If I may trust the flattering truth of sleep,
My dreams presage some joyful news at hand.
My bosom's lord sits lightly in his throne;
And all this day an unaccustomed spirit
Lifts me above the ground with cheerful thoughts.
I dreamt my lady came and found me dead
(Strange dream, that gives a dead man leave to think!)
And breathed such life with kisses in my lips
That I revived, and was an emperor.
Ah me! How sweet is love itself possessed,
When but love's shadows are so rich in joy!

Enter BALTHASAR, *booted*

News from Verona! How now, Balthasar!
Dost thou not bring me letters from the friar?
How doth my lady? Is my father well?
How fares my Juliet? That I ask again;
For nothing can be ill, if she be well.
BALTHASAR. Then she is well, and nothing can be ill.
Her body sleeps in Capels' monument,
And her immortal part with angels lives.
I saw her laid low in her kindred's vault,
And presently took post to tell it you.
O, pardon me for bringing these ill news,
Since you did leave it for my office, sir.
ROMEO. Is it even so? Then I defy you, stars!
Thou know'st my lodging—get me ink and paper,
And hire posthorses; I will hence tonight.
BALTHASAR. I do beseech you, sir, have patience.
Your looks are pale and wild, and do import
Some misadventure.
ROMEO.   Tush, thou art deceived.
Leave me, and do the thing I bid thee do.
Hast thou no letters to me from the friar?
BALTHASAR. No, my good lord.
ROMEO.   No matter. Get thee gone,
And hire those horses; I'll be with thee straight.
                                        Exit BALTHASAR
Well, Juliet, I will lie with thee tonight.
Let's see for means. O mischief, thou art swift
To enter in the thoughts of desperate men!
I do remember an apothecary,
And hereabouts he dwells, which late I noted
In tattered weeds, with overwhelming brows,
Culling of simples; meagre were his looks,
Sharp misery had worn him to the bones;
And in his needy shop a tortoise hung,
An alligator stuffed, and other skins
Of ill-shaped fishes; and about his shelves
A beggarly account of empty boxes,
Green earthen pots, bladders and musty seeds,

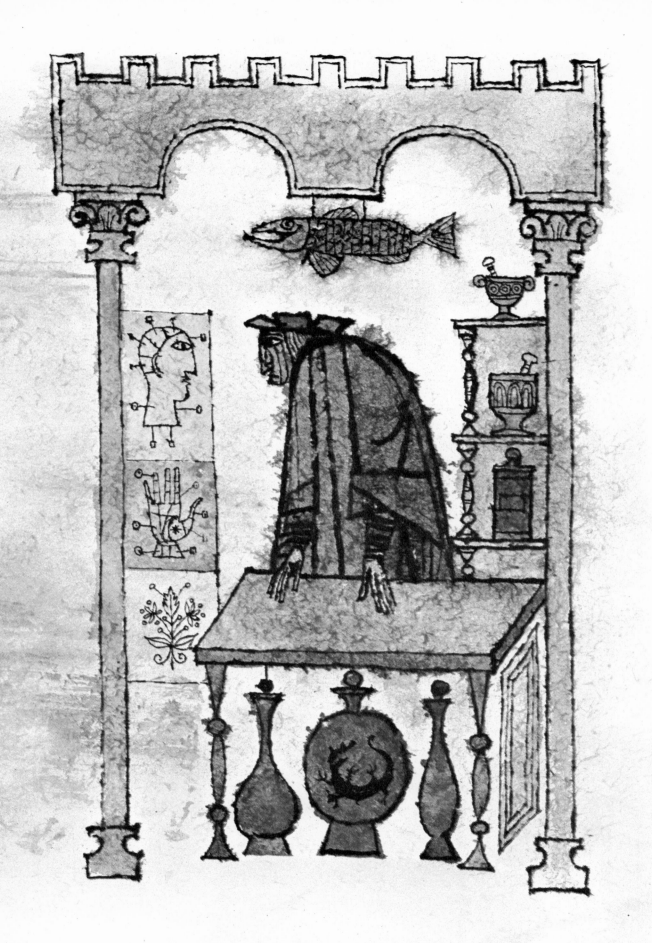

Remnants of packthread and old cakes of roses,
Were thinly scattered, to make up a show.
Noting this penury, to myself I said,
"An if a man did need a poison now,
Whose sale is present death in Mantua,
Here lives a caitiff wretch would sell it him."
O, this same thought did but forerun my need;
And this same needy man must sell it me.
As I remember, this should be the house.
Being holiday, the beggar's shop is shut.
What, ho! apothecary!

Enter Apothecary

APOTHECARY.   Who calls so loud?
ROMEO. Come hither, man. I see that thou art poor.
    Hold, there is forty ducats. Let me have
    A dram of poison, such soon-speeding gear
    As will disperse itself through all the veins
    That the life-weary taker may fall dead
    And that the trunk may be discharged of breath
    As violently as hasty powder fired
    Doth hurry from the fatal cannon's womb.

APOTHECARY. Such mortal drugs I have; but Mantua's
    law
    Is death to any he that utters them.
ROMEO. Art thou so bare and full of wretchedness,
    And fear'st to die? Famine is in thy cheeks,
    Need and oppression starveth in thine eyes,
    Contempt and beggary hangs upon thy back;
    The world is not thy friend nor the world's law;
    The world affords no law to make thee rich;
    Then be not poor, but break it, and take this.
APOTHECARY. My poverty, but not my will, consents.
ROMEO. I pay thy poverty, and not thy will.
APOTHECARY. Put this in any liquid thing you will,
    And drink it off; and, if you had the strength
    Of twenty men, it would dispatch you straight.
ROMEO. There is thy gold, worse poison to men's souls,
    Doing more murders in this loathsome world,
    Than these poor compounds that thou mayst not sell.
    I sell thee poison; thou hast sold me none.
    Farewell. Buy food, and get thyself in flesh.
    Come, cordial and not poison, go with me
    To Juliet's grave; for there must I use thee.   *Exeunt*

SCENE II *Friar Laurence's cell*

Enter FRIAR JOHN

FRIAR JOHN. Holy Franciscan friar! Brother, ho!
            Enter FRIAR LAURENCE
FRIAR LAURENCE. This same should be the voice of
    Friar John.
    Welcome from Mantua. What says Romeo?
    Or, if his mind be writ, give me his letter.
FRIAR JOHN. Going to find a barefoot brother out,
    One of our order, to associate me,
    Here in this city visiting the sick,
    And finding him, the searchers of the town,
    Suspecting that we both were in a house
    Where the infectious pestilence did reign,
    Sealed up the doors, and would not let us forth;
    So that my speed to Mantua there was stayed.
FRIAR LAURENCE. Who bare my letter, then, to Romeo?
FRIAR JOHN. I could not send it—here it is again—
    Nor get a messenger to bring it thee,

    So fearful were they of infection.
FRIAR LAURENCE. Unhappy fortune! By my brother-
    hood,
    The letter was not nice but full of charge
    Of dear import, and the neglecting it
    May do much danger. Friar John, go hence;
    Get me an iron crow, and bring it straight
    Unto my cell.
FRIAR JOHN.   Brother, I'll go and bring it thee. *Exit*
FRIAR LAURENCE. Now must I to the monument
    alone;
    Within this three hours will fair Juliet wake.
    She will beshrew me much that Romeo
    Hath had no notice of these accidents;
    But I will write again to Mantua,
    And keep her at my cell till Romeo come;
    Poor living corpse, closed in a dead man's tomb! *Exit*

SCENE III *A churchyard; in it a tomb belonging to the Capulets*

Enter PARIS, *and his Page bearing flowers and a torch*

PARIS. Give me thy torch, boy. Hence, and stand aloof.
    Yet put it out, for I would not be seen.
    Under yond yew trees lay thee all along,
    Holding thine ear close to the hollow ground,
    So shall no foot upon the churchyard tread,
    Being loose, unfirm, with digging up of graves,

    But thou shalt hear it. Whistle then to me,
    As signal that thou hear'st something approach.
    Give me those flowers. Do as I bid thee, go.
PAGE. [*Aside*] I am almost afraid to stand alone
    Here in the churchyard; yet I will adventure.
                                                    Retires

PARIS. Sweet flower, with flowers thy bridal bed I
    strew—
      O woe! thy canopy is dust and stones—
    Which with sweet water nightly I will dew,
      Or, wanting that, with tears distilled by
        moans.
    The obsequies that I for thee will keep
    Nightly shall be to strew thy grave and weep.
                         The Page *whistles*
  The boy gives warning something doth approach.
  What cursed foot wanders this way tonight,
  To cross my obsequies and true love's rite?
  What, with a torch! Muffle me, night, awhile. *Retires*

Enter ROMEO *and* BALTHASAR, *with a torch, mattock,* &c.

ROMEO. Give me that mattock and the wrenching iron.
  Hold, take this letter; early in the morning
  See thou deliver it to my lord and father.
  Give me the light. Upon thy life, I charge thee,
  Whate'er thou hear'st or seest, stand all aloof,
  And do not interrupt me in my course.
  Why I descend into this bed of death,
  Is partly to behold my lady's face;
  But chiefly to take thence from her dead finger
  A precious ring, a ring that I must use
  In dear employment. Therefore hence, be gone.
  But if thou, jealous, dost return to pry
  In what I further shall intend to do,
  By heaven, I will tear thee joint by joint
  And strew this hungry churchyard with thy limbs.
  The time and my intents are savage-wild,
  More fierce and more inexorable far
  Than empty tigers or the roaring sea.
BALTHASAR. I will be gone, sir, and not trouble you.
ROMEO. So shalt thou show me friendship. Take thou
    that.
  Live, and be prosperous, and farewell, good fellow.
BALTHASAR. [*Aside*] For all this same, I'll hide me here-
    about.
  His looks I fear, and his intents I doubt. *Retires*
ROMEO. Thou detestable maw, thou womb of death,
  Gorged with the dearest morsel of the earth,
  Thus I enforce thy rotten jaws to open,
  And, in despite, I'll cram thee with more food!
                        Opens the tomb
PARIS. This is that banished haughty Montague,
  That murdered my love's cousin, with which grief,
  It is supposed, the fair creature died;
  And here is come to do some villainous shame
  To the dead bodies. I will apprehend him.
                        Comes forward
  Stop thy unhallowed toil, vile Montague!
  Can vengeance be pursued further than death?
  Condemned villain, I do apprehend thee.
  Obey, and go with me; for thou must die.
ROMEO. I must indeed; and therefore came I hither.

Good gentle youth, tempt not a desperate man;
  Fly hence, and leave me. Think upon these gone;
  Let them affright thee. I beseech thee, youth,
  Put not another sin upon my head,
  By urging me to fury. O, be gone!
  By heaven, I love thee better than myself;
  For I come hither armed against myself.
  Stay not, be gone; live, and hereafter say,
  A madman's mercy bade thee run away.
PARIS. I do defy thy conjurations,
  And apprehend thee for a felon here.
ROMEO. Wilt thou provoke me? Then have at thee, boy!
                        They fight
PAGE. O Lord, they fight! I will go call the watch. *Exit*
PARIS. O, I am slain! [*Falls*] If thou be merciful,
  Open the tomb, lay me with Juliet.   *Dies*
ROMEO. In faith, I will. Let me peruse this face.
  Mercutio's kinsman, noble County Paris!
  What said my man, when my betossed soul
  Did not attend him as we rode? I think
  He told me Paris should have married Juliet.
  Said he not so? Or did I dream it so?
  Or am I mad, hearing him talk of Juliet,
  To think it was so? O, give me thy hand,
  One writ with me in sour misfortune's book!
  I'll bury thee in a triumphant grave.
  A grave? O, no! A lantern, slaughtered youth,
  For here lies Juliet, and her beauty makes
  This vault a feasting presence full of light.
  Death, lie thou there, by a dead man interred.
                  Laying PARIS *in the tomb*
  How oft when men are at the point of death
  Have they been merry! which their keepers call
  A lightning before death. O, how may I
  Call this a lightning? O my love! my wife!
  Death, that hath sucked the honey of thy breath,
  Hath had no power yet upon thy beauty.
  Thou art not conquered; beauty's ensign yet
  Is crimson in thy lips and in thy cheeks,
  And death's pale flag is not advanced there.
  Tybalt, liest thou there in thy bloody sheet?
  O, what more favour can I do to thee,
  Than with that hand that cut thy youth in twain
  To sunder his that was thine enemy?
  Forgive me, cousin! Ah, dear Juliet,
  Why art thou yet so fair? Shall I believe
  That unsubstantial death is amorous,
  And that the lean abhorred monster keeps
  Thee here in dark to be his paramour?
  For fear of that, I still will stay with thee;
  And never from this palace of dim night
  Depart again. Here, here will I remain
  With worms that are thy chambermaids; O, here
  Will I set up my everlasting rest,
  And shake the yoke of inauspicious stars
  From this world-wearied flesh. Eyes, look your last!

Arms, take your last embrace! And, lips, O you
The doors of breath, seal with a righteous kiss
A dateless bargain to engrossing death!
Come, bitter conduct, come, unsavoury guide!
Thou desperate pilot, now at once run on
The dashing rocks thy seasick weary bark!
Here's to my love! [*Drinks*] O true apothecary!
Thy drugs are quick. Thus with a kiss I die.   *Dies*

Enter, at the other end of the churchyard,
FRIAR LAURENCE,
with a lantern, crow, and spade

FRIAR LAURENCE. Saint Francis be my speed! How oft
          tonight
     Have my old feet stumbled at graves! Who's there?
BALTHASAR. Here's one, a friend, and one that knows
          you well.
FRIAR LAURENCE. Bliss be upon you! Tell me, good my
          friend,
     What torch is yond, that vainly lends his light
     To grubs and eyeless skulls? As I discern,
     It burneth in the Capels' monument.
BALTHASAR. It doth so, holy sir; and there's my master,
     One that you love.
FRIAR LAURENCE.   Who is it?
BALTHASAR.   Romeo.
FRIAR LAURENCE. How long hath he been there?
BALTHASAR.   Full half an hour.
FRIAR LAURENCE. Go with me to the vault.
BALTHASAR.   I dare not, sir.
     My master knows not but I am gone hence;
     And fearfully did menace me with death,
     If I did stay to look on his intents.
FRIAR LAURENCE. Stay, then; I'll go alone. Fear comes
          upon me.
     O, much I fear some ill unlucky thing.
BALTHASAR. As I did sleep under this yew tree here,
     I dreamt my master and another fought,
     And that my master slew him.
FRIAR LAURENCE.   Romeo!   *Advances*
     Alack, alack, what blood is this, which stains
     The stony entrance of this sepulchre?
     What mean these masterless and gory swords
     To lie discoloured by this place of peace?
                              Enters the tomb
     Romeo! O, pale! Who else? What, Paris too?
     And steeped in blood? Ah, what an unkind hour
     Is guilty of this lamentable chance!
     The lady stirs.   JULIET *wakes*
JULIET. O comfortable friar! Where is my lord?
     I do remember well where I should be,
     And there I am. Where is my Romeo?   *Noise within*
FRIAR LAURENCE. I hear some noise. Lady, come from
          that nest
     Of death, contagion, and unnatural sleep.
     A greater power than we can contradict

Hath thwarted our intents. Come, come away.
Thy husband in thy bosom there lies dead;
And Paris too. Come, I'll dispose of thee
Among a sisterhood of holy nuns.
Stay not to question, for the watch is coming;
Come, go, good Juliet [*Noise again*], I dare no longer
 stay.
JULIET. Go, get thee hence, for I will not away.
         Exit FRIAR LAURENCE
What's here? A cup, closed in my true love's hand?
Poison, I see, hath been his timeless end.
O churl! drunk all, and left no friendly drop
To help me after? I will kiss thy lips;
Haply some poison yet doth hang on them,
To make me die with a restorative. [*Kisses him*]
Thy lips are warm.
FIRST WATCHMAN. [*Within*] Lead, boy. Which way?
JULIET. Yea, noise? Then I'll be brief. O happy dagger!
      Snatching ROMEO's *dagger*
This is thy sheath [*Stabs herself*]; there rust, and let
 me die.   *Falls on* ROMEO's *body, and dies*

   Enter Watch, *with the* Page *of* PARIS

PAGE. This is the place; there, where the torch doth
 burn.
FIRST WATCHMAN. The ground is bloody; search about
 the churchyard.
Go, some of you, whoe'er you find attach.
Pitiful sight! Here lies the County slain;
And Juliet bleeding, warm, and newly dead,
Who here hath lain these two days buried.
Go, tell the Prince; run to the Capulets;
Raise up the Montagues; some others search.
We see the ground whereon these woes do lie;
But the true ground of all these piteous woes
We cannot without circumstance descry.

  Re-enter some of the Watch, *with* BALTHASAR

SECOND WATCHMAN. Here's Romeo's man; we found
 him in the churchyard.
FIRST WATCHMAN. Hold him in safety, till the Prince
 come hither.

  Re-enter others of the Watch, *with* FRIAR LAURENCE

THIRD WATCHMAN. Here is a friar, that trembles, sighs,
 and weeps.
We took this mattock and this spade from him,
As he was coming from this churchyard side.
FIRST WATCHMAN. A great suspicion. Stay the friar too.

   Enter the PRINCE *and* Attendants

PRINCE. What misadventure is so early up,
That calls our person from our morning's rest?

  Enter CAPULET, LADY CAPULET, *and others*

CAPULET. What should it be, that they so shriek abroad?

LADY CAPULET. The people in the street cry "Romeo,"
Some "Juliet," and some "Paris"; and all run,
With open outcry, toward our monument.
PRINCE. What fear is this which startles in our ears?
FIRST WATCHMAN. Sovereign, here lies the County Paris
 slain;
And Romeo dead; and Juliet, dead before,
Warm and new killed.
PRINCE. Search, seek, and know how this foul murder
 comes.
FIRST WATCHMAN. Here is a friar, and slaughtered
 Romeo's man;
With instruments upon them, fit to open
These dead men's tombs.
CAPULET. O heavens! O wife, look how our daughter
 bleeds!
This dagger hath mista'en—for, lo, his house
Is empty on the back of Montague—
And it mis-sheathed in my daughter's bosom!
LADY CAPULET. O me! this sight of death is as a bell,
That warns my old age to a sepulchre.

   Enter MONTAGUE *and others*

PRINCE. Come, Montague; for thou art early up,
To see thy son and heir more early down.
MONTAGUE. Alas, my liege, my wife is dead tonight;
Grief of my son's exile hath stopped her breath.
What further woe conspires against mine age?
PRINCE. Look, and thou shalt see.
MONTAGUE. O thou untaught! what manners is in this,
To press before thy father to a grave?
PRINCE. Seal up the mouth of outrage for a while,
Till we can clear these ambiguities,
And know their spring, their head, their true descent;
And then will I be general of your woes,
And lead you even to death. Meantime forbear,
And let mischance be slave to patience.
Bring forth the parties of suspicion.
FRIAR LAURENCE. I am the greatest, able to do least,
Yet most suspected, as the time and place
Doth make against me, of this direful murder;
And here I stand, both to impeach and purge
Myself condemned and myself excused.
PRINCE. Then say at once what thou dost know in this.
FRIAR LAURENCE. I will be brief, for my short date of
 breath
Is not so long as is a tedious tale.
Romeo, there dead, was husband to that Juliet;
And she, there dead, that Romeo's faithful wife.
I married them; and their stol'n marriage day
Was Tybalt's doomsday, whose untimely death
Banished the new-made bridegroom from this city;
For whom, and not for Tybalt, Juliet pined.
You, to remove that siege of grief from her,
Betrothed and would have married her perforce
To County Paris. Then comes she to me,

And, with wild looks, bid me devise some mean
To rid her from this second marriage,
Or in my cell there would she kill herself.
Then gave I her, so tutored by my art,
A sleeping potion; which so took effect
As I intended, for it wrought on her
The form of death. Meantime I writ to Romeo,
That he should hither come as this dire night,
To help to take her from her borrowed grave,
Being the time the potion's force should cease.
But he which bore my letter, Friar John,
Was stayed by accident, and yesternight
Returned my letter back. Then all alone
At the prefixed hour of her waking,
Came I to take her from her kindred's vault;
Meaning to keep her closely at my cell,
Till I conveniently could send to Romeo.
But when I came, some minute ere the time
Of her awaking, here untimely lay
The noble Paris and true Romeo dead.
She wakes; and I entreated her come forth,
And bear this work of heaven with patience;
But then a noise did scare me from the tomb;
And she, too desperate, would not go with me,
But, as it seems, did violence on herself.
All this I know; and to the marriage
Her nurse is privy; and, if aught in this
Miscarried by my fault, let my old life
Be sacrificed, some hour before his time,
Unto the rigour of severest law.
PRINCE. We still have known thee for a holy man.
    Where's Romeo's man? What can he say in this?
BALTHASAR. I brought my master news of Juliet's death;
    And then in post he came from Mantua
    To this same place, to this same monument.
    This letter he early bid me give his father,

And threatened me with death, going in the vault,
    If I departed not and left him there.
PRINCE. Give me the letter; I will look on it.
    Where is the County's page, that raised the watch?
    Sirrah, what made your master in this place?
PAGE. He came with flowers to strew his lady's grave;
    And bid me stand aloof, and so I did.
    Anon comes one with light to ope the tomb;
    And by and by my master drew on him;
    And then I ran away to call the watch.
PRINCE. This letter doth make good the friar's words,
    Their course of love, the tidings of her death;
    And here he writes that he did buy a poison
    Of a poor 'pothecary, and therewithal
    Came to this vault to die, and lie with Juliet.
    Where be these enemies? Capulet! Montague!
    See, what a scourge is laid upon your hate,
    That heaven finds means to kill your joys with love.
    And I for winking at your discords too
    Have lost a brace of kinsmen. All are punished.
CAPULET. O brother Montague, give me thy hand.
    This is my daughter's jointure, for no more
    Can I demand.
MONTAGUE.   But I can give thee more:
    For I will raise her statue in pure gold;
    That while Verona by that name is known,
    There shall no figure at such rate be set
    As that of true and faithful Juliet.
CAPULET. As rich shall Romeo's by his lady's lie;
    Poor sacrifices of our enmity!
PRINCE. A glooming peace this morning with it brings;
    The sun, for sorrow, will not show his head.
    Go hence, to have more talk of these sad things;
    Some shall be pardoned, and some punished.
    For never was a story of more woe
    Than this of Juliet and her Romeo.   *Exeunt*

A MIDSUMMER NIGHT'S DREAM

A Midsummer Night's Dream is a trinity: three stories, involving three different sets of characters, are woven into one.

There are the grand people, Theseus, duke of Athens, and his bride, the Amazon queen, Hippolyta, and the four lovers. The second element is the group of Athenian workmen, who are preparing an amateur dramatic production in honour of the royal marriage. Finally, there are the fairies.

It is essentially an artificial comedy. Its arrangement makes no pretense at telling a true, or even probable, story. On the contrary, it aims to increase our enjoyment by drawing attention to its own artificial and symmetrical design. The lovers' scenes cannot possibly be read, or played, as naturalistic comedy, as an imitation of what happens in real life. They must be considered as exhibitions of style, considered, that is, not so much for what is said and done as the way it is said and done.

Perhaps a word should be said about the acting of artificial comedy, or, as it is sometimes called, "comedy of style".

Some actors, particularly in America, imagine that to play this kind of comedy you must assume a lot of elegant attitudes, derived from pictures of whatever age is being represented, and speak in a specially elegant and highly unnatural manner. This, I think, is a mistake. Acting should always bear a recognizable resemblance to real life.

This is where "style" comes in. Neither the lines nor the action of the lovers' scenes in the wood are in the least "naturalistic". The lines are in verse, of a deliberately and extremely artificial character; the action has to suggest, upon the virtually bare and cramped space of a stage, flight and pursuit through a forest. The problem for the actor is to handle the diction and the mime with such style that an audience will be "convinced" that Lysander and Hermia, Demetrius and Helena are four credible and amusing young people in a credible and amusing predicament, that the emotions which they express are real, and the lines they utter spontaneous.

At the same time their feelings must be expressed more lightly than if they were characters in a tragedy. The jealous anger of Lysander and Demetrius must differ in quality from that, for instance, of Othello. For one thing, they are supposed to be two quite ordinary young fellows not subject to the great passions which rage in the breasts of monumental tragic characters. For another, their emotions are supposed to evoke amused sympathy rather than the pity and terror aroused by tragic agony.

It has been said that comedy is harder for young people to act than tragedy. I think this is true. Tragedy can be carried off by a youngster of talent on a torrent of feeling *and energy*. On the other hand, in comedy part of the

actor's energy must be spent on comment, and that comment in *A Midsummer Night's Dream* ought to be subtle, witty and sympathetic. Therefore a sophisticated intelligence must be brought to bear. Further, playing comedy requires considerable experience in handling an audience; getting laughs is a matter of "know-how": when to move, when to keep still, when to hurry, when to pause, where to look, how to pitch the voice, which syllable to stress—considerable command, in short, of the niceties of technique.

While the four lovers in this play do not demand actors of the most outstanding talent, they do call for four young people who really know their job. That is why in amateur performances of *A Midsummer Night's Dream* the lovers' scenes so often fall flat. Looks and charm are not enough; the parts call for skill.

The Workmen: it is important that they should be amusing. It is even more important that they should be true and touching. All too often actors bent on extracting the last ounce of fun lose the humanity and gentleness of these characters and present "comics" out of Vaudeville.

It is vital that the right degree of contrast be marked, not merely between the sophistication of the upper class lovers and the simplicity of the hempen homespuns, but also between artificial and naturalistic comedy: a difference implied by Shakespeare in the use of verse for the one, prose for the other.

Bottom is the part usually assigned in professional productions to a leading comic actor. In consequence, in many productions Bottom is far too old, since young leading actors tend to be more interested in the Hamlets, Romeos and so on, and too loudly and dominantly funny. It is not funny if Bottom seems to push his partners around and force himself into the leading position. He is admittedly the best actor in Peter Quince's little amateur group and, on the evidence of the lines, enormously keen. The absurd enthusiasm which he brings to the proceedings should be touching as well as funny, and suggests that he is quite a young man.

The Masque at the end should not be farcical. But audiences make it so. They laugh so heartily and so obtusely when things go wrong with the *Tragedy of Pyramus and Thisbe* that it is all but impossible for the actors to keep the scene in its intended key. It slips into uproarious farce and all idea is lost of a desperately serious amateur group—real people—struggling to stave off a disaster which is obviously inevitable.

The Fairies: here is where illustration, untrammelled by the necessity to cooperate with flesh and blood, is at a great advantage over the theatre. The illustrator can allow his imagination to embody what Shakespeare has suggested—tiny beings who can creep into an acorn cup, who can merge into the woodland landscape and pass for moths, cobwebs or mustard seeds.

In the theatre these creatures have to be impersonated by life-sized men and women, or possibly by children. We know that in the theatre of Shakespeare's time boys were attached to the companies of players. It may sensibly be assumed that the fairy parts in this play were written for such youngsters. Titania and Oberon will have been taller, older and more advanced in understanding and accomplishment than their attendant fairies, some of whom may have been little more than toddlers. But even Oberon and Titania will have been notably smaller than the grown-up actors.

In practical terms the theatrical dilemma is this: whether to employ grown-up fairies who can act the part but look all wrong; or whether to use children who can look the parts but not act them. In an amateur production it will probably be best to have children and rely on their endearing lack of artifice to carry the day. But a professional production would be forced to rely on the cooperation of professional children, neither endearing nor artless, but rather little monsters, weaned on the harshest realities of showbiz.

The professional producer is therefore usually constrained to employ grown-ups. So, since the fairies are going to look very much the same size and of the same kind as the mortals, the difference between them must be made by the interpretation of the actors.

In these days when ideas spread mostly from highly urbanized centres, there is a tendency to sentimentalize most of the traditions which belong to our more rural past. In this category are our conceptions of fairies and all other personifications of nature. About fairies we are especially and vulgarly sentimental.

In the case of *A Midsummer Night's Dream,* sentimentality has found a powerful ally in Mendelssohn. His justly celebrated *Incidental Music* has proved good enough to impose a particular conception of the play upon at least three generations. Mendelssohn's Fairy Music is exquisitely pretty, but it is impossible to associate it with any kind of fairies except exquisitely pretty, tiny, female things, tippeting about in white muslin ballet skirts with tinsel stars on the ends of their "wands". It is all a long way from Shakespeare's idea of fairyland.

Oberon is certainly a mischievous, if not a malevolent, creature, interfering quite unwarrantably with his love-juice in the affairs of the young Athenians and prepared to go to cruel lengths to get the better of Titania. He is addressed by Puck as "King of Shadows" and, in the same scene, it emerges that fairies, like ghosts in the churchyard, must shun the approach of day. When Puck hears the morning lark, it is the signal for Oberon and Titania to trip in silence after night's shade. They compass the globe "following darkness like a dream".

In the fairy scenes the "beautiful" scenes are offset by others. Fairyland is just *not* all sweetness and charm. For example: the first little fairy's speech about cowslips and dewdrops is followed by the speeches of the Puck in his disguise as Robin Goodfellow. These exploits are not pretty at all; they are not even funny. It is not in the least amusing to mislead night-wanderers laughing at their harm; nor to make wise old aunts miss their stools and hurt their poor old bums. Laughter at pranks like these is not the tinkle of silvery fairy bells, but the guffaw of an ill-conditioned lout or the snigger of a malevolent eld.

Similarly a dainty, doll-like fairy queen just does not square with the lines. Titania sends her elves to "war with rere-mice for their leathern wings"; she commands them not merely to steal the honey-bags from Humble Bees, but to crop the poor insects' thighs for night-tapers which are to be lighted at fiery glowworms' eyes—incitement not merely to theft but to gross cruelty, described in glowing terms. And, if this were not enough, they are to pluck the wings from painted butterflies to fan the moonbeam from her lover's eyes. The play is not well served if the ferocity, the greed, the sensuality and mischievous silliness of the fairies is played down in favour of daintiness and respectability.

Theseus and Hippolyta, like so many of the great personages in Shakespeare, have little else to do but be graciously authoritative, to suggest—an idea heavily stressed in many of Shakespeare's works—that society is a hierarchy, that "togetherness" does not work without due observance of "degree"; and, at the end, to be Master and Mistress of the Revels. This, I suspect, is a more important function than is admitted in the modern world. The Master and Mistress, the presiding figures over a ceremony in time past, were felt to have more than human significance. Whoever they were, maybe no more than some provincial mayor and his fat dame, they represented Father and Mother, thence King and Queen, thence the presence, even at quite humble little events, of that God who is concerned with the fall of a sparrow. I believe that it dignified an occasion to be reminded that God is interested and indeed symbolically present.

To Theseus is given the splendid crown of an otherwise dull part: the moment when, at the end of the Bergomask, which—according to tradition—gentle and simple should dance *together,* he says, "The iron tongue of midnight hath told twelve". It is time for the masquers to return to their life of everyday; time for the lovers to go to bed; fairy time. "Fairies now are frolic". But now, instead of spite and mischief, they are intent upon blessing every room of the palace with "sweet peace".

This benevolence, presumably, is the result of the reconciliation of Oberon and Titania. The lovers, who all unwittingly have brought this about, are to be treated as friends. One of the dangers of sentimentalizing the fairy scenes is that this denouement is then robbed both of meaning and surprise. It should be an unexpected, but fortunate, result of the events of the play, not just one more instance of the fairies' "sweetness".

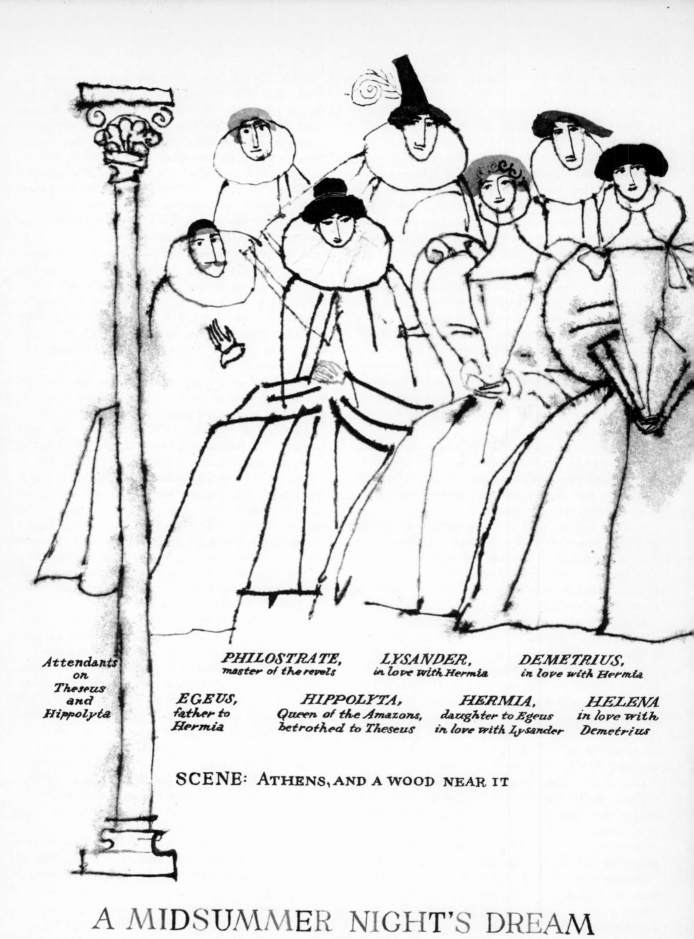

Attendants
on
Theseus
and
Hippolyta

PHILOSTRATE,
master of the revels

LYSANDER,
in love with Hermia

DEMETRIUS,
in love with Hermia

EGEUS,
father to
Hermia

HIPPOLYTA,
Queen of the Amazons,
betrothed to Theseus

HERMIA,
daughter to Egeus
in love with Lysander

HELENA
in love with
Demetrius

SCENE: ATHENS, AND A WOOD NEAR IT

A MIDSUMMER NIGHT'S DREAM

DRAMATIS PERSONAE

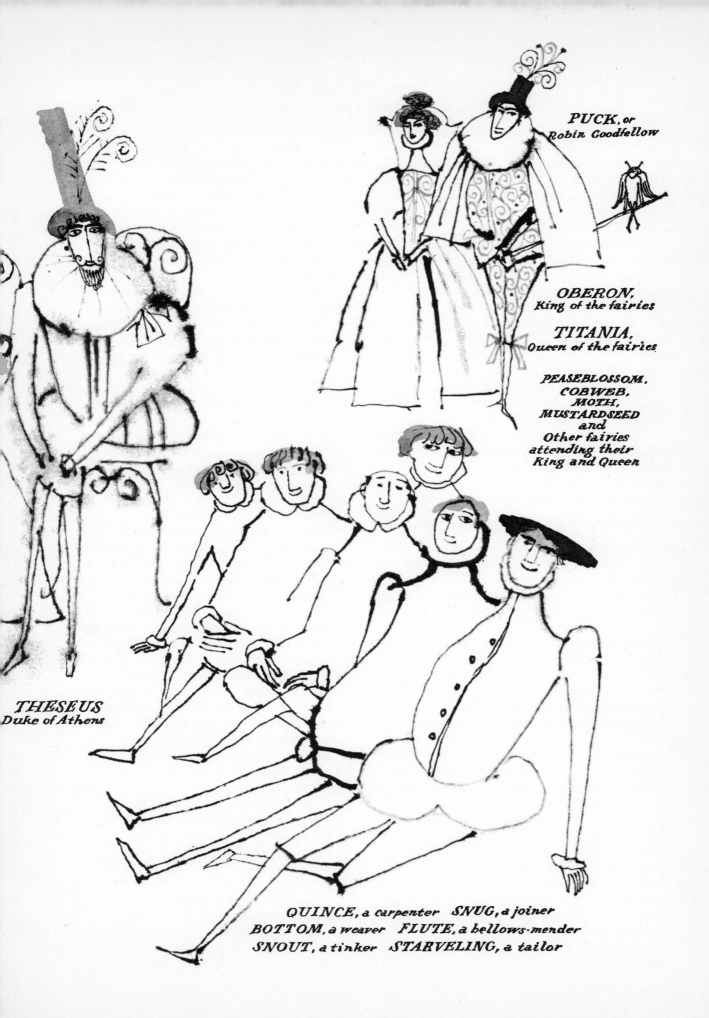

PUCK, or
Robin Goodfellow

OBERON,
King of the fairies

TITANIA,
Queen of the fairies

PEASEBLOSSOM,
COBWEB,
MOTH,
MUSTARDSEED
and
Other fairies
attending their
King and Queen

THESEUS
Duke of Athens

QUINCE, a carpenter   SNUG, a joiner
BOTTOM, a weaver   FLUTE, a bellows-mender
SNOUT, a tinker   STARVELING, a tailor

ACT I

Scene I *Athens. The palace of* Theseus

Enter Theseus, Hippolyta, Philostrate, *and* Attendants

Theseus. Now, fair Hippolyta, our nuptial hour
  Draws on apace; four happy days bring in
  Another moon: but, O, methinks, how slow
  This old moon wanes! She lingers my desires,
  Like to a stepdame or a dowager
  Long withering out a young man's revenue.
Hippolyta. Four days will quickly steep themselves in
      night;
  Four nights will quickly dream away the time;
  And then the moon, like to a silver bow
  New-bent in heaven, shall behold the night
  Of our solemnities.
Theseus.   Go, Philostrate,
  Stir up the Athenian youth to merriments;
  Awake the pert and nimble spirit of mirth;
  Turn melancholy forth to funerals;
  The pale companion is not for our pomp.

                                Exit Philostrate

  Hippolyta, I wooed thee with my sword,
  And won thy love, doing thee injuries;
  But I will wed thee in another key,
  With pomp, with triumph and with revelling.

Enter Egeus, Hermia, Lysander, *and* Demetrius

Egeus. Happy be Theseus, our renowned duke!
Theseus. Thanks, good Egeus: what's the news with
      thee?
Egeus. Full of vexation come I, with complaint
  Against my child, my daughter Hermia.
  Stand forth, Demetrius. My noble lord,
  This man hath my consent to marry her.
  Stand forth, Lysander—and, my gracious Duke,
  This man hath bewitched the bosom of my child.
  Thou, thou, Lysander, thou hast given her rhymes
  And interchanged lovetokens with my child;
  Thou hast by moonlight at her window sung
  With feigning voice verses of feigning love,
  And stolen the impression of her fantasy
  With bracelets of thy hair, rings, gawds, conceits,
  Knacks, trifles, nosegays, sweetmeats, messengers
  Of strong prevailment in unhardened youth;
  With cunning hast thou filched my daughter's heart,
  Turned her obedience, which is due to me,
  To stubborn harshness. And, my gracious Duke,
  Be it so she will not here before your grace
  Consent to marry with Demetrius,
  I beg the ancient privilege of Athens,
  As she is mine, I may dispose of her:
  Which shall be either to this gentleman
  Or to her death, according to our law
  Immediately provided in that case.

Theseus. What say you, Hermia? Be advised, fair maid:
  To you your father should be as a god;
  One that composed your beauties, yea, and one
  To whom you are but as a form in wax
  By him imprinted and within his power
  To leave the figure or disfigure it.
  Demetrius is a worthy gentleman.
Hermia. So is Lysander.
Theseus.   In himself he is;
  But in this kind, wanting your father's voice,
  The other must be held the worthier.
Hermia. I would my father looked but with my eyes.
Theseus. Rather your eyes must with his judgement
      look.
Hermia. I do entreat your grace to pardon me.
  I know not by what power I am made bold,
  Nor how it may concern my modesty,
  In such a presence here to plead my thoughts;
  But I beseech your grace that I may know
  The worst that may befall me in this case,
  If I refuse to wed Demetrius.
Theseus. Either to die the death or to abjure
  For ever the society of men.
  Therefore, fair Hermia, question your desires;
  Know of your youth, examine well your blood,
  Whether, if you yield not to your father's choice,
  You can endure the livery of a nun,
  For aye to be in shady cloister mewed,
  To live a barren sister all your life,
  Chanting faint hymns to the cold fruitless moon.
  Thrice-blessed they that master so their blood,
  To undergo such maiden pilgrimage;
  But earthlier happy is the rose distilled,
  Than that which withering on the virgin thorn
  Grows, lives and dies in single blessedness.
Hermia. So will I grow, so live, so die, my lord,
  Ere I will yield my virgin patent up
  Unto his lordship, whose unwished yoke
  My soul consents not to give sovereignty.
Theseus. Take time to pause; and, by the next new
      moon—
  The sealing-day betwixt my love and me,
  For everlasting bond of fellowship—
  Upon that day either prepare to die
  For disobedience to your father's will,
  Or else to wed Demetrius, as he would;
  Or on Diana's altar to protest
  For aye austerity and single life.
Demetrius. Relent, sweet Hermia; and, Lysander, yield
  Thy crazed title to my certain right.
Lysander. You have her father's love, Demetrius;

Let me have Hermia's: do you marry him.

EGEUS. Scornful Lysander! True, he hath my love,
And what is mine my love shall render him.
And she is mine, and all my right of her
I do estate unto Demetrius.

LYSANDER. I am, my lord, as well derived as he,
As well possessed; my love is more than his;
My fortunes every way as fairly ranked,
If not with vantage, as Demetrius';
And, which is more than all these boasts can be,
I am beloved of beauteous Hermia.
Why should not I then prosecute my right?
Demetrius, I'll avouch it to his head,
Made love to Nedar's daughter, Helena,
And won her soul; and she, sweet lady, dotes,
Devoutly dotes, dotes in idolatry,
Upon this spotted and inconstant man.

THESEUS. I must confess that I have heard so much,
And with Demetrius thought to have spoke thereof;
But, being over-full of self-affairs,
My mind did lose it. But, Demetrius, come;
And come, Egeus; you shall go with me,
I have some private schooling for you both.
For you, fair Hermia, look you arm yourself
To fit your fancies to your father's will;
Or else the law of Athens yields you up—
Which by no means we may extenuate—
To death, or to a vow of single life.
Come, my Hippolyta: what cheer, my love?
Demetrius and Egeus, go along.
I must employ you in some business
Against our nuptial and confer with you
Of something nearly that concerns yourselves.

EGEUS. With duty and desire we follow you.

Exeunt all but LYSANDER *and* HERMIA

LYSANDER. How now, my love! why is your cheek so
pale?
How chance the roses there do fade so fast?

HERMIA. Belike for want of rain, which I could well
Beteem them from the tempest of my eyes.

LYSANDER. Ay me! For aught that I could ever read,
Could ever hear by tale or history,
The course of true love never did run smooth;
But, either it was different in blood—

HERMIA. O cross! too high to be enthralled to low.

LYSANDER. Or else misgraffed in respect of years—

HERMIA. O spite! too old to be engaged to young.

LYSANDER. Or else it stood upon the choice of friends—

HERMIA. O hell! to choose love by another's eyes.

LYSANDER. Or, if there were a sympathy in choice,
War, death, or sickness did lay siege to it,
Making it momentary as a sound,
Swift as a shadow, short as any dream;
Brief as the lightning in the collied night,
That, in a spleen, unfolds both heaven and earth,
And ere a man hath power to say "Behold!"

The jaws of darkness do devour it up:
So quick bright things come to confusion.

HERMIA. If then true lovers have been ever crossed,
It stands as an edict in destiny.
Then let us teach our trial patience,
Because it is a customary cross,
As due to love as thoughts and dreams and sighs,
Wishes and tears, poor fancy's followers.

LYSANDER. A good persuasion; therefore, hear me,
Hermia.
I have a widow aunt, a dowager
Of great revenue, and she hath no child:
From Athens is her house remote seven leagues;
And she respects me as her only son.
There, gentle Hermia, may I marry thee;
And to that place the sharp Athenian law
Cannot pursue us. If thou lovest me then,
Steal forth thy father's house tomorrow night;
And in the wood, a league without the town,
Where I did meet thee once with Helena,
To do observance to a morn of May,
There will I stay for thee.

HERMIA.   My good Lysander!
I swear to thee, by Cupid's strongest bow,
By his best arrow with the golden head,
By the simplicity of Venus' doves,
By that which knitteth souls and prospers loves,
And by that fire which burned the Carthage queen,
When the false Troyan under sail was seen,
By all the vows that ever men have broke,
In number more than ever women spoke,
In that same place thou hast appointed me,
Tomorrow truly will I meet with thee.

LYSANDER. Keep promise, love. Look, here comes
Helena.

Enter HELENA

HERMIA. God speed fair Helena! whither away?

HELENA. Call you me fair? That fair again unsay.
Demetrius loves your fair: O happy fair!
Your eyes are lodestars; and your tongue's sweet air
More tuneable than lark to shepherd's ear,
When wheat is green, when hawthorn buds appear.
Sickness is catching. O, were favour so,
Yours would I catch, fair Hermia, ere I go;
My ear should catch your voice, my eye your eye,
My tongue should catch your tongue's sweet melody.
Were the world mine, Demetrius being bated,
The rest I'd give to be to you translated.
O, teach me how you look, and with what art
You sway the motion of Demetrius' heart.

HERMIA. I frown upon him, yet he loves me still.

HELENA. O that your frowns would teach my smiles
such skill!

HERMIA. I give him curses, yet he gives me love.

HELENA. O that my prayers could such affection move!

HERMIA. The more I hate, the more he follows me.
HELENA. The more I love, the more he hateth me.
HERMIA. His folly, Helena, is no fault of mine.
HELENA. None, but your beauty: would that fault were
    mine!
HERMIA. Take comfort; he no more shall see my face;
    Lysander and myself will fly this place.
    Before the time I did Lysander see,
    Seemed Athens as a paradise to me.
    O, then, what graces in my love do dwell,
    That he hath turned a heaven unto a hell!
LYSANDER. Helen, to you our minds we will unfold:
    Tomorrow night, when Phœbe doth behold
    Her silver visage in the watery glass,
    Decking with liquid pearl the bladed grass,
    A time that lovers' flights doth still conceal,
    Through Athens' gates have we devised to steal.
HERMIA. And in the wood, where often you and I
    Upon faint primrose beds were wont to lie,
    Emptying our bosoms of their counsel sweet,
    There my Lysander and myself shall meet;
    And thence from Athens turn away our eyes,
    To seek new friends and stranger companies.
    Farewell, sweet playfellow; pray thou for us;
    And good luck grant thee thy Demetrius!
    Keep word, Lysander; we must starve our sight
    From lovers' food till morrow deep midnight.
LYSANDER. I will, my Hermia.   *Exit* HERMIA
                    Helena, adieu;
    As you on him, Demetrius dote on you!   *Exit*
HELENA. How happy some o'er other some can be!
    Through Athens I am thought as fair as she.
    But what of that? Demetrius thinks not so;
    He will not know what all but he do know;
    And as he errs, doting on Hermia's eyes,
    So I, admiring of his qualities.
    Things base and vile, holding no quantity,
    Love can transpose to form and dignity;
    Love looks not with the eyes, but with the mind;
    And therefore is winged Cupid painted blind.
    Nor hath Love's mind of any judgement taste;
    Wings and no eyes figure unheedy haste;
    And therefore is Love said to be a child,
    Because in choice he is so oft beguiled.
    As waggish boys in game themselves forswear,
    So the boy Love is perjured every where:
    For ere Demetrius looked on Hermia's eyne,
    He hailed down oaths that he was only mine;
    And when this hail some heat from Hermia felt,
    So he dissolved, and showers of oaths did melt.
    I will go tell him of fair Hermia's flight.
    Then to the wood will he tomorrow night
    Pursue her; and for this intelligence
    If I have thanks, it is a dear expense.
    But herein mean I to enrich my pain,
    To have his sight thither and back again.   *Exit*

SCENE II *Athens.* QUINCE's *house*

Enter QUINCE, SNUG, BOTTOM, FLUTE, SNOUT, *and* STARVELING

QUINCE. Is all our company here?

BOTTOM. You were best to call them generally, man by man, according to the scrip.

QUINCE. Here is the scroll of every man's name, which is thought fit, through all Athens, to play in our interlude before the Duke and the Duchess, on his wedding day at night.

BOTTOM. First, good Peter Quince, say what the play treats on, then read the names of the actors, and so grow to a point.

QUINCE. Marry, our play is: The most lamentable comedy, and most cruel death of Pyramus and Thisby.

BOTTOM. A very good piece of work, I assure you, and a merry. Now, good Peter Quince, call forth your actors by the scroll. Masters, spread yourselves.

QUINCE. Answer as I call you. Nick Bottom, the weaver.

BOTTOM. Ready. Name what part I am for, and proceed.

QUINCE. You, Nick Bottom, are set down for Pyramus.

BOTTOM. What is Pyramus? a lover, or a tyrant?

QUINCE. A lover, that kills himself most gallant for love.

BOTTOM. That will ask some tears in the true performing of it. If I do it, let the audience look to their eyes; I will move storms, I will condole in some measure. To the rest. Yet my chief humour is for a tyrant: I could play Ercles rarely, or a part to tear a cat in, to make all split.

> The raging rocks
> And shivering shocks
> Shall break the locks
>   Of prison gates;
> And Phibbus' car
> Shall shine from far
> And make and mar
>   The foolish Fates.

This was lofty! Now name the rest of the players. This is Ercles' vein, a tyrant's vein; a lover is more condoling.

QUINCE. Francis Flute, the bellows-mender.

FLUTE. Here, Peter Quince.

QUINCE. Flute, you must take Thisby on you.

FLUTE. What is Thisby? a wandering knight?

QUINCE. It is the lady that Pyramus must love.

FLUTE. Nay, faith, let not me play a woman; I have a beard coming.

QUINCE. That's all one; you shall play it in a mask, and you may speak as small as you will.

BOTTOM. An I may hide my face, let me play Thisby too, I'll speak in a monstrous little voice, "Thisne, Thisne"; "Ah Pyramus, my lover dear! thy Thisby dear, and lady dear!"

QUINCE. No, no! You must play Pyramus; and, Flute, you Thisby.

BOTTOM. Well, proceed.

QUINCE. Robin Starveling, the tailor.

STARVELING. Here, Peter Quince.

QUINCE. Robin Starveling, you must play Thisby's mother. Tom Snout, the tinker.

SNOUT. Here, Peter Quince.

QUINCE. You, Pyramus' father; myself, Thisby's father. Snug, the joiner; you, the lion's part. And, I hope, here is a play fitted.

SNUG. Have you the lion's part written? Pray you, if it be, give it me, for I am slow of study.

QUINCE. You may do it extempore, for it is nothing but roaring.

BOTTOM. Let me play the lion too. I will roar, that I will do any man's heart good to hear me; I will roar, that I will make the Duke say "Let him roar again, let him roar again."

QUINCE. An you should do it too terribly, you would fright the Duchess and the ladies, that they would shriek; and that were enough to hang us all.

ALL. That would hang us, every mother's son.

BOTTOM. I grant you, friends, if that you should fright the ladies out of their wits, they would have no more discretion but to hang us; but I will aggravate my voice so that I will roar you as gently as any sucking dove. I will roar you an 'twere any nightingale.

QUINCE. You can play no part but Pyramus; for Pyramus is a sweet-faced man; a proper man, as one shall see in a summer's day; a most lovely gentleman-like man. Therefore you must needs play Pyramus.

BOTTOM. Well, I will undertake it. What beard were I best to play it in?

QUINCE. Why, what you will.

BOTTOM. I will discharge it in either your straw-colour beard, your orange-tawny beard, your purple-in-grain beard, or your French-crown-colour beard, your perfect yellow.

QUINCE. Some of your French crowns have no hair at all, and then you will play barefaced. But, masters, here are your parts: and I am to entreat you, request you and desire you, to con them by tomorrow night; and meet me in the palace wood, a mile without the town, by moonlight; there will we rehearse, for if we meet in the city, we shall be dogged with company, and our devices known. In the meantime I will draw a bill of properties, such as our play wants. I pray you, fail me not.

BOTTOM. We will meet; and there we may rehearse most obscenely and courageously. Take pains; be perfect. Adieu.

QUINCE. At the Duke's oak we meet.

BOTTOM. Enough; hold or cut bowstrings.

Exeunt

ACT II

ACT II

SCENE I *A wood near Athens*

Enter, from opposite sides, a Fairy, *and* Puck

Puck. How now, spirit! whither wander you?
Fairy. Over hill, over dale,
    Through bush, through brier,
  Over park, over pale,
    Through flood, through fire,
I do wander every where,
Swifter than the moon's sphere;
And I serve the Fairy Queen,
To dew her orbs upon the green.
    The cowslips tall her pensioners be:
    In their gold coats spots you see;
    Those be rubies, fairy favours,
    In those freckles live their savours.
  I must go seek some dewdrops here
  And hang a pearl in every cowslip's ear.
  Farewell, thou lob of spirits; I'll be gone.
  Our Queen and all her elves come here anon.
Puck. The King doth keep his revels here tonight;
  Take heed the Queen come not within his sight;
  For Oberon is passing fell and wrath,
  Because that she, as her attendant, hath
  A lovely boy, stolen from an Indian king—
  She never had so sweet a changeling—
  And jealous Oberon would have the child
  Knight of his train, to trace the forests wild.
  But she perforce withholds the loved boy,
  Crowns him with flowers and makes him all her joy.
  And now they never meet in grove or green,
  By fountain clear, or spangled starlight sheen,
  But they do square, that all their elves for fear
  Creep into acorn cups and hide them there.
Fairy. Either I mistake your shape and making quite,
  Or else you are that shrewd and knavish sprite
  Called Robin Goodfellow. Are not you he
  That frights the maidens of the villagery;
  Skim milk, and sometimes labour in the quern
  And bootless make the breathless housewife churn;
  And sometime make the drink to bear no barm;
  Mislead night wanderers, laughing at their harm?
  Those that Hobgoblin call you, and sweet Puck,
  You do their work, and they shall have good luck:
  Are not you he?
Puck.   Thou speak'st aright;
  I am that merry wanderer of the night.
  I jest to Oberon and make him smile
  When I a fat and bean-fed horse beguile,
  Neighing in likeness of a filly foal;
  And sometime lurk I in a gossip's bowl,
  In very likeness of a roasted crab,
  And when she drinks, against her lips I bob
  And on her withered dewlap pour the ale.
  The wisest aunt, telling the saddest tale,
  Sometime for three foot stool mistaketh me;
  Then slip I from her bum, down topples she,
  And "tailor" cries, and falls into a cough;
  And then the whole quire hold their hips and laugh,
  And waxen in their mirth and sneeze and swear
  A merrier hour was never wasted there.
  But, room, fairy! here comes Oberon.
Fairy. And here my mistress. Would that he were gone!
    Enter, from one side, Oberon, *with his train;*
      from the other, Titania, *with hers*

OBERON. Ill met by moonlight, proud Titania.

TITANIA. What, jealous Oberon! Fairies, skip hence;
  I have forsworn his bed and company.

OBERON. Tarry, rash wanton: am not I thy lord?

TITANIA. Then I must be thy lady; but I know
  When thou hast stolen away from fairyland,
  And in the shape of Corin sat all day,
  Playing on pipes of corn and versing love
  To amorous Phillida. Why art thou here,
  Come from the farthest steppe of India?
  But that, forsooth, the bouncing Amazon,
  Your buskined mistress and your warrior love,
  To Theseus must be wedded, and you come
  To give their bed joy and prosperity.

OBERON. How canst thou thus for shame, Titania,
  Glance at my credit with Hippolyta,
  Knowing I know thy love to Theseus?
  Didst thou not lead him through the glimmering night
  From Perigenia, whom he ravished?
  And make him with fair Aegle break his faith,
  With Ariadne and Antiopa?

TITANIA. These are the forgeries of jealousy;
  And never, since the middle summer's spring,
  Met we on hill, in dale, forest or mead,
  By paved fountain or by rushy brook,
  Or in the beached margent of the sea,
  To dance our ringlets to the whistling wind,
  But with thy brawls thou hast disturbed our sport.
  Therefore the winds, piping to us in vain,
  As in revenge, have sucked up from the sea
  Contagious fogs; which falling in the land
  Have every pelting river made so proud
  That they have overborne their continents.
  The ox hath therefore stretched his yoke in vain,
  The ploughman lost his sweat, and the green corn
  Hath rotted ere his youth attained a beard;
  The fold stands empty in the drowned field,
  And crows are fatted with the murrain flock;
  The nine men's morris is filled up with mud,
  And the quaint mazes in the wanton green
  For lack of tread are undistinguishable.
  The human mortals want their winter cheer;
  No night is now with hymn or carol blest;
  Therefore the moon, the governess of floods,
  Pale in her anger, washes all the air,
  That rheumatic diseases do abound.
  And through this distemperature we see
  The seasons alter. Hoary-headed frosts
  Fall in the fresh lap of the crimson rose,
  And on old Hiems' thin and icy crown
  An odorous chaplet of sweet summer buds
  Is, as in mockery, set; the spring, the summer,
  The childing autumn, angry winter, change
  Their wonted liveries, and the mazed world,
  By their increase, now knows not which is which.
  And this same progeny of evils comes

From our debate, from our dissension;
  We are their parents and original.

OBERON. Do you amend it then; it lies in you.
  Why should Titania cross her Oberon?
  I do but beg a little changeling boy,
  To be my henchman.

TITANIA.   Set your heart at rest:
  The fairyland buys not the child of me.
  His mother was a votaress of my order;
  And, in the spiced Indian air, by night,
  Full often hath she gossiped by my side,
  And sat with me on Neptune's yellow sands,
  Marking the embarked traders on the flood,
  When we have laughed to see the sails conceive
  And grow big-bellied with the wanton wind;
  Which she, with pretty and with swimming gait
  Following—her womb then rich with my young
    squire—
  Would imitate, and sail upon the land,
  To fetch me trifles, and return again,
  As from a voyage, rich with merchandise.
  But she, being mortal, of that boy did die;
  And for her sake do I rear up her boy,
  And for her sake I will not part with him.

OBERON. How long within this wood intend you stay?

TITANIA. Perchance till after Theseus' wedding day.
  If you will patiently dance in our round
  And see our moonlight revels, go with us;
  If not, shun me, and I will spare your haunts.

OBERON. Give me that boy, and I will go with thee.

TITANIA. Not for thy fairy kingdom. Fairies, away!
  We shall chide downright, if I longer stay.

                              Exit TITANIA *with her train*

OBERON. Well, go thy way; thou shalt not from this
    grove
  Till I torment thee for this injury.
  My gentle Puck, come hither. Thou rememberest
  Since once I sat upon a promontory,
  And heard a mermaid on a dolphin's back
  Uttering such dulcet and harmonious breath
  That the rude sea grew civil at her song
  And certain stars shot madly from their spheres,
  To hear the sea-maid's music.

PUCK.   I remember.

OBERON. That very time I saw, but thou couldst not,
  Flying between the cold moon and the earth,
  Cupid all armed. A certain aim he took
  At a fair vestal throned by the west,
  And loosed his love-shaft smartly from his bow,
  As it should pierce a hundred thousand hearts;
  But I might see young Cupid's fiery shaft
  Quenched in the chaste beams of the watery moon,
  And the imperial votaress passed on,
  In maiden meditation, fancy-free.
  Yet marked I where the bolt of Cupid fell.
  It fell upon a little western flower,

Before milk-white, now purple with love's wound,
And maidens call it love-in-idleness.
Fetch me that flower; the herb I shewed thee once.
The juice of it on sleeping eyelids laid
Will make or man or woman madly dote
Upon the next live creature that it sees.
Fetch me this herb; and be thou here again
Ere the leviathan can swim a league.

PUCK. I'll put a girdle round about the earth
In forty minutes.   *Exit*

OBERON.   Having once this juice,
I'll watch Titania when she is asleep,
And drop the liquor of it in her eyes.
The next thing then she waking looks upon,
Be it on lion, bear, or wolf, or bull,
On meddling monkey, or on busy ape,
She shall pursue it with the soul of love.
And ere I take this charm from off her sight,
As I can take it with another herb,
I'll make her render up her page to me.
But who comes here? I am invisible;
And I will overhear their conference.

Enter DEMETRIUS,
HELENA *following him*

DEMETRIUS. I love thee not, therefore pursue me not.
Where is Lysander and fair Hermia?
The one I'll slay, the other slayeth me.
Thou told'st me they were stolen unto this wood;
And here am I, and wood within this wood,
Because I cannot meet my Hermia.
Hence, get thee gone, and follow me no more.

HELENA. You draw me, you hard-hearted adamant;
But yet you draw not iron, for my heart
Is true as steel. Leave you your power to draw,
And I shall have no power to follow you.

DEMETRIUS. Do I entice you? Do I speak you fair?
Or, rather, do I not in plainest truth
Tell you, I do not, nor I cannot love you?

HELENA. And even for that do I love you the more.
I am your spaniel; and, Demetrius,
The more you beat me, I will fawn on you.
Use me but as your spaniel, spurn me, strike me,
Neglect me, lose me; only give me leave,
Unworthy as I am, to follow you.
What worser place can I beg in your love—
And yet a place of high respect with me—
Than to be used as you use your dog?

DEMETRIUS. Tempt not too much the hatred of my
spirit,
For I am sick when I do look on thee.

HELENA. And I am sick when I look not on you.

DEMETRIUS. You do impeach your modesty too much,
To leave the city and commit yourself
Into the hands of one that loves you not;
To trust the opportunity of night

And the ill counsel of a desert place
With the rich worth of your virginity.

HELENA. Your virtue is my privilege. For that
It is not night when I do see your face,
Therefore I think I am not in the night;
Nor doth this wood lack worlds of company,
For you in my respect are all the world.
Then how can it be said I am alone,
When all the world is here to look on me?

DEMETRIUS. I'll run from thee and hide me in the brakes,
And leave thee to the mercy of wild beasts.

HELENA. The wildest hath not such a heart as you.
Run when you will, the story shall be changed:
Apollo flies, and Daphne holds the chase;
The dove pursues the griffin; the mild hind
Makes speed to catch the tiger; bootless speed,
When cowardice pursues and valour flies.

DEMETRIUS. I will not stay thy questions; let me go.
Or, if thou follow me, do not believe
But I shall do thee mischief in the wood.

HELENA. Ay, in the temple, in the town, the field,
You do me mischief. Fie, Demetrius!
Your wrongs do set a scandal on my sex:
We cannot fight for love, as men may do;
We should be wooed and were not made to woo.
                                                    Exit DEMETRIUS
I'll follow thee and make a heaven of hell,
To die upon the hand I love so well.   *Exit*

OBERON. Fare thee well, nymph; ere he do leave this
grove,
Thou shalt fly him and he shall seek thy love.

Re-enter PUCK
Hast thou the flower there? Welcome, wanderer.

PUCK. Ay, there it is.

OBERON.   I pray thee, give it me.
I know a bank where the wild thyme blows,
Where oxlips and the nodding violet grows,
Quite over-canopied with luscious woodbine,
With sweet musk-roses and with eglantine.
There sleeps Titania sometime of the night,
Lulled in these flowers with dances and delight;
And there the snake throws her enamelled skin,
Weed wide enough to wrap a fairy in;
And with the juice of this I'll streak her eyes,
And make her full of hateful fantasies.
Take thou some of it, and seek through this grove.
A sweet Athenian lady is in love
With a disdainful youth. Anoint his eyes;
But do it when the next thing he espies
May be the lady. Thou shalt know the man
By the Athenian garments he hath on.
Effect it with some care that he may prove
More fond on her than she upon her love;
And look thou meet me ere the first cock crow.

PUCK. Fear not, my lord, your servant shall do so.
                                                    Exeunt

SCENE II *Another part of the wood*

Enter TITANIA *with her train*

TITANIA. Come, now a roundel and a fairy song;
  Then, for the third part of a minute, hence;
  Some to kill cankers in the musk-rose buds,
  Some war with reremice for their leathern wings,
  To make my small elves coats, and some keep back
  The clamorous owl that nightly hoots and wonders
  At our quaint spirits. Sing me now asleep;
  Then to your offices and let me rest.

The Fairies *sing*

You spotted snakes with double tongue,
  Thorny hedgehogs, be not seen;
Newts and blind-worms, do no wrong,
  Come not near our Fairy Queen.
    Philomel, with melody
    Sing in our sweet lullaby;
Lulla, lulla, lullaby, lulla, lulla, lullaby;
    Never harm,
    Nor spell nor charm,
  Come our lovely lady nigh;
  So, good night, with lullaby.

Weaving spiders, come not here;
  Hence, you long-legged spinners, hence!
Beetles black, approach not near;
  Worm nor snail, do no offence.
    Philomel, with melody
    Sing in our sweet lullaby;
Lulla, lulla, lullaby, lulla, lulla, lullaby;
    Never harm,
    Nor spell nor charm,
  Come our lovely lady nigh;
  So, good night, with lullaby.

A FAIRY. Hence, away! now all is well;
  One aloof stand sentinel.
                              Exeunt Fairies. TITANIA *sleeps*

Enter OBERON, *and squeezes the flower on* TITANIA'S *eyelids*

OBERON. What thou seest when thou dost wake,
  Do it for thy true-love take,
  Love and languish for his sake.
  Be it ounce, or cat, or bear,
  Pard, or boar with bristled hair,
  In thy eye that shall appear
  When thou wakest, it is thy dear.
  Wake when some vile thing is near.   *Exit*

Enter LYSANDER *and* HERMIA

LYSANDER. Fair love, you faint with wandering in the
    wood;
  And to speak troth, I have forgot our way.
  We'll rest us, Hermia, if you think it good,
  And tarry for the comfort of the day.

HERMIA. Be it so, Lysander. Find you out a bed;
  For I upon this bank will rest my head.
LYSANDER. One turf shall serve as pillow for us both;
  One heart, one bed, two bosoms and one troth.
HERMIA. Nay, good Lysander; for my sake, my dear,
  Lie further off yet, do not lie so near.
LYSANDER. O, take the sense, sweet, of my innocence!
  Love takes the meaning in love's conference.
  I mean, that my heart unto yours is knit
  So that but one heart we can make of it;
  Two bosoms interchained with an oath;
  So then two bosoms and a single troth.
  Then by your side no bed-room me deny;
  For lying so, Hermia, I do not lie.
HERMIA. Lysander riddles very prettily.
  Now much beshrew my manners and my pride,
  If Hermia meant to say Lysander lied.
  But, gentle friend, for love and courtesy
  Lie further off. In human modesty,
  Such separation as may well be said
  Becomes a virtuous bachelor and a maid,
  So far be distant; and, good night, sweet friend,
  Thy love ne'er alter till thy sweet life end!
LYSANDER. Amen, amen, to that fair prayer, say I;
  And then end life when I end loyalty!
  Here is my bed; sleep give thee all his rest!
HERMIA. With half that wish the wisher's eyes be
    pressed!   *They sleep*

Enter PUCK

PUCK. Through the forest have I gone,
  But Athenian found I none,
  On whose eyes I might approve
  This flower's force in stirring love.
  Night and silence!—Who is here?
  Weeds of Athens he doth wear:
  This is he, my master said,
  Despised the Athenian maid;
  And here the maiden, sleeping sound,
  On the dank and dirty ground.
  Pretty soul! She durst not lie
  Near this lack-love, this kill-courtesy.
  Churl, upon thy eyes I throw
  All the power this charm doth owe.
  When thou wakest, let love forbid
  Sleep his seat on thy eyelid.
  So awake when I am gone;
  For I must now to Oberon.   *Exit*

Enter DEMETRIUS *and* HELENA, *running*

HELENA. Stay, though thou kill me, sweet Demetrius.
DEMETRIUS. I charge thee, hence, and do not haunt me
    thus.
HELENA. O, wilt thou darkling leave me? Do not so.

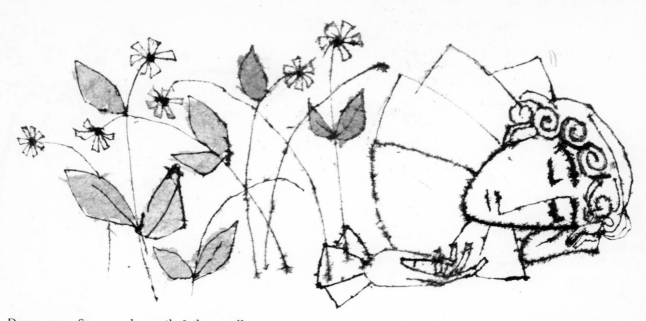

DEMETRIUS. Stay, on thy peril; I alone will go. *Exit*

HELENA. O, I am out of breath in this fond chase!
  The more my prayer, the lesser is my grace.
  Happy is Hermia, wheresoe'er she lies;
  For she hath blessed and attractive eyes.
  How came her eyes so bright? Not with salt tears;
  If so, my eyes are oftener washed than hers.
  No, no, I am as ugly as a bear;
  For beasts that meet me run away for fear.
  Therefore no marvel though Demetrius
  Do, as a monster, fly my presence thus.
  What wicked and dissembling glass of mine
  Made me compare with Hermia's sphery eyne?
  But who is here? Lysander! on the ground!
  Dead? or asleep? I see no blood, no wound.
  Lysander, if you live, good sir, awake.

LYSANDER. [*Awaking*] And run through fire I will for
    thy sweet sake.
  Transparent Helena! Nature shows her art,
  That through thy bosom makes me see thy heart.
  Where is Demetrius? O, how fit a word
  Is that vile name to perish on my sword!

HELENA. Do not say so, Lysander; say not so.
  What though he love your Hermia? Lord, what though?
  Yet Hermia still loves you; then be content.

LYSANDER. Content with Hermia! No; I do repent
  The tedious minutes I with her have spent.
  Not Hermia but Helena I love—
  Who will not change a raven for a dove?
  The will of man is by his reason swayed;
  And reason says you are the worthier maid.
  Things growing are not ripe until their season:
  So I, being young, till now ripe not to reason;
  And touching now the point of human skill,
  Reason becomes the marshal to my will
  And leads me to your eyes, where I o'erlook
  Love's stories written in love's richest book.

HELENA. Wherefore was I to this keen mockery born?
  When at your hands did I deserve this scorn?
  Is't not enough, is't not enough, young man,
  That I did never, no, nor never can,
  Deserve a sweet look from Demetrius' eye,
  But you must flout my insufficiency?
  Good troth, you do me wrong, good sooth, you do,
  In such disdainful manner me to woo.
  But fare you well. Perforce I must confess
  I thought you lord of more true gentleness.
  O, that a lady, of one man refused,
  Should of another therefore be abused! *Exit*

LYSANDER. She sees not Hermia. Hermia, sleep thou
    there;
  And never mayst thou come Lysander near!
  For as a surfeit of the sweetest things
  The deepest loathing to the stomach brings,
  Or as the heresies that men do leave
  Are hated most of those they did deceive,
  So thou, my surfeit and my heresy,
  Of all be hated, but the most of me!
  And, all my powers, address your love and might
  To honour Helen and to be her knight! *Exit*

HERMIA. [*Awaking*] Help me, Lysander, help me! Do
    thy best
  To pluck this crawling serpent from my breast!
  Ay me, for pity! What a dream was here!
  Lysander, look how I do quake with fear:
  Methought a serpent eat my heart away,
  And you sat smiling at his cruel prey.
  Lysander! What, removed? Lysander! Lord!
  What, out of hearing? Gone? No sound, no word?
  Alack, where are you? Speak, an if you hear;
  Speak, of all loves! I swoon almost with fear.
  No? Then I well perceive you are not nigh:
  Either death or you I'll find immediately. *Exit*

ACT III

SCENE I *The wood.* TITANIA *lying asleep*

Enter QUINCE, SNUG, BOTTOM, FLUTE,
SNOUT, *and* STARVELING

BOTTOM. Are we all met?

QUINCE. Pat, pat; and here's a marvellous convenient
place for our rehearsal. This green plot shall be our
stage, this hawthorn brake our tiring-house; and we
will do it in action as we will do it before the Duke.

BOTTOM. Peter Quince—

QUINCE. What sayest thou, bully Bottom?

BOTTOM. There are things in this comedy of Pyramus
and Thisby that will never please. First, Pyramus must
draw a sword to kill himself; which the ladies cannot
abide. How answer you that?

SNOUT. By'r lakin, a parlous fear.

STARVELING. I believe we must leave the killing out,
when all is done.

BOTTOM. Not a whit: I have a device to make all well.
Write me a prologue; and let the prologue seem to
say, we will do no harm with our swords and that
Pyramus is not killed indeed; and, for the more better
assurance, tell them that I Pyramus am not Pyramus,
but Bottom the weaver. This will put them out of fear.

QUINCE. Well, we will have such a prologue; and it
shall be written in eight and six.

BOTTOM. No, make it two more; let it be written in
eight and eight.

SNOUT. Will not the ladies be afeard of the lion?

STARVELING. I fear it, I promise you.

BOTTOM. Masters, you ought to consider with yourselves: to bring in—God shield us!—a lion among
ladies, is a most dreadful thing; for there is not a more
fearful wild-fowl than your lion living; and we ought
to look to 't.

SNOUT. Therefore another prologue must tell he is not
a lion.

BOTTOM. Nay, you must name his name, and half his
face must be seen through the lion's neck; and he himself must speak through, saying thus, or to the same
defect: "Ladies,"— or "Fair ladies, I would wish
you,"—or "I would request you,"—or "I would
entreat you—not to fear, not to tremble: my life for
yours. If you think I come hither as a lion, it were
pity of my life. No, I am no such thing; I am a man as
other men are''; and there indeed let him name his
name, and tell them plainly he is Snug the joiner.

QUINCE. Well, it shall be so. But there is two hard
things: that is, to bring the moonlight into a chamber;
for, you know, Pyramus and Thisby meet by moonlight.

SNOUT. Doth the moon shine that night we play our
play?

BOTTOM. A calendar, a calendar! Look in the almanac;
find out moonshine, find out moonshine.

QUINCE. Yes, it doth shine that night.

BOTTOM. Why, then may you leave a casement of the
great chamber window, where we play, open, and
the moon may shine in at the casement.

QUINCE. Ay; or else one must come in with a bush of
thorns and a lantern, and say he comes to disfigure,

or to present, the person of Moonshine. Then, there is another thing: we must have a wall in the great chamber; for Pyramus and Thisby, says the story, did talk through the chink of a wall.

SNOUT. You can never bring in a wall. What say you, Bottom?

BOTTOM. Some man or other must present Wall; and let him have some plaster, or some loam, or some rough-cast about him, to signify wall; and let him hold his fingers thus, and through that cranny shall Pyramus and Thisby whisper.

QUINCE. If that may be, then all is well. Come, sit down, every mother's son, and rehearse your parts. Pyramus, you begin: when you have spoken your speech, enter into that brake; and so every one according to his cue.

Enter PUCK *behind*

PUCK. What hempen homespuns have we swaggering here,
So near the cradle of the Fairy Queen?
What, a play toward! I'll be an auditor;
An actor too perhaps, if I see cause.

QUINCE. Speak, Pyramus. Thisby, stand forth.

BOTTOM. Thisby, the flowers of odious savours sweet—

QUINCE. Odours, odours.

BOTTOM. ——odours savours sweet;
So hath thy breath, my dearest Thisby dear.
But hark, a voice! Stay thou but here awhile,
And by and by I will to thee appear.   *Exit*

PUCK. A stranger Pyramus than e'er played here.   *Exit*

FLUTE. Must I speak now?

QUINCE. Ay, marry, must you; for you must understand he goes but to see a noise that he heard, and is to come again.

FLUTE. Most radiant Pyramus, most lily-white of hue,
Of color like the red rose on triumphant brier,
Most brisky juvenal and eke most lovely Jew,
As true as truest horse that yet would never tire.
I'll meet thee, Pyramus, at Ninny's tomb.

QUINCE. Ninus' tomb, man. Why, you must not speak that yet; that you answer to Pyramus. You speak all your part at once, cues and all. Pyramus, enter. Your cue is past; it is, "never tire."

FLUTE. O—As true as truest horse, that yet would never tire.

Re-enter PUCK, *and* BOTTOM *with an ass's head*

BOTTOM. If I were fair, Thisby, I were only thine.

QUINCE. O monstrous! O strange! we are haunted. Pray, masters! Fly, masters! Help!   *Exeunt* QUINCE,
SNUG, FLUTE, SNOUT, *and* STARVELING

PUCK. I'll follow you, I'll lead you about a round,
    Through bog, through bush, through brake, through
        brier:
    Sometime a horse I'll be, sometime a hound,
        A hog, a headless bear, sometime a fire;
    And neigh, and bark, and grunt, and roar, and burn,
    Like horse, hound, hog, bear, fire, at every turn.
                                            Exit

BOTTOM. Why do they run away? This is a knavery of
    them to make me afeard.

Re-enter SNOUT

SNOUT. O Bottom, thou art changed! What do I see
    on thee?
BOTTOM. What do you see? You see an ass-head of your
    own, do you?   *Exit* SNOUT

Re-enter QUINCE

QUINCE. Bless thee, Bottom! Bless thee! thou art trans-
    lated.   *Exit*
BOTTOM. I see their knavery: this is to make an ass of
    me; to fright me, if they could. But I will not stir
    from this place, do what they can. I will walk up and
    down here, and I will sing, that they shall hear I am
    not afraid.   *Sings*
        The ousel cock so black of hue,
            With orange-tawny bill,
        The throstle with his note so true,
            The wren with little quill—
TITANIA. [*Awaking*] What angel wakes me from my
    flowery bed?
BOTTOM. [*Sings*]
        The finch, the sparrow and the lark,
            The plain-song cuckoo gray,
        Whose note full many a man doth mark,
            And dares not answer nay—
    for, indeed, who would set his wit to so foolish a bird?
    Who would give a bird the lie, though he cry
    "cuckoo" never so?
TITANIA. I pray thee, gentle mortal, sing again.
    Mine ear is much enamoured of thy note;
    So is mine eye enthralled to thy shape;
    And thy fair virtue's force perforce doth move me
    On the first view to say, to swear, I love thee.
BOTTOM. Methinks, mistress, you should have little
    reason for that. And yet, to say the truth, reason and
    love keep little company together nowadays; the
    more the pity that some honest neighbours will not
    make them friends. Nay, I can gleek upon occasion.
TITANIA. Thou art as wise as thou art beautiful.
BOTTOM. Not so, neither; but if I had wit enough to
    get out of this wood, I have enough to serve mine
    own turn.
TITANIA. Out of this wood do not desire to go;
    Thou shalt remain here, whether thou wilt or no.
    I am a spirit of no common rate:

The summer still doth tend upon my state;
And I do love thee. Therefore, go with me;
I'll give thee fairies to attend on thee,
And they shall fetch thee jewels from the deep,
And sing while thou on pressed flowers dost sleep.
And I will purge thy mortal grossness so
That thou shalt like an airy spirit go.
Peaseblossom! Cobweb! Moth! and Mustardseed!

Enter PEASEBLOSSOM, COBWEB, MOTH, *and* MUSTARDSEED

PEASEBLOSSOM. Ready.
COBWEB.   And I.
MOTH.   And I.
MUSTARDSEED.   And I.
ALL.   Where shall we go?
TITANIA. Be kind and courteous to this gentleman;
    Hop in his walks and gambol in his eyes;
    Feed him with apricots and dewberries,
    With purple grapes, green figs, and mulberries;
    The honey-bags steal from the humble-bees,
    And for night tapers crop their waxen thighs
    And light them at the fiery glow-worm's eyes,
    To have my love to bed and to arise;
    And pluck the wings from painted butterflies
    To fan the moonbeams from his sleeping eyes.
    Nod to him, elves, and do him courtesies.
PEASEBLOSSOM. Hail, mortal!
COBWEB. Hail!
MOTH. Hail!
MUSTARDSEED. Hail!
BOTTOM. I cry your worships mercy, heartily; I be-
    seech your worship's name.
COBWEB. Cobweb.
BOTTOM. I shall desire you of more acquaintance, good
    Master Cobweb; if I cut my finger, I shall make bold
    with you. Your name, honest gentleman?
PEASEBLOSSOM. Peaseblossom.

BOTTOM. I pray you, commend me to Mistress Squash, your mother, and to Master Peascod, your father. Good Master Peaseblossom, I shall desire you of more acquaintance too. Your name, I beseech you, sir?

MUSTARDSEED. Mustardseed.

BOTTOM. Good Master Mustardseed, I know your patience well: that same cowardly, giant-like ox-beef hath devoured many a gentleman of your house. I promise you your kindred hath made my eyes water ere now. I desire your more acquaintance, good Master Mustardseed.

TITANIA. Come, wait upon him; lead him to my bower.
The moon methinks looks with a watery eye;
And when she weeps, weeps every little flower,
Lamenting some enforced chastity.
Tie up my love's tongue, bring him silently.

Exeunt

SCENE II *Another part of the wood*

Enter OBERON

OBERON. I wonder if Titania be awaked;
   Then, what it was that next came in her eye,
   Which she must dote on in extremity.

Enter PUCK

Here comes my messenger.
                    How now, mad spirit!
   What night-rule now about this haunted grove?
PUCK. My mistress with a monster is in love.
   Near to her close and consecrated bower,
   While she was in her dull and sleeping hour,
   A crew of patches, rude mechanicals,
   That work for bread upon Athenian stalls,
   Were met together to rehearse a play
   Intended for great Theseus' nuptial day.
   The shallowest thick-skin of that barren sort,
   Who Pyramus presented, in their sport
   Forsook his scene and entered in a brake.
   When I did him at this advantage take,
   An ass's nole I fixed on his head.

   Anon his Thisbe must be answered,
   And forth my mimic comes. When they him spy,
   As wild geese that the creeping fowler eye,
   Or russet-pated choughs, many in sort,
   Rising and cawing at the gun's report,
   Sever themselves and madly sweep the sky,
   So, at his sight, away his fellows fly;
   And, at our stamp, here o'er and o'er one falls;
   He murder cries and help from Athens calls.
   Their sense thus weak, lost with their fears thus strong,
   Made senseless things begin to do them wrong;
   For briers and thorns at their apparel snatch;
   Some sleeves, some hats, from yielders all things catch.
   I led them on in this distracted fear,
   And left sweet Pyramus translated there.
   When in that moment, so it came to pass,
   Titania waked and straightway loved an ass.
OBERON. This falls out better than I could devise.
   But hast thou yet latched the Athenian's eyes
   With the love-juice, as I did bid thee do?

82

PUCK. I took him sleeping—that is finished too—
    And the Athenian woman by his side;
    That, when he waked, of force she must be eyed.

Enter HERMIA *and* DEMETRIUS

OBERON. Stand close; this is the same Athenian.
PUCK. This is the woman, but not this the man.
DEMETRIUS. O, why rebuke you him that loves you so?
    Lay breath so bitter on your bitter foe.
HERMIA. Now I but chide; but I should use thee worse,
    For thou, I fear, hast given me cause to curse.
    If thou hast slain Lysander in his sleep,
    Being o'er shoes in blood, plunge in the deep,
    And kill me too.
    The sun was not so true unto the day
    As he to me. Would he have stolen away
    From sleeping Hermia? I'll believe as soon
    This whole earth may be bored and that the moon
    May through the centre creep and so displease
    Her brother's noontide with the Antipodes.
    It cannot be but thou hast murdered him;
    So should a murderer look, so dead, so grim.
DEMETRIUS. So should the murdered look, and so
        should I,
    Pierced through the heart with your stern cruelty.
    Yet you, the murderer, look as bright, as clear,
    As yonder Venus in her glimmering sphere.
HERMIA. What's this to my Lysander? Where is he?
    Ah, good Demetrius, wilt thou give him me?
DEMETRIUS. I had rather give his carcass to my hounds.
HERMIA. Out, dog! Out, cur! Thou drivest me past
        the bounds
    Of maiden's patience. Hast thou slain him, then?
    Henceforth be never numbered among men!
    O, once tell true, tell true, even for my sake!
    Durst thou have looked upon him being awake,
    And hast thou killed him sleeping? O brave touch!
    Could not a worm, an adder, do so much?
    An adder did it; for with doubler tongue
    Than thine, thou serpent, never adder stung.
DEMETRIUS. You spend your passion on a misprised
        mood:
    I am not guilty of Lysander's blood,
    Nor is he dead, for aught that I can tell.
HERMIA. I pray thee, tell me then that he is well.
DEMETRIUS. An if I could, what should I get therefore?
HERMIA. A privilege never to see me more.
    And from thy hated presence part I so:
    See me no more, whether he be dead or no.   *Exit*
DEMETRIUS. There is no following her in this fierce vein.
    Here therefore for a while I will remain.
    So sorrow's heaviness doth heavier grow
    For debt that bankrupt sleep doth sorrow owe;
    Which now in some slight measure it will pay,
    If for his tender here I make some stay.
                                Lies down and sleeps

OBERON. What hast thou done? Thou hast mistaken
        quite
    And laid the love-juice on some true-love's sight.
    Of thy misprision must perforce ensue
    Some true love turned and not a false turned true.
PUCK. Then fate o'er-rules, that, one man holding troth,
    A million fail, confounding oath on oath.
OBERON. About the wood go swifter than the wind,
    And Helena of Athens look thou find.
    All fancy-sick she is and pale of cheer,
    With sighs of love, that costs the fresh blood dear.
    By some illusion see thou bring her here;
    I'll charm his eyes against she do appear.
PUCK. I go, I go; look how I go,
    Swifter than arrow from the Tartar's bow.   *Exit*

OBERON.   Flower of this purple dye,
        Hit with Cupid's archery,
        Sink in apple of his eye.
        When his love he doth espy,
        Let her shine as gloriously
        As the Venus of the sky.
        When thou wak'st, if she be by,
        Beg of her for remedy.

Re-enter PUCK

PUCK.   Captain of our fairy band,
        Helena is here at hand;
        And the youth, mistook by me,
        Pleading for a lover's fee.
        Shall we their fond pageant see?
        Lord, what fools these mortals be!
OBERON.   Stand aside: the noise they make
        Will cause Demetrius to awake.
PUCK.   Then will two at once woo one;
        That must needs be sport alone;
        And those things do best please me
        That befall preposterously.

Enter LYSANDER *and* HELENA

LYSANDER. Why should you think that I should woo in
        scorn?
    Scorn and derision never come in tears.
    Look, when I vow, I weep; and vows so born,
    In their nativity all truth appears.
    How can these things in me seem scorn to you,
    Bearing the badge of faith, to prove them true?
HELENA. You do advance your cunning more and more.
    When truth kills truth, O devilish-holy fray!
    These vows are Hermia's: will you give her o'er?
    Weigh oath with oath, and you will nothing weigh.
    Your vows to her and me, put in two scales,
    Will even weigh, and both as light as tales.
LYSANDER. I had no judgement when to her I swore.
HELENA. Nor none, in my mind, now you give her o'er.
LYSANDER. Demetrius loves her, and he loves not you.

DEMETRIUS. [*Awaking*] O Helen, goddess, nymph, per-
    fect, divine!
  To what, my love, shall I compare thine eyne?
  Crystal is muddy. O, how ripe in show
  Thy lips, those kissing cherries, tempting grow!
  That pure congealed white, high Taurus' snow,
  Fanned with the eastern wind, turns to a crow
  When thou hold'st up thy hand. O, let me kiss
  This princess of pure white, this seal of bliss!
HELENA. O spite! O hell! I see you all are bent
  To set against me for your merriment.
  If you were civil and knew courtesy,
  You would not do me thus much injury.
  Can you not hate me, as I know you do,
  But you must join in souls to mock me too?
  If you were men, as men you are in show,
  You would not use a gentle lady so;
  To vow, and swear, and superpraise my parts,
  When I am sure you hate me with your hearts.
  You both are rivals, and love Hermia;
  And now both rivals, to mock Helena.
  A trim exploit, a manly enterprise,
  To conjure tears up in a poor maid's eyes
  With your derision! None of noble sort
  Would so offend a virgin and extort
  A poor soul's patience, all to make you sport.
LYSANDER. You are unkind, Demetrius; be not so;
  For you love Hermia, this you know I know.
  And here, with all good will, with all my heart,
  In Hermia's love I yield you up my part;
  And yours of Helena to me bequeath,
  Whom I do love and will do till my death.
HELENA. Never did mockers waste more idle breath.
DEMETRIUS. Lysander, keep thy Hermia; I will none.
  If e'er I loved her, all that love is gone.
  My heart to her but as guest-wise sojourned,
  And now to Helen is it home returned,
  There to remain.
LYSANDER.   Helen, it is not so.
DEMETRIUS. Disparage not the faith thou dost not know,
  Lest, to thy peril, thou aby it dear.
  Look, where thy love comes; yonder is thy dear.

            Re-enter HERMIA

HERMIA. Dark night, that from the eye his function takes,
  The ear more quick of apprehension makes;
  Wherein it doth impair the seeing sense,
  It pays the hearing double recompense.
  Thou art not by mine eye, Lysander, found;
  Mine ear, I thank it, brought me to thy sound.
  But why unkindly didst thou leave me so?
LYSANDER. Why should he stay, whom love doth press
    to go?
HERMIA. What love could press Lysander from my side?
LYSANDER. Lysander's love, that would not let him bide,
  Fair Helena, who more engilds the night
  Than all yon fiery oes and eyes of light.

  Why seek'st thou me? Could not this make thee know,
  The hate I bear thee made me leave thee so?
HERMIA. You speak not as you think; it cannot be.
HELENA. Lo, she is one of this confederacy!
  Now I perceive they have conjoined all three
  To fashion this false sport, in spite of me.
  Injurious Hermia! Most ungrateful maid!
  Have you conspired, have you with these contrived
  To bait me with this foul derision?
  Is all the counsel that we two have shared,
  The sisters' vows, the hours that we have spent,
  When we have chid the hasty-footed time
  For parting us—O, is it all forgot?
  All schooldays' friendship, childhood innocence?
  We, Hermia, like two artificial gods,
  Have with our needles created both one flower,
  Both on one sampler, sitting on one cushion,
  Both warbling of one song, both in one key,
  As if our hands, our sides, voices and minds,
  Had been incorporate. So we grew together,
  Like to a double cherry, seeming parted,
  But yet an union in partition;
  Two lovely berries moulded on one stem;
  So, with two seeming bodies, but one heart;
  Two of the first, like coats in heraldry,
  Due but to one and crowned with one crest.
  And will you rent our ancient love asunder,
  To join with men in scorning your poor friend?
  It is not friendly, 'tis not maidenly.
  Our sex, as well as I, may chide you for it,
  Though I alone do feel the injury.
HERMIA. I am amazed at your passionate words.
  I scorn you not; it seems that you scorn me.
HELENA. Have you not set Lysander, as in scorn,
  To follow me and praise my eyes and face?
  And made your other love, Demetrius,
  Who even but now did spurn me with his foot,
  To call me goddess, nymph, divine and rare,
  Precious, celestial? Wherefore speaks he this
  To her he hates? And wherefore doth Lysander
  Deny your love, so rich within his soul,
  And tender me, forsooth, affection,
  But by your setting on, by your consent?
  What though I be not so in grace as you,
  So hung upon with love, so fortunate,
  But miserable most, to love unloved?
  This you should pity rather than despise.
HERMIA. I understand not what you mean by this.
HELENA. Ay, do, persevere, counterfeit sad looks,
  Make mouths upon me when I turn my back;
  Wink each at other; hold the sweet jest up:
  This sport, well carried, shall be chronicled.
  If you have any pity, grace, or manners,
  You would not make me such an argument.
  But fare ye well: 'tis partly my own fault;
  Which death or absence soon shall remedy.

LYSANDER. Stay, gentle Helena; hear my excuse.
My love, my life, my soul, fair Helena!
HELENA. O excellent!
HERMIA. Sweet, do not scorn her so.
DEMETRIUS. If she cannot entreat, I can compel.
LYSANDER. Thou canst compel no more than she entreat;
Thy threats have no more strength than her weak
prayers.
Helen, I love thee; by my life, I do.
I swear by that which I will lose for thee,
To prove him false that says I love thee not.
DEMETRIUS. I say I love thee more than he can do.
LYSANDER. If thou say so, withdraw, and prove it too.
DEMETRIUS. Quick, come!
HERMIA. Lysander, whereto tends all this?
LYSANDER. Away, you Ethiope!
DEMETRIUS. No, no, sir! You
Seem to break loose, take on as you would follow,
But yet come not. You are a tame man, go!
LYSANDER. Hang off, thou cat, thou bur! Vile thing,
let loose,
Or I will shake thee from me like a serpent!
HERMIA. Why are you grown so rude? What change is
this?
Sweet love—
LYSANDER. Thy love! Out, tawny Tartar, out!
Out, loathed medicine! Hated potion, hence!
HERMIA. Do you not jest?
HELENA. Yes, sooth; and so do you.
LYSANDER. Demetrius, I will keep my word with thee.
DEMETRIUS. I would I had your bond, for I perceive
A weak bond holds you; I'll not trust your word.
LYSANDER. What, should I hurt her, strike her, kill
her dead?
Although I hate her, I'll not harm her so.
HERMIA. What, can you do me greater harm than hate?
Hate me! Wherefore? O me! what news, my love!
Am not I Hermia? Are not you Lysander?
I am as fair now as I was erewhile.
Since night you loved me; yet since night you left me.
Why, then you left me—O, the gods forbid!—
In earnest, shall I say?
LYSANDER. Ay, by my life;
And never did desire to see thee more.
Therefore be out of hope, of question, of doubt;
Be certain, nothing truer; 'tis no jest
That I do hate thee and love Helena.
HERMIA. O me! You juggler! You cankerblossom!
You thief of love! What, have you come by night
And stolen my love's heart from him?
HELENA. Fine, i' faith!
Have you no modesty, no maiden shame,
No touch of bashfulness? What, will you tear
Impatient answers from my gentle tongue?
Fie, fie! you counterfeit, you puppet, you!
HERMIA. Puppet? Why so? Ay, that way goes the game.

Now I perceive that she hath made compare
Between our statures; she hath urged her height;
And with her personage, her tall personage,
Her height, forsooth, she hath prevailed with him.
And are you grown so high in his esteem,
Because I am so dwarfish and so low?
How low am I, thou painted maypole? Speak;
How low am I? I am not yet so low
But that my nails can reach unto thine eyes.
HELENA. I pray you, though you mock me, gentlemen,
Let her not hurt me. I was never curst;
I have no gift at all in shrewishness;
I am a right maid for my cowardice.
Let her not strike me. You perhaps may think,
Because she is something lower than myself,
That I can match her.
HERMIA. Lower! Hark, again.
HELENA. Good Hermia, do not be so bitter with me.
I evermore did love you, Hermia,
Did ever keep your counsels, never wronged you;
Save that, in love unto Demetrius,
I told him of your stealth unto this wood.
He followed you; for love I followed him;
But he hath chid me hence and threatened me
To strike me, spurn me, nay, to kill me too.
And now, so you will let me quiet go,
To Athens will I bear my folly back
And follow you no further. Let me go;
You see how simple and how fond I am.
HERMIA. Why, get you gone; who is 't that hinders you?
HELENA. A foolish heart, that I leave here behind.
HERMIA. What, with Lysander?
HELENA. With Demetrius.
LYSANDER. Be not afraid; she shall not harm thee,
Helena.
DEMETRIUS. No, sir, she shall not, though you take her
part.
HELENA. O, when she's angry, she is keen and shrewd!
She was a vixen when she went to school;
And though she be but little, she is fierce.
HERMIA. "Little" again! Nothing but "low" and
"little"!
Why will you suffer her to flout me thus?
Let me come to her.
LYSANDER. Get you gone, you dwarf;
You minimus, of hindering knot-grass made;
You bead, you acorn.
DEMETRIUS. You are too officious
In her behalf that scorns your services.
Let her alone; speak not of Helena;
Take not her part; for, if thou dost intend
Never so little show of love to her,
Thou shalt aby it.
LYSANDER. Now she holds me not;
Now follow, if thou darest, to try whose right,
Of thine or mine, is most in Helena.

DEMETRIUS. Follow! nay, I'll go with thee, cheek by
    jowl. *Exeunt* LYSANDER *and* DEMETRIUS
HERMIA. You, mistress, all this coil is 'long of you.
    Nay, go not back.
HELENA.   I will not trust you, I,
    Nor longer stay in your curst company.
    Your hands than mine are quicker for a fray,
    My legs are longer though, to run away. *Exit*
HERMIA. I am amazed, and know not what to say. *Exit*
OBERON. This is thy negligence; still thou mistak'st,
    Or else committ'st thy knaveries wilfully.
PUCK. Believe me, King of Shadows, I mistook.
    Did not you tell me I should know the man
    By the Athenian garments he had on?
    And so far blameless proves my enterprise,
    That I have 'nointed an Athenian's eyes;
    And so far am I glad it so did sort
    As this their jangling I esteem a sport.
OBERON. Thou see'st these lovers seek a place to fight.
    Hie therefore, Robin, overcast the night;
    The starry welkin cover thou anon
    With drooping fog as black as Acheron,
    And lead these testy rivals so astray
    As one come not within another's way.
    Like to Lysander sometime frame thy tongue,
    Then stir Demetrius up with bitter wrong;
    And sometime rail thou like Demetrius;
    And from each other look thou lead them thus,
    Till o'er their brows death-counterfeiting sleep
    With leaden legs and batty wings doth creep.
    Then crush this herb into Lysander's eye;
    Whose liquor hath this virtuous property,
    To take from thence all error with his might,
    And make his eyeballs roll with wonted sight.
    When they next wake, all this derision
    Shall seem a dream and fruitless vision,
    And back to Athens shall the lovers wend,
    With league whose date till death shall never end.
    Whiles I in this affair do thee employ,
    I'll to my Queen and beg her Indian boy;
    And then I will her charmed eye release
    From monster's view, and all things shall be peace.
PUCK. My fairy lord, this must be done with haste,
    For night's swift dragons cut the clouds full fast,
    And yonder shines Aurora's harbinger;
    At whose approach, ghosts, wandering here and there,
    Troop home to churchyards. Damned spirits all,
    That in crossways and floods have burial,
    Already to their wormy beds are gone;
    For fear lest day should look their shames upon,
    They wilfully themselves exile from light
    And must for aye consort with black-browed night.
OBERON. But we are spirits of another sort.
    I with the morning's love have oft made sport,
    And, like a forester, the groves may tread,
    Even till the eastern gate, all fiery-red,

Opening on Neptune with fair blessed beams,
    Turns into yellow gold his salt green streams.
    But, notwithstanding, haste; make no delay.
    We may effect this business yet ere day. *Exit*
PUCK. Up and down, up and down,
    I will lead them up and down:
    I am feared in field and town:
    Goblin, lead them up and down.
    Here comes one.

Re-enter LYSANDER

LYSANDER. Where art thou, proud Demetrius? Speak
    thou now.
PUCK. Here, villain; drawn and ready. Where art thou?
LYSANDER. I will be with thee straight.
PUCK.   Follow me, then,
    To plainer ground. *Exit* LYSANDER

Re-enter DEMETRIUS

DEMETRIUS.   Lysander! Speak again.
    Thou runaway, thou coward, art thou fled?
    Speak! In some bush? Where dost thou hide thy head?
PUCK. Thou coward, art thou bragging to the stars,
    Telling the bushes that thou look'st for wars,
    And wilt not come? Come, recreant; come, thou
    child,
    I'll whip thee with a rod. He is defiled
    That draws a sword on thee.
DEMETRIUS.   Yea, art thou there?
PUCK. Follow my voice; we'll try no manhood here.
                  Exeunt

Re-enter LYSANDER

LYSANDER. He goes before me and still dares me on.
    When I come where he calls, then he is gone.
    The villain is much lighter-heeled than I,
    I followed fast, but faster he did fly;
    That fallen am I in dark uneven way,
    And here will rest me. [*Lies down*] Come, thou gentle
    day!
    For if but once thou show me thy grey light,
    I'll find Demetrius and revenge this spite. *Sleeps*

Re-enter PUCK *and* DEMETRIUS

PUCK. Ho, ho, ho! Coward, why com'st thou not?
DEMETRIUS. Abide me, if thou dar'st; for well I wot
    Thou runn'st before me, shifting every place,
    And darest not stand, nor look me in the face.
    Where art thou now?
PUCK.   Come hither; I am here.
DEMETRIUS. Nay, then, thou mock'st me. Thou shalt
    buy this dear,
    If ever I thy face by daylight see.
    Now, go thy way. Faintness constraineth me
    To measure out my length on this cold bed.
    By day's approach look to be visited.
              Lies down and sleeps

Re-enter HELENA

HELENA. O weary night, O long and tedious night,
   Abate thy hours! Shine comforts from the east,
That I may back to Athens by daylight,
   From these that my poor company detest:
And sleep, that sometimes shuts up sorrow's eye,
Steal me awhile from mine own company.
                                    Lies down and sleeps

PUCK. Yet but three? Come one more;
   Two of both kinds makes up four.
   Here she comes, curst and sad.
   Cupid is a knavish lad,
   Thus to make poor females mad.

Re-enter HERMIA

HERMIA. Never so weary, never so in woe,
   Bedabbled with the dew and torn with briers,
I can no further crawl, no further go;
   My legs can keep no pace with my desires.
Here will I rest me till the break of day.
Heavens shield Lysander, if they mean a fray!
                                    Lies down and sleeps

PUCK.   On the ground
             Sleep sound;
             I'll apply
             To your eye,
         Gentle lover, remedy.
                 Squeezing the juice on LYSANDER's *eyes*
             When thou wak'st,
             Thou tak'st
             True delight
             In the sight
         Of thy former lady's eye.
         And the country proverb known,
         That every man should take his own,
         In your waking shall be shown:
             Jack shall have Jill;
             Nought shall go ill;
The man shall have his mare again, and all shall be well.
                                    Exit

ACT IV

SCENE I *The same.* LYSANDER, DEMETRIUS, HELENA, *and* HERMIA *lying asleep*

Enter TITANIA *and* BOTTOM; PEASEBLOSSOM, COBWEB, MOTH, MUSTARDSEED, *and other* Fairies *attending;* OBERON *behind unseen*

TITANIA. Come, sit thee down upon this flowery bed,
    While I thy amiable cheeks do coy,
  And stick musk-roses in thy sleek smooth head,
    And kiss thy fair large ears, my gentle joy.
BOTTOM. Where's Peaseblossom?
PEASEBLOSSOM. Ready.

BOTTOM. Scratch my head, Peaseblossom. Where's Mounsieur Cobweb?
COBWEB. Ready.
BOTTOM. Mounsieur Cobweb, good mounsieur, get you your good dry oats. Methinks I have a great desire to a humble-bee on the top of a thistle; and, good moun-

sieur, bring me the honey-bag. Do not fret yourself
too much in the action, mounsieur; and, good mounsieur, have a care the honey-bag break not; I would
be loath to have you overflown with a honey-bag,
signior. Where's Mounsieur Mustardseed?

MUSTARDSEED. Ready.

BOTTOM. Give me your neaf, Mounsieur Mustardseed.
Pray you, leave your courtesy, good mounsieur.

MUSTARDSEED. What's your will?

BOTTOM. Nothing, good mounsieur, but to help Cavalery
Cobweb to scratch. I must to the barber's, mounsieur;
for methinks I am marvellous hairy about the face;
and I am such a tender ass, if my hair do but tickle me,
I must scratch.

TITANIA. What, wilt thou hear some music, my sweet
love?

BOTTOM. I have a reasonable good ear in music. Let's
have the tongs and the bones.

TITANIA. Or say, sweet love, what thou desir'st to eat.

BOTTOM. Truly, a peck of provender; I could munch
your good dry oats. Methinks I have a great desire to a
bottle of hay: good hay, sweet hay, hath no fellow.

TITANIA. I have a venturous fairy that shall seek
The squirrel's hoard, and fetch thee new nuts.

BOTTOM. I had rather have a handful or two of dried
peas. But, I pray you, let none of your people stir me;
I have an exposition of sleep come upon me.

TITANIA. Sleep thou, and I will wind thee in my arms.
Fairies, be gone, and be all ways away. *Exeunt* Fairies
So doth the woodbine, the sweet honeysuckle,
Gentle entwist; the female ivy so
Enrings the barky fingers of the elm.
O, how I love thee! how I dote on thee!   *They sleep*

Enter PUCK

OBERON. [*Advancing*] Welcome, good Robin. See'st
thou this sweet sight?
Her dotage now I do begin to pity;
For, meeting her of late behind the wood,
Seeking sweet favours for this hateful fool,
I did upbraid her and fall out with her;
For she his hairy temples then had rounded
With coronet of fresh and fragrant flowers;
And that same dew, which sometime on the buds
Was wont to swell like round and orient pearls,
Stood now within the pretty flowerets' eyes
Like tears that did their own disgrace bewail.
When I had at my pleasure taunted her
And she in mild terms begged my patience,
I then did ask of her her changeling child;
Which straight she gave me, and her fairy sent
To bear him to my bower in fairyland.
And now I have the boy, I will undo
This hateful imperfection of her eyes.
And, gentle Puck, take this transformed scalp
From off the head of this Athenian swain;
That, he awaking when the other do,

May all to Athens back again repair
And think no more of this night's accidents
But as the fierce vexation of a dream.
But first I will release the Fairy Queen.
    Be as thou wast wont to be;
    See as thou wast wont to see:
    Dian's bud o'er Cupid's flower
    Hath such force and blessed power.
Now, my Titania; wake you, my sweet Queen.

TITANIA. My Oberon! what visions have I seen!
Methought I was enamoured of an ass.

OBERON. There lies your love.

TITANIA.   How came these things to pass?
O, how mine eyes do loathe his visage now!

OBERON. Silence awhile. Robin, take off this head.
Titania, music call; and strike more dead
Than common sleep of all these five the sense.

TITANIA. Music, ho! Music, such as charmeth sleep!
                                                Music

PUCK. Now, when thou wak'st, with thine own fool's
eyes peep.

OBERON. Sound, music! Come, my Queen, take hands
with me,
And rock the ground whereon these sleepers be.
Now thou and I are new in amity
And will tomorrow midnight solemnly
Dance in Duke Theseus' house triumphantly
And bless it to all fair prosperity.
There shall the pairs of faithful lovers be
Wedded, with Theseus, all in jollity.

PUCK.   Fairy King, attend, and mark:
          I do hear the morning lark.

OBERON.   Then, my Queen, in silence sad,
          Trip we after night's shade;
          We the globe can compass soon,
          Swifter than the wandering moon.

TITANIA. Come, my lord, and in our flight
          Tell me how it came this night
          That I sleeping here was found
          With these mortals on the ground.   *Exeunt*
                                        Horns sound offstage

Enter THESEUS, HIPPOLYTA, EGEUS, *and train*

THESEUS. Go, one of you, find out the forester;
For now our observation is performed;
And since we have the vanguard of the day,
My love shall hear the music of my hounds,
Uncouple in the western valley; let them go.
Dispatch, I say, and find the forester.
                            Exit an Attendant
We will, fair Queen, up to the mountain's top
And mark the musical confusion
Of hounds and echo in conjunction.

HIPPOLYTA. I was with Hercules and Cadmus once,
When in a wood of Crete they bayed the bear
With hounds of Sparta. Never did I hear
Such gallant chiding; for, besides the groves,

The skies, the fountains, every region near
Seemed all one mutual cry. I never heard
So musical a discord, such sweet thunder.

THESEUS. My hounds are bred out of the Spartan kind,
So flewed, so sanded, and their heads are hung
With ears that sweep away the morning dew;
Crook-kneed, and dewlapped like Thessalian bulls;
Slow in pursuit, but matched in mouth like bells,
Each under each. A cry more tuneable
Was never holla'd to, nor cheered with horn,
In Crete, in Sparta, nor in Thessaly.
Judge when you hear. But, soft! What nymphs are
    these?

EGEUS. My lord, this is my daughter here asleep;
And this, Lysander; this Demetrius is;
This Helena, old Nedar's Helena.
I wonder of their being here together.

THESEUS. No doubt they rose up early to observe
The rite of May, and, hearing our intent,
Came here in grace of our solemnity.
But speak, Egeus; is not this the day
That Hermia should give answer of her choice?

EGEUS. It is, my lord.

THESEUS. Go, bid the huntsmen wake them with their
    horns.   *Horns and shouts offstage.* LYSANDER,
        DEMETRIUS, HELENA, *and* HERMIA *wake up*
Good morrow, friends. Saint Valentine is past.
Begin these woodbirds but to couple now?

LYSANDER. Pardon, my lord.

THESEUS.   I pray you all, stand up.
I know you two are rival enemies.
How comes this gentle concord in the world,
That hatred is so far from jealousy,
To sleep by hate, and fear no enmity?

LYSANDER. My lord, I shall reply amazedly,
Half sleep, half waking; but as yet, I swear,
I cannot truly say how I came here.
But, as I think—for truly would I speak,
And now I do bethink me, so it is—
I came with Hermia hither. Our intent
Was to be gone from Athens, where we might,
Without the peril of the Athenian law.

EGEUS. Enough, enough, my lord; you have enough.
I beg the law, the law, upon his head.
They would have stolen away; they would, Demetrius,
Thereby to have defeated you and me,
You of your wife and me of my consent,
Of my consent that she should be your wife.

DEMETRIUS. My lord, fair Helen told me of their stealth,
Of this their purpose hither to this wood;
And I in fury hither followed them,
Fair Helena in fancy following me.
But, my good lord, I wot not by what power—
But by some power it is—my love to Hermia,
Melted as the snow, seems to me now
As the remembrance of an idle gawd

    Which in my childhood I did dote upon;
    And all the faith, the virtue of my heart,
    The object and the pleasure of mine eye,
    Is only Helena. To her, my lord,
    Was I betrothed ere I saw Hermia;
    But, like in sickness, did I loathe this food;
    But, as in health, come to my natural taste,
    Now I do wish it, love it, long for it,
    And will for evermore be true to it.

THESEUS. Fair lovers, you are fortunately met:
    Of this discourse we more will hear anon.
    Egeus, I will overbear your will;
    For in the temple, by and by, with us
    These couples shall eternally be knit.
    And, for the morning now is something worn,
    Our purposed hunting shall be set aside.
    Away with us to Athens; three and three,
    We'll hold a feast in great solemnity.
    Come, Hippolyta.   *Exeunt* THESEUS, HIPPOLYTA,
                              EGEUS, *and train*

DEMETRIUS. These things seem small and undistinguish-
    able,
    Like far-off mountains turned into clouds.

HERMIA. Methinks I see these things with parted eye,
    When every thing seems double.

HELENA.   So methinks;
    And I have found Demetrius like a jewel,
    Mine own, and not mine own.

DEMETRIUS.   Are you sure
    That we are awake? It seems to me
    That yet we sleep, we dream. Do not you think
    The Duke was here, and bid us follow him?

HERMIA. Yea; and my father.

HELENA.   And Hippolyta.

LYSANDER. And he did bid us follow to the temple.

DEMETRIUS. Why, then, we are awake: let's follow him;
    And by the way let us recount our dreams.   *Exeunt*

BOTTOM. [*Awaking*] When my cue comes, call me, and
    I will answer; my next is, "Most fair Pyramus."
    Heigh-ho! Peter Quince! Flute, the bellows-mender!
    Snout, the tinker! Starveling! God's my life, stolen
    hence, and left me asleep! I have had a most rare vision.
    I have had a dream, past the wit of man to say what
    dream it was: man is but an ass, if he go about to ex-
    pound this dream. Methought I was—there is no man
    can tell what. Methought I was—and methought I
    had—but man is but a patched fool, if he will offer to
    say what methought I had. The eye of man hath not
    heard, the ear of man hath not seen, man's hand is
    not able to taste, his tongue to conceive, nor his heart
    to report, what my dream was. I will get Peter Quince
    to write a ballad of this dream: it shall be called
    Bottom's Dream, because it hath no bottom; and I
    will sing it in the latter end of a play, before the Duke.
    Peradventure, to make it the more gracious, I shall
    sing it at her death.   *Exit*

SCENE II *Athens*. QUINCE's *house*

Enter QUINCE, FLUTE, SNOUT, *and* STARVELING

QUINCE. Have you sent to Bottom's house? Is he come home yet?

STARVELING. He cannot be heard of. Out of doubt he is transported.

FLUTE. If he come not, then the play is marred; it goes not forward, doth it?

QUINCE. It is not possible; you have not a man in all Athens able to discharge Pyramus but he.

FLUTE. No, he hath simply the best wit of any handicraft man in Athens.

QUINCE. Yea, and the best person too; and he is a very paramour for a sweet voice.

FLUTE. You must say "paragon." A paramour is, God bless us, a thing of naught.

Enter SNUG

SNUG. Masters, the Duke is coming from the temple, and there is two or three lords and ladies more married. If our sport had gone forward, we had all been made men.

FLUTE. O sweet bully Bottom! Thus hath he lost sixpence a day during his life; he could not have 'scaped sixpence a day. An the Duke had not given him sixpence a day for playing Pyramus, I'll be hanged; he would have deserved it: sixpence a day in Pyramus, or nothing.

Enter BOTTOM

BOTTOM. Where are these lads? Where are these hearts?

QUINCE. Bottom! O most courageous day! O most happy hour!

BOTTOM. Masters, I am to discourse wonders. But ask me not what; for if I tell you, I am no true Athenian. I will tell you everything, right as it fell out.

QUINCE. Let us hear, sweet Bottom.

BOTTOM. Not a word of me. All that I will tell you is, that the Duke hath dined. Get your apparel together, good strings to your beards, new ribbons to your pumps; meet presently at the palace; every man look o'er his part; for the short and the long is, our play is preferred. In any case, let Thisby have clean linen; and let not him that plays the lion pare his nails, for they shall hang out for the lion's claws. And, most dear actors, eat no onions nor garlic, for we are to utter sweet breath; and I do not doubt but to hear them say, it is a sweet comedy. No more words: away! go, away!

Exeunt

ACT V

SCENE I *Athens. The palace of* THESEUS

Enter THESEUS, HIPPOLYTA, PHILOSTRATE, Lords, *and* Attendants

HIPPOLYTA. 'Tis strange, my Theseus, that these lovers
  speak of.
THESEUS. More strange than true; I never may believe
  These antique fables, nor these fairy toys.
  Lovers and madmen have such seething brains,
  Such shaping fantasies, that apprehend
  More than cool reason ever comprehends.
  The lunatic, the lover and the poet
  Are of imagination all compact.
  One sees more devils than vast Hell can hold,
  That is, the madman. The lover, all as frantic,
  Sees Helen's beauty in a brow of Egypt.
  The poet's eye, in a fine frenzy rolling,
  Doth glance from heaven to earth, from earth to
    heaven;
  And as imagination bodies forth
  The forms of things unknown, the poet's pen
  Turns them to shapes and gives to airy nothing
  A local habitation and a name.
  Such tricks hath strong imagination,
  That, if it would but apprehend some joy,
  It comprehends some bringer of that joy;
  Or in the night, imagining some fear,
  How easy is a bush supposed a bear!
HIPPOLYTA. But all the story of the night told over,
  And all their minds transfigured so together,
  More witnesseth than fancy's images
  And grows to something of great constancy;
  But, howsoever, strange and admirable.
THESEUS. Here come the lovers, full of joy and mirth.

Enter LYSANDER, DEMETRIUS, HERMIA, *and* HELENA

Joy, gentle friends! joy and fresh days of love
Accompany your hearts!
LYSANDER.   More than to us
  Wait in your royal walks, your board, your bed!
THESEUS. Come now; what masques, what dances shall
    we have,
  To wear away this long age of three hours
  Between our after-supper and bedtime?
  Where is our usual manager of mirth?
  What revels are in hand? Is there no play,
  To ease the anguish of a torturing hour?
  Call Philostrate.
PHILOSTRATE.   Here, mighty Theseus.
THESEUS. Say, what abridgement have you for this
    evening?
  What masque? What music? How shall we beguile
  The lazy time, if not with some delight?
PHILOSTRATE. There is a brief how many sports are ripe;

Make choice of which your highness will see first.
                                    Giving a paper
THESEUS. [*Reads*] "The battle with the Centaurs, to be
    sung
  By an Athenian eunuch to the harp."
  We'll none of that: that have I told my love,
  In glory of my kinsman Hercules.
  [*Reads*] "The riot of the tipsy Bacchanals,
  Tearing the Thracian singer in their rage."
  That is an old device; and it was played
  When I from Thebes came last a conqueror.
  [*Reads*] "The thrice three Muses mourning for the
    death
  Of Learning, late deceased in beggary."
  That is some satire, keen and critical,
  Not sorting with a nuptial ceremony.
  [*Reads*] "A tedious brief scene of young Pyramus
  And his love Thisbe; very tragical mirth."
  Merry and tragical! Tedious and brief!
  That is, hot ice and wondrous strange snow.
  How shall we find the concord of this discord?
PHILOSTRATE. A play there is, my lord, some ten words
    long,
  Which is as brief as I have known a play;
  But by ten words, my lord, it is too long,
  Which makes it tedious; for in all the play
  There is not one word apt, one player fitted.
  And tragical, my noble lord, it is;
  For Pyramus therein doth kill himself.
  Which, when I saw rehearsed, I must confess,
  Made mine eyes water; but more merry tears
  The passion of loud laughter never shed.
THESEUS. What are they that do play it?
PHILOSTRATE. Hard-handed men that work in Athens
    here,
  Which never laboured in their minds till now
  And now have toiled their unbreathed memories
  With this same play, against your nuptial.
THESEUS. And we will hear it.
PHILOSTRATE.   No, my noble lord;
  It is not for you. I have heard it over,
  And it is nothing, nothing in the world;
  Unless you can find sport in their intents,
  Extremely stretched and conned with cruel pain,
  To do you service.
THESEUS.   I will hear that play;
  For never anything can be amiss,
  When simpleness and duty tender it.
  Go, bring them in; and take your places, ladies.
                                    Exit PHILOSTRATE

HIPPOLYTA. I love not to see wretchedness o'ercharged
  And duty in his service perishing.
THESEUS. Why, gentle sweet, you shall see no such thing.
HIPPOLYTA. He says they can do nothing in this kind.
THESEUS. The kinder we, to give them thanks for
    nothing.
  Our sport shall be to take what they mistake;
  And what poor duty cannot do, noble respect
  Takes it in might, not merit.
  Where I have come, great clerks have purposed
  To greet me with premeditated welcomes;
  Where I have seen them shiver and look pale,
  Make periods in the midst of sentences,
  Throttle their practised accent in their fears
  And in conclusion dumbly have broke off,
  Not paying me a welcome. Trust me, sweet,
  Out of this silence yet I picked a welcome;
  And in the modesty of fearful duty
  I read as much as from the rattling tongue
  Of saucy and audacious eloquence.
  Love, therefore, and tongue-tied simplicity
  In least speak most, to my capacity.

Re-enter PHILOSTRATE

PHILOSTRATE. So please your grace, the Prologue is
    addressed.
THESEUS. Let him approach.   *Flourish of trumpets*

Enter QUINCE *as the* Prologue

PROLOGUE. If we offend, it is with our good will.
  That you should think, we come not to offend,
  But with good will. To show our simple skill,
  That is the true beginning of our end.
  Consider then we come but in despite.
  We do not come as minding to content you,
  Our true intent is. All for your delight
  We are not here. That you should here repent you,
  The actors are at hand and by their show
  You shall know all that you are like to know.
THESEUS. This fellow doth not stand upon points.
LYSANDER. He hath rid his prologue like a rough colt;
  he knows not the stop. A good moral, my lord: it is
  not enough to speak, but to speak true.
HIPPOLYTA. Indeed he hath played on his prologue like
  a child on a recorder; a sound, but not in government.
THESEUS. His speech was like a tangled chain; nothing
  impaired, but all disordered. Who is next?

Enter PYRAMUS *and* THISBE, WALL,
MOONSHINE, *and* LION

PROLOGUE. Gentles, perchance you wonder at this
    show;
  But wonder on, till truth make all things plain.
  This man is Pyramus, if you would know;
  This beauteous lady Thisby is certain.
  This man, with lime and rough-cast, doth present

Wall, that vile Wall which did these lovers sunder;
  And through Wall's chink, poor souls, they are content
    To whisper. At the which let no man wonder.
  This man, with lantern, dog, and bush of thorn,
    Presenteth Moonshine; for, if you will know,
  By moonshine did these lovers think no scorn
  To meet at Ninus' tomb, there, there to woo.
  This grisly beast, which Lion hight by name,
  The trusty Thisby, coming first by night,
  Did scare away, or rather did affright;
  And, as she fled, her mantle she did fall,
    Which Lion vile with bloody mouth did stain.
  Anon comes Pyramus, sweet youth and tall,
    And finds his trusty Thisby's mantle slain;
  Whereat, with blade, with bloody blameful blade,
    He bravely broached his boiling bloody breast;
  And Thisby, tarrying in mulberry shade,
    His dagger drew, and died. For all the rest,
  Let Lion, Moonshine, Wall, and lovers twain
  At large discourse, while here they do remain.
            Exeunt Prologue, PYRAMUS, THISBE,
                    LION, *and* MOONSHINE
THESEUS. I wonder if the lion be to speak.
DEMETRIUS. No wonder, my lord; one lion may, when
  many asses do.
WALL. In this same interlude it doth befall
  That I, one Snout by name, present a wall;
  And such a wall, as I would have you think,
  That had in it a crannied hole or chink,
  Through which the lovers, Pyramus and Thisby,
  Did whisper often very secretly.
  This loam, this rough-cast and this stone doth show
  That I am that same wall; the truth is so.
  And this the cranny is, right and sinister,
  Through which the fearful lovers are to whisper.
THESEUS. Would you desire lime and hair to speak
  better?
DEMETRIUS. It is the wittiest partition that ever I heard
  discourse, my lord.

Re-enter PYRAMUS

THESEUS. Pyramus draws near the wall. Silence!
PYRAMUS. O grim-looked night! O night with hue so
    black!
  O night, which ever art when day is not!
  O night, O night! Alack, alack, alack,
    I fear my Thisby's promise is forgot!
  And thou, O wall, O sweet, O lovely wall,
    That stand'st between her father's ground and mine!
  Thou wall, O wall, O sweet and lovely wall,
    Show me thy chink, to blink through with mine
      eyne!   WALL *holds up his fingers*
  Thanks, courteous wall; Jove shield thee well for this!
  But what see I? No Thisby do I see.
  O wicked wall, through whom I see no bliss!
    Cursed be thy stones for thus deceiving me!

THESEUS. The wall, methinks, being sensible, should curse again.

PYRAMUS. No, in truth, sir, he should not. "Deceiving me" is Thisby's cue. She is to enter now, and I am to spy her through the wall. You shall see, it will fall pat as I told you. Yonder she comes.

Re-enter THISBE

THISBE. O wall, full often hast thou heard my moans,
    For parting my fair Pyramus and me!
My cherry lips have often kissed thy stones,
    Thy stones with lime and hair knit up in thee.

PYRAMUS. I see a voice; now will I to the chink,
    To spy an I can hear my Thisby's face.
    Thisby!

THISBE. My love thou art, my love I think.

PYRAMUS. Think what thou wilt, I am thy lover's grace;
    And, like Limander, am I trusty still.

THISBE. And I like Helen, till the Fates me kill.

PYRAMUS. Not Shafalus to Procrus was so true.

THISBE. As Shafalus to Procrus, I to you.

PYRAMUS. O, kiss me through the hole of this vile wall!

THISBE. I kiss the wall's hole, not your lips at all.

PYRAMUS. Wilt thou at Ninny's tomb meet me straightway?

THISBE. 'Tide life, 'tide death, I come without delay.

Exeunt PYRAMUS *and* THISBE

WALL. Thus have I, Wall, my part discharged so;
    And, being done, thus Wall away doth go.   *Exit*

THESEUS. Now is the moon to see between the two neighbours.

DEMETRIUS. No remedy, my lord, when walls are so
  wilful to hear without warning.
HIPPOLYTA. This is the silliest stuff that ever I heard.
THESEUS. The best in this kind are but shadows; and the
  worst are no worse, if imagination amend them.
HIPPOLYTA. It must be your imagination then, and not
  theirs.
THESEUS. If we imagine no worse of them than they of
  themselves, they may pass for excellent men. Here
  come two noble beasts in, a man and a lion.

  Re-enter LION *and* MOONSHINE

LION. You, ladies, you, whose gentle hearts do fear
    The smallest monstrous mouse that creeps on floor,
  May now perchance both quake and tremble here,
    When lion rough in wildest rage doth roar.
  Then know that I, as Snug the joiner, am
  A lion fell, nor else no lion's dam;
  For, if I should as lion come in strife
  Into this place, 'twere pity on my life.

THESEUS. A very gentle beast, and of a good conscience.
DEMETRIUS. The very best at a beast, my lord, that e'er I saw.
LYSANDER. This lion is a very fox for his valour.
THESEUS. True; and a goose for his discretion.
DEMETRIUS. Not so, my lord; for his valour cannot carry his discretion; and the fox carries the goose.
THESEUS. His discretion, I am sure, cannot carry his valour; for the goose carries not the fox. It is well; leave it to his discretion, and let us listen to the moon.
MOONSHINE. This lantern doth the horned moon present—
DEMETRIUS. He should have worn the horns on his head.
THESEUS. He is no crescent, and his horns are invisible within the circumference.
MOONSHINE. This lantern doth the horned moon present;
  Myself the man i' the moon do seem to be.
THESEUS. This is the greatest error of all the rest; the man should be put into the lantern. How is it else the man i' the moon?
DEMETRIUS. He dares not come there for the candle; for, you see, it is already in snuff.
HIPPOLYTA. I am aweary of this moon; would he would change!
THESEUS. It appears, by his small light of discretion, that he is in the wane; but yet, in courtesy, in all reason, we must stay the time.
LYSANDER. Proceed, Moon.
MOONSHINE. All that I have to say, is, to tell you that the lantern is the moon; I, the man in the moon; this thorn-bush, my thorn-bush; and this dog, my dog.
DEMETRIUS. Why, all these should be in the lantern; for all these are in the moon. But, silence! here comes Thisbe.

Re-enter THISBE

THISBE. This is old Ninny's tomb. Where is my love?
LION. [Roaring] Oh——   THISBE runs off
DEMETRIUS. Well roared, Lion.
THESEUS. Well run, Thisbe.
HIPPOLYTA. Well shone, Moon. Truly, the moon shines with a good grace.
        The LION shakes THISBE's mantle, and exits

THESEUS. Well moused, Lion.

LYSANDER. And so the lion vanished.

DEMETRIUS. And then came Pyramus.

Re-enter PYRAMUS

PYRAMUS. Sweet Moon, I thank thee for thy sunny
    beams;
  I thank thee, Moon, for shining now so bright;
  For, by thy gracious, golden, glittering beams,
    I trust to take of truest Thisby sight.
        But stay, O spite!
        But mark, poor knight,
    What dreadful dole is here!
        Eyes, do you see?
        How can it be?
    O dainty duck! O dear!
        Thy mantle good,
    What, stained with blood!
    Approach, ye Furies fell!
        O Fates, come, come,
        Cut thread and thrum;
    Quail, crush, conclude, and quell!

THESEUS. This passion, and the death of a dear friend,
  would go near to make a man look sad.

HIPPOLYTA. Beshrew my heart, but I pity the man.

PYRAMUS. O wherefore, Nature, didst thou lions frame?
  Since lion vile hath here deflowered my dear;
  Which is—no, no—which was the fairest dame
    That lived, that loved, that liked, that looked with
    cheer.
        Come, tears, confound;
        Out, sword, and wound
    The pap of Pyramus;
        Ay, that left pap,
        Where heart doth hop.   *Stabs himself*
    Thus die I, thus, thus, thus.
        Now am I dead,
        Now am I fled;
    My soul is in the sky.
        Tongue, lose thy light;
        Moon, take thy flight.   *Exit* MOONSHINE
    Now die, die, die, die, die.   *Dies*

DEMETRIUS. No die, but an ace, for him; for he is but
  one.

LYSANDER. Less than an ace, man; for he is dead; he is
  nothing.

THESEUS. With the help of a surgeon he might yet recover, and prove an ass.

HIPPOLYTA. How chance Moonshine is gone before
  Thisbe comes back and finds her lover?

THESEUS. She will find him by starlight. Here she
  comes; and her passion ends the play.

Re-enter THISBE

HIPPOLYTA. Methinks she should not use a long one for
  such a Pyramus. I hope she will be brief.

DEMETRIUS. A mote will turn the balance, which
  Pyramus, which Thisbe, is the better; he for a man,
  God warrant us; she for a woman, God bless us.

LYSANDER. She hath spied him already with those
  sweet eyes.

DEMETRIUS. And thus she means, videlicet—

THISBE.   Asleep, my love?
        What, dead, my dove?
    O Pyramus, arise!
        Speak, speak. Quite dumb?
        Dead, dead? A tomb
    Must cover thy sweet eyes.
        These lily lips,
        This cherry nose,
    These yellow cowslip cheeks,
        Are gone, are gone.
        Lovers, make moan
    His eyes were green as leeks.
        O Sisters Three,
        Come, come to me,
    With hands as pale as milk;
        Lay them in gore,
        Since you have shore
    With shears his thread of silk.
        Tongue, not a word;
        Come, trusty sword;
    Come, blade, my breast imbrue; *Stabs herself*
        And, farewell, friends;
        Thus Thisby ends.
    Adieu, adieu, adieu.   *Dies*

THESEUS. Moonshine and Lion are left to bury the dead.

DEMETRIUS. Ay, and Wall too.

BOTTOM. [*Starting up*] No, I assure you; the wall is
  down that parted their fathers. Will it please you to
  see the epilogue, or to hear a Bergomask dance between two of our company?

THESEUS. No epilogue, I pray you; for your play
  needs no excuse. Never excuse; for when the players
  are all dead, there need none to be blamed. Marry,
  if he that writ it had played Pyramus and hanged himself in Thisbe's garter, it would have been a fine
  tragedy; and so it is, truly; and very notably dis-
  charged. But, come, your Bergomask: let your epi-
  logue alone.   *A dance*
  The iron tongue of midnight hath told twelve.
  Lovers, to bed; 'tis almost fairy time.
  I fear we shall outsleep the coming morn
  As much as we this night have overwatched.
  This palpable-gross play hath well beguiled
  The heavy gait of night. Sweet friends, to bed.
  A fortnight hold we this solemnity,
  In nightly revels and new jollity.   *Exeunt*

Enter PUCK

PUCK.   Now the hungry lion roars,
    And the wolf behowls the moon;

Whilst the heavy ploughman snores,
   All with weary task fordone.
Now the wasted brands do glow,
   Whilst the screech-owl, screeching loud,
Puts the wretch that lies in woe
   In remembrance of a shroud.
Now it is the time of night
   That the graves all gaping wide,
Every one lets forth his sprite,
   In the church-way paths to glide.
And we fairies, that do run
   By the triple Hecate's team,
From the presence of the sun,
   Following darkness like a dream,
Now are frolic. Not a mouse
Shall disturb this hallowed house.
I am sent with broom before,
To sweep the dust behind the door.

Enter OBERON *and* TITANIA *with their train*

OBERON. Through the house give glimmering light,
   By the dead and drowsy fire;
   Every elf and fairy sprite
     Hop as light as bird from brier;
   And this ditty, after me,
   Sing, and dance it trippingly.
TITANIA. First rehearse your song by rote,
   To each word a warbling note.
   Hand in hand, with fairy grace,
   Will we sing, and bless this place.

Song and dance

OBERON. Now, until the break of day,
   Through this house each fairy stray.
   To the best bride-bed will we,
   Which by us shall blessed be;

And the issue there create
Ever shall be fortunate.
So shall all the couples three
Ever true in loving be;
And the blots of Nature's hand
Shall not in their issue stand;
Never mole, hare-lip, nor scar,
Nor mark prodigious, such as are
Despised in nativity,
Shall upon their children be.
With this field-dew consecrate,
Every fairy take his gait;
And each several chamber bless,
Through this palace, with sweet peace;
And the owner of it blest
Ever shall in safety rest.
Trip away; make no stay;
Meet me all by break of day.

Exeunt OBERON, TITANIA, *and train*

PUCK. If we shadows have offended,
Think but this, and all is mended:
That you have but slumbered here
While these visions did appear.
And this weak and idle theme,
No more yielding but a dream,
Gentles, do not reprehend:
If you pardon, we will mend.
And, as I am an honest Puck,
If we have unearned luck
Now to 'scape the serpent's tongue,
We will make amends ere long;
Else the Puck a liar call.
So, good night unto you all.
Give me your hands, if we be friends,
And Robin shall restore amends.   *Exit*

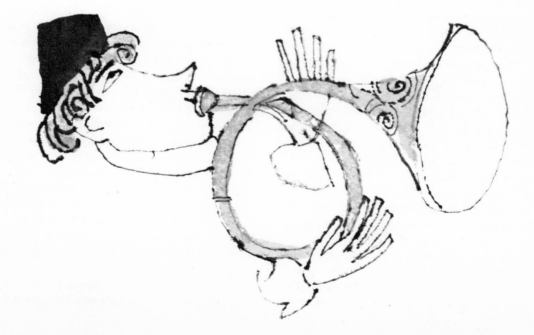

THE MERCHANT OF VENICE

Who is the Merchant of Venice? Shylock's part is the most striking and effective, and he is arguably *a* merchant. However, he is absolutely not a Venetian. I think Shakespeare referred in the title not to Shylock but to Antonio. He is the pivot of the story; his kindness enables Bassanio to woo Portia; to make the loan to Bassanio he puts himself in the power of Shylock; he is an example of gentleness and unselfishness in striking contrast to all the other principal masculine characters. But even Antonio's gentleness does not extend to Shylock, the Jew. Like all the other Venetians in the play, not excluding the Duke at the extremely irregular trial, he shows marked anti-Semitic prejudice.

On this account it has been argued that the play is an anti-Semitic document. But surely, to conclude that the attitude of his Venetians represents Shakespeare's own attitude is as wild as to assume that, because he wrote *Macbeth, Hamlet* or *Richard the Third,* he condoned regicide. The Venetian attitude in this respect is stressed to show the moral climate in which Shylock had to live, and which conditions, and to a great extent excuses, both his and Jessica's conduct.

Several factors, although his is the title role, combine to put Antonio in the shade. First, Shylock is a much better part—a highly colored portrait in Shakespeare's most exciting vein. Second, the relation between Antonio and Bassanio is not meant to suggest that of uncle and nephew, or just two friends, but that Antonio is in love with the younger man. I will argue this case more fully in a moment, but, granting it temporarily, it is obvious that the idea is expressed between the lines, not baldly and explicitly. In epochs when conventional respectability was of great importance—the nineteenth century, for example—the hint of an "irregular" relationship will have been studiously ignored. Thus this theme will have been omitted from the play and the character of Antonio will therefore have been rendered more simple. He just becomes an entirely uninteresting "good" man.

The third reason why Antonio, from reading the text, does not seem a very important or interesting character is that in two of the play's important scenes, though he is absolutely central to the meaning of both, he hardly speaks: I refer to the Trial Scene and the Finale.

When you read the Trial Scene it is the duel between Shylock and Portia that almost exclusively occupies the attention. Gratiano and Bassanio have "moments". The Duke, as the president of the court, must be accorded a certain prominence. But what of the prisoner?

Frequently, even in the theatre, the prisoner passes almost unnoticed. Very often, I think, the set-up and opening moments of the scene are mishandled. The Duke's entrance is importantly arranged, and when he

has reached his place he speaks the appointed line: "What is Antonio here?" Antonio, already in place, and usually a rather inconspicuous place since the most effective acting positions are held in reserve for Shylock and Portia, answers, "Ready, so please your Grace".

I believe that it is not only Shakespeare's intention, but also theatrical common sense, that since this is Antonio's trial, he should be, if not the principal figure, at least one of the focal points of interest. Shylock and Portia have well-prepared, effective entrances. Common sense dictates this; but it is also apparent from the text.

Antonio, I contend, should also have an important entrance. This is less apparent from the text, but it can very easily be contrived and with no detriment to the entrance of the Duke. The Duke must, of course, have a pompous entrance with procession, fanfare and so on to the limits of the production's budget. He has to represent the pomp, might, majesty, dominion and power of Venice at the height of her greatness. Besides, the more this entrance is built up, the better by contrast will be that of Antonio, *provided that it precedes Antonio's.* Let the Duke enter with all the theatrical pomp that can be contrived. Let him ask, "What is Antonio here?" Then let a small and dismal door open from the cells, possibly a trap-door from below, and let Antonio appear between officers, in prison dress, pale, nervous, the very antithesis of the sleek, prosperous merchant we knew before his ruin; and let him be conducted to a dock so placed that constantly throughout the scene the focus may be thrown onto his reaction to proceedings that to him are of literally vital importance.

The Trial Scene then becomes for Antonio an important acting scene, and when his turn comes to speak, it is not an interpolation by a half-forgotten personage, but an utterance for which the audience is waiting.

Antonio's speech, when it comes, seems at first glance to be disappointing. It is, to use professional jargon, emphatically "cued-in" by Portia: "You, merchant," ("Merchant", note, apropos of the title) "have you anything to say?" One expects a tirade of some kind; a burning self-justification, a thrilling defiance of Shylock, even a monumental farewell like Cardinal Wolsey's. But no. At first glance, and even at second, the speech seems strangely lacking in dramatic impact.

What is the explanation? Did Homer nod? Did Shakespeare try, and fail, to write a movingly eloquent speech? Is the speech—this, I think, is the customary interpretation—a deliberately dull utterance to suggest a dull character? I cannot see what possible advantage Shakespeare could have had in making Antonio a bore. Nor is he so in other parts of the play. Nor, were he intended as a bore, would the play's title be what it is. It would be called *Shylock* or *Portia*—on the analogy that in all the others of Shakespeare's plays that bear the name of a character, the title-part is the central figure.

What then?

I think the significance lies in the fact that Antonio's Last Words are addressed to Bassanio and in open court. Bassanio is the person who means most to him in the life he is just about to forfeit. He is in no position to pour out intimate, passionate thoughts and feelings. It is a constrained, stiff-upper-lip speech, but nevertheless a final protestation of love, ending with a gallant little attempt at a joke. If an actor playing Antonio keeps this in mind, I believe that the effect can be moving; and the more constrained and embarrassed the manner of delivery, the more moving the speech can be.

I am sure that the intention of the speech is to be moving from the fact that Bassanio's answering protest draws from Portia an "aside" which is undoubtedly meant to make the audience laugh. The theatrical structure is a poignant tension broken by a laugh; and any experienced comedian will confirm that the laugh will come only if the preceding tension has been achieved.

It was consideration of this speech which convinced me that Antonio's relation to Bassanio is what out grandparents called a "tender" one. Granted this, his loan of the money for Bassanio to go to woo the heiress of Belmont becomes much more than the rather easy gesture of a very rich man. And it is ironic that it is his very generosity that brings about his downfall.

Further, it gives infinitely more point to the final scene. Instead of being just an elegant frolic, in verse of incomparable elegance, by the four young people, it is immensely enriched by the presence of the solitary figure of the older man. Not only Bassanio but, on the evidence of the aside in the Trial Scene, which we have just discussed, Portia, too, is aware that he loves Bassanio.

I have seen an effectively contrived ending to the play, when the lovers went in to bed, with their jokes and rhymes and laughter still echoing in the garden, where Antonio is left solitary, the papers that confirm the safety of his argosies in his hand. As the lights faded, he slowly let the papers fall at his feet.

Nevertheless, when all is said and done, in the theatre it is almost impossible to make Antonio dominate the play. Although he is the pivot of its plot, and although theoretically it seems to be planned as a conflict between Justice and Mercy, of which the two protagonists are Shylock and Antonio, it does not work out that way. At the culminating scene of the Trial, it is Portia, not Antonio, who is the advocate of Mercy; Antonio is relegated to the passive role of Shylock's victim.

It is not generally realized what a long part Portia's is. She is in more scenes than any of the other characters and must dominate each scene she plays. I had not realized how important the part was until I directed a production in which Portia was entirely miscast—a sweet, motherly young woman, the epitome of middle-class respectability. The more we stuck her with jewels and decked her up in pink satin, the more she resembled the Railway Queen of some remote junction; the harder she tried to be witty and sophisticated, the more she sounded like a hospital nurse reading a script prepared for somebody else. At the other end of the scale is the star actress who brings a battery of accomplishment to bear and suddenly turns Portia into a wily mantrap, mangling poor Bassanio in her rusty jaws, while, at the Trial Scene, everyone's sympathy instinctively transfers itself to Shylock as he gets hell beaten out of him by the most formidable female advocate of all time.

The truth is that the part was written for a boy, and exploits both the attributes and the limitations of a gifted boy-player. The companies with which Shakespeare was associated trained youngsters for the stage from a very early age. And the best evidence to their capacity is the fact that Shakespeare was willing to write Viola, Imogen, Rosalind and Portia, knowing that there would be boys fit to interpret them.

The masquerade of Portia and Nerissa in the Trial Scene really makes sense only when the girls are played by boys. Two boys are no more, and no less, convincing as Doctor and Doctor's Clerk than as Portia and Nerissa; whereas in the modern theatre, two actresses, who seemed credible as Portia and Nerissa, appear at the trial disguised in a manner which makes us feel either that the play has suddenly changed into operetta, or else that the Duke must be a dim old personage indeed not to see that they are a pair of young ladies and have them arrested for contempt of court.

Shylock has been the subject of so much comment and controversy that little more need be added here. It is my view that Shakespeare's portrait is not anti-Semitic; that the pound of flesh wager was entered upon as a jest and only turns to vengeance in earnest after Shylock has been robbed and his daughter abducted by young Venetians of Antonio's "set". In fact, after the trial, and after Portia's great invocation of mercy, it is the Christians who lack all mercy toward their enemy. The sadistic vengeance taken upon Shylock is as offensive to Christianity as it is legally outrageous. To say this to Jews in the present epoch is as useless as to beg the rain not to fall. There is a rooted tradition among Jews that the play is an anti-Semitic document, and it is indeed true that many Jewish boys at school have, through generations, been taunted and execrated as "Shylock". This is to the shame of all humanity. But the remedy is not, I sincerely believe, to boycott Shakespeare's play and pretend that it does not exist, but to interpret it so that it becomes, as its author intended, a fantasia on the twin themes of Mercy and Justice, in which none of the characters fully exemplify either, in which none of the characters are either wholly good or wholly evil, and in which his rightful place is accorded to the Merchant of Venice.

LAUNCELOT GOBBO, the clown, servant to Shylock
OLD GOBBO, father to Launcelot
LORENZO, in love with Jessica
JESSICA, daughter to Shylock
TUBAL, a Jew, friend to Shylock

SHYLOCK,
a rich Jew

BASSANIO, suitor to Portia,
friend to Antonio
LEONARDO,
servant to
Bassanio

ANTONIO,
a merchant
of Venice

SALANIO,
SALARINO,
GRATIANO,
SALERIO,
friends to
Antonio
and
Bassanio

THE MERCHANT OF VENICE
DRAMATIS PERSONAE

THE
PRINCE
OF
MOROCCO,

THE
PRINCE
OF
ARRAGON,
suitors to Portia

BALTHASAR, STEPHANO
servants to Portia

THE DUKE OF VENICE

Magnificoes of Venice,
Officers of
The Court of Justice,
Gaoler,
servants to Portia,
And other Attendants

PORTIA, *a rich heiress*
NERISSA, *her waiting-maid*

SCENE:
PARTLY AT VENICE, AND PARTLY
AT BELMONT, *the seat of Portia,
on the Continent.*

ACT I

SCENE I *Venice: a street*

Enter ANTONIO, SALARINO, *and* SALANIO

ANTONIO. In sooth, I know not why I am so sad.
   It wearies me; you say it wearies you;
   But how I caught it, found it, or came by it,
   What stuff 'tis made of, whereof it is born,
   I am to learn.
   And such a want-wit sadness makes of me,
   That I have much ado to know myself.
SALARINO. Your mind is tossing on the ocean.
   There, where your argosies with portly sail—

Like signiors and rich burghers on the flood,
Or, as it were, the pageants of the sea—
Do overpeer the petty traffickers,
That curtsy to them, do them reverence,
As they fly by them with their woven wings.

SALANIO. Believe me, sir, had I such venture forth,
The better part of my affections would
Be with my hopes abroad. I should be still
Plucking the grass, to know where sits the wind,
Peering in maps for ports and piers and roads;
And every object that might make me fear
Misfortune to my ventures, out of doubt
Would make me sad.

SALARINO.　　　　　　　My wind cooling my broth
Would blow me to an ague, when I thought
What harm a wind too great at sea might do.
I should not see the sandy hour-glass run,
But I should think of shallows and of flats,
And see my wealthy Andrew docked in sand,
Vailing her high top lower than her ribs
To kiss her burial. Should I go to church
And see the holy edifice of stone,
And not bethink me straight of dangerous rocks,
Which touching but my gentle vessel's side,
Would scatter all her spices on the stream,
Enrobe the roaring waters with my silks,
And, in a word, but even now worth this,
And now worth nothing? Shall I have the thought
To think on this, and shall I lack the thought
That such a thing bechanced would make me sad?
But tell not me; I know, Antonio
Is sad to think upon his merchandise.

ANTONIO. Believe me, no. I thank my fortune for it,
My ventures are not in one bottom trusted,
Nor to one place; nor is my whole estate
Upon the fortune of this present year.
Therefore my merchandise makes me not sad.

SALARINO. Why, then you are in love.

ANTONIO.　　　　　　　　　　　　Fie, fie!

SALARINO. Not in love neither? Then let us say you
are sad,
Because you are not merry; and 'twere as easy
For you to laugh and leap and say you are merry,
Because you are not sad. Now, by two-headed Janus,
Nature hath framed strange fellows in her time:
Some that will evermore peep through their eyes
And laugh like parrots at a bagpiper,
And other of such vinegar aspect
That they'll not show their teeth in way of smile,
Though Nestor swear the jest be laughable.

Enter BASSANIO, LORENZO, *and* GRATIANO

SALANIO. Here comes Bassanio, your most noble kins-
man,
Gratiano and Lorenzo. Fare ye well;
We leave you now with better company.

SALARINO. I would have stayed till I had made you
merry,
If worthier friends had not prevented me.

ANTONIO. Your worth is very dear in my regard.
I take it, your own business calls on you
And you embrace the occasion to depart.

SALARINO. Good morrow, my good lords.

BASSANIO. Good signiors both, when shall we laugh?
Say, when?
You grow exceeding strange; must it be so?

SALARINO. We'll make our leisures to attend on yours.
　　　　　　　　　　Exeunt SALARINO *and* SALANIO

LORENZO. My Lord Bassanio, since you have found
Antonio,
We two will leave you; but at dinner-time,
I pray you, have in mind where we must meet.

BASSANIO. I will not fail you.

GRATIANO. You look not well, Signior Antonio;
You have too much respect upon the world—
They lose it that do buy it with much care.
Believe me, you are marvellously changed.

ANTONIO. I hold the world but as the world, Gratiano;
A stage where every man must play a part,
And mine a sad one.

GRATIANO.　　　　　　　Let me play the fool;
With mirth and laughter let old wrinkles come,
And let my liver rather heat with wine
Than my heart cool with mortifying groans.
Why should a man, whose blood is warm within,
Sit like his grandsire cut in alabaster?
Sleep when he wakes and creep into the jaundice
By being peevish? I tell thee what, Antonio—
I love thee, and it is my love that speaks—
There are a sort of men whose visages
Do cream and mantle like a standing pond,
And do a wilful stillness entertain,
With purpose to be dressed in an opinion
Of wisdom, gravity, profound conceit,
As who should say "I am Sir Oracle,
And when I ope my lips let no dog bark!"
O my Antonio, I do know of these
That therefore only are reputed wise
For saying nothing, when, I am very sure,
If they should speak, would almost damn those ears
Which, hearing them, would call their brothers fools.
I'll tell thee more of this another time—
But fish not, with this melancholy bait,
For this fool gudgeon, this opinion.
Come, good Lorenzo. Fare ye well awhile;
I'll end my exhortation after dinner.

LORENZO. Well, we will leave you then till dinner-time.
I must be one of these same dumb wise men,
For Gratiano never lets me speak.

GRATIANO. Well, keep me company but two years
more,
Thou shalt not know the sound of thine own tongue.

ANTONIO. Farewell; I'll grow a talker for this gear.
GRATIANO. Thanks, i' faith, for silence is only com-
    mendable
    In a neat's tongue dried and a maid not vendible.

Exeunt GRATIANO *and* LORENZO

ANTONIO. Is that anything now?
BASSANIO. Gratiano speaks an infinite deal of nothing,
    more than any man in all Venice. His reasons are as
    two grains of wheat hid in two bushels of chaff: you
    shall seek all day ere you find them, and when you
    have them, they are not worth the search.
ANTONIO. Well, tell me now what lady is the same
    To whom you swore a secret pilgrimage,
    That you today promised to tell me of?
BASSANIO. 'Tis not unknown to you, Antonio,
    How much I have disabled mine estate,
    By something showing a more swelling port
    Than my faint means would grant continuance;
    Nor do I now make moan to be abridged
    From such a noble rate; but my chief care
    Is to come fairly off from the great debts
    Wherein my time something too prodigal
    Hath left me gaged. To you, Antonio,
    I owe the most, in money and in love,
    And from your love I have a warranty
    To unburden all my plots and purposes
    How to get clear of all the debts I owe.
ANTONIO. I pray you, good Bassanio, let me know it;
    And if it stand, as you yourself still do,
    Within the eye of honour, be assured,
    My purse, my person, my extremest means,
    Lie all unlocked to your occasions.
BASSANIO. In my schooldays, when I had lost one shaft,
    I shot his fellow of the selfsame flight
    The selfsame way with more advised watch,
    To find the other forth, and by adventuring both
    I oft found both. I urge this childhood proof,
    Because what follows is pure innocence.
    I owe you much, and, like a wilful youth,

That which I owe is lost; but if you please
To shoot another arrow that self way
Which you did shoot the first, I do not doubt,
As I will watch the aim, or to find both
Or bring your latter hazard back again
And thankfully rest debtor for the first.
ANTONIO. You know me well, and herein spend but
    time
    To wind about my love with circumstance;
    And out of doubt you do me now more wrong
    In making question of my uttermost
    Than if you had made waste of all I have.
    Then do but say to me what I should do
    That in your knowledge may by me be done,
    And I am prest unto it; therefore, speak.
BASSANIO. In Belmont is a lady richly left;
    And she is fair and, fairer than that word,
    Of wondrous virtues—sometimes from her eyes
    I did receive fair speechless messages.
    Her name is Portia, nothing undervalued
    To Cato's daughter, Brutus' Portia;
    Nor is the wide world ignorant of her worth,
    For the four winds blow in from every coast
    Renowned suitors, and her sunny locks
    Hang on her temples like a golden fleece,
    Which makes her seat of Belmont Colchos' strand,
    And many Jasons come in quest of her.
    O my Antonio, had I but the means
    To hold a rival place with one of them,
    I have a mind presages me such thrift,
    That I should questionless be fortunate!
ANTONIO. Thou know'st that all my fortunes are at sea;
    Neither have I money nor commodity
    To raise a present sum. Therefore go forth;
    Try what my credit can in Venice do.
    That shall be racked, even to the uttermost,
    To furnish thee to Belmont, to fair Portia.
    Go, presently inquire, and so will I,
    Where money is, and I no question make
    To have it of my trust or for my sake.   *Exeunt*

SCENE II *Belmont: a room in* PORTIA'S *house*

Enter PORTIA *and* NERISSA

PORTIA. By my troth, Nerissa, my little body is aweary
    of this great world.
NERISSA. You would be, sweet madam, if your miseries
    were in the same abundance as your good fortunes
    are; and yet, for aught I see, they are as sick that
    surfeit with too much as they that starve with nothing.
    It is no mean happiness therefore, to be seated in the
    mean. Superfluity comes sooner by white hairs, but
    competency lives longer.
PORTIA. Good sentences and well pronounced.
NERISSA. They would be better, if well followed.

PORTIA. If to do were as easy as to know what were
    good to do, chapels had been churches and poor men's
    cottages princes' palaces. It is a good divine that fol-
    lows his own instructions. I can easier teach twenty
    what were good to be done, than be one of the twenty
    to follow mine own teaching. The brain may devise
    laws for the blood, but a hot temper leaps o'er a
    cold decree; such a hare is madness the youth, to
    skip o'er the meshes of good counsel the cripple.
    But this reasoning is not in the fashion to choose me a
    husband. O me, the word "choose!" I may neither

choose whom I would nor refuse whom I dislike; so is the will of a living daughter curbed by the will of a dead father. Is it not hard, Nerissa, that I cannot choose one nor refuse none?

NERISSA. Your father was ever virtuous; and holy men at their death have good inspirations. Therefore the lottery, that he hath devised in these three chests of gold, silver and lead, whereof who chooses his meaning chooses you, will, no doubt, never be chosen by any rightly but one who shall rightly love. But what warmth is there in your affection towards any of these princely suitors that are already come?

PORTIA. I pray thee, over-name them; and as thou namest them, I will describe them; and, according to my description, level at my affection.

NERISSA. First, there is the Neapolitan prince.

PORTIA. Ay, that's a colt indeed, for he doth nothing but talk of his horse; and he makes it a great appropriation to his own good parts, that he can shoe him himself. I am much afeard my lady his mother played false with a smith.

NERISSA. Then there is the County Palatine.

PORTIA. He doth nothing but frown, as who should say "If you will not have me, choose." He hears merry tales and smiles not; I fear he will prove the weeping philosopher when he grows old, being so full of unmannerly sadness in his youth. I had rather be married to a death's-head with a bone in his mouth than to either of these. God defend me from these two!

NERISSA. How say you by the French lord, Monsieur Le Bon?

PORTIA. God made him, and therefore let him pass for a man. In truth, I know it is a sin to be a mocker; but, he! why, he hath a horse better than the Neapolitan's, a better bad habit of frowning than the Count Palatine; he is every man in no man; if a throstle sing, he falls straight a-capering; he will fence with his own shadow. If I should marry him, I should marry twenty husbands. If he would despise me, I would forgive him, for if he love me to madness I shall never requite him.

NERISSA. What say you, then, to Falconbridge, the young baron of England?

PORTIA. You know I say nothing to him, for he understands not me, nor I him. He hath neither Latin, French, nor Italian, and you will come into the court and swear that I have a poor pennyworth in the English. He is a proper man's picture, but, alas, who can converse with a dumb show? How oddly he is suited! I think he bought his doublet in Italy, his round hose in France, his bonnet in Germany and his behaviour everywhere.

NERISSA. What think you of the Scottish lord, his neighbour?

PORTIA. That he hath a neighbourly charity in him, for he borrowed a box of the ear of the Englishman

and swore he would pay him again when he was able. I think the Frenchman became his surety and sealed under for another.

NERISSA. How like you the young German, the Duke of Saxony's nephew?

PORTIA. Very vilely in the morning, when he is sober, and most vilely in the afternoon, when he is drunk. When he is best, he is a little worse than a man, and when he is worst, he is little better than a beast. An the worst fall that ever fell, I hope I shall make shift to go without him.

NERISSA. If he should offer to choose, and choose the right casket, you should refuse to perform your father's will, if you should refuse to accept him.

PORTIA. Therefore, for fear of the worst, I pray thee, set a deep glass of Rhenish wine on the contrary casket, for if the devil be within and that temptation without, I know he will choose it. I will do anything, Nerissa, ere I'll be married to a sponge.

NERISSA. You need not fear, lady, the having any of these lords. They have acquainted me with their determinations; which is, indeed, to return to their home and to trouble you with no more suit, unless you may be won by some other sort than your father's imposition depending on the caskets.

PORTIA. If I live to be as old as Sibylla, I will die as chaste as Diana, unless I be obtained by the manner of my father's will. I am glad this parcel of wooers are so reasonable, for there is not one among them but I dote on his very absence, and I pray God grant them a fair departure.

NERISSA. Do you not remember, lady, in your father's time, a Venetian, a scholar and a soldier, that came hither in company of the Marquis of Montferrat?

PORTIA. Yes, yes, it was Bassanio; as I think, he was so called.

NERISSA. True, madam. He, of all the men that ever my foolish eyes looked upon, was the best deserving a fair lady.

PORTIA. I remember him well, and I remember him worthy of thy praise.

Enter a Servingman

How now! what news?

SERVINGMAN. The four strangers seek for you, madam, to take their leave; and there is a forerunner come from a fifth, the Prince of Morocco, who brings word the Prince his master will be here tonight.

PORTIA. If I could bid the fifth welcome with so good a heart as I can bid the other four farewell, I should be glad of his approach. If he have the condition of a saint and the complexion of a devil, I had rather he should shrive me than wive me.

Come, Nerissa. Sirrah, go before.

Whiles we shut the gates upon one wooer, another knocks at the door.   *Exeunt*

SCENE III *Venice: a public place*

Enter BASSANIO *and* SHYLOCK

SHYLOCK. Three thousand ducats; well.

BASSANIO. Ay, sir, for three months.

SHYLOCK. For three months; well.

BASSANIO. For the which, as I told you, Antonio shall
be bound.

SHYLOCK. Antonio shall become bound; well.

BASSANIO. May you stead me? Will you pleasure me?
Shall I know your answer?

SHYLOCK. Three thousand ducats for three months and
Antonio bound.

BASSANIO. Your answer to that.

SHYLOCK. Antonio is a good man.

BASSANIO. Have you heard any imputation to the contrary?

SHYLOCK. Oh, no, no, no, no; my meaning in saying
he is a good man is to have you understand me that
he is sufficient. Yet his means are in supposition:
he hath an argosy bound to Tripolis, another to the
Indies; I understand, moreover, upon the Rialto, he
hath a third at Mexico, a fourth for England, and
other ventures he hath, squandered abroad. But ships
are but boards, sailors but men: there be land-rats
and water-rats, water-thieves and land-thieves—I
mean pirates; and then there is the peril of waters,
winds and rocks. The man is, notwithstanding, sufficient. Three thousand ducats; I think I may take
his bond.

BASSANIO. Be assured you may.

SHYLOCK. I will be assured I may; and, that I may be
assured, I will bethink me. May I speak with Antonio?

BASSANIO. If it please you to dine with us.

SHYLOCK. Yes, to smell pork; to eat of the habitation
which your prophet the Nazarite conjured the devil
into. I will buy with you, sell with you, talk with you,
walk with you, and so following, but I will not eat
with you, drink with you, nor pray with you. What
news on the Rialto? Who is he comes here?

Enter ANTONIO

BASSANIO. This is Signior Antonio.

SHYLOCK. [*Aside*] How like a fawning publican he
looks!
I hate him for he is a Christian,
But more for that in low simplicity
He lends out money gratis and brings down
The rate of usance here with us in Venice.
If I can catch him once upon the hip,
I will feed fat the ancient grudge I bear him.
He hates our sacred nation, and he rails,
Even there where merchants most do congregate,
On me, my bargains and my well-won thrift,
Which he calls interest. Cursed be my tribe,
If I forgive him!

BASSANIO.   Shylock, do you hear?

SHYLOCK. I am debating of my present store,
And, by the near guess of my memory,
I cannot instantly raise up the gross
Of full three thousand ducats. What of that?
Tubal, a wealthy Hebrew of my tribe,
Will furnish me. But soft! how many months
Do you desire? [*To Antonio*] Rest you fair, good
signior;
Your worship was the last man in our mouths.

ANTONIO. Shylock, although I neither lend nor borrow
By taking nor by giving of excess,
Yet, to supply the ripe wants of my friend,
I'll break a custom. Is he yet possessed
How much ye would?

SHYLOCK.   Ay, ay, three thousand ducats.

ANTONIO. And for three months.

SHYLOCK. I had forgot; three months; you told me so.
Well then, your bond; and let me see. But hear you:
Methought you said you neither lend nor borrow
Upon advantage.

ANTONIO.   I do never use it.

SHYLOCK. When Jacob grazed his uncle Laban's sheep—
This Jacob from our holy Abram was,
As his wise mother wrought in his behalf,
The third possessor; ay, he was the third—

ANTONIO. And what of him? Did he take interest?

SHYLOCK. No, not take interest, not, as you would say,

Directly interest. Mark what Jacob did.
When Laban and himself were compromised
That all the eanlings which were streaked and pied
Should fall as Jacob's hire, the ewes, being rank,
In the end of autumn turned to the rams,
And, when the work of generation was
Between these woolly breeders in the act,
The skilful shepherd peeled me certain wands
And, in the doing of the deed of kind,
He stuck them up before the fulsome ewes,
Who then conceiving did in eaning time
Fall parti-coloured lambs, and those were Jacob's.
This was a way to thrive, and he was blest;
And thrift is blessing, if men steal it not.

ANTONIO. This was a venture, sir, that Jacob served for;
A thing not in his power to bring to pass,
But swayed and fashioned by the hand of heaven.
Was this inserted to make interest good?
Or is your gold and silver ewes and rams?

SHYLOCK. I cannot tell; I make it breed as fast.
But note me, signior.

ANTONIO.   Mark you this, Bassanio,
The devil can cite Scripture for his purpose.
An evil soul producing holy witness
Is like a villain with a smiling cheek,
A goodly apple rotten at the heart:
O, what a goodly outside falsehood hath!

SHYLOCK. Three thousand ducats; 'tis a good round
    sum.
Three months from twelve; then, let me see; the
    rate—

ANTONIO. Well, Shylock, shall we be beholding to you?

SHYLOCK. Signior Antonio, many a time and oft
In the Rialto you have rated me
About my moneys and my usances.
Still have I borne it with a patient shrug,
For sufferance is the badge of all our tribe.
You call me misbeliever, cut-throat dog,
And spit upon my Jewish gaberdine,
And all for use of that which is mine own.
Well then, it now appears you need my help.
Go to, then; you come to me, and you say
"Shylock, we would have moneys." You say so;
You, that did void your rheum upon my beard
And foot me as you spurn a stranger cur
Over your threshold. Moneys is your suit.
What should I say to you? Should I not say
"Hath a dog money? Is it possible
A cur can lend three thousand ducats?" Or
Shall I bend low and in a bondman's key,
With bated breath and whispering humbleness,
Say this:
"Fair sir, you spit on me on Wednesday last;
You spurned me such a day; another time
You called me dog; and for these courtesies
I'll lend you thus much moneys"?

ANTONIO. I am as like to call thee so again,
To spit on thee again, to spurn thee too.
If thou wilt lend this money, lend it not
As to thy friends; for when did friendship take
A breed for barren metal of his friend?
But lend it rather to thine enemy,
Who, if he break, thou mayst with better face
Exact the penalty.

SHYLOCK.   Why, look you, how you storm!
I would be friends with you and have your love,
Forget the shames that you have stained me with,
Supply your present wants and take no doit
Of usance for my moneys, and you'll not hear me.
This is kind I offer.

BASSANIO. This were kindness.

SHYLOCK.   This kindness will I show.
Go with me to a notary, seal me there
Your single bond; and, in a merry sport,
If you repay me not on such a day,
In such a place, such sum or sums as are
Expressed in the condition, let the forfeit
Be nominated for an equal pound
Of your fair flesh, to be cut off and taken
In what part of your body pleaseth me.

ANTONIO. Content, i' faith; I'll seal to such a bond
And say there is much kindness in the Jew.

BASSANIO. You shall not seal to such a bond for me;
I'll rather dwell in my necessity.

ANTONIO. Why, fear not, man; I will not forfeit it.
Within these two months—that's a month before
This bond expires—I do expect return
Of thrice three times the value of this bond.

SHYLOCK. O father Abram, what these Christians are,
Whose own hard dealings teaches them suspect
The thoughts of others! Pray you, tell me this:
If he should break his day, what should I gain
By the exaction of the forfeiture?
A pound of man's flesh taken from a man
Is not so estimable, profitable neither,
As flesh of muttons, beefs, or goats. I say,
To buy his favour, I extend this friendship.
If he will take it, so; if not, adieu;
And, for my love, I pray you wrong me not.

ANTONIO. Yes, Shylock, I will seal unto this bond.

SHYLOCK. Then meet me forthwith at the notary's;
Give him direction for this merry bond,
And I will go and purse the ducats straight,
See to my house, left in the fearful guard
Of an unthrifty knave, and presently
I will be with you.

ANTONIO. Hie thee, gentle Jew.   *Exit* SHYLOCK
The Hebrew will turn Christian; he grows kind.

BASSANIO. I like not fair terms and a villain's mind.

ANTONIO. Come on; in this there can be no dismay;
My ships come home a month before the day.
                                        Exeunt

ACT II

SCENE I *Belmont: A room in* PORTIA'S *house*

Flourish of cornets. Enter the PRINCE OF MOROCCO *and his train;* PORTIA, NERISSA, *and Attendants*

MOROCCO. Mislike me not for my complexion,
  The shadowed livery of the burnished sun,
  To whom I am a neighbour and near bred.
  Bring me the fairest creature northward born,
  Where Phœbus' fire scarce thaws the icicles,
  And let us make incision for your love,
  To prove whose blood is reddest, his or mine.
  I tell thee, lady, this aspect of mine
  Hath feared the valiant: by my love, I swear
  The best-regarded virgins of our clime
  Have loved it too. I would not change this hue,
  Except to steal your thoughts, my gentle queen.

PORTIA. In terms of choice I am not solely led
  By nice direction of a maiden's eyes;
  Besides, the lottery of my destiny
  Bars me the right of voluntary choosing.
  But if my father had not scanted me
  And hedged me by his wit, to yield myself
  His wife who wins me by that means I told you,
  Yourself, renowned Prince, then stood as fair
  As any comer I have looked on yet
  For my affection.

MOROCCO.   Even for that I thank you.
  Therefore, I pray you, lead me to the caskets
  To try my fortune. By this scimitar
  That slew the Sophy and a Persian prince
  That won three fields of Sultan Solyman,
  I would outstare the sternest eyes that look,
  Outbrave the heart most daring on the earth,
  Pluck the young sucking cubs from the she-bear,
  Yea, mock the lion when he roars for prey,
  To win thee, lady. But, alas the while!
  If Hercules and Lichas play at dice
  Which is the better man, the greater throw
  May turn by fortune from the weaker hand.
  So is Alcides beaten by his page;
  And so may I, blind fortune leading me,
  Miss that which one unworthier may attain,
  And die with grieving.

PORTIA.   You must take your chance,
  And either not attempt to choose at all
  Or swear before you choose, if you choose wrong
  Never to speak to lady afterward
  In way of marriage; therefore be advised.

MOROCCO. Nor will not. Come, bring me unto my
    chance.

PORTIA. First, forward to the temple; after dinner
  Your hazard shall be made.

MOROCCO.   Good fortune then!
  To make me blest or cursed'st among men.

                              Cornets, and exeunt

Enter LAUNCELOT

LAUNCELOT. Certainly my conscience will serve me to run from this Jew my master. The fiend is at mine elbow and tempts me saying to me "Gobbo, Launcelot Gobbo, good Launcelot," or "good Gobbo," or "good Launcelot Gobbo, use your legs, take the start, run away." My conscience says "No; take heed, honest Launcelot; take heed, honest Gobbo," or, as aforesaid, "honest Launcelot Gobbo; do not run; scorn running with thy heels." Well, the most courageous fiend bids me pack: "Via!" says the fiend; "away!" says the fiend; "for the heavens, rouse up a brave mind," says the fiend, "and run." Well, my conscience, hanging about the neck of my heart, says very wisely to me, "My honest friend Launcelot, being

an honest man's son,'' or rather an honest woman's son; for, indeed, my father did something smack, something grow to, he had a kind of taste—well, my conscience says ''Launcelot, budge not.'' ''Budge,'' says the fiend. ''Budge not,'' says my conscience. ''Conscience,'' say I, ''you counsel well.'' ''Fiend,'' say I, ''you counsel well.'' To be ruled by my conscience, I should stay with the Jew my master, who, God bless the mark, is a kind of devil; and, to run away from the Jew, I should be ruled by the fiend, who, saving your reverence, is the devil himself. Certainly the Jew is the very devil incarnation; and, in my conscience, my conscience is but a kind of hard conscience, to offer to counsel me to stay with the Jew. The fiend gives the more friendly counsel: I will run, fiend; my heels are at your command; I will run.

Enter Old GOBBO, *with a basket*

GOBBO. Master young man, you, I pray you, which is the way to master Jew's?

LAUNCELOT. [*Aside*] O heavens, this is my true-begotten father! who, being more than sand-blind, high-gravel blind, knows me not. I will try confusions with him.

GOBBO. Master young gentleman, I pray you, which is the way to master Jew's?

LAUNCELOT. Turn up on your right hand at the next turning, but, at the next turning of all, on your left; marry, at the very next turning, turn of no hand, but turn down indirectly to the Jew's house.

GOBBO. By God's sonties, 'twill be a hard way to hit. Can you tell me whether one Launcelot, that dwells with him, dwell with him or no?

LAUNCELOT. Talk you of young Master Launcelot? [*Aside*] Mark me now; now will I raise the waters. Talk you of young Master Launcelot?

GOBBO. No master, sir, but a poor man's son. His father, though I say it, is an honest exceeding poor man and, God be thanked, well to live.

LAUNCELOT. Well, let his father be what a' will, we talk of young Master Launcelot.

GOBBO. Your worship's friend and Launcelot, sir.

LAUNCELOT. But I pray you, ergo, old man, ergo, I beseech you, talk you of young Master Launcelot?

GOBBO. Of Launcelot, an't please your mastership.

LAUNCELOT. Ergo, Master Launcelot. Talk not of Master Launcelot, father; for the young gentleman, according to Fates and Destinies and such odd sayings, the Sisters Three and such branches of learning, is indeed deceased, or, as you would say in plain terms, gone to Heaven.

GOBBO. Marry, God forbid! The boy was the very staff of my age, my very prop.

LAUNCELOT. Do I look like a cudgel or a hovel-post, a staff or a prop? Do you know me, father?

GOBBO. Alack the day, I know you not, young gentleman; but, I pray you, tell me, is my boy, God rest his soul, alive or dead?

LAUNCELOT. Do you not know me, father?

GOBBO. Alack, sir, I am sand-blind; I know you not.

LAUNCELOT. Nay, indeed, if you had your eyes, you might fail of the knowing me. It is a wise father that knows his own child. Well, old man, I will tell you news of your son. Give me your blessing. Truth will come to light; murder cannot be hid long; a man's son may, but at the length truth will out.

GOBBO. Pray you, sir, stand up; I am sure you are not Launcelot, my boy.

LAUNCELOT. Pray you, let's have no more fooling about it, but give me your blessing. I am Launcelot, your boy that was, your son that is, your child that shall be.

GOBBO. I cannot think you are my son.

LAUNCELOT. I know not what I shall think of that; but I am Launcelot, the Jew's man, and I am sure Margery your wife is my mother.

GOBBO. Her name is Margery, indeed. I'll be sworn, if thou be Launcelot, thou art mine own flesh and blood. Lord worshipped might he be, what a beard hast thou got! Thou hast got more hair on thy chin than Dobbin my fill-horse has on his tail.

LAUNCELOT. It should seem, then, that Dobbin's tail grows backward. I am sure he had more hair of his tail than I have of my face when I last saw him.

GOBBO. Lord, how art thou changed! How dost thou and thy master agree? I have brought him a present. How 'gree you now?

LAUNCELOT. Well, well; but, for mine own part, as I have set up my rest to run away, so I will not rest till I have run some ground. My master's a very Jew.

Give him a present! Give him a halter! I am famished in his service; you may tell every finger I have with my ribs. Father, I am glad you are come. Give me your present to one Master Bassanio, who, indeed, gives rare new liveries. If I serve not him, I will run as far as God has any ground. O rare fortune! here comes the man. To him, father, for I am a Jew if I serve the Jew any longer.

Enter BASSIANO,
with LEONARDO *and other followers*

BASSANIO. You may do so; but let it be so hasted that supper be ready at the farthest by five of the clock. See these letters delivered; put the liveries to making, and desire Gratiano to come anon to my lodging.

Exit a Servant

LAUNCELOT. To him, father.

GOBBO. God bless your worship!

BASSANIO. Gramercy! Wouldst thou aught with me?

GOBBO. Here's my son, sir, a poor boy—

LAUNCELOT. Not a poor boy, sir, but the rich Jew's man; that would, sir, as my father shall specify—

GOBBO. He hath a great infection, sir, as one would say, to serve—

LAUNCELOT. Indeed, the short and the long is, I serve the Jew, and have a desire, as my father shall specify—

GOBBO. His master and he, saving your worship's reverence, are scarce cater-cousins—

LAUNCELOT. To be brief, the very truth is that the Jew, having done me wrong, doth cause me, as my father, being, I hope, an old man, shall frutify unto you—

GOBBO. I have here a dish of doves that I would bestow upon your worship, and my suit is—

LAUNCELOT. In very brief, the suit is impertinent to myself, as your worship shall know by this honest old man; and, though I say it, though old man, yet poor man, my father.

BASSANIO. One speak for both. What would you?

LAUNCELOT. Serve you, sir.

GOBBO. That is the very defect of the matter, sir.

BASSANIO. I know thee well; thou hast obtained thy suit;
Shylock thy master spoke with me this day,
And hath preferred thee, if it be preferment
To leave a rich Jew's service, to become
The follower of so poor a gentleman.

LAUNCELOT. The old proverb is very well parted between my master Shylock and you, sir: you have the grace of God, sir, and he hath enough.

BASSANIO. Thou speak'st it well. Go, father, with thy son.
Take leave of thy old master and inquire
My lodging out. Give him a livery
More guarded than his fellows'. See it done.

LAUNCELOT. Father, in. I cannot get a service, no; I have ne'er a tongue in my head. Well [*examining his palm*],

if any man in Italy have a fairer table which doth offer to swear upon a book, I shall have good fortune. Go to, here's a simple line of life; here's a small trifle of wives! Alas, fifteen wives is nothing! Eleven widows and nine maids is a simple coming-in for one man; and then to 'scape drowning thrice, and to be in peril of my life with the edge of a feather-bed; here are simple scapes. Well, if Fortune be a woman, she's a good wench for this gear. Father, come; I'll take my leave of the Jew in the twinkling of an eye.

Exeunt LAUNCELOT *and* OLD GOBBO

BASSANIO. I pray thee, good Leonardo, think on this:
These things being bought and orderly bestowed,
Return in haste, for I do feast tonight
My best-esteemed acquaintance: hie thee, go.

LEONARDO. My best endeavours shall be done herein.

Enter GRATIANO

GRATIANO. Where is your master?

LEONARDO.   Yonder, sir, he walks.   *Exit*

GRATIANO. Signior Bassanio!

BASSANIO. Gratiano!

GRATIANO. I have a suit to you.

BASSANIO.   You have obtained it.

GRATIANO. You must not deny me: I must go with you to Belmont.

BASSANIO. Why, then you must. But hear thee, Gratiano;
Thou art too wild, too rude and bold of voice:
Parts that become thee happily enough
And in such eyes as ours appear not faults.
But where thou art not known, why, there they show
Something too liberal. Pray thee, take pain
To allay with some cold drops of modesty
Thy skipping spirit, lest through thy wild behaviour
I be misconstrued in the place I go to
And lose my hopes.

GRATIANO.   Signior Bassanio, hear me:
If I do not put on a sober habit,
Talk with respect and swear but now and then,
Wear Prayer Books in my pocket, look demurely,
Nay more, while grace is saying, hood mine eyes
Thus with my hat, and sigh and say "amen,"
Use all the observance of civility,
Like one well studied in a sad ostent
To please his grandam, never trust me more.

BASSANIO. Well, we shall see your bearing.

GRATIANO. Nay, but I bar tonight; you shall not gauge me
By what we do tonight.

BASSANIO.   No, that were pity.
I would entreat you rather to put on
Your boldest suit of mirth, for we have friends
That purpose merriment. But fare you well;
I have some business.

GRATIANO. And I must to Lorenzo and the rest;
But we will visit you at supper-time.   *Exeunt*

SCENE IV *The same: a street*

Enter GRATIANO, LORENZO, SALARINO, *and* SALANIO

LORENZO. Nay, we will slink away in supper-time,
Disguise us at my lodging and return,
All in an hour.
GRATIANO. We have not made good preparation.
SALARINO. We have not spoke us yet of torch-bearers.
SALANIO. 'Tis vile, unless it may be quaintly ordered,
And better in my mind not undertook.
LORENZO. 'Tis now but four o'clock: we have two hours
To furnish us.

Enter LAUNCELOT, *with a letter*

Friend Launcelot, what's the news?

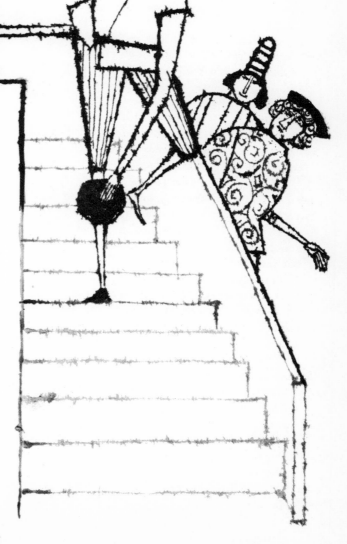

SCENE III *The same: a room in* SHYLOCK's *house*

Enter JESSICA *and* LAUNCELOT

JESSICA. I am sorry thou wilt leave my father so.
Our house is hell, and thou, a merry devil,
Didst rob it of some taste of tediousness.
But fare thee well, there is a ducat for thee.
And, Launcelot, soon at supper shalt thou see
Lorenzo, who is thy new master's guest.
Give him this letter—do it secretly—
And so farewell; I would not have my father
See me in talk with thee.
LAUNCELOT. Adieu! tears exhibit my tongue, most
beautiful pagan, most sweet Jew! If a Christian did
not play the knave and get thee, I am much deceived.
But, adieu; these foolish drops do something drown
my manly spirit; adieu.
JESSICA. Farewell, good Launcelot.   *Exit* LAUNCELOT
Alack, what heinous sin is it in me
To be ashamed to be my father's child!
But though I am a daughter to his blood,
I am not to his manners. O Lorenzo,
If thou keep promise, I shall end this strife,
Become a Christian and thy loving wife.   *Exit*

LAUNCELOT. An it shall please you to break up this, it shall seem to signify.

LORENZO. I know the hand. In faith, 'tis a fair hand;
And whiter than the paper it writ on
Is the fair hand that writ.

GRATIANO.   Love-news, in faith.

LAUNCELOT. By your leave, sir.

LORENZO. Whither goest thou?

LAUNCELOT. Marry, sir, to bid my old master the Jew to sup tonight with my new master the Christian.

LORENZO. Hold here, take this; tell gentle Jessica
I will not fail her; speak it privately.

Exit LAUNCELOT

Go, gentlemen,
Will you prepare you for this masque tonight?
I am provided of a torch-bearer.

SALARINO. Ay, marry, I'll be gone about it straight.

SALANIO. And so will I.

LORENZO.   Meet me and Gratiano
At Gratiano's lodging some hour hence.

SALARINO. 'Tis good we do so.

Exeunt SALARINO *and* SALANIO

GRATIANO. Was not that letter from fair Jessica?

LORENZO. I must needs tell thee all. She hath directed
How I shall take her from her father's house,
What gold and jewels she is furnished with,
What page's suit she hath in readiness.
If e'er the Jew her father come to heaven,
It will be for his gentle daughter's sake.
And never dare misfortune cross her foot,
Unless she do it under this excuse,
That she is issue to a faithless Jew.
Come, go with me; peruse this as thou goest.
Fair Jessica shall be my torch-bearer.   *Exeunt*

SCENE V *The same: before* SHYLOCK's *house*

Enter SHYLOCK *and* LAUNCELOT

SHYLOCK. Well, thou shalt see, thy eyes shall be thy judge,
The difference of old Shylock and Bassanio—
What, Jessica!—thou shalt not gormandise,
As thou hast done with me—What, Jessica!—
And sleep and snore, and rend apparel out—
Why, Jessica, I say!

LAUNCELOT.   Why, Jessica!

SHYLOCK. Who bids thee call? I do not bid thee call.

LAUNCELOT. Your worship was wont to tell me that I could do nothing without bidding.

Enter JESSICA

JESSICA. Call you? What is your will?

SHYLOCK. I am bid forth to supper, Jessica;
There are my keys. But wherefore should I go?
I am not bid for love; they flatter me;
But yet I'll go in hate, to feed upon
The prodigal Christian. Jessica, my girl,
Look to my house. I am right loath to go:
There is some ill a-brewing towards my rest,
For I did dream of money bags tonight.

LAUNCELOT. I beseech you, sir, go; my young master doth expect your reproach.

SHYLOCK. So do I his.

LAUNCELOT. And they have conspired together, I will not say you shall see a masque; but if you do, then it was not for nothing that my nose fell a-bleeding on Black Monday last at six o'clock i' the morning, falling out that year on Ash Wednesday was four year, in the afternoon.

SHYLOCK. What, are there masques? Hear you me, Jessica:

Lock up my doors; and when you hear the drum
And the vile squealing of the wry-necked fife,
Clamber not you up to the casements then,
Nor thrust your head into the public street
To gaze on Christian fools with varnished faces,
But stop my house's ears, I mean my casements.
Let not the sound of shallow foppery enter
My sober house. By Jacob's staff, I swear,
I have no mind of feasting forth tonight;
But I will go. Go you before me, sirrah;
Say I will come.

LAUNCELOT. I will go before, sir. Mistress, look out at window, for all this;

There will come a Christian by,
Will be worth a Jewess' eye.   *Exit*

SHYLOCK. What says that fool of Hagar's offspring, ha?

JESSICA. His words were "Farewell, mistress"; nothing else.

SHYLOCK. The patch is kind enough, but a huge feeder;
Snail-slow in profit, and he sleeps by day
More than the wild cat. Drones hive not with me;
Therefore I part with him, and part with him
To one that I would have him help to waste
His borrowed purse. Well, Jessica, go in—
Perhaps I will return immediately—
Do as I bid you; shut doors after you.
Fast bind, fast find;
A proverb never stale in thrifty mind.   *Exit*

JESSICA. Farewell; and if my fortune be not crossed,
I have a father, you a daughter, lost.   *Exit*

SCENE VI *The same*

Enter GRATIANO *and* SALARINO, *masked*

GRATIANO. This is the penthouse under which Lorenzo
  Desired us to make stand.
SALARINO.   His hour is almost past.
GRATIANO. And it is marvel he out-dwells his hour,
  For lovers ever run before the clock.
SALARINO. O, ten times faster Venus' pigeons fly
  To seal love's bonds new-made, than they are wont
  To keep obliged faith unforfeited!
GRATIANO. That ever holds: who riseth from a feast
  With that keen appetite that he sits down?
  Where is the horse that doth untread again
  His tedious measures with the unbated fire
  That he did pace them first? All things that are,
  Are with more spirit chased than enjoyed.
  How like a younker or a prodigal
  The scarfed bark puts from her native bay,
  Hugged and embraced by the strumpet wind!
  How like the prodigal doth she return,
  With over-weathered ribs and ragged sails,
  Lean, rent and beggared by the strumpet wind!
SALARINO. Here comes Lorenzo—more of this here-
  after.

Enter LORENZO

LORENZO. Sweet friends, your patience for my long
  abode;
  Not I, but my affairs, have made you wait.
  When you shall please to play the thieves for wives,
  I'll watch as long for you then. Approach;
  Here dwells my father Jew. Ho! who's within?

Enter JESSICA, *above, in boy's clothes*

JESSICA. Who are you? Tell me, for more certainty,
  Albeit I'll swear that I do know your tongue.
LORENZO. Lorenzo, and thy love.
JESSICA. Lorenzo, certain, and my love indeed,
  For who love I so much? And now who knows
  But you, Lorenzo, whether I am yours?
LORENZO. Heaven and thy thoughts are witness that
  thou art.
JESSICA. Here, catch this casket; it is worth the pains.
  I am glad 'tis night, you do not look on me,
  For I am much ashamed of my exchange.
  But love is blind and lovers cannot see
  The pretty follies that themselves commit;
  For if they could, Cupid himself would blush
  To see me thus transformed to a boy.
LORENZO. Descend, for you must be my torch-bearer.
JESSICA. What, must I hold a candle to my shames?
  They in themselves, good sooth, are too too light.
  Why, 'tis an office of discovery, love;
  And I should be obscured.
LORENZO.   So are you, sweet,

Even in the lovely garnish of a boy.
  But come at once;
  For the close night doth play the runaway,
  And we are stayed for at Bassanio's feast.
JESSICA. I will make fast the doors, and gild myself
  With some more ducats, and be with you straight.
                                        Exit above
GRATIANO. Now, by my hood, a Gentile and no Jew.
LORENZO. Beshrew me but I love her heartily;
  For she is wise, if I can judge of her,
  And fair she is, if that mine eyes be true,
  And true she is, as she hath proved herself,
  And therefore, like herself, wise, fair and true,
  Shall she be placed in my constant soul.

Enter JESSICA, *below*

What, art thou come? On, gentlemen; away!
Our masquing mates by this time for us stay.
                    Exit with JESSICA *and* SALARINO

Enter ANTONIO

ANTONIO. Who's there?
GRATIANO. Signior Antonio!
ANTONIO. Fie, fie, Gratiano! Where are all the rest?
  'Tis nine o'clock; our friends all stay for you.
  No masque tonight: the wind is come about;
  Bassanio presently will go aboard.
  I have sent twenty out to seek for you.
GRATIANO. I am glad on 't. I desire no more delight
  Than to be under sail and gone tonight.   *Exeunt*

117

SCENE VII *Belmont: a room in* PORTIA'S *house*

Flourish of cornets. Enter PORTIA, *with the* PRINCE OF MOROCCO, *and their trains*

PORTIA. Go draw aside the curtains and discover
  The several caskets to this noble prince.
  Now make your choice.
MOROCCO. The first, of gold, who this inscription bears,
  "Who chooseth me shall gain what many men desire";
  The second, silver, which this promise carries,
  "Who chooseth me shall get as much as he deserves";
  This third, dull lead, with warning all as blunt,
  "Who chooseth me must give and hazard all he hath."
  How shall I know if I do choose the right?
PORTIA. The one of them contains my picture, Prince.
  If you choose that, then I am yours withal.
MOROCCO. Some god direct my judgement! Let me see;
  I will survey the inscriptions back again.
  What says this leaden casket?
  "Who chooseth me must give and hazard all he hath."
  Must give: for what? for lead? hazard for lead?
  This casket threatens. Men that hazard all
  Do it in hope of fair advantages.
  A golden mind stoops not to shows of dross.
  I'll then nor give nor hazard aught for lead.
  What says the silver with her virgin hue?
  "Who chooseth me shall get as much as he deserves."
  As much as he deserves! Pause there, Morocco,
  And weigh thy value with an even hand:
  If thou be'st rated by thy estimation,
  Thou dost deserve enough; and yet enough
  May not extend so far as to the lady.
  And yet to be afeard of my deserving
  Were but a weak disabling of myself.
  As much as I deserve! Why, that's the lady;
  I do in birth deserve her, and in fortunes,
  In graces and in qualities of breeding.
  But more than these, in love I do deserve.
  What if I strayed no further, but chose here?
  Let's see once more this saying graved in gold;
  "Who chooseth me shall gain what many men desire."
  Why, that's the lady; all the world desires her;
  From the four corners of the earth they come,
  To kiss this shrine, this mortal-breathing saint.
  The Hyrcanian deserts and the vasty wilds

Of wide Arabia are as throughfares now
For princes to come view fair Portia.
The watery kingdom, whose ambitious head
Spits in the face of heaven, is no bar
To stop the foreign spirits, but they come,
As o'er a brook, to see fair Portia.
One of these three contains her heavenly picture.
Is't like that lead contains her? 'Twere damnation
To think so base a thought: it were too gross
To rib her cerecloth in the obscure grave.
Or shall I think in silver she's immured,
Being ten times undervalued to tried gold?
O sinful thought! Never so rich a gem
Was set in worse than gold. They have in England
A coin that bears the figure of an angel
Stamped in gold, but that's insculped upon;
But here an angel in a golden bed
Lies all within. Deliver me the key:
Here do I choose, and thrive I as I may!
PORTIA. There, take it, prince; and if my form lie there,
  Then I am yours.   *He unlocks the golden casket*
MOROCCO.   O hell! what have we here?
  A carrion Death, within whose empty eye
  There is a written scroll! I'll read the writing.

  [*Reads*] All that glisters is not gold;
       Often have you heard that told.
       Many a man his life hath sold
       But my outside to behold.
       Gilded tombs do worms infold.
       Had you been as wise as bold,
       Young in limbs, in judgement old,
       Your answer had not been inscrolled.
       Fare you well; your suit is cold.

    Cold, indeed; and labour lost;
    Then, farewell, heat, and welcome, frost!
  Portia, adieu. I have too grieved a heart
  To take a tedious leave: thus losers part.
                    Exit with his train; flourish of cornets
PORTIA. A gentle riddance. Draw the curtains, go.
  Let all of his complexion choose me so.   *Exeunt*

SCENE VIII *Venice: a street*

Enter SALARINO *and* SALANIO

SALARINO. Why, man, I saw Bassanio under sail.
  With him is Gratiano gone along;
  And in their ship I am sure Lorenzo is not.
SALANIO. The villain Jew with outcries raised the Duke,
  Who went with him to search Bassanio's ship.
SALARINO. He came too late, the ship was under sail.
  But there the Duke was given to understand

That in a gondola were seen together
Lorenzo and his amorous Jessica.
Besides, Antonio certified the Duke
They were not with Bassanio in his ship.
SALANIO. I never heard a passion so confused,
  So strange, outrageous, and so variable,
  As the dog Jew did utter in the streets:

"My daughter! O my ducats! O my daughter!
Fled with a Christian! O my Christian ducats!
Justice! the law! my ducats, and my daughter!
A sealed bag, two sealed bags of ducats,
Of double ducats, stolen from me by my daughter!
And jewels, two stones, two rich and precious stones,
Stolen by my daughter! Justice! find the girl;
She hath the stones upon her, and the ducats."
SALARINO. Why, all the boys in Venice follow him,
  Crying, his stones, his daughter, and his ducats.
SALANIO. Let good Antonio look he keep his day,
  Or he shall pay for this.
SALARINO.   Marry, well remembered.
  I reasoned with a Frenchman yesterday,
  Who told me, in the narrow seas that part
  The French and English, there miscarried
  A vessel of our country richly fraught.
  I thought upon Antonio when he told me;
  And wished in silence that it were not his.
SALANIO. You were best to tell Antonio what you hear;
  Yet do not suddenly, for it may grieve him.

SALARINO. A kinder gentleman treads not the earth.
  I saw Bassanio and Antonio part.
  Bassanio told him he would make some speed
  Of his return; he answered, "Do not so;
  Slubber not business for my sake, Bassanio,
  But stay the very riping of the time;
  And for the Jew's bond which he hath of me,
  Let it not enter in your mind of love.
  Be merry, and employ your chiefest thoughts
  To courtship and such fair ostents of love
  As shall conveniently become you there."
  And even there, his eye being big with tears,
  Turning his face, he put his hand behind him,
  And with affection wondrous sensible
  He wrung Bassanio's hand; and so they parted.
SALANIO. I think he only loves the world for him.
  I pray thee, let us go and find him out
  And quicken his embraced heaviness
  With some delight or other.
SALARINO.   Do we so.

Exeunt

SCENE IX *Belmont: a room in* PORTIA'S *house*

Enter NERISSA *with a* Servitor

NERISSA. Quick, quick, I pray thee; draw the curtain
    straight.
  The Prince of Arragon hath ta'en his oath,
  And comes to his election presently.

Flourish of cornets. Enter the PRINCE OF ARRAGON, PORTIA,
    and their trains

PORTIA. Behold, there stand the caskets, noble Prince.
  If you choose that wherein I am contained,
  Straight shall our nuptial rites be solemnized:
  But if you fail, without more speech, my lord,
  You must be gone from hence immediately.
ARRAGON. I am enjoined by oath to observe three things:
  First, never to unfold to anyone
  Which casket 'twas I chose; next, if I fail
  Of the right casket, never in my life
  To woo a maid in way of marriage;
  Lastly,
  If I do fail in fortune of my choice,
  Immediately to leave you and be gone.
PORTIA. To these injunctions everyone doth swear
  That comes to hazard for my worthless self.
ARRAGON. And so have I addressed me. Fortune now
  To my heart's hope! Gold; silver; and base lead.
  "Who chooseth me must give and hazard all he hath."
  You shall look fairer, ere I give or hazard.
  What says the golden chest? ha! let me see:
  "Who chooseth me shall gain what many men desire."

What many men desire! that "many" may be meant
By the fool multitude, that choose by show,
Not learning more than the fond eye doth teach;
Which pries not to the interior, but, like the martlet,
Builds in the weather on the outward wall,
Even in the force and road of casualty.
I will not choose what many men desire,
Because I will not jump with common spirits
And rank me with the barbarous multitudes.
Why, then to thee, thou silver treasure-house;
Tell me once more what title thou dost bear:
"Who chooseth me shall get as much as he deserves."
And well said too; for who shall go about
To cozen fortune and be honourable
Without the stamp of merit? Let none presume
To wear an undeserved dignity.
O, that estates, degrees and offices
Were not derived corruptly, and that clear honour
Were purchased by the merit of the wearer!
How many then should cover that stand bare!
How many be commanded that command!
How much low peasantry would then be gleaned
From the true seed of honour! and how much honour
Picked from the chaff and ruin of the times
To be new-varnished! Well, but to my choice:
"Who chooseth me shall get as much as he deserves."
I will assume desert. Give me a key for this,
And instantly unlock my fortunes here.

He opens the silver casket

PORTIA. Too long a pause for that which you find there.

ARRAGON. What's here? The portrait of a blinking idiot,
  Presenting me a schedule! I will read it.
  How much unlike art thou to Portia!
  How much unlike my hopes and my deservings!
  "Who chooseth me shall have as much as he deserves."
  Did I deserve no more than a fool's head?
  Is that my prize? Are my deserts no better?

PORTIA. To offend, and judge, are distinct offices
  And of opposed natures.

ARRAGON.   What is here?

  "The fire seven times tried this;
  Seven times tried that judgement is,
  That did never choose amiss.
  Some there be that shadows kiss;
  Such have but a shadow's bliss.
  There be fools alive, iwis,
  Silvered o'er; and so was this.
  Take what wife you will to bed,
  I will ever be your head.
  So be gone; you are sped."

  Still more fool I shall appear
  By the time I linger here.
  With one fool's head I came to woo,
  But I go away with two.
  Sweet, adieu. I'll keep my oath,
  Patiently to bear my wroth.

Exeunt ARRAGON *and train*

PORTIA. Thus hath the candle singed the moth.
  O, these deliberate fools! When they do choose,
  They have the wisdom by their wit to lose.

NERISSA. The ancient saying is no heresy,
  Hanging and wiving goes by destiny.

PORTIA. Come, draw the curtain, Nerissa.

Enter a Servant

SERVANT. Where is my lady?

PORTIA.   Here; what would my lord?

SERVANT. Madam, there is alighted at your gate
  A young Venetian, one that comes before
  To signify the approaching of his lord;
  From whom he bringeth sensible regreets,
  To wit, besides commends and courteous breath,
  Gifts of rich value. Yet I have not seen
  So likely an ambassador of love:
  A day in April never came so sweet,
  To show how costly summer was at hand,
  As this fore-spurrer comes before his lord.

PORTIA. No more, I pray thee; I am half afeard
  Thou wilt say anon he is some kin to thee,
  Thou spend'st such high-day wit in praising him.
  Come, come, Nerissa; for I long to see
  Quick Cupid's post that comes so mannerly.

NERISSA. Bassanio, lord Love, if thy will it be!   *Exeunt*

ACT III

SCENE I *Venice: a street*

Enter SALANIO *and* SALARINO

SALANIO. Now, what news on the Rialto?

SALARINO. Why, yet it lives there unchecked that Antonio hath a ship of rich lading wrecked on the narrow seas; the Goodwins, I think they call the place; a very dangerous flat, and fatal, where the carcases of many a tall ship lie buried, as they say, if my gossip Report be an honest woman of her word.

SALANIO. I would she were as lying a gossip in that as ever knapped ginger or made her neighbours believe she wept for the death of a third husband. But it is true, without any slips of prolixity or crossing the plain highway of talk, that the good Antonio, the honest Antonio——O that I had a title good enough to keep his name company!—

SALARINO. Come, the full stop.

SALANIO. Ha! what sayest thou? Why, the end is, he hath lost a ship.

SALARINO. I would it might prove the end of his losses.

SALANIO. Let me say "amen" betimes, lest the Devil cross my prayer, for here he comes in the likeness of a Jew.

Enter SHYLOCK

How now, Shylock! what news among the merchants?

SHYLOCK. You knew, none so well, none so well as you, of my daughter's flight.

SALARINO. That's certain; I, for my part, knew the tailor that made the wings she flew withal.

SALANIO. And Shylock, for his own part, knew the bird was fledged; and then it is the complexion of them all to leave the dam.

SHYLOCK. She is damned for it.

SALARINO. That's certain, if the Devil may be her judge.

SHYLOCK. My own flesh and blood to rebel!

SALANIO. Out upon it, old carrion! rebels it at these years?

SHYLOCK. I say, my daughter is my flesh and blood.

SALARINO. There is more difference between thy flesh and hers than between jet and ivory; more between your bloods than there is between red wine and Rhenish. But tell us, do you hear whether Antonio have had any loss at sea or no?

SHYLOCK. There I have another bad match: a bankrupt, a prodigal, who dare scarce show his head on the Rialto; a beggar, that was used to come so smug upon the mart; let him look to his bond. He was wont to call me usurer; let him look to his bond. He was wont to lend money for a Christian courtesy; let him look to his bond.

SALARINO. Why, I am sure, if he forfeit, thou wilt not take his flesh; what's that good for?

SHYLOCK. To bait fish withal; if it will feed nothing else, it will feed my revenge. He hath disgraced me, and hindered me half a million; laughed at my losses, mocked at my gains, scorned my nation, thwarted my bargains, cooled my friends, heated mine enemies; and what's his reason? I am a Jew. Hath not a Jew eyes? Hath not a Jew hands, organs, dimensions, senses, affections, passions? Fed with the same food, hurt with the same weapons, subject to the same diseases, healed by the same means, warmed and cooled by the same winter and summer, as a Christian is? If you prick us, do we not bleed? If you tickle us, do we not laugh? If you poison us, do we not die? And if you wrong us, shall we not revenge? If we are like you in the rest, we will resemble you in that. If a Jew wrong a Christian, what is his humility? Revenge. If a Christian wrong a Jew, what should his sufferance be by Christian example? Why, revenge. The villainy you teach me, I will execute, and it shall go hard but I will better the instruction.

Enter a Servant

SERVANT. Gentlemen, my master Antonio is at his house and desires to speak with you both.

SALARINO. We have been up and down to seek him.

Enter TUBAL

SALANIO. Her comes another of the tribe. A third cannot be matched, unless the devil himself turn Jew.

Exeunt SALANIO, SALARINO, *and* Servant

SHYLOCK. How now, Tubal! What news from Genoa? Hast thou found my daughter?

TUBAL. I often came where I did hear of her, but cannot find her.

SHYLOCK. Why, there, there, there, there! A diamond gone, cost me two thousand ducats in Frankfort! The curse never fell upon our nation till now; I never felt it till now. Two thousand ducats in that; and other precious, precious jewels. I would my daughter were dead at my foot, and the jewels in her ear! Would she were hearsed at my foot, and the ducats in her coffin! No news of them? Why, so—and I know not what's spent in the search—why, thou loss upon loss! The thief gone with so much, and so much to find the thief; and no satisfaction, no revenge; nor no ill luck stirring but what lights on my shoulders; no sighs but of my breathing; no tears but of my shedding.

TUBAL. Yes, other men have ill luck too: Antonio, as I heard in Genoa—

SHYLOCK. What, what, what? Ill luck, ill luck?

TUBAL. Hath an argosy cast away, coming from Tripolis.

SHYLOCK. I thank God, I thank God. Is't true, is't true?

TUBAL. I spoke with some of the sailors that escaped the wreck.

SHYLOCK. I thank thee, good Tubal. Good news, good news! ha, ha! where? in Genoa?

TUBAL. Your daughter spent in Genoa, as I heard, in one night fourscore ducats.

SHYLOCK. Thou stickest a dagger in me—I shall never see my gold again. Fourscore ducats at a sitting! Fourscore ducats!

TUBAL. There came divers of Antonio's creditors in my company to Venice, that swear he cannot choose but break.

SHYLOCK. I am very glad of it. I'll plague him; I'll torture him. I am glad of it.

TUBAL. One of them showed me a ring that he had of your daughter for a monkey.

SHYLOCK. Out upon her! Thou torturest me, Tubal; it was my turquoise; I had it of Leah when I was a bachelor. I would not have given it for a wilderness of monkeys.

TUBAL. But Antonio is certainly undone.

SHYLOCK. Nay, that's true, that's very true. Go, Tubal, fee me an officer; bespeak him a fortnight before. I will have the heart of him, if he forfeit; for, were he out of Venice, I can make what merchandise I will. Go, go, Tubal, and meet me at our synagogue; go, good Tubal; at our synagogue, Tubal.   *Exeunt*

SCENE II *Belmont: a room in* PORTIA'S *house*

Enter BASSANIO, PORTIA, GRATIANO, NERISSA, *and* Attendants

PORTIA. I pray you, tarry; pause a day or two
Before you hazard; for, in choosing wrong,
I lose your company. Therefore forbear awhile.
There's something tells me, but it is not love,
I would not lose you; and you know yourself,
Hate counsels not in such a quality.
But lest you should not understand me well—
And yet a maiden hath no tongue but thought—
I would detain you here some month or two
Before you venture for me. I could teach you
How to choose right, but I am then forsworn;
So will I never be; so may you miss me;
But if you do, you'll make me wish a sin,
That I had been forsworn. Beshrew your eyes,
They have o'erlooked me and divided me;
One half of me is yours, the other half yours,
Mine own, I would say; but if mine, then yours,
And so all yours. O, these naughty times
Put bars between the owners and their rights!
And so, though yours, not yours. Prove it so,
Let fortune go to hell for it, not I.
I speak too long; but 'tis to peize the time,
To eke it and to draw it out in length,
To stay you from election.

BASSANIO.   Let me choose;
For as I am, I live upon the rack.

PORTIA. Upon the rack, Bassanio! Then confess
What treason there is mingled with your love.

BASSANIO. None but that ugly treason of mistrust,
Which makes me fear the enjoying of my love.
There may as well be amity and life
'Tween snow and fire, as treason and my love.

PORTIA. Ay, but I fear you speak upon the rack,
Where men enforced do speak anything.

BASSANIO. Promise me life, and I'll confess the truth.

PORTIA. Well then, confess and live.

BASSANIO.   "Confess" and "love"
Had been the very sum of my confession.
O happy torment, when my torturer
Doth teach me answers for deliverance!
But let me to my fortune and the caskets.

PORTIA. Away, then! I am locked in one of them.
If you do love me, you will find me out.
Nerissa and the rest, stand all aloof.
Let music sound while he doth make his choice;
Then, if he lose, he makes a swan-like end,
Fading in music. That the comparison
May stand more proper, my eye shall be the stream
And watery death-bed for him. He may win;
And what is music then? Then music is
Even as the flourish when true subjects bow
To a new-crowned monarch. Such it is
As are those dulcet sounds in break of day
That creep into the dreaming bridegroom's ear
And summon him to marriage. Now he goes,
With no less presence, but with much more love,
Than young Alcides, when he did redeem
The virgin tribute paid by howling Troy
To the sea-monster. I stand for sacrifice;
The rest aloof are the Dardanian wives,
With bleared visages, come forth to view
The issue of the exploit. Go, Hercules!
Live thou, I live; with much much more dismay
I view the fight than thou that mak'st the fray.

Music, whilst BASSANIO *comments on the caskets to himself*

SONG

        Tell me where is fancy bred,
        Or in the heart or in the head?
        How begot, how nourished?
              Reply, reply.
        It is engendered in the eyes,
        With gazing fed; and fancy dies
        In the cradle where it lies.
            Let us all ring fancy's knell.
            I'll begin it—Ding, dong, bell.

ALL. Ding, dong, bell.

BASSANIO. So may the outward shows be least them-
    selves;
  The world is still deceived with ornament.
  In law, what plea so tainted and corrupt
  But, being seasoned with a gracious voice,
  Obscures the show of evil? In religion,
  What damned error, but some sober brow
  Will bless it and approve it with a text,
  Hiding the grossness with fair ornament?
  There is no vice so simple but assumes
  Some mark of virtue on his outward parts.
  How many cowards, whose hearts are all as false
  As stairs of sand, wear yet upon their chins
  The beards of Hercules and frowning Mars,
  Who, inward searched, have livers white as milk;
  And these assume but valour's excrement
  To render them redoubted! Look on beauty,
  And you shall see 'tis purchased by the weight;
  Which therein works a miracle in nature,
  Making them lightest that wear most of it.
  So are those crisped snaky golden locks
  Which make such wanton gambols with the wind,
  Upon supposed fairness, often known
  To be the dowry of a second head,
  The skull that bred them in the sepulchre.
  Thus ornament is but the guiled shore
  To a most dangerous sea; the beauteous scarf
  Veiling an Indian beauty; in a word,
  The seeming truth which cunning times put on
  To entrap the wisest. Therefore, thou gaudy gold,
  Hard food for Midas, I will none of thee;
  Nor none of thee, thou pale and common drudge
  'Tween man and man. But thou, thou meagre lead,
  Which rather threatenest than dost promise aught,
  Thy paleness moves me more than eloquence;
  And here choose I: joy be the consequence!

PORTIA. [*Aside*] How all the other passions fleet to air,
  As doubtful thoughts, and rash-embraced despair,
  And shuddering fear, and green-eyed jealousy!
  O love,
  Be moderate; allay thy ecstasy;
  In measure rein thy joy; scant this excess.
  I feel too much thy blessing. Make it less,
  For fear I surfeit.

BASSANIO.   What find I here?

Opening the leaden casket

Fair Portia's counterfeit! What demigod
Hath come so near creation? Move these eyes?
Or whether, riding on the balls of mine,
Seem they in motion? Here are severed lips,
Parted with sugar breath—so sweet a bar
Should sunder such sweet friends. Here in her hairs
The painter plays the spider and hath woven
A golden mesh to entrap the hearts of men
Faster than gnats in cobwebs. But her eyes—
How could he see to do them? Having made one,
Methinks it should have power to steal both his
And leave itself unfurnished. Yet look, how far
The substance of my praise doth wrong this shadow
In underprizing it, so far this shadow
Doth limp behind the substance. Here's the scroll.
The continent and summary of my fortune.
[*Reads*] You that choose not by the view,
      Chance as fair and choose as true!
      Since this fortune falls to you,
      Be content and seek no new.
      If you be well pleased with this
      And hold your fortune for your bliss,
      Turn you where your lady is
      And claim her with a loving kiss.
A gentle scroll. Fair lady, by your leave; *kissing her*
I come by note, to give and to receive.
Like one of two contending in a prize,
That thinks he hath done well in people's eyes,
Hearing applause and universal shout,
Giddy in spirit, still gazing in a doubt
Whether those peals of praise be his or no;
So, thrice-fair lady, stand I, even so;
As doubtful whether what I see be true,
Until confirmed, signed, ratified by you.
PORTIA. You see me, Lord Bassanio, where I stand,
Such as I am—though for myself alone
I would not be ambitious in my wish,
To wish myself much better. Yet, for you
I would be trebled twenty times myself;
A thousand times more fair, ten thousand times
More rich;
That only to stand high in your account,
I might in virtues, beauties, livings, friends,
Exceed account; but the full sum of me
Is sum of something, which, to term in gross,
Is an unlessoned girl, unschooled, unpractised;
Happy in this, she is not yet so old
But she may learn; happier than this,
She is not bred so dull but she can learn;
Happiest of all is that her gentle spirit
Commits itself to yours to be directed,
As from her lord, her governor, her king.
Myself and what is mine to you and yours
Is now converted. But now I was the lord
Of this fair mansion, master of my servants,
Queen o'er myself; and even now, but now,
This house, these servants and this same myself
Are yours, my lord. I give them with this ring;
Which when you part from, lose, or give away,
Let it presage the ruin of your love
And be my vantage to exclaim on you.
BASSANIO. Madam, you have bereft me of all words,
Only my blood speaks to you in my veins;
And there is such confusion in my powers,
As, after some oration fairly spoke
By a beloved prince, there doth appear
Among the buzzing pleased multitude;
Where every something, being blent together,
Turns to a wild of nothing, save of joy,
Expressed and not expressed. But when this ring
Parts from this finger, then parts life from hence—
O, then be bold to say Bassanio's dead!
NERISSA. My lord and lady, it is now our time,
That have stood by and seen our wishes prosper,
To cry, good joy: good joy, my lord and lady!
GRATIANO. My lord Bassanio and my gentle lady,
I wish you all the joy that you can wish;
For I am sure you can wish none from me.
And when your honours mean to solemnize
The bargain of your faith, I do beseech you,
Even at that time I may be married too.
BASSANIO. With all my heart, so thou canst get a wife.
GRATIANO. I thank your lordship, you have got me one.
My eyes, my lord, can look as swift as yours.
You saw the mistress, I beheld the maid;
You loved, I loved for intermission
No more pertains to me, my lord, than you.
Your fortune stood upon the casket there,
And so did mine too, as the matter falls;
For wooing here until I sweat again,
And swearing till my very roof was dry
With oaths of love, at last, if promise last,
I got a promise of this fair one here
To have her love, provided that your fortune
Achieved her mistress.
PORTIA.   Is this true, Nerissa?
NERISSA. Madam, it is, so you stand pleased withal.
BASSANIO. And do you, Gratiano, mean good faith?
GRATIANO. Yes, faith, my lord.
BASSANIO. Our feast shall be much honoured in your
   marriage.
GRATIANO. We'll play with them the first boy for a
   thousand ducats.
NERISSA. What, and stake down?
GRATIANO. No; we shall ne'er win at that sport, and
   stake down.
But who comes here? Lorenzo and his infidel?
What, and my old Venetian friend Salerio?

Enter LORENZO, JESSICA, *and* SALERIO,
a Messenger from Venice

BASSANIO. Lorenzo and Salerio, welcome hither;
  If that the youth of my new interest here
  Have power to bid you welcome. By your leave,
  I bid my very friends and countrymen,
  Sweet Portia, welcome.
PORTIA.   So do I, my lord;
  They are entirely welcome.
LORENZO. I thank your honour. For my part, my lord,
  My purpose was not to have seen you here;
  But meeting with Salerio by the way,
  He did intreat me, past all saying nay,
  To come with him along.
SALERIO.   I did, my lord;
  And I have reason for it. Signior Antonio
  Commends him to you.

Gives BASSANIO *a letter*

BASSANIO.   Ere I ope his letter,
  I pray you, tell me how my good friend doth.
SALERIO. Not sick, my lord, unless it be in mind;
  Nor well, unless in mind. His letter there
  Will show you his estate.
GRATIANO. Nerissa, cheer yon stranger; bid her welcome.
  Your hand, Salerio; what's the news from Venice?
  How doth that royal merchant, good Antonio?
  I know he will be glad of our success;
  We are the Jasons, we have won the fleece.
SALERIO. I would you had won the fleece that he hath
  lost.
PORTIA. There are some shrewd contents in yon same
    paper,
  That steals the colour from Bassanio's cheek:
  Some dear friend dead; else nothing in the world
  Could turn so much the constitution
  Of any constant man. What, worse and worse!
  With leave, Bassanio; I am half yourself,
  And I must freely have the half of anything
  That this same paper brings you.
BASSANIO.   O sweet Portia,
  Here are a few of the unpleasantest words
  That ever blotted paper! Gentle lady,
  When I did first impart my love to you,
  I freely told you, all the wealth I had
  Ran in my veins, I was a gentleman;
  And then I told you true. And yet, dear lady,
  Rating myself at nothing, you shall see
  How much I was a braggart. When I told you
  My state was nothing, I should then have told you
  That I was worse than nothing; for, indeed,
  I have engaged myself to a dear friend,
  Engaged my friend to his mere enemy,
  To feed my means. Here is a letter, lady;
  The paper as the body of my friend,
  And every word in it a gaping wound,
  Issuing life-blood. But is it true, Salerio?
  Have all his ventures failed? What, not one hit?

From Tripolis, from Mexico and England,
  From Lisbon, Barbary and India?
  And not one vessel 'scape the dreadful touch
  Of merchant-marring rocks?
SALERIO.   Not one, my lord.
  Besides, it should appear, that if he had
  The present money to discharge the Jew,
  He would not take it. Never did I know
  A creature, that did bear the shape of man,
  So keen and greedy to confound a man.
  He plies the Duke at morning and at night,
  And doth impeach the freedom of the state,
  If they deny him justice. Twenty merchants,
  The Duke himself, and the magnificoes
  Of greatest port, have all persuaded with him;
  But none can drive him from the envious plea
  Of forfeiture, of justice and his bond.
JESSICA. When I was with him I have heard him swear
  To Tubal and to Chus, his countrymen,
  That he would rather have Antonio's flesh
  Than twenty times the value of the sum
  That he did owe him; and I know, my lord,
  If law, authority and power deny not,
  It will go hard with poor Antonio.
PORTIA. Is it your dear friend that is thus in trouble?
BASSANIO. The dearest friend to me, the kindest man,
  The best-conditioned and unwearied spirit
  In doing courtesies, and one in whom
  The ancient Roman honour more appears
  Than any that draws breath in Italy.
PORTIA. What sum owes he the Jew?
BASSANIO. For me three thousand ducats.
PORTIA.   What, no more?
  Pay him six thousand, and deface the bond;
  Double six thousand, and then treble that,
  Before a friend of this description
  Shall lose a hair through Bassanio's fault.
  First go with me to church and call me wife,
  And then away to Venice to your friend;
  For never shall you lie by Portia's side
  With an unquiet soul. You shall have gold
  To pay the petty debt twenty times over.
  When it is paid, bring your true friend along.
  My maid Nerissa and myself meantime
  Will live as maids and widows. Come, away!
  For you shall hence upon your wedding day:
  Bid your friends welcome, show a merry cheer:
  Since you are dear bought, I will love you dear.
  But let me hear the letter of your friend.
BASSANIO. [*Reads*] Sweet Bassanio, my ships have all
  miscarried, my creditors grow cruel, my estate is
  very low, my bond to the Jew is forfeit; and since in
  paying it, it is impossible I should live, all debts are
  cleared between you and I, if I might but see you at
  my death. Notwithstanding, use your pleasure: if your
  love do not persuade you to come, let not my letter.

SCENE III *Venice: a street*

Enter SHYLOCK, SALARINO, ANTONIO, *and* Gaoler

SHYLOCK. Gaoler, look to him; tell not me of mercy;
  This is the fool that lent out money gratis.
  Gaoler, look to him.
ANTONIO.   Hear me yet, good Shylock.
SHYLOCK. I'll have my bond; speak not against my bond.
  I have sworn an oath that I will have my bond.
  Thou calledst me dog before thou hadst a cause;
  But, since I am a dog, beware my fangs.
  The Duke shall grant me justice. I do wonder,
  Thou naughty gaoler, that thou art so fond
  To come abroad with him at his request.
ANTONIO. I pray thee, hear me speak.
SHYLOCK. I'll have my bond; I will not hear thee speak.
  I'll have my bond; and therefore speak no more.
  I'll not be made a soft and dull-eyed fool,
  To shake the head, relent, and sigh, and yield
  To Christian intercessors. Follow not;
  I'll have no speaking. I will have my bond.   *Exit*

PORTIA. O love, dispatch all business, and be gone!
BASSANIO. Since I have your good leave to go away,
  I will make haste. But, till I come again,
  No bed shall e'er be guilty of my stay,
  No rest be interposer 'twixt us twain.   *Exeunt*

SALARINO. It is the most impenetrable cur
  That ever kept with men.
ANTONIO.   Let him alone.
  I'll follow him no more with bootless prayers.
  He seeks my life; his reason well I know:
  I oft delivered from his forfeitures
  Many that have at times made moan to me;
  Therefore he hates me.
SALARINO.   I am sure the Duke
  Will never grant this forfeiture to hold.
ANTONIO. The Duke cannot deny the course of law;

For the commodity that strangers have
With us in Venice, if it be denied,
Will much impeach the justice of his state;
Since that the trade and profit of the city
Consisteth of all nations. Therefore, go;
These griefs and losses have so bated me,
That I shall hardly spare a pound of flesh
Tomorrow to my bloody creditor.
Well, gaoler, on. Pray God, Bassanio come
To see me pay his debt, and then I care not!

                               Exeunt

SCENE IV *Belmont: a room in* PORTIA'S *house*

Enter PORTIA, NERISSA, LORENZO, JESSICA, *and* BALTHASAR

LORENZO. Madam, although I speak it in your presence,
  You have a noble and a true conceit
  Of god-like amity; which appears most strongly
  In bearing thus the absence of your lord.
  But if you knew to whom you show this honour,
  How true a gentleman you send relief,
  How dear a lover of my lord your husband,
  I know you would be prouder of the work
  Than customary bounty can enforce you.
PORTIA. I never did repent for doing good,
  Nor shall not now; for in companions
  That do converse and waste the time together,
  Whose souls do bear an equal yoke of love,
  There must be needs a like proportion
  Of lineaments, of manners and of spirit;
  Which makes me think that this Antonio,
  Being the bosom lover of my lord,
  Must needs be like my lord. If it be so,
  How little is the cost I have bestowed
  In purchasing the semblance of my soul
  From out the state of hellish misery!
  This comes too near the praising of myself;
  Therefore no more of it. Hear other things.
  Lorenzo, I commit into your hands
  The husbandry and manage of my house
  Until my lord's return. For mine own part,
  I have toward heaven breathed a secret vow
  To live in prayer and contemplation,
  Only attended by Nerissa here,
  Until her husband and my lord's return.
  There is a monastery two miles off;
  And there will we abide. I do desire you
  Not to deny this imposition;
  The which my love and some necessity
  Now lays upon you.
LORENZO.   Madam, with all my heart;
  I shall obey you in all fair commands.
PORTIA. My people do already know my mind,
  And will acknowledge you and Jessica
  In place of Lord Bassanio and myself.

And so farewell, till we shall meet again.
LORENZO. Fair thoughts and happy hours attend on you!
JESSICA. I wish your ladyship all heart's content.
PORTIA. I thank you for your wish, and am well pleased
  To wish it back on you. Fare you well, Jessica.
                    Exeunt JESSICA *and* LORENZO
  Now, Balthasar,
  As I have ever found thee honest-true,
  So let me find thee still. Take this same letter,
  And use thou all the endeavour of a man
  In speed to Padua. See thou render this
  Into my cousin's hand, Doctor Bellario;
  And, look, what notes and garments he doth give thee,
  Bring them, I pray thee, with imagined speed
  Unto the traject, to the common ferry
  Which trades to Venice. Waste no time in words,
  But get thee gone; I shall be there before thee.
BALTHASAR. Madam, I go with all convenient speed.
                             Exit
PORTIA. Come on, Nerissa; I have work in hand
  That you yet know not of. We'll see our husbands
  Before they think of us.
NERISSA.   Shall they see us?
PORTIA. They shall, Nerissa; but in such a habit,
  That they shall think we are accomplished
  With that we lack. I'll hold thee any wager,
  When we are both accoutred like young men,
  I'll prove the prettier fellow of the two,
  And wear my dagger with the braver grace,
  And speak between the change of man and boy
  With a reed voice, and turn two mincing steps
  Into a manly stride, and speak of frays
  Like a fine bragging youth, and tell quaint lies,
  How honourable ladies sought my love,
  Which I denying, they fell sick and died;
  I could not do withal; then I'll repent,
  And wish, for all that, that I had not killed them;
  And twenty of these puny lies I'll tell,
  That men shall swear I have discontinued school
  Above a twelvemonth. I have within my mind

A thousand raw tricks of these bragging Jacks,
Which I will practise.
NERISSA.   Why, shall we turn to men?
PORTIA. Fie, what a question's that,
If thou wert near a lewd interpreter!

But come, I'll tell thee all my whole device
When I am in my coach, which stays for us
At the park gate; and therefore haste away,
For we must measure twenty miles today.

Exeunt

SCENE V *The same: A garden*

Enter LAUNCELOT *and* JESSICA

LAUNCELOT. Yes, truly; for, look you, the sins of the father are to be laid upon the children. Therefore, I promise ye, I fear you. I was always plain with you, and so now I speak my agitation of the matter. Therefore be of good cheer, for truly I think you are damned. There is but one hope in it that can do you any good; and that is but a kind of bastard hope neither.

JESSICA. And what hope is that, I pray thee?

LAUNCELOT. Marry, you may partly hope that your father got you not, that you are not the Jew's daughter.

JESSICA. That were a kind of bastard hope, indeed; so the sins of my mother should be visited upon me.

LAUNCELOT. Truly then I fear you are damned both by father and mother. Thus when I shun Scylla, your father, I fall into Charybdis, your mother. Well, you are gone both ways.

JESSICA. I shall be saved by my husband; he hath made me a Christian.

LAUNCELOT. Truly, the more to blame he. We were Christians enow before; e'en as many as could well live, one by another. This making of Christians will raise the price of hogs; if we grow all to be pork-eaters, we shall not shortly have a rasher on the coals for money.

Enter LORENZO

JESSICA. I'll tell my husband, Launcelot, what you say; here he comes.

LORENZO. I shall grow jealous of you shortly, Launcelot, if you thus get my wife into corners.

JESSICA. Nay, you need not fear us, Lorenzo; Launcelot and I are out. He tells me flatly, there is no mercy for me in Heaven, because I am a Jew's daughter; and, he says, you are no good member of the commonwealth, for in converting Jews to Christians, you raise the price of pork.

LORENZO. I shall answer that better to the commonwealth than you can the getting up of the Negro's belly: the Moor is with child by you, Launcelot.

LAUNCELOT. It is much that the Moor should be more than reason; but if she be less than an honest woman, she is indeed more than I took her for.

LORENZO. How every fool can play upon the word! I think the best grace of wit will shortly turn into silence, and discourse grow commendable in none

only but parrots. Go in, sirrah; bid them prepare for dinner.

LAUNCELOT. That is done, sir; they have all stomachs.

LORENZO. Goodly Lord, what a wit-snapper are you! Then bid them prepare dinner.

LAUNCELOT. That is done too, sir; only "cover" is the word.

LORENZO. Will you cover then, sir?

LAUNCELOT. Not so, sir, neither; I know my duty.

LORENZO. Yet more quarrelling with occasion! Wilt thou show the whole wealth of thy wit in an instant? I pray thee, understand a plain man in his plain meaning: go to thy fellows; bid them cover the table, serve in the meat, and we will come in to dinner.

LAUNCELOT. For the table, sir, it shall be served in; for the meat, sir, it shall be covered; for your coming in to dinner, sir, why, let it be as humours and conceits shall govern.   *Exit*

LORENZO. O dear discretion, how his words are suited!
The fool hath planted in his memory
An army of good words; and I do know
A many fools, that stand in better place,
Garnished like him, that for a tricksy word
Defy the matter. How cheer'st thou, Jessica?
And now, good sweet, say thy opinion,
How dost thou like the Lord Bassanio's wife?

JESSICA. Past all expressing. It is very meet
The Lord Bassanio live an upright life;
For, having such a blessing in his lady,
He finds the joys of Heaven here on earth;
And if on earth he do not mean it, then
In reason he should never come to Heaven.
Why, if two gods should play some Heavenly match
And on the wager lay two earthly women,
And Portia one, there must be something else
Pawned with the other, for the poor rude world
Hath not her fellow.

LORENZO.   Even such a husband
Hast thou of me as she is for a wife.

JESSICA. Nay, but ask my opinion too of that.

LORENZO. I will anon; first, let us go to dinner.

JESSICA. Nay, let me praise you while I have a stomach.

LORENZO. No, pray thee, let it serve for table-talk;
Then, howsoe'er thou speak'st, 'mong other things
I shall digest it.

JESSICA.   Well, I'll set you forth.   *Exeunt*

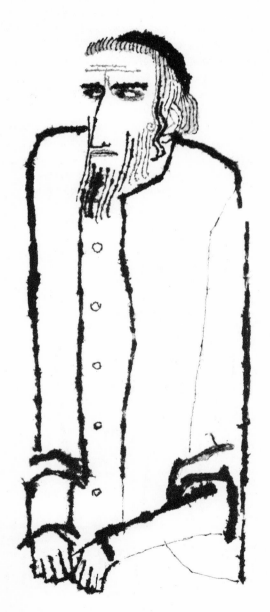

ACT IV

SCENE I *Venice: a court of justice*

Enter the DUKE, *the* Magnificoes, ANTONIO, BASSANIO.
GRATIANO, SALERIO, *and others*

DUKE. What, is Antonio here?
ANTONIO. Ready, so please your grace.
DUKE. I am sorry for thee. Thou art come to answer
  A stony adversary, an inhuman wretch
  Uncapable of pity, void and empty
  From any dram of mercy.
ANTONIO.   I have heard
  Your grace hath ta'en great pains to qualify
  His rigorous course; but since he stands obdurate
  And that no lawful means can carry me
  Out of his envy's reach, I do oppose
  My patience to his fury, and am armed
  To suffer, with a quietness of spirit,
  The very tyranny and rage of his.
DUKE. Go one, and call the Jew into the court.
SALERIO. He is ready at the door; he comes, my lord.

Enter SHYLOCK

DUKE. Make room, and let him stand before our face.
  Shylock, the world thinks, and I think so too,
  That thou but lead'st this fashion of thy malice
  To the last hour of act; and then 'tis thought
  Thou'lt show thy mercy and remorse more strange
  Than is thy strange apparent cruelty;
  And where thou now exact'st the penalty,
  Which is a pound of this poor merchant's flesh,
  Thou wilt not only loose the forfeiture,
  But, touched with human gentleness and love,
  Forgive a moiety of the principal;
  Glancing an eye of pity on his losses,
  That have of late so huddled on his back,
  Enow to press a royal merchant down
  And pluck commiseration of his state
  From brassy bosoms and rough hearts of flint,
  From stubborn Turks and Tartars, never trained
  To offices of tender courtesy.
  We all expect a gentle answer, Jew.
SHYLOCK. I have possessed your grace of what I purpose;
  And by our holy Sabbath have I sworn
  To have the due and forfeit of my bond.
  If you deny it, let the danger light
  Upon your charter and your city's freedom.
  You'll ask me, why I rather choose to have
  A weight of carrion flesh than to receive
  Three thousand ducats. I'll not answer that;
  But, say, it is my humour: is it answered?
  What if my house be troubled with a rat
  And I be pleased to give ten thousand ducats
  To have it baned? What, are you answered yet?
  Some men there are love not a gaping pig;

BASSANIO. Do all men kill the things they do not love?

SHYLOCK. Hates any man the thing he would not kill?

BASSANIO. Every offence is not a hate at first.

SHYLOCK. What, wouldst thou have a serpent sting thee
    twice?

ANTONIO. I pray you, think you question with the Jew.
  You may as well go stand upon the beach
  And bid the main flood bate his usual height;
  You may as well use question with the wolf
  Why he hath made the ewe bleat for the lamb;
  You may as well forbid the mountain pines
  To wag their high tops and to make no noise,
  When they are fretten with the gusts of heaven;
  You may as well do anything most hard,
  As seek to soften that—than which what's harder?—
  His Jewish heart. Therefore, I do beseech you,
  Make no more offers, use no farther means,
  But with all brief and plain conveniency
  Let me have judgement and the Jew his will.

BASSANIO. For thy three thousand ducats here is six.

SHYLOCK. If every ducat in six thousand ducats
  Were in six parts and every part a ducat,
  I would not draw them; I would have my bond.

DUKE. How shalt thou hope for mercy, rendering none?

SHYLOCK. What judgement shall I dread, doing no
    wrong?
  You have among you many a purchased slave,
  Which, like your asses and your dogs and mules,
  You use in abject and in slavish parts,

Some, that are mad if they behold a cat;
And others, when the bagpipe sings i' the nose,
Cannot contain their urine; for affection,
Mistress of passion, sways it to the mood
Of what it likes or loathes. Now, for your answer:
As there is no firm reason to be rendered,
Why he cannot abide a gaping pig;
Why he, a harmless necessary cat;
Why he, a woolen bagpipe; but of force
Must yield to such inevitable shame
As to offend, himself being offended;
So can I give no reason, nor I will not,
More than a lodged hate and a certain loathing
I bear Antonio, that I follow thus
A losing suit against him. Are you answered?

BASSANIO. This is no answer, thou unfeeling man,
  To excuse the current of thy cruelty.

SHYLOCK. I am not bound to please thee with my
    answers.

Because you bought them. Shall I say to you,
Let them be free, marry them to your heirs?
Why sweat they under burthens? Let their beds
Be made as soft as yours and let their palates
Be seasoned with such viands? You will answer
"The slaves are ours." So do I answer you:
The pound of flesh, which I demand of him,
Is dearly bought; 'tis mine and I will have it.
If you deny me, fie upon your law!
There is no force in the decrees of Venice.
I stand for judgement. Answer: shall I have it?

DUKE. Upon my power I may dismiss this court,
Unless Bellario, a learned doctor,
Whom I have sent for to determine this,
Come here today.

SALERIO.   My lord, here stays without
A messenger with letters from the doctor,
New come from Padua.

DUKE. Bring us the letters; call the messenger.

BASSANIO. Good cheer, Antonio! What, man, courage
    yet!
The Jew shall have my flesh, blood, bones and all,
Ere thou shalt loose for me one drop of blood.

ANTONIO. I am a tainted wether of the flock,
Meetest for death; the weakest kind of fruit
Drops earliest to the ground; and so let me.
You cannot better be employed, Bassanio,
Than to live still and write mine epitaph.

Enter NERISSA, dressed like a lawyer's clerk

DUKE. Came you from Padua, from Bellario?

NERISSA. From both, my lord. Bellario greets your
    grace.   *Presenting a letter*

BASSANIO. Why dost thou whet thy knife so earnestly?

SHYLOCK. To cut the forfeiture from that bankrupt
    there.

GRATIANO. Not on thy sole, but on thy soul, harsh Jew
Thou makest thy knife keen; but no metal can,
No, not the hangman's axe, bear half the keenness
Of thy sharp envy. Can no prayers pierce thee?

SHYLOCK. No, none that thou hast wit enough to make.

GRATIANO. O, be thou damned, inexecrable dog!
And for thy life let justice be accused.
Thou almost mak'st me waver in my faith
To hold opinion with Pythagoras,
That souls of animals infuse themselves
Into the trunks of men. Thy currish spirit
Governed a wolf, who, hanged for human slaughter,
Even from the gallows did his fell soul fleet,
And, whilst thou lay'st in thy unhallowed dam,
Infused itself in thee; for thy desires
Are wolvish, bloody, starved and ravenous.

SHYLOCK. Till thou canst rail the seal from off my bond,
Thou but offend'st thy lungs to speak so loud.
Repair thy wit, good youth, or it will fall
To cureless ruin. I stand here for law.

DUKE. This letter from Bellario doth commend
A young and learned doctor to our court.
Where is he?

NERISSA.   He attendeth here hard by,
To know your answer, whether you'll admit him.

DUKE. With all my heart. Some three or four of you
Go give him courteous conduct to this place.
Meantime the court shall hear Bellario's letter.

CLERK. [*Reads*] Your grace shall understand that at the
receipt of your letter I am very sick; but in the instant that your messenger came, in loving visitation
was with me a young doctor of Rome; his name is
Balthasar. I acquainted him with the cause in controversy between the Jew and Antonio the merchant.
We turned o'er many books together. He is furnished

with my opinion; which, bettered with his own learning, the greatness whereof I cannot enough commend,
comes with him, at my importunity, to fill up your
grace's request in my stead. I beseech you, let his
lack of years be no impediment to let him lack a
reverend estimation; for I never knew so young a
body with so old a head. I leave him to your gracious
acceptance, whose trial shall better publish his commendation.

DUKE. You hear the learned Bellario, what he writes;
   And here, I take it, is the doctor come.

Enter PORTIA, *dressed like a doctor of laws*

Give me your hand. Come you from old Bellario?
PORTIA. I did, my lord.
DUKE. You are welcome; take your place.
   Are you acquainted with the difference
   That holds this present question in the court?
PORTIA. I am informed throughly of the cause.
   Which is the merchant here, and which the Jew?
DUKE. Antonio and old Shylock, both stand forth.
PORTIA. Is your name Shylock?
SHYLOCK.   Shylock is my name.
PORTIA. Of a strange nature is the suit you follow;
   Yet in such rule that the Venetian law
   Cannot impugn you as you do proceed.
   You stand within his danger, do you not?
ANTONIO. Ay, so he says.
PORTIA.   Do you confess the bond?
ANTONIO. I do.
PORTIA.   Then must the Jew be merciful.
SHYLOCK. On what compulsion must I? Tell me that.
PORTIA. The quality of mercy is not strained,
   It droppeth as the gentle rain from heaven
   Upon the place beneath. It is twice blest:
   It blesseth him that gives and him that takes.
   'Tis mightiest in the mightiest; it becomes
   The thronèd monarch better than his crown;
   His sceptre shows the force of temporal power,
   The attribute to awe and majesty,
   Wherein doth sit the dread and fear of kings.
   But mercy is above this sceptred sway;
   It is enthronèd in the hearts of kings,
   It is an attribute to God himself;
   And earthly power doth then show likest God's
   When mercy seasons justice. Therefore, Jew,
   Though justice be thy plea, consider this,
   That, in the course of justice, none of us
   Should see salvation. We do pray for mercy;
   And that same prayer doth teach us all to render
   The deeds of mercy. I have spoke thus much
   To mitigate the justice of thy plea;
   Which if thou follow, this strict court of Venice
   Must needs give sentence 'gainst the merchant there.
SHYLOCK. My deeds upon my head! I crave the law,
   The penalty and forfeit of my bond.

PORTIA. Is he not able to discharge the money?
BASSANIO. Yes, here I tender it for him in the court;
   Yea, twice the sum. If that will not suffice,
   I will be bound to pay it ten times o'er,
   On forfeit of my hands, my head, my heart.
   If this will not suffice, it must appear
   That malice bears down truth. And I beseech you,
   Wrest once the law to your authority.
   To do a great right, do a little wrong,
   And curb this cruel devil of his will.
PORTIA. It must not be; there is no power in Venice
   Can alter a decree established.
   'Twill be recorded for a precedent,
   And many an error by the same example
   Will rush into the state. It cannot be.
SHYLOCK. A Daniel come to judgement! yea, a Daniel!
   O wise young judge, how I do honour thee!
PORTIA. I pray you, let me look upon the bond.
SHYLOCK. Here 'tis, most reverend doctor, here it is.
PORTIA. Shylock, there's thrice thy money offered thee.
SHYLOCK. An oath, an oath, I have an oath in heaven.
   Shall I lay perjury upon my soul?
   No, not for Venice.
PORTIA.   Why, this bond is forfeit;
   And lawfully by this the Jew may claim
   A pound of flesh, to be by him cut off
   Nearest the merchant's heart. Be merciful.
   Take thrice thy money; bid me tear the bond,
SHYLOCK. When it is paid according to the tenor.
   It doth appear you are a worthy judge;
   You know the law, your exposition
   Hath been most sound. I charge you by the law,
   Whereof you are a well-deserving pillar,
   Proceed to judgement. By my soul I swear
   There is no power in the tongue of man
   To alter me. I stay here on my bond.
ANTONIO. Most heartily I do beseech the court
   To give the judgement.
PORTIA.   Why then, thus it is:
   You must prepare your bosom for his knife.
SHYLOCK. O noble judge! O excellent young man!
PORTIA. For the intent and purpose of the law
   Hath full relation to the penalty,
   Which here appeareth due upon the bond.
SHYLOCK. 'Tis very true. O wise and upright judge!
   How much more elder art thou than thy looks!
PORTIA. Therefore lay bare your bosom.
SHYLOCK.   Ay, his breast—
   So says the bond, doth it not, noble judge?
   "Nearest his heart." Those are the very words.
PORTIA. It is so. Are there balance here to weigh
   The flesh?
SHYLOCK.   I have them ready.
PORTIA. Have by some surgeon, Shylock, on your
   charge,
   To stop his wounds, lest he do bleed to death.

SHYLOCK. Is it so nominated in the bond?

PORTIA. It is not so expressed; but what of that?
'Twere good you do so much for charity.

SHYLOCK. I cannot find it; 'tis not in the bond.

PORTIA. You, merchant, have you anything to say?

ANTONIO. But little; I am armed and well prepared.
Give me your hand, Bassanio; fare you well!
Grieve not that I am fallen to this for you;
For herein Fortune shows herself more kind
Than is her custom: it is still her use
To let the wretched man outlive his wealth,
To view with hollow eye and wrinkled brow
An age of poverty; from which lingering penance
Of such misery doth she cut me off.
Commend me to your honourable wife.
Tell her the process of Antonio's end;
Say how I loved you, speak me fair in death;
And, when the tale is told, bid her be judge
Whether Bassanio had not once a love.
Repent but you that you shall lose your friend,
And he repents not that he pays your debt;
For if the Jew do cut but deep enough,
I'll pay it presently with all my heart.

BASSANIO. Antonio, I am married to a wife
Which is as dear to me as life itself;
But life itself, my wife, and all the world,
Are not with me esteemed above thy life.
I would lose all, ay, sacrifice them all
Here to this devil, to deliver you.

PORTIA. Your wife would give you little thanks for that,
If she were by, to hear you make the offer.

GRATIANO. I have a wife, whom, I protest, I love.
I would she were in heaven, so she could
Entreat some power to change this currish Jew.

NERISSA. 'Tis well you offer it behind her back;
The wish would make else an unquiet house.

SHYLOCK. [Aside] These be the Christian husbands. I
have a daughter;
Would any of the stock of Barrabas
Had been her husband rather than a Christian!
We trifle time; I pray thee, pursue sentence.

PORTIA. A pound of that same merchant's flesh is thine;
The court awards it, and the law doth give it.

SHYLOCK. Most rightful judge!

PORTIA. And you must cut this flesh from off his breast;
The law allows it, and the court awards it.

SHYLOCK. Most learned judge! A sentence! Come, prepare!

PORTIA. Tarry a little; there is something else.
This bond doth give thee here no jot of blood;
The words expressly are "a pound of flesh."
Take then thy bond, take thou thy pound of flesh;
But, in the cutting it, if thou dost shed
One drop of Christian blood, thy lands and goods
Are, by the laws of Venice, confiscate
Unto the state of Venice.

GRATIANO. O upright judge! Mark, Jew: O learned
Judge!

SHYLOCK. Is that the law?

PORTIA.   Thyself shalt see the act;
For, as thou urgest justice, be assured
Thou shalt have justice, more than thou desirest.

GRATIANO. O learned judge! Mark, Jew: a learned
judge!

SHYLOCK. I take this offer, then; pay the bond thrice
And let the Christian go.

BASSANIO.   Here is the money.

PORTIA. Soft!
The Jew shall have all justice; soft! no haste.
He shall have nothing but the penalty.

GRATIANO. O Jew! an upright judge, a learned judge!

PORTIA. Therefore prepare thee to cut off the flesh.
Shed thou no blood, nor cut thou less nor more
But just a pound of flesh. If thou cut'st more
Or less than a just pound, be it but so much
As makes it light or heavy in the substance,
Or the division of the twentieth part
Of one poor scruple, nay, if the scale do turn
But in the estimation of a hair,
Thou diest and all thy goods are confiscate.

GRATIANO. A second Daniel, a Daniel, Jew!
Now, infidel, I have you on the hip.

PORTIA. Why doth the Jew pause? Take thy forfeiture.

SHYLOCK. Give me my principal, and let me go.

BASSANIO. I have it ready for thee; here it is.

PORTIA. He hath refused it in the open court.
He shall have merely justice and his bond.

GRATIANO. A Daniel, still say I, a second Daniel!
I thank thee, Jew, for teaching me that word.

SHYLOCK. Shall I not have barely my principal?

PORTIA. Thou shalt have nothing but the forfeiture,
To be so taken at thy peril, Jew.

SHYLOCK. Why, then the devil give him good of it!
I'll stay no longer question.

PORTIA.   Tarry, Jew.
The law hath yet another hold on you.
It is enacted in the laws of Venice,
If it be proved against an alien
That by direct or indirect attempts
He seek the life of any citizen,
The party 'gainst the which he doth contrive
Shall seize one half his goods; the other half
Comes to the privy coffer of the state;
And the offender's life lies in the mercy
Of the Duke only, 'gainst all other voice.
In which predicament, I say, thou stand'st;
For it appears, by manifest proceeding,
That indirectly and directly too
Thou hast contrived against the very life
Of the defendant; and thou hast incurred
The danger formerly by me rehearsed.
Down therefore and beg mercy of the Duke.

GRATIANO. Beg that thou mayst have leave to hang
    thyself.
  And yet, thy wealth being forfeit to the state,
  Thou hast not left the value of a cord;
  Therefore thou must be hanged at the state's charge.
DUKE. That thou shalt see the difference of our spirits,
  I pardon thee thy life before thou ask it.
  For half thy wealth, it is Antonio's;
  The other half comes to the general state,
  Which humbleness may drive unto a fine.

PORTIA. Ay, for the state, not for Antonio.
SHYLOCK. Nay, take my life and all. Pardon not that.
  You take my house when you do take the prop
  That doth sustain my house; you take my life
  When you do take the means whereby I live.
PORTIA. What mercy can you render him, Antonio?
GRATIANO. A halter gratis; nothing else, for God's
    sake.
ANTONIO. So please my lord the Duke and all the court
  To quit the fine for one half of his goods,
  I am content; so he will let me have
  The other half in use, to render it,
  Upon his death, unto the gentleman
  That lately stole his daughter.
  Two things provided more, that, for this favour,
  He presently become a Christian;
  The other, that he do record a gift,
  Here in the court, of all he dies possessed,
  Unto his son Lorenzo and his daughter.
DUKE. He shall do this, or else I do recant
  The pardon that I late pronounced here.

PORTIA. Art thou contented, Jew? What dost thou say?

SHYLOCK. I am content.

PORTIA.   Clerk, draw a deed of gift.

SHYLOCK. I pray you, give me leave to go from hence.
I am not well; send the deed after me,
And I will sign it.

DUKE.   Get thee gone, but do it.

GRATIANO. In christening shalt thou have two god-
fathers:
Had I been judge, thou shouldst have had ten more,
To bring thee to the gallows, not the font.

Exit SHYLOCK

DUKE. Sir, I entreat you home with me to dinner.

PORTIA. I humbly do desire your grace of pardon:
I must away this night toward Padua,
And it is meet I presently set forth.

DUKE. I am sorry that your leisure serves you not.
Antonio, gratify this gentleman,
For, in my mind, you are much bound to him.

Exeunt DUKE *and his train*

BASSANIO. Most worthy gentleman, I and my friend
Have by your wisdom been this day acquitted
Of grievous penalties; in lieu whereof,
Three thousand ducats, due unto the Jew,
We freely cope your courteous pains withal.

ANTONIO. And stand indebted, over and above,
In love and service to you evermore.

PORTIA. He is well paid that is well satisfied;
And I, delivering you, am satisfied
And therein do account myself well paid.
My mind was never yet more mercenary.
I pray you, know me when we meet again.
I wish you well, and so I take my leave.

BASSANIO. Dear sir, of force I must attempt you further.
Take some remembrance of us, as a tribute,
Not as a fee. Grant me two things, I pray you,
Not to deny me, and to pardon me.

PORTIA. You press me far, and therefore I will yield.
[*To Antonio*] Give me your gloves, I'll wear them for
your sake;
[*To Bassanio*] And, for your love, I'll take this ring
from you.
Do not draw back your hand; I'll take no more;
And you in love shall not deny me this.

BASSANIO. This ring, good sir, alas, it is a trifle!
I will not shame myself to give you this.

PORTIA. I will have nothing else but only this;
And now methinks I have a mind to it.

BASSANIO. There's more depends on this than on the
value.
The dearest ring in Venice will I give you,
And find it out by proclamation:
Only for this, I pray you, pardon me.

PORTIA. I see, sir, you are liberal in offers:
You taught me first to beg; and now methinks
You teach me how a beggar should be answered.

BASSANIO. Good sir, this ring was given me by my wife;
And when she put it on, she made me vow
That I should neither sell nor give nor lose it.

PORTIA. That 'scuse serves many men to save their gifts.
An if your wife be not a madwoman,
And know how well I have deserved the ring,
She would not hold out enemy for ever,
For giving it to me. Well, peace be with you!

Exeunt PORTIA *and* NERISSA

ANTONIO. My Lord Bassanio, let him have the ring.
Let his deservings and my love withal
Be valued 'gainst your wife's commandment.

BASSANIO. Go, Gratiano, run and overtake him;
Give him the ring, and bring him, if thou canst,
Unto Antonio's house; away! make haste.

Exit GRATIANO

Come, you and I will thither presently;
And in the morning early will we both
Fly toward Belmont. Come, Antonio.   *Exeunt*

SCENE II *The same: a street*

Enter PORTIA *and* NERISSA

PORTIA. Inquire the Jew's house out, give him this deed
And let him sign it. We'll away tonight
And be a day before our husbands home.
This deed will be well welcome to Lorenzo.

Enter GRATIANO

GRATIANO. Fair sir, you are well o'erta'en.
My Lord Bassanio upon more advice
Hath sent you here this ring, and doth entreat
Your company at dinner.

PORTIA.   That cannot be—
His ring I do accept most thankfully;
And so, I pray you, tell him. Furthermore,
I pray you, show my youth old Shylock's house.

GRATIANO. That will I do.

NERISSA.   Sir, I would speak with you.
[*Aside to Portia*] I'll see if I can get my husband's ring,
Which I did make him swear to keep for ever.

PORTIA. [*Aside to Nerissa*] Thou mayst, I warrant. We
shall have old swearing
That they did give the rings away to men;
But we'll outface them, and outswear them too.
[*Aloud*] Away! make haste; thou know'st where I
will tarry.

NERISSA. Come, good sir, will you show me to this
house?   *Exeunt*

ACT V

SCENE I *Belmont: avenue to* PORTIA'S *house*

Enter LORENZO *and* JESSICA

LORENZO. The moon shines bright; in such a night
   as this,
   When the sweet wind did gently kiss the trees
   And they did make no noise, in such a night
   Troilus methinks mounted the Troyan walls
   And sighed his soul toward the Grecian tents,
   Where Cressid lay that night.
JESSICA.   In such a night
   Did Thisbe fearfully o'ertrip the dew
   And saw the lion's shadow ere himself
   And ran dismayed away.
LORENZO.   In such a night
   Stood Dido with a willow in her hand
   Upon the wild sea banks and waft her love
   To come again to Carthage.
JESSICA.   In such a night
   Medea gathered the enchanted herbs
   That did renew old Aeson.
LORENZO.   In such a night
   Did Jessica steal from the wealthy Jew
   And with an unthrift love did run from Venice
   As far as Belmont.
JESSICA.   In such a night
   Did young Lorenzo swear he loved her well,
   Stealing her soul with many vows of faith
   And ne'er a true one.
LORENZO.   In such a night
   Did pretty Jessica, like a little shrew,
   Slander her love, and he forgave it her.
JESSICA. I would out-night you, did nobody come;
   But, hark, I hear the footing of a man.

Enter STEPHANO

LORENZO. Who comes so fast in silence of the night?
STEPHANO. A friend.
LORENZO. A friend! What friend? Your name, I pray
   you, friend?
STEPHANO. Stephano is my name; and I bring word
   My mistress will before the break of day
   Be here at Belmont. She doth stray about
   By holy crosses, where she kneels and prays
   For happy wedlock hours.
LORENZO.   Who comes with her?
STEPHANO. None but a holy hermit and her maid.
   I pray you, is my master yet returned?
LORENZO. He is not, nor we have not heard from him.
   But go we in, I pray thee, Jessica,
   And ceremoniously let us prepare
   Some welcome for the mistress of the house.

Enter LAUNCELOT

LAUNCELOT. Sola, sola! wo ha, ho! sola, sola!
LORENZO. Who calls?
LAUNCELOT. Sola! did you see Master Lorenzo?
   Master Lorenzo, sola, sola!
LORENZO. Leave hollaing, man; here.
LAUNCELOT. Sola! where? where?
LORENZO. Here.
LAUNCELOT. Tell him there's a post come from my
   master, with his horn full of good news: my master
   will be here ere morning.   *Exit*
LORENZO. Sweet soul, let's in, and there expect their
   coming.
   And yet no matter; why should we go in?
   My friend Stephano, signify, I pray you,
   Within the house, your mistress is at hand;
   And bring your music forth into the air.

                                  Exit STEPHANO

   How sweet the moonlight sleeps upon this bank!
   Here will we sit and let the sounds of music
   Creep in our ears: soft stillness and the night
   Become the touches of sweet harmony.
   Sit, Jessica. Look how the floor of heaven
   Is thick inlaid with patens of bright gold.
   There's not the smallest orb which thou behold'st
   But in his motion like an angel sings,
   Still quiring to the young-eyed cherubins.
   Such harmony is in immortal souls;
   But whilst this muddy vesture of decay
   Doth grossly close it in, we cannot hear it.

Enter Musicians

   Come, ho! and wake Diana with a hymn;
   With sweetest touches pierce your mistress' ear
   And draw her home with music.   *Music*
JESSICA. I am never merry when I hear sweet music.
LORENZO. The reason is, your spirits are attentive;
   For do but note a wild and wanton herd,
   Or race of youthful and unhandled colts,
   Fetching mad bounds, bellowing and neighing loud,
   Which is the hot condition of their blood;
   If they but hear perchance a trumpet sound,
   Or any air of music touch their ears,
   You shall perceive them make a mutual stand,
   Their savage eyes turned to a modest gaze
   By the sweet power of music. Therefore the poet
   Did feign that Orpheus drew trees, stones and floods;
   Since nought so stockish, hard and full of rage,
   But music for the time doth change his nature.
   The man that hath no music in himself,
   Nor is not moved with concord of sweet sounds,
   Is fit for treasons, stratagems and spoils;

    The motions of his spirit are dull as night
    And his affections dark as Erebus:
    Let no such man be trusted. Mark the music.

Enter PORTIA *and* NERISSA

PORTIA. That light we see is burning in my hall.
    How far that little candle throws his beams!
    So shines a good deed in a naughty world.
NERISSA. When the moon shone, we did not see the
    candle.
PORTIA. So doth the greater glory dim the less:
    A substitute shines brightly as a king
    Until a king be by, and then his state
    Empties itself, as doth an inland brook
    Into the main of waters. Music! hark!
NERISSA. It is your music, madam, of the house.
PORTIA. Nothing is good, I see, without respect;
    Methinks it sounds much sweeter than by day.
NERISSA. Silence bestows that virtue on it, madam.
PORTIA. The crow doth sing as sweetly as the lark
    When neither is attended, and I think
    The nightingale, if she should sing by day,
    When every goose is cackling, would be thought
    No better a musician than the wren.
    How many things by season seasoned are
    To their right praise and true perfection!
    Peace, ho! the moon sleeps with Endymion
    And would not be awaked.   *Music ceases*
LORENZO.   That is the voice,
    Or I am much deceived, of Portia.
PORTIA. He knows me as the blind man knows the
    cuckoo,
    By the bad voice.
LORENZO.   Dear lady, welcome home.
PORTIA. We have been praying for our husbands' healths,
    Which speed, we hope, the better for our words.
    Are they returned?
LORENZO.   Madam, they are not yet;
    But there is come a messenger before,
    To signify their coming.
PORTIA.   Go in, Nerissa;
    Give order to my servants that they take
    No note at all of our being absent hence;
    Nor you, Lorenzo; Jessica, nor you.   *A tucket sounds*
LORENZO. Your husband is at hand; I hear his trumpet.
    We are no tell-tales, madam; fear you not.
PORTIA. This night methinks is but the daylight sick;
    It looks a little paler; 'tis a day,
    Such as the day is when the sun is hid.

Enter BASSANIO, ANTONIO, GRATIANO, *and their followers*

BASSANIO. We should hold day with the Antipodes,
    If you would walk in absence of the sun.
PORTIA. Let me give light, but let me not be light;
    For a light wife doth make a heavy husband,
    And never be Bassanio so for me.

But God sort all! You are welcome home, my lord.

BASSANIO. I thank you, madam. Give welcome to my
    friend.
This is the man, this is Antonio,
To whom I am so infinitely bound.

PORTIA. You should in all sense be much bound to him,
For, as I hear, he was much bound for you.

ANTONIO. No more than I am well acquitted of.

PORTIA. Sir, you are very welcome to our house.
It must appear in other ways than words,
Therefore I scant this breathing courtesy.

GRATIANO. [*To Nerissa*] By yonder moon I swear you
    do me wrong;
In faith, I gave it to the judge's clerk.
Would.he were gelt that had it, for my part,
Since you do take it, love, so much at heart.

PORTIA. A quarrel, ho, already! What's the matter?

GRATIANO. About a hoop of gold, a paltry ring
That she did give me, whose posy was
For all the world like cutler's poetry
Upon a knife, "Love me, and leave me not."

NERISSA. What talk you of the posy or the value?
You swore to me, when I did give it you,
That you would wear it till your hour of death
And that it should lie with you in your grave.
Though not for me, yet for your vehement oaths,
You should have been respective and have kept it.
Gave it a judge's clerk! No, God's my judge,
The clerk will ne'er wear hair on's face that had it.

GRATIANO. He will, an if he live to be a man.

NERISSA. Ay, if a woman live to be a man.

GRATIANO. Now, by this hand, I gave it to a youth,
A kind of boy, a little scrubbed boy,
No higher than thyself, the judge's clerk,
A prating boy, that begged it as a fee.
I could not for my heart deny it him.

PORTIA. You were to blame, I must be plain with you,
To part so slightly with your wife's first gift;
A thing stuck on with oaths upon your finger
And so riveted with faith unto your flesh.
I gave my love a ring and made him swear
Never to part with it; and here he stands;
I dare be sworn for him he would not leave it
Nor pluck it from his finger, for the wealth
That the world masters. Now, in faith, Gratiano,
You give your wife too unkind a cause of grief.
An 'twere to me, I should be mad at it.

BASSANIO. [*Aside*] Why, I were best to cut my left
    hand off
And swear I lost the ring defending it.

GRATIANO. My Lord Bassanio gave his ring away
Unto the judge that begged it and indeed
Deserved it too; and then the boy, his clerk,
That took some pains in writing, he begged mine;
And neither man nor master would take aught
But the two rings.

PORTIA.   What ring gave you, my lord?
  Not that, I hope, which you received of me.
BASSANIO. If I could add a lie unto a fault,
  I would deny it; but you see my finger
  Hath not the ring upon it; it is gone.
PORTIA. Even so void is your false heart of truth.
  By heaven, I will ne'er come in your bed
  Until I see the ring.
NERISSA.   Nor I in yours
  Till I again see mine.
BASSANIO.   Sweet Portia,
  If you did know to whom I gave the ring,
  If you did know for whom I gave the ring
  And would conceive for what I gave the ring
  And how unwillingly I left the ring,
  When nought would be accepted but the ring,
  You would abate the strength of your displeasure.
PORTIA. If you had known the virtue of the ring,
  Or half her worthiness that gave the ring,
  Or your own honour to contain the ring,
  You would not then have parted with the ring.
  What man is there so much unreasonable,
  If you had pleased to have defended it
  With any terms of zeal, wanted the modesty
  To urge the thing held as a ceremony?
  Nerissa teaches me what to believe:
  I'll die for't but some woman had the ring.
BASSANIO. No, by my honour, madam, by my soul,
  No woman had it, but a civil doctor,
  Which did refuse three thousand ducats of me
  And begged the ring; the which I did deny him
  And suffered him to go displeased away;
  Even he that did uphold the very life
  Of my dear friend. What should I say, sweet lady?
  I was enforced to send it after him;
  I was beset with shame and courtesy;
  My honour would not let ingratitude
  So much besmear it. Pardon me, good lady;
  For, by these blessed candles of the night,
  Had you been there, I think you would have begged
  The ring of me to give the worthy doctor.
PORTIA. Let not that doctor e'er come near my house:
  Since he hath got the jewel that I loved,
  And that which you did swear to keep for me,
  I will become as liberal as you;
  I'll not deny him anything I have,
  No, not my body nor my husband's bed.
  Know him I shall, I am well sure of it.
  Lie not a night from home; watch me like Argus:
  If you do not, if I be left alone,
  Now, by mine honour, which is yet mine own,
  I'll have that doctor for my bedfellow.
NERISSA. And I his clerk; therefore be well advised
  How you do leave me to mine own protection.
GRATIANO. Well, do you so. Let not me take him, then;
  For if I do, I'll mar the young clerk's pen.

ANTONIO. I am the unhappy subject of these quarrels.
PORTIA. Sir, grieve not you; you are welcome notwithstanding.
BASSANIO. Portia, forgive me this enforced wrong;
  And, in the hearing of these many friends,
  I swear to thee, even by thine own fair eyes,
  Wherein I see myself—
PORTIA.   Mark you but that!
  In both my eyes he doubly sees himself;
  In each eye, one. Swear by your double self,
  And there's an oath of credit.
BASSANIO.   Nay, but hear me:
  Pardon this fault, and by my soul I swear
  I never more will break an oath with thee.
ANTONIO. I once did lend my body for his wealth;
  Which, but for him that had your husband's ring,
  Had quite miscarried. I dare be bound again,
  My soul upon the forfeit, that your lord
  Will never more break faith advisedly.
PORTIA. Then you shall be his surety. Give him this
  And bid him keep it better than the other.
ANTONIO. Here, Lord Bassanio; swear to keep this ring.
BASSANIO. By heaven, it is the same I gave the doctor!
PORTIA. I had it of him. Pardon me, Bassanio;
  For, by this ring, the doctor lay with me.
NERISSA. And pardon me, my gentle Gratiano;
  For that same scrubbed boy, the doctor's clerk,
  In lieu of this last night did lie with me.
GRATIANO. Why, this is like the mending of highways
  In summer, where the ways are fair enough.
  What, are we cuckolds ere we have deserved it?
PORTIA. Speak not so grossly. You are all amazed.
  Here is a letter; read it at your leisure;
  It comes from Padua, from Bellario.
  There you shall find that Portia was the doctor,
  Nerissa there her clerk. Lorenzo here
  Shall witness I set forth as soon as you
  And even but now returned; I have not yet
  Entered my house. Antonio, you are welcome;
  And I have better news in store for you
  Than you expect: unseal this letter soon;
  There you shall find three of your argosies
  Are richly come to harbour suddenly.
  You shall not know by what strange accident
  I chanced on this letter.
ANTONIO.   I am dumb.
BASSANIO. Were you the doctor and I knew you not?
GRATIANO. Were you the clerk that is to make me
    cuckold?
NERISSA. Ay, but the clerk that never means to do it,
  Unless he live until he be a man.
BASSANIO. Sweet doctor, you shall be my bedfellow.
  When I am absent, then lie with my wife.
ANTONIO. Sweet lady, you have given me life and living;
  For here I read for certain that my ships
  Are safely come to road.

PORTIA.   How now, Lorenzo!
  My clerk hath some good comforts too for you.
NERISSA. Ay, and I'll give them him without a fee.
  There do I give to you and Jessica,
  From the rich Jew, a special deed of gift,
  After his death, of all he dies possessed of.
LORENZO. Fair ladies, you drop manna in the way
  Of starved people.
PORTIA.   It is almost morning,
  And yet I am sure you are not satisfied
  Of these events at full. Let us go in;
  And charge us there upon inter'gatories,
  And we will answer all things faithfully.
GRATIANO. Let it be so. The first inter'gatory
  That my Nerissa shall be sworn on is,
  Whether till the next night she had rather stay
  Or go to bed now, being two hours to day.
  But were the day come, I should wish it dark,
  That I were couching with the doctor's clerk.
  Well, while I live I'll fear no other thing
  So sore as keeping safe Nerissa's ring.   *Exeunt*

This is certainly the most popular of Shakespeare's plays. In the theatre it offers opportunity for ringing, thrilling declamation, pageantry, and comedy scenes which play a great deal better than they read. Alternation of grave and gay, lively and quiet, fast and slow, majestic and vulgar is, as always with Shakespeare, arranged with immense skill and aplomb.

In our epoch, it is hard to feel much affection for, or sympathy with, Henry. War has ceased to have the thrill and glamour which young men still felt it to have even as late as 1914. But it does not require too great a stretch of imagination to feel that, to high-spirited young fellows, it was not only a dangerous but splendidly thrilling sport and a challenge to display the qualities which the society of their day considered most admirable, but was also infinitely the surest and fastest way to financial, political and social advancement.

Granting all that, can we really admire the Henry whom Shakespeare presents?

No serious attempt is made to justify Henry's claim to the throne of France. I think the scene which opens the play, between the Archbishop of Canterbury and the Bishop of Ely, is intended satirically. These are two extremely sophisticated, worldly prelates. The Church is threatened by a bill which, if ratified by Parliament, will strip it of more than half its property and a great deal of power. Their tactics to defeat this bill are to create a diversion; they will back the young king heavily with legal, moral and financial support to press a claim on the French throne which will, they know, lead to war.

In the light of this first scene, which is virtually a Prologue, we are warned by the author clearly enough that the Archbishop's subsequent expounding of the Salic Law is not to be regarded as the impartial summary of a just judge; there follows his celebrated discourse upon the diverse functions of society. This turns out to be not so much a politico-moral homily as a propaganda piece in favour of war.

Once embarked on the war, is Henry such an admirable hero as, dazzled by the play's glittering rhetoric, we might at first suppose?

He plays cat and mouse with the three traitors, Cambridge, Scroop and Gray, in a manner which makes a highly theatrical scene (Act II, scene 2), but which does not reveal him as at all a likeable person.

His next appearance (Act III, scene 1) is at the breach in the walls of Harfleur. Again the marvelous trumpet-music of the speech is so thrilling, the scene, if well directed and powerfully delivered by a heroic actor, carries one along with such impetus that, in the theatre, as Shakespeare well knew, no one can question it or analyze its meaning. But in fact it is simply an exhortation to the soldiers to forget their humanity and act like wild beasts. Questionably this is good generalship, more questionably good kingship; there can be no question at all that it is at complete odds with a Christianity which, elsewhere in the play, Henry sanctimoniously professes.

Next we see him before the gates of Harfleur (Act III, scene 3) warning the governor of the town what he and his citizens may expect if they do not offer immediate and unconditional surrender. The speech, by changing the proper names and by downgrading the language from that of genius to that of the gutter, might have been uttered by Hitler to Benes before the gates of Prague in 1939. It is a series of gloating threats, uttered by a bully, in order to get what he wants by inspiring fear.

King Henry's next scene (Act III, scene 6) is unexceptionable; he is sensible with Fluellen, kingly with the French Herald.

Then comes the scene where he moves about the camp at night, wearing a borrowed cloak, listening, unrecognized, to the talk of his soldiers. This is very sneaky behavior. It is the Headmaster spying on the Boys, the Managing Director taking an unauthorized tape-recording of the shop-stewards' meeting. It is true that, in the splendid and moving argument with Williams, he makes some just and telling points and, after the soldiers have gone, the soliloquy upon ceremony and the heavy load of responsibility which royalty must bear is very fine stuff, and shows King Henry in a sympathetic light. But then it is followed by a prayer addressed, significantly enough, not to God the Father of all Humanity and of Jesus Christ, but to the God of Battles. This deity is besought to steel the hearts of Henry's soldiers, to take from them the sense of reckoning so that they shall not recognize how terribly they are outnumbered, and is finally reminded, in chaffering, niggling and superstitious terms, of various acts which are supposed to incline this God to grant Henry's prayers.

Again the theatrical context—midnight on the eve of battle, the lonely figure oppressed with its burden of responsibility—the appeal to patriotism and the tenderly majestic music of the verse all invest an unpleasant, even sickening, speech with such glamour that its content passes unexamined.

Then comes the morning of Agincourt (Act IV, scene 3) and the famous speech about Saint Crispian's Day. The rhetoric is simply irresistible and I think it would be unduly censorious to fault the King at this point for trying to cheer hearts fainter than his own at the eleventh hour. It seems to me, however, that this speech rather takes the glory from the scene's second great speech, to the French Herald, Montjoy. The good wine is not kept till the end of the feast; or rather an adequately good wine, tasted second, seems flavourless when the first draught has been so superb.

Henry's next scene (Act IV, scene 6) must be imagined to occur in the course of the battle. I suspect that the text at the end of this scene is corrupt, since little as I believe Shakespeare liked Henry, I cannot conceive that the order to kill the French prisoners would be given on such slight provocation. It seems much more reasonable that this command would be given *after* the audience knows, as it does from Fluellen at the beginning of the next scene (Act IV, scene 7) that the boys who were guarding the luggage had been killed. (I would have Fluellen carry the dead body of the boy whom the audience knows from his earlier and very winning appearances.) Then Henry's fury: "I was not angry since I came to France . . ." is intelligible.

Also in this same speech he again speaks of killing the prisoners as though the idea were occurring to him for the first time and in words which, if the lines at the end of the previous scene are not corrupt, would be dramatically redundant.

The quiet end of the scene, when the casualty lists are read, with the victims too exhausted for noisy or exuberant rejoicing, is superb playwriting; but again I think Henry emerges in an unsympathetic light. His quiet, humble religiosity does not ring true. In the theatre the moment passes because the context is so moving. But in cold blood, could anyone place any confidence in the piety of the boastful victor of Harfleur, the young general who put heart into his cousin, Westmoreland, and who defied the French Herald in such ringing terms? Could anyone really believe that he means a word of it when he says:

And be it death proclaimed through our host
To boast of this or take that praise from God
Which is his only.

This is the mock-modesty of the sports champion or the opera diva, acknowledging, with bowed head and lowered eyes, the plaudits of the fans.

Finally, in the last scene of the play, our hero squeezes the last drop of political and financial advantage out of the defeated and humiliated enemy and makes it perfectly clear to the young princess, a helpless pawn in the game of power politics, that she had better put a good face on their marriage. In the theatre this scene passes off charmingly because the Princess plays it in a pretty daze of girlish hero-worship for a matinee-idol king. But it is thin ice. Imagine the same scene with a frightened, reluctant girl and the swaggering, vulgar bully whom she is compelled to accept.

Did Shakespeare intend the audience to think Henry a vulgar, swaggering bully? Absolutely not.

But I think he thought him so, and was well aware that,

with the aid of theatrical glamour, it would be possible to conceal his opinion from all who did not seek for it with diligence. Most of the people can be fooled the whole of the time. May it be that Shakespeare, not very much interested in or attracted by the character of the fifth Henry, but nevertheless pledged to a historical series from which this monarch could not be omitted, amused himself by achieving this crypto-satirical portrait? He was certain of his ability to disguise the satire under a splendid "smothering sauce" of rhetoric, certain too, as the good businessman we know him to have been, of the public's insatiable appetite for ringing patriotism. This appetite, we may note, has persisted down the centuries. Our generation has supped its full on Churchillian rhetoric of a not dissimilar vintage, and *Henry the Fifth* remains, of all Shakespeare's plays, one of the most certain "draws" at the box office.

The experiment of presenting a production in which Henry should be unsympathetically portrayed would be bound to fail. It would not be a wise idea to present a version of *Jack the Giantkiller*—and *Henry the Fifth* is just that—in which the character of Jack was to be debunked, when the text allows no possibility of swinging the sympathy over to the poor old defeated Giant. One of Shakespeare's devices for making Henry acceptable to the audience is to make his adversaries even more unpleasant than is Henry. The French swagger even more insolently. In a production which tried to debunk Henry, there would be no one and nothing in which an audience could take a sympathetic interest; victory could be wished to neither side.

Shakespeare knew that an audience will always range itself passionately on the side of Jack. If Jack can be a spendidly handsome, attractive fellow, and not only that, if he can also be a personification of the audience's feelings about Home and Country, and if expression can be given to thoroughly popular sentiments in ringing trumpet-tones, no one is going to bother about moral issues or think too precisely on what may be the real nature of so spanking a giant-killer.

A final word, about the Chorus. As a device it triumphantly succeeds in its job of scene-setting, of excusing inevitable shortcomings, of kindling the imagination of an audience and of briskly conveying information. The various set-pieces are instances of Shakespeare's blank verse at its most pictorially vivid and rhythmically flexible. They are probably the most "speakable" poetry in our language. To the historian, the antiquary and the theatre-technician, they are the most valuable single piece of evidence which we possess as to how Shakespeare's plays were staged and what his theatrical philosophy was.

EARL OF SALISBURY.
EARL OF WESTMORELAND
EARL OF WARWICK

SIR THOMAS ERPINGHAM,
GOWER, FLUELLEN, JAMY,
MACMORRIS, officers in King
Henry's army. BATES, COURT,
WILLIAMS, soldiers in the same.

A Boy
and
A Herald

ARCHBISHOP
OF CANTERBURY
and the
BISHOP OF ELY

DUKES OF GLOUCESTER AND BEDFORD,
brothers to the King
DUKE OF EXETER, uncle to the King
DUKE OF YORK, cousin to the King

KING
HENRY
the Fifth

EARL OF CAMBRIDGE
LORD SCROOP
SIR THOMAS GREY

PISTOL
NYM
BARDOLPH

Mistress of a tavern
in Eastcheap,
formerly Mistress Quickly,
and now married
to Pistol

CHORUS

SCENE:
ENGLAND;

HENRY THE FIFTH
PERSONAE

RAMBURES
and
GRANDPRE
French Lords
MONTJOY,
a French Herald

The Constable of France
The Governor of Harfleur
and
Ambassadors
to the
King of England

LEWIS,
the
Dauphin

CHARLES the Sixth,
King of France
ISABEL, Queen of France

DUKES OF BURGUNDY,
ORLEANS AND BOURBON

KATHERINE
daughter to
Charles and Isabel
ALICE, a lady
attending on her.

Lords, Ladies,
Officers, Soldiers
Citizens, Messengers,
and Attendants

fterwards FRANCE

PROLOGUE

Enter Chorus

CHORUS. O for a Muse of fire, that would ascend
  The brightest heaven of invention!
  A kingdom for a stage, princes to act
  And monarchs to behold the swelling scene!
  Then should the warlike Harry, like himself,
  Assume the port of Mars; and at his heels,
  Leashed in like hounds, should famine, sword and fire
  Crouch for employment. But pardon, gentles all,
  The flat unraised spirits that have dared
  On this unworthy scaffold to bring forth
  So great an object. Can this cockpit hold
  The vasty fields of France? Or may we cram
  Within this wooden O the very casques
  That did affright the air at Agincourt?
  O, pardon! since a crooked figure may
  Attest in little place a million;
  And let us, ciphers to this great accompt,
On your imaginary forces work.
Suppose within the girdle of these walls
Are now confined two mighty monarchies,
Whose high upreared and abutting fronts
The perilous narrow ocean parts asunder.
Piece out our imperfections with your thoughts—
Into a thousand parts divide one man,
And make imaginary puissance;
Think, when we talk of horses, that you see them
Printing their proud hoofs i' the receiving earth—
For 'tis your thoughts that now must deck our kings,
Carry them here and there, jumping o'er times,
Turning the accomplishment of many years
Into an hour-glass. For the which supply,
Admit me Chorus to this history,
Who prologue-like your humble patience pray,
Gently to hear, kindly to judge, our play.   *Exit*

ACT I

SCENE I *London: an ante-chamber in the* KING'S *palace*

Enter the ARCHBISHOP OF CANTERBURY *and the* BISHOP OF ELY

CANTERBURY. My lord, I'll tell you: that self bill is
    urged,
  Which in the eleventh year of the last King's reign
  Was like, and had indeed against us passed,
  But that the scambling and unquiet time
  Did push it out of farther question.
ELY. But how, my lord, shall we resist it now?
CANTERBURY. It must be thought on. If it pass against us,
  We lose the better half of our possession;
  For all the temporal lands which men devout
  By testament have given to the Church
  Would they strip from us, being valued thus:
  As much as would maintain, to the King's honour,
  Full fifteen earls and fifteen hundred knights,
  Six thousand and two hundred good esquires;
  And, to relief of lazars and weak age,
  Of indigent faint souls past corporal toil,
  A hundred almshouses right well supplied;
  And to the coffers of the King beside,
  A thousand pounds by the year. Thus runs the bill.
ELY. This would drink deep.
CANTERBURY.   'Twould drink the cup and all.
ELY. But what prevention?
CANTERBURY. The King is full of grace and fair regard.
ELY. And a true lover of the holy Church.
CANTERBURY. The courses of his youth promised it not.
  The breath no sooner left his father's body,
  But that his wildness, mortified in him,
  Seemed to die too; yea, at that very moment
Consideration, like an angel, came
And whipped the offending Adam out of him,
Leaving his body as a paradise,
To envelop and contain celestial spirits.
Never was such a sudden scholar made;
Never came reformation in a flood,
With such a heady currance, scouring faults;
Nor never Hydra-headed wilfulness
So soon did lose his seat—and all at once—
As in this King.
ELY.   We are blessed in the change.
CANTERBURY. Hear him but reason in divinity,
  And, all-admiring, with an inward wish
  You would desire the King were made a prelate;
  Hear him debate of commonwealth affairs,
  You would say it hath been all in all his study;
  List his discourse of war, and you shall hear
  A fearful battle rendered you in music;
  Turn him to any cause of policy,
  The Gordian knot of it he will unloose,
  Familiar as his garter—that, when he speaks,
  The air, a chartered libertine, is still,
  And the mute wonder lurketh in men's ears,
  To steal his sweet and honeyed sentences;
  So that the art and practic part of life
  Must be the mistress to this theoric—
  Which is a wonder how his grace should glean it,
  Since his addiction was to courses vain,
  His companies unlettered, rude and shallow,

His hours filled up with riots, banquets, sports,
And never noted in him any study,
Any retirement, any sequestration
From open haunts and popularity.
ELY. The strawberry grows underneath the nettle,
And wholesome berries thrive and ripen best
Neighboured by fruit of baser quality.
And so the Prince obscured his contemplation
Under the veil of wildness, which, no doubt,
Grew like the summer grass, fastest by night,
Unseen, yet crescive in his faculty.
CANTERBURY. It must be so, for miracles are ceased;
And therefore we must needs admit the means
How things are perfected.
ELY.   But, my good lord,
How now for mitigation of this bill
Urged by the Commons? Doth his majesty
Incline to it, or no?
CANTERBURY.   He seems indifferent,
Or rather swaying more upon our part
Than cherishing the exhibiters against us;
For I have made an offer to his majesty,
Upon our spiritual convocation

And in regard of causes now in hand,
Which I have opened to his grace at large,
As touching France, to give a greater sum
Than ever at one time the clergy yet
Did to his predecessors part withal.
ELY. How did this offer seem received, my lord?
CANTERBURY. With good acceptance of his majesty;
Save that there was not time enough to hear,
As I perceived his grace would fain have done,
The severals and unhidden passages
Of his true titles to some certain dukedoms
And generally to the crown and seat of France
Derived from Edward, his great-grandfather.
ELY. What was the impediment that broke this off?
CANTERBURY. The French ambassador upon that instant
Craved audience; and the hour, I think, is come
To give him hearing. Is it four o'clock?
ELY. It is.
CANTERBURY. Then go we in, to know his embassy;
Which I could with a ready guess declare,
Before the Frenchman speak a word of it.
ELY. I'll wait upon you, and I long to hear it.

Exeunt

SCENE II *The same: the Presence Chamber*

Enter KING HENRY, GLOUCESTER, BEDFORD, EXETER, WARWICK, WESTMORELAND, *and* Attendants

KING HENRY. Where is my gracious Lord of Canterbury?
EXETER. Not here in presence.
KING HENRY.   Send for him, good uncle.
WESTMORELAND. Shall we call in the ambassador, my
liege?
KING HENRY. Not yet, my cousin; we would be
resolved,
Before we hear him, of some things of weight
That task our thoughts, concerning us and France.
Enter the ARCHBISHOP OF CANTERBURY *and the*
BISHOP OF ELY
CANTERBURY. God and his angels guard your sacred
throne
And make you long become it!
KING HENRY.   Sure, we thank you.
My learned lord, we pray you to proceed
And justly and religiously unfold
Why the law Salique that they have in France
Or should, or should not, bar us in our claim.
And God forbid, my dear and faithful lord,
That you should fashion, wrest, or bow your reading,
Or nicely charge your understanding soul
With opening titles miscreate, whose right
Suits not in native colours with the truth;
For God doth know how many now in health
Shall drop their blood in approbation
Of what your reverence shall incite us to.

Therefore take heed how you impawn our person,
How you awake our sleeping sword of war.
We charge you, in the name of God, take heed;
For never two such kingdoms did contend
Without much fall of blood, whose guiltless drops
Are every one a woe, a sore complaint
'Gainst him whose wrongs give edge unto the swords
That make such waste in brief mortality.
Under this conjuration speak, my lord;
For we will hear, note, and believe in heart
That what you speak is in your conscience washed
As pure as sin with baptism.
CANTERBURY. Then hear me, gracious sovereign, and
you peers,
That owe yourselves, your lives, and services
To this imperial throne. There is no bar
To make against your highness' claim to France
But this, which they produce from Pharamond,
In terram Salicam mulieres ne succedant,
"No woman shall succeed in Salique land";
Which Salique land the French unjustly gloze
To be the realm of France, and Pharamond
The founder of this law and female bar.
Yet their own authors faithfully affirm
That the land Salique is in Germany,
Between the floods of Sala and of Elbe;
Where Charles the Great, having subdued the Saxons,

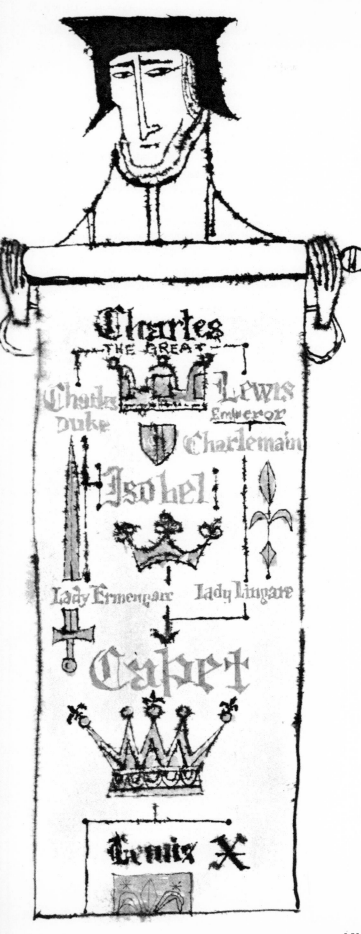

There left behind and settled certain French;
Who, holding in disdain the German women
For some dishonest manners of their life,
Established then this law: to wit, no female
Should be inheritrix in Salique land;
Which Salique, as I said, 'twixt Elbe and Sala,
Is at this day in Germany called Meisen.
Then doth it well appear the Salique law
Was not devised for the realm of France;
Nor did the French possess the Salique land
Until four hundred one and twenty years
After defunction of King Pharamond,
Idly supposed the founder of this law,
Who died within the year of our redemption
Four hundred twenty-six; and Charles the Great
Subdued the Saxons, and did seat the French
Beyond the river Sala, in the year
Eight hundred five. Besides, their writers say,
King Pepin, which deposed Childeric,
Did, as heir general, being descended
Of Blithild, which was daughter to King Clothair,
Make claim and title to the crown of France.
Hugh Capet also, who usurped the crown
Of Charles the Duke of Lorraine, sole heir male
Of the true line and stock of Charles the Great,
To find his title with some shows of truth,
Though, in pure truth, it was corrupt and naught,
Conveyed himself as heir to the Lady Lingare,
Daughter to Charlemain, who was the son
To Lewis the Emperor, and Lewis the son
Of Charles the Great. Also King Lewis the Tenth,
Who was sole heir to the usurper Capet,
Could not keep quiet in his conscience,
Wearing the crown of France, till satisfied
That fair Queen Isabel, his grandmother,
Was lineal of the Lady Ermengare,
Daughter to Charles the foresaid Duke of Lorraine;
By the which marriage the line of Charles the Great
Was reunited to the crown of France.
So that, as clear as is the summer's sun,
King Pepin's title and Hugh Capet's claim,
King Lewis his satisfaction, all appear
To hold in right and title of the female.
So do the kings of France unto this day,
Howbeit they would hold up this Salique law
To bar your highness claiming from the female,
And rather choose to hide them in a net
Than amply to imbar their crooked titles
Usurped from you and your progenitors.

KING HENRY. May I with right and conscience make
    this claim?

CANTERBURY. The sin upon my head, dread sovereign!
    For in the book of Numbers is it writ:
    "When the man dies, let the inheritance
    Descend unto the daughter." Gracious lord,
    Stand for your own; unwind your bloody flag;

151

Look back into your mighty ancestors:
Go, my dread lord, to your great-grandsire's tomb,
From whom you claim; invoke his warlike spirit,
And your great-uncle's, Edward the Black Prince,
Who on the French ground played a tragedy,
Making defeat on the full power of France,
Whiles his most mighty father on a hill
Stood smiling to behold his lion's whelp
Forage in blood of French nobility.
O noble English, that could entertain
With half their forces the full pride of France
And let another half stand laughing by,
All out of work and cold for action!

ELY. Awake remembrance of these valiant dead
And with your puissant arm renew their feats!
You are their heir; you sit upon their throne;
The blood and courage that renowned them
Runs in your veins; and my thrice-puissant liege
Is in the very May-morn of his youth,
Ripe for exploits and mighty enterprises.

EXETER. Your brother kings and monarchs of the earth
Do all expect that you should rouse yourself,
As did the former lions of your blood.

WESTMORELAND. They know your grace hath cause and
    means and might;
So hath your highness; never king of England
Had nobles richer and more loyal subjects,
Whose hearts have left their bodies here in England
And lie pavilioned in the fields of France.

CANTERBURY. O, let their bodies follow, my dear liege,
With blood and sword and fire to win your right;
In aid whereof we of the spiritualty
Will raise your highness such a mighty sum
As never did the clergy at one time
Bring in to any of your ancestors.

KING HENRY. We must not only arm to invade the
    French,
But lay down our proportions to defend
Against the Scot, who will make road upon us
With all advantages.

CANTERBURY. They of those marches, gracious sov-
    ereign,
Shall be a wall sufficient to defend
Our inland from the pilfering borderers.

KING HENRY. We do not mean the coursing snatchers
    only,
But fear the main intendment of the Scot,
Who hath been still a giddy neighbour to us;
For you shall read that my great-grandfather
Never went with his forces into France
But that the Scot on his unfurnished kingdom
Came pouring, like the tide into a breach,
With ample and brim fullness of his force,
Calling the gleaned land with hot assays,
Girding with grievous siege castles and towns,
That England, being empty of defence,

Hath shook and trembled at the ill neighbourhood.

CANTERBURY. She hath been then more feared than
    harmed, my liege;
For hear her but exampled by herself:
When all her chivalry hath been in France
And she a mourning widow of her nobles,
She hath herself not only well defended
But taken and impounded as a stray
The King of Scots; whom she did send to France,
To fill King Edward's fame with prisoner kings
And make her chronicle as rich with praise
As is the ooze and bottom of the sea
With sunken wreck and sumless treasuries.

WESTMORELAND. But there's a saying very old and true,
    "If that you will France win,
        Then with Scotland first begin";
For once the eagle England being in prey,
To her unguarded nest the weasel Scot
Comes sneaking and so sucks her princely eggs,
Playing the mouse in absence of the cat,
To tear and havoc more than she can eat.

EXETER. It follows then the cat must stay at home.
Yet that is but a crushed necessity,
Since we have locks to safeguard necessaries,
And pretty traps to catch the petty thieves.
While that the armed hand doth fight abroad,
The advised head defends itself at home;
For government, though high and low and lower,
Put into parts, doth keep in one consent,
Congreeing in a full and natural close,
Like music.

CANTERBURY. Therefore doth heaven divide
The state of man in divers functions,
Setting endeavour in continual motion;
To which is fixed, as an aim or butt,
Obedience. For so work the honey-bees,
Creatures that by a rule in nature teach
The act of order to a peopled kingdom:
They have a king and officers of sorts;
Where some, like magistrates, correct at home,
Others, like merchants, venture trade abroad,
Others, like soldiers, armed in their stings,
Make boot upon the summer's velvet buds;
Which pillage they with merry march bring home
To the tent-royal of their emperor;
Who, busied in his majesty, surveys
The singing masons building roofs of gold,
The civil citizens kneading up the honey,
The poor mechanic porters crowding in
Their heavy burdens at his narrow gate,
The sad-eyed justice, with his surly hum,
Delivering o'er to executors pale
The lazy yawning drone. I this infer,
That many things, having full reference
To one consent, may work contrariously:
As many arrows, loosed several ways,

Come to one mark; as many ways meet in one town;
As many fresh streams meet in one salt sea;
As many lines close in the dial's centre;
So may a thousand actions, once afoot,
End in one purpose, and be all well borne
Without defeat. Therefore to France, my liege.
Divide your happy England into four,
Whereof take you one quarter into France,
And you withal shall make all Gallia shake.
If we, with thrice such powers left at home,
Cannot defend our own doors from the dog,
Let us be worried and our nation lose
The name of hardiness and policy.

KING HENRY. Call in the messengers sent from the
    Dauphin.   *Exeunt some* Attendants
Now are we well resolved; and, by God's help,
And yours, the noble sinews of our power,
France being ours, we'll bend it to our awe
Or break it all to pieces; or there we'll sit,
Ruling in large and ample empery
O'er France and all her almost kingly dukedoms,
Or lay these bones in an unworthy urn,
Tombless, with no remembrance over them;
Either our history shall with full mouth
Speak freely of our acts, or else our grave,
Like Turkish mute, shall have a tongueless mouth,
Not worshipped with a waxen epitaph.

Enter Ambassadors *of France*

Now are we well prepared to know the pleasure
Of our fair cousin Dauphin; for we hear
Your greeting is from him, not from the King.

FIRST AMBASSADOR.   May 't please your majesty to give
    us leave
Freely to render what we have in charge;
Or shall we sparingly show you far off
The Dauphin's meaning and our embassy?

KING HENRY. We are no tyrant, but a Christian king,
Unto whose grace our passion is as subject
As are our wretches fettered in our prisons.
Therefore with frank and with uncurbed plainness
Tell us the Dauphin's mind.

FIRST AMBASSADOR.   Thus, then, in few.
Your highness, lately sending into France,
Did claim some certain dukedoms, in the right
Of your great predecessor, King Edward the Third.
In answer of which claim, the Prince our master
Says that you savour too much of your youth,
And bids you be advised there's nought in France
That can be with a nimble galliard won;
You cannot revel into dukedoms there.
He therefore sends you, meeter for your spirit,
This tun of treasure; and, in lieu of this,
Desires you let the dukedoms that you claim
Hear no more of you. This the Dauphin speaks.

KING HENRY. What treasure, uncle?

EXETER.   Tennis balls, my liege.

KING HENRY. We are glad the Dauphin is so pleasant
    with us;
His present and your pains we thank you for.
When we have matched our rackets to these balls,
We will, in France, by God's grace, play a set
Shall strike his father's crown into the hazard.
Tell him he hath made a match with such a wrangler
That all the courts of France will be disturbed
With chases. And we understand him well,
How he comes o'er us with our wilder days,
Not measuring what use we made of them.
We never valued this poor seat of England;
And therefore, living hence, did give ourself
To barbarous license, as 'tis ever common
That men are merriest when they are from home.
But tell the Dauphin I will keep my state,
Be like a king and show my sail of greatness
When I do rouse me in my throne of France;
For that I have laid by my majesty
And plodded like a man for working-days,
But I will rise there with so full a glory
That I will dazzle all the eyes of France,
Yea, strike the Dauphin blind to look on us.
And tell the pleasant prince this mock of his
Hath turned his balls to gun-stones; and his soul
Shall stand sore charged for the wasteful vengeance
That shall fly with them: for many a thousand widows
Shall this his mock mock out of their dear husbands;
Mock mothers from their sons, mock castles down;
And some are yet ungotten and unborn
That shall have cause to curse the Dauphin's scorn.
But this lies all within the will of God,
To whom I do appeal; and in whose name
Tell you the Dauphin I am coming on,
To venge me as I may and to put forth
My rightful hand in a well-hallowed cause.
So get you hence in peace; and tell the Dauphin
His jest will savour but of shallow wit,
When thousands weep more than did laugh at it.
Convey them with safe conduct. Fare you well.
                                Exeunt Ambassadors

EXETER. This was a merry message.

KING HENRY. We hope to make the sender blush at it.
Therefore, my lords, omit no happy hour
That may give furtherance to our expedition;
For we have now no thought in us but France,
Save those to God, that run before our business.
Therefore let our proportions for these wars
Be soon collected and all things thought upon
That may with reasonable swiftness add
More feathers to our wings; for, God before,
We'll chide this Dauphin at his father's door.
Therefore let every man now task his thought,
That this fair action may on foot be brought.
                                Exeunt. Flourish

ACT II

PROLOGUE

Flourish. Enter Chorus

CHORUS. Now all the youth of England are on fire,
And silken dalliance in the wardrobe lies;
Now thrive the armourers, and honour's thought
Reigns solely in the breast of every man;
They sell the pasture now to buy the horse,
Following the mirror of all Christian kings,
With winged heels, as English Mercuries.
For now sits Expectation in the air,
And hides a sword from hilts unto the point
With crowns imperial, crowns and coronets,
Promised to Harry and his followers.
The French, advised by good intelligence
Of this most dreadful preparation,
Shake in their fear and with pale policy
Seek to divert the English purposes.
O England! model to thy inward greatness,
Like little body with a mighty heart,
What mightst thou do, that honour would thee do,
Were all thy children kind and natural!
But see thy fault! France hath in thee found out
A nest of hollow bosoms, which he fills
With treacherous crowns; and three corrupted men,
One, Richard Earl of Cambridge, and the second,
Henry Lord Scroop of Masham, and the third,
Sir Thomas Grey, knight, of Northumberland,
Have, for the gilt of France—O guilt indeed!—
Confirmed conspiracy with fearful France;
And by their hands this grace of kings must die,
If hell and treason hold their promises,
Ere he take ship for France, and in Southampton.
Linger your patience on; and we'll digest
The abuse of distance; force a play.
The sum is paid; the traitors are agreed;
The King is set from London; and the scene
Is now transported, gentles, to Southampton.
There is the playhouse now, there must you sit;
And thence to France shall we convey you safe,
And bring you back, charming the narrow seas
To give you gentle pass; for, if we may,
We'll not offend one stomach with our play.
But, till the King come forth, and not till then,
Unto Southampton do we shift our scene.   *Exit*

SCENE I *London: a street*

Enter Corporal NYM *and Lieutenant* BARDOLPH

BARDOLPH. Well met, Corporal Nym.

NYM. Good morrow, Lieutenant Bardolph.

BARDOLPH. What, are Ancient Pistol and you friends yet?

NYM. For my part, I care not. I say little; but when time shall serve, there shall be smiles. But that shall be as it may. I dare not fight, but I will wink and hold out mine iron. It is a simple one, but what though? It will toast cheese, and it will endure cold as another man's sword will. And there's an end.

BARDOLPH. I will bestow a breakfast to make you friends; and we'll be all three sworn brothers to France. Let it be so, good Corporal Nym.

NYM. Faith, I will live so long as I may, that's the certain of it; and when I cannot live any longer, I will do as I may. That is my rest, that is the rendezvous of it.

BARDOLPH. It is certain, corporal, that he is married to Nell Quickly; and certainly she did you wrong, for you were troth-plight to her.

NYM. I cannot tell; things must be as they may. Men may sleep, and they may have their throats about them at that time; and some say knives have edges. It must be as it may. Though patience be a tired mare, yet she will plod. There must be conclusions. Well, I cannot tell.

Enter PISTOL *and* HOSTESS

BARDOLPH. Here comes Ancient Pistol and his wife. Good corporal, be patient here. How now, mine host Pistol!

PISTOL. Base tike, call'st thou me host?
Now, by this hand, I swear, I scorn the term;
Nor shall my Nell keep lodgers.

HOSTESS. No, by my troth, not long; for we cannot lodge and board a dozen or fourteen gentlewomen that live honestly by the prick of their needles, but it will be thought we keep a bawdy house straight. [*Nym and Pistol draw*] O well-a-day, Lady, if he be not drawn now! We shall see willful adultery and murder committed.

BARDOLPH. Good lieutenant! good corporal! offer nothing here.

NYM. Pish!

PISTOL. Pish for thee, Iceland dog! thou prickeared cur of Iceland!

HOSTESS. Good Corporal Nym, show thy valour, and put up your sword.

NYM. Will you shog off? I would have you solus.

PISTOL. "Solus," egregious dog? O viper vile!
The "solus" in thy most mervailous face;
The "solus" in thy teeth, and in thy throat,
And in thy hateful lungs, yea, in thy maw, perdy,
And, which is worse, within thy nasty mouth!
I do retort the "solus" in thy bowels;

For I can take, and Pistol's cock is up,
And flashing fire will follow.

NYM. I am not Barbason; you cannot conjure me. I have an humour to knock you indifferently well. If you grow foul with me, Pistol, I will scour you with my rapier, as I may, in fair terms; if you would walk off, I would prick your guts a little, in good terms, as I may. And that's the humour of it.

PISTOL. O braggart vile and damned furious wight!
The grave doth gape, and doting death is near;
Therefore exhale.

BARDOLPH. Hear me, hear me what I say: he that strikes the first stroke, I'll run him up to the hilts, as I am a soldier.   *Draws*

PISTOL. An oath of mickle might; and fury shall abate.
Give me thy fist, thy fore-foot to me give;
Thy spirits are most tall.

NYM. I will cut thy throat, one time or other, in fair terms; that is the humour of it.

PISTOL. "Couple a gorge!"
That is the word. I thee defy again.
O hound of Crete, think'st thou my spouse to get?
No; to the spital go,
And from the powdering-tub of infamy
Fetch forth the lazar kite of Cressid's kind,
Doll Tearsheet she by name, and her espouse.
I have, and I will hold, the quondam Quickly
For the only she; and—pauca, there's enough.
Go to.

Enter the Boy

BOY. Mine host Pistol, you must come to my master, and you, hostess; he is very sick, and would to bed. Good Bardolph, put thy face between his sheets, and do the office of a warming-pan. Faith, he 's very ill.

BARDOLPH. Away, you rogue!

HOSTESS. By my troth, he'll yield the crow a pudding one of these days. The King has killed his heart. Good husband, come home presently. *Exeunt* Hostess *and* Boy

BARDOLPH. Come, shall I make you two friends? We must to France together. Why the devil should we keep knives to cut one another's throats?

PISTOL. Let floods o'erswell, and fiends for food howl on!

NYM. You'll pay me the eight shillings I won of you at betting?

PISTOL. Base is the slave that pays.

NYM. That now I will have; that's the humour of it.

PISTOL. As manhood shall compound; push home.

They draw

BARDOLPH. By this sword, he that makes the first thrust, I'll kill him; by this sword, I will.

PISTOL. Sword is an oath, and oaths must have their course.

BARDOLPH. Corporal Nym, an thou wilt be friends, be friends; an thou wilt not, why, then, be enemies with me too. Prithee, put up.

NYM. I shall have my eight shillings I won of you at betting?

PISTOL. A noble shalt thou have, and present pay;
And liquor likewise will I give to thee,
And friendship shall combine, and brotherhood.
I'll live by Nym, and Nym shall live by me.
Is not this just? for I shall sutler be
Unto the camp, and profits will accrue.
Give me thy hand.

NYM. I shall have my noble?

PISTOL. In cash most justly paid.

NYM. Well, then, that's the humour of 't.

Re-enter HOSTESS

HOSTESS. As ever you came of women, come in quickly to Sir John. Ah, poor heart! he is so shaked of a burning quotidian tertian, that it is most lamentable to behold. Sweet men, come to him.

NYM. The King hath run bad humours on the knight; that's the even of it.

PISTOL. Nym, thou hast spoke the right;
His heart is fracted and corroborate.

NYM. The King is a good king, but it must be as it may; he passes some humours and careers.

PISTOL. Let us condole the knight; for, lambkins, we will live.   *Exeunt*

SCENE II *Southampton: a council-chamber*

Enter EXETER, BEDFORD, *and* WESTMORELAND

BEDFORD. 'Fore God, his grace is bold, to trust these traitors.

EXETER. They shall be apprehended by and by.

WESTMORELAND. How smooth and even they do bear themselves!
As if allegiance in their bosoms sat,
Crowned with faith and constant loyalty.

BEDFORD. The King hath note of all that they intend,
By interception which they dream not of.

EXETER. Nay, but the man that was his bedfellow,
Whom he hath dulled and cloyed with gracious favours,
That he should, for a foreign purse, so sell
His sovereign's life to death and treachery.

Trumpets sound.
Enter KING HENRY, SCROOP, CAMBRIDGE,
GREY, *and* Attendants

KING HENRY. Now sits the wind fair, and we will aboard.
My Lord of Cambridge, and my kind Lord of Masham,
And you, my gentle knight, give me your thoughts.
Think you not that the powers we bear with us
Will cut their passage through the force of France,
Doing the execution and the act
For which we have in head assembled them?

SCROOP. No doubt, my liege, if each man do his best.

KING HENRY. I doubt not that; since we are well persuaded
We carry not a heart with us from hence
That grows not in a fair consent with ours,
Nor leave not one behind that doth not wish
Success and conquest to attend on us.

CAMBRIDGE. Never was monarch better feared and loved
Than is your majesty. There's not, I think, a subject
That sits in heart-grief and uneasiness
Under the sweet shade of your government.

GREY. True! Those that were your father's enemies

Have steeped their galls in honey and do serve you
With hearts create of duty and of zeal.

KING HENRY. We therefore have great cause of thankfulness;
And shall forget the office of our hand,
Sooner than quittance of desert and merit
According to the weight and worthiness.

SCROOP. So service shall with steeled sinews toil,
And labour shall refresh itself with hope,
To do your grace incessant services.

KING HENRY. We judge no less. Uncle of Exeter,
Enlarge the man committed yesterday,
That railed against our person; we consider
It was excess of wine that set him on,
And on his more advice we pardon him.

SCROOP. That's mercy, but too much security.
Let him be punished, sovereign, lest example
Breed, by his sufferance, more of such a kind.

KING HENRY. O, let us yet be merciful.

CAMBRIDGE. So may your highness, and yet punish too.

GREY. Sir,
You show great mercy, if you give him life,
After the taste of much correction.

KING HENRY. Alas, your too much love and care of me
Are heavy orisons 'gainst this poor wretch!
If little faults, proceeding on distemper,
Shall not be winked at, how shall we stretch our eye
When capital crimes, chewed, swallowed and digested,
Appear before us? We'll yet enlarge that man,
Though Cambridge, Scroop, and Grey, in their dear care
And tender preservation of our person,
Would have him punished. And now to our French causes:
Who are the late commissioners?

CAMBRIDGE. I one, my lord.
Your highness bade me ask for it today.

SCROOP. So did you me, my liege.

GREY. And I, my royal sovereign.

KING HENRY. Then, Richard Earl of Cambridge, there
   is yours;
   There yours, Lord Scroop of Masham; and, sir knight,
   Grey of Northumberland, this same is yours.
   Read them; and know, I know your worthiness.
   My Lord of Westmoreland, and uncle Exeter,
   We will aboard tonight. Why, how now, gentlemen!
   What see you in those papers that you lose
   So much complexion? Look ye, how they change!
   Their cheeks are paper. Why, what read you there,
   That hath so cowarded and chased your blood
   Out of appearance?

CAMBRIDGE.   I do confess my fault;
   And do submit me to your highness' mercy.

GREY.
      ⎱ To which we all appeal.
SCROOP. ⎰

KING HENRY. The mercy that was quick in us but late,
   By your own counsel is suppressed and killed.
   You must not dare, for shame, to talk of mercy;
   For your own reasons turn into your bosoms,
   As dogs upon their masters, worrying you.
   See you, my princes and my noble peers,
   These English monsters! My Lord of Cambridge here,
   You know how apt our love was to accord
   To furnish him with all appertinents
   Belonging to his honour; and this man
   Hath, for a few light crowns, lightly conspired,
   And sworn unto the practices of France,
   To kill us here in Hampton; to the which
   This knight, no less for bounty bound to us
   Than Cambridge is, hath likewise sworn. But, O,
   What shall I say to thee, Lord Scroop? thou cruel,
   Ingrateful, savage and inhuman creature!
   Thou that didst bear the key of all my counsels,
   That knew'st the very bottom of my soul,
   That almost mightst have coined me into gold,
   Wouldst thou have practised on me for thy use!
   May it be possible, that foreign hire
   Could out of thee extract one spark of evil
   That might annoy my finger? 'tis so strange,
   That, though the truth of it stands off as gross
   As black and white, my eye will scarcely see it.
   Treason and murder ever kept together,
   As two yoke-devils sworn to either's purpose,
   Working so grossly in a natural cause,
   That admiration did not hoop at them.
   But thou, 'gainst all proportion, didst bring in
   Wonder to wait on treason and on murder;
   And whatsoever cunning fiend it was
   That wrought upon thee so preposterously
   Hath got the voice in Hell for excellence!
   All other devils that suggest by treasons
   Do botch and bungle up damnation
   With patches, colours, and with forms being fetched

From glistering semblances of piety;
   But he that tempered thee bade thee stand up,
   Gave thee no instance why thou shouldst do treason,
   Unless to dub thee with the name of traitor.
   If that same demon that hath gulled thee thus
   Should with his lion gait walk the whole world,
   He might return to vasty Tartar back,
   And tell the legions ''I can never win
   A soul so easy as that Englishman's.''
   O, how hast thou with jealousy infected
   The sweetness of affiance! Show men dutiful?
   Why, so didst thou. Seem they grave and learned?
   Why, so didst thou. Come they of noble family?
   Why, so didst thou. Seem they religious?

Why, so didst thou. Or are they spare in diet,
   Free from gross passion or of mirth or anger,
   Constant in spirit, not swerving with the blood,
   Garnished and decked in modest complement,
   Not working with the eye without the ear,
   And but in purged judgement trusting neither?
   Such and so finely bolted didst thou seem;
   And thus thy fall hath left a kind of blot,
   To mark the full-fraught man and best indued
   With some suspicion. I will weep for thee;
   For this revolt of thine, methinks, is like
   Another fall of man. Their faults are open;
   Arrest them to the answer of the law.
   And God acquit them of their practices!

EXETER. I arrest thee of high treason, by the name of
   Richard Earl of Cambridge.
   I arrest thee of high treason, by the name of Henry
   Lord Scroop of Masham.
   I arrest thee of high treason, by the name of Thomas
   Grey, knight, of Northumberland.

SCROOP. Our purposes God justly hath discovered,
   And I repent my fault more than my death;
   Which I beseech your highness to forgive,
   Although my body pay the price of it.

CAMBRIDGE. For me, the gold of France did not seduce,
   Although I did admit it as a motive
   The sooner to effect what I intended.

But God be thanked for prevention;
Which I in sufferance heartily will rejoice,
Beseeching God and you to pardon me.
GREY. Never did faithful subject more rejoice
At the discovery of most dangerous treason
Than I do at this hour joy o'er myself,
Prevented from a damned enterprise.
My fault, but not my body, pardon, sovereign.
KING HENRY. God quit you in his mercy! Hear your
    sentence.
You have conspired against our royal person,
Joined with an enemy proclaimed and from his coffers
Received the golden earnest of our death;
Wherein you would have sold your king to slaughter,
His princes and his peers to servitude,
His subjects to oppression and contempt
And his whole kingdom into desolation.
Touching our person seek we no revenge;
But we our kingdom's safety must so tender,

Whose ruin you have sought, that to her laws
We do deliver you. Get you therefore hence,
Poor miserable wretches, to your death;
The taste whereof, God of his mercy give
You patience to endure, and true repentance
Of all your dear offences! Bear them hence.
        Exeunt CAMBRIDGE, SCROOP, *and* GREY, *guarded*
Now, lords, for France; the enterprise whereof
Shall be to you, as us, like glorious.
We doubt not of a fair and lucky war,
Since God so graciously hath brought to light
This dangerous treason lurking in our way
To hinder our beginnings. We doubt not now
But every rub is smoothed on our way.
Then forth, dear countrymen! Let us deliver
Our puissance into the hand of God,
Putting it straight in expedition.
Cheerly to sea; the signs of war advance;
No king of England, if not king of France.   *Exeunt*

SCENE III *London: before a tavern*

Enter PISTOL, HOSTESS, NYM, BARDOLPH, *and* Boy

HOSTESS. Prithee, honey-sweet husband, let me bring thee to Staines.
PISTOL. No; for my manly heart doth yearn.
    Bardolph, be blithe; Nym, rouse thy vaunting veins;
    Boy, bristle thy courage up; for Falstaff he is dead,
    And we must yearn therefore.
BARDOLPH. Would I were with him, wheresome'er he is, either in Heaven or in Hell!
HOSTESS. Nay, sure, he's not in Hell. He's in Arthur's bosom, if ever man went to Arthur's bosom. A' made a finer end and went away an it had been any christom child. A' parted even just between twelve and one, even at the turning o' the tide, for after I saw him fumble with the sheets and play with flowers and smile upon his fingers' ends, I knew there was but one way; for his nose was as sharp as a pen, and a' babbled of green fields. "How now, Sir John!" quoth I. "What, man! be o' good cheer." So a' cried out "God, God, God!" three or four times. Now I, to comfort him, bid him a' should not think of God; I hoped there was no need to trouble himself with any such thoughts yet. So a' bade me lay more clothes on his feet. I put my hand into the bed and felt them, and they were as cold as any stone; then I felt to his knees, and they were as cold as any stone, and so upward and upward, and all was as cold as any stone.
NYM. They say he cried out of sack.
HOSTESS. Ay, that a' did.
BARDOLPH. And of women.
HOSTESS. Nay, that a' did not.
BOY. Yes, that a' did; and said they were devils incarnate.

HOSTESS. A' could never abide carnation; 'twas a colour he never liked.
BOY. A' said once, the devil would have him about women.
HOSTESS. A' did in some sort, indeed, handle women; but then he was rheumatic, and talked of the whore of Babylon.
BOY. Do you not remember, a' saw a flea stick upon Bardolph's nose, and a' said it was a black soul burning in hell-fire?
BARDOLPH. Well, the fuel is gone that maintained that fire; that's all the riches I got in his service.
NYM. Shall we shog? The King will be gone from Southampton.
PISTOL. Come, let's away. My love, give me thy lips.
    Look to my chattels and my movables.
    Let senses rule; the word is "Pitch and Pay."
    Trust none;
    For oaths are straws, men's faiths are wafercakes,
    And hold-fast is the only dog, my duck;
    Therefore, Caveto be thy counsellor.
    Go, clear thy crystals. Yoke-fellows in arms,
    Let us to France; like horse-leeches, my boys,
    To suck, to suck, the very blood to suck!
BOY. And that's but unwholesome food, they say.
PISTOL. Touch her soft mouth, and march.
BARDOLPH. Farewell, hostess.
                                            Kissing her
NYM. I cannot kiss, that is the humour of it; but, adieu.
PISTOL. Let housewifery appear; keep close, I thee command.
HOSTESS. Farewell; adieu.   *Exeunt*

SCENE IV *France: the* KING'S *palace*

Flourish. Enter the FRENCH KING, *the* DAUPHIN, *the* DUKES OF BERRI *and* BRETAGNE, *the* CONSTABLE, *and others*

FRENCH KING. Thus comes the English with full power
   upon us;
  And more than carefully it us concerns
  To answer royally in our defences.
  Therefore the Dukes of Berri and of Bretagne,
  Of Brabant and of Orleans, shall make forth,
  And you, Prince Dauphin, with all swift dispatch,
  To line and new repair our towns of war
  With men of courage and with means defendant;
  For England his approaches makes as fierce
  As waters to the sucking of a gulf.
  It fits us then to be as provident
  As fear may teach us out of late examples
  Left by the fatal and neglected English
  Upon our fields.
DAUPHIN.   My most redoubted father,
  It is most meet we arm us 'gainst the foe;
  For peace itself should not so dull a kingdom,
  Though war nor no known quarrel were in question,
  But that defences, musters, preparations,
  Should be maintained, assembled and collected,
  As were a war in expectation.
  Therefore, I say 'tis meet we all go forth
  To view the sick and feeble parts of France.
  And let us do it with no show of fear;
  No, with no more than if we heard that England
  Were busied with a Whitsun morris-dance;
  For, my good liege, she is so idly kinged,
  Her sceptre so fantastically borne
  By a vain, giddy, shallow, humorous youth,
  That fear attends her not.
CONSTABLE.   O peace, Prince Dauphin!
  You are too much mistaken in this King.
  Question your grace the late ambassadors,
  With what great state he heard their embassy,
  How well supplied with noble counsellors,
  How modest in exception, and withal
  How terrible in constant resolution,
  And you shall find his vanities forespent
  Were but the outside of the Roman Brutus,
  Covering discretion with a coat of folly;
  As gardeners do with ordure hide those roots
  That shall first spring and be most delicate.
DAUPHIN. Well, 'tis not so, my lord high Constable;
  But though we think it so, it is no matter.
  In cases of defence 'tis best to weigh
  The enemy more mighty than he seems.
  So the proportions of defence are filled;
  Which of a weak and niggardly projection
  Doth, like a miser, spoil his coat with scanting
  A little cloth.
FRENCH KING. Think we King Harry strong;
  And, princes, look you strongly arm to meet him.

  The kindred of him hath been fleshed upon us;
  And he is bred out of that bloody strain
  That haunted us in our familiar paths.
  Witness our too much memorable shame
  When Cressy battle fatally was struck,
  And all our princes captived by the hand
  Of that black name, Edward, Black Prince of Wales;
  Whiles that his mountain sire, on mountain standing,
  Up in the air, crowned with the golden sun,
  Saw his heroical seed, and smiled to see him,
  Mangle the work of nature and deface
  The patterns that by God and by French fathers
  Had twenty years been made. This is a stem
  Of that victorious stock; and let us fear
  The native mightiness and fate of him.

Enter a Messenger

MESSENGER. Ambassadors from Harry, King of England
  Do crave admittance to your majesty.
FRENCH KING. We'll give them present audience.
  Go, and bring them.

Exeunt Messenger and certain Lords

  You see this chase is hotly followed, friends.
DAUPHIN. Turn head, and stop pursuit; for coward dogs
  Most spend their mouths when what they seem to
    threaten
  Runs far before them. Good my sovereign,
  Take up the English short, and let them know
  Of what a monarchy you are the head.
  Self-love, my liege, is not so vile a sin
  As self-neglecting.

Re-enter Lords, with EXETER *and train*

FRENCH KING.   From our brother England?
EXETER. From him; and thus he greets your majesty:
  He wills you, in the name of God Almighty,
  That you divest yourself, and lay apart
  The borrowed glories that by gift of heaven,
  By law of nature and of nations, 'long
  To him and to his heirs; namely, the crown
  And all wide-stretched honours that pertain
  By custom and the ordinance of times
  Unto the crown of France. That you may know
  'Tis no sinister nor no awkward claim,
  Picked from the worm-holes of long-vanished days,
  Nor from the dust of old oblivion raked,
  He sends you this most memorable line,
  In every branch truly demonstrative,
  Willing you overlook this pedigree.
  And when you find him evenly derived
  From his most famed of famous ancestors,
  Edward the Third, he bids you then resign

Your crown and kingdom, indirectly held
From him the native and true challenger.
FRENCH KING. Or else what follows?
EXETER. Bloody constraint; for if you hide the crown
Even in your hearts, there will he rake for it.
Therefore in fierce tempest is he coming,
In thunder and in earthquake, like a Jove,
That, if requiring fail, he will compel;
And bids you, in the bowels of the Lord,
Deliver up the crown, and to take mercy
On the poor souls for whom this hungry war
Opens his vasty jaws; and on your head
Turning the widows' tears, the orphans' cries,
The dead men's blood, the pining maidens' groans,
For husbands, fathers and betrothed lovers,
That shall be swallowed in this controversy.
This is his claim, his threatening, and my message;
Unless the Dauphin be in presence here,
To whom expressly I bring greeting too.
FRENCH KING. For us, we will consider of this further.
Tomorrow shall you bear our full intent
Back to our brother England.
DAUPHIN.   For the Dauphin,
I stand here for him. What to him from England?
EXETER. Scorn and defiance; slight regard, contempt,
And anything that may not misbecome
The mighty sender, doth he prize you at.
Thus says my King; an if your father's highness
Do not, in grant of all demands at large,
Sweeten the bitter mock you sent his majesty,
He'll call you to so hot an answer of it,
That caves and womby vaultages of France
Shall chide your trespass and return your mock
In second accent of his ordinance.
DAUPHIN. Say, if my father render fair return,
It is against my will; for I desire
Nothing but odds with England. To that end,
As matching to his youth and vanity,
I did present him with the Paris balls.
EXETER. He'll make your Paris Louvre shake for it,
Were it the mistress-court of mighty Europe;
And, be assured, you'll find a difference,
As we his subjects have in wonder found,
Between the promise of his greener days
And these he masters now. Now he weighs time
Even to the utmost grain; that you shall read
In your own losses, if he stay in France.
FRENCH KING. Tomorrow shall you know our mind
    at full.
EXETER. Dispatch us with all speed, lest that our King
Come here himself to question our delay;
For he is footed in this land already.
FRENCH KING. You shall be soon dispatched with fair
    conditions;
A night is but small breath and little pause
To answer matters of this consequence.   *Exeunt*

ACT III

PROLOGUE

Enter Chorus

CHORUS. Thus with imagined wing our swift scene flies
In motion of no less celerity
Than that of thought. Suppose that you have seen
The well-appointed King at Hampton pier
Embark his royalty; and his brave fleet
With silken streamers the young Phœbus fanning.
Play with your fancies, and in them behold
Upon the hempen tackle ship-boys climbing;
Hear the shrill whistle which doth order give
To sounds confused; behold the threaden sails,
Borne with the invisible and creeping wind,
Draw the huge bottoms through the furrowed sea,
Breasting the lofty surge. O, do but think
You stand upon the rivage and behold
A city on the inconstant billows dancing;
For so appears this fleet majestical,
Holding due course to Harfleur. Follow, follow!
Grapple your minds to sternage of this navy,
And leave your England, as dead midnight still,
Guarded with grandsires, babies and old women,
Either past or not arrived to pith and puissance;
For who is he, whose chin is but enriched
With one appearing hair, that will not follow
These culled and choice-drawn cavaliers to France?
Work, work your thoughts, and therein see a siege;
Behold the ordnance on their carriages,
With fatal mouths gaping on girded Harfleur.
Suppose the ambassador from the French comes back;
Tells Harry that the King doth offer him
Katharine his daughter, and with her, to dowry,
Some petty and unprofitable dukedoms.
The offer likes not; and the nimble gunner
With linstock now the devilish cannon touches,
          Alarum, and chambers go off
And down goes all before them. Still be kind,
And eke out our performance with your mind.   *Exit*

SCENE I *France: before Harfleur*

Alarum. Enter KING HENRY, EXETER, BEDFORD, GLOU-
CESTER, *and* Soldiers, *with scaling-ladders*

KING HENRY. Once more unto the breach, dear friends,
   once more;
  Or close the wall up with our English dead.
  In peace there's nothing so becomes a man
  As modest stillness and humility.
  But when the blast of war blows in our ears,
  Then imitate the action of the tiger;
  Stiffen the sinews, summon up the blood,
  Disguise fair nature with hard-favoured rage;
  Then lend the eye a terrible aspect;
  Let it pry through the portage of the head
  Like the brass cannon; let the brow o'erwhelm it
  As fearfully as doth a galled rock
  O'erhang and jutty his confounded base,
  Swilled with the wild and wasteful ocean.
  Now set the teeth and stretch the nostril wide,
  Hold hard the breath and bend up every spirit
  To his full height. On, on, you noblest English,
  Whose blood is fet from fathers of war-proof!
  Fathers that, like so many Alexanders,
  Have in these parts from morn till even fought
  And sheathed their swords for lack of argument.
  Dishonour not your mothers; now attest
  That those whom you called fathers did beget you.
  Be copy now to men of grosser blood,
  And teach them how to war. And you, good yeomen
  Whose limbs were made in England, show us here
  The mettle of your pasture; let us swear
  That you are worth your breeding—which I doubt
    not—
  For there is none of you so mean and base,
  That hath not noble lustre in your eyes.
  I see you stand like greyhounds in the slips,
  Straining upon the start. The game's afoot;
  Follow your spirit, and upon this charge
  Cry "God for Harry, England, and Saint George!"
       Exeunt. Alarum, and chambers go off

SCENE II *The same*

Enter NYM, BARDOLPH, PISTOL, *and* Boy

BARDOLPH. On, on, on, on, on! to the breach, to the breach!

NYM. Pray thee, corporal, stay; the knocks are too hot. And, for mine own part, I have not a case of lives. The humour of it is too hot, that is the very plain-song of it.

PISTOL. The plain-song is most just; for humours do abound.

Knocks go and come; God's vassals drop and die;
        And sword and shield,
        In bloody field,
    Doth win immortal fame.

BOY. Would I were in an alehouse in London! I would give all my fame for a pot of ale and safety.

PISTOL.   And I:
    If wishes would prevail with me,
    My purpose should not fail with me,
        But thither would I hie.

BOY.   As duly, but not as truly,
        As bird doth sing on bough.

Enter FLUELLEN

FLUELLEN. Up to the breach, you dogs! avaunt, you cullions!   *Driving them forward*

PISTOL. Be merciful, great duke, to men of mould.
    Abate thy rage, abate thy manly rage,
    Abate thy rage, great duke!
    Good bawcock, bate thy rage; use lenity, sweet chuck!

NYM. These be good humours! your honour wins bad humours.   *Exeunt all but Boy*

BOY. As young as I am, I have observed these three swashers. I am boy to them all three, but all they three, though they would serve me, could not be man to me; for indeed three such antics do not amount to a man. For Bardolph, he is white-livered and red-faced; by the means whereof a' faces it out, but fights not. For Pistol, he hath a killing tongue and a quiet sword; by the means whereof a' breaks words, and keeps whole weapons. For Nym, he hath heard that men of few words are the best men; and therefore he scorns to say his prayers, lest a' should be thought a coward. But his few bad words are matched with as few good deeds; for a' never broke any man's head but his own, and that was against a post when he was drunk. They will steal anything, and call it purchase. Bardolph stole a lute-case, bore it twelve leagues, and sold it for three half-pence. Nym and Bardolph are sworn brothers in filching, and in Calais they stole a fire-shovel; I knew by that piece of service the men would carry coals. They would have me as familiar with men's pockets as their gloves or their handkerchers; which makes much against my manhood, if I should take from another's pocket to put into mine, for it is plain pocketing up of wrongs. I must leave them, and seek some better service; their villainy goes against my weak stomach, and therefore I must cast it up.   *Exit*

Re-enter FLUELLEN, GOWER *following*

GOWER. Captain Fluellen, you must come presently to the mines; the Duke of Gloucester would speak with you.

FLUELLEN. To the mines! Tell you the Duke, it is not so good to come to the mines; for, look you, the mines is not according to the disciplines of the war—the concavities of it is not sufficient; for, look you, th' athversary, you may discuss unto the Duke, look you, is digt himself four yard under the countermines. By Cheshu, I think a' will plow up all, if there is not better directions.

GOWER. The Duke of Gloucester, to whom the order of the siege is given, is altogether directed by an Irishman, a very valiant gentleman, i' faith.

FLUELLEN. It is Captain Macmorris, is it not?

GOWER. I think it be.

FLUELLEN. By Cheshu, he is an ass, as in the world—I will verify as much in his beard—he has no more directions in the true disciplines of the wars, look you, of the Roman disciplines, than is a puppy-dog.

Enter MACMORRIS *and* Captain JAMY

GOWER. Here a' comes; and the Scots captain, Captain Jamy, with him.

FLUELLEN. Captain Jamy is a marvellous falorous gentleman, that is certain; and of great expedition and knowledge in th' aunchient wars, upon my particular knowledge of his directions. By Cheshu, he will maintain his argument as well as any military man in the world, in the disciplines of the pristine wars of the Romans.

JAMY. I say gud-day, Captain Fluellen.

FLUELLEN. God-den to your worship, good Captain James.

GOWER. How now, Captain Macmorris! have you quit the mines? Have the pioners given o'er?

MACMORRIS. By Chrish, la! tish ill done! The work ish give over, the trompet sound the retreat. By my hand, I swear, and my father's soul, the work ish ill done; it ish give over. I would have blowed up the town, so Chrish save me, la! in an hour. O, tish ill done, tish ill done; by my hand, tish ill done!

FLUELLEN. Captain Macmorris, I beseech you now, will you voutsafe me, look you, a few disputations with you, as partly touching or concerning the disciplines of the war, the Roman wars, in the way of argument, look you, and friendly communication; partly to satisfy my opinion, and partly for the satisfaction, look you, of my mind, as touching the direction of the military discipline; that is the point.

JAMY. It sall be vary gud, gud feith, gud captains bath; and I sall quit you with gud leve, as I may pick occasion. That sall I, marry.

MACMORRIS. It is no time to discourse, so Chrish save me. The day is hot, and the weather, and the wars, and the King, and the Dukes; it is no time to discourse. The town is beseeched, and the trumpet call us to the breach; and we talk, and, be Chrish, do nothing. 'Tis shame for us all, so God sa' me, 'tis shame to stand still. It is shame, by my hand; and there is throats to be cut, and works to be done; and there ish nothing done, so Chrish sa' me, la!

JAMY. By the mess, ere theise eyes of mine take themselves to slomber, ay 'll de gud service, or ay 'll lig i' the grund for it; ay, or go to death; and ay 'll pay 't as valorously as I may, that sall I suerly do, that is the breff and the long. Marry, I wad full fain hear some question 'tween you tway.

FLUELLEN. Captain Macmorris, I think, look you, under your correction, there is not many of your nation—

MACMORRIS. Of my nation! What ish my nation? Ish a villain, and a bastard, and a knave, and a rascal— What ish my nation? Who talks of my nation?

FLUELLEN. Look you, if you take the matter otherwise than is meant, Captain Macmorris, peradventure I shall think you do not use me with that affability as in discretion you ought to use me, look you; being as good a man as yourself, both in the disciplines of war, and in the derivation of my birth, and in other particularities.

MACMORRIS. I do not know you so good a man as myself. So Chrish save me, I will cut off your head.

GOWER. Gentlemen both, you will mistake each other.

JAMY. A! that's a foul fault.   *A parley sounded*

GOWER. The town sounds a parley.

FLUELLEN. Captain Macmorris, when there is more better opportunity to be required, look you, I will be so bold as to tell you I know the disciplines of war; and there is an end.   *Exeunt*

SCENE III *The same: before the gates*

The Governor *and some* Citizens *on the walls; the English forces below. Enter* KING HENRY *and his train*

KING HENRY. How yet resolves the governor of the town?
This is the latest parle we will admit.
Therefore to our best mercy give yourselves,
Or like to men proud of destruction
Defy us to our worst; for, as I am a soldier,
A name that in my thoughts becomes me best,
If I begin the battery once again,
I will not leave the half-achieved Harfleur
Till in her ashes she lie buried.
The gates of mercy shall be all shut up,
And the fleshed soldier, rough and hard of heart,
In liberty of bloody hand shall range
With conscience wide as hell, mowing like grass
Your fresh-fair virgins and your flowering infants.
What is it then to me, if impious war,
Arrayed in flames like to the prince of fiends,
Do, with his smirched complexion, all fell feats
Enlinked to waste and desolation?
What is 't to me, when you yourselves are cause,
If your pure maidens fall into the hand
Of hot and forcing violation?
What rein can hold licentious wickedness
When down the hill he holds his fierce career?
We may as bootless spend our vain command
Upon the enraged soldiers in their spoil
As send precepts to the leviathan
To come ashore. Therefore, you men of Harfleur,
Take pity of your town and of your people,
Whiles yet my soldiers are in my command;

Whiles yet the cool and temperate wind of grace
O'erblows the filthy and contagious clouds
Of heady murder, spoil and villainy.
If not, why, in a moment look to see
The blind and bloody soldier with foul hand
Defile the locks of your shrill-shrieking daughters;
Your fathers taken by the silver beards,
And their most reverend heads dashed to the walls;
Your naked infants spitted upon pikes,
Whiles the mad mothers with their howls confused
Do break the clouds, as did the wives of Jewry
At Herod's bloody-hunting slaughtermen.
What say you? will you yield, and this avoid,
Or, guilty in defence, be thus destroyed?

GOVERNOR. Our expectation hath this day an end.
The Dauphin, whom of succours we entreated,
Returns us that his powers are yet not ready
To raise so great a siege. Therefore, great King,
We yield our town and lives to thy soft mercy.
Enter our gates, dispose of us and ours;
For we no longer are defensible.

KING HENRY. Open your gates. Come, uncle Exeter,
Go you and enter Harfleur; there remain,
And fortify it strongly 'gainst the French.
Use mercy to them all. For us, dear uncle,
The winter coming on and sickness growing
Upon our soldiers, we will retire to Calais.
Tonight in Harfleur will we be your guest;
Tomorrow for the march are we addrest.

Flourish. The KING *and his train enter the town*

SCENE IV

The FRENCH KING'S *palace*

Enter KATHARINE *and* ALICE

KATHARINE. Alice, tu as été en Angleterre, et tu parles bien le langage.

ALICE. Un peu, madame.

KATHARINE. Je te prie, m'enseignez; il faut que j'apprenne à parler. Comment appelez-vous la main en Anglois?

ALICE. La main? elle est appelée de hand.

KATHARINE. De hand. Et les doigts?

ALICE. Les doigts? ma foi, j'oublie les doigts, mais je me souviendrai. Les doigts? je pense qu'ils sont appelés de fingres; oui, de fingres.

KATHARINE. La main, de hand; les doigts, de fingres. Je pense que je suis le bon écolier; j'ai gagné deux mots d'Anglois vîtement. Comment appelez-vous les ongles?

ALICE. Les ongles? nous les appelons de nails.

KATHARINE. De nails. Ecoutez; dites-moi, si je parle bien: de hand, de fingres, et de nails.

ALICE. C'est bien dit, madame; il est fort bon Anglois.

KATHARINE. Dites-moi l'Anglois pour le bras.

ALICE. De arm, madame.

KATHARINE. Et le coude?

ALICE. De elbow.

KATHARINE. De elbow. Je m'en fais la répétition de tous les mots que vous m'avez appris dès à présent.

ALICE. Il est trop difficile, madame, comme je pense.

KATHARINE. Excusez-moi, Alice; écoutez; de hand, de fingres, de nails, de arma, de bilbow.

ALICE. De elbow, madame.

KATHARINE. O Seigneur Dieu, je m'en oublie! de elbow. Comment appelez-vous le col?

ALICE. De neck, madame.

KATHARINE. De nick. Et le menton?

ALICE. De chin.

KATHARINE. De sin. Le col, de nick; le menton, de sin.

ALICE. Oui. Sauf votre honneur, en vérité, vous prononcez les mots aussi droit que les natifs d'Angleterre.

KATHARINE. Je ne doute point d'apprendre, par la grace de Dieu, et en peu de temps.

ALICE. N'avez vous pas déjà oublié ce que je vous ai enseigné?

KATHARINE. Non, je réciterai à vous promptement: de hand, de fingres, de mails,—

ALICE. De nails, madame.

KATHARINE. De nails, de arm, de ilbow.

ALICE. Sauf votre honneur, de elbow.

KATHARINE. Ainsi dis-je; de elbow, de nick, et de sin. Comment appelez-vous le pied et la robe?

ALICE. De foot, madame; et de coun.

KATHARINE. De foot et de coun! O Seigneur Dieu! ce sont mots de son mauvais, corruptible, gros, et impudique, et non pour les dames d'honneur d'user.

Je ne voudrais prononcer ces mots devant les seigneurs de France pour tout le monde. Foh! le foot et le coun! Néanmoins, je réciterai une autre fois ma leçon ensemble: de hand, de fingres, de nails, de arm, de elbow, de nick, de sin, de foot, de coun.

ALICE. Excellent, madame!

KATHARINE. C'est assez pour une fois. Allons-nous à dîner. *Exeunt*

SCENE V *The same*

Enter the KING OF FRANCE,
the DAUPHIN, *the* DUKE OF BOURBON,
the CONSTABLE OF FRANCE, *and others*

FRENCH KING. 'Tis certain he hath passed the river
    Somme.
CONSTABLE. And if he be not fought withal, my lord,
    Let us not live in France; let us quit all
    And give our vineyards to a barbarous people.
DAUPHIN. O Dieu vivant! shall a few sprays of us,
    The emptying of our fathers' luxury,
    Our scions, put in wild and savage stock,
    Spirt up so suddenly into the clouds,
    And overlook their grafters?
BOURBON. Normans, but bastard Normans, Norman
    bastards!
    Mort de ma vie! if they march along
    Unfought withal, but I will sell my dukedom,
    To buy a slobbery and a dirty farm
    In that nook-shotten isle of Albion.
CONSTABLE. Dieu de batailles! where have they this
    mettle?
    Is not their climate foggy, raw and dull,
    On whom, as in despite, the sun looks pale,
    Killing their fruit with frowns? Can sodden water,
    A drench for sur-reined jades, their barleybroth,
    Decoct their cold blood to such valiant heat?
    And shall our quick blood, spirited with wine,
    Seem frosty? O, for honour of our land,
    Let us not hang like roping icicles
    Upon our houses' thatch, whiles a more frosty people
    Sweat drops of gallant youth in our rich fields!
    Poor we may call them in their native lords.
DAUPHIN. By faith and honour,
    Our madams mock at us, and plainly say
    Our mettle is bred out; and they will give
    Their bodies to the lust of English youth
    To new-store France with bastard warriors.
BOURBON. They bid us to the English dancing-schools,
    And teach lavoltas high and swift corantos;
    Saying our grace is only in our heels,
    And that we are most lofty runaways.
FRENCH KING. Where is Montjoy the herald? speed
    him hence!
    Let him greet England with our sharp defiance.
    Up, princes! and, with spirit of honour edged
    More sharper than your swords, hie to the field!
    Charles Delabreth, high constable of France;
    You Dukes of Orleans, Bourbon, and of Berri,
    Alençon, Brabant, Bar, and Burgundy;
    Jaques Chatillon, Rambures, Vaudemont
    Beaumont, Grandpré, Roussi, and Fauconberg,
    Foix, Lestrale, Bouciqualt, and Charolois;
    High dukes, great princes, barons, lords and knights,

For your great seats now quit you of great shames.
Bar Harry England, that sweeps through our land
With pennons painted in the blood of Harfleur!
Rush on his host, as doth the melted snow
Upon the valleys, whose low vassal seat
The Alps doth spit and void his rheum upon!
Go down upon him, you have power enough,
And in a captive chariot into Rouen
Bring him our prisoner!
CONSTABLE.   This becomes the great.
Sorry am I his numbers are so few,
His soldiers sick and famished in their march,

For I am sure, when he shall see our army,
He'll drop his heart into the sink of fear
And for achievement offer us his ransom.
FRENCH KING. Therefore, lord Constable, haste on
Montjoy,
And let him say to England that we send
To know what willing ransom he will give.
Prince Dauphin, you shall stay with us in Rouen.
DAUPHIN. Not so, I do beseech your majesty.
FRENCH KING. Be patient, for you shall remain with us.
Now forth, lord Constable and princes all,
And quickly bring us word of England's fall. *Exeunt*

SCENE VI *The English camp in Picardy*

Enter GOWER and FLUELLEN, *meeting*

GOWER. How now, Captain Fluellen! come you from
the bridge?
FLUELLEN. I assure you, there is very excellent services
committed at the bridge.
GOWER. Is the Duke of Exeter safe?
FLUELLEN. The Duke of Exeter is as magnanimous as
Agamemnon; and a man that I love and honour with
my soul, and my heart, and my duty, and my life,
and my living, and my uttermost power. He is not—
God be praised and blessed!—any hurt in the world;
but keeps the bridge most valiantly, with excellent
discipline. There is an aunchient lieutenant there at
the pridge; I think in my very conscience he is as
valiant a man as Mark Antony; and he is a man of no
estimation in the world; but I did see him do as
gallant service.
GOWER. What do you call him?
FLUELLEN. He is called Aunchient Pistol.
GOWER. I know him not.

Enter PISTOL

FLUELLEN. Here is the man.
PISTOL. Captain, I thee beseech to do me favours.
The Duke of Exeter doth love thee well.
FLUELLEN. Ay, I praise God; and I have merited some
love at his hands.
PISTOL. Bardolph, a soldier, firm and sound of heart,
And of buxom valour, hath, by cruel fate,
And giddy Fortune's furious fickle wheel,
That goddess blind,
That stands upon the rolling restless stone—
FLUELLEN. By your patience, Aunchient Pistol. For-
tune is painted blind, with a muffler afore her eyes,
to signify to you that Fortune is blind; and she is
painted also with a wheel, to signify to you, which is
the moral of it, that she is turning, and inconstant,
and mutability, and variation; and her foot, look you,

is fixed upon a spherical stone, which rolls, and rolls,
and rolls. In good truth, the poet makes a most ex-
cellent description of it; Fortune is an excellent
moral.
PISTOL. Fortune is Bardolph's foe, and frowns on him;
For he hath stolen a pax, and hanged must a' be.
A damned death!
Let gallows gape for dog; let man go free
And let not hemp his wind-pipe suffocate.
But Exeter hath given the doom of death
For pax of little price.
Therefore, go speak; the Duke will hear thy voice;
And let not Bardolph's vital thread be cut
With edge of penny cord and vile reproach.
Speak, captain, for his life, and I will thee requite.
FLUELLEN. Aunchient Pistol, I do partly understand your
meaning.
PISTOL. Why then, rejoice therefore.
FLUELLEN. Certainly, aunchient, it is not a thing to re-
joice at; for if, look you, he were my brother, I would
desire the Duke to use his good pleasure, and put him
to execution; for discipline ought to be used.
PISTOL. Die and be damned! and figo for thy friendship!
FLUELLEN. It is well.
PISTOL. The fig of Spain!   *Exit*
FLUELLEN. Very good.
GOWER. Why, this is an arrant counterfeit rascal. I remember him now; a bawd, a cutpurse.
FLUELLEN. I'll assure you, a' uttered as prave words at
the pridge as you shall see in a summer's day. But it is
very well; what he has spoke to me, that is well,
I warrant you, when time is serve.
GOWER. Why, 'tis a gull, a fool, a rogue, that now and
then goes to the wars, to grace himself at his return
into London under the form of a soldier. And such
fellows are perfect in the great commanders' names,
and they will learn you by rote where services were

done—at such and such a sconce, at such a breach, at such a convoy; who came off bravely, who was shot, who disgraced, what terms the enemy stood on; and this they con perfectly in the phrase of war, which they trick up with new-tuned oaths—and what a beard of the general's cut and a horrid suit of the camp will do among foaming bottles and ale-washed wits, is wonderful to be thought on. But you must learn to know such slanders of the age, or else you may be marvellously mistook.

FLUELLEN. I tell you what, Captain Gower; I do perceive he is not the man that he would gladly make show to the world he is. If I find a hole in his coat, I will tell him my mind. [*Drum heard*] Hark you, the King is coming, and I must speak with him from the pridge.

Drum and colours.
Enter KING HENRY, GLOUCESTER, *and* SOLDIERS

God pless your majesty!

KING HENRY. How now, Fluellen! camest thou from the bridge?

FLUELLEN. Ay, so please your majesty. The Duke of Exeter has very gallantly maintained the pridge. The French is gone off, look you; and there is gallant and most prave passages. Marry, th' athversary was have possession of the pridge; but he is enforced to retire, and the Duke of Exeter is master of the pridge. I can tell your majesty, the Duke is a prave man.

KING HENRY. What men have you lost, Fluellen?

FLUELLEN. The perdition of th' athversary hath been very great, reasonable great. Marry, for my part, I think the Duke hath lost never a man, but one that is like to be executed for robbing a church, one Bardolph, if your majesty know the man. His face is all bubukles, and whelks, and knobs, and flames o' fire; and his lips blows at his nose, and it is like a coal of fire, sometimes plue and sometimes red; but his nose is executed, and his fire's out.

KING HENRY. We would have all such offenders so cut off. And we give express charge, that in our marches through the country, there be nothing compelled from the villages, nothing taken but paid for, none of the French upbraided or abused in disdainful language; for when lenity and cruelty play for a kingdom, the gentler gamester is the soonest winner.

Tucket. Enter MONTJOY

MONTJOY. You know me by my habit.

KING HENRY. Well then I know thee. What shall I know of thee?

MONTJOY. My master's mind.

KING HENRY. Unfold it.

MONTJOY. Thus says my King: Say thou to Harry of England: Though we seemed dead, we did but sleep; advantage is a better soldier than rashness. Tell him

we could have rebuked him at Harfleur, but that we thought not good to bruise an injury till it were full ripe. Now we speak upon our cue, and our voice is imperial. England shall repent his folly, see his weakness, and admire our sufferance. Bid him therefore consider of his ransom; which must proportion the losses we have borne, the subjects we have lost, the disgrace we have digested; which in weight to reanswer, his pettiness would bow under. For our losses, his exchequer is too poor; for the effusion of our blood, the muster of his kingdom too faint a number; and for our disgrace, his own person, kneeling at our feet, but a weak and worthless satisfaction. To this add defiance; and tell him, for conclusion, he hath betrayed his followers, whose condemnation is pronounced. So far my King and master, so much my office.

KING HENRY. What is thy name? I know thy quality.

MONTJOY. Montjoy.

KING HENRY. Thou dost thy office fairly. Turn thee back,
And tell thy King I do not seek him now,
But could be willing to march on to Calais
Without impeachment; for, to say the sooth,
Though 'tis no wisdom to confess so much
Unto an enemy of craft and vantage,
My people are with sickness much enfeebled,
My numbers lessened, and those few I have
Almost no better than so many French;
Who when they were in health, I tell thee, herald,
I thought upon one pair of English legs
Did march three Frenchmen. Yet, forgive me, God,
That I do brag thus! This your air of France
Hath blown that vice in me; I must repent.
Go therefore, tell thy master here I am;
My ransom is this frail and worthless trunk,
My army but a weak and sickly guard;
Yet, God before, tell him we will come on,
Though France himself and such another neighbour
Stand in our way. There's for thy labour, Montjoy.
Go, bid thy master well advise himself.
If we may pass, we will; if we be hindered,
We shall your tawny ground with your red blood
Discolour. And so, Montjoy, fare you well.
The sum of all our answer is but this:
We would not seek a battle, as we are;
Nor, as we are, we say we will not shun it.
So tell your master.

MONTJOY. I shall deliver so. Thanks to your highness.

Exit

GLOUCESTER. I hope they will not come upon us now.

KING HENRY. We are in God's hand, brother, not in theirs.
March to the bridge; it now draws toward night.
Beyond the river we'll encamp ourselves,
And on tomorrow bid them march away.

Exeunt

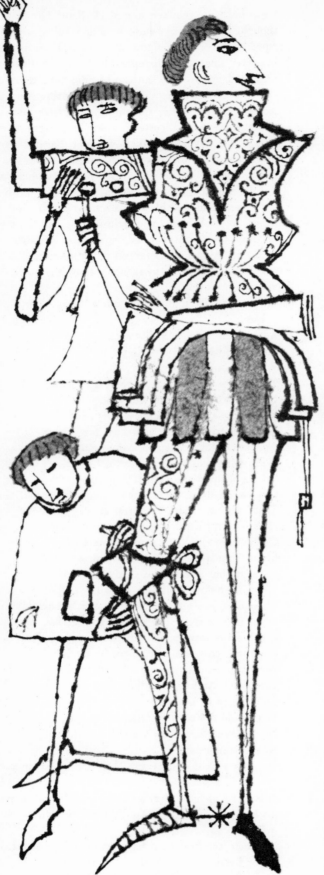

SCENE VII

The French camp, near Agincourt

Enter the CONSTABLE OF FRANCE, *the* LORD RAMBURES, ORLEANS, DAUPHIN, *with others*

CONSTABLE. Tut! I have the best armour of the world. Would it were day!

ORLEANS. You have an excellent armour; but let my horse have his due.

CONSTABLE. It is the best horse of Europe.

ORLEANS. Will it never be morning?

DAUPHIN. My Lord of Orleans, and my lord high Constable, you talk of horse and armour?

ORLEANS. You are as well provided of both as any prince in the world.

DAUPHIN. What a long night is this! I will not change my horse with any that treads but on four pasterns. Ça, ha! he bounds from the earth, as if his entrails were hairs; le cheval volant, the Pegasus, chez les narines de feu! When I bestride him, I soar, I am a hawk. He trots the air; the earth sings when he touches it; the basest horn of his hoof is more musical than the pipe of Hermes.

ORLEANS. He's of the colour of the nutmeg.

DAUPHIN. And of the heat of the ginger. It is a beast for Perseus. He is pure air and fire; and the dull elements of earth and water never appear in him, but only in patient stillness while his rider mounts him. He is indeed a horse; and all other jades you may call beasts.

CONSTABLE. Indeed, my lord, it is a most absolute and excellent horse.

DAUPHIN. It is the prince of palfreys; his neigh is like the bidding of a monarch and his countenance enforces homage.

ORLEANS. No more, cousin.

DAUPHIN. Nay, the man hath no wit that cannot, from the rising of the lark to the lodging of the lamb, vary deserved praise on my palfrey. It is a theme as fluent as the sea; turn the sands into eloquent tongues, and my horse is argument for them all. 'Tis a subject for a sovereign to reason on, and for a sovereign's sovereign to ride on; and for the world, familiar to us and unknown, to lay apart their particular functions and wonder at him. I once writ a sonnet in his praise and began thus: "Wonder of nature,"—

ORLEANS. I have heard a sonnet begin so to one's mistress.

DAUPHIN. Then did they imitate that which I composed to my courser, for my horse is my mistress.

ORLEANS. Your mistress bears well.

DAUPHIN. Me well; which is the prescript praise and perfection of a good and particular mistress.

CONSTABLE. Nay, for methought yesterday your mistress shrewdly shook your back.

DAUPHIN. So perhaps did yours.

CONSTABLE. Mine was not bridled.

DAUPHIN. O then belike she was old and gentle; and
you rode, like a kern of Ireland, your French hose off,
and in your strait strossers.

CONSTABLE. You have good judgement in horsemanship.

DAUPHIN. Be warned by me, then: they that ride so and
ride not warily, fall into foul bogs. I had rather have
my horse to my mistress.

CONSTABLE. I had as lief have my mistress a jade.

DAUPHIN. I tell thee, constable, my mistress wears his
own hair.

CONSTABLE. I could make as true a boast as that, if I
had a sow to my mistress.

DAUPHIN. Le chien est retourné à son propre vomisse-
ment, et la truie lavée au bourbier: thou makest use
of anything.

CONSTABLE. Yet do I not use my horse for my mistress,
or any such proverb so little kin to the purpose.

RAMBURES. My lord Constable, the armour that I saw
in your tent tonight, are those stars or suns upon it?

CONSTABLE. Stars, my lord.

DAUPHIN. Some of them will fall tomorrow, I hope.

CONSTABLE. And yet my sky shall not want.

DAUPHIN. That may be, for you bear a many super-
fluously, and 'twere more honour some were away.

CONSTABLE. Even as your horse bears your praises; who
would trot as well, were some of your brags dis-
mounted.

DAUPHIN. Would I were able to load him with his
desert! Will it never be day? I will trot tomorrow a
mile, and my way shall be paved with English faces.

CONSTABLE. I will not say so, for fear I should be faced
out of my way. But I would it were morning; for I
would fain be about the ears of the English.

RAMBURES. Who will go to hazard with me for twenty
prisoners?

CONSTABLE. You must first go yourself to hazard, ere
you have them.

DAUPHIN. 'Tis midnight; I'll go arm myself.   *Exit*

ORLEANS. The Dauphin longs for morning.

RAMBURES. He longs to eat the English.

CONSTABLE. I think he will eat all he kills.

ORLEANS. By the white hand of my lady, he's a gallant
prince.

CONSTABLE. Swear by her foot, that she may tread out
the oath.

ORLEANS. He is simply the most active gentleman of
France.

CONSTABLE. Doing is activity; and he will still be doing.

ORLEANS. He never did harm, that I heard of.

CONSTABLE. Nor will do none tomorrow. He will keep
that good name still.

ORLEANS. I know him to be valiant.

CONSTABLE. I was told that by one that knows him better
than you.

ORLEANS. What's he?

CONSTABLE. Marry, he told me so himself; and he said
he cared not who knew it.

ORLEANS. He needs not; it is no hidden virtue in him.

CONSTABLE. By my faith, sir, but it is; never anybody
saw it but his lackey. 'Tis a hooded valour; and when
it appears, it will bate.

ORLEANS. Ill will never said well.

CONSTABLE. I will cap that proverb with ''There is
flattery in friendship.''

ORLEANS. And I will take up that with ''Give the devil
his due.''

CONSTABLE. Well placed; there stands your friend for
the devil. Have at the very eye of that proverb with
''A pox of the devil.''

ORLEANS. You are the better at proverbs, by how much
''A fool's bolt is soon shot.''

CONSTABLE. You have shot over.

ORLEANS. 'Tis not the first time you were overshot.

Enter a Messenger

MESSENGER. My lord high Constable, the English lie
within fifteen hundred paces of your tents.

CONSTABLE. Who hath measured the ground?

MESSENGER. The Lord Grandpré.

CONSTABLE. A valiant and most expert gentleman.
Would it were day! Alas, poor Harry of England! he
longs not for the dawning as we do.

ORLEANS. What a wretched and peevish fellow is this
King of England, to mope with his fatbrained followers so far out of his knowledge!

CONSTABLE. If the English had any apprehension, they
would run away.

ORLEANS. That they lack; for if their heads had any
intellectual armour, they could never wear such
heavy head-pieces.

RAMBURES. That island of England breeds very valiant
creatures; their mastiffs are of unmatchable courage.

ORLEANS. Foolish curs, that run winking into the
mouth of a Russian bear and have their heads crushed
like rotten apples! You may as well say, that's a
valiant flea that dare eat his breakfast on the lip of a
lion.

CONSTABLE. Just, just; and the men do sympathize with
the mastiffs in robustious and rough coming on, leaving their wits with their wives. And then give them
great meals of beef and iron and steel, they will eat
like wolves and fight like devils.

ORLEANS. Ay, but these English are shrewdly out of
beef.

CONSTABLE. Then shall we find tomorrow they have
only stomachs to eat and none to fight. Now is it
time to arm; come, shall we about it?

ORLEANS. It is now two o'clock; but, let me see, by ten
We shall have each a hundred Englishmen.

                                                    Exeunt

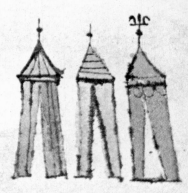

ACT IV

PROLOGUE

Enter Chorus

CHORUS. Now entertain conjecture of a time
When creeping murmur and the poring dark
Fills the wide vessel of the universe.
From camp to camp through the foul womb of night
The hum of either army stilly sounds,
That the fixed sentinels almost receive
The secret whispers of each other's watch.
Fire answers fire, and through their paly flames
Each battle sees the other's umbered face;
Steed threatens steed, in high and boastful neighs
Piercing the night's dull ear; and from the tents
The armourers, accomplishing the knights,
With busy hammers closing rivets up,
Give dreadful note of preparation.
The country cocks do crow, the clocks do toll,
And the third hour of drowsy morning name.
Proud of their numbers and secure in soul,
The confident and over-lusty French
Do the low-rated English play at dice;
And chide the cripple tardy-gaited night
Who, like a foul and ugly witch, doth limp
So tediously away. The poor condemned English,
Like sacrifices, by their watchful fires
Sit patiently and inly ruminate
The morning's danger, and their gesture sad
Investing lank-lean cheeks and war-worn coats
Presenteth them unto the gazing moon
So many horrid ghosts. O now, who will behold
The royal captain of this ruined band
Walking from watch to watch, from tent to tent,
Let him cry "Praise and glory on his head!"
For forth he goes and visits all his host,
Bids them good morrow with a modest smile
And calls them brothers, friends and countrymen.
Upon his royal face there is no note
How dread an army hath enrounded him;
Nor doth he dedicate one jot of colour
Unto the weary and all-watched night,
But freshly looks and over-bears attaint
With cheerful semblance and sweet majesty;
That every wretch, pining and pale before,
Beholding him, plucks comfort from his looks.
A largess universal like the sun
His liberal eye doth give to every one,
Thawing cold fear, that mean and gentle all
Behold, as may unworthiness define,
A little touch of Harry in the night.
And so our scene must to the battle fly;
Where—O for pity!—we shall much disgrace
With four or five most vile and ragged foils,
Right ill-disposed in brawl ridiculous,
The name of Agincourt. Yet sit and see
Minding true things by what their mockeries be.
Exit

SCENE I *The English camp at Agincourt*

Enter KING HENRY, BEDFORD, *and* GLOUCESTER

KING HENRY. Gloucester, 'tis true that we are in great
    danger;
  The greater therefore should our courage be.
  Good morrow, brother Bedford. God Almighty!
  There is some soul of goodness in things evil,
  Would men observingly distil it out;
  For our bad neighbour makes us early stirrers,
  Which is both healthful and good husbandry.
  Besides, they are our outward consciences,
  And preachers to us all, admonishing
  That we should dress us fairly for our end.
  Thus may we gather honey from the weed,
  And make a moral of the devil himself.

Enter ERPINGHAM

  Good morrow, old Sir Thomas Erpingham!
  A good soft pillow for that good white head
  Were better than a churlish turf of France.
ERPINGHAM. Not so, my liege. This lodging likes me
    better,
  Since I may say "Now lie I like a king."
KING HENRY. 'Tis good for men to love their present
    pains
  Upon example; so the spirit is eased.
  And when the mind is quickened, out of doubt,
  The organs, though defunct and dead before,
  Break up their drowsy grave and newly move,
  With casted slough and fresh legerity.
  Lend me thy cloak, Sir Thomas. Brothers both,
  Commend me to the princes in our camp;
  Do my good morrow to them, and anon
  Desire them all to my pavilion.
GLOUCESTER. We shall, my liege.
ERPINGHAM. Shall I attend your grace?
KING HENRY.   No, my good knight;
  Go with my brothers to my lords of England.
  I and my bosom must debate awhile,
  And then I would no other company.
ERPINGHAM. The Lord in heaven bless thee, noble
    Harry!   *Exeunt all but* KING
KING HENRY. God-a-mercy, old heart! thou speak'st
  cheerfully.

Enter PISTOL

PISTOL. Qui va la?
KING HENRY. A friend.
PISTOL. Discuss unto me; art thou officer?
  Or art thou base, common and popular?
KING HENRY. I am a gentleman of a company.
PISTOL. Trail'st thou the puissant pike?
KING HENRY. Even so. What are you?
PISTOL. As good a gentleman as the emperor.
KING HENRY. Then you are a better than the King.

PISTOL. The King 's a bawcock, and a heart of gold,
  A lad of life, an imp of fame;
  Of parents good, of fist most valiant.
  I kiss his dirty shoe, and from heart-string
  I love the lovely bully. What is thy name?
KING HENRY. Harry le Roy.
PISTOL. Le Roy! a Cornish name; art thou of Cornish
  crew?
KING HENRY. No, I am a Welshman.
PISTOL. Know'st thou Fluellen?
KING HENRY. Yes.
PISTOL. Tell him, I 'll knock his leek about his pate
  Upon Saint Davy's day.
KING HENRY. Do not you wear your dagger in your cap
  that day, lest he knock that about yours.
PISTOL. Art thou his friend?
KING HENRY. And his kinsman too.
PISTOL. The figo for thee, then!
KING HENRY. I thank you. God be with you!
PISTOL. My name is Pistol called.   *Exit*
KING HENRY. It sorts well with your fierceness.

Enter FLUELLEN *and* GOWER

GOWER. Captain Fluellen!
FLUELLEN. So! in the name of Jesu Christ, speak lower.
  It is the greatest admiration in the universal world,
  when the true and aunchient prerogatifes and laws of
  the wars is not kept. If you would take the pains but
  to examine the wars of Pompey the Great, you shall
  find, I warrant you, that there is no tiddle taddle nor
  pibble pabble in Pompey's camp; I warrant you, you
  shall find the ceremonies of the wars, and the cares
  of it, and the forms of it, and the sobriety of it, and
  the modesty of it, to be otherwise.
GOWER. Why, the enemy is loud; you hear him all
  night.
FLUELLEN. If the enemy is an ass and a fool and a prating
  coxcomb, is it meet, think you, that we should also,
  look you, be an ass and a fool and a prating coxcomb?
  In your own conscience, now?
GOWER. I will speak lower.
FLUELLEN. I pray you and beseech you that you will.
             Exeunt GOWER *and* FLUELLEN
KING HENRY. Though it appear a little out of fashion,
  There is much care and valour in this Welshman.

Enter three soldiers,
JOHN BATES, ALEXANDER COURT,
and MICHAEL WILLIAMS

COURT. Brother John Bates, is not that the morning
  which breaks yonder?
BATES. I think it be; but we have no great cause to desire
  the approach of day.

WILLIAMS. We see yonder the beginning of the day, but I think we shall never see the end of it. Who goes there?

KING HENRY. A friend.

WILLIAMS. Under what captain serve you?

KING HENRY. Under Sir Thomas Erpingham.

WILLIAMS. A good old commander and a most kind gentleman. I pray you, what thinks he of our estate?

KING HENRY. Even as men wrecked upon a sand, that look to be washed off the next tide.

BATES. He hath not told his thought to the King?

KING HENRY. No; nor it is not meet he should. For, though I speak it to you, I think the King is but a man, as I am—the violet smells to him as it doth to me; the element shows to him as it doth to me; all his senses have but human conditions—his ceremonies laid by, in his nakedness he appears but a man; and though his affections are higher mounted than ours, yet, when they stoop, they stoop with the like wing. Therefore when he sees reason of fears, as we do, his fears, out of doubt, be of the same relish as ours are. Yet, in reason, no man should possess him with any appearance of fear, lest he, by showing it, should dishearten his army.

BATES. He may show what outward courage he will, but I believe, as cold a night as 'tis, he could wish himself in Thames up to the neck; and so I would he were, and I by him, at all adventures, so we were quit here.

KING HENRY. By my troth, I will speak my conscience of the King. I think he would not wish himself anywhere but where he is.

BATES. Then I would he were here alone; so should he be sure to be ransomed, and a many poor men's lives saved.

KING HENRY. I dare say you love him not so ill, to wish him here alone, howsoever you speak this to feel other men's minds. Methinks I could not die anywhere so contented as in the King's company, his cause being just and his quarrel honourable.

WILLIAMS. That's more than we know.

BATES. Ay, or more than we should seek after; for we know enough, if we know we are the King's subjects. If his cause be wrong, our obedience to the King wipes the crime of it out of us.

WILLIAMS. But if the cause be not good, the King himself hath a heavy reckoning to make, when all those legs and arms and heads, chopped off in a battle, shall join together at the latter day and cry all "We died at such a place"; some swearing, some crying for a surgeon, some upon their wives left poor behind them, some upon the debts they owe, some upon their children rawly left. I am afeard there are few die well that die in a battle; for how can they charitably dispose of anything, when blood is their argument? Now, if these men do not die well, it will be a black

matter for the king that led them to it; whom to disobey were against all proportion of subjection.

KING HENRY. So, if a son that is by his father sent about merchandise do sinfully miscarry upon the sea, the imputation of his wickedness, by your rule, should be imposed upon his father that sent him; or if a servant, under his master's command transporting a sum of money, be assailed by robbers and die in many irreconciled iniquities, you may call the business of the master the author of the servant's damnation. But this is not so. The king is not bound to answer the particular endings of his soldiers, the father of his son, nor the master of his servant; for they purpose not their death, when they purpose their services. Besides, there is no king, be his cause never so spotless, if it come to the arbitrement of swords, can try it out with all unspotted soldiers. Some peradventure have on them the guilt of premeditated and contrived murder; some, of beguiling virgins with the broken seals of perjury; some, making the wars their bulwark, that have before gored the gentle bosom of peace with pillage and robbery. Now, if these men have defeated the law and outrun native punishment, though they can outstrip men, they have no wings to fly from God. War is his beadle, war is his vengeance; so that here men are punished for before-breach of the king's laws in now the king's quarrel. Where they feared the death, they have borne life away; and where they would be safe, they perish. Then if they die unprovided, no more is the king guilty of their damnation than he was before guilty of those impieties for the which they are now visited. Every subject's duty is the king's; but every subject's soul is his own. Therefore should every soldier in the wars do as every sick man in his bed, wash every mote out of his conscience; and dying so, death is to him advantage; or not dying, the time was blessedly lost wherein such preparation was gained. And in him that escapes, it were not sin to think that, making God so free an offer, He let him outlive that day to see His greatness and to teach others how they should prepare.

WILLIAMS. 'Tis certain, every man that dies ill, the ill upon his own head, the King is not to answer it.

BATES. I do not desire he should answer for me; and yet I determine to fight lustily for him.

KING HENRY. I myself heard the King say he would not be ransomed.

WILLIAMS. Ay, he said so, to make us fight cheerfully; but when our throats are cut, he may be ransomed, and we ne'er the wiser.

KING HENRY. If I live to see it, I will never trust his word after.

WILLIAMS. You pay him then. That's a perilous shot out of an elder-gun, that a poor and a private displeasure can do against a monarch! You may as well go about to turn the sun to ice with fanning in his face with a peacock's feather. You'll never trust his word after! Come, 'tis a foolish saying.

KING HENRY. Your reproof is something too round. I should be angry with you, if the time were convenient.

WILLIAMS. Let it be a quarrel between us, if you live.

KING HENRY. I embrace it.

WILLIAMS. How shall I know thee again?

KING HENRY. Give me any gage of thine, and I will wear it in my bonnet; then, if ever thou darest acknowledge it, I will make it my quarrel.

WILLIAMS. Here's my glove; give me another of thine.

KING HENRY. There.

WILLIAMS. This will I also wear in my cap. If ever thou come to me and say, after tomorrow, "This is my glove," by this hand, I will take thee a box on the ear.

KING HENRY. If ever I live to see it, I will challenge it.

WILLIAMS. Thou darest as well be hanged.

KING HENRY. Well, I will do it, though I take thee in the King's company.

WILLIAMS. Keep thy word; fare thee well.

BATES. Be friends, you English fools, be friends; we have French quarrels enow, if you could tell how to reckon.

KING HENRY. Indeed, the French may lay twenty French crowns to one, they will beat us; for they bear them on their shoulders. But it is no English treason to cut French crowns, and tomorrow the King himself will be a clipper.

Exeunt Soldiers

Upon the King! let us our lives, our souls,
Our debts, our careful wives,
Our children and our sins lay on the King!
We must bear all. O hard condition,
Twin-born with greatness, subject to the breath
Of every fool, whose sense no more can feel
But his own wringing! What infinite heart's-ease
Must kings neglect, that private men enjoy!
And what have kings, that privates have not too,
Save ceremony, save general ceremony?
And what art thou, thou idol ceremony?
What kind of god art thou, that suffer'st more
Of mortal griefs than do thy worshippers?
What are thy rents? what are thy comings in?
O ceremony, show me but thy worth!
What is thy soul of adoration?
Art thou aught else but place, degree and form,
Creating awe and fear in other men?
Wherein thou art less happy being feared
Than they in fearing.
What drink'st thou oft, instead of homage sweet,
But poisoned flattery? O, be sick, great greatness,
And bid thy ceremony give thee cure!
Think'st thou the fiery fever will go out
With titles blown from adulation?
Will it give place to flexure and low bending?

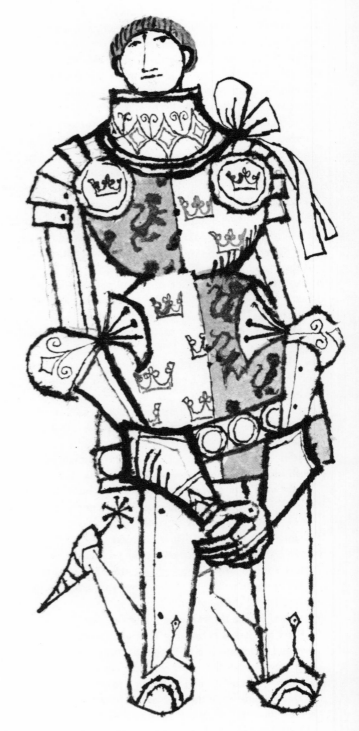

Canst thou, when thou command'st the beggar's knee,
Command the health of it? No, thou proud dream,
That play'st so subtly with a king's repose;
I am a king that find thee, and I know
'Tis not the balm, the sceptre and the ball,
The sword, the mace, the crown imperial,
The intertissued robe of gold and pearl,
The farced title running 'fore the king,
The throne he sits on, nor the tide of pomp
That beats upon the high shore of this world,
No, not all these, thrice-gorgeous ceremony,
Not all these, laid in bed majestical,
Can sleep so soundly as the wretched slave,
Who with a body filled and vacant mind
Gets him to rest, crammed with distressful bread;
Never sees horrid night, the child of hell,
But, like a lackey, from the rise to set
Sweats in the eye of Phœbus and all night
Sleeps in Elysium; next day after dawn
Doth rise and help Hyperion to his horse,
And follows so the ever-running year,
With profitable labour, to his grave.
And, but for ceremony, such a wretch,
Winding up days with toil and nights with sleep,
Had the fore-hand and vantage of a king.
The slave, a member of the country's peace,
Enjoys it; but in gross brain little wots
What watch the king keeps to maintain the peace,
Whose hours the peasant best advantages.

Re-enter ERPINGHAM

ERPINGHAM. My lord, your nobles, jealous of your
   absence,
   Seek through your camp to find you.
KING HENRY.   Good old knight,
   Collect them all together at my tent;
   I 'll be before thee.
ERPINGHAM.   I shall do 't, my lord.   *Exit*
KING HENRY. O God of battles! steel my soldiers'
   hearts;
   Possess them not with fear; take from them now
   The sense of reckoning, if the opposed numbers
   Pluck their hearts from them. Not today, O Lord,
   O, not today, think not upon the fault
   My father made in compassing the crown!
   I Richard's body have interred new,
   And on it have bestowed more contrite tears
   Than from it issued forced drops of blood.
   Five hundred poor I have in yearly pay,
   Who twice a day their withered hands hold up
   Toward heaven, to pardon blood; and I have built
   Two chantries, where the sad and solemn priests
   Sing still for Richard's soul. More will I do;
   Though all that I can do is nothing worth,
   Since that my penitence comes after all,
   Imploring pardon.

Re-enter GLOUCESTER

GLOUCESTER. My liege!
KING HENRY. My brother Gloucester's voice? Ay;
   I know thy errand, I will go with thee;
   The day, my friends and all things stay for me. *Exeunt*

SCENE II *The French camp*

Enter the DAUPHIN, ORLEANS, RAMBURES, *and others*

ORLEANS. The sun doth gild our armour; up, my lords!
DAUPHIN. Montez à cheval! My horse! varlet! laquais!
   ha!
ORLEANS. O brave spirit!
DAUPHIN. Via! les eaux et la terre.
ORLEANS. Rien puis? l'air et le feu.
DAUPHIN. Ciel, cousin Orleans.

Enter CONSTABLE

Now, my lord Constable!
CONSTABLE. Hark, how our steeds for present service
   neigh!
DAUPHIN. Mount them, and make incision in their
   hides,
   That their hot blood may spin in English eyes,
   And dout them with superfluous courage, ha!
RAMBURES. What, will you have them weep our horses'
   blood?
   How shall we, then, behold their natural tears?

Enter Messenger

MESSENGER. The English are embattled, you French
   peers.
CONSTABLE. To horse, you gallant princes! straight to
   horse!
   Do but behold yon poor and starved band,
   And your fair show shall suck away their souls,
   Leaving them but the shales and husks of men.
   There is not work enough for all our hands;
   Scarce blood enough in all their sickly veins
   To give each naked curtle-axe a stain,
   That our French gallants shall today draw out,
   And sheathe for lack of sport. Let us but blow on
   them;
   The vapour of our valour will o'erturn them.
   'Tis positive 'gainst all exceptions, lords,
   That our superfluous lackeys and our peasants,
   Who in unnecessary action swarm
   About our squares of battle, were enow
   To purge this field of such a hilding foe,
   Though we upon this mountain's basis by
   Took stand for idle speculation.

But that our honours must not. What's to say?
A very little little let us do,
And all is done. Then let the trumpets sound
The tucket sonance and the note to mount;
For our approach shall so much dare the field
That England shall couch down in fear and yield.

Enter GRANDPRE

GRANDPRE. Why do you stay so long, my lords of
    France?
Yon island carrions, desperate of their bones,
Ill-favouredly become the morning field;
Their ragged curtains poorly are let loose,
And our air shakes them passing scornfully;
Big Mars seems bankrupt in their beggared host
And faintly through a rusty beaver peeps;
The horsemen sit like fixed candlesticks,
With torch-staves in their hand; and their poor jades
Lob down their heads, dropping the hides and hips,
The gum down-roping from their pale-dead eyes,
And in their pale dull mouths the gimmal bit
Lies foul with chewed grass, still and motionless;
And their executors, the knavish crows,
Fly o'er them, all impatient for their hour.
Description cannot suit itself in words
To demonstrate the life of such a battle
In life so lifeless as it shows itself.
CONSTABLE. They have said their prayers, and they stay
    for death.
DAUPHIN. Shall we go send them dinners and fresh
    suits
And give their fasting horses provender,
And after fight with them?
CONSTABLE. I stay but for my guidon. To the field!
I will the banner from a trumpet take,
And use it for my haste. Come, come, away!
The sun is high, and we outwear the day.

Exeunt

SCENE III *The English camp*

Enter GLOUCESTER, BEDFORD, EXETER, ERPINGHAM, *with all his host;* SALISBURY *and* WESTMORELAND

GLOUCESTER. Where is the King?
BEDFORD. The King himself is rode to view their battle.
WESTMORELAND. Of fighting men they have full three
    score thousand.
EXETER. There's five to one; besides, they all are fresh.
SALISBURY. God's arm strike with us! 'tis a fearful odds.
God be wi' you, princes all; I'll to my charge.
If we no more meet till we meet in heaven,
Then, joyfully, my noble Lord of Bedford,
My dear Lord Gloucester, and my good Lord Exeter,
And my kind kinsman, warriors all, adieu!
BEDFORD. Farewell, good Salisbury; and good luck go
    with thee!
EXETER. Farewell, kind lord. Fight valiantly today;
And yet I do thee wrong to mind thee of it,
For thou art framed of the firm truth of valour.

Exit SALISBURY

BEDFORD. He is as full of valour as of kindness;
Princely in both.

Enter the KING

WESTMORELAND.   O that we now had here
But one ten thousand of those men in England
That do no work today!
KING HENRY.   What's he that wishes so?
My cousin Westmoreland? No, my fair cousin,
If we are marked to die, we are enow
To do our country loss; and if to live,
The fewer men, the greater share of honour.
God's will! I pray thee, wish not one man more.
By Jove, I am not covetous for gold,
Nor care I who doth feed upon my cost;
It yearns me not if men my garments wear—
Such outward things dwell not in my desires.
But if it be a sin to covet honour,
I am the most offending soul alive.
No, faith, my coz, wish not a man from England.
God's peace! I would not lose so great an honour
As one man more, methinks, would share from me
For the best hope I have. O, do not wish one more!
Rather proclaim it, Westmoreland, through my host,
That he which hath no stomach to this fight,
Let him depart; his passport shall be made
And crowns for convoy put into his purse.
We would not die in that man's company
That fears his fellowship to die with us.
This day is called the feast of Crispian.
He that outlives this day, and comes safe home,
Will stand a tip-toe when this day is named,
And rouse him at the name of Crispian.
He that shall live this day, and see old age,
Will yearly on the vigil feast his neighbours,
And say "Tomorrow is Saint Crispian."
Then will he strip his sleeve and show his scars,
And say "These wounds I had on Crispin's day."
Old men forget; yet all shall be forgot,
But he'll remember with advantages
What feats he did that day. Then shall our names,
Familiar in his mouth as household words,
Harry the King, Bedford and Exeter,
Warwick and Talbot, Salisbury and Gloucester,
Be in their flowing cups freshly remembered.
This story shall the good man teach his son;
And Crispin Crispian shall ne'er go by,

ACT IV, SCENE III

From this day to the ending of the world,
But we in it shall be remembered,
We few, we happy few, we band of brothers;
For he today that sheds his blood with me
Shall be my brother. Be he ne'er so vile,
This day shall gentle his condition;
And gentlemen in England now a-bed
Shall think themselves accursed they were not here,
And hold their manhoods cheap whiles any speaks
That fought with us upon Saint Crispin's day.

Re-enter SALISBURY

SALISBURY. My sovereign lord, bestow yourself with
    speed!
  The French are bravely in their battles set,
  And will with all expedience charge on us.
KING HENRY. All things are ready, if our minds be so.
WESTMORELAND. Perish the man whose mind is back-
    ward now!
KING HENRY. Thou dost not wish more help from Eng-
    land, coz?
WESTMORELAND. God's will! my liege, would you and
    I alone,
  Without more help, could fight this royal battle!
KING HENRY. Why, now thou hast unwished five thou-
    sand men;
  Which likes me better than to wish us one.
  You know your places; God be with you all!

Tucket. Enter MONTJOY

MONTJOY. Once more I come to know of thee, King
    Harry,
  If for thy ransom thou wilt now compound,
  Before thy most assured overthrow;
  For certainly thou art so near the gulf,
  Thou needs must be englutted. Besides, in mercy,
  The Constable desires thee thou wilt mind
  Thy followers of repentance; that their souls
  May make a peaceful and a sweet retire
  From off these fields, where, wretches, their poor
    bodies
  Must lie and fester.
KING HENRY.   Who hath sent thee now?
MONTJOY. The Constable of France.
KING HENRY. I pray thee, bear my former answer back.
  Bid them achieve me and then sell my bones.
  Good God! why should they mock poor fellows thus?
  The man that once did sell the lion's skin
  While the beast lived, was killed with hunting him.
  A many of our bodies shall no doubt
  Find native graves; upon the which, I trust,
  Shall witness live in brass of this day's work;
  And those that leave their valiant bones in France,
  Dying like men, though buried in your dunghills,
  They shall be famed; for there the sun shall greet them,
  And draw their honours reeking up to heaven,
  Leaving their earthly parts to choke your clime,
  The smell whereof shall breed a plague in France.
  Mark then abounding valour in our English,
  That being dead, like to the bullet's grazing,
  Break out into a second course of mischief,
  Killing in relapse of mortality.
  Let me speak proudly: tell the Constable
  We are but warriors for the working-day;
  Our gayness and our gilt are all besmirched
  With rainy marching in the painful field;
  There's not a piece of feather in our host—
  Good argument, I hope, we will not fly—

And time hath worn us into slovenry.
But, by the mass, our hearts are in the trim;
And my poor soldiers tell me, yet ere night
They'll be in fresher robes, or they will pluck
The gay new coats o'er the French soldiers' heads
And turn them out of service. If they do this—
As, if God please, they shall—my ransom then
Will soon be levied. Herald, save thou thy labour;
Come thou no more for ransom, gentle herald.
They shall have none, I swear, but these my joints;
Which if they have as I will leave 'em them,

Shall yield them little, tell the Constable.
MONTJOY. I shall, King Harry. And so fare thee well.
 Thou never shalt hear herald any more.   *Exit*
KING HENRY. I fear thou 'lt once more come again for
 ransom.

Enter YORK

YORK. My lord, most humbly on my knee I beg
 The leading of the vaward.
KING HENRY. Take it, brave York. Now, soldiers,
 march away!
 And how thou pleasest, God, dispose the day! *Exeunt*

SCENE IV *The field of battle*

Alarum. Excursions. Enter PISTOL, French Soldier, *and* Boy

PISTOL. Yield, cur!
FRENCH SOLDIER. Je pense que vous êtes gentilhomme
 de bonne qualité.
PISTOL. Qualtitie calmie custure me! Art thou a gentle-
 man? What is thy name? Discuss!
FRENCH SOLDIER. O Seigneur Dieu!
PISTOL. O, Signieur Dew should be a gentleman.
 Perpend my words, O Signieur Dew, and mark:
 O Signieur Dew, thou diest on point of fox,
 Except, O signieur, thou do give to me
 Egregious ransom.
FRENCH SOLDIER. O, prenez miséricorde! ayez pitié de
 moi!
PISTOL. Moy shall not serve; I will have forty moys,
 Or I will fetch thy rim out at thy throat
 In drops of crimson blood.
FRENCH SOLDIER. Est-il impossible d'échapper la force
 de ton bras?
PISTOL. Brass, cur!
 Thou damned and luxurious mountain goat,
 Offer'st me brass?
FRENCH SOLDIER. O pardonnez moi!
PISTOL. Say'st thou me so? Is that a ton of moys?
 Come hither, boy! Ask me this slave in French
 What is his name.
BOY. Ecoutez: comment êtes-vous appelé?
FRENCH SOLDIER. Monsieur le Fer.
BOY. He says his name is Master Fer.
PISTOL. Master Fer! I'll fer him, and firk him, and
 ferret him. Discuss the same in French unto him.
BOY. I do not know the French for fer, and ferret,
 and firk.
PISTOL. Bid him prepare; for I will cut his throat.
FRENCH SOLDIER. Que dit-il, monsieur?
BOY. Il me commande de vous dire que vous faites
 vous prêt; car ce soldat ici est disposé tout à cette
 heure de couper votre gorge.
PISTOL. Owy, cuppele gorge, permafoy,
 Peasant, unless thou give me crowns, brave crowns;
 Or mangled shalt thou be by this my sword.

FRENCH SOLDIER. O, je vous supplie, pour l'amour de
 Dieu, me pardonner! Je suis gentilhomme de bonne
 maison. Gardez ma vie, et je vous donnerai deux
 cents écus.
PISTOL. What are his words?
BOY. He prays you to save his life. He is a gentleman of a
 good house; and for his ransom he will give you two
 hundred crowns.
PISTOL. Tell him my fury shall abate, and I
 The crowns will take.
FRENCH SOLDIER. Petit monsieur, que dit-il?
BOY. Encore qu'il est contre son jurement de pardonner
 aucun prisonnier, néanmoins, pour les écus que vous
 l'avez promis, il est content de vous donner la
 liberté, le franchisement.
FRENCH SOLDIER. Sur mes genoux je vous donne mille
 remercîments; et je m'estime heureux que je suis
 tombé entre les mains d'un chevalier, je pense, le
 plus brave, vaillant, et très distingué seigneur
 d'Angleterre.
PISTOL. Expound unto me, boy.
BOY. He gives you, upon his knees, a thousand thanks;
 and he esteems himself happy that he hath fallen into
 the hands of one, as he thinks, the most brave, valor-
 ous, and thrice-worthy signieur of England.
PISTOL. As I suck blood, I will some mercy show.
 Follow me!
BOY. Suivez-vous le grand capitaine.

Exeunt PISTOL *and* French Soldier

I did never know so full a voice issue from so empty a
heart; but the saying is true, "The empty vessel
makes the greatest sound." Bardolph and Nym had
ten times more valour than this roaring devil i' the
old play, that every one may pare his nails with a
wooden dagger; and they are both hanged; and so
would this be, if he durst steal anything adventurously.
I must stay with the lackeys, with the luggage of our
camp. The French might have a good prey of us, if
he knew of it; for there is none to guard it but boys.

Exit

SCENE V *Another part of the field*

Enter CONSTABLE, ORLEANS, BOURBON, DAUPHIN, *and* RAMBURES

CONSTABLE. O diable!

ORLEANS. O seigneur! le jour est perdu, tout est perdu!

DAUPHIN. Mort de ma vie! all is confounded, all!
  Reproach and everlasting shame
  Sits mocking in our plumes. O méchante fortune!
  Do not run away.   *A short alarum*

CONSTABLE.   Why, all our ranks are broke.

DAUPHIN. O perdurable shame! let's stab ourselves.
  Be these the wretches that we played at dice for?

ORLEANS. Is this the king we sent to for his ransom?

BOURBON. Shame and eternal shame, nothing but
  shame!
  Let us die in honour; once more back again!

And he that will not follow Bourbon now,
  Let him go hence, and with his cap in hand,
  Like a base pandar, hold the chamber-door
  Whilst by a slave, no gentler than my dog,
  His fairest daughter is contaminated.

CONSTABLE. Disorder, that hath spoiled us, friend us
  now!
  Let us on heaps go offer up our lives.

ORLEANS. We are enow yet living in the field
  To smother up the English in our throngs,
  If any order might be thought upon.

BOURBON. The devil take order now! I'll to the throng;
  Let life be short, else shame will be too long. *Exeunt*

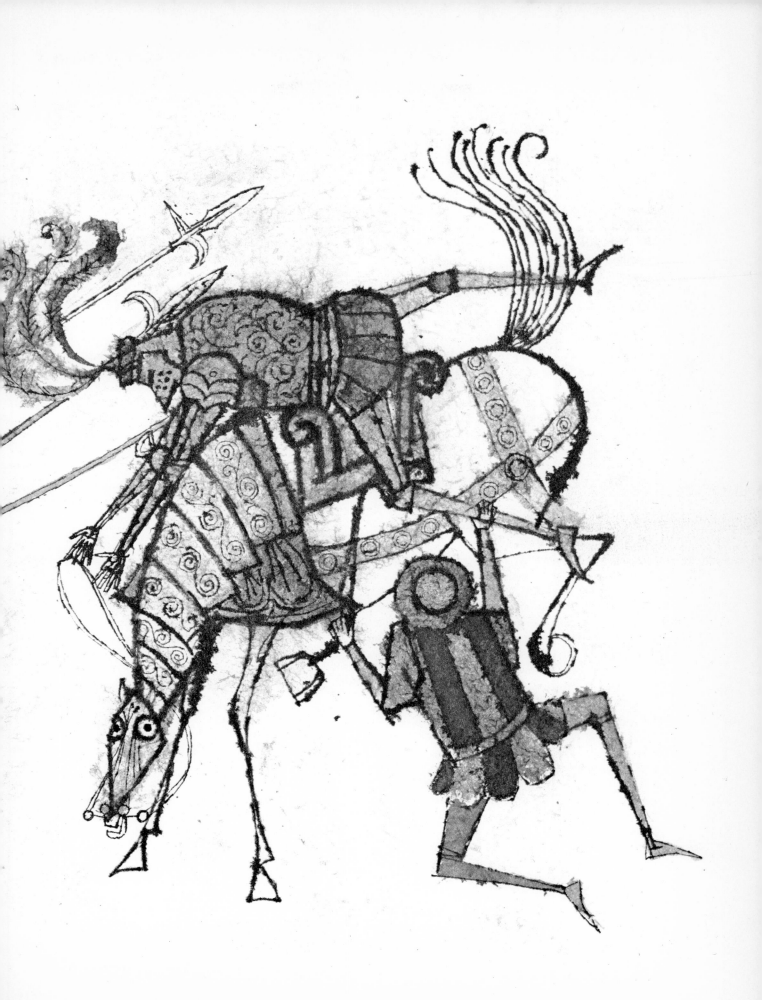

SCENE VI *Another part of the field*

Alarums. Enter KING HENRY *and forces,* EXETER, *and others*

KING HENRY. Well have we done, thrice vailant countrymen,
But all's not done; yet keep the French the field.

EXETER. The Duke of York commends him to your majesty.

KING HENRY. Lives he, good uncle? Thrice within this hour
I saw him down, thrice up again and fighting;
From helmet to the spur all blood he was.

EXETER. In which array, brave soldier, doth he lie,
Larding the plain; and by his bloody side,
Yoke-fellow to his honour-owing wounds,
The noble Earl of Suffolk also lies.
Suffolk first died; and York, all haggled over,
Comes to him, where in gore he lay insteeped,
And takes him by the beard, kisses the gashes
That bloodily did yawn upon his face,
And cries aloud "Tarry, dear cousin Suffolk!
My soul shall thine keep company to heaven;
Tarry, sweet soul, for mine, then fly abreast,
As in this glorious and well-foughten field
We kept together in our chivalry!"
Upon these words I came and cheered him up;
He smiled me in the face, raught me his hand,
And, with a feeble gripe, says "Dear my lord,
Commend my service to my sovereign."
So did he turn and over Suffolk's neck
He threw his wounded arm and kissed his lips;
And so espoused to death, with blood he sealed
A testament of noble-ending love.
The pretty and sweet manner of it forced
Those waters from me which I would have stopped;
But I had not so much of man in me,
And all my mother came into mine eyes
And gave me up to tears.

KING HENRY.   I blame you not;
For, hearing this, I must perforce compound
With mistful eyes, or they will issue too.   *Alarum*
But, hark! what new alarum is this same?
The French have reinforced their scattered men;
Then every soldier kill his prisoners!
Give the word through.   *Exeunt*

SCENE VII *Another part of the field*

Enter FLUELLEN *and* GOWER

FLUELLEN. Kill the poys and the luggage! 'tis expressly against the law of arms; 'tis as arrant a piece of knavery, mark you now, as can be offer't. In your conscience, now, is it not?

GOWER. 'Tis certain there's not a boy left alive; and the cowardly rascals that ran from the battle ha' done this slaughter. Besides, they have burned and carried away all that was in the King's tent; wherefore the King, most worthily, hath caused every soldier to cut his prisoner's throat. O, 'tis a gallant king!

FLUELLEN. Ay, he was porn at Monmouth, Captain Gower. What call you the town's name where Alexander the Pig was born?

GOWER. Alexander the Great.

FLUELLEN. Why, I pray you, is not pig great? the pig, or the great, or the mighty, or the huge, or the magnanimous, are all one reckonings, save the phrase is a little variations.

GOWER. I think Alexander the Great was born in Macedon; his father was called Philip of Macedon, as I take it.

FLUELLEN. I think it is in Macedon where Alexander is porn. I tell you, captain, if you look in the maps of the 'orld, I warrant you sall find, in the comparisons between Macedon and Monmouth, that the situations, look you, is both alike. There is a river in Macedon; and there is also moreover a river at Monmouth. It is called Wye at Monmouth, but it is out of my prains what is the name of the other river; but 'tis all one, 'tis alike as my fingers is to my fingers, and there is salmons in both. If you mark Alexander's life well, Harry of Monmouth's life is come after it indifferent well; for there is figures in all things. Alexander, God knows, and you know, in his rages, and his furies, and his wraths, and his cholers, and his moods, and his displeasures, and his indignations, and also being a little intoxicates in his prains, did, in his ales and his angers, look you, kill his best friend, Cleitus.

GOWER. Our king is not like him in that; he never killed any of his friends.

FLUELLEN. It is not well done, mark you now, to take the tales out of my mouth, ere it is made and finished. I speak but in the figures and comparisons of it. As Alexander killed his friend Cleitus, being in his ales and his cups, so also Harry Monmouth, being in his right wits and his good judgments, turned away the fat knight with the great-belly doublet. He was full of jests, and gipes, and knaveries, and mocks; I have forgot his name.

GOWER. Sir John Falstaff.

FLUELLEN. That is he. I 'll tell you there is good men porn at Monmouth.

GOWER. Here comes his majesty.

Alarum. Enter KING HENRY, *and forces;* WARWICK,
GLOUCESTER, EXETER, *and others*

KING HENRY. I was not angry since I came to France
  Until this instant. Take a trumpet, herald;
  Ride thou unto the horsemen on yon hill.
  If they will fight with us, bid them come down,
  Or void the field; they do offend our sight.
  If they'll do neither, we will come to them,
  And make them skirr away, as swift as stones
  Enforced from the old Assyrian slings.
  Besides, we'll cut the throats of those we have,
  And not a man of them that we shall take
  Shall taste our mercy. Go and tell them so.

Enter MONTJOY

EXETER. Here comes the herald of the French, my liege.
GLOUCESTER. His eyes are humbler than they used to be.
KING HENRY. How now! what means this, herald?
    Know'st thou not
  That I have fined these bones of mine for ransom?
  Com'st thou again for ransom?
MONTJOY.   No, great King,
  I come to thee for charitable license,
  That we may wander o'er this bloody field
  To look our dead, and then to bury them;
  To sort our nobles from our common men,
  For many of our princes—woe the while!—
  Lie drowned and soaked in mercenary blood;
  So do our vulgar drench their peasant limbs
  In blood of princes; and their wounded steeds
  Fret fetlock deep in gore and with wild rage
  Yerk out their armed heels at their dead masters,
  Killing them twice. O, give us leave, great King,
  To view the field in safety and dispose
  Of their dead bodies!
KING HENRY.   I tell thee truly, herald,
  I know not if the day be ours or no;
  For yet a many of your horsemen peer
  And gallop o'er the field.
MONTJOY.   The day is yours.
KING HENRY. Praised be God, and not our strength,
    for it!
  What is this castle called that stands hard by?
MONTJOY. They call it Agincourt.
KING HENRY. Then call we this the field of Agincourt,
  Fought on the day of Crispin Crispianus.
FLUELLEN. Your grandfather of famous memory, an 't
  please your majesty, and your great-uncle Edward the
  Plack Prince of Wales, as I have read in the chronicles,
  fought a most prave pattle here in France.
KING HENRY. They did, Fluellen.
FLUELLEN. Your majesty says very true. If your majesties
  is remembered of it, the Welshmen did good service
  in a garden where leeks did grow, wearing leeks in

their Monmouth caps; which, your majesty know,
to this hour is an honourable badge of the service;
and I do believe your majesty takes no scorn to wear
the leek upon Saint Tavy's day.
KING HENRY. I wear it for a memorable honour;
  For I am Welsh, you know, good countryman.
FLUELLEN. All the water in Wye cannot wash your
  majesty's Welsh plood out of your pody, I can tell
  you that. God pless it and preserve it, as long as it
  pleases his grace, and his majesty too!
KING HENRY. Thanks, good my countryman.
FLUELLEN. By Jeshu, I am your majesty's countryman,
  I care not who know it; I will confess it to all the
  'orld. I need not to be ashamed of your majesty,
  praised be God, so long as your majesty is an honest
  man.
KING HENRY. God keep me so! Our heralds go with
  him.

Bring me just notice of the numbers dead
On both our parts. Call yonder fellow hither.

    Points to WILLIAMS. *Exeunt* Heralds *with* MONTJOY

EXETER. Soldier, you must come to the King.

KING HENRY. Soldier, why wearest thou that glove in thy cap?

WILLIAMS. An 't please your majesty, 'tis the gage of one that I should fight withal, if he be alive.

KING HENRY. An Englishman?

WILLIAMS. An 't please your majesty, a rascal that swaggered with me last night; who, if alive and ever dare to challenge this glove, I have sworn to take him a box o' th' ear; or if I can see my glove in his cap, which he swore, as he was a soldier, he would wear if alive, I will strike it out soundly.

KING HENRY. What think you, Captain Fluellen? Is it fit this soldier keep his oath?

FLUELLEN. He is a craven and a villain else, an 't please your majesty, in my conscience.

KING HENRY. It may be his enemy is a gentleman of great sort, quite from the answer of his degree.

FLUELLEN. Though he be as good a gentleman as the devil is, as Lucifer and Belzebub himself, it is necessary, look your grace, that he keep his vow and his oath. If he be perjured, see you now, his reputation is as arrant a villain and a Jacksauce as ever his black shoe trod upon God's ground and his earth, in my conscience, la!

KING HENRY. Then keep thy vow, sirrah, when thou meetest the fellow.

WILLIAMS. So I will, my liege, as I live.

KING HENRY. Who servest thou under?

WILLIAMS. Under Captain Gower, my liege.

FLUELLEN. Gower is a good captain, and is good knowledge and literatured in the wars.

KING HENRY. Call him hither to me, soldier.

WILLIAMS. I will, my liege.   *Exit*

KING HENRY. Here, Fluellen, wear thou this favour for me and stick it in thy cap. When Alençon and myself were down together, I plucked this glove from his helm. If any man challenge this, he is a friend to Alençon, and an enemy to our person; if thou encounter any such, apprehend him, an thou dost me love.

FLUELLEN. Your grace doo's me as great honours as can be desired in the hearts of his subjects. I would fain see the man, that has but two legs, that shall find himself aggriefed at this glove, that is all; but I would fain see it once, an please God of his grace that I might see.

KING HENRY. Knowest thou Gower?

FLUELLEN. He is my dear friend, an please you.

KING HENRY. Pray thee, go seek him, and bring him to my tent.

FLUELLEN. I will fetch him.   *Exit*

KING HENRY. My Lord of Warwick, and my brother Gloucester,
Follow Fluellen closely at the heels.
The glove which I have given him for a favour
May haply purchase him a box o' th' ear;
It is the soldier's; I by bargain should
Wear it myself. Follow, good cousin Warwick.
If that the soldier strike him, as I judge
By his blunt bearing he will keep his word,
Some sudden mischief may arise of it;
For I do know Fluellen valiant
And, touched with choler, hot as gunpowder,
And quickly will return an injury.
Follow, and see there be no harm between them.
Go you with me, uncle of Exeter.   *Exeunt*

SCENE VIII *Before* KING HENRY's *pavilion*

Enter GOWER *and* WILLIAMS

WILLIAMS. I warrant it is to knight you, captain.

Enter FLUELLEN

FLUELLEN. God's will and his pleasure, captain, I beseech you now, come apace to the King. There is more good toward you peradventure than is in your knowledge to dream of.

WILLIAMS. Sir, know you this glove?

FLUELLEN. Know the glove! I know the glove is a glove.

WILLIAMS. I know this; and thus I challenge it.

    Strikes him

FLUELLEN. 'Sblood! an arrant traitor as any is in the universal world, or in France, or in England!

GOWER. How now, sir! you villain!

WILLIAMS. Do you think I 'll be forsworn?

FLUELLEN. Stand away, Captain Gower; I will give treason his payment into plows, I warrant you.

WILLIAMS. I am no traitor.

FLUELLEN. That's a lie in thy throat. I charge you in his majesty's name, apprehend him. He's a friend of the Duke Alençon's.

Enter WARWICK *and* GLOUCESTER

WARWICK. How now, how now! what's the matter?

FLUELLEN. My Lord of Warwick, here is—praised be God for it!—a most contagious treason come to light, look you, as you shall desire in a summer's day. Here is his majesty.

Enter KING HENRY *and* EXETER

KING HENRY. How now! what's the matter?

FLUELLEN. My liege, here is a villain and a traitor, that, look your grace, has struck the glove which your majesty is take out of the helmet of Alençon.

WILLIAMS. My liege, this was my glove; here is the fellow of it; and he that I gave it to in change promised to wear it in his cap. I promised to strike him, if he did. I met this man with my glove in his cap, and I have been as good as my word.

FLUELLEN. Your majesty hear now, saving your majesty's manhood, what an arrant, rascally, beggarly, lousy knave it is. I hope your majesty is pear me testimony and witness, and will avouchment, that this is the glove of Alençon, that your majesty is give me; in your conscience, now.

KING HENRY. Give me thy glove, soldier; look, here is the fellow of it.
    'Twas I, indeed, thou promised'st to strike;
    And thou hast given me most bitter terms.

FLUELLEN. And please your majesty, let his neck answer for it, if there is any martial law in the world.

KING HENRY. How canst thou make me satisfaction?

WILLIAMS. All offences, my lord, come from the heart. Never came any from mine that might offend your majesty.

KING HENRY. It was ourself thou didst abuse.

WILLIAMS. Your majesty came not like yourself; you appeared to me but as a common man. Witness the night, your garments, your lowliness; and what your highness suffered under that shape, I beseech you take it for your own fault and not mine; for had you been as I took you for, I made no offence; therefore, I beseech your highness, pardon me.

KING HENRY. Here, uncle Exeter, fill this glove with crowns,
    And give it to this fellow. Keep it, fellow;
    And wear it for an honour in thy cap
    Till I do challenge it. Give him the crowns.
    And, captain, you must needs be friends with him.

FLUELLEN. By this day and this light, the fellow has mettle enough in his belly. Hold, there is twelve pence for you; and I pray you to serve God, and keep you out of prawls, and prabbles, and quarrels, and dissensions, and, I warrant you, it is the better for you.

WILLIAMS. I will none of your money.

FLUELLEN. It is with a good will; I can tell you, it will serve you to mend your shoes. Come, wherefore should you be so pashful? Your shoes is not so good. 'Tis a good silling, I warrant you, or I will change it.

Enter an English Herald

KING HENRY. Now, herald, are the dead numbered?

HERALD. Here is the number of the slaughtered French.

KING HENRY. What prisoners of good sort are taken, uncle?

EXETER. Charles Duke of Orleans, nephew to the King;

John Duke of Bourbon, and Lord Bouciqualt;
    Of other lords and barons, knights and squires,
    Full fifteen hundred, besides common men.

KING HENRY. This note doth tell me of ten thousand French
    That in the field lie slain. Of princes, in this number,
    And nobles bearing banners, there lie dead
    One hundred twenty six; added to these,
    Of knights, esquires, and gallant gentlemen,
    Eight thousand and four hundred, of the which,
    Five hundred were but yesterday dubbed knights.
    So that, in these ten thousand they have lost,
    There are but sixteen hundred mercenaries;
    The rest are princes, barons, lords, knights, squires,
    And gentlemen of blood and quality.
    The names of those their nobles that lie dead:
    Charles Delabreth, high Constable of France;
    Jaques of Chatillon, admiral of France;
    The master of the cross-bows, Lord Rambures;
    Great Master of France, the brave Sir Guichard Dauphin;
    John Duke of Alençon; Anthony Duke of Brabant,
    The brother to the Duke of Burgundy;
    And Edward Duke of Bar; of lusty earls,
    Grandpré and Roussi, Fauconberg and Foix,
    Beaumont and Marle, Vaudemont and Lestrale.
    Here was a royal fellowship of death!
    Where is the number of our English dead?

                    Herald *shows him another paper*
    Edward the Duke of York, the Earl of Suffolk,
    Sir Richard Ketly, Davy Gam, esquire;
    None else of name; and of all other men
    But five and twenty. O God, thy arm was here;
    And not to us, but to thy arm alone,
    Ascribe we all! When, without stratagem,
    But in plain shock and even play of battle,
    Was ever known so great and little loss
    On one part and on the other? Take it, God,
    For it is none but thine!

EXETER.   'Tis wonderful!

KING HENRY. Come, go we in procession to the village.
    And be it death proclaimed through our host
    To boast of this or take that praise from God
    Which is his only.

FLUELLEN. Is it not lawful, an please your majesty, to tell how many is killed?

KING HENRY. Yes, captain; but with this acknowledgment,
    That God fought for us.

FLUELLEN. Yes, my conscience, he did us great good.

KING HENRY. Do we all holy rites:
    Let there be sung "Non nobis," and "Te Deum";
    The dead with charity enclosed in clay.
    And then to Calais; and to England then,
    Where ne'er from France arrived more happy men.
                                            Exeunt

ACT V

PROLOGUE

Enter Chorus

CHORUS. Vouchsafe to those that have not read the
    story,
  That I may prompt them; and of such as have,
  I humbly pray them to admit the excuse
  Of time, of numbers, and due course of things,
  Which cannot in their huge and proper life
  Be here presented. Now we bear the King
  Toward Calais. Grant him there; there seen,
  Heave him away upon your winged thoughts
  Athwart the sea. Behold, the English beach
  Pales in the flood with men, with wives and boys,
  Whose shouts and claps out-voice the deep-mouthed
    sea,
  Which like a mighty whiffler 'fore the King
  Seems to prepare his way. So let him land,
  And solemnly see him set on to London.
  So swift a pace hath thought that even now
  You may imagine him upon Blackheath;
  Where that his lords desire him to have borne
  His bruised helmet and his bended sword
  Before him through the city. He forbids it,
  Being free from vainness and self-glorious pride;
  Giving full trophy, signal and ostent
  Quite from himself to God. But now behold,
  In the quick forge and working-house of thought,
  How London doth pour out her citizens!
  The mayor and all his brethren in best sort,
  Like to the senators of the antique Rome,
  With the plebeians swarming at their heels,
  Go forth and fetch their conquering Cæsar in—
  As by a lower but loving likelihood,
  Were now the general of our gracious empress,
  As in good time he may, from Ireland coming,
  Bringing rebellion broached on his sword,
  How many would the peaceful city quit,
  To welcome him! much more, and much more cause,
  Did they this Harry. Now in London place him,
  As yet the lamentation of the French
  Invites the King of England's stay at home.
  The emperor's coming in behalf of France,
  To order peace between them; and omit
  All the occurrences, whatever chanced,
  Till Harry's back-return again to France.
  There must we bring him; and myself have played
  The interim, by remembering you 'tis past.
  Then brook abridgement, and your eyes advance,
  After your thoughts, straight back again to France.

Exit

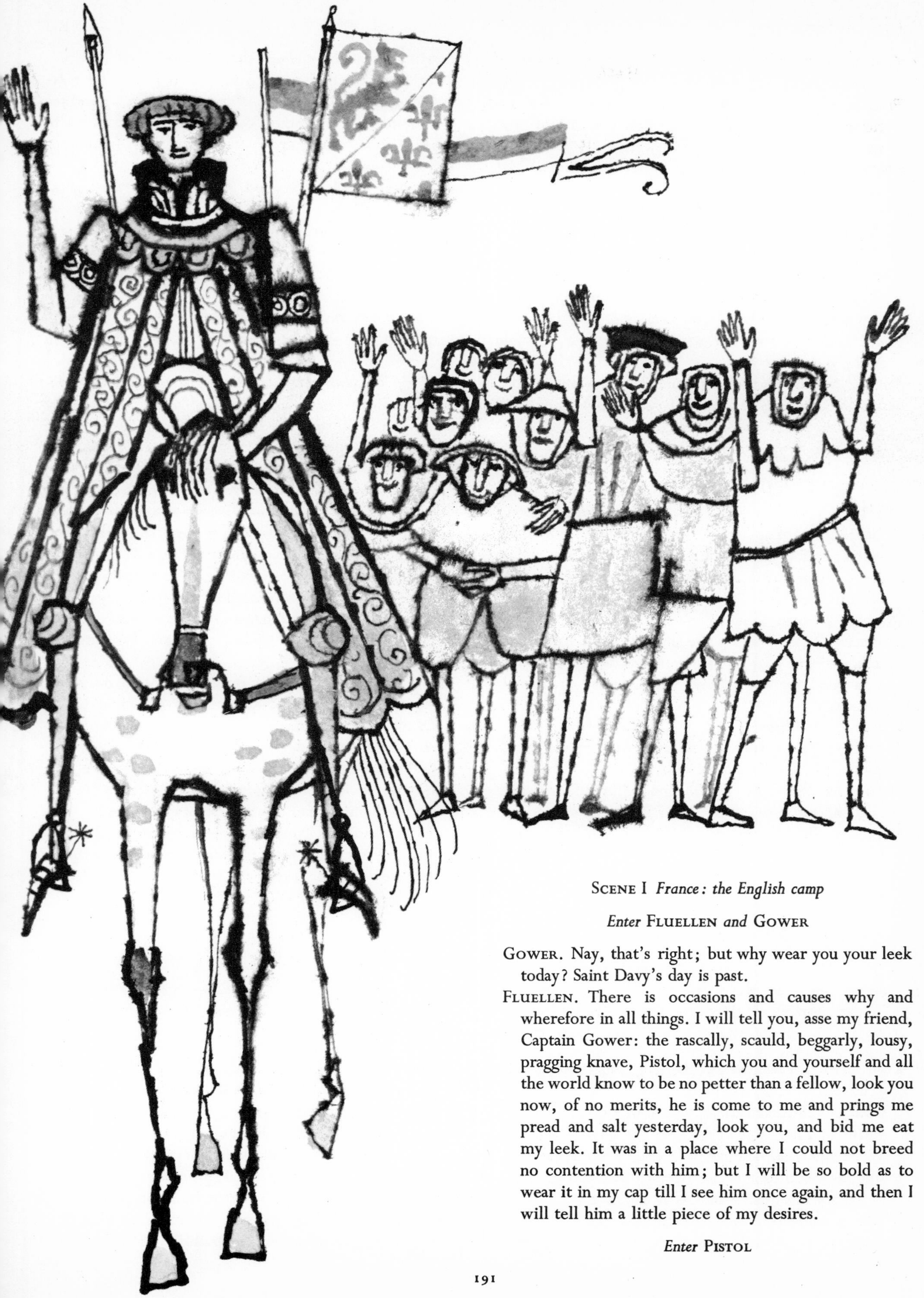

SCENE I *France: the English camp*

Enter FLUELLEN *and* GOWER

GOWER. Nay, that's right; but why wear you your leek today? Saint Davy's day is past.

FLUELLEN. There is occasions and causes why and wherefore in all things. I will tell you, asse my friend, Captain Gower: the rascally, scauld, beggarly, lousy, pragging knave, Pistol, which you and yourself and all the world know to be no petter than a fellow, look you now, of no merits, he is come to me and prings me pread and salt yesterday, look you, and bid me eat my leek. It was in a place where I could not breed no contention with him; but I will be so bold as to wear it in my cap till I see him once again, and then I will tell him a little piece of my desires.

Enter PISTOL

GOWER. Why, here he comes, swelling like a turkey-cock.

FLUELLEN. 'Tis no matter for his swellings nor his turkey-cocks. God pless you, Aunchient Pistol! you scurvy, lousy knave, God pless you!

PISTOL. Ha! art thou bedlam? Dost thou thirst, base Trojan,
To have me fold up Parca's fatal web?
Hence! I am qualmish at the smell of leek.

FLUELLEN. I peseech you heartily, scurvy, lousy knave, at my desires, and my requests, and my petitions, to eat, look you, this leek; because, look you, you do not love it, nor your affections and your appetites and your digestions doo's not agree with it, I would desire you to eat it.

PISTOL. Not for Cadwallader and all his goats.

FLUELLEN. There is one goat for you. [Strikes him] Will you be so good, scauld knave, as eat it?

PISTOL. Base Trojan, thou shalt die.

FLUELLEN. You say very true, scauld knave, when God's will is. I will desire you to live in the mean time, and eat your victuals; come, there is sauce for it. [Strikes him] You called me yesterday mountain-squire; but I will make you today a squire of low degree. I pray you, fall to. If you can mock a leek, you can eat a leek.

GOWER. Enough, captain, you have astonished him.

FLUELLEN. I say, I will make him eat some part of my leek, or I will peat his pate four days. Bite, I pray you; it is good for your green wound and your ploody coxcomb.

PISTOL. Must I bite?

FLUELLEN. Yes, certainly, and out of doubt and out of question too, and ambiguities.

PISTOL. By this leek, I will most horribly revenge. I eat and eat, I swear—

FLUELLEN. Eat, I pray you. Will you have some more sauce to your leek? There is not enough leek to swear by.

PISTOL. Quiet thy cudgel; thou dost see I eat.

FLUELLEN. Much good do you, scauld knave, heartily. Nay, pray you, throw none away; the skin is good for your broken coxcomb. When you take occasions to see leeks hereafter, I pray you, mock at 'em; that is all.

PISTOL. Good.

FLUELLEN. Ay, leeks is good. Hold you, there is a groat to heal your pate.

PISTOL. Me a groat!

FLUELLEN. Yes, verily and in truth, you shall take it; or I have another leek in my pocket, which you shall eat.

PISTOL. I take thy groat in earnest of revenge.

FLUELLEN. If I owe you anything, I will pay you in cudgels; you shall be a woodmonger, and buy nothing of me but cudgels. God b' wi' you, and keep you, and heal your pate.   Exit

PISTOL. All hell shall stir for this.

GOWER. Go, go; you are a counterfeit cowardly knave. Will you mock at an ancient tradition, begun upon an honourable respect, and worn as a memorable trophy of predeceased valour and dare not avouch in your deeds any of your words? I have seen you gleeking and galling at this gentleman twice or thrice. You thought, because he could not speak English in the native garb, he could not therefore handle an English cudgel. You find it otherwise; and henceforth let a Welsh correction teach you a good English condition. Fare ye well.
                                                        Exit

PISTOL. Doth Fortune play the huswife with me now?
News have I, that my Nell is dead i' the spital
Of malady of France;
And there my rendezvous is quite cut off.
Old I do wax; and from my weary limbs
Honour is cudgelled. Well, bawd I 'll turn,
And something lean to cutpurse of quick hand.
To England will I steal, and there I 'll steal,
And patches will I get unto these cudgelled scars,
And swear I got them in the Gallia wars.   Exit

SCENE II *France: a royal palace*

Enter, at one door, KING HENRY, EXETER, BEDFORD, GLOUCESTER, WARWICK, WESTMORELAND, *and other* Lords;
at another, the FRENCH KING, QUEEN ISABEL, *the* PRINCESS KATHARINE, ALICE *and other* Ladies;
the DUKE OF BURGUNDY, *and his train*

KING HENRY. Peace to this meeting, wherefore we are met!
Unto our brother France, and to our sister,
Health and fair time of day; joy and good wishes
To our most fair and princely cousin Katharine;
And, as a branch and member of this royalty,
By whom this great assembly is contrived,
We do salute you, Duke of Burgundy;
And, princes French, and peers, health to you all!

FRENCH KING. Right joyous are we to behold your face,
Most worthy brother England; fairly met.
So are you, princes English, every one.

QUEEN ISABEL. So happy be the issue, brother England,
Of this good day and of this gracious meeting,
As we are now glad to behold your eyes;
Your eyes, which hitherto have borne in them
Against the French, that met them in their bent,
The fatal balls of murdering basilisks.

The venom of such looks, we fairly hope,
Have lost their quality, and that this day
Shall change all griefs and quarrels into love.
KING HENRY. To cry amen to that, thus we appear.
QUEEN ISABEL. You English princes all, I do salute you.
BURGUNDY. My duty to you both, on equal love,
  Great Kings of France and England! That I have
    laboured,
  With all my wits, my pains, and strong endeavours,
  To bring your most imperial majesties
  Unto this bar and royal interview,
  Your mightiness on both parts best can witness.
  Since then my office hath so far prevailed
  That, face to face and royal eye to eye,
  You have congreeted, let it not disgrace me
  If I demand before this royal view,
  What rub or what impediment there is,
  Why that the naked, poor, and mangled Peace,
  Dear nurse of arts, plenties and joyful births,
  Should not in this best garden of the world,
  Our fertile France, put up her lovely visage?
  Alas, she hath from France too long been chased,
  And all her husbandry doth lie on heaps,
  Corrupting in it own fertility.
  Her vine, the merry cheerer of the heart,
  Unpruned dies; her hedges even-pleached,
  Like prisoners wildly overgrown with hair,
  Put forth disordered twigs; her fallow leas
  The darnel, hemlock and rank fumitory
  Doth root upon, while that the coulter rusts
  That should deracinate such savagery;
  The even mead, that erst brought sweetly forth
  The freckled cowslip, burnet and green clover,
  Wanting the scythe, all uncorrected, rank,
  Conceives by idleness, and nothing teems
  But hateful docks, rough thistles, kecksies, burs,
  Losing both beauty and utility.
  And as our vineyards, fallows, meads, and hedges,
  Defective in their natures, grow to wildness,
  Even so our houses and ourselves and children
  Have lost, or do not learn for want of time,
  The sciences that should become our country,
  But grow like savages—as soldiers will
  That nothing do but meditate on blood—
  To swearing and stern looks, defused attire
  And everything that seems unnatural.
  Which to reduce into our former favour
  You are assembled; and my speech entreats
  That I may know the let, why gentle Peace
  Should not expel these inconveniences
  And bless us with her former qualities.
KING HENRY. If, Duke of Burgundy, you would the
    peace,
  Whose want gives growth to the imperfections
  Which you have cited, you must buy that peace
  With full accord to all our just demands;

Whose tenours and particular effects
You have enscheduled briefly in your hands.
BURGUNDY. The King hath heard them; to the which
    as yet
  There is no answer made.
KING HENRY.   Well then the peace,
  Which you before so urged, lies in his answer.
FRENCH KING. I have but with a cursorary eye
  O'erglanced the articles. Pleaseth your grace
  To appoint some of your council presently
  To sit with us once more, with better heed
  To re-survey them, we will suddenly
  Pass our accept and peremptory answer.
KING HENRY. Brother, we shall. Go, uncle Exeter,
  And brother Clarence, and you, brother Gloucester,
  Warwick and Huntingdon, go with the King;
  And take with you free power to ratify,
  Augment, or alter, as your wisdoms best
  Shall see advantageable for our dignity,
  Anything in or out of our demands,
  And we'll consign thereto. Will you, fair sister,
  Go with the princes, or stay here with us?
QUEEN ISABEL. Our gracious brother, I will go with
    them.
  Haply a woman's voice may do some good,
  When articles too nicely urged be stood on.
KING HENRY. Yet leave our cousin Katharine here with
  us.
  She is our capital demand, comprised
  Within the fore-rank of our articles.
QUEEN ISABEL. She hath good leave.
                Exeunt all except
        HENRY, KATHARINE, *and* ALICE
KING HENRY.   Fair Katharine, and most fair,
  Will you vouchsafe to teach a soldier terms
  Such as will enter at a lady's ear
  And plead his love-suit to her gentle heart?
KATHARINE. Your majesty shall mock at me; I cannot
  speak your England.
KING HENRY. O fair Katharine, if you will love me
  soundly with your French heart, I will be glad to hear
  you confess it brokenly with your English tongue.
  Do you like me, Kate?
KATHARINE. Pardonnez-moi, I cannot tell vat is "like
  me."
KING HENRY. An angel is like you, Kate, and you are
  like an angel.
KATHARINE. Que dit-il? que je suis semblable à les
  anges?
ALICE. Oui, vraiment, sauf votre grace, ainsi dit-il.
KING HENRY. I said so, dear Katharine; and I must not
  blush to affirm it.
KATHARINE. O bon Dieu! les langues des hommes sont
  pleines de tromperies.
KING HENRY. What says she, fair one? that the tongues
  of men are full of deceits?

ALICE. Oui, dat de tongues of de mans is be full of deceits; dat is de princess.

KING HENRY. The princess is the better Englishwoman. I' faith, Kate, my wooing is fit for thy understanding; I am glad thou canst speak no better English; for, if thou couldst, thou wouldst find me such a plain king that thou wouldst think I had sold my farm to buy my crown. I know no ways to mince it in love, but directly to say "I love you"; then if you urge me farther than to say "Do you in faith?" I wear out my suit. Give me your answer; i' faith, do; and so clap hands and a bargain. How say you, lady?

KATHARINE. Sauf votre honneur, me understand vell.

KING HENRY. Marry, if you would put me to verses or to dance for your sake, Kate, why you undid me. For the one, I have neither words nor measure, and for the other, I have no strength in measure, yet a reasonable measure in strength. If I could win a lady at leap-frog, or by vaulting into my saddle with my armour on my back, under the correction of bragging be it spoken, I should quickly leap into a wife. Or if I might buffet for my love, or bound my horse for her favours, I could lay on like a butcher and sit like a jack-an-apes, never off. But, before God, Kate, I cannot look greenly nor gasp out my eloquence, nor I have no cunning in protestation; only downright oaths, which I never use till urged, nor never break for urging. If thou canst love a fellow of this temper, Kate, whose face is not worth sunburning, that never looks in his glass for love of anything he sees there, let thine eye be thy cook. I speak to thee plain soldier: if thou canst love me for this, take me; if not, to say to thee that I shall die, is true; but for thy love, by the Lord, no; yet I love thee too. And while thou livest, dear Kate, take a fellow of plain and uncoined constancy; for he perforce must do thee right, because he hath not the gift to woo in other places; for these fellows of infinite tongue, that can rhyme themselves into ladies' favours, they do always reason themselves out again. What! a speaker is but a prater; a rhyme is but a ballad. A good leg will fall, a straight back will stoop, a black beard will turn white, a curled pate will grow bald, a fair face will wither, a full eye will wax hollow; but a good heart, Kate, is the sun and the moon; or rather the sun and not the moon; for it shines bright and never changes, but keeps his course truly. If thou would have such a one, take me; and take me, take a soldier; take a soldier, take a King. And what sayest thou then to my love? speak, my fair, and fairly, I pray thee.

KATHARINE. Is it possible dat I sould love de enemy of France?

KING HENRY. No; it is not possible you should love the enemy of France, Kate; but, in loving me, you should love the friend of France; for I love France so well that I will not part with a village of it; I will

have it all mine; and, Kate, when France is mine and I am yours, then yours is France and you are mine.

KATHARINE. I cannot tell vat is dat.

KING HENRY. No, Kate? I will tell thee in French, which I am sure will hang upon my tongue like a new-married wife about her husband's neck, hardly to be shook off. Je quand sur le possession de France, et quand vous avez le possession de moi—let me see, what then? Saint Denis be my speed!—donc votre est France et vous êtes mienne. It is as easy for me, Kate, to conquer the kingdom as to speak so much more French. I shall never move thee in French, unless it be to laugh at me.

KATHARINE. Sauf votre honneur, le François que vous parlez, il est meilleur que l'Anglois lequel je parle.

KING HENRY. No, faith, is 't not, Kate; but thy speaking of my tongue, and I thine, most truly-falsely, must needs be granted to be much at one. But, Kate, dost thou understand thus much English, canst thou love me?

KATHARINE. I cannot tell.

KING HENRY. Can any of your neighbours tell, Kate? I 'll ask them. Come, I know thou lovest me; and at night, when you come into your closet, you'll question this gentlewoman about me; and I know, Kate, you will to her dispraise those parts in me that you love with your heart; but, good Kate, mock me mercifully; the rather, gentle princess, because I love thee cruelly. If ever thou beest mine, Kate, as I have a saving faith within me tells me thou shalt, I get thee with scambling, and thou must therefore needs prove a good soldier-breeder. Shall not thou and I, between Saint Denis and Saint George, compound a boy, half French, half English, that shall go to Constantinople and take the Turk by the beard? Shall we not? What sayest thou, my fair flower-de-luce?

KATHARINE. I do not know dat.

KING HENRY. No; 'tis hereafter to know, but now to

promise. Do but now promise, Kate, you will endeavour for your French part of such a boy, and for my English moiety take the word of a king and a bachelor. How answer you, la plus belle Katharine du monde, mon très cher et devin déesse?

KATHARINE. Your majestee ave fausse French enough to deceive de most sage demoiselle dat is en France.

KING HENRY. Now, fie upon my false French! By mine honour, in true English, I love thee, Kate; by which honour I dare not swear thou lovest me; yet my blood begins to flatter me that thou dost, notwithstanding the poor and untempering effect of my visage. Now, beshrew my father's ambition! he was thinking of civil wars when he got me; therefore was I created with a stubborn outside, with an aspect of iron, that, when I come to woo ladies, I fright them. But, in faith, Kate, the elder I wax, the better I shall appear. My comfort is, that old age, that ill layer up of beauty, can do no more spoil upon my face. Thou hast me, if thou hast me, at the worst; and thou shalt wear me, if thou wear me, better and better. And therefore tell me, most fair Katharine, will you have me? Put off your maiden blushes; avouch the thoughts of your heart with the looks of an empress; take me by the hand, and say "Harry of England, I am thine"; which word thou shalt no sooner bless mine ear withal, but I will tell thee aloud "England is thine, Ireland is thine, France is thine, and Henry Plantagenet is thine"; who, though I speak it before his face, if he be not fellow with the best king, thou shalt find the best king of good fellows. Come, your answer in broken music; for thy voice is music and thy English broken; therefore, queen of all, Katharine, break thy mind to me in broken English. Wilt thou have me?

KATHARINE. Dat is as it sall please de roi mon père.

KING HENRY. Nay, it will please him well, Kate; it shall please him, Kate.

KATHARINE. Den it sall also content me.

KING HENRY. Upon that I kiss your hand, and I call you my Queen.

KATHARINE. Laissez, mon seigneur, laissez, laissez! Ma foi, je ne veux point que vous abaissiez votre grandeur en baisant la main d'une de votre siegneurie indigne serviteur; excusez-moi, je vous supplie, mon très-puissant seigneur.

KING HENRY. Then I will kiss your lips, Kate.

KATHARINE. Les dames et demoiselles pour être baisées devant leur noces, il n'est pas la coutume de France.

KING HENRY. Madam my interpreter, what says she?

ALICE. Dat it is not be de fashion pour les ladies of France—I cannot tell vat is baiser en Anglish.

KING HENRY. To kiss.

ALICE. Your majesty entendre bettre que moi.

KING HENRY. It is not a fashion for the maids in France to kiss before they are married, would she say?

ALICE. Oui, vraiment.

KING HENRY. O Kate, nice customs curtsy to great kings. Dear Kate, you and I cannot be confined within the weak list of a country's fashion. We are the makers of manners, Kate; and the liberty that follows our places stops the mouth of all find-faults, as I will do yours, for upholding the nice fashion of your country in denying me a kiss; therefore, patiently and yielding. [*Kissing her*] You have witchcraft in your lips, Kate; there is more eloquence in a sugar touch of them than in the tongues of the French council; and they should sooner persuade Harry of England than a general petition of monarchs. Here comes your father.

Re-enter the FRENCH KING *and his* QUEEN, BURGUNDY, *and other* Lords

BURGUNDY. God save your majesty! My royal cousin, teach you our princess English?

KING HENRY. I would have her learn, my fair cousin, how perfectly I love her; and that is good English.

BURGUNDY. Is she not apt?

KING HENRY. Our tongue is rough, coz, and my condition is not smooth; so that, having neither the voice nor the heart of flattery about me, I cannot so conjure up the spirit of love in her, that he will appear in his true likeness.

BURGUNDY. Pardon the frankness of my mirth, if I answer you for that. If you would conjure in her, you must make a circle; if conjure up love in her in his true likeness, he must appear naked and blind. Can you blame her then, being a maid yet rosed over with the virgin crimson of modesty, if she deny the appearance of a naked blind boy in her naked seeing self? It were, my lord, a hard condition for a maid to consign to.

KING HENRY. Yet they do wink and yield, as love is blind and enforces.

BURGUNDY. They are then excused, my lord, when they see not what they do.

KING HENRY. Then, good my lord, teach your cousin to consent winking.

BURGUNDY. I will wink on her to consent, my lord, if you will teach her to know my meaning; for maids, well summered and warm kept, are like flies at Bartholomew-tide, blind, though they have their eyes; and then they will endure handling, which before would not abide looking on.

KING HENRY. This moral ties me over to time and a hot summer; and so I shall catch the fly, your cousin, in the latter end and she must be blind too.

BURGUNDY. As love is, my lord, before it loves.

KING HENRY. It is so; and you may, some of you, thank love for my blindness, who cannot see many a fair French city for one fair French maid that stands in my way.

FRENCH KING. Yes, my lord, you see them perspectively, the cities turned into a maid; for they are all girdled with maiden walls that war hath never entered.

KING HENRY. Shall Kate be my wife?

FRENCH KING. So please you.

KING HENRY. I am content; so the maiden cities you talk of may wait on her. So the maid that stood in the way for my wish shall show me the way to my will.

FRENCH KING. We have consented to all terms of reason.

KING HENRY. Is 't so, my lords of England?

WESTMORELAND. The King hath granted every article:
His daughter first, and then in sequel all,
According to their firm proposed natures.

EXETER. Only he hath not yet subscribed this: Where your majesty demands, that the King of France, having any occasion to write for matter of grant, shall name your highness in this form and with this addition, in French, Notre très-cher fils Henri, Roi d'Angleterre, Héritier de France; and thus in Latin, Præclarissimus filius noster Henricus, Rex Angliæ, et Hæres Franciæ.

FRENCH KING. Nor this I have not, brother, so denied,
But your request shall make me let it pass.

KING HENRY. I pray you then, in love and dear alliance,
Let that one article rank with the rest;
And thereupon give me your daughter.

FRENCH KING. Take her, fair son, and from her blood raise up
Issue to me; that the contending kingdoms
Of France and England, whose very shores look pale
With envy of each other's happiness,
May cease their hatred, and this dear conjunction
Plant neighbourhood and Christian-like accord
In their sweet bosoms, that never war advance
His bleeding sword 'twixt England and fair France.

ALL. Amen!

KING HENRY. Now, welcome, Kate; and bear me witness all,
That here I kiss her as my sovereign Queen. *Flourish*

QUEEN ISABEL. God, the best maker of all marriages,
Combine your hearts in one, your realms in one!
As man and wife, being two, are one in love,
So be there 'twixt your kingdoms such a spousal,
That never may ill office, or fell jealousy,
Which troubles oft the bed of blessed marriage,
Thrust in between the paction of these kingdoms,
To make divorce of their incorporate league;
That English may as French, French Englishmen,
Receive each other. God speak this Amen!

ALL. Amen!

KING HENRY. Prepare we for our marriage; on which day,
My Lord of Burgundy, we'll take your oath,
And all the peers', for surety of our leagues.
Then shall I swear to Kate, and you to me;
And may our oaths well kept and prosperous be!
Sennet. Exeunt

EPILOGUE

Enter Chorus

CHORUS. Thus far, with rough and all-unable pen,
    Our bending author hath pursued the story,
  In little room confining mighty men,
    Mangling by starts the full course of their glory.
  Small time, but in that small most greatly lived
    This star of England. Fortune made his sword;
  By which the world's best garden he achieved,

And of it left his son imperial lord.
  Henry the Sixth, in infant bands crowned King
    Of France and England, did this King succeed;
  Whose state so many had the managing,
    That they lost France and made his England bleed—
  Which oft our stage hath shown; and, for their sake,
  In your fair minds let this acceptance take.   *Exit*

JULIUS CAESAR

What is this play about?

The title of a Shakespearian play often offers a key to its meaning. It is surely an odd but significant thing that in this play the part of Julius Caesar, though very effective, is very short. He is killed around half-time; and even while he is still alive he is never the chief character. Clearly, then, it is not about the *life* of Julius Caesar. But, arguably, it is about his *death* and, I suggest, it is about the reasons for his death, the death itself, and then, most importantly, the consequences of his death.

This is a case where the plot, or story, of the play can be clearly differentiated from the theme. By the story I mean the sequence of events which occur to the characters of the play, either before our eyes in action, or else, like Casca's description of the offering of the crown to Caesar, in narration. By the theme I mean the idea, or complex of ideas, which are the author's comment upon the story.

Remember that it is not possible, it simply is not possible, to tell even the simplest story without some kind of comment. Such comment need not be conscious. Often it is made when the teller, or author, of the story quite unconsciously omits some element, or stresses another, or invents something on the spur of the moment. Such omissions, emphases and inventions give to the story the particular slant which the author requires it to have, usually for reasons of which he is unaware.

In this case, however, comment is very conscious. Let us consider what Shakespeare means to imply, by considering very briefly the structure of the play.

The first scenes establish the situation: Caesar is likely to assume absolute power in Rome. A group of aristocrats, for various reasons, feels so strongly opposed to this that each of them is prepared to go to the length of assassinating the would-be dictator. Of this group the principal figure is Brutus, a man moved by no personal hostility to Caesar, but only by consideration of the public good. Brutus, at the beginning of the play, is uncertain where he stands. He hesitates to upset the regime, recoils in horror from the act of murder. The murder-plot is the conception of the clever and ambitious Cassius, who brings to bear on Brutus every influence he can. By the end of the fourth scene Brutus has been persuaded to head the conspiracy.

The assassination takes place.

Then Brutus makes the fatal political mistake of allowing Antony, a handsome young friend of Caesar, to make the Funeral Oration over Caesar's body. Antony uses the occasion to inflame the anger of the Roman populace against the aristocratic conspirators; Brutus and Cassius are forced to fly from the city; Antony joins forces with Octavius, Caesar's nephew and heir. The removal of the dictator has been achieved, but at the cost of civil war.

At this point we are only about two-thirds of the way through the play. It is now clear that Brutus, not Julius Caesar, is the play's central figure. Clear, too, that the play is less concerned with the actual murder than with its consequences.

The remaining scenes show the Caesarian Party, led by Octavius and Antony, defeating the Conspirators Party. This defeat is the more inevitable because of the disaffection between Brutus and Cassius. At the same time we are shown that all is not well between the victors either: Octavius and Antony are quarrelling too.

Side by side with this picture of political and military disintegration is shown the personal disintegration of Brutus. Like Macbeth, he is a great man, haunted, sapped and finally destroyed by the guilt of murder.

In performance, as in so many of Shakespeare's plays, it is easier to hold an audience in the early and middle parts of the play than in the last third. This is not, I think, that the author's work deteriorates. The difficulty arises because the final scenes of Shakespearian tragedy show the conflict resolved in combat; but action of a kind— battles, suicides, violence of all sorts—which cannot be made convincing by the naturalistic methods which have for some generations now dominated theatrical presentation.

The final impression created by the pell-mell sequence of disasters, culminating in the defeat and death of Brutus and the uneasy triumph of Octavius and Antony, should be one of disintegration, the falling apart of what the whole conspiracy had been designed to protect: the body-politic of Rome.

This is not an easy effect to achieve because, again, it is at odds with customary theatrical procedure. Usually plays are designed so that the end brings all the loose ends of the story together and offers them to the audience tied with a neat bow of silver ribbon—the happy-ever-after convention. Or, where a "happy" ending is quite out of the question—as in *Hamlet, Macbeth* or *King Lear*—the ending shows the tragic events of the play irradiated by the hope of a more auspicious future.

Here, however, the whole point is lost if the future is indicated to be anything but gloomy and confused. Like Sophocles' *Oedipus Rex,* this is a tragedy where the good intentions of the central figure are rewarded with nothing but disaster; and, at the end, the audience is left to take what consolation it can, not from virtue rewarded and vice punished, but merely from the fact that the chief character has steadfastly done what he *believed* to be right.

This is what I believe to be the conscious comment of the author.

There is a further comment, of which he may also have been conscious, but of which he was more probably only partly aware. It is a hidden theme of many, perhaps most, of his serious plays. Brutus, like Macbeth, murdered a man who stood to him in the relation of king, or father —for a king is a symbolical father, what psychologists call a Father Figure. Julius Caesar, like King Duncan, like Hamlet's father, is one more of the great, so-called archetypal figures which haunt the frontiers of human consciousness: the Murdered Father.

Julius Caesar is one of the more popular and frequently performed of Shakespeare's plays, and very rightly so. In it are endless felicities of expression, moments of insight, exhibitions of those qualities of mind and heart which stamp the author as a master-artist, and those qualities of theatrical workmanship which likewise stamp him as a master-craftsman. His accomplishment in many fields is displayed especially, perhaps, in the scene immediately after Caesar's murder (Act III, scene 2). The murder itself has been a "big scene"; whatever follows runs some risk of anti-climax. Shakespeare sets Antony to work upon the Roman populace in a scene which has two of the great rhetorical set-pieces in our language, which is an absolute model of plot-manipulation. The scene, instead of being itself an anti-climax, makes it very hard to avoid anti-climax in the rest of the play. Indeed, in the theatre I have often known performances to decline from this point on. The only way to guard against this is to find the intention and the pattern, both far from obvious, of the later scenes.

As I have indicated, the intention is to show disintegration, both of the Body Politic and of the principal personages of the play. It is expressed in a series of brief, highly condensed episodes, which demand a great deal both from the skill of the performers and from the imagination of the audience. It is easy for the long series of deaths and disasters to seem not only monotonous but a little absurd, especially to audiences accustomed to television and movies. In these media the mechanics and outward appearance of death and violence are treated with respectful realism; whereas the ideas and passions involved—cops versus robbers, good versus bad—are extremely obvious as a rule, and are treated with contemptuous triviality.

The final scenes of *Julius Caesar* deal with ideas which are neither trivial nor obvious, and in the expression of which realism would be as out of place as a rhetorical finale in blank verse would be in the last ninety seconds of a crime serial.

Because the pattern is one to which we are not accustomed, we are apt to express it clumsily, or indeed even to fail to see that it exists.

The women's parts are small and comparatively unimportant. I have never been able to find Cato's daughter other than a noble bore, one more instance of the extreme difficulty of making unadulterated goodness acceptable in fiction. Calpurnia's scene with Caesar is far more interesting and unconventional. But her part in the drama is all too soon over.

The fact that in *Julius Caesar* the sex interest is so marginal and so tepid has been, paradoxically, a major factor in the high estimation which the play enjoys in the English-speaking world. In the theatre it is one of the most frequently revived of all Shakespeare's plays and is known to be one of the very soundest at the box-office. It is the play which recurs most frequently in the exam syllabus at every level and in every corner of the educational field. This is because it is a "safe" play for youngsters. Teachers and parents can expose them to it without anxiety about awkward questions or unsuitable giggles or, worse still, the possibility that Horrid Ideas may have been indelibly imprinted upon the impressionable wax of the young mind.

For this reason, *Julius Caesar,* masterpiece though it be, has resulted in so many young people being "put off" Shakespeare for life that, laid end to end they would stretch . . . the notion is too sad and painful to pursue.

Shakespeare is not a kiddy's playwright. It is no service to Shakespeare, to education nor to anything else to expose children to an adult masterpiece before they can possibly be ready for it. *Julius Caesar,* for all it contains scenes of obviously exciting drama and rabble-rousing popular rhetoric, is a work of highly sophisticated and grown-up values. The mere absence of sex, even if it were absent, does not make it more understandable by, nor more suitable for, the inexperienced young.

JULIUS CAESAR
DRAMATIS PERSONAE

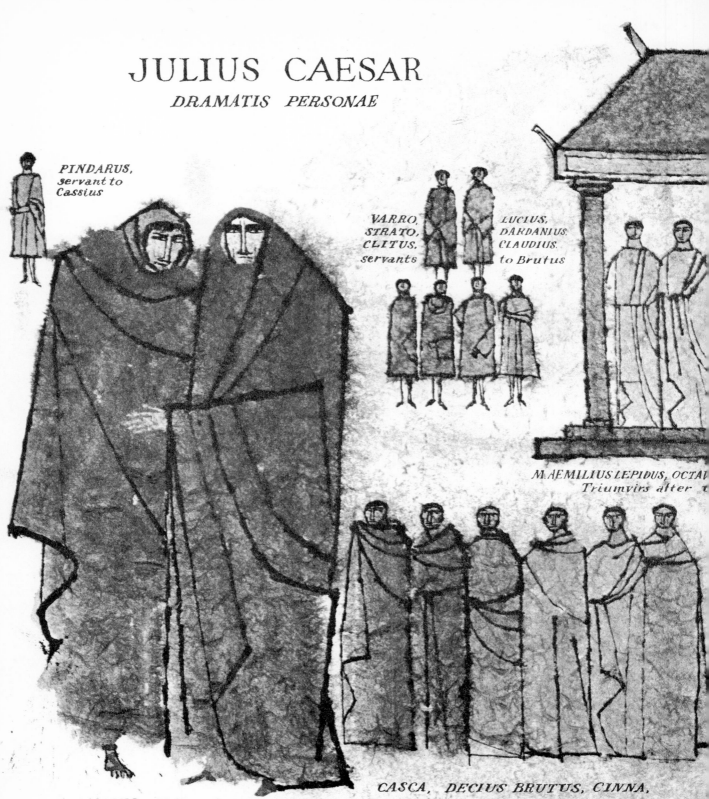

PINDARUS,
servant to
Cassius

VARRO,
STRATO,
CLITUS,
servants

LUCIUS,
DARDANIUS,
CLAUDIUS,
to Brutus

M. AEMILIUS LEPIDUS, OCTAV
Triumvirs after t

CASCA, DECIUS BRUTUS, CINNA,
CASSIUS, MARCUS BRUTUS, METELLUS CIMBER, TREBONIUS, LIGARIUS,
Conspirators against Julius Caesar

SAR, MARCUS ANTONIUS
th of Julius Caesar

JULIUS
CAESAR

POPILIUS LENA,
PUBLIUS,
CICERO,
Senators

FLAVIUS
and
MARULLUS,
Tribunes

CALPURNIA,
wife to Caesar
PORTIA,
wife to Brutus

VOLUMNIUS, LUCILIUS,
TITINIUS, MESSALA, Young CATO,
Friends to Brutus and Cassius

ARTEMIDORUS of Cnidos,
A teacher of rhetoric.
CINNA,
A poet.
A soothsayer,   Another Poet
Senators, Citizens, Guards,
Attendants, et cetera.

SCENE: ROME;
The neighbourhood of SARDIS,
The neighbourhood of PHILIPPI.

ACT I

SCENE I *Rome: a street*

Enter FLAVIUS, MARULLUS, *and certain* Commoners

FLAVIUS. Hence! Home, you idle creatures, get you home.
  Is this a holiday? What! know you not,
  Being mechanical, you ought not walk
  Upon a labouring day without the sign
  Of your profession? Speak, what trade art thou?
FIRST COMMONER. Why, sir, a carpenter.
MARULLUS. Where is thy leather apron and thy rule?
  What dost thou with thy best apparel on?
  You sir, what trade are you?
SECOND COMMONER. Truly, sir, in respect of a fine workman, I am but, as you would say, a cobbler.
MARULLUS. But what trade art thou? Answer me directly.
SECOND COMMONER. A trade, sir, that, I hope, I may use with a safe conscience; which is, indeed, sir, a mender of bad soles.
MARULLUS. What trade, thou knave? Thou naughty knave, what trade?
SECOND COMMONER. Nay, I beseech you, sir, be not out with me. Yet, if you be out, sir, I can mend you.
MARULLUS. What meanest thou by that? Mend me, thou saucy fellow?
SECOND COMMONER. Why, sir, cobble you.
FLAVIUS. Thou art a cobbler, art thou?
SECOND COMMONER. Truly, sir, all that I live by is with the awl. I meddle with no tradesman's matters, nor women's matters, but with all. I am, indeed, sir, a surgeon to old shoes; when they are in great

danger, I recover them. As proper men as ever trod
upon neat's leather have gone upon my handiwork.

FLAVIUS. But wherefore art not in thy shop today?
   Why dost thou lead these men about the streets?

SECOND COMMONER. Truly, sir, to wear out their shoes,
   to get myself into more work. But, indeed, sir, we
   make holiday, to see Cæsar and to rejoice in his
   triumph.

MARULLUS. Wherefore rejoice? What conquest brings
   he home?
   What tributaries follow him to Rome,
   To grace in captive bonds his chariot wheels?
   You blocks, you stones, you worse than senseless
      things!
   O you hard hearts, you cruel men of Rome,
   Knew you not Pompey? Many a time and oft
   Have you climbed up to walls and battlements,
   To towers and windows, yea, to chimney-tops,
   Your infants in your arms, and there have sat
   The live-long day, with patient expectation,
   To see great Pompey pass the streets of Rome.
   And when you saw his chariot but appear,

Have you not made an universal shout,
That Tiber trembled underneath her banks,
To hear the replication of your sounds
Made in her concave shores?
And do you now put on your best attire?
And do you now cull out a holiday?
And do you now strew flowers in his way
That comes in triumph over Pompey's blood?
Be gone!
Run to your houses, fall upon your knees,
Pray to the gods to intermit the plague
That needs must light on this ingratitude.

FLAVIUS. Go, go, good countrymen, and, for this fault,
   Assemble all the poor men of your sort;
   Draw them to Tiber banks, and weep your tears
   Into the channel, till the lowest stream
   Do kiss the most exalted shores of all.

                              Exeunt all the Commoners
   See, whether their basest metal be not moved;
   They vanish tongue-tied in their guiltiness.
   Go you down that way towards the Capitol;
   This way will I. Disrobe the images,
   If you do find them decked with ceremonies.

MARULLUS. May we do so?
   You know it is the feast of Lupercal.

FLAVIUS. It is no matter; let no images
   Be hung with Cæsar's trophies. I'll about,
   And drive away the vulgar from the streets.
   So do you too, where you perceive them thick.
   These growing feathers plucked from Cæsar's wing
   Will make him fly an ordinary pitch,
   Who else would soar above the view of men
   And keep us all in servile fearfulness.   *Exeunt*

SCENE II *A public place*

Flourish. Enter CÆSAR; ANTONY, *for the course;* CALPURNIA, PORTIA, DECIUS, CICERO, BRUTUS, CASSIUS, *and* CASCA;
a great crowd following, among them a Soothsayer

CÆSAR. Calpurnia!

CASCA.　　　　　　Peace, ho! Cæsar speaks.

CÆSAR.　　　　　　　　　　　　Calpurnia!

CALPURNIA. Here, my lord.

CÆSAR. Stand you directly in Antonius' way,
　When he doth run his course. Antonius!

ANTONY. Cæsar, my lord?

CÆSAR. Forget not, in your speed, Antonius,
　To touch Calpurnia; for our elders say,
　The barren, touched in this holy chase,
　Shake off their sterile curse.

ANTONY.　　　　　　　　　I shall remember;
　When Cæsar says "do this," it is performed.

CÆSAR. Set on; and leave no ceremony out.　*Flourish*

SOOTHSAYER. Cæsar!

CÆSAR. Ha! who calls?

CASCA. Bid every noise be still. Peace yet again!

CÆSAR. Who is it in the press that calls on me?
　I hear a tongue, shriller than all the music,
　Cry "Cæsar!" Speak; Cæsar is turned to hear.

SOOTHSAYER. Beware the ides of March.

CÆSAR.　　　　　　　　　What man is that?

BRUTUS. A soothsayer bids you beware the ides of
　March.

CÆSAR. Set him before me; let me see his face.

Thoughts of great value, worthy cogitations.
Tell me, good Brutus, can you see your face?
BRUTUS. No, Cassius; for the eye sees not itself,
But by reflection, by some other things.
CASSIUS. 'Tis just;
And it is very much lamented, Brutus,
That you have no such mirrors as will turn
Your hidden worthiness into your eye,
That you might see your shadow. I have heard,
Where many of the best respect in Rome,
Except immortal Cæsar, speaking of Brutus
And groaning underneath this age's yoke,
Have wished that noble Brutus had his eyes.
BRUTUS. Into what dangers would you lead me, Cassius,
That you would have me seek into myself
For that which is not in me?
CASSIUS. Therefore, good Brutus, be prepared to hear;
And since you know you cannot see yourself
So well as by reflection, I, your glass,
Will modestly discover to yourself
That of yourself which you yet know not of.
And be not jealous on me, gentle Brutus;
Were I a common laughter, or did use
To stale with ordinary oaths my love
To every new protester; if you know
That I do fawn on men and hug them hard
And after scandal them, or if you know
That I profess myself in banqueting
To all the rout, then hold me dangerous.
                    Flourish, and shout
BRUTUS. What means this shouting? I do fear, the people
Choose Cæsar for their king.
CASSIUS.   Ay, do you fear it?
Then must I think you would not have it so.
BRUTUS. I would not, Cassius; yet I love him well.
But wherefore do you hold me here so long?
What is it that you would impart to me?
If it be aught toward the general good,
Set honour in one eye and death i' the other,
And I will look on both indifferently;
For let the gods so speed me as I love
The name of honour more than I fear death.
CASSIUS. I know that virtue to be in you, Brutus,
As well as I do know your outward favour.
Well, honour is the subject of my story.
I cannot tell what you and other men
Think of this life; but, for my single self,
I had as lief not be as live to be
In awe of such a thing as I myself.
I was born free as Cæsar; so were you.
We both have fed as well, and we can both
Endure the winter's cold as well as he.
For once, upon a raw and gusty day,
The troubled Tiber chafing with her shores,
Cæsar said to me, "Darest thou, Cassius, now
Leap in with me into this angry flood,

CASSIUS. Fellow, come from the throng; look upon
    Cæsar.
CÆSAR. What say'st thou to me now? Speak once again.
SOOTHSAYER. Beware the ides of March.
CÆSAR. He is a dreamer; let us leave him: pass.
            Trumpet call. Exeunt all except BRUTUS *and* CASSIUS
CASSIUS. Will you go see the order of the course?
BRUTUS. Not I.
CASSIUS. I pray you, do.
BRUTUS. I am not gamesome. I do lack some part
    Of that quick spirit that is in Antony.
    Let me not hinder, Cassius, your desires;
    I 'll leave you.
CASSIUS. Brutus, I do observe you now of late.
    I have not from your eyes that gentleness
    And show of love as I was wont to have.
    You bear too stubborn and too strange a hand
    Over your friend that loves you.
BRUTUS.   Cassius,
    Be not deceived; if I have veiled my look,
    I turn the trouble of my countenance
    Merely upon myself. Vexed I am
    Of late with passions of some difference,
    Conceptions only proper to myself,
    Which give some soil perhaps to my behaviours.
    But let not therefore my good friends be grieved—
    Among which number, Cassius, be you one—
    Nor construe any further my neglect,
    Than that poor Brutus, with himself at war,
    Forgets the shows of love to other men.
CASSIUS. Then, Brutus, I have much mistook your
        passion;
    By means whereof this breast of mine hath buried

And swim to yonder point?" Upon the word,
Accoutred as I was, I plunged in
And bade him follow. So indeed he did.
The torrent roared, and we did buffet it
With lusty sinews, throwing it aside
And stemming it with hearts of controversy;
But ere we could arrive the point proposed,
Cæsar cried, "Help me, Cassius, or I sink!"
I, as Aeneas, our great ancestor,
Did from the flames of Troy upon his shoulder
The old Anchises bear, so from the waves of Tiber
Did I the tired Cæsar. And this man
Is now become a god, and Cassius is
A wretched creature and must bend his body,
If Cæsar carelessly but nod on him.
He had a fever when he was in Spain,
And when the fit was on him, I did mark
How he did shake—'tis true, this god did shake—
His coward lips did from their colour fly,
And that same eye whose bend doth awe the world
Did lose his lustre. I did hear him groan;
Ay, and that tongue of his that bade the Romans
Mark him and write his speeches in their books,
Alas, it cried, "Give me some drink, Titinius,"
As a sick girl. Ye gods, it doth amaze me
A man of such a feeble temper should
So get the start of the majestic world
And bear the palm alone.   *Shout; flourish*
BRUTUS. Another general shout!
  I do believe that these applauses are
  For some new honours that are heaped on Cæsar.
CASSIUS. Why, man, he doth bestride the narrow world
  Like a Colossus, and we petty men
  Walk under his huge legs and peep about
  To find ourselves dishonourable graves.
  Men at some time are masters of their fates.
  The fault, dear Brutus, is not in our stars,
  But in ourselves, that we are underlings.
  Brutus and Cæsar—what should be in that "Cæsar"?
  Why should that name be sounded more than yours?
  Write them together, yours is as fair a name;
  Sound them, it doth become the mouth as well;
  Weigh them, it is as heavy; conjure with 'em,
  Brutus will start a spirit as soon as Cæsar.
  Now, in the names of all the gods at once,
  Upon what meat doth this our Cæsar feed,
  That he is grown so great? Age, thou art shamed!
  Rome, thou hast lost the breed of noble bloods!
  When went there by an age, since the great flood,
  But it was famed with more than with one man?
  When could they say till now, that talked of Rome,
  That her wide walls encompassed but one man?
  Now is it Rome indeed and room enough,
  When there is in it but one only man.
  O, you and I have heard our fathers say,
  There was a Brutus once that would have brooked

The eternal devil to keep his state in Rome
  As easily as a king.
BRUTUS. That you do love me, I am nothing jealous;
  What you would work me to, I have some aim.
  How I have thought of this and of these times,
  I shall recount hereafter; for this present,
  I would not, so with love I might entreat you,
  Be any further moved. What you have said
  I will consider; what you have to say
  I will with patience hear, and find a time
  Both meet to hear and answer such high things.
  Till then, my noble friend, chew upon this:
  Brutus had rather be a villager
  Than to repute himself a son of Rome
  Under these hard conditions as this time
  Is like to lay upon us.
CASSIUS. I am glad that my weak words
  Have struck but thus much show of fire from Brutus.
BRUTUS. The games are done and Cæsar is returning.
CASSIUS. As they pass by, pluck Casca by the sleeve;
  And he will, after his sour fashion, tell you
  What hath proceeded worthy note today.

Re-enter CÆSAR and his Train

BRUTUS. I will do so. But, look you, Cassius,
  The angry spot doth glow on Cæsar's brow,
  And all the rest look like a chidden train.
  Calpurnia's cheek is pale; and Cicero
  Looks with such ferret and such fiery eyes
  As we have seen him in the Capitol,
  Being crossed in conference by some senators.
CASSIUS. Casca will tell us what the matter is.
CÆSAR. Antonius!
ANTONY. Cæsar?
CÆSAR. Let me have men about me that are fat;
  Sleek-headed men and such as sleep o' nights.
  Yond Cassius has a lean and hungry look;
  He thinks too much: such men are dangerous.
ANTONY. Fear him not, Cæsar; he's not dangerous;
  He is a noble Roman and well given.
CÆSAR. Would he were fatter! But I fear him not.
  Yet if my name were liable to fear,
  I do not know the man I should avoid
  So soon as that spare Cassius. He reads much;
  He is a great observer and he looks
  Quite through the deeds of men. He loves no plays,
  As thou dost, Antony; he hears no music;
  Seldom he smiles, and smiles in such a sort
  As if he mocked himself and scorned his spirit
  That could be moved to smile at anything.
  Such men as he be never at heart's ease
  Whiles they behold a greater than themselves,
  And therefore are they very dangerous.
  I rather tell thee what is to be feared
  Than what I fear; for always I am Cæsar.
  Come on my right hand, for this ear is deaf,

And tell me truly what thou think'st of him.
Trumpet call.
Exeunt CÆSAR *and all his Train, but* CASCA

CASCA. You pulled me by the cloak; would you speak
with me?

BRUTUS. Ay, Casca; tell us what hath chanced today,
That Cæsar looks so sad.

CASCA. Why, you were with him, were you not?

BRUTUS. I should not then ask Casca what had chanced.

CASCA. Why, there was a crown offered him; and being
offered him, he put it by with the back of his hand,
thus; and then the people fell a-shouting.

BRUTUS. What was the second noise for?

CASCA. Why, for that too.

CASSIUS. They shouted thrice; what was the last cry for?

CASCA. Why, for that too.

BRUTUS. Was the crown offered him thrice?

CASCA. Ay, marry, was 't, and he put it by thrice, every
time gentler than other, and at every putting-by mine
honest neighbours shouted.

CASSIUS. Who offered him the crown?

CASCA. Why, Antony.

BRUTUS. Tell us the manner of it, gentle Casca.

CASCA. I can as well be hanged as tell the manner of it.
It was mere foolery; I did not mark it. I saw Mark
Antony offer him a crown—yet 'twas not a crown
neither, 'twas one of these coronets—and, as I told
you, he put it by once; but, for all that, to my thinking, he would fain have had it. Then he offered it to
him again; then he put it by again; but, to my thinking,
he was very loath to lay his fingers off it. And then he
offered it the third time; he put it the third time by;
and still as he refused it, the rabblement hooted and
clapped their chopped hands and threw up their
sweaty night-caps and uttered such a deal of stinking
breath because Cæsar refused the crown that it had
almost choked Cæsar; for he swounded and fell down
at it; and for mine own part, I durst not laugh, for
fear of opening my lips and receiving the bad air.

CASSIUS. But, soft, I pray you. What, did Cæsar swound?

CASCA. He fell down in the market-place, and foamed
at mouth, and was speechless.

BRUTUS. 'Tis very like he hath the falling sickness.

CASSIUS. No, Cæsar hath it not; but you and I
And honest Casca, we have the falling sickness.

CASCA. I know not what you mean by that; but, I am
sure, Cæsar fell down. If the tag-rag people did not
clap him and hiss him, according as he pleased and
displeased them, as they use to do the players in the
theatre, I am no true man.

BRUTUS. What said he when he came unto himself?

CASCA. Marry, before he fell down, when he perceived
the common herd was glad he refused the crown, he
plucked me ope his doublet and offered them his
throat to cut. An I had been a man of any occupation,
if I would not have taken him at a word, I would I

might go to hell among the rogues. And so he fell.
When he came to himself again, he said: If he had
done or said any thing amiss, he desired their worships
to think it was his infirmity. Three or four wenches,
where I stood, cried "Alas, good soul!" and forgave
him with all their hearts. But there's no heed to be
taken of them; if Cæsar had stabbed their mothers,
they would have done no less.

BRUTUS. And after that, he came, thus sad, away?

CASCA. Ay.

CASSIUS. Did Cicero say any thing?

CASCA. Ay, he spoke Greek.

CASSIUS. To what effect?

CASCA. Nay, an I tell you that, I 'll ne'er look you i'
the face again; but those that understood him smiled
at one another and shook their heads; but, for mine
own part, it was Greek to me. I could tell you more
news too: Marullus and Flavius, for pulling scarfs off
Cæsar's images, are put to silence. Fare you well.
There was more foolery yet, if I could remember it.

CASSIUS. Will you sup with me tonight, Casca?

CASCA. No, I am promised forth.

CASSIUS. Will you dine with me tomorrow?

CASCA. Ay, if I be alive and your mind hold and your
dinner worth the eating.

CASSIUS. Good; I will expect you.

CASCA. Do so. Farewell, both.						*Exit*

BRUTUS. What a blunt fellow is this grown to be!
He was quick mettle when he went to school.

CASSIUS. So is he now in execution
Of any bold or noble enterprise,
However he puts on this tardy form.
This rudeness is a sauce to his good wit,
Which gives men stomach tò digest his words
With better appetite.

BRUTUS. And so it is. For this time I will leave you.
Tomorrow, if you please to speak with me,
I will come home to you; or, if you will,
Come home to me, and I will wait for you.

CASSIUS. I will do so; till then, think of the world.
Exit BRUTUS

Well, Brutus, thou art noble; yet, I see,
Thy honourable metal may be wrought
From that it is disposed. Therefore it is meet
That noble minds keep ever with their likes;
For who so firm that cannot be seduced?
Cæsar doth bear me hard; but he loves Brutus.
If I were Brutus now and he were Cassius,
He should not humour me. I will this night,
In several hands, in at his windows throw,
As if they came from several citizens,
Writings all tending to the great opinion
That Rome holds of his name; wherein obscurely
Cæsar's ambition shall be glanced at;
And after this let Cæsar seat him sure;
For we will shake him, or worse days endure.		*Exit*

SCENE III *The same: a street*

Thunder and lightning. Enter, from opposite sides, CASCA,
with his sword drawn, and CICERO

CICERO. Good even, Casca; brought you Cæsar home?
  Why are you breathless? And why stare you so?
CASCA. Are not you moved, when all the sway of earth
  Shakes like a thing unfirm? O Cicero,
  I have seen tempests, when the scolding winds
  Have rived the knotty oaks, and I have seen
  The ambitious ocean swell and rage and foam,
  To be exalted with the threatening clouds;
  But never till tonight, never till now,
  Did I go through a tempest dropping fire.

208

Either there is a civil strife in heaven,
Or else the world, too saucy with the gods,
Incenses them to send destruction.

CICERO. Why, saw you anything more wonderful?

CASCA. A common slave—you know him well by sight—
Held up his left hand, which did flame and burn
Like twenty torches joined, and yet his hand,
Not sensible of fire, remained unscorched.
Besides—I ha' not since put up my sword—
Against the Capitol I met a lion,
Who glazed upon me, and went surly by,
Without annoying me. And there were drawn
Upon a heap a hundred ghastly women,
Transformed with their fear; who swore they saw
Men all in fire walk up and down the streets.
And yesterday the bird of night did sit
Even at noonday upon the market-place,
Hooting and shrieking. When these prodigies
Do so conjointly meet, let not men say,
"These are their reasons; they are natural";
For, I believe, they are portentous things
Unto the climate that they point upon.

CICERO. Indeed, it is a strange-disposed time;
But men may construe things after their fashion,
Clean from the purpose of the things themselves.
Comes Cæsar to the Capitol tomorrow?

CASCA. He doth; for he did bid Antonius
Send word to you he would be there tomorrow.

CICERO. Good night then, Casca. This disturbed sky
Is not to walk in.

CASCA. Farewell, Cicero.   Exit CICERO

Enter CASSIUS

CASSIUS. Who 's there?

CASCA.   A Roman.

CASSIUS.   Casca, by your voice.

CASCA. Your ear is good. Cassius, what night is this!

CASSIUS. A very pleasing night to honest men.

CASCA. Who ever knew the heavens menace so?

CASSIUS. Those that have known the earth so full of
    faults.
For my part, I have walked about the streets,
Submitting me unto the perilous night,
And, thus unbraced, Casca, as you see,
Have bared my bosom to the thunder-stone;
And when the cross blue lightning seemed to open
The breast of heaven, I did present myself
Even in the aim and very flash of it.

CASCA. But wherefore did you so much tempt the
    heavens?
It is the part of men to fear and tremble,
When the most mighty gods by tokens send
Such dreadful heralds to astonish us.

CASSIUS. You are dull, Casca, and those sparks of life
That should be in a Roman you do want,
Or else you use not. You look pale and gaze

And put on fear and cast yourself in wonder,
To see the strange impatience of the heavens.
But if you would consider the true cause
Why all these fires, why all these gliding ghosts,
Why birds and beasts from quality and kind,
Why old men, fools, and children calculate,
Why all these things change from their ordinance
Their natures and preformed faculties
To monstrous quality—why, you shall find
That heaven hath infused them with these spirits,
To make them instruments of fear and warning
Unto some monstrous state.
Now could I, Casca, name to thee a man
Most like this dreadful night,
That thunders, lightens, opens graves, and roars
As doth the lion in the Capitol,
A man no mightier than thyself or me
In personal action, yet prodigious grown
And fearful, as these strange eruptions are.

CASCA. 'Tis Cæsar that you mean; is it not, Cassius?

CASSIUS. Let it be who it is; for Romans now
Have thews and limbs like to their ancestors.
But, woe the while! Our fathers' minds are dead,
And we are governed with our mothers' spirits;
Our yoke and sufferance show us womanish.

CASCA. Indeed, they say the senators tomorrow
Mean to establish Cæsar as a king;
And he shall wear his crown by sea and land,
In every place, save here in Italy.

CASSIUS. I know where I will wear this dagger then;
Cassius from bondage will deliver Cassius.
Therein, ye gods, you make the weak most strong;
Therein, ye gods, you tyrants do defeat;
Nor stony tower, nor walls of beaten brass,
Nor airless dungeon, nor strong links of iron,
Can be retentive to the strength of spirit;
But life, being weary of these worldly bars,
Never lacks power to dismiss itself.
If I know this, know all the world besides,
That part of tyranny that I do bear
I can shake off at pleasure.   *Thunder*

CASCA.   So can I:
So every bondman in his own hand bears
The power to cancel his captivity.

CASSIUS. And why should Cæsar be a tyrant then?
Poor man! I know he would not be a wolf,
But that he sees the Romans are but sheep;
He were no lion, were not Romans hinds.
Those that with haste will make a mighty fire
Begin it with weak straws. What trash is Rome,
What rubbish and what offal, when it serves
For the base matter to illuminate
So vile a thing as Cæsar! But, O grief,
Where hast thou led me? I perhaps speak this
Before a willing bondman; then I know
My answer must be made. But I am armed,

And dangers are to me indifferent.

CASCA. You speak to Casca, and to such a man
   That is no fleering tell-tale. Hold, my hand.
   Be factious for redress of all these griefs,
   And I will set this foot of mine as far
   As who goes farthest.

CASSIUS.   There's a bargain made.
   Now know you, Casca, I have moved already
   Some certain of the noblest-minded Romans
   To undergo with me an enterprise
   Of honourable-dangerous consequence.
   And I do know, by this, they stay for me
   In Pompey's porch; for now, this fearful night,
   There is no stir or walking in the streets;
   And the complexion of the element
   Is favoured like the work we have in hand,
   Most bloody, fiery, and most terrible.

CASCA. Stand close awhile, for here comes one in haste.

CASSIUS. 'Tis Cinna; I do know him by his gait.
   He is a friend.

Enter CINNA

               Cinna, where haste you so?

CINNA. To find out you. Who's that? Metellus Cimber?

CASSIUS. No, it is Casca; one incorporate
   To our attempts. Am I not stayed for, Cinna?

CINNA. I am glad on 't. What a fearful night is this!
   There's two or three of us have seen strange sights.

CASSIUS. Am I not stayed for? Tell me.

CINNA.   Yes, you are.
   O Cassius, if you could
   But win the noble Brutus to our party—

CASSIUS. Be you content. Good Cinna, take this paper,
   And look you lay it in the praetor's chair,
   Where Brutus may but find it; and throw this
   In at his window; set this up with wax
   Upon old Brutus' statue. All this done,
   Repair to Pompey's porch, where you shall find us.
   Is Decius Brutus and Trebonius there?

CINNA. All but Metellus Cimber; and he's gone
   To seek you at your house. Well, I will hie,
   And so bestow these papers as you bade me.

CASSIUS. That done, repair to Pompey's theatre.

Exit CINNA

   Come, Casca, you and I will yet ere day
   See Brutus at his house. Three parts of him
   Is ours already, and the man entire
   Upon the next encounter yields him ours.

CASCA. O, he sits high in all the people's hearts;
   And that which would appear offence in us,
   His countenance, like richest alchemy,
   Will change to virtue and to worthiness.

CASSIUS. Him and his worth and our great need of him
   You have right well conceited. Let us go,
   For it is after midnight; and ere day
   We will awake him and be sure of him.   Exeunt

ACT II

Enter BRUTUS

BRUTUS. What, Lucius, ho!
I cannot, by the progress of the stars,
Give guess how near to day. Lucius, I say!
I would it were my fault to sleep so soundly.
When, Lucius, when? Awake, I say! What, Lucius!

Enter LUCIUS

LUCIUS. Called you, my lord?
BRUTUS. Get me a taper in my study, Lucius.
When it is lighted, come and call me here.
LUCIUS. I will, my lord.   *Exit*
BRUTUS. It must be by his death: and for my part,
I know no personal cause to spurn at him,
But for the general. He would be crowned:
How that might change his nature, there's the
question.
It is the bright day that brings forth the adder;
And that craves wary walking. Crown him that,
And then, I grant, we put a sting in him,
That at his will he may do danger with.
The abuse of greatness is, when it disjoins
Remorse from power. And, to speak truth of Cæsar,
I have not known when his affections swayed
More than his reason. But 'tis a common proof,
That lowliness is young ambition's ladder,
Whereto the climber-upward turns his face;
But when he once attains the upmost round,
He then unto the ladder turns his back,
Looks in the clouds, scorning the base degrees
By which he did ascend. So Cæsar may.
Then, lest he may, prevent. And, since the quarrel
Will bear no colour for the thing he is,
Fashion it thus; that what he is, augmented,
Would run to these and these extremities.
And therefore think him as a serpent's egg
Which, hatched, would, as his kind, grow mischievous,
And kill him in the shell.

Re-enter LUCIUS

LUCIUS. The taper burneth in your closet, sir.
Searching the window for a flint, I found
This paper, thus sealed up; and, I am sure,
It did not lie there when I went to bed.
                                        Gives him the letter
BRUTUS. Get you to bed again; it is not day.
Is not tomorrow, boy, the ides of March?
LUCIUS. I know not, sir.
BRUTUS. Look in the calendar, and bring me word.
LUCIUS. I will, sir.   *Exit*
BRUTUS. The exhalations whizzing in the air

Give so much light that I may read by them.
                                        Opens the letter and reads
"Brutus, thou sleep'st; awake, and see thyself.
Shall Rome, &c. Speak, strike, redress!"
"Brutus, thou sleep'st; awake!"
Such instigations have been often dropped
Where I have took them up.
"Shall Rome, &c." Thus must I piece it out:
Shall Rome stand under one man's awe? What, Rome?
My ancestors did from the streets of Rome
The Tarquin drive, when he was called a king.
"Speak, strike, redress!" Am I entreated
To speak and strike? O Rome, I make thee promise;
If the redress will follow, thou receivest
Thy full petition at the hand of Brutus!

Re-enter LUCIUS

LUCIUS. Sir, March is wasted fourteen days.
                                        Knocking within
BRUTUS. 'Tis good. Go to the gate; somebody knocks.
                                        Exit LUCIUS
Since Cassius first did whet me against Cæsar,
I have not slept.
Between the acting of a dreadful thing
And the first motion, all the interim is
Like a phantasma, or a hideous dream.
The Genius and the mortal instruments
Are then in council; and the state of man,
Like to a little kingdom, suffers then
The nature of an insurrection.

Re-enter LUCIUS

LUCIUS. Sir, 'tis your brother Cassius at the door,
Who doth desire to see you.
BRUTUS.   Is he alone?
LUCIUS. No, sir, there are more with him.
BRUTUS.   Do you know them?
LUCIUS. No, sir; their hats are plucked about their ears,
And half their faces buried in their cloaks,
That by no means I may discover them
By any mark of favour.
BRUTUS.   Let 'em enter.   *Exit* LUCIUS
They are the faction. O conspiracy,
Shamest thou to show thy dangerous brow by night,
When evils are most free? O, then by day
Where wilt thou find a cavern dark enough
To mask thy monstrous visage? Seek none, conspiracy;
Hide it in smiles and affability;
For if thou put thy native semblance on,
Not Erebus itself were dim enough
To hide thee from prevention.

Enter the conspirators, CASSIUS, CASCA, DECIUS, CINNA,
    METELLUS CIMBER, *and* TREBONIUS

CASSIUS. I think we are too bold upon your rest.
  Good morrow, Brutus; do we trouble you?
BRUTUS. I have been up this hour, awake all night.
  Know I these men that come along with you?
CASSIUS. Yes, every man of them, and no man here
  But honours you; and every one doth wish
  You had but that opinion of yourself
  Which every noble Roman bears of you.
  This is Trebonius.
BRUTUS.   He is welcome hither.
CASSIUS. This, Decius Brutus.
BRUTUS.   He is welcome too.
CASSIUS. This, Casca; this, Cinna; and this, Metellus
    Cimber.
BRUTUS. They are all welcome.
  What watchful cares do interpose themselves
  Betwixt your eyes and night?
CASSIUS. Shall I entreat a word?
                    BRUTUS *and* CASSIUS *whisper*
DECIUS. Here lies the east; doth not the day break here?
CASCA. No.
CINNA. O, pardon, sir, it doth; and yon gray lines
  That fret the clouds are messengers of day.
CASCA. You shall confess that you are both deceived.
  Here, as I point my sword, the sun arises,
  Which is a great way growing on the south,
  Weighing the youthful season of the year.
  Some two months hence up higher toward the north
  He first presents his fire; and the high east
  Stands, as the Capitol, directly here.
BRUTUS. Give me your hands all over, one by one.
CASSIUS. And let us swear our resolution.
BRUTUS. No, not an oath; if not the face of men,
  The sufferance of our souls, the time's abuse—

If these be motives weak, break off betimes,
And every man hence to his idle bed.
So let high-sighted tyranny range on,
Till each man drop by lottery. But if these,
As I am sure they do, bear fire enough
To kindle cowards and to steel with valour
The melting spirits of women, then, countrymen,
What need we any spur but our own cause,
To prick us to redress? What other bond
Than secret Romans, that have spoke the word,
And will not palter? And what other oath
Than honesty to honesty engaged,
That this shall be, or we will fall for it?
Swear priests and cowards and men cautelous,
Old feeble carrions and such suffering souls
That welcome wrongs; unto bad causes swear
Such creatures as men doubt; but do not stain
The even virtue of our enterprise,
Nor the insuppressive mettle of our spirits,
To think that or our cause or our performance
Did need an oath; when every drop of blood
That every Roman bears, and nobly bears,
Is guilty of a several bastardy,
If he do break the smallest particle
Of any promise that hath passed from him.

CASSIUS. But what of Cicero? Shall we sound him?
I think he will stand very strong with us.

CASCA. Let us not leave him out.

CINNA.   No, by no means.

METELLUS. O, let us have him, for his silver hairs
Will purchase us a good opinion
And buy men's voices to commend our deeds.
It shall be said, his judgement ruled our hands;
Our youths and wildness shall no whit appear,
But all be buried in his gravity.

BRUTUS. O, name him not. Let us not break with him;
For he will never follow anything
That other men begin.

CASSIUS.   Then leave him out.

CASCA. Indeed he is not fit.

DECIUS. Shall no man else be touched but only Cæsar?

CASSIUS. Decius, well urged. I think it is not meet,
Mark Antony, so well beloved of Cæsar,
Should outlive Cæsar. We shall find of him
A shrewd contriver; and, you know, his means,
If he improve them, may well stretch so far
As to annoy us all; which to prevent,
Let Antony and Cæsar fall together.

BRUTUS. Our course will seem too bloody, Caius
    Cassius,
To cut the head off and then hack the limbs,
Like wrath in death and envy afterwards;
For Antony is but a limb of Cæsar.
Let us be sacrificers, but not butchers, Caius.
We all stand up against the spirit of Cæsar;
And in the spirit of men there is no blood.

O, that we then could come by Cæsar's spirit,
And not dismember Cæsar! But, alas,
Cæsar must bleed for it! And, gentle friends,
Let's kill him boldly, but not wrathfully;
Let's carve him as a dish fit for the gods,
Not hew him as a carcass fit for hounds.
And let our hearts, as subtle masters do,
Stir up their servants to an act of rage,
And after seem to chide 'em. This shall make
Our purpose necessary and not envious;
Which so appearing to the common eyes,
We shall be called purgers, not murderers.
And for Mark Antony, think not of him;
For he can do no more than Cæsar's arm
When Cæsar's head is off.

CASSIUS.   Yet I fear him;
For in the ingrafted love he bears to Cæsar—

BRUTUS. Alas, good Cassius, do not think of him:
If he love Cæsar, all that he can do
Is to himself, take thought and die for Cæsar.
And that were much he should; for he is given
To sports, to wildness and much company.

TREBONIUS. There is no fear in him; let him not die;
For he will live, and laugh at this hereafter.

                                        Clock strikes

BRUTUS. Peace! Count the clock.

CASSIUS.   The clock hath stricken three.

TREBONIUS. 'Tis time to part.

CASSIUS.   But it is doubtful yet,
Whether Cæsar will come forth today, or no;
For he is superstitious grown of late,
Quite from the main opinion he held once
Of fantasy, of dreams and ceremonies.
It may be, these apparent prodigies,
The unaccustomed terror of this night,
And the persuasion of his augurers,
May hold him from the Capitol today.

DECIUS. Never fear that. If he be so resolved,
I can o'ersway him; for he loves to hear
That unicorns may be betrayed with trees,
And bears with glasses, elephants with holes,
Lions with toils and men with flatterers;
But when I tell him he hates flatterers,
He says he does, being then most flattered.
Let me work;
For I can give his humour the true bent,
And I will bring him to the Capitol.

CASSIUS. Nay, we will all of us be there to fetch him.

BRUTUS. By the eighth hour; is that the uttermost?

CINNA. Be that the uttermost, and fail not then.

METELLUS. Caius Ligarius doth bear Cæsar hard,
Who rated him for speaking well of Pompey.
I wonder none of you have thought of him.

BRUTUS. Now, good Metellus, go along by him.
He loves me well, and I have given him reasons;
Send him but hither, and I'll fashion him.

CASSIUS. The morning comes upon 's. We'll leave you,
    Brutus.
  And, friends, disperse yourselves; but all remember
  What you have said, and show yourselves true Romans.
BRUTUS. Good gentlemen, look fresh and merrily;
  Let not our looks put on our purposes,
  But bear it as our Roman actors do,
  With untired spirits and formal constancy.
  And so good morrow to you every one.

               Exeunt all but BRUTUS

  Boy! Lucius! Fast asleep? It is no matter;
  Enjoy the honey-heavy dew of slumber.
  Thou hast no figures nor no fantasies,
  Which busy care draws in the brains of men;
  Therefore thou sleep'st so sound.

Enter PORTIA

PORTIA.   Brutus, my lord!
BRUTUS. Portia, what mean you? Wherefore rise you
    now?
  It is not for your health thus to commit
  Your weak condition to the raw cold morning.
PORTIA. Nor for yours neither. You've ungently,
    Brutus,
  Stole from my bed; and yesternight, at supper,
  You suddenly arose, and walked about,
  Musing and sighing, with your arms across,
  And when I asked you what the matter was,
  You stared upon me with ungentle looks;
  I urged you further; then you scratched your head,
  And too impatiently stamped with your foot.
  Yet I insisted, yet you answered not,
  But, with an angry wafture of your hand,
  Gave sign for me to leave you. So I did,
  Fearing to strengthen that impatience
  Which seemed too much enkindled, and withal
  Hoping it was but an effect of humour,
  Which sometime hath his hour with every man.
  It will not let you eat, nor talk, nor sleep,
  And could it work so much upon your shape
  As it hath much prevailed on your condition,
  I should not know you, Brutus. Dear my lord,
  Make me acquainted with your cause of grief.
BRUTUS. I am not well in health, and that is all.
PORTIA. Brutus is wise, and, were he not in health,
  He would embrace the means to come by it.
BRUTUS. Why, so I do. Good Portia, go to bed.
PORTIA. Is Brutus sick? And is it physical
  To walk unbraced and suck up the humours
  Of the dank morning? What, is Brutus sick,
  And will he steal out of his wholesome bed,
  To dare the vile contagion of the night
  And tempt the rheumy and unpurged air
  To add unto his sickness? No, my Brutus;
  You have some sick offence within your mind,
  Which, by the right and virtue of my place,

  I ought to know of; and, upon my knees,
  I charm you, by my once-commended beauty,
  By all your vows of love and that great vow
  Which did incorporate and make us one,
  That you unfold to me, yourself, your half,
  Why you are heavy, and what men tonight
  Have had resort to you; for here have been
  Some six or seven, who did hide their faces
  Even from darkness.
BRUTUS.   Kneel not, gentle Portia.
PORTIA. I should not need, if you were gentle Brutus.
  Within the bond of marriage, tell me, Brutus,
  Is it excepted I should know no secrets
  That appertain to you? Am I yourself
  But, as it were, in sort or limitation,
  To keep with you at meals, comfort your bed,
  And talk to you sometimes? Dwell I but in the suburbs
  Of your good pleasure? If it be no more,
  Portia is Brutus' harlot, not his wife.
BRUTUS. You are my true and honourable wife,
  As dear to me as are the ruddy drops
  That visit my sad heart.
PORTIA. If this were true, then should I know this
    secret.
  I grant I am a woman; but withal
  A woman that Lord Brutus took to wife.
  I grant I am a woman; but withal
  A woman well-reputed, Cato's daughter.
  Think you I am no stronger than my sex,
  Being so fathered and so husbanded?
  Tell me your counsels, I will not disclose 'em;
  I have made strong proof of my constancy,
  Giving myself a voluntary wound
  Here, in the thigh. Can I bear that with patience,
  And not my husband's secrets?
BRUTUS.   O ye gods,
  Render me worthy of this noble wife!

                   Knocking within

  Hark, hark! One knocks. Portia, go in awhile;
  And by and by thy bosom shall partake
  The secrets of my heart.
  All my engagements I will construe to thee,
  All the charactery of my sad brows.
  Leave me with haste. [*Exit Portia*] Lucius, who's that
    knocks?

Re-enter LUCIUS *with* LIGARIUS

LUCIUS. Here is a sick man that would speak with you.
BRUTUS. Caius Ligarius, that Metellus spake of.
  Boy, stand aside. Caius Ligarius! how?
LIGARIUS. Vouchsafe good morrow from a feeble tongue.
BRUTUS. O, what a time have you chose out, brave
    Caius,
  To wear a kerchief! Would you were not sick!
LIGARIUS. I am not sick, if Brutus have in hand
  Any exploit worthy the name of honour.

BRUTUS. Such an exploit have I in hand, Ligarius,
Had you a healthful ear to hear of it.
LIGARIUS. By all the gods that Romans bow before,
I here discard my sickness! Soul of Rome!
Brave son, derived from honourable loins!
Thou, like an exorcist, hast conjured up
My mortified spirit. Now bid me run,
And I will strive with things impossible;
Yea, get the better of them. What's to do?
BRUTUS. A piece of work that will make sick men whole.

LIGARIUS. But are not some whole that we must make
sick?
BRUTUS. That must we also. What it is, my Caius,
I shall unfold to thee, as we are going
To whom it must be done.
LIGARIUS.   Set on your foot,
And with a heart new-fired I follow you,
To do I know not what; but it sufficeth
That Brutus leads me on.
BRUTUS.   Follow me, then.   *Exeunt*

SCENE II *Cæsar's house*

Thunder and lightning. Enter CÆSAR, *in his night-gown*

CÆSAR. Nor heaven nor earth have been at peace
tonight.
Thrice hath Calpurnia in her sleep cried out,
"Help, ho! they murder Cæsar!" Who's within?

Enter a Servant

SERVANT. My lord?
CÆSAR. Go bid the priests do present sacrifice
And bring me their opinions of success.
SERVANT. I will, my lord.   *Exit*

Enter CALPURNIA

CALPURNIA. What mean you, Cæsar? Think you to
walk forth?
You shall not stir out of your house today.
CÆSAR. Cæsar shall forth. The things that threatened me
Ne'er looked but on my back; when they shall see
The face of Cæsar, they are vanished.
CALPURNIA. Cæsar, I never stood on ceremonies,
Yet now they fright me. There is one within,
Besides the things that we have heard and seen,
Recounts most horrid sights seen by the watch.
A lioness hath whelped in the streets;
And graves have yawned, and yielded up their dead;
Fierce fiery warriors fought upon the clouds,
In ranks and squadrons and right form of war,
Which drizzled blood upon the Capitol;
The noise of battle hurtled in the air,
Horses did neigh, and dying men did groan,
And ghosts did shriek and squeal about the streets.
O Cæsar! these things are beyond all use,
And I do fear them.
CÆSAR.   What can be avoided
Whose end is purposed by the mighty gods?
Yet Cæsar shall go forth; for these predictions
Are to the world in general as to Cæsar.
CALPURNIA. When beggars die, there are no comets
seen;
The heavens themselves blaze forth the death of
princes.
CÆSAR. Cowards die many times before their deaths;
The valiant never taste of death but once.

Of all the wonders that I yet have heard,
It seems to me most strange that men should fear;
Seeing that death, a necessary end,
Will come when it will come.

Re-enter Servant

                              What say the augurers?
SERVANT. They would not have you to stir forth today.
Plucking the entrails of an offering forth,
They could not find a heart within the beast.
CÆSAR. The gods do this in shame of cowardice.
Cæsar should be a beast without a heart,
If he should stay at home today for fear.
No, Cæsar shall not; danger knows full well
That Cæsar is more dangerous than he.
We are two lions littered in one day,
And I the elder and more terrible;
And Cæsar shall go forth.
CALPURNIA.   Alas, my lord,
Your wisdom is consumed in confidence.
Do not go forth today. Call it my fear
That keeps you in the house, and not your own.
We'll send Mark Antony to the Senate House;
And he shall say you are not well today.
Let me, upon my knee, prevail in this.
CÆSAR. Mark Antony shall say I am not well;
And, for thy humour, I will stay at home.

Enter DECIUS

Here's Decius Brutus, he shall tell them so.
DECIUS. Cæsar, all hail! Good morrow, worthy Cæsar;
I come to fetch you to the Senate House.
CÆSAR. And you are come in very happy time,
To bear my greeting to the senators
And tell them that I will not come today.
Cannot, is false, and that I dare not, falser.
I will not come today; tell them so, Decius.
CALPURNIA. Say he is sick.
CÆSAR.   Shall Cæsar send a lie?
Have I in conquest stretched mine arm so far,
To be afeared to tell graybeards the truth?
Decius, go tell them Cæsar will not come.

DECIUS. Most mighty Cæsar, let me know some cause,
    Lest I be laughed at when I tell them so.
CÆSAR. The cause is in my will. I will not come;
    That is enough to satisfy the senate.
    But for your private satisfaction,
    Because I love you, I will let you know:
    Calpurnia here, my wife, stays me at home;
    She dreamt tonight she saw my statue,
    Which like a fountain with an hundred spouts,
    Did run pure blood; and many lusty Romans
    Came smiling, and did bathe their hands in it.
    And these does she apply for warnings, and portents,
    And evils imminent; and on her knee
    Hath begged that I will stay at home today.
DECIUS. This dream is all amiss interpreted;
    It was a vison fair and fortunate:
    Your statue spouting blood in many pipes,
    In which so many smiling Romans bathed,
    Signifies that from you great Rome shall suck
    Reviving blood, and that great men shall press
    For tinctures, stains, relics and cognizance.
    This by Calpurnia's dream is signified.
CÆSAR. And this way have you well expounded it.
DECIUS. I have, when you have heard what I can say:
    And know it now—the senate have concluded
    To give this day a crown to mighty Cæsar.
    If you shall send them word you will not come,
    Their minds may change. Besides, it were a mock
    Apt to be rendered, for some one to say
    "Break up the senate till another time,
    When Cæsar's wife shall meet with better dreams."
    If Cæsar hide himself, shall they not whisper
    "Lo, Cæsar is afraid"?
    Pardon me, Cæsar; for my dear dear love
    To your proceeding bids me tell you this;
    And reason to my love is liable.

CÆSAR. How foolish do your fears seem now, Calpurnia!
    I am ashamed I did yield to them.
    Give me my robe, for I will go.

Enter PUBLIUS, BRUTUS, LIGARIUS, METELLUS, CASCA,
TREBONIUS, *and* CINNA

    And look where Publius is come to fetch me.
PUBLIUS. Good morrow, Cæsar.
CÆSAR.   Welcome, Publius.
    What, Brutus, are you stirred so early too?
    Good morrow, Casca. Caius Ligarius,
    Cæsar was ne'er so much your enemy
    As that same ague which has made you lean.
    What is 't o'clock?
BRUTUS.   Cæsar, 'tis strucken eight.
CÆSAR. I thank you for your pains and courtesy.

Enter ANTONY

    See! Antony, that revels long o' nights,
    Is notwithstanding up. Good morrow, Antony.
ANTONY. So to most noble Cæsar.
CÆSAR.   Bid them prepare within.
    I am to blame to be thus waited for.
    Now, Cinna; now, Metellus; what, Trebonius!
    I have an hour's talk in store for you;
    Remember that you call on me today.
    Be near me, that I may remember you.
TREBONIUS. Cæsar, I will. [*Aside*] And so near will
    I be,
    That your best friends shall wish I had been further.
CÆSAR. Good friends, go in, and taste some wine with
    me;
    And we, like friends, will straightway go together.
BRUTUS. [*Aside*] That every like is not the same, O
    Cæsar,
    The heart of Brutus yearns to think upon!   *Exeunt*

SCENE III *A street near the Capitol*

Enter ARTEMIDORUS, *reading a paper*

ARTEMIDORUS. "Cæsar, beware of Brutus; take heed
    of Cassius; come not near Casca; have an eye to
    Cinna; trust not Trebonius; mark well Metellus
    Cimber; Decius Brutus loves thee not; thou hast
    wronged Caius Ligarius. There is but one mind in all
    these men, and it is bent against Cæsar. If thou beest
    not immortal, look about you: security gives way to
    conspiracy. The mighty gods defend thee! Thy lover,
                                    "ARTEMIDORUS."
    Here will I stand till Cæsar pass along,
    And as a suitor will I give him this.
    My heart laments that virtue cannot live
    Out of the teeth of emulation.
    If thou read this, O Cæsar, thou mayst live;
    If not, the Fates with traitors do contrive.   *Exit*

ACT II, SCENE IV

SCENE IV *Another part of the same street, before the house of Brutus*

Enter PORTIA *and* LUCIUS

PORTIA. I prithee, boy, run to the Senate House;
  Stay not to answer me, but get thee gone.
  Why dost thou stay?
LUCIUS.   To know my errand, madam.
PORTIA. I would have had thee there, and here again,
  Ere I can tell thee what thou shouldst do there.
  O constancy, be strong upon my side,
  Set a huge mountain 'tween my heart and tongue!
  I have a man's mind, but a woman's might.
  How hard it is for women to keep counsel!
  Art thou here yet?
LUCIUS.   Madam, what should I do?
  Run to the Capitol, and nothing else?
  And so return to you, and nothing else?
PORTIA. Yes, bring me word, boy, if thy lord look well,
  For he went sickly forth; and take good note
  What Cæsar doth, what suitors press to him.
  Hark, boy! what noise is that?
LUCIUS. I hear none, madam.
PORTIA.   Prithee, listen well;
  I heard a bustling rumour, like a fray,
  And the wind brings it from the Capitol.
LUCIUS. Sooth, madam, I hear nothing.

Enter the Soothsayer

PORTIA. Come hither, fellow. Which way hast thou
  been?
SOOTHSAYER. At mine own house, good lady.

PORTIA. What is 't o'clock?
SOOTHSAYER.   About the ninth hour, lady.
PORTIA. Is Cæsar yet gone to the Capitol?
SOOTHSAYER. Madam, not yet. I go to take my stand,
  To see him pass on to the Capitol.
PORTIA. Thou hast some suit to Cæsar, hast thou not?
SOOTHSAYER. That I have, lady. If it will please Cæsar
  To be so good to Cæsar as to hear me,
  I shall beseech him to befriend himself.
PORTIA. Why, know'st thou any harm's intended to-
  wards him?
SOOTHSAYER. None that I know will be, much that I
  fear may chance.
  Good morrow to you. Here the street is narrow;
  The throng that follows Cæsar at the heels,
  Of senators, of praetors, common suitors,
  Will crowd a feeble man almost to death.
  I'll get me to a place more void, and there
  Speak to great Cæsar as he comes along.   *Exit*
PORTIA. I must go in. Ay me, how weak a thing
  The heart of woman is! O Brutus,
  The heavens speed thee in thine enterprise!
  Sure, the boy heard me; Brutus hath a suit
  That Cæsar will not grant. O, I grow faint.
  Run, Lucius, and commend me to my lord;
  Say I am merry. Come to me again,
  And bring me word what he doth say to thee.
                                      Exeunt

ACT III

SCENE I *Rome. Before the Capitol; the Senate sitting above*

A crowd of people; among them ARTEMIDORUS *and the* Soothsayer. *Flourish. Enter* CÆSAR, BRUTUS, CASSIUS, CASCA, DECIUS, METELLUS, TREBONIUS, CINNA, ANTONY, LEPIDUS, POPILIUS, PUBLIUS, *and others*

CÆSAR. [*To the Soothsayer*] The ides of March are come.
SOOTHSAYER. Ay, Cæsar; but not gone.
ARTEMIDORUS. Hail, Cæsar! Read this schedule.
DECIUS. Trebonius doth desire you to o'er-read,
  At your best leisure, this his humble suit.
ARTEMIDORUS. O Cæsar, read mine first; for mine's a
  suit
  That touches Cæsar nearer. Read it, great Cæsar.
CÆSAR. What touches us ourself shall be last served.
ARTEMIDORUS. Delay not, Cæsar; read it instantly.
CÆSAR. What, is the fellow mad?
PUBLIUS.   Sirrah, give place.
CASSIUS. What, urge you your petitions in the street?
  Come to the Capitol.
      CÆSAR *goes up to the Senate House, the rest following*

POPILIUS. I wish your enterprise today may thrive.
CASSIUS. What enterprise, Popilius?
POPILIUS.   Fare you well.
                      Advances to CÆSAR
BRUTUS. What said Popilius Lena?
CASSIUS. He wished today our enterprise might thrive.
  I fear our purpose is discovered.
BRUTUS. Look, how he makes to Cæsar; mark him.
CASSIUS. Casca, be sudden, for we fear prevention.
  Brutus, what shall be done? If this be known,
  Cassius or Cæsar never shall turn back,
  For I will slay myself.
BRUTUS.   Cassius, be constant.
  Popilius Lena speaks not of our purposes;
  For, look, he smiles, and Cæsar doth not change.

CASSIUS. Trebonius knows his time; for, look you, Brutus,
   He draws Mark Antony out of the way.
                    Exeunt ANTONY *and* TREBONIUS

DECIUS. Where is Metellus Cimber? Let him go,
   And presently prefer his suit to Cæsar.

BRUTUS. He is addressed; press near and second him.

CINNA. Casca, you are the first that rears your hand.

CÆSAR. Are we all ready? What is now amiss
   That Cæsar and his senate must redress?

METELLUS. Most high, most mighty, and most puissant
   Cæsar,
   Metellus Cimber throws before thy seat
   An humble heart—   *Kneeling*

CÆSAR.   I must prevent thee, Cimber.
   These couchings and these lowly courtesies
   Might fire the blood of ordinary men,
   And turn pre-ordinance and first decree
   Into the law of children. Be not fond,
   To think that Cæsar bears such rebel blood
   That will be thawed from the true quality
   With that which melteth fools; I mean, sweet words,
   Low-crooked curtsies and base spaniel-fawning.
   Thy brother by decree is banished.
   If thou dost bend and pray and fawn for him,
   I spurn thee like a cur out of my way.
   Know, Cæsar doth not wrong, nor without cause
   Will he be satisfied.

METELLUS. Is there no voice more worthy than my own,
   To sound more sweetly in great Cæsar's ear
   For the repealing of my banished brother?

BRUTUS. I kiss thy hand, but not in flattery, Cæsar;
   Desiring thee that Publius Cimber may
   Have an immediate freedom of repeal.

CÆSAR. What, Brutus!

CASSIUS.   Pardon, Cæsar; Cæsar, pardon.
   As low as to thy foot doth Cassius fall,
   To beg enfranchisement for Publius Cimber.

CÆSAR. I could be well moved, if I were as you;
   If I could pray to move, prayers would move me.
   But I am constant as the northern star,
   Of whose true-fixed and resting quality
   There is no fellow in the firmament.
   The skies are painted with unnumbered sparks,
   They are all fire and every one doth shine,
   But there's but one in all doth hold his place.
   So in the world; 'tis furnished well with men,
   And men are flesh and blood, and apprehensive;
   Yet in the number I do know but one
   That unassailable holds on his rank,
   Unshaked of motion: and that I am he,
   Let me a little show it, even in this;
   That I was constant Cimber should be banished,
   And constant do remain to keep him so.

CINNA. O Cæsar—

CÆSAR.   Hence! Wilt thou lift up Olympus?

DECIUS. Great Cæsar—

CÆSAR.   Doth not Brutus bootless kneel?

CASCA. Speak, hands, for me!
        CASCA *first, then the other* CONSPIRATORS *and*
            MARCUS BRUTUS *stab* CÆSAR

CÆSAR. Et tu, Brute! Then fall, Cæsar!   *Dies*

CINNA. Liberty! Freedom! Tyranny is dead!
  Run hence, proclaim, cry it about the streets.
CASSIUS. Some to the common pulpits, and cry out
  "Liberty, freedom, and enfranchisement!"
BRUTUS. People and senators, be not affrighted;
  Fly not; stand still; ambition's debt is paid.
CASCA. Go to the pulpit, Brutus.
DECIUS.   And Cassius too.
BRUTUS. Where's Publius?
CINNA. Here, quite confounded with this mutiny.
METELLUS. Stand fast together, lest some friend of
    Cæsar's
  Should chance—
BRUTUS. Talk not of standing. Publius, good cheer;
  There is no harm intended to your person,
  Nor to no Roman else. So tell them, Publius.
CASSIUS. And leave us, Publius; lest that the people,
  Rushing on us, should do your age some mischief.
BRUTUS. Do so; and let no man abide this deed,
  But we the doers.

Re-enter TREBONIUS

CASSIUS.   Where is Antony?
TREBONIUS. Fled to his house amazed.
  Men, wives and children stare, cry out and run
  As it were Doomsday.
BRUTUS.   Fates, we will know your pleasures:
  That we shall die, we know; 'tis but the time
  And drawing days out, that men stand upon.
CASCA. Why, he that cuts off twenty years of life
  Cuts off so many years of fearing death.
BRUTUS. Grant that, and then is death a benefit.
  So are we Cæsar's friends, that have abridged
  His time of fearing death. Stoop, Romans, stoop,
  And let us bathe our hands in Cæsar's blood
  Up to the elbows, and besmear our swords.
  Then walk we forth, even to the market-place,
  And, waving our red weapons o'er our heads,
  Let's all cry "Peace, freedom and liberty!"
CASSIUS. Stoop, then, and wash. How many ages hence
  Shall this our lofty scene be acted over
  In states unborn and accents yet unknown!
BRUTUS. How many times shall Cæsar bleed in sport,
  That now on Pompey's basis lies along
  No worthier than the dust!
CASSIUS.   So oft as that shall be,
  So often shall the knot of us be called
  The men that gave their country liberty.
DECIUS. What, shall we forth?
CASSIUS.   Ay, every man away.
  Brutus shall lead; and we will grace his heels
  With the most boldest and best hearts of Rome.

Enter a Servant

BRUTUS. Soft! who comes here? A friend of Antony's.
SERVANT. Thus, Brutus, did my master bid me kneel;

Thus did Mark Antony bid me fall down;
And, being prostrate, thus he bade me say:
Brutus is noble, wise, valiant, and honest;
Cæsar was mighty, bold, royal, and loving.
Say I love Brutus, and I honour him;
Say I feared Cæsar, honoured him and loved him.
If Brutus will vouchsafe that Antony
May safely come to him, and be resolved
How Cæsar hath deserved to lie in death,
Mark Antony shall not love Cæsar dead
So well as Brutus living; but will follow
The fortunes and affairs of noble Brutus
Through the hazards of this untrod state
With all true faith. So says my master Antony.
BRUTUS. Thy master is a wise and valiant Roman;
  I never thought him worse.
  Tell him, so please him come unto this place,
  He shall be satisfied; and, by my honour,
  Depart untouched.
SERVANT.   I'll fetch him presently.   *Exit*
BRUTUS. I know that we shall have him well to friend.
CASSIUS. I wish we may; but yet have I a mind
  That fears him much; and my misgiving still
  Falls shrewdly to the purpose.
BRUTUS. But here comes Antony.

Re-enter ANTONY

                    Welcome, Mark Antony.

ANTONY. O mighty Cæsar! dost thou lie so low?
  Are all thy conquests, glories, triumphs, spoils,
  Shrunk to this little measure? Fare thee well.
  I know not, gentlemen, what you intend,
  Who else must be let blood, who else is rank.
  If I myself, there is no hour so fit
  As Cæsar's death's hour, nor no instrument
  Of half that worth as those your swords, made rich
  With the most noble blood of all this world.
  I do beseech ye, if you bear me hard,
  Now, whilst your purpled hands do reek and smoke,
  Fulfil your pleasure. Live a thousand years,
  I shall not find myself so apt to die;
  No place will please me so, no mean of death,
  As here by Cæsar, and by you cut off,
  The choice and master spirits of this age.
BRUTUS. O Antony, beg not your death of us.
  Though now we must appear bloody and cruel,
  As, by our hands and this our present act,
  You see we do, yet see you but our hands
  And this the bleeding business they have done.
  Our hearts you see not; they are pitiful;
  And pity to the general wrong of Rome—
  As fire drives out fire, so pity pity—
  Hath done this deed on Cæsar. For your part,
  To you our swords have leaden points, Mark Antony.
  Our arms, in strength of malice, and our hearts
  Of brothers' temper, do receive you in
  With all kind love, good thoughts, and reverence.
CASSIUS. Your voice shall be as strong as any man's
  In the disposing of new dignities.

BRUTUS. Only be patient till we have appeased
　The multitude, beside themselves with fear,
　And then we will deliver you the cause,
　Why I, that did love Cæsar when I struck him,
　Have thus proceeded.
ANTONY.　　　　　I doubt not of your wisdom.
　Let each man render me his bloody hand.
　First, Marcus Brutus, will I shake with you;
　Next, Caius Cassius, do I take your hand;
　Now, Decius Brutus, yours; now yours, Metellus;
　Yours, Cinna; and, my valiant Casca, yours;
　Though last, not least in love, yours, good Trebonius.
　Gentlemen all—alas, what shall I say?
　My credit now stands on such slippery ground,
　That one of two bad ways you must conceit me,
　Either a coward or a flatterer.
　That I did love thee, Cæsar, O, 'tis true.
　If then thy spirit look upon us now,
　Shall it not grieve thee dearer than thy death,
　To see thy Antony making his peace,
　Shaking the bloody fingers of thy foes,
　Most noble! in the presence of thy corpse?
　Had I as many eyes as thou hast wounds,
　Weeping as fast as they stream forth thy blood,
　It would become me better than to close
　In terms of friendship with thine enemies.
　Pardon me, Julius! Here wast thou bayed, brave hart;
　Here didst thou fall; and here thy hunters stand,
　Signed in thy spoil, and crimsoned in thy lethe.
　O world, thou wast the forest to this hart;
　And this, indeed, O world, the heart of thee.
　How like a deer, strucken by many princes,
　Dost thou here lie!
CASSIUS. Mark Antony—
ANTONY.　　　　　Pardon me, Caius Cassius.
　The enemies of Cæsar shall say this;
　Then, in a friend, it is cold modesty.
CASSIUS. I blame you not for praising Cæsar so;
　But what compact mean you to have with us?
　Will you be pricked in number of our friends;
　Or shall we on, and not depend on you?
ANTONY. Therefore I took your hands, but was, indeed,
　Swayed from the point, by looking down on Cæsar.
　Friends am I with you all and love you all,
　Upon this hope, that you shall give me reasons
　Why and wherein Cæsar was dangerous.
BRUTUS. Or else were this a savage spectacle.
　Our reasons are so full of good regard
　That were you, Antony, the son of Cæsar,
　You should be satisfied.
ANTONY.　　　　　That's all I seek;
　And am moreover suitor that I may
　Produce his body to the market-place;
　And in the pulpit, as becomes a friend,
　Speak in the order of his funeral.
BRUTUS. You shall, Mark Antony.

CASSIUS.　　　　　Brutus, a word with you.
　[Aside to Brutus] You know not what you do. Do not
　　consent
　That Antony speak in his funeral.
　Know you how much the people may be moved
　By that which he will utter?
BRUTUS.　　　　　By your pardon;
　I will myself into the pulpit first,
　And show the reason of our Cæsar's death.
　What Antony shall speak, I will protest
　He speaks by leave and by permission,
　And that we are contented Cæsar shall
　Have all true rites and lawful ceremonies.
　It shall advantage more than do us wrong.
CASSIUS. I know not what may fall; I like it not.
BRUTUS. Mark Antony, here, take you Cæsar's body.
　You shall not in your funeral speech blame us,
　But speak all good you can devise of Cæsar,
　And say you do 't by our permission;
　Else shall you not have any hand at all
　About his funeral. And you shall speak
　In the same pulpit whereto I am going,
　After my speech is ended.
ANTONY.　　　　　Be it so;
　I do desire no more.
BRUTUS. Prepare the body then, and follow us.
　　　　　　　　　　　　　　Exeunt all but ANTONY
ANTONY. O, pardon me, thou bleeding piece of earth,
　That I am meek and gentle with these butchers!
　Thou art the ruins of the noblest man
　That ever lived in the tide of times.
　Woe to the hand that shed this costly blood!
　Over thy wounds now do I prophesy—
　Which, like dumb mouths, do ope their ruby lips,
　To beg the voice and utterance of my tongue—
　A curse shall light upon the limbs of men;
　Domestic fury and fierce civil strife
　Shall cumber all the parts of Italy;
　Blood and destruction shall be so in use
　And dreadful objects so familiar
　That mothers shall but smile when they behold
　Their infants quartered with the hands of war;
　All pity choked with custom of fell deeds;
　And Cæsar's spirit, ranging for revenge,
　With Ate by his side come hot from hell,
　Shall in these confines with a monarch's voice
　Cry "Havoc," and let slip the dogs of war,
　That this foul deed shall smell above the earth
　With carrion men, groaning for burial.
　　　　　　　　　　　Enter a Servant
　You serve Octavius Cæsar, do you not?
SERVANT. I do, Mark Antony.
ANTONY. Cæsar did write for him to come to Rome.
SERVANT. He did receive his letters, and is coming;
　And bid me say to you by word of mouth—
　O Cæsar!—　　　　　　　　Seeing the body

ANTONY. Thy heart is big, get thee apart and weep.
　Passion, I see, is catching; for mine eyes,
　Seeing those beads of sorrow stand in thine,
　Began to water. Is thy master coming?
SERVANT. He lies tonight within seven leagues of Rome.
ANTONY. Post back with speed, and tell him what hath
　　chanced.
　Here is a mourning Rome, a dangerous Rome,
　No Rome of safety for Octavius yet.

Hie hence, and tell him so. Yet, stay awhile;
Thou shalt not back till I have borne this corpse
Into the market-place. There shall I try,
In my oration, how the people take
The cruel issue of these bloody men;
According to the which, thou shalt discourse
To young Octavius of the state of things.
Lend me your hand.

　　　　　　　　　　　　　　　Exeunt with CÆSAR's *body*

Scene II *The Forum*

Enter BRUTUS *and* CASSIUS, *and a throng of* Citizens

CITIZENS. We will be satisfied; let us be satisfied.
BRUTUS. Then follow me, and give me audience, friends.
　Cassius, go you into the other street,
　And part the numbers.
　Those that will hear me speak, let 'em stay here;
　Those that will follow Cassius, go with him;
　And public reasons shall be rendered
　Of Cæsar's death.
FIRST CITIZEN.　　　　I will hear Brutus speak.
SECOND CITIZEN. I will hear Cassius; and compare
　　their reasons,
　When severally we hear them rendered.

　　　Exit CASSIUS, *with some of the* Citizens
　　　BRUTUS *goes into the pulpit*

THIRD CITIZEN. The noble Brutus is ascended. Silence!
BRUTUS. Be patient till the last.

　Romans, countrymen, and lovers! Hear me for my
cause, and be silent, that you may hear. Believe me for
mine honour, and have respect to mine honour, that
you may believe. Censure me in your wisdom, and
awake your senses, that you may the better judge. If
there be any in this assembly, any dear friend of
Cæsar's, to him I say, that Brutus' love to Cæsar was
no less than his. If then that friend demand why
Brutus rose against Cæsar, this is my answer: Not
that I loved Cæsar less, but that I loved Rome more.
Had you rather Cæsar were living and die all slaves,
than that Cæsar were dead, to live all free men? As
Cæsar loved me, I weep for him; as he was fortunate,
I rejoice at it; as he was valiant, I honour him: but,
as he was ambitious, I slew him. There is tears for
his love; joy for his fortune; honour for his valour;
and death for his ambition. Who is here so base that
would be a bondman? If any, speak; for him have I
offended. Who is here so rude that would not be a
Roman? If any, speak; for him have I offended. Who
is here so vile that will not love his country? If any,
speak; for him have I offended. I pause for a reply.
ALL. None, Brutus, none.
BRUTUS. Then none have I offended. I have done no
more to Cæsar than you shall do to Brutus. The
question of his death is enrolled in the Capitol; his

glory not extenuated, wherein he was worthy, nor his
offences enforced, for which he suffered death.

Enter ANTONY *and others, with* CÆSAR's *body*

Here comes his body, mourned by Mark Antony;
who, though he had no hand in his death, shall re-
ceive the benefit of his dying, a place in the common-
wealth; as which of you shall not? With this I depart—
that, as I slew my best lover for the good of Rome,
I have the same dagger for myself, when it shall please
my country to need my death.
ALL. Live, Brutus! Live, live!
FIRST CITIZEN. Bring him with triumph home unto his
　house.
SECOND CITIZEN. Give him a statue with his ancestors.
THIRD CITIZEN. Let him be Cæsar.
FOURTH CITIZEN.　　　　　　　　Cæsar's better parts
　Shall be crowned in Brutus.
FIRST CITIZEN.　　　　　　We'll bring him to his house
　With shouts and clamours.
BRUTUS.　　　　　　　　My countrymen—
SECOND CITIZEN. Peace, silence! Brutus speaks.
FIRST CITIZEN.　　　　　　　　　　　　Peace, ho!
BRUTUS. Good countrymen, let me depart alone,
　And, for my sake, stay here with Antony.
　Do grace to Cæsar's corpse, and grace his speech
　Tending to Cæsar's glories; which Mark Antony,
　By our permission, is allowed to make.
　I do entreat you, not a man depart,
　Save I alone, till Antony have spoke.　　　*Exit*
FIRST CITIZEN. Stay, ho! and let us hear Mark Antony.
THIRD CITIZEN. Let him go up into the public chair;
　We'll hear him. Noble Antony, go up.
ANTONY. For Brutus' sake, I am beholding to you.

　　　　　　　　　　　　　　Goes into the pulpit

FOURTH CITIZEN. What does he say of Brutus?
THIRD CITIZEN.　　　　　　　He says, for Brutus' sake,
　He finds himself beholding to us all.
FOURTH CITIZEN. 'Twere best he speak no harm of
　Brutus here.
FIRST CITIZEN. This Cæsar was a tyrant.
THIRD CITIZEN.　　　　　　　　Nay, that's certain;
　We are blest that Rome is rid of him.

SECOND CITIZEN. Peace! Let us hear what Antony can
    say.
ANTONY. You gentle Romans—
CITIZENS.   Peace, ho! Let us hear him.
ANTONY. Friends, Romans, countrymen, lend me your
    ears;
  I come to bury Cæsar, not to praise him.
  The evil that men do lives after them;
  The good is oft interred with their bones:
  So let it be with Cæsar. The noble Brutus
  Hath told you Cæsar was ambitious.
  If it were so, it was a grievous fault,
  And grievously hath Cæsar answered it.
  Here, under leave of Brutus and the rest—
  For Brutus is an honourable man;
  So are they all, all honourable men—
  Come I to speak in Cæsar's funeral.
  He was my friend, faithful and just to me—
  But Brutus says he was ambitious;
  And Brutus is an honourable man.

He hath brought many captives home to Rome,
Whose ransoms did the general coffers fill.
Did this in Cæsar seem ambitious?
When that the poor have cried, Cæsar hath wept;
Ambition should be made of sterner stuff.
Yet Brutus says he was ambitious;
And Brutus is an honourable man.
You all did see that on the Lupercal
I thrice presented him a kingly crown,
Which he did thrice refuse. Was this ambition?
Yet Brutus says he was ambitious;
And, sure, he is an honourable man.
I speak not to disprove what Brutus spoke,
But here I am to speak what I do know.
You all did love him once, not without cause.
What cause withholds you then, to mourn for him?
O judgement! thou art fled to brutish beasts,
And men have lost their reason. Bear with me,
My heart is in the coffin there with Cæsar,
And I must pause till it come back to me.

FIRST CITIZEN. Methinks there is much reason in his
   sayings.
SECOND CITIZEN. If thou consider rightly of the matter,
   Cæsar has had great wrong.
THIRD CITIZEN.   Has he, masters?
   I fear there will a worse come in his place.
FOURTH CITIZEN. Marked ye his words? He would not
      take the crown;
   Therefore 'tis certain he was not ambitious.
FIRST CITIZEN. If it be found so, some will dear abide it.
SECOND CITIZEN. Poor soul! His eyes are red as fire
   with weeping.
THIRD CITIZEN. There's not a nobler man in Rome than
   Antony.
FOURTH CITIZEN. Now mark him, he begins again to
   speak.
ANTONY. But yesterday the word of Cæsar might
   Have stood against the world; now lies he there,
   And none so poor to do him reverence.
   O masters, if I were disposed to stir
   Your hearts and minds to mutiny and rage,
   I should do Brutus wrong, and Cassius wrong,
   Who, you all know, are honourable men.
   I will not do them wrong; I rather choose
   To wrong the dead, to wrong myself and you,
   Than I will wrong such honourable men.
   But here's a parchment with the seal of Cæsar;
   I found it in his closet, 'tis his will.
   Let but the commons hear this testament—
   Which, pardon me, I do not mean to read—
   And they would go and kiss dead Cæsar's wounds
   And dip their napkins in his sacred blood,
   Yea, beg a hair of him for memory,
   And, dying, mention it within their wills,
   Bequeathing it as a rich legacy
   Unto their issue.
FOURTH CITIZEN. We'll hear the will. Read it, Mark
   Antony.
ALL. The will, the will! We will hear Cæsar's will.
ANTONY. Have patience, gentle friends, I must not
      read it;
   It is not meet you know how Cæsar loved you.
   You are not wood, you are not stones, but men;
   And, being men, hearing the will of Cæsar,
   It will inflame you, it will make you mad.
   'Tis good you know not that you are his heirs;
   For, if you should, O, what would come of it!
FOURTH CITIZEN. Read the will; we'll hear it, Antony;
   You shall read us the will, Cæsar's will.
ANTONY. Will you be patient? Will you stay awhile?
   I have o'ershot myself to tell you of it.
   I fear I wrong the honourable men
   Whose daggers have stabbed Cæsar; I do fear it.
FOURTH CITIZEN. They were traitors. Honourable men!
ALL. The will! The testament!
SECOND CITIZEN. They were villains, murderers. The
   will! Read the will.

ANTONY. You will compel me, then, to read the will?
   Then make a ring about the corpse of Cæsar,
   And let me show you him that made the will.
   Shall I descend? And will you give me leave?
SEVERAL CITIZENS. Come down.
SECOND CITIZEN. Descend.
THIRD CITIZEN. You shall have leave. ANTONY comes down
FOURTH CITIZEN. A ring; stand round.
FIRST CITIZEN. Stand from the hearse, stand from the
   body.
SECOND CITIZEN. Room for Antony, most noble Antony.
ANTONY. Nay, press not so upon me; stand far off.
SEVERAL CITIZENS. Stand back; room; bear back.
ANTONY. If you have tears, prepare to shed them now.
   You all do know this mantle. I remember
   The first time ever Cæsar put it on;
   'Twas on a summer's evening, in his tent,
   That day he overcame the Nervii.
   Look, in this place ran Cassius' dagger through;
   See what a rent the envious Casca made;
   Through this the well-beloved Brutus stabbed;
   And as he plucked his cursed steel away,
   Mark how the blood of Cæsar followed it,
   As rushing out of doors, to be resolved
   If Brutus so unkindly knocked, or no;
   For Brutus, as you know, was Cæsar's angel.
   Judge, O you gods, how dearly Cæsar loved him!
   This was the most unkindest cut of all;
   For when the noble Cæsar saw him stab,
   Ingratitude, more strong than traitors' arms,
   Quite vanquished him. Then burst his mighty heart;
   And, in his mantle muffling up his face,
   Even at the base of Pompey's statue,
   Which all the while ran blood, great Cæsar fell.
   O, what a fall was there, my countrymen!
   Then I, and you, and all of us fell down,
   Whilst bloody treason flourished over us.
   O, now you weep; and, I perceive, you feel
   The dint of pity. These are gracious drops.
   Kind souls, what, weep you when you but behold
   Our Cæsar's vesture wounded? Look you here,
   Here is himself, marred, as you see, with traitors.
FIRST CITIZEN. O piteous spectacle!
SECOND CITIZEN. O noble Cæsar!
THIRD CITIZEN. O woeful day!
FOURTH CITIZEN. O traitors, villains!
FIRST CITIZEN. O most bloody sight!
SECOND CITIZEN. We will be revenged.
ALL. Revenge! About! Seek! Burn! Fire! Kill! Slay!
   Let not a traitor live!
ANTONY. Stay, countrymen.
FIRST CITIZEN. Peace there! hear the noble Antony.
SECOND CITIZEN. We'll hear him, we'll follow him,
   we'll die with him.
ANTONY. Good friends, sweet friends, let me not stir
      you up
   To such a sudden flood of mutiny.

They that have done this deed are honourable.
What private griefs they have, alas, I know not,
That made them do it. They are wise and honourable,
And will, no doubt, with reasons answer you.
I come not, friends, to steal away your hearts.
I am no orator, as Brutus is;
But, as you know me all, a plain blunt man,
That love my friend; and that they know full well
That gave me public leave to speak of him.
For I have neither wit, nor words, nor worth,
Action, nor utterance, nor the power of speech,
To stir men's blood. I only speak right on;
I tell you that which you yourselves do know;
Show you sweet Cæsar's wounds, poor poor dumb
   mouths,
And bid them speak for me. But were I Brutus,
And Brutus Antony, there were an Antony
Would ruffle up your spirits and put a tongue
In every wound of Cæsar that should move
The stones of Rome to rise and mutiny.
ALL. We'll mutiny.
FIRST CITIZEN. We'll burn the house of Brutus.
THIRD CITIZEN. Away, then! Come, seek the con-
   spirators.
ANTONY. Yet hear me, countrymen; yet hear me speak.
ALL. Peace, ho! Hear Antony. Most noble Antony!
ANTONY. Why, friends, you go to do you know not
   what.
   Wherein hath Cæsar thus deserved your loves?
   Alas, you know not—I must tell you, then—
   You have forgot the will I told you of.
ALL. Most true. The will! Let's stay and hear the will.
ANTONY. Here is the will, and under Cæsar's seal.
   To every Roman citizen he gives,
   To every several man, seventy-five drachmas.

SECOND CITIZEN. Most noble Cæsar! We'll revenge his
   death.
THIRD CITIZEN. O royal Cæsar!
ANTONY. Hear me with patience.
ALL. Peace, ho!
ANTONY. Moreover, he hath left you all his walks,
   His private arbours and new-planted orchards,
   On this side Tiber. He hath left them you,
   And to your heirs for ever, common pleasures,
   To walk abroad, and recreate yourselves.
   Here was a Cæsar! When comes such another?
FIRST CITIZEN. Never, never. Come, away, away!
   We'll burn his body in the holy place,
   And with the brands fire the traitors' houses.
   Take up the body.
SECOND CITIZEN. Go fetch fire.
THIRD CITIZEN. Pluck down benches.
FOURTH CITIZEN. Pluck down forms, windows, any-
   thing.   *Exeunt* Citizens *with the body*
ANTONY. Now let it work. Mischief, thou art afoot,
   Take thou what course thou wilt!

Enter a Servant
                                   How now, fellow!
SERVANT. Sir, Octavius is already come to Rome.
ANTONY. Where is he?
SERVANT. He and Lepidus are at Cæsar's house.
ANTONY. And thither will I straight to visit him;
   He comes upon a wish. Fortune is merry,
   And in this mood will give us anything.
SERVANT. I heard him say, Brutus and Cassius
   Are rid like madmen through the gates of Rome.
ANTONY. Belike they had some notice of the people,
   How I had moved them. Bring me to Octavius.
                                                Exeunt

SCENE III *A street*

Enter CINNA *the poet*

CINNA. I dreamt tonight that I did feast with Cæsar,
  And things unluckily charge my fantasy:
  I have no will to wander forth of doors,
  Yet something leads me forth.
              Enter Citizens
FIRST CITIZEN. What is your name?
SECOND CITIZEN. Whither are you going?
THIRD CITIZEN. Where do you dwell?
FOURTH CITIZEN. Are you a married man or a bachelor?
SECOND CITIZEN. Answer every man directly.
FIRST CITIZEN. Ay, and briefly.
FOURTH CITIZEN. Ay, and wisely.
THIRD CITIZEN. Ay, and truly, you were best.
CINNA. What is my name? Whither am I going? Where
  do I dwell? Am I a married man or a bachelor? Then,
  to answer every man directly and briefly, wisely and
  truly: wisely I say, I am a bachelor.
SECOND CITIZEN. That's as much as to say, they are
  fools that marry. You'll bear me a bang for that,
  I fear. Proceed; directly.

CINNA. Directly, I am going to Cæsar's funeral.
FIRST CITIZEN. As a friend or an enemy?
CINNA. As a friend.
SECOND CITIZEN. That matter is answered directly.
FOURTH CITIZEN. For your dwelling—briefly.
CINNA. Briefly, I dwell by the Capitol.
THIRD CITIZEN. Your name, sir, truly.
CINNA. Truly, my name is Cinna.
FIRST CITIZEN. Tear him to pieces; he's a conspirator.
CINNA. I am Cinna the poet, I am Cinna the poet.
FOURTH CITIZEN. Tear him for his bad verses, tear him
  for his bad verses.
CINNA. I am not Cinna the conspirator.
FOURTH CITIZEN. It is no matter, his name's Cinna;
  pluck but his name out of his heart, and turn him
  going.
THIRD CITIZEN. Tear him, tear him! Come, brands, ho!
  fire-brands! To Brutus', to Cassius'; burn all! Some to
  Decius' house, and some to Casca's; some to Ligarius'.
  Away, go!
                                        Exeunt

ACT IV

Scene I *A house in Rome*

Antony, Octavius, *and* Lepidus, *seated at a table*

Antony. These many, then, shall die; their names are
    pricked.
Octavius. Your brother too must die; consent you,
    Lepidus?
Lepidus. I do consent—
Octavius.   Prick him down, Antony.
Lepidus. Upon condition Publius shall not live,
    Who is your sister's son, Mark Antony.
Antony. He shall not live; look, with a spot I damn
    him.
    But, Lepidus, go you to Cæsar's house;
    Fetch the will hither, and we shall determine
    How to cut off some charge in legacies.
Lepidus. What, shall I find you here?
Octavius. Or here, or at the Capitol.
                                    Exit Lepidus

Antony. This is a slight unmeritable man,
    Meet to be sent on errands. Is it fit,
    The three-fold world divided, he should stand
    One of the three to share it?
Octavius.   So you thought him;
    And took his voice who should be pricked to die,
    In our black sentence and proscription.
Antony. Octavius, I have seen more days than you;
    And though we lay these honours on this man,
    To ease ourselves of divers slanderous loads,
    He shall but bear them as the ass bears gold,
    To groan and sweat under the business,
    Either led or driven, as we point the way;

And having brought our treasure where we will,
    Then take we down his load, and turn him off,
    Like to the empty ass, to shake his ears,
    And graze in commons.
Octavius.   You may do your will;
    But he's a tried and valiant soldier.
Antony. So is my horse, Octavius; and for that
    I do appoint him store of provender.
    It is a creature that I teach to fight,
    To wind, to stop, to run directly on,
    His corporal motion governed by my spirit.
    And, in some taste, is Lepidus but so;
    He must be taught and trained and bid go forth;
    A barren-spirited fellow; one that feeds
    On objects, arts and imitations,
    Which, out of use and staled by other men,
    Begin his fashion. Do not talk of him,
    But as a property. And now, Octavius,
    Listen great things: Brutus and Cassius
    Are levying powers; we must straight make head.
    Therefore let our alliance be combined,
    Our best friends made, our means stretched;
    And let us presently go sit in council,
    How covert matters may be best disclosed,
    And open perils surest answered.
Octavius. Let us do so; for we are at the stake,
    And bayed about with many enemies.
    And some that smile have in their hearts, I fear,
    Millions of mischiefs.   *Exeunt*

Scene II *Camp near Sardis. Before Brutus' tent*

Drum. Enter Brutus, Lucilius, Lucius, *and* Soldiers; Titinius *and* Pindarus *meeting them*

Brutus. Stand, ho!
Lucilius. Give the word, ho! and stand.
Brutus. What now, Lucilius! is Cassius near?
Lucilius. He is at hand; and Pindarus is come
    To do you salutation from his master.
Brutus. He greets me well. Your master, Pindarus,
    In his own change, or by ill officers,
    Hath given me some worthy cause to wish
    Things done, undone. But, if he be at hand,
    I shall be satisfied.
Pindarus.   I do not doubt
    But that my noble master will appear
    Such as he is, full of regard and honour.
Brutus. He is not doubted. A word, Lucilius;
    How he received you, let me be resolved.
Lucilius. With courtesy and with respect enough;
    But not with such familiar instances,

Nor with such free and friendly conference,
    As he hath used of old.
Brutus.   Thou hast described
    A hot friend cooling. Ever note, Lucilius,
    When love begins to sicken and decay,
    It useth an enforced ceremony.
    There are no tricks in plain and simple faith;
    But hollow men, like horses hot at hand,
    Make gallant show and promise of their mettle;
    But when they should endure the bloody spur,
    They fall their crests, and, like deceitful jades,
    Sink in the trial. Comes his army on?
Lucilius. They mean this night in Sardis to be quartered;
    The greater part, the horse in general,
    Are come with Cassius.   *March within*
Brutus.   Hark! He is arrived.
    March gently on to meet him.

Enter CASSIUS *and his powers*

CASSIUS. Stand, ho!

BRUTUS. Stand, ho! Speak the word along.

FIRST SOLDIER. Stand!

SECOND SOLDIER. Stand!

THIRD SOLDIER. Stand!

CASSIUS. Most noble brother, you have done me wrong.

BRUTUS. Judge me, you gods! Wrong I mine enemies?
    And, if not so, how should I wrong a brother?

CASSIUS. Brutus, this sober form of yours hides wrongs;
    And when you do them—

BRUTUS.   Cassius, be content;
    Speak your griefs softly. I do know you well.
    Before the eyes of both our armies here,
    Which should perceive nothing but love from us,
    Let us not wrangle. Bid them move away;
    Then in my tent, Cassius, enlarge your griefs,
    And I will give you audience.

CASSIUS.   Pindarus,
    Bid our commanders lead their charges off
    A little from this ground.

BRUTUS. Lucilius, do you the like; and let no man
    Come to our tent till we have done our conference.
    Let Lucius and Titinius guard our door.   *Exeunt*

SCENE III *Brutus' tent*

Enter BRUTUS *and* CASSIUS

CASSIUS. That you have wronged me doth appear in this:
    You have condemned and noted Lucius Pella
    For taking bribes here of the Sardians;
    Wherein my letters, praying on his side,
    Because I knew the man, were slighted off.

BRUTUS. You wronged yourself to write in such a case.

CASSIUS. In such a time as this it is not meet
    That every nice offence should bear his comment.

BRUTUS. Let me tell you, Cassius, you yourself
    Are much condemned to have an itching palm;
    To sell and mart your offices for gold
    To undeservers.

CASSIUS.   I an itching palm!
    You know that you are Brutus that speak this,
    Or, by the gods, this speech were else your last.

BRUTUS. The name of Cassius honours this corruption,
    And chastisement doth therefore hide his head.

CASSIUS. Chastisement!

BRUTUS. Remember March, the ides of March re-
    member.
    Did not great Julius bleed for justice' sake?
    What villain touched his body, that did stab,
    And not for justice? What, shall one of us,
    That struck the foremost man of all this world
    But for supporting robbers, shall we now
    Contaminate our fingers with base bribes,
    And sell the mighty space of our large honours
    For so much trash as may be grasped thus?
    I had rather be a dog, and bay the moon,
    Than such a Roman.

CASSIUS.   Brutus, bait not me;
    I'll not endure it. You forget yourself,
    To hedge me in; I am a soldier, I,
    Older in practice, abler than yourself
    To make conditions.

BRUTUS.   Go to; you are not, Cassius.

CASSIUS. I am.

BRUTUS. I say you are not.

CASSIUS. Urge me no more, I shall forget myself;
    Have mind upon your health, tempt me no farther.

BRUTUS. Away, slight man!

CASSIUS. Is 't possible?

BRUTUS.   Hear me, for I will speak.
    Must I give way and room to your rash choler?
    Shall I be frighted when a madman stares?

CASSIUS. O ye gods, ye gods! Must I endure all this?

BRUTUS. All this! ay, more. Fret till your proud heart
    break;
    Go show your slaves how choleric you are,
    And make your bondmen tremble. Must I budge?
    Must I observe you? Must I stand and crouch
    Under your testy humour? By the gods,
    You shall digest the venom of your spleen,
    Though it do split you; for, from this day forth,
    I'll use you for my mirth, yea, for my laughter,
    When you are waspish.

CASSIUS.   Is it come to this?

BRUTUS. You say you are a better soldier:
    Let it appear so; make your vaunting true,
    And it shall please me well. For mine own part,
    I shall be glad to learn of noble men.

CASSIUS. You wrong me every way; you wrong me,
    Brutus;
    I said, an elder soldier, not a better.
    Did I say "better"?

BRUTUS.   If you did, I care not.

CASSIUS. When Cæsar lived, he durst not thus have
    moved me.

BRUTUS. Peace, peace! You durst not so have tempted
    him.

CASSIUS. I durst not!

BRUTUS. No.

CASSIUS. What, durst not tempt him!

BRUTUS.   For your life you durst not.

CASSIUS. Do not presume too much upon my love;
    I may do that I shall be sorry for.

BRUTUS. You have done that you should be sorry for.
  There is no terror, Cassius, in your threats,
  For I am armed so strong in honesty
  That they pass by me as the idle wind,
  Which I respect not. I did send to you
  For certain sums of gold, which you denied me—
  For I can raise no money by vile means—
  By heaven, I had rather coin my heart,
  And drop my blood for drachmas, than to wring
  From the hard hands of peasants their vile trash
  By any indirection. I did send
  To you for gold to pay my legions,
  Which you denied me. Was that done like Cassius?
  Should I have answered Caius Cassius so?
  When Marcus Brutus grows so covetous,
  To lock such rascal counters from his friends,
  Be ready, gods, with all your thunderbolts;
  Dash him to pieces!
CASSIUS.   I denied you not.
BRUTUS. You did.
CASSIUS. I did not. He was but a fool that brought
  My answer back. Brutus hath rived my heart.
  A friend should bear his friend's infirmities,
  But Brutus makes mine greater than they are.
BRUTUS. I do not, till you practise them on me.
CASSIUS. You love me not.
BRUTUS.   I do not like your faults.
CASSIUS. A friendly eye could never see such faults.
BRUTUS. A flatterer's would not, though they do appear
  As huge as high Olympus.
CASSIUS. Come, Antony, and young Octavius, come,
  Revenge yourselves alone on Cassius,
  For Cassius is aweary of the world;
  Hated by one he loves; braved by his brother;
  Checked like a bondman; all his faults observed,
  Set in a notebook, learned, and conned by rote,
  To cast into my teeth. O, I could weep
  My spirit from mine eyes! There is my dagger,
  And here my naked breast; within, a heart
  Dearer than Pluto's mine, richer than gold.
  If that thou be'st a Roman, take it forth;
  I, that denied thee gold, will give my heart.
  Strike, as thou didst at Cæsar; for, I know,
  When thou didst hate him worst, thou lovedst him
    better
  Than ever thou lovedst Cassius.
BRUTUS.   Sheathe your dagger.
  Be angry when you will, it shall have scope;
  Do what you will, dishonour shall be humour.
  O Cassius, you are yoked with a lamb
  That carries anger as the flint bears fire;
  Who, much enforced, shows a hasty spark,
  And straight is cold again.
CASSIUS.   Hath Cassius lived
  To be but mirth and laughter to his Brutus,
  When grief, and blood ill-tempered, vexeth him?

BRUTUS. When I spoke that, I was ill-tempered too.
CASSIUS. Do you confess so much? Give me your hand.
BRUTUS. And my heart too.
CASSIUS.   O Brutus!
BRUTUS.   What's the matter?
CASSIUS. Have not you love enough to bear with me,
  When that rash humour which my mother gave me
Makes me forgetful?
BRUTUS. Yes, Cassius; and, from henceforth,
  When you are over-earnest with your Brutus,
  He'll think your mother chides, and leave you so.
POET [Within] Let me go in to see the generals;
  There is some grudge between 'em, 'tis not meet
  They be alone.
LUCILIUS. [Within] You shall not come to them.
POET [Within] Nothing but death shall stay me.

Enter Poet, *followed by* LUCILIUS, TITINIUS, *and* LUCIUS

CASSIUS. How now! What's the matter?
POET. For shame, you generals! What do you mean?
  Love, and be friends, as two such men should be;
  For I have seen more years, I 'm sure, than ye.
CASSIUS. Ha, ha! How vilely doth this cynic rhyme!
BRUTUS. Get you hence, sirrah; saucy fellow, hence!
CASSIUS. Bear with him, Brutus; 'tis his fashion.
BRUTUS. I 'll know his humour, when he knows his time.
  What should the wars do with these jigging fools?
  Companion, hence!
CASSIUS.   Away, away, be gone!
                              Exit Poet

BRUTUS. Lucilius and Titinius, bid the commanders
  Prepare to lodge their companies tonight.
CASSIUS. And come yourselves, and bring Messala with
    you
  Immediately to us.   *Exeunt* LUCILIUS *and* TITINIUS
BRUTUS. Lucius, a bowl of wine!   *Exit* LUCIUS
CASSIUS. I did not think you could have been so angry.
BRUTUS. O Cassius, I am sick of many griefs.
CASSIUS. Of your philosophy you make no use,
  If you give place to accidental evils.
BRUTUS. No man bears sorrow better. Portia is dead.
CASSIUS. Ha! Portia!
BRUTUS. She is dead.
CASSIUS. How 'scaped I killing when I crossed you so?
  O insupportable and touching loss!
  Upon what sickness?
BRUTUS.   Impatient of my absence,
  And grief that young Octavius with Mark Antony
  Have made themselves so strong—for with her death
  That tidings came—with this she fell distract,
  And, her attendants absent, swallowed fire.
CASSIUS. And died so?
BRUTUS.   Even so.
CASSIUS.   O ye immortal gods!

Re-enter LUCIUS, *with wine and taper*

BRUTUS. Speak no more of her. Give me a bowl of wine.
  In this I bury all unkindness, Cassius.
CASSIUS. My heart is thirsty for that noble pledge.
  Fill, Lucius, till the wine o'erswell the cup;
  I cannot drink too much of Brutus' love.
BRUTUS. Come in, Titinius!   *Exit* LUCIUS
    Re-enter TITINIUS, *with* MESSALA
                         Welcome, good Messala.
  Now sit we close about this taper here,
  And call in question our necessities.
CASSIUS. Portia, art thou gone?
BRUTUS.   No more, I pray you.
  Messala, I have here received letters,
  That young Octavius and Mark Antony
  Come down upon us with a mighty power,
  Bending their expedition toward Philippi.
MESSALA. Myself have letters of the selfsame tenor.
BRUTUS. With what addition?
MESSALA. That by proscription and bills of outlawry,
  Octavius, Antony, and Lepidus,
  Have put to death an hundred senators.
BRUTUS. Therein our letters do not well agree;
  Mine speak of seventy senators that died
  By their proscriptions, Cicero being one.
CASSIUS. Cicero one!
MESSALA.   Cicero is dead,
  And by that order of proscription.
  Had you your letters from your wife, my lord?
BRUTUS. No, Messala.
MESSALA. Nor nothing in your letters writ of her?
BRUTUS. Nothing, Messala.
MESSALA.   That, methinks, is strange.
BRUTUS. Why ask you? Hear you aught of her in yours?
MESSALA. No, my lord.
BRUTUS. Now, as you are a Roman, tell me true.
MESSALA. Then like a Roman bear the truth I tell:
  For certain she is dead, and by strange manner.
BRUTUS. Why, farewell, Portia. We must die, Messala.
  With meditating that she must die once,
  I have the patience to endure it now.
MESSALA. Even so great men great losses should endure.
CASSIUS. I have as much of this in art as you,
  But yet my nature could not bear it so.
BRUTUS. Well, to our work alive. What do you think
  Of marching to Philippi presently?
CASSIUS. I do not think it good.
BRUTUS.   Your reason?
CASSIUS.   This it is:
  'Tis better that the enemy seek us;
  So shall he waste his means, weary his soldiers,
  Doing himself offence; whilst we, lying still,
  Are full of rest, defence, and nimbleness.
BRUTUS. Good reasons must, of force, give place to
    better.
  The people 'twixt Philippi and this ground
  Do stand but in a forced affection;

For they have grudged us contribution.
The enemy, marching along by them,
By them shall make a fuller number up,
Come on refreshed, new-added, and encouraged;
From which advantage shall we cut him off,
If at Philippi we do face him there,
These people at our back.
CASSIUS.   Hear me, good brother.
BRUTUS. Under your pardon. You must note beside,
    That we have tried the utmost of our friends,
    Our legions are brim-full, our cause is ripe.
    The enemy increaseth every day;
    We, at the height, are ready to decline.
    There is a tide in the affairs of men,
    Which, taken at the flood, leads on to fortune;
    Omitted, all the voyage of their life
    Is bound in shallows and in miseries.
    On such a full sea are we now afloat;
    And we must take the current when it serves,
    Or lose our ventures.
CASSIUS.   Then, with your will, go on;
    We'll along ourselves, and meet them at Philippi.
BRUTUS. The deep of night is crept upon our talk,
    And nature must obey necessity;
    Which we will niggard with a little rest.
    There is no more to say?
CASSIUS.   No more. Good night.
    Early tomorrow will we rise, and hence.
BRUTUS. Lucius! [Enter Lucius] My gown.   Exit Lucius
    Farewell, good Messala;
    Good night, Titinius. Noble, noble Cassius,
    Good night, and good repose.
CASSIUS.   O my dear brother!
    This was an ill beginning of the night.
    Never come such division 'tween our souls!
    Let it not, Brutus.
BRUTUS.   Everything is well.
CASSIUS. Good night, my lord.
BRUTUS.   Good night, good brother.
TITINIUS. ⎱
MESSALA. ⎰ Good night, Lord Brutus.
BRUTUS.   Farewell, every one.
                          Exeunt all but BRUTUS
        Re-enter LUCIUS, with the gown
    Give me the gown. Where is thy instrument?
LUCIUS. Here in the tent.
BRUTUS.   What, thou speak'st drowsily?
    Poor knave, I blame thee not; thou art o'erwatched.
    Call Claudius and some other of my men;
    I'll have them sleep on cushions in my tent.
LUCIUS. Varro and Claudius!
        Enter VARRO and CLAUDIUS
VARRO. Calls my lord?
BRUTUS. I pray you, sirs, lie in my tent and sleep;
    It may be I shall raise you by and by
    On business to my brother Cassius.

VARRO. So please you, we will stand and watch your
    pleasure.
BRUTUS. I will not have it so. Lie down, good sirs;
    It may be I shall otherwise bethink me.
    Look, Lucius, here's the book I sought for so;
    I put it in the pocket of my gown.
                    VARRO and CLAUDIUS lie down
LUCIUS. I was sure your lordship did not give it me.
BRUTUS. Bear with me, good boy, I am much forgetful.
    Canst thou hold up thy heavy eyes awhile,
    And touch thy instrument a strain or two?
LUCIUS. Ay, my lord, an 't please you.
BRUTUS.   It does, my boy.
    I trouble thee too much, but thou art willing.
LUCIUS. It is my duty, sir.
BRUTUS. I should not urge thy duty past thy might;
    I know young bloods look for a time of rest.
LUCIUS. I have slept, my lord, already.
BRUTUS. It was well done; and thou shalt sleep again;
    I will not hold thee long. If I do live,
    I will be good to thee.   Music, and a song
    This is a sleepy tune. O murderous slumber,
    Lay'st thou thy leaden mace upon my boy,
    That plays thee music? Gentle knave, good night;
    I will not do thee so much wrong to wake thee.
    If thou dost nod, thou break'st thy instrument;
    I'll take it from thee; and, good boy, good night.
    Let me see, let me see; is not the leaf turned down
    Where I left reading? Here it is, I think.

        Enter the Ghost of CÆSAR

    How ill this taper burns! Ha! who comes here?
    I think it is the weakness of mine eyes
    That shapes this monstrous apparition.
    It comes upon me. Art thou any thing?
    Art thou some god, some angel, or some devil,
    That mak'st my blood cold and my hair to stare?
    Speak to me what thou art.
GHOST. Thy evil spirit, Brutus.
BRUTUS. Why comest thou?
GHOST. To tell thee thou shalt see me at Philippi.
BRUTUS. Well; then I shall see thee again?
GHOST. Ay, at Philippi.
BRUTUS. Why, I will see thee at Philippi, then.
                              Exit Ghost
    Now I have taken heart thou vanishest.
    Ill spirit, I would hold more talk with thee.
    Boy, Lucius! Varro! Claudius! Sirs, awake!
    Claudius!
LUCIUS. The strings, my lord, are false.
BRUTUS. He thinks he still is at his instrument. Lucius,
    awake!
LUCIUS. My lord?
BRUTUS. Didst thou dream, Lucius, that thou so criedst
    out?
LUCIUS. My lord, I do not know that I did cry.

BRUTUS. Yes, that thou didst. Didst thou see anything?
LUCIUS. Nothing, my lord.
BRUTUS. Sleep again, Lucius. Sirrah Claudius! [*To Varro*] Fellow thou, awake!
VARRO. My lord?
CLAUDIUS. My lord?
BRUTUS. Why did you so cry out, sirs, in your sleep?
VARRO. ⎫
CLAUDIUS. ⎭ Did we, my lord?
BRUTUS.   Ay; saw you anything?
VARRO. No, my lord, I saw nothing.
CLAUDIUS.   Nor I, my lord.
BRUTUS. Go and commend me to my brother Cassius;
    Bid him set on his powers betimes before,
    And we will follow.
VARRO. ⎫
CLAUDIUS. ⎭ It shall be done, my lord.

                                                            Exeunt

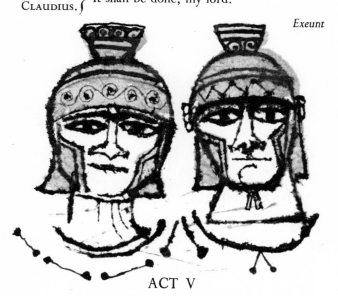

ACT V

SCENE I *The plains of Philippi*

Enter OCTAVIUS, ANTONY, *and their army*

OCTAVIUS. Now, Antony, our hopes are answered.
    You said the enemy would not come down,
    But keep the hills and upper regions;
    It proves not so. Their battles are at hand;
    They mean to warn us at Philippi here,
    Answering before we do demand of them.
ANTONY. Tut, I am in their bosoms, and I know
    Wherefore they do it. They could be content
    To visit other places; and come down
    With fearful bravery, thinking by this face
    To fasten in our thoughts that they have courage;
    But 'tis not so.

Enter a Messenger

MESSENGER.   Prepare you, generals:
    The enemy comes on in gallant show;
    Their bloody sign of battle is hung out,
    And something to be done immediately.

ANTONY. Octavius, lead your battle softly on,
    Upon the left hand of the even field.
OCTAVIUS. Upon the right hand I; keep thou the left.
ANTONY. Why do you cross me in this exigent?
OCTAVIUS. I do not cross you; but I will do so.   *March*

Drum; enter BRUTUS, CASSIUS, *and their* Army; LUCILIUS,
    TITINIUS, MESSALA, *and others*

BRUTUS. They stand, and would have parley.
CASSIUS. Stand fast, Titinius; we must out and talk.
OCTAVIUS. Mark Antony, shall we give sign of battle?
ANTONY. No, Cæsar, we will answer on their charge.
    Make forth; the generals would have some words.
OCTAVIUS. Stir not until the signal.
BRUTUS. Words before blows; is it so, countrymen?
OCTAVIUS. Not that we love words better, as you do.
BRUTUS. Good words are better than bad strokes,
    Octavius.
ANTONY. In your bad strokes, Brutus, you give good
    words.
    Witness the hole you made in Cæsar's heart,
    Crying "Long live! Hail, Cæsar!"
CASSIUS.   Antony,
    The posture of your blows are yet unknown;
    But for your words, they rob the Hybla bees,
    And leave them honeyless.
ANTONY.   Not stingless too.
BRUTUS. O, yes, and soundless too;
    For you have stol'n their buzzing, Antony,
    And very wisely threat before you sting.
ANTONY. Villains, you did not so, when your vile
    daggers
    Hacked one another in the sides of Cæsar.
    You showed your teeth like apes, and fawned like
    hounds,
    And bowed like bondmen, kissing Cæsar's feet;
    Whilst damned Casca, like a cur, behind
    Struck Cæsar on the neck. O you flatterers!
CASSIUS. Flatterers! Now, Brutus, thank yourself:
    This tongue had not offended so today,
    If Cassius might have ruled.
OCTAVIUS. Come, come, the cause. If arguing make us
    sweat,
    The proof of it will turn to redder drops.
    Look;
    I draw a sword against conspirators;
    When think you that the sword goes up again?
    Never, till Cæsar's three and thirty wounds
    Be well avenged; or till another Cæsar
    Have added slaughter to the sword of traitors.
BRUTUS. Cæsar, thou canst not die by traitors' hands,
    Unless thou bring'st them with thee.
OCTAVIUS.   So I hope;
    I was not born to die on Brutus' sword.
BRUTUS. O, if thou wert the noblest of thy strain,
    Young man, thou couldst not die more honourable.

CASSIUS. A peevish schoolboy, worthless of such honour,
   Joined with a masker and a reveller!
ANTONY. Old Cassius still!
OCTAVIUS.   Come, Antony, away!
   Defiance, traitors, hurl we in your teeth.
   If you dare fight today, come to the field;
   If not, when you have stomachs.
                    Exeunt OCTAVIUS, ANTONY, *and their army*
CASSIUS. Why, now, blow wind, swell billow and swim
   bark!
   The storm is up, and all is on the hazard.
BRUTUS. Ho, Lucilius! Hark, a word with you.
LUCILIUS.   [*Standing forth*] My lord?
                    BRUTUS *and* LUCILIUS *converse apart*
CASSIUS. Messala!
MESSALA. [*Standing forth*] What says my general?
CASSIUS. Messala,
   This is my birthday; as this very day
   Was Cassius born. Give me thy hand, Messala.
   Be thou my witness that against my will
   As Pompey was, am I compelled to set
   Upon one battle all our liberties.
   You know that I held Epicurus strong
   And his opinion. Now I change my mind,
   And partly credit things that do presage.
   Coming from Sardis, on our former ensign
   Two mighty eagles fell, and there they perched,
   Gorging and feeding from our soldiers' hands;
   Who to Philippi here consorted us.
   This morning are they fled away and gone;
   And in their steads do ravens, crows and kites,
   Fly o'er our heads and downward look on us,
   As we were sickly prey. Their shadows seem
   A canopy most fatal, under which
   Our army lies, ready to give up the ghost.
MESSALA. Believe not so.
CASSIUS.   I but believe it partly;
   For I am fresh of spirit and resolved
   To meet all perils very constantly.
BRUTUS. Even so, Lucilius.
CASSIUS.   Now, most noble Brutus,
   The gods today stand friendly, that we may,
   Lovers in peace, lead on our days to age!
   But since the affairs of men rest still incertain,
   Let's reason with the worst that may befall.
   If we do lose this battle, then is this
   The very last time we shall speak together.
   What are you then determined to do?
BRUTUS. Even by the rule of that philosophy
   By which I did blame Cato for the death
   Which he did give himself, I know not how,
   But I do find it cowardly and vile,
   For fear of what might fall, so to prevent
   The time of life: arming myself with patience
   To stay the providence of some high powers
   That govern us below.

CASSIUS.   Then, if we lose this battle,
   You are contented to be led in triumph
   Thorough the streets of Rome?
BRUTUS. No, Cassius, no. Think not, thou noble Roman,
   That ever Brutus will go bound to Rome;
   He bears too great a mind. But this same day
   Must end that work the ides of March begun;
   And whether we shall meet again I know not.
   Therefore our everlasting farewell take.
   For ever, and for ever, farewell, Cassius!
   If we do meet again, why, we shall smile;
   If not, why then, this parting was well made.
CASSIUS. For ever, and for ever, farewell, Brutus!
   If we do meet again, we'll smile indeed;
   If not, 'tis true this parting was well made.
BRUTUS. Why, then, lead on. O, that a man might know
   The end of this day's business ere it come!
   But it sufficeth that the day will end,
   And then the end is known. Come, ho! Away!
                                                      Exeunt

SCENE II *The same. The field of battle*

Alarum. Enter BRUTUS *and* MESSALA

BRUTUS. Ride, ride, Messala, ride, and give these bills
   Unto the legions on the other side.   *Loud alarum*
   Let them set on at once; for I perceive
   But cold demeanour in Octavius' wing,
   And sudden push gives them the overthrow.
   Ride, ride, Messala; let them all come down.
                                                      Exeunt

SCENE III *Another part of the field*

Alarums. Enter CASSIUS *and* TITINIUS

CASSIUS. O, look, Titinius, look, the villains fly!
   Myself have to mine own turned enemy.
   This ensign here of mine was turning back;
   I slew the coward, and did take it from him.
TITINIUS. O Cassius, Brutus gave the word too early;
   Who, having some advantage on Octavius,
   Took it too eagerly. His soldiers fell to spoil,
   Whilst we by Antony are all enclosed.

Enter PINDARUS

PINDARUS. Fly further off, my lord, fly further off;
   Mark Antony is in your tents, my lord.
   Fly, therefore, noble Cassius, fly far off.
CASSIUS. This hill is far enough. Look, look, Titinius;
   Are those my tents where I perceive the fire?
TITINIUS. They are, my lord.
CASSIUS.   Titinius, if thou lovest me,
   Mount thou my horse, and hide thy spurs in him,

Till he have brought thee up to yonder troops,
And here again; that I may rest assured
Whether yond troops are friend or enemy.
TITINIUS. I will be here again, even with a thought.

Exit

CASSIUS. Go, Pindarus, get higher on that hill;
My sight was ever thick; regard Titinius,
And tell me what thou notest about the field.

PINDARUS *ascends the hill*

This day I breathed first; time is come round,
And where I did begin, there shall I end;
My life is run his compass. Sirrah, what news?
PINDARUS. [*Above*] O my lord!
CASSIUS. What news?
PINDARUS. [*Above*] Titinius is enclosed round about
With horsemen, that make to him on the spur;
Yet he spurs on. Now they are almost on him.
Now, Titinius! Now some light. O, he lights too.
He's ta'en. [*Shout*] And, hark! they shout for joy.
CASSIUS. Come down, behold no more.
O, coward that I am, to live so long,
To see my best friend ta'en before my face!

PINDARUS *descends*

Come hither, sirrah.
In Parthia did I take thee prisoner;
And then I swore thee, saving of thy life,
That whatsoever I did bid thee do,
Thou shouldst attempt it. Come now, keep thine oath.
Now be a freeman; and with this good sword,
That ran through Cæsar's bowels, search this bosom.
Stand not to answer; here, take thou the hilts;
And, when my face is covered, as 'tis now,
Guide thou the sword.   PINDARUS *stabs him*
Cæsar, thou art revenged,
Even with the sword that killed thee.   *Dies*
PINDARUS. So, I am free; yet would not so have been,
Durst I have done my will. O Cassius,
Far from this country Pindarus shall run,
Where never Roman shall take note of him.   *Exit*

Re-enter TITINIUS *with* MESSALA

MESSALA. It is but change, Titinius; for Octavius
Is overthrown by noble Brutus' power,
As Cassius' legions are by Antony.
TITINIUS. These tidings will well comfort Cassius.
MESSALA. Where did you leave him?
TITINIUS.   All disconsolate,
With Pindarus his bondman, on this hill.
MESSALA. Is not that he that lies upon the ground?
TITINIUS. He lies not like the living. O my heart!
MESSALA. Is not that he?
TITINIUS.   No, this was he, Messala,
But Cassius is no more. O setting sun,
As in thy red rays thou dost sink to night,
So in his red blood Cassius' day is set;
The sun of Rome is set! Our day is gone;

Clouds, dews, and dangers come; our deeds are done!
Mistrust of my success hath done this deed.
MESSALA. Mistrust of good success hath done this deed.
O hateful error, melancholy's child,
Why dost thou show to the apt thoughts of men
The things that are not? O error, soon conceived,
Thou never comest unto a happy birth,
But kill'st the mother that engendered thee!
TITINIUS. What, Pindarus! Where art thou, Pindarus?
MESSALA. Seek him, Titinius, whilst I go to meet
The noble Brutus, thrusting this report
Into his ears; I may say, thrusting it;
For piercing steel and darts envenomed
Shall be as welcome to the ears of Brutus
As tidings of this sight.
TITINIUS.   Hie you, Messala,
And I will seek for Pindarus the while.

Exit MESSALA

Why didst thou send me forth, brave Cassius?
Did I not meet thy friends? And did not they
Put on my brows this wreath of victory,
And bid me give it thee? Didst thou not hear their
shouts?
Alas, thou hast misconstrued everything!
But, hold thee, take this garland on thy brow;
Thy Brutus bid me give it thee, and I
Will do his bidding. Brutus, come apace,
And see how I regarded Caius Cassius.
By your leave, gods—this is a Roman's part—
Come, Cassius' sword, and find Titinius' heart.

Kills himself

Alarum. Re-enter MESSALA, *with* BRUTUS, *young* CATO,
STRATO, VOLUMNIUS, *and* LUCILIUS

BRUTUS. Where, where, Messala, doth his body lie?
MESSALA. Lo, yonder, and Titinius mourning it.
BRUTUS. Titinius' face is upward.
CATO.   He is slain.
BRUTUS. O Julius Cæsar, thou art mighty yet!
Thy spirit walks abroad, and turns our swords
In our own proper entrails.   *Low alarums*
CATO.   Brave Titinius!
Look, whether he have not crowned dead Cassius!
BRUTUS. Are yet two Romans living such as these?
The last of all the Romans, fare thee well!
It is impossible that ever Rome
Should breed thy fellow. Friends, I owe more tears
To this dead man than you shall see me pay.
I shall find time, Cassius, I shall find time.
Come, therefore, and to Thasos send his body.
His funerals shall not be in our camp,
Lest it discomfort us. Lucilius, come;
And come, young Cato; let us to the field.
Labeo and Flavius, set our battles on.
'Tis three o'clock; and, Romans, yet ere night
We shall try fortune in a second fight.   *Exeunt*

SCENE IV *Another part of the field*

Alarum. Enter fighting, Soldiers *of both armies; then* BRUTUS, *young* CATO, LUCILIUS, *and others*

BRUTUS. Yet, countrymen, O, yet hold up your heads!

Exit

CATO. What bastard doth not? Who will go with me?
  I will proclaim my name about the field:
  I am the son of Marcus Cato, ho!
  A foe to tyrants, and my country's friend;
  I am the son of Marcus Cato, ho!

LUCILIUS. And I am Brutus, Marcus Brutus, I;
  Brutus, my country's friend; know me for Brutus!
  O young and noble Cato, art thou down?
  Why, now thou diest as bravely as Titinius;
  And mayst be honoured, being Cato's son.

FIRST SOLDIER. Yield, or thou diest.

LUCILIUS.   Only I yield to die.
  There is so much that thou wilt kill me straight;

Offering money

  Kill Brutus, and be honoured in his death.

FIRST SOLDIER. We must not. A noble prisoner!

SECOND SOLDIER. Room, ho! Tell Antony, Brutus is
  ta'en.

FIRST SOLDIER. I'll tell the news. Here comes the
  general.

Enter ANTONY

  Brutus is ta'en, Brutus is ta'en, my lord.

ANTONY. Where is he?

LUCILIUS. Safe, Antony; Brutus is safe enough.
  I dare assure thee that no enemy
  Shall ever take alive the noble Brutus.
  The gods defend him from so great a shame!
  When you do find him, or alive or dead,
  He will be found like Brutus, like himself.

ANTONY. This is not Brutus, friend; but, I assure you,
  A prize no less in worth. Keep this man safe;
  Give him all kindness. I had rather have
  Such men my friends than enemies. Go on,
  And see whether Brutus be alive or dead;
  And bring us word unto Octavius' tent
  How everything is chanced.

Exeunt

SCENE V *Another part of the field*

Enter BRUTUS, DARDANIUS, CLITUS, STRATO, *and* VOLUMNIUS

BRUTUS. Come, poor remains of friends, rest on this
    rock.

CLITUS. Statilius showed the torch-light, but, my lord,
    He came not back; he is or ta'en or slain.

BRUTUS. Sit thee down, Clitus. Slaying is the word;
    It is a deed in fashion. Hark thee, Clitus.   *Whispers*

CLITUS. What, I, my lord? No, not for all the world.

BRUTUS. Peace then! No words.

CLITUS.   I'll rather kill myself.

BRUTUS. Hark thee, Dardanius.   *Whispers*

DARDANIUS.   Shall I do such a deed?

CLITUS. O Dardanius!

DARDANIUS. O Clitus!

CLITUS. What ill request did Brutus make to thee?

DARDANIUS. To kill him, Clitus. Look, he meditates.

CLITUS. Now is that noble vessel full of grief,
    That it runs over even at his eyes.

BRUTUS. Come hither, good Volumnius; list a word.

VOLUMNIUS. What says my lord?

BRUTUS.   Why, this, Volumnius:
    The ghost of Cæsar hath appeared to me
    Two several times by night; at Sardis once,
    And, this last night, here in Philippi fields.
    I know my hour is come.

VOLUMNIUS.   Not so, my lord.

BRUTUS. Nay, I am sure it is, Volumnius.
    Thou seest the world, Volumnius, how it goes;
    Our enemies have beat us to the pit.   *Low alarums*
    It is more worthy to leap in ourselves,
    Than tarry till they push us. Good Volumnius,
    Thou know'st that we two went to school together.
    Even for that our love of old, I prithee,
    Hold thou my sword-hilts, whilst I run on it.

VOLUMNIUS. That's not an office for a friend, my lord.
                          Alarum still

CLITUS. Fly, fly, my lord; there is no tarrying here.

BRUTUS. Farewell to you; and you; and you, Volumnius.
    Strato, thou hast been all this while asleep;
    Farewell to thee too, Strato. Countrymen,
    My heart doth joy that yet in all my life
    I found no man but he was true to me.
    I shall have glory by this losing day
    More than Octavius and Mark Antony
    By this vile conquest shall attain unto.
    So fare you well at once; for Brutus' tongue
    Hath almost ended his life's history.
    Night hangs upon mine eyes; my bones would rest,
    That have but laboured to attain this hour.
         Alarum. Cry within: "Fly, fly, fly!"

CLITUS. Fly, my lord, fly.

BRUTUS.   Hence! I will follow.
      Exeunt CLITUS, DARDANIUS, *and* VOLUMNIUS
    I prithee, Strato, stay thou by thy lord.
    Thou art a fellow of a good respect;
    Thy life hath had some smatch of honour in it.
    Hold then my sword, and turn away thy face,
    While I do run upon it. Wilt thou, Strato?

STRATO. Give me your hand first. Fare you well, my
    lord.

BRUTUS. Farewell, good Strato. [*Runs on his sword*]
    Cæsar, now be still;
    I killed not thee with half so good a will.   [*Dies*]

Alarum. Retreat

Enter OCTAVIUS, ANTONY, MESSALA,
LUCILIUS, *and the army*

OCTAVIUS. What man is that?

MESSALA. My master's man. Strato, where is thy master?

STRATO. Free from the bondage you are in, Messala.
    The conquerors can but make a fire of him;
    For Brutus only overcame himself,
    And no man else hath honour by his death.

LUCILIUS. So Brutus should be found. I thank thee,
    Brutus,
    That thou hast proved Lucilius' saying true.

OCTAVIUS. All that served Brutus, I will entertain them.
    Fellow, wilt thou bestow thy time with me?

STRATO. Ay, if Messala will prefer me to you.

OCTAVIUS. Do so, good Messala.

MESSALA. How died my master, Strato?

STRATO. I held the sword, and he did run on it.

MESSALA. Octavius, then take him to follow thee,
    That did the latest service to my master.

ANTONY. This was the noblest Roman of them all.
    All the conspirators save only he
    Did that they did in envy of great Cæsar;
    He only, in a general honest thought
    And common good to all, made one of them.
    His life was gentle, and the elements
    So mixed in him that Nature might stand up
    And say to all the world, "This was a man!"

OCTAVIUS. According to his virtue let us use him,
    With all respect and rites of burial.
    Within my tent his bones tonight shall lie,
    Most like a soldier, ordered honourably.
    So call the field to rest; and let's away,
    To part the glories of this happy day.   *Exeunt*

AS YOU LIKE IT

There is not much to say about this comedy since it speaks for itself so eloquently, so charmingly, and is so easy to understand. I have seen it most happily and aptly produced in decors based on Watteau or Fragonard.

The play is so artificial that no one need be expected to take it seriously. I daresay that that is why Shakespeare entitled it ''As You Like It''. As an experienced man of theatrical affairs he knew well that audiences prefer, above everything else, to be gently, good-humoredly, amused. Of course, it is possible to raise an eyebrow at the extreme implausibility of Oliver's character—a villainy of fairy-tale blackness suddenly transformed to

purest white. It is possible to regret that Celia, the loyal, charming, sensible Celia, should be palmed off in such a perfunctory style on such an unsatisfactory mate.

You may feel that, even at the highly artificial close, with Hymen in command of a highly artificial comedy, the arrival of the second son of old Sir Rowland and the speech in which he informs Duke Senior of his brother's sudden conversion (almost as improbable as the parallel conversion of Orlando's wicked brother) is carrying artlessness to the verge of impudence. This part, Jacques de Boys, is considered among actors to be one of the worst and most difficult to act with credit in the entire classic repertoire. And what an odd, confusing little lapse—or is there some "meaning" in it?—that this character, as well as the melancholy lord, should be called Jacques.

However, at the end of a gay evening, all these blemishes are calculated to produce only the indulgent smiles of a happy audience. Of course, if the play has gone badly it is another matter altogether. But, if half-decently produced, which is not an easy feat to achieve, this play cannot go badly. The cunning old pro who wrote it put into it too many things which audiences the world over have loved from the beginning of time, and will love till the human race is either extinguished or else evolved out of all recognizable resemblance to the species as it now exists.

Rosalind, of course, is the play's crown. I suppose the comedy can only be fully realized if the part is played by a boy. With an intelligent, lively little boy pretending to be a girl who is dressed up and pretending to be a boy, the part would be irresistible, and the whole play would move into a more fantastic key than can ever be possible when it is played, however well, by a woman.

I saw Edith Evans play Rosalind at the Old Vic, in London. It is many years ago, but I remember moments in the performance as vividly as the liveliest remembrances of my life. She was already a mature woman, twenty-five years or more older than Rosalind is supposed to be. For five minutes this was disconcerting. Then the magic of great acting transformed the middle-aged actress into a young girl madly, joyously in love. The performance was all the better because here was the comment of a wise and mature woman upon young girlhood and young love, and because a battery of technical accomplishment was brought into play, such as only a mature actress can command.

But, wonderful as was this performance, I do not think it was the *kind* of contribution which Shakespeare meant Rosalind to make to the evening's entertainment. Evans made the play a deeper, more moving, more important experience than was, I think, intended. But this was achieved at the expense of simplicity, fantasy and of a merriment unclouded by intimations of mortality.

Touchstone and Jacques are evidently meant to offer a contrast in humour to match with the other contrasts and symmetries of this formal piece. There are two brother-dukes, one benevolent, one villain, to match with those other brothers, good Orlando and bad Oliver. There are two humble, "real" pastoral lovers, Silvius and Phoebe, to match the pastoral masquerade of Orlando and Rosalind; Corin matches Adam; and, finally, Touchstone, the simple-witted clown and would-be nobleman, matches Jacques, the sophisticated nobleman and would-be jester.

Both of these latter two parts have suffered in the passage of time. They are a sad little commentary on the fact that nothing is less durable, more brittle, than satirical humour. It is funny only so long as that which is being satirized remains contemporary.

What will posterity make of the satirical humour of our own day? Mort Sahl, for instance, a lugubrious and rather aristocratic clown, quite after the fashion of the melancholy Jacques. And what of the satirists of yester-year? Leaf over the pages of the *New Yorker* for 1932. Where be its quips and its quiddities now?

I have read in the commentaries that Touchstone's lines are both funny and pathetic. But for my own part, I can get little pleasure out of stuff like, for example, his long rigmarole about gentlemanly quarrelling (Act V, scene 4), even after I have read in the notes that "Shakespeare almost certainly had in mind Vincentio Saviolo's book on duelling, the title of which was translated into English as *Of Honour and Honourable Quarrels.*"

I only know that I have seen Touchstone played by the late Morland Graham, the best Shakespearian clown on the British stage and one of the finest character actors of our time. He was sweet, he was sad, he made something touching out of a town-dweller incongruously and miserably stranded in the depths of a forest. But even he was unable to make of those dreadful "jokes" anything but an abstruse bore.

Jacques is often considered by actors to be a good part; and many is the ham I've seen putting on finical airs, which were meant to be aristocratic, and handing out the Seven Ages of Man at dictation speed. But, alas, the humour of the part has faded with the context of its day. And the Seven Ages speech, like the Quality of Mercy and various other Gems from Shakespeare, has become so rubbed and worn through use that it is as hard to recapture its meaning as it is to hear afresh such over-familiar words as the General Confession of the Anglican Church.

Do people still, I wonder, buy for one another Shakespearian Calendars—an inspiring quotation for every single day of the year? Or Shakespearian Birthday Books—"To thine own self be true and it must follow as the night the day thou canst not then be false to any man"? That was the quotation for June 11th and there follow the signatures of Aunt Carrie and, lower down, Mr. Bowker, who kept the store on the corner of Linden and Hazel and who drank, which accounts for the oddness of the signature.

I think, and hope, that such homage to the Bard has gone "out", like Touchstone's jokes. Perhaps a generation is going to grow up to whom the speech about the Seven Ages of Man will seem as fresh, as wise, as amusing as no doubt it seemed to its first audiences. Then, once again, the melancholy Jacques will be a part worth playing. Indeed, how much more enchanting in every way Shakespeare's work will be when we have a chance to "discover" it, instead of having it rammed down our throats, a vile-tasting Bolus which is Good For Us, the dreadful counterpart of Quadratic Equations and French Irregular Verbs.

SIR
OLIVER
MARTEXT,
a vicar

JAQUES, son to Sir
Rowland de Boys. LEBEAU,
a courtier attending on
Frederick, CHARLES,
wrestler to Frederick

CORIN, PHEBE, SILVIUS,
shepherds and shepherdess

WILLIAM, a country
fellow, in love with
AUDREY,
a country wench.

OLIVER, son to Sir Rowland de Boys

FREDERICK, brother to the Duke, and usurper of his dominions

SCENE: OLIVER'S HOUSE;
DUKE FREDERICK'S COURT;
and the
FOREST OF ARDEN

ADAM,

DENNIS,
servants to
Oliver

ORLANDO,
son of Sir Rowland de Boys,
brother to Oliver and Jaques

JAQUES, ~ lords
AMIENS, attending on the
banished Duke

ROSALIND,
daughter to the
banished Duke

CELIA,
daughter to
Frederick

TOUCHSTONE,
a clown

DUKE, living in banishment
A person representing Hymen; Lords, pages and attendants.

AS YOU LIKE IT
DRAMATIS PERSONAE

he keeps me rustically at home, or, to speak more properly, stays me here at home unkept; for call you that keeping for a gentleman of my birth, that differs not from the stalling of an ox? His horses are bred better; for, besides that they are fair with their feeding, they are taught their manage, and to that end riders dearly hired. But I, his brother, gain nothing under him but growth; for the which his animals on his dunghills are as much bound to him as I. Besides this nothing that he so plentifully gives me, the something that nature gave me his countenance seems to take from me. He lets me feed with his hinds, bars me the place of a brother, and, as much as in him lies, mines my gentility with my education. This is it, Adam, that grieves me; and the spirit of my father, which I think is within me, begins to mutiny against this servitude. I will no longer endure it, though yet I know no wise remedy how to avoid it.

ADAM. Yonder comes my master, your brother.

ORLANDO. Go apart, Adam, and thou shalt hear how he will shake me up.

Enter OLIVER

OLIVER. Now, sir! What make you here?

ORLANDO. Nothing; I am not taught to make anything.

OLIVER. What mar you then, sir?

ORLANDO. Marry, sir, I am helping you to mar that which God made, a poor unworthy brother of yours, with idleness.

OLIVER. Marry, sir, be better employed, and be naught awhile.

ORLANDO. Shall I keep your hogs and eat husks with them? What prodigal portion have I spent, that I should come to such penury?

OLIVER. Know you where you are, sir?

ORLANDO. O, sir, very well: here in your orchard.

OLIVER. Know you before whom, sir?

ORLANDO. Ay, better than him I am before knows me. I know you are my eldest brother; and, in the gentle condition of blood, you should so know me. The courtesy of nations allows you my better, in that you are the first-born; but the same tradition takes not away my blood, were there twenty brothers betwixt us. I have as much of my father in me as you; albeit, I confess, your coming before me is nearer to his reverence.

OLIVER. What, boy!

ORLANDO. Come, come, elder brother, you are too young in this.

OLIVER. Wilt thou lay hands on me, villain?

ORLANDO. I am no villain; I am the youngest son of Sir Rowland de Boys. He was my father, and he is thrice a villain that says such a father begot villains. Wert thou not my brother, I would not take this hand from thy throat till this other had pulled out thy tongue for saying so. Thou hast railed on thyself.

ACT I

SCENE I *Orchard of* OLIVER's *house*

Enter ORLANDO and ADAM

ORLANDO. As I remember, Adam, it was upon this fashion bequeathed me by will but poor a thousand crowns, and, as thou sayest, charged my brother, on his blessing, to breed me well: and there begins my sadness. My brother Jaques he keeps at school, and report speaks goldenly of his profit. For my part,

ADAM. Sweet masters, be patient. For your father's remembrance, be at accord.

OLIVER. Let me go, I say.

ORLANDO. I will not, till I please. You shall hear me. My father charged you in his will to give me good education. You have trained me like a peasant, obscuring and hiding from me all gentlemanlike qualities. The spirit of my father grows strong in me, and I will no longer endure it. Therefore allow me such exercises as may become a gentleman, or give me the poor allottery my father left me by testament; with that I will go buy my fortunes.

OLIVER. And what wilt thou do? Beg, when that is spent? Well, sir, get you in. I will not long be troubled with you; you shall have some part of your will. I pray you, leave me.

ORLANDO. I will no further offend you than becomes me for my good.

OLIVER. Get you with him, you old dog.

ADAM. Is "old dog" my reward? Most true, I have lost my teeth in your service. God be with my old master! He would not have spoke such a word.

Exeunt ORLANDO *and* ADAM

OLIVER. Is it even so? Begin you to grow upon me? I will physic your rankness, and yet give no thousand crowns neither. Holla, Dennis!

Enter DENNIS

DENNIS. Calls your worship?

OLIVER. Was not Charles, the Duke's wrestler, here to speak with me?

DENNIS. So please you, he is here at the door and importunes access to you.

OLIVER. Call him in. [*Exit Dennis*] 'Twill be a good way; and tomorrow the wrestling is.

Enter CHARLES

CHARLES. Good morrow to your worship.

OLIVER. Good Monsieur Charles, what 's the new news at the new court?

CHARLES. There's no news at the court, sir, but the old news. That is, the old Duke is banished by his younger brother the new Duke; and three or four loving lords have put themselves into voluntary exile with him, whose lands and revenues enrich the new Duke; therefore he gives them good leave to wander.

OLIVER. Can you tell if Rosalind, the Duke's daughter, be banished with her father?

CHARLES. O, no; for the Duke's daughter, her cousin, so loves her, being ever from their cradles bred together, that she would have followed her exile, or have died to stay behind her. She is at the court, and no less beloved of her uncle than his own daughter; and never two ladies loved as they do.

OLIVER. Where will the old Duke live?

CHARLES. They say he is already in the forest of Arden, and a many merry men with him; and there they live like the old Robin Hood of England. They say many young gentlemen flock to him every day, and fleet the time carelessly, as they did in the golden world.

OLIVER. What, you wrestle tomorrow before the new Duke?

CHARLES. Marry, do I, sir; and I came to acquaint you with a matter. I am given, sir, secretly to understand that your younger brother Orlando hath a disposition to come in disguised against me to try a fall. Tomorrow, sir, I wrestle for my credit; and he that escapes me without some broken limb shall acquit him well. Your brother is but young and tender; and, for your love, I would be loath to foil him, as I must, for my own honour, if he come in. Therefore, out of my love to you, I came hither to acquaint you withal, that either you might stay him from his intendment or brook such disgrace well as he shall run into, in that it is a thing of his own search and altogether against my will.

OLIVER. Charles, I thank thee for thy love to me, which thou shalt find I will most kindly requite. I had myself notice of my brother's purpose herein and have by underhand means laboured to dissuade him from it, but he is resolute. I'll tell thee, Charles: it is the stubbornest young fellow of France, full of ambition, an envious emulator of every man's good parts, a secret and villainous contriver against me his natural brother. Therefore use thy discretion; I had as lief thou didst break his neck as his finger. And thou wert best look to 't; for if thou dost him any slight disgrace or if he do not mightily grace himself on thee, he will practise against thee by poison, entrap thee by some treacherous device and never leave thee till he hath ta'en thy life by some indirect means or other; for, I assure thee, and almost with tears I speak it, there is not one so young and so villainous this day living. I speak but brotherly of him; but should I anatomize him to thee as he is, I must blush and weep and thou must look pale and wonder.

CHARLES. I am heartily glad I came hither to you. If he come tomorrow, I'll give him his payment. If ever he go alone again, I'll never wrestle for prize more; and so God keep your worship!

OLIVER. Farewell, good Charles. [*Exit Charles*] Now will I stir this gamester. I hope I shall see an end of him; for my soul, yet I know not why, hates nothing more than he. Yet he's gentle, never schooled and yet learned, full of noble device, of all sorts enchantingly beloved, and indeed so much in the heart of the world, and especially of my own people, who best know him, that I am altogether misprised. But it shall not be so long; this wrestler shall clear all. Nothing remains but that I kindle the boy thither; which now I'll go about. *Exit*

CELIA. Marry, I prithee do, to make sport withal. But love no man in good earnest; nor no further in sport neither than with safety of a pure blush thou mayst in honour come off again.

ROSALIND. What shall be our sport, then?

CELIA. Let us sit and mock the good housewife Fortune from her wheel, that her gifts may henceforth be bestowed equally.

ROSALIND. I would we could do so, for her benefits are mightily misplaced, and the bountiful blind woman doth most mistake in her gifts to women.

CELIA. 'Tis true; for those that she makes fair she scarce makes honest, and those that she makes honest she makes very ill-favouredly.

ROSALIND. Nay, now thou goest from Fortune's office to Nature's. Fortune reigns in gifts of the world, not in the lineaments of Nature.

Enter TOUCHSTONE

CELIA. No? When Nature hath made a fair creature, may she not by Fortune fall into the fire? Though Nature hath given us wit to flout at Fortune, hath not Fortune sent in this fool to cut off the argument?

ROSALIND. Indeed, there is Fortune too hard for Nature, when Fortune makes Nature's natural the cutter-off of Nature's wit.

CELIA. Peradventure this is not Fortune's work neither, but Nature's; who perceiveth our natural wits too dull to reason of such goddesses and hath sent this natural for our whetstone; for always the dullness of the fool is the whetstone of the wits. How now, wit! Whither wander you?

TOUCHSTONE. Mistress, you must come away to your father.

CELIA. Were you made the messenger?

TOUCHSTONE. No, by mine honour, but I was bid to come for you.

ROSALIND. Where learned you that oath, fool?

TOUCHSTONE. Of a certain knight that swore by his honour they were good pancakes and swore by his honour the mustard was naught. Now I 'll stand to it, the pancakes were naught and the mustard was good, and yet was not the knight forsworn.

CELIA. How prove you that, in the great heap of your knowledge?

ROSALIND. Ay, marry, now unmuzzle your wisdom.

TOUCHSTONE. Stand you both forth now. Stroke your chins, and swear by your beards that I am a knave.

CELIA. By our beards, if we had them, thou art.

TOUCHSTONE. By my knavery, if I had it, then I were; but if you swear by that that is not, you are not forsworn. No more was this knight, swearing by his honour, for he never had any; or if he had, he had sworn it away before ever he saw those pancakes or that mustard.

SCENE II *Lawn before the* DUKE'S *palace*

Enter CELIA *and* ROSALIND

CELIA. I pray thee, Rosalind, sweet my coz, be merry.

ROSALIND. Dear Celia, I show more mirth than I am mistress of; and would you yet I were merrier? Unless you could teach me to forget a banished father, you must not learn me how to remember any extraordinary pleasure.

CELIA. Herein I see thou lovest me not with the full weight that I love thee. If my uncle, thy banished father, had banished thy uncle, the Duke my father, so thou hadst been still with me, I could have taught my love to take thy father for mine. So wouldst thou, if the truth of thy love to me were so righteously tempered as mine is to thee.

ROSALIND. Well, I will forget the condition of my estate, to rejoice in yours.

CELIA. You know my father hath no child but I, nor none is like to have. And, truly, when he dies, thou shalt be his heir, for what he hath taken away from thy father perforce, I will render thee again in affection; by mine honour, I will; and when I break that oath, let me turn monster. Therefore, my sweet Rose, my dear Rose, be merry.

ROSALIND. From henceforth I will, coz, and devise sports. Let me see; what think you of falling in love?

CELIA. Prithee, who is 't that thou meanest?

TOUCHSTONE. One that old Frederick, your father, loves.

CELIA. My father's love is enough to honour him. Enough! Speak no more of him; you'll be whipped for taxation one of these days.

TOUCHSTONE. The more pity, that fools may not speak wisely what wise men do foolishly.

CELIA. By my troth, thou sayest true; for since the little wit that fools have was silenced, the little foolery that wise men have makes a great show. Here comes Monsieur Le Beau.

ROSALIND. With his mouth full of news.

CELIA. Which he will put on us, as pigeons feed their young.

ROSALIND. Then shall we be news-crammed.

CELIA. All the better; we shall be the more marketable.

Enter LE BEAU

Bonjour, Monsieur Le Beau; what's the news?

LE BEAU. Fair princess, you have lost much good sport.

CELIA. Sport? Of what colour?

LE BEAU. What colour, madam? How shall I answer you?

ROSALIND. As wit and fortune will.

TOUCHSTONE. Or as the Destinies decree.

CELIA. Well said. That was laid on with a trowel.

TOUCHSTONE. Nay, if I keep not my rank—

ROSALIND. Thou losest thy old smell.

LE BEAU. You amaze me, ladies. I would have told you of good wrestling, which you have lost the sight of.

ROSALIND. Yet tell us the manner of the wrestling.

LE BEAU. I will tell you the beginning; and, if it please your ladyships, you may see the end; for the best is yet to do; and here, where you are, they are coming to perform it.

CELIA. Well, the beginning, that is dead and buried.

LE BEAU. There comes an old man and his three sons—

CELIA. I could match this beginning with an old tale.

LE BEAU. Three proper young men, of excellent growth and presence.

ROSALIND. With bills on their necks, "Be it known unto all men by these presents."

LE BEAU. The eldest of the three wrestled with Charles, the Duke's wrestler; which Charles in a moment threw him and broke three of his ribs, that there is little hope of life in him. So he served the second, and so the third. Yonder they lie; the poor old man, their father, making such pitiful dole over them that all the beholders take his part with weeping.

ROSALIND. Alas!

TOUCHSTONE. But what is the sport, monsieur, that the ladies have lost?

LE BEAU. Why, this that I speak of.

TOUCHSTONE. Thus men may grow wiser every day.

It is the first time that ever I heard breaking of ribs was sport for ladies.

CELIA. Or I, I promise thee.

ROSALIND. But is there any else longs to see this broken music in his sides? Is there yet another dotes upon rib-breaking? Shall we see this wrestling, cousin?

LE BEAU. You must, if you stay here. For here is the place appointed for the wrestling, and they are ready to perform it.

CELIA. Yonder, sure, they are coming. Let us now stay and see it.

Flourish. Enter DUKE FREDERICK, Lords, ORLANDO, CHARLES, *and* Attendants

DUKE FREDERICK. Come on. Since the youth will not be entreated, his own peril on his forwardness.

ROSALIND. Is yonder the man?

LE BEAU. Even he, madam.

CELIA. Alas, he is too young! Yet he looks successfully.

DUKE FREDERICK. How now, daughter and cousin! Are you crept hither to see the wrestling?

ROSALIND. Ay, my liege, so please you give us leave.

DUKE FREDERICK. You will take little delight in it, I can tell you; there is such odds in the man. In pity of the challenger's youth I would fain dissuade him, but he will not be entreated. Speak to him, ladies; see if you can move him.

CELIA. Call him hither, good Monsieur Le Beau.

DUKE FREDERICK. Do so. I 'll not be by.

LE BEAU. Monsieur the challenger, the Princess calls for you.

ORLANDO. I attend them with all respect and duty.

ROSALIND. Young man, have you challenged Charles the wrestler?

ORLANDO. No, fair Princess; he is the general challenger. I come but in, as others do, to try with him the strength of my youth.

CELIA. Young gentleman, your spirits are too bold for your years. You have seen cruel proof of this man's strength. If you saw yourself with your eyes or knew yourself with your judgement, the fear of your adventure would counsel you to a more equal enterprise. We pray you, for your own sake, to embrace your own safety and give over this attempt.

ROSALIND. Do, young sir; your reputation shall not therefore be misprised. We will make it our suit to the Duke that the wrestling might not go forward.

ORLANDO. I beseech you, punish me not with your hard thoughts; wherein I confess me much guilty, to deny so fair and excellent ladies anything. But let your fair eyes and gentle wishes go with me to my trial; wherein if I be foiled, there is but one shamed that was never gracious; if killed, but one dead that is willing to be so. I shall do my friends no wrong, for I have none to lament me, the world no injury, for in it I have nothing; only in the world I fill up a

place, which may be better supplied when I have made
it empty.

ROSALIND. The little strength that I have, I would it
were with you.

CELIA. And mine, to eke out hers.

ROSALIND. Fare you well. Pray Heaven I be deceived
in you!

CELIA. Your heart's desires be with you!

CHARLES. Come, where is this young gallant that is so
desirous to lie with his mother earth?

ORLANDO. Ready, sir; but his will hath in it a more
modest working.

DUKE FREDERICK. You shall try but one fall.

CHARLES. No, I warrant your grace, you shall not entreat him to a second, that have so mightily persuaded
him from a first.

ORLANDO. An you mean to mock me after, you should
not have mocked me before. But come your ways.

ROSALIND. Now Hercules be thy speed, young man!

CELIA. I would I were invisible, to catch the strong
fellow by the leg.   *They wrestle*

ROSALIND. O excellent young man!

CELIA. If I had a thunderbolt in mine eye, I can tell
who should down.   *Shout:* CHARLES *is thrown*

DUKE FREDERICK. No more, no more.

ORLANDO. Yes, I beseech your grace. I am not yet well
breathed.

DUKE FREDERICK. How dost thou, Charles?

LE BEAU. He cannot speak, my lord.

DUKE FREDERICK. Bear him away. What is thy name,
young man?   CHARLES *is carried out*

ORLANDO. Orlando, my liege; the youngest son of Sir
Rowland de Boys.

DUKE FREDERICK. I would thou hadst been son to some
man else.

The world esteemed thy father honourable,
But I did find him still mine enemy.
Thou shouldst have better pleased me with this deed,
Hadst thou descended from another house.
But fare thee well; thou art a gallant youth:
I would thou hadst told me of another father.
            Exeunt DUKE FREDERICK, *train, and* LE BEAU

CELIA. Were I my father, coz, would I do this?

ORLANDO. I am more proud to be Sir Rowland's son,
His youngest son; and would not change that calling,
To be adopted heir to Frederick.

ROSALIND. My father loved Sir Rowland as his soul,
And all the world was of my father's mind.
Had I before known this young man his son,
I should have given him tears unto entreaties,
Ere he should thus have ventured.

CELIA.   Gentle cousin,
Let us go thank him and encourage him.
My father's rough and envious disposition
Sticks me at heart. Sir, you have well deserved.
If you do keep your promises in love

But justly, as you have exceeded all promise,
Your mistress shall be happy.

ROSALIND.   Gentleman,
            Giving him a chain from her neck
Wear this for me, one out of suits with fortune,
That could give more, but that her hand lacks means.
Shall we go, coz?

CELIA.   Ay. Fare you well, fair gentleman.

ORLANDO. Can I not say, I thank you? My better parts
Are all thrown down, and that which here stands up
Is but a quintain, a mere lifeless block.

ROSALIND. He calls us back: my pride fell with my
fortunes;
I'll ask him what he would. Did you call, sir?
Sir, you have wrestled well and overthrown
More than your enemies.

CELIA.   Will you go, coz?

ROSALIND. Have with you. Fare you well.
                       Exeunt ROSALIND *and* CELIA

ORLANDO. What passion hangs these weights upon my
tongue?
I cannot speak to her, yet she urged conference.
O poor Orlando, thou art overthrown!
Or Charles or something weaker masters thee.

Re-enter LE BEAU

LE BEAU. Good sir, I do in friendship counsel you
To leave this place. Albeit you have deserved
High commendation, true applause and love,
Yet such is now the Duke's condition
That he misconstrues all that you have done.
The Duke is humorous: what he is indeed,
More suits you to conceive than I to speak of.

ORLANDO. I thank you, sir. And, pray you, tell me this;
Which of the two was daughter of the Duke
That here was at the wrestling?

LE BEAU. Neither his daughter, if we judge by manners.
But yet indeed the smaller is his daughter;
The other is daughter to the banished Duke,
And here detained by her usurping uncle,
To keep his daughter company; whose loves
Are dearer than the natural bond of sisters.
But I can tell you that of late this Duke
Hath ta'en displeasure 'gainst his gentle niece,
Grounded upon no other argument
But that the people praise her for her virtues
And pity her for her good father's sake;
And, on my life, his malice 'gainst the lady
Will suddenly break forth. Sir, fare you well:
Hereafter, in a better world than this,
I shall desire more love and knowledge of you.

ORLANDO. I rest much bounden to you; fare you well.
                                        Exit LE BEAU

Thus must I from the smoke into the smother;
From tyrant Duke unto a tyrant brother.
But heavenly Rosalind!   *Exit*

SCENE III *A room in the palace*

Enter CELIA *and* ROSALIND

CELIA. Why, cousin! Why, Rosalind! Cupid have mercy! Not a word?

ROSALIND. Not one to throw at a dog.

CELIA. No, thy words are too precious to be cast away upon curs; throw some of them at me. Come, lame me with reasons.

ROSALIND. Then there were two cousins laid up; when the one should be lamed with reasons and the other mad without any.

CELIA. But is all this for your father?

ROSALIND. No, some of it is for my child's father. O, how full of briers is this working-day world!

CELIA. They are but burs, cousin, thrown upon thee in holiday foolery. If we walk not in the trodden paths, our very petticoats will catch them.

ROSALIND. I could shake them off my coat. These burs are in my heart.

CELIA. Hem them away.

ROSALIND. I would try, if I could cry "hem" and have him.

CELIA. Come, come, wrestle with thy affections.

ROSALIND. O, they take the part of a better wrestler than myself!

CELIA. O, a good wish upon you! You will cry in time, in despite of a fall. But, turning these jests out of service, let us talk in good earnest. Is it possible, on such a sudden, you should fall into so strong a liking with old Sir Rowland's youngest son?

ROSALIND. The Duke my father loved his father dearly.

CELIA. Doth it therefore ensue that you should love his son dearly? By this kind of chase, I should hate him, for my father hated his father dearly; yet I hate not Orlando.

ROSALIND. No, faith, hate him not, for my sake.

CELIA. Why should I not? Doth he not deserve well?

ROSALIND. Let me love him for that, and do you love him because I do. Look, here comes the Duke.

CELIA. With his eyes full of anger.

Enter DUKE FREDERICK, *with* Lords

DUKE FREDERICK. Mistress, dispatch you with your safest haste

And get you from our court.

ROSALIND.   Me, uncle?

DUKE FREDERICK.   You, cousin.
  Within these ten days if that thou be'st found
  So near our public court as twenty miles,
  Thou diest for it.

ROSALIND.   I do beseech your grace,
  Let me the knowledge of my fault bear with me.
  If with myself I hold intelligence
  Or have acquaintance with mine own desires,
  If that I do not dream or be not frantic—
  As I do trust I am not—then, dear uncle,
  Never so much as in a thought unborn
  Did I offend your highness.

DUKE FREDERICK.   Thus do all traitors:
  If their purgation did consist in words,
  They are as innocent as grace itself.
  Let it suffice thee that I trust thee not.

ROSALIND. Yet your mistrust cannot make me a traitor.
  Tell me whereon the likelihood depends.

DUKE FREDERICK. Thou art thy father's daughter; there's
    enough.

ROSALIND. So was I when your highness took his duke-
    dom;
  So was I when your highness banished him.
  Treason is not inherited, my lord;
  Or, if we did derive it from our friends,
  What's that to me? My father was no traitor.
  Then, good my liege, mistake me not so much
  To think my poverty is treacherous.

CELIA. Dear sovereign, hear me speak.

DUKE FREDERICK. Ay, Celia; we stayed her for your
    sake,
  Else had she with her father ranged along.

CELIA. I did not then entreat to have her stay;
  It was your pleasure and your own remorse.
  I was too young that time to value her;
  But now I know her. If she be a traitor,
  Why so am I; we still have slept together,
  Rose at an instant, learned, played, eat together,
  And wheresoe'er we went, like Juno's swans,
  Still we went coupled and inseparable.

DUKE FREDERICK. She is too subtle for thee; and her
    smoothness,
  Her very silence and her patience
  Speak to the people, and they pity her.
  Thou art a fool. She robs thee of thy name;
  And thou wilt show more bright and seem more
    virtuous
  When she is gone. Then open not thy lips:
  Firm and irrevocable is my doom
  Which I have passed upon her; she is banished.

CELIA. Pronounce that sentence then on me, my liege.
  I cannot live out of her company.

DUKE FREDERICK. You are a fool. You, niece, provide
    yourself.

If you outstay the time, upon mine honour,
And in the greatness of my word, you die.
                  Exeunt DUKE FREDERICK *and* Lords

CELIA. O my poor Rosalind, whither wilt thou go?
  Wilt thou change fathers? I will give thee mine.
  I charge thee, be not thou more grieved than I am.

ROSALIND. I have more cause.

CELIA.   Thou hast not, cousin;
  Prithee, be cheerful. Know'st thou not, the Duke
  Hath banished me, his daughter?

ROSALIND.   That he hath not.

CELIA. No, hath not? Rosalind lacks then the love
  Which teacheth thee that thou and I am one.
  Shall we be sundered? Shall we part, sweet girl?
  No! Let my father seek another heir.
  Therefore devise with me how we may fly,
  Whither to go and what to bear with us;
  And do not seek to take your change upon you,
  To bear your griefs yourself and leave me out;
  For, by this heaven, now at our sorrows pale,
  Say what thou canst, I'll go along with thee.

ROSALIND. Why, whither shall we go?

CELIA. To seek my uncle in the forest of Arden.

ROSALIND. Alas, what danger will it be to us,
  Maids as we are, to travel forth so far!
  Beauty provoketh thieves sooner than gold.

CELIA. I'll put myself in poor and mean attire
  And with a kind of umber smirch my face;
  The like do you. So shall we pass along
  And never stir assailants.

ROSALIND.   Were it not better,
  Because that I am more than common tall,
  That I did suit me all points like a man?
  A gallant curtle-axe upon my thigh,
  A boar-spear in my hand; and—in my heart
  Lie there what hidden woman's fear there will—
  We'll have a swashing and a martial outside,
  As many other mannish cowards have
  That do outface it with their semblances.

CELIA. What shall I call thee when thou art a man?

ROSALIND. I'll have no worse a name than Jove's own
    page;
  And therefore look you call me Ganymede.
  But what will you be called?

CELIA. Something that hath a reference to my state;
  No longer Celia, but Aliena.

ROSALIND. But, cousin, what if we assayed to steal
  The clownish fool out of your father's court?
  Would he not be a comfort to our travel?

CELIA. He'll go along o'er the wide world with me;
  Leave me alone to woo him. Let's away,
  And get our jewels and our wealth together,
  Devise the fittest time and safest way
  To hide us from pursuit that will be made
  After my flight. Now go we in content
  To liberty and not to banishment.   *Exeunt*

ACT II

SCENE I *The Forest of Arden*

Enter DUKE SENIOR, AMIENS, *and two or three* Lords,
dressed as foresters

DUKE SENIOR. Now, my co-mates and brothers in exile,
  Hath not old custom made this life more sweet
  Than that of painted pomp? Are not these woods
  More free from peril than the envious court?
  Here feel we but the penalty of Adam,
  The seasons' difference, as the icy fang
  And churlish chiding of the winter's wind,
  Which, when it bites and blows upon my body,

Even till I shrink with cold, I smile and say
"This is no flattery: these are counsellors
That feelingly persuade me what I am."
Sweet are the uses of adversity,
Which, like the toad, ugly and venomous,
Wears yet a precious jewel in his head;
And this our life exempt from public haunt
Finds tongues in trees, books in the running brooks,
Sermons in stones and good in everything.
AMIENS. I would not change it. Happy is your grace.
That can translate the stubbornness of fortune
Into so quiet and so sweet a style.
DUKE SENIOR. Come, shall we go and kill us venison?
And yet it irks me the poor dappled fools,

Being native burghers of this desert city,
Should in their own confines with forked heads
Have their round haunches gored.
FIRST LORD.   Indeed, my lord,
The melancholy Jaques grieves at that,
And, in that kind, swears you do more usurp
Than doth your brother that hath banished you.
Today my Lord of Amiens and myself
Did steal behind him as he lay along
Under an oak whose antique root peeps out
Upon the brook that brawls along this wood:
To the which place a poor sequestered stag,
That from the hunter's aim had ta'en a hurt,
Did come to languish, and indeed, my lord,

The wretched animal heaved forth such groans
That their discharge did stretch his leathern coat
Almost to bursting, and the big round tears
Coursed one another down his innocent nose
In piteous chase; and thus the hairy fool,
Much marked of the melancholy Jaques,
Stood on the extremest verge of the swift brook,
Augmenting it with tears.
DUKE SENIOR.   But what said Jaques?
Did he not moralize this spectacle?
FIRST LORD. O, yes, into a thousand similes.
First, for his weeping into the needless stream;
"Poor deer," quoth he, "thou makest a testament
As worldlings do, giving thy sum of more
To that which had too much." Then, being there
  alone,
Left and abandoned of his velvet friend,
" 'Tis right," quoth he; "thus misery doth part
The flux of company." Anon a careless herd,
Full of the pasture, jumps along by him

And never stays to greet him. "Ay," quoth Jaques,
"Sweep on, you fat and greasy citizens;
'Tis just the fashion: wherefore do you look
Upon that poor and broken bankrupt there?"
Thus most invectively he pierceth through
The body of the country, city, court,
Yea, and of this our life, swearing that we
Are mere usurpers, tyrants and what 's worse,
To fright the animals and to kill them up
In their assigned and native dwelling-place.
DUKE SENIOR. And did you leave him in this con-
  templation?
SECOND LORD. We did, my lord, weeping and com-
  menting
Upon the sobbing deer.
DUKE SENIOR.   Show me the place.
I love to cope him in these sullen fits,
For then he's full of matter.
FIRST LORD. I'll bring you to him straight.

Exeunt

SCENE II *A room in the palace*

Enter DUKE FREDERICK, *with* Lords

DUKE FREDERICK. Can it be possible that no man saw
  them?
It cannot be: some villains of my court
Are of consent and sufferance in this.
FIRST LORD. I cannot hear of any that did see her.
The ladies, her attendants of her chamber,
Saw her abed, and in the morning early
They found the bed untreasured of their mistress.
SECOND LORD. My lord, the roynish clown, at whom
  so oft
Your grace was wont to laugh, is also missing.
Hisperia, the princess' gentlewoman,

Confesses that she secretly o'erheard
Your daughter and her cousin much commend
The parts and graces of the wrestler
That did but lately foil the sinewy Charles;
And she believes, wherever they are gone,
That youth is surely in their company.
DUKE FREDERICK. Send to his brother; fetch that gal-
  lant hither;
If he be absent, bring his brother to me;
I 'll make him find him. Do this suddenly,
And let not search and inquisition quail
To bring again these foolish runaways.   *Exeunt*

SCENE III *Before* OLIVER'S *house*

Enter ORLANDO *and* ADAM, *meeting*

ORLANDO. Who's there?
ADAM. What, my young master? O my gentle master!
O my sweet master! O you memory
Of old Sir Rowland! Why, what make you here?
Why are you virtuous? Why do people love you?
And wherefore are you gentle, strong and valiant?
Why would you be so fond to overcome
The bonny prizer of the humorous Duke?
Your praise is come too swiftly home before you.
Know you not, master, to some kind of men
Their graces serve them but as enemies?
No more do yours: your virtues, gentle master,
Are sanctified and holy traitors to you.

O, what a world is this, when what is comely
Envenoms him that bears it!
ORLANDO. Why, what's the matter?
ADAM.   O unhappy youth!
Come not within these doors; within this roof
The enemy of all your graces lives.
Your brother—no, no brother; yet the son—
Yet not the son, I will not call him son
Of him I was about to call his father—
Hath heard your praises, and this night he means
To burn the lodging where you use to lie
And you within it. If he fail of that,
He will have other means to cut you off.

258

I overheard him and his practices.
This is no place; this house is but a butchery.
Abhor it, fear it, do not enter it.

ORLANDO. Why, whither, Adam, wouldst thou have
me go?

ADAM. No matter whither, so you come not here.

ORLANDO. What, wouldst thou have me go and beg my
food?

Or with a base and boisterous sword enforce
A thievish living on the common road?
This I must do, or know not what to do.
Yet this I will not do, do how I can;
I rather will subject me to the malice
Of a diverted blood and bloody brother.

ADAM. But do not so. I have five hundred crowns,
The thrifty hire I saved under your father,
Which I did store to be my foster-nurse
When service should in my old limbs lie lame
And unregarded age in corners thrown.
Take that, and He that doth the ravens feed,
Yea, providently caters for the sparrow,
Be comfort to my age! Here is the gold;
All this I give you. Let me be your servant.
Though I look old, yet I am strong and lusty;
For in my youth I never did apply
Hot and rebellious liquors in my blood,
Nor did not with unbashful forehead woo

The means of weakness and debility;
Therefore my age is as a lusty winter,
Frosty, but kindly. Let me go with you;
I'll do the service of a younger man
In all your business and necessities.

ORLANDO. O good old man, how well in thee appears
The constant service of the antique world,
When service sweat for duty, not for meed!
Thou art not for the fashion of these times,
Where none will sweat but for promotion,
And having that, do choke their service up
Even with the having: it is not so with thee.
But, poor old man, thou prunest a rotten tree,
That cannot so much as a blossom yield
In lieu of all thy pains and husbandry.
But come thy ways; we'll go along together,
And ere we have thy youthful wages spent,
We'll light upon some settled low content.

ADAM. Master, go on, and I will follow thee,
To the last gasp, with truth and loyalty.
From seventeen years till now almost fourscore
Here lived I, but now live here no more.
At seventeen years many their fortunes seek;
But at fourscore it is too late a week.
Yet fortune cannot recompense me better
Than to die well and not my master's debtor.

Exeunt

SCENE IV *The Forest of Arden*

Enter ROSALIND *as* GANYMEDE, CELIA *as* ALIENA, *and* TOUCHSTONE

ROSALIND. O Jupiter, how weary are my spirits!

TOUCHSTONE. I care not for my spirits, if my legs were
not weary.

ROSALIND. I could find in my heart to disgrace my man's
apparel and to cry like a woman; but I must comfort
the weaker vessel, as doublet and hose ought to show
itself courageous to petticoat: therefore courage, good
Aliena!

CELIA. I pray you, bear with me; I cannot go no further.

TOUCHSTONE. For my part, I had rather bear with you
than bear you: yet I should bear no cross if I did bear
you, for I think you have no money in your purse.

ROSALIND. Well, this is the forest of Arden.

TOUCHSTONE. Ay, now am I in Arden; the more fool I;
when I was at home, I was in a better place. But
travellers must be content.

ROSALIND. Ay, be so, good Touchstone.

Enter CORIN *and* SILVIUS

Look you, who comes here; a young man and an old
in solemn talk.

CORIN. That is the way to make her scorn you still.

SILVIUS. O Corin, that thou knew'st how I do love her!

CORIN. I partly guess; for I have loved ere now.

SILVIUS. No, Corin, being old, thou canst not guess,

Though in thy youth thou wast as true a lover
As ever sighed upon a midnight pillow.
But if thy love were ever like to mine—
As sure I think did never man love so—
How many actions most ridiculous
Hast thou been drawn to by thy fantasy?

CORIN. Into a thousand that I have forgotten.

SILVIUS. O, thou didst then ne'er love so heartily!
If thou remember'st not the slightest folly
That ever love did make thee run into,
Thou hast not loved;
Or if thou hast not sat as I do now,
Wearying thy hearer in thy mistress' praise,
Thou hast not loved;
Or if thou hast not broke from company
Abruptly, as my passion now makes me,
Thou hast not loved.
O Phebe, Phebe, Phebe!   *Exit*

ROSALIND. Alas, poor shepherd! Searching of thy wound,
I have by hard adventure found mine own.

TOUCHSTONE. And I mine. I remember, when I was in
love I broke my sword upon a stone and bid him take
that for coming a-night to Jane Smile; and I remember
the kissing of her batlet and the cow's dugs that her
pretty chopt hands had milked; and I remember the

wooing of a peascod instead of her, from whom I took two cods and, giving her them again, said with weeping tears "Wear these for my sake." We that are true lovers run into strange capers; but as all is mortal in nature, so is all nature in love mortal in folly.

ROSALIND. Thou speakest wiser than thou art ware of.

TOUCHSTONE. Nay, I shall ne'er be ware of mine own wit till I break my shins against it.

ROSALIND. Jove, Jove! This shepherd's passion
    Is much upon my fashion.

TOUCHSTONE. And mine; but it grows something stale with me.

CELIA. I pray you, one of you question yon man
    If he for gold will give us any food.
    I faint almost to death.

TOUCHSTONE.   Holla, you clown!

ROSALIND. Peace, fool. He's not thy kinsman.

CORIN.   Who calls?

TOUCHSTONE. Your betters, sir.

CORIN.   Else are they very wretched.

ROSALIND. Peace, I say. Good even to you, friend.

CORIN. And to you, gentle sir, and to you all.

ROSALIND. I prithee, shepherd, if that love or gold
    Can in this desert place buy entertainment,
    Bring us where we may rest ourselves and feed.
    Here's a young maid with travel much oppressed
    And faints for succour.

CORIN.   Fair sir, I pity her
    And wish, for her sake more than for mine own,
    My fortunes were more able to relieve her;
    But I am shepherd to another man
    And do not shear the fleeces that I graze.
    My master is of churlish disposition
    And little recks to find the way to heaven
    By doing deeds of hospitality.
    Besides, his cote, his flocks and bounds of feed
    Are now on sale, and at our sheepcote now,
    By reason of his absence, there is nothing
    That you will feed on; but what is, come see,
    And in my voice most welcome shall you be.

ROSALIND. What is he that shall buy his flock and pasture?

CORIN. That young swain that you saw here but erewhile,
    That little cares for buying anything.

ROSALIND. I pray thee, if it stand with honesty,
    Buy thou the cottage, pasture and the flock,
    And thou shalt have to pay for it of us.

CELIA. And we will mend thy wages. I like this place,
    And willingly could waste my time in it.

CORIN. Assuredly the thing is to be sold.
    Go with me: if you like upon report
    The soil, the profit and this kind of life,
    I will your very faithful feeder be
    And buy it with your gold right suddenly.   *Exeunt*

SCENE V *The forest*

Enter AMIENS, JAQUES, *and others*

SONG

AMIENS.   Under the greenwood tree
             Who loves to lie with me,
             And turn his merry note
             Unto the sweet bird's throat,
    Come hither, come hither, come hither:
             Here shall he see
             No enemy
        But winter and rough weather.

JAQUES. More, more, I prithee, more.

AMIENS. It will make you melancholy, Monsieur Jaques.

JAQUES. I thank it. More, I prithee, more. I can suck melancholy out of a song, as a weasel sucks eggs. More, I prithee, more.

AMIENS. My voice is ragged; I know I cannot please you.

JAQUES. I do not desire you to please me; I do desire you to sing. Come, more; another stanzo. Call you 'em stanzos?

AMIENS. What you will, Monsieur Jaques.

JAQUES. Nay, I care not for their names; they owe me nothing. Will you sing?

AMIENS. More at your request than to please myself.

JAQUES. Well then, if ever I thank any man, I 'll thank you; but that they call compliment is like the encounter of two dog-apes, and when a man thanks me heartily, methinks I have given him a penny and he renders me the beggarly thanks. Come, sing; and you that will not, hold your tongues.

AMIENS. Well, I 'll end the song. Sirs, cover the while; the Duke will drink under this tree. He hath been all this day to look you.

JAQUES. And I have been all this day to avoid him. He is too disputable for my company. I think of as many

matters as he, but I give heaven thanks and make no boast of them. Come, warble, come.

SONG

Who doth ambition shun   [*All together here*]
And loves to live i' the sun,
Seeking the food he eats
And pleased with what he gets,
Come hither, come hither, come hither:
      Here shall he see
      No enemy
But winter and rough weather.

JAQUES. I 'll give you a verse to this note that I made yesterday in despite of my invention.
AMIENS. And I 'll sing it.
JAQUES. Thus it goes—   *hands him a paper*

SONG

AMIENS.
            If it do come to pass
            That any man turn ass,
            Leaving his wealth and ease,
            A stubborn will to please,
      Ducdame, ducdame, ducdame:
            Here shall he see
            Gross fools as he,
      An if he will come to me.

AMIENS. What's that ''ducdame''?
JAQUES. 'Tis a Greek invocation, to call fools into a circle. I'll go sleep, if I can; if I cannot, I'll rail against all the first-born of Egypt.
AMIENS. And I'll go seek the Duke. His banquet is prepared.   *Exeunt severally*

SCENE VI *The forest*

Enter ORLANDO *and* ADAM

ADAM. Dear master, I can go no further. O, I die for food! Here lie I down, and measure out my grave. Farewell, kind master.
ORLANDO. Why, how now, Adam! no greater heart in thee? Live a little; comfort a little; cheer thyself a little. If this uncouth forest yield anything savage, I will either be food for it or bring it for food to thee. Thy conceit is nearer death than thy powers. For my sake be comfortable; hold death awhile at the arm's end. I will here be with thee presently; and if I bring thee not something to eat, I will give thee leave to die. But if thou diest before I come, thou art a mocker of my labour. Well said! Thou lookest cheerly, and I'll be with thee quickly. Yet thou liest in the bleak air. Come, I will bear thee to some shelter; and thou shalt not die for lack of a dinner, if there live anything in this desert. Cheerly, good Adam!   *Exeunt*

SCENE VII *The forest*

A table set out. Enter DUKE SENIOR, AMIENS, *and* Lords *like outlaws*

DUKE SENIOR. I think he be transformed into a beast;
  For I can nowhere find him like a man.
FIRST LORD. My lord, he is but even now gone hence:
  Here was he merry, hearing of a song.
DUKE SENIOR. If he, compact of jars, grow musical,
  We shall have shortly discord in the spheres.
  Go, seek him; tell him I would speak with him.

Enter JAQUES

FIRST LORD. He saves my labour by his own approach.
DUKE SENIOR. Why, how now, monsieur! What a life
    is this,
  That your poor friends must woo your company?
  What, you look merrily!
JAQUES. A fool, a fool! I met a fool i' the forest,
  A motley fool; a miserable world!
  As I do live by food, I met a fool;
  Who laid him down and basked him in the sun,
  And railed on Lady Fortune in good terms,
  In good set terms and yet a motley fool.
  "Good morrow, fool," quoth I. "No, sir," quoth he,
  "Call me not fool till Heaven hath sent me fortune."
  And then he drew a dial from his poke,
  And, looking on it with lack-lustre eye,
  Says very wisely, "It is ten o'clock:
  Thus we may see," quoth he, "how the world wags.
  'Tis but an hour ago since it was nine,
  And after one hour more 'twill be eleven;
  And so, from hour to hour, we ripe and ripe,
  And then, from hour to hour, we rot and rot;
  And thereby hangs a tale." When I did hear
  The motley fool thus moral on the time,
  My lungs began to crow like chanticleer,
  That fools should be so deep-contemplative,
  And I did laugh sans intermission
  An hour by his dial. O noble fool!
  A worthy fool! Motley 's the only wear.
DUKE SENIOR. What fool is this?
JAQUES. O worthy fool! One that hath been a courtier,
  And says, if ladies be but young and fair,
  They have the gift to know it; and in his brain,
  Which is as dry as the remainder biscuit
  After a voyage, he hath strange places crammed
  With observation, the which he vents
  In mangled forms. O that I were a fool!
  I am ambitious for a motley coat.
DUKE SENIOR. Thou shalt have one.
JAQUES.   It is my only suit;
  Provided that you weed your better judgements
  Of all opinion that grows rank in them
  That I am wise. I must have liberty
  Withal, as large a charter as the wind,
  To blow on whom I please; for so fools have;

And they that are most galled with my folly,
  They most must laugh. And why, sir, must they so?
  The "why" is plain as way to parish church:
  He that a fool doth very wisely hit
  Doth very foolishly, although he smart,
  Not to seem senseless of the bob. If not,
  The wise man's folly is anatomized
  Even by the squandering lances of the fool.
  Invest me in my motley; give me leave
  To speak my mind, and I will through and through
  Cleanse the foul body of the infected world,
  If they will patiently receive my medicine.
DUKE SENIOR. Fie on thee! I can tell what thou wouldst
    do.
JAQUES. What, for a counter, would I do but good?
DUKE SENIOR. Most mischievous foul sin, in chiding sin:
  For thou thyself hast been a libertine,
  As sensual as the brutish sting itself;
  And all the embossed sores and headed evils,
  That thou with license of free foot hast caught,
  Wouldst thou disgorge into the general world.
JAQUES. Why, who cries out on pride,
  That can therein tax any private party?
  Doth it not flow as hugely as the sea,
  Till that the weary very means do ebb?
  What woman in the city do I name,
  When that I say the city-woman bears
  The cost of princes on unworthy shoulders?
  Who can come in and say that I mean her,
  When such a one as she, such is her neighbour?
  Or what is he of basest function
  That says his bravery is not on my cost,
  Thinking that I mean him, but therein suits
  His folly to the mettle of my speech?
  There then; how then? What then? Let me see wherein
  My tongue hath wronged him. If it do him right,
  Then he hath wronged himself; if he be free,
  Why then my taxing like a wild goose flies,
  Unclaimed of any man. But who comes here?

Enter ORLANDO, *with his sword drawn*

ACT II, SCENE VII

ORLANDO. Forbear, and eat no more.
JAQUES.   Why, I have eat none yet.
ORLANDO. Nor shalt not, till necessity be served.
JAQUES. Of what kind should this cock come of?
DUKE SENIOR. Art thou thus boldened, man, by thy
    distress,
  Or else a rude despiser of good manners,
  That in civility thou seem'st so empty?
ORLANDO. You touched my vein at first. The thorny
    point
  Of bare distress hath ta'en from me the show
  Of smooth civility. Yet am I inland bred
  And know some nurture. But forbear, I say:
  He dies that touches any of this fruit
  Till I and my affairs are answered.
JAQUES. An you will not be answered with reason, I
  must die.

DUKE SENIOR. What would you have? Your gentleness
    shall force
  More than your force move us to gentleness.
ORLANDO. I almost die for food; and let me have it.
DUKE SENIOR. Sit down and feed, and welcome to our
    table.
ORLANDO. Speak you so gently? Pardon me, I pray you.
  I thought that all things had been savage here;
  And therefore put I on the countenance
  Of stern commandment. But whate'er you are
  That in this desert inaccessible,
  Under the shade of melancholy boughs,
  Lose and neglect the creeping hours of time;
  If ever you have looked on better days,
  If ever been where bells have knolled to church,
  If ever sat at any good man's feast,
  If ever from your eyelids wiped a tear
  And know what 'tis to pity and be pitied,
  Let gentleness my strong enforcement be:
  In the which hope I blush, and hide my sword.
DUKE SENIOR. True is it that we have seen better days,
  And have with holy bell been knolled to church
  And sat at good men's feasts and wiped our eyes
  Of drops that sacred pity hath engendered;
  And therefore sit you down in gentleness
  And take upon command what help we have
  That to your wanting may be ministered.
ORLANDO. Then but forbear your food a little while,
  Whiles, like a doe, I go to find my fawn
  And give it food. There is an old poor man,
  Who after me hath many a weary step
  Limped in pure love. Till he be first sufficed,
  Oppressed with two weak evils, age and hunger,
  I will not touch a bit.
DUKE SENIOR.   Go find him out,
  And we will nothing waste till you return.
ORLANDO. I thank ye; and be blest for your good com-
    fort!   Exit
DUKE SENIOR. Thou seest we are not all alone unhappy:
  This wide and universal theatre
  Presents more woeful pageants than the scene
  Wherein we play in.
JAQUES.   All the world 's a stage,
  And all the men and women merely players:
  They have their exits and their entrances;
  And one man in his time plays many parts,
  His acts being seven ages. At first the infant,
  Mewling and puking in the nurse's arms.
  And then the whining schoolboy, with his satchel
  And shining morning face, creeping like snail
  Unwillingly to school. And then the lover,
  Sighing like furnace, with a woeful ballad
  Made to his mistress' eyebrow. Then a soldier,
  Full of strange oaths and bearded like the pard,
  Jealous in honour, sudden and quick in quarrel,
  Seeking the bubble reputation

Even in the cannon's mouth. And then the justice,
In fair round belly with good capon lined,
With eyes severe and beard of formal cut,
Full of wise saws and modern instances;
And so he plays his part. The sixth age shifts
Into the lean and slippered pantaloon,
With spectacles on nose and pouch on side,
His youthful hose, well saved, a world too wide
For his shrunk shank; and his big manly voice,
Turning again toward childish treble, pipes
And whistles in his sound. Last scene of all,
That ends this strange eventful history,
Is second childishness and mere oblivion,
Sans teeth, sans eyes, sans taste, sans everything.

Re-enter ORLANDO, *with* ADAM

DUKE SENIOR. Welcome. Set down your venerable
    burden
  And let him feed.
ORLANDO. I thank you most for him.
ADAM.   So had you need.
  I scarce can speak to thank you for myself.
DUKE SENIOR. Welcome; fall to. I will not trouble you
  As yet, to question you about your fortunes.
  Give us some music; and, good cousin, sing.

SONG

AMIENS.   Blow, blow, thou winter wind,
        Thou art not so unkind
           As man's ingratitude;
        Thy tooth is not so keen,
        Because thou art not seen,
           Although thy breath be rude.
Heigh-ho! sing, heigh-ho! unto the green holly.
Most friendship is feigning, most loving mere folly.
        Then, heigh-ho, the holly!
          This life is most jolly.

        Freeze, freeze, thou bitter sky,
        That dost not bite so nigh
          As benefits forgot:
        Though thou the waters warp,
        Thy sting is not so sharp
          As friend remembered not.
Heigh-ho! sing, heigh-ho! unto the green holly.
Most friendship is feigning, most loving mere folly.

DUKE SENIOR. If that you were the good Sir Rowland's
    son,
  As you have whispered faithfully you were,
  And as mine eye doth his effigies witness
  Most truly limned and living in your face,
  Be truly welcome hither. I am the duke
  That loved your father. The residue of your fortune,
  Go to my cave and tell me. Good old man,
  Thou art right welcome as thy master is.
  Support him by the arm. Give me your hand,
  And let me all your fortunes understand.   *Exeunt*

ACT III

SCENE I *A room in the palace*

Enter DUKE FREDERICK, Lords, *and* OLIVER

DUKE FREDERICK. Not see him since? Sir, sir, that can-
    not be.
  But were I not the better part made mercy,
  I should not seek an absent argument
  Of my revenge, thou present. But look to it:
  Find out thy brother, wheresoe'er he is;
  Seek him with candle; bring him dead or living
  Within this twelvemonth, or turn thou no more
  To seek a living in our territory.
  Thy lands and all things that thou dost call thine

Worth seizure do we seize into our hands,
  Till thou canst quit thee by thy brother's mouth
  Of what we think against thee.
OLIVER. O that your highness knew my heart in this!
  I never loved my brother in my life.
DUKE FREDERICK. More villain thou. Well, push him
    out of doors;
  And let my officers of such a nature
  Make an extent upon his house and lands.
  Do this expediently and turn him going.   *Exeunt*

SCENE II *The forest*

Enter ORLANDO, *with a paper*

ORLANDO. Hang there, my verse, in witness of my love.
  And thou, thrice-crowned queen of night, survey
  With thy chaste eye, from thy pale sphere above,
  Thy huntress' name that my full life doth sway.
  O Rosalind! These trees shall be my books
  And in their barks my thoughts I'll character;
  That every eye which in this forest looks
  Shall see thy virtue witnessed everywhere.
  Run, run, Orlando; carve on every tree
  The fair, the chaste and unexpressive she.   *Exit*

Enter CORIN *and* TOUCHSTONE

CORIN. And how like you this shepherd's life, Master
  Touchstone?
TOUCHSTONE. Truly, shepherd, in respect of itself, it is
  a good life; but in respect that it is a shepherd's life,
  it is naught. In respect that it is solitary, I like it
  very well; but in respect that it is private, it is a
  very vile life. Now, in respect it is in the fields, it
  pleaseth me well; but in respect it is not in the court,
  it is tedious. As it is a spare life, look you, it fits my
  humour well; but as there is no more plenty in it, it
  goes much against my stomach. Hast any philosophy
  in thee, shepherd?
CORIN. No more but that I know the more one sickens
  the worse at ease he is; and that he that wants money,
  means and content is without three good friends;
  that the property of rain is to wet and fire to burn;
  that good pasture makes fat sheep, and that a great
  cause of the night is lack of the sun; that he that hath
  learned no wit by nature nor art may complain of
  good breeding or comes of a very dull kindred.
TOUCHSTONE. Such a one is a natural philosopher.
  Wast ever in court, shepherd?
CORIN. No, truly.
TOUCHSTONE. Then thou art damned.
CORIN. Nay, I hope.

TOUCHSTONE. Truly, thou art damned, like an ill-
  roasted egg all on one side.
CORIN. For not being at court? Your reason.
TOUCHSTONE. Why, if thou never wast at court, thou
  never sawest good manners; if thou never sawest good
  manners, then thy manners must be wicked; and
  wickedness is sin, and sin is damnation. Thou art in a
  parlous state, shepherd.
CORIN. Not a whit, Touchstone. Those that are good
  manners at the court are as ridiculous in the country
  as the behaviour of the country is most mockable at
  the court. You told me you salute not at the court,
  but you kiss your hands. That courtesy would be uncleanly, if courtiers were shepherds.
TOUCHSTONE. Instance, briefly; come, instance.
CORIN. Why, we are still handling our ewes, and their
  fells, you know, are greasy.
TOUCHSTONE. Why, do not your courtier's hands
  sweat? And is not the grease of a mutton as wholesome as the sweat of a man? Shallow, shallow. A better
  instance, I say; come.
CORIN. Besides, our hands are hard.
TOUCHSTONE. Your lips will feel them the sooner.
  Shallow again. A more sounder instance, come.
CORIN. And they are often tarred over with the surgery
  of our sheep; and would you have us kiss tar? The
  courtier's hands are perfumed with civet.
TOUCHSTONE. Most shallow man! Thou wormsmeat,
  in respect of a good piece of flesh indeed! Learn of the
  wise, and perpend: civet is of a baser birth than tar,
  the very uncleanly flux of a cat. Mend the instance,
  shepherd.
CORIN. You have too courtly a wit for me. I'll rest.
TOUCHSTONE. Wilt thou rest damned? God help thee,
  shallow man! God make incision in thee! thou art
  raw.
CORIN. Sir, I am a true labourer: I earn that I eat,

get that I wear, owe no man hate, envy no man's happiness, glad of other men's good, content with my harm, and the greatest of my pride is to see my ewes graze and my lambs suck.

TOUCHSTONE. That is another simple sin in you, to bring the ewes and the rams together and to offer to get your living by the copulation of cattle; to be bawd to a bell-wether, and to betray a she-lamb of a twelvemonth to a crooked-pated, old, cuckoldly ram, out of all reasonable match. If thou beest not damned for this, the devil himself will have no shepherds; I cannot see else how thou shouldst 'scape.

CORIN. Here comes young Master Ganymede, my new mistress' brother.

If the cat will after kind,
So be sure will Rosalind.
Wintred garments must be lined,
So must slender Rosalind.
They that reap must sheaf and bind;
Then to cart with Rosalind.
Sweetest nut hath sourest rind,
Such a nut is Rosalind.
He that sweetest rose will find
Must find love's prick and Rosalind.

This is the very false gallop of verses. Why do you infect yourself with them?

ROSALIND. Peace, you dull fool! I found them on a tree.

TOUCHSTONE. Truly, the tree yields bad fruit.

ROSALIND. I 'll graff it with you, and then I shall graff it with a medlar. Then it will be the earliest fruit i' the country; for you 'll be rotten ere you be half ripe, and that's the right virtue of the medlar.

TOUCHSTONE. You have said; but whether wisely or no, let the forest judge.

Enter CELIA, *with a writing*

ROSALIND. Peace!
Here comes my sister, reading: stand aside.

CELIA. [*Reads*]
Why should this a desert be?
For it is unpeopled? No;
Tongues I 'll hang on every tree,
That shall civil sayings show:
Some, how brief the life of man
Runs his erring pilgrimage,
That the stretching of a span
Buckles in his sum of age.
Some, of violated vows
'Twixt the souls of friend and friend;
But upon the fairest boughs,
Or at every sentence end,
Will I Rosalinda write,
Teaching all that read to know
The quintessence of every sprite
Heaven would in little show.
Therefore Heaven Nature charged
That one body should be filled
With all graces wide-enlarged:
Nature presently distilled
Helen's cheek, but not her heart,
Cleopatra's majesty,
Atalanta's better part,
Sad Lucretia's modesty.
Thus Rosalind of many parts
By heavenly synod was devised,
Of many faces, eyes and hearts,
To have the touches dearest prized.
Heaven would that she these gifts should have,
And I to live and die her slave.

Enter ROSALIND, *reading a paper*

ROSALIND. From the east to western Ind,
No jewel is like Rosalind.
Her worth, being mounted on the wind,
Through all the world bears Rosalind.
All the pictures fairest lined
Are but black to Rosalind.
Let no fair be kept in mind
But the fair of Rosalind.

TOUCHSTONE. I'll rhyme you so eight years together, dinners and suppers and sleeping-hours excepted. It is the right butter-women's rank to market.

ROSALIND. Out, fool!

TOUCHSTONE. For a taste:
If a hart do lack a hind,
Let him seek out Rosalind.

ROSALIND. O most gentle Jupiter! What tedious homily of love have you wearied your parishioners withal, and never cried "Have patience, good people!"

CELIA. How now! Back, friends! Shepherd, go off a little. Go with him, sirrah.

TOUCHSTONE. Come, shepherd, let us make an honourable retreat; though not with bag and baggage, yet with scrip and scrippage.

Exeunt CORIN *and* TOUCHSTONE

CELIA. Didst thou hear these verses?

ROSALIND. O, yes, I heard them all, and more too; for some of them had in them more feet than the verses would bear.

CELIA. That's no matter: the feet might bear the verses.

ROSALIND. Ay, but the feet were lame and could not bear themselves without the verse and therefore stood lamely in the verse.

CELIA. But didst thou hear without wondering how thy name should be hanged and carved upon these trees?

ROSALIND. I was seven of the nine days out of the wonder before you came; for look here what I found on a palm-tree. I was never so berhymed since Pythagoras' time, that I was an Irish rat, which I can hardly remember.

CELIA. Trow you who hath done this?

ROSALIND. Is it a man?

CELIA. And a chain, that you once wore, about his neck. Change you colour?

ROSALIND. I prithee, who?

CELIA. O Lord, Lord! It is a hard matter for friends to meet; but mountains may be removed with earthquakes and so encounter.

ROSALIND. Nay, but who is it?

CELIA. Is it possible?

ROSALIND. Nay, I prithee now with most petitionary vehemence, tell me who it is.

CELIA. O wonderful, wonderful, and most wonderful wonderful! And yet again wonderful, and after that, out of all hooping!

ROSALIND. Good my complexion! Dost thou think, though I am caparisoned like a man, I have a doublet and hose in my disposition? One inch of delay more is a South Sea of discovery; I prithee, tell me who is it quickly, and speak apace. I would thou couldst stammer, that thou mightst pour this concealed man out of thy mouth, as wine comes out of a narrow-mouthed bottle, either too much at once, or none at all. I prithee, take the cork out of thy mouth that I may drink thy tidings.

CELIA. So you may put a man in your belly.

ROSALIND. Is he of God's making? What manner of man? Is his head worth a hat, or his chin worth a beard?

CELIA. Nay, he hath but a little beard.

ROSALIND. Why, God will send more, if the man will be thankful. Let me stay the growth of his beard, if thou delay me not the knowledge of his chin.

CELIA. It is young Orlando, that tripped up the wrestler's heels and your heart both in an instant.

ROSALIND. Nay, but the devil take mocking. Speak, sad brow and true maid.

CELIA. I' faith, coz, 'tis he.

ROSALIND. Orlando?

CELIA. Orlando.

ROSALIND. Alas the day! What shall I do with my doublet and hose? What did he when thou sawest him? What said he? How looked he? Wherein went he? What makes he here? Did he ask for me? Where remains he? How parted he with thee? And when shalt thou see him again? Answer me in one word.

CELIA. You must borrow me Gargantua's mouth first: 'tis a word too great for any mouth of this age's size. To say ay and no to these particulars is more than to answer in a catechism.

ROSALIND. But doth he know that I am in this forest and in man's apparel? Looks he as freshly as he did the day he wrestled?

CELIA. It is as easy to count atomies as to resolve the propositions of a lover; but take a taste of my finding him, and relish it with good observance. I found him under a tree, like a dropped acorn.

ROSALIND. It may well be called Jove's tree, when it drops forth such fruit.

CELIA. Give me audience, good madam.

ROSALIND. Proceed.

CELIA. There lay he, stretched along, like a wounded knight.

ROSALIND. Though it be pity to see such a sight, it well becomes the ground.

CELIA. Cry "holla" to thy tongue, I prithee; it curvets unseasonably. He was furnished like a hunter.

ROSALIND. O, ominous! He comes to kill my heart.

CELIA. I would sing my song without a burden: thou bringest me out of tune.

ROSALIND. Do you not know I am a woman? When I think, I must speak. Sweet, say on.

CELIA. You bring me out. Soft! comes he not here?

Enter
ORLANDO *and* JAQUES

ROSALIND. 'Tis he. Slink by, and note him.

JAQUES. I thank you for your company; but, good faith, I had as lief have been myself alone.

ORLANDO. And so had I; but yet, for fashion sake, I thank you too for your society.

JAQUES. God be wi' you. Let's meet as little as we can.

ORLANDO. I do desire we may be better strangers.

JAQUES. I pray you, mar no more trees with writing love-songs in their barks.

ORLANDO. I pray you, mar no more of my verses with reading them ill-favouredly.

JAQUES. Rosalind is your love's name?

ORLANDO. Yes, just.

JAQUES. I do not like her name.

ORLANDO. There was no thought of pleasing you when she was christened.

JAQUES. What stature is she of?

ORLANDO. Just as high as my heart.

JAQUES. You are full of pretty answers. Have you not been acquainted with goldsmiths' wives, and conned them out of rings?

ORLANDO. Not so; but I answer you right painted cloth, from whence you have studied your questions.

JAQUES. You have a nimble wit. I think 'twas made of Atalanta's heels. Will you sit down with me? And we two will rail against our mistress the world and all our misery.

ORLANDO. I will chide no breather in the world but myself, against whom I know most faults.

JAQUES. The worst fault you have is to be in love.

ORLANDO. 'Tis a fault I will not change for your best virtue. I am weary of you.

JAQUES. By my troth, I was seeking for a fool when I found you.

ORLANDO. He is drowned in the brook. Look but in, and you shall see him.

JAQUES. There I shall see mine own figure.

ORLANDO. Which I take to be either a fool or a cipher.

JAQUES. I 'll tarry no longer with you. Farewell, good Signior Love.

ORLANDO. I am glad of your departure. Adieu, good Monsieur Melancholy.   *Exit* JAQUES

ROSALIND. [*Aside to Celia*] I will speak to him like a saucy lackey and under that habit play the knave with him. Do you hear, forester?

ORLANDO. Very well. What would you?

ROSALIND. I pray you, what is 't o'clock?

ORLANDO. You should ask me what time o' day: there's no clock in the forest.

ROSALIND. Then there is no true lover in the forest; else sighing every minute and groaning every hour would detect the lazy foot of Time as well as a clock.

ORLANDO. And why not the swift foot of Time? Had not that been as proper?

ROSALIND. By no means, sir: Time travels in divers paces with divers persons. I'll tell you who Time ambles withal, who Time trots withal, who Time gallops withal and who he stands still withal.

ORLANDO. I prithee, who doth he trot withal?

ROSALIND. Marry, he trots hard with a young maid between the contract of her marriage and the day it is solemnized. If the interim be but a se'nnight, Time's pace is so hard that it seems the length of seven year.

ORLANDO. Who ambles Time withal?

ROSALIND. With a priest that lacks Latin and a rich man that hath not the gout, for the one sleeps easily because he cannot study and the other lives merrily because he feels no pain, the one lacking the burden of lean and wasteful learning, the other knowing no burden of heavy tedious penury; these Time ambles withal.

ORLANDO. Who doth he gallop withal?

ROSALIND. With a thief to the gallows, for though he go as softly as foot can fall, he thinks himself too soon there.

ORLANDO. Who stays it still withal?

ROSALIND. With lawyers in the vacation; for they sleep between term and term and then they perceive not how Time moves.

ORLANDO. Where dwell you, pretty youth?

ROSALIND. With this shepherdess, my sister; here in the skirts of the forest, like fringe upon a petticoat.

ORLANDO. Are you native of this place?

ROSALIND. As the cony that you see dwell where she is kindled.

ORLANDO. Your accent is something finer than you could purchase in so removed a dwelling.

ROSALIND. I have been told so of many. But indeed an old religious uncle of mine taught me to speak, who was in his youth an inland man; one that knew courtship too well, for there he fell in love. I have heard him read many lectures against it, and I thank God I am not a woman, to be touched with so many giddy offences as he hath generally taxed their whole sex withal.

ORLANDO. Can you remember any of the principal evils that he laid to the charge of women?

ROSALIND. There were none principal; they were all like one another as halfpence are, every one fault seeming monstrous till his fellow-fault came to match it.

ORLANDO. I prithee, recount some of them.

ROSALIND. No, I will not cast away my physic but on those that are sick. There is a man haunts the forest, that abuses our young plants with carving ''Rosalind'' on their barks; hangs odes upon hawthorns and elegies on brambles, all, forsooth, deifying the name of Rosalind. If I could meet that fancy-monger, I would give him some good counsel, for he seems to have the quotidian of love upon him.

ORLANDO. I am he that is so love-shaked. I pray you, tell me your remedy.

ROSALIND. There is none of my uncle's marks upon you. He taught me how to know a man in love; in which cage of rushes I am sure you are not prisoner.

ORLANDO. What were his marks?

ROSALIND. A lean cheek, which you have not, a blue eye and sunken, which you have not, an unquestionable spirit, which you have not, a beard neglected, which you have not; but I pardon you for that, for simply your having in beard is a younger brother's revenue. Then your hose should be ungartered, your bonnet unbanded, your sleeve unbuttoned, your shoe untied and everything about you demonstrating a careless desolation; but you are no such man; you are rather point-device in your accoutrements as loving yourself than seeming the lover of any other.

ORLANDO. Fair youth, I would I could make thee believe I love.

ROSALIND. Me believe it! You may as soon make her that you love believe it; which, I warrant, she is apter to do than to confess she does. That is one of the points in the which women still give the lie to their consciences. But, in good sooth, are you he that hangs the verses on the trees, wherein Rosalind is so admired?

ORLANDO. I swear to thee, youth, by the white hand of Rosalind, I am that he, that unfortunate he.

ROSALIND. But are you so much in love as your rhymes speak?

ORLANDO. Neither rhyme nor reason can express how much.

ROSALIND. Love is merely a madness, and, I tell you, deserves as well a dark house and a whip as madmen do. And the reason why they are not so punished and cured is, that the lunacy is so ordinary that the whippers are in love too. Yet I profess curing it by counsel.

ORLANDO. Did you ever cure any so?

ROSALIND. Yes, one, and in this manner. He was to imagine me his love, his mistress; and I set him every day to woo me: at which time would I, being but a moonish youth, grieve, be effeminate, changeable, longing and liking, proud, fantastical, apish, shallow, inconstant, full of tears, full of smiles, for every passion something and for no passion truly anything, as boys and women are for the most part cattle of this colour; would now like him, now loathe him; then entertain him, then forswear him; now weep for him, then spit at him; that I drave my suitor from his mad humour of love to a living humour of madness; which was, to forswear the full stream of the world and to live in a nook merely monastic. And thus I cured him; and this way will I take upon me to wash your liver as clean as a sound sheep's heart, that there shall not be one spot of love in 't.

ORLANDO. I would not be cured, youth.

ROSALIND. I would cure you, if you would but call me Rosalind and come every day to my cote and woo me.

ORLANDO. Now, by the faith of my love, I will. Tell me where it is.

ROSALIND. Go with me to it and I'll show it you. And by the way you shall tell me where in the forest you live. Will you go?

ORLANDO. With all my heart, good youth.

ROSALIND. Nay, you must call me Rosalind. Come, sister, will you go? *Exeunt*

SCENE III *The forest*

Enter TOUCHSTONE *and* AUDREY; JAQUES *behind*

TOUCHSTONE. Come apace, good Audrey; I will fetch up your goats, Audrey. And how, Audrey? Am I the man yet? Doth my simple feature content you?

AUDREY. Your features! Lord warrant us! What features?

TOUCHSTONE. I am here with thee and thy goats, as the most capricious poet, honest Ovid, was among the Goths.

JAQUES. [*Aside*] O knowledge ill-inhabited, worse than Jove in a thatched house!

TOUCHSTONE. When a man's verses cannot be understood, nor a man's good wit seconded with the forward child Understanding, it strikes a man more dead than a great reckoning in a little room. Truly, I would the gods had made thee poetical.

AUDREY. I do not know what "poetical" is. Is it honest in deed and word? Is it a true thing?

TOUCHSTONE. No, truly; for the truest poetry is the most feigning; and lovers are given to poetry, and what they swear in poetry may be said as lovers they do feign.

AUDREY. Do you wish then that the gods had made me poetical?

TOUCHSTONE. I do, truly; for thou swearest to me thou art honest. Now, if thou wert a poet, I might have some hope thou didst feign.

AUDREY. Would you not have me honest?

TOUCHSTONE. No, truly, unless thou wert hard-favoured; for honesty coupled to beauty is to have honey a sauce to sugar.

JAQUES. [*Aside*] A material fool!

AUDREY. Well, I am not fair; and therefore I pray the gods make me honest.

TOUCHSTONE. Truly, and to cast away honesty upon a foul slut were to put good meat into an unclean dish.

AUDREY. I am not a slut, though I thank the gods I am foul.

TOUCHSTONE. Well, praised be the gods for thy foulness! Sluttishness may come hereafter. But be it as it may be, I will marry thee, and to that end I have been with Sir Oliver Martext, the vicar of the next village, who hath promised to meet me in this place of the forest and to couple us.

JAQUES. [*Aside*] I would fain see this meeting.

AUDREY. Well, the gods give us joy!

TOUCHSTONE. Amen. A man may, if he were of a fearful heart, stagger in this attempt; for here we have no temple but the wood, no assembly but horn-beasts. But what though? Courage! As horns are odious, they are necessary. It is said, "many a man knows no end of his goods." Right; many a man has good horns,

and knows no end of them. Well, that is the dowry of his wife; 'tis none of his own getting. Horns? Even so. Poor men alone? No, no; the noblest deer hath them as huge as the rascal. Is the single man therefore blessed? No: as a walled town is more worthier than a village, so is the forehead of a married man more honourable than the bare brow of a bachelor; and by how much defence is better than no skill, by so much is a horn more precious than to want. Here comes Sir Oliver.

Enter SIR OLIVER MARTEXT

SIR Oliver Martext, you are well met. Will you dispatch us here under this tree, or shall we go with you to your chapel?

SIR OLIVER MARTEXT. Is there none here to give the woman?

TOUCHSTONE. I will not take her on gift of any man.

SIR OLIVER MARTEXT. Truly, she must be given, or the marriage is not lawful.

JAQUES. [*Advancing*] Proceed, proceed. I 'll give her.

TOUCHSTONE. Good even, good Master What-ye-call 't. How do you, sir? You are very well met. God 'ild you for your last company. I am very glad to see you— even a toy in hand here, sir—nay, pray be covered.

JAQUES. Will you be married, motley?

TOUCHSTONE. As the ox hath his bow, sir, the horse his curb and the falcon her bells, so man hath his de-

sires; and as pigeons bill, so wedlock would be nibbling.

JAQUES. And will you, being a man of your breeding, be married under a bush like a beggar? Get you to church, and have a good priest that can tell you what marriage is. This fellow will but join you together as they join wainscot; then one of you will prove a shrunk panel and, like green timber, warp, warp.

TOUCHSTONE. [*Aside*] I am not in the mind but I were better to be married of him than of another: for he is not like to marry me well; and not being well married, it will be a good excuse for me hereafter to leave my wife.

JAQUES. Go thou with me, and let me counsel thee.

TOUCHSTONE. Come, sweet Audrey.
  We must be married, or we must live in bawdry.
  Farewell, good Master Oliver: not—
        O sweet Oliver,
        O brave Oliver,
     Leave me not behind thee:

but—

        Wind away,
        Begone, I say,
     I will not to wedding with thee.

Exeunt JAQUES, TOUCHSTONE *and* AUDREY

SIR OLIVER MARTEXT. 'Tis no matter. Ne'er a fantastical knave of them all shall flout me out of my calling. *Exit*

SCENE IV *The forest*

Enter ROSALIND *and* CELIA

ROSALIND. Never talk to me; I will weep.

CELIA. Do, I prithee; but yet have the grace to consider that tears do not become a man.

ROSALIND. But have I not cause to weep?

CELIA. As good cause as one would desire; therefore weep.

ROSALIND. His very hair is of the dissembling colour.

CELIA. Something browner than Judas's. Marry, his kisses are Judas's own children.

ROSALIND. I' faith, his hair is of a good colour.

CELIA. An excellent colour. Your chestnut was ever the only colour.

ROSALIND. And his kissing is as full of sanctity as the touch of holy bread.

CELIA. He hath bought a pair of cast lips of Diana. A nun of winter's sisterhood kisses not more religiously; the very ice of chastity is in them.

ROSALIND. But why did he swear he would come this morning, and comes not?

CELIA. Nay, certainly, there is no truth in him.

ROSALIND. Do you think so?

CELIA. Yes; I think he is not a pick-purse nor a horse-stealer, but for his verity in love, I do think him as concave as a covered goblet or a worm-eaten nut.

ROSALIND. Not true in love?

CELIA. Yes, when he is in; but I think he is not in.

ROSALIND. You have heard him swear downright he was.

CELIA. "Was" is not "is." Besides, the oath of a lover is no stronger than the word of a tapster; they are both the confirmer of false reckonings. He attends here in the forest on the Duke your father.

ROSALIND. I met the Duke yesterday and had much question with him. He asked me of what parentage I was; I told him, of as good as he; so he laughed and let me go. But what talk we of fathers, when there is such a man as Orlando?

CELIA. O, that 's a brave man! He writes brave verses, speaks brave words, swears brave oaths and breaks them bravely, quite traverse, athwart the heart of his lover; as a puny tilter, that spurs his horse but on one side, breaks his staff like a noble goose. But all's brave that youth mounts and folly guides. Who comes here?

Enter CORIN

CORIN. Mistress and master, you have oft inquired
After the shepherd that complained of love,
Who you saw sitting by me on the turf,
Praising the proud disdainful shepherdess
That was his mistress.

CELIA.   Well, and what of him?

CORIN. If you will see a pageant truly played,
Between the pale complexion of true love
And the red glow of scorn and proud disdain,
Go hence a little and I shall conduct you,
If you will mark it.

ROSALIND.   O, come, let us remove:
The sight of lovers feedeth those in love.
Bring us to this sight, and you shall say
I'll prove a busy actor in their play.   *Exeunt*

SCENE V *Another part of the forest*

Enter SILVIUS *and* PHEBE

SILVIUS. Sweet Phebe, do not scorn me; do not, Phebe;
Say that you love me not, but say not so
In bitterness. The common executioner,
Whose heart the accustomed sight of death makes hard,
Falls not the axe upon the humbled neck
But first begs pardon. Will you sterner be
Than he that dies and lives by bloody drops?

Enter ROSALIND, CELIA, *and* CORIN, *behind*

PHEBE. I would not be thy executioner.
I fly thee, for I would not injure thee.
Thou tell'st me there is murder in mine eye.
'Tis pretty, sure, and very probable,
That eyes, that are the frail'st and softest things,
Who shut their coward gates on atomies,
Should be called tyrants, butchers, murderers!
Now I do frown on thee with all my heart;
And if mine eyes can wound, now let them kill thee:
Now counterfeit to swoon; why now fall down;
Or if thou canst not, O, for shame, for shame,
Lie not, to say mine eyes are murderers!
Now show the wound mine eye hath made in thee.
Scratch thee but with a pin, and there remains
Some scar of it; lean but upon a rush,
The cicatrice and capable impressure
Thy palm some moment keeps; but now mine eyes,
Which I have darted at thee, hurt thee not,
Nor, I am sure, there is no force in eyes
That can do hurt.

SILVIUS.   O dear Phebe,
If ever—as that ever may be near—
You meet in some fresh cheek the power of fancy,
Then shall you know the wounds invisible
That love's keen arrows make.

PHEBE.   But till that time
Come not thou near me. And when that time comes,
Afflict me with thy mocks, pity me not;

As till that time I shall not pity thee.

ROSALIND. And why, I pray you? Who might be your
    mother,
That you insult, exult, and all at once,
Over the wretched? What though you have no
    beauty—
As, by my faith, I see no more in you
Than without candle may go dark to bed—
Must you be therefore proud and pitiless?
Why, what means this? Why do you look on me?
I see no more in you than in the ordinary
Of nature's sale-work. 'Od's my little life,
I think she means to tangle my eyes too!
No, faith, proud mistress, hope not after it.
'Tis not your inky brows, your black silk hair,
Your bugle eyeballs, nor your cheek of cream,
That can entame my spirits to your worship.
You foolish shepherd, wherefore do you follow her,
Like foggy south puffing with wind and rain?
You are a thousand times a properer man
Than she a woman. 'Tis such fools as you
That makes the world full of ill-favoured children.
'Tis not her glass, but you, that flatters her;
And out of you she sees herself more proper
Than any of her lineaments can show her.
But, mistress, know yourself: down on your knees,
And thank heaven, fasting, for a good man's love;
For I must tell you friendly in your ear,
Sell when you can—you are not for all markets.
Cry the man mercy; love him; take his offer:
Foul is most foul, being foul to be a scoffer.
So take her to thee, shepherd. Fare you well.

PHEBE. Sweet youth, I pray you, chide a year together.
I had rather hear you chide than this man woo.

ROSALIND. He's fallen in love with your foulness and
    she'll fall in love with my anger. If it be so, as fast
    as she answers thee with frowning looks, I'll sauce
    her with bitter words. Why look you so upon me?

PHEBE. For no ill will I bear you.

ROSALIND. I pray you, do not fall in love with me,
For I am falser than vows made in wine.
Besides, I like you not. If you will know my house,
'Tis at the tuft of olives here hard by.
Will you go, sister? Shepherd, ply her hard.
Come, sister. Shepherdess, look on him better,
And be not proud: though all the world could see,
None could be so abused in sight as he.
Come, to our flock.

                    Exeunt ROSALIND, CELIA *and* CORIN

PHEBE. Dead shepherd, now I find thy saw of might,
    "Who ever loved that loved not at first sight?"

SILVIUS. Sweet Phebe—

PHEBE.   Ha, what say'st thou, Silvius?

SILVIUS. Sweet Phebe, pity me.

PHEBE. Why, I am sorry for thee, gentle Silvius.

SILVIUS. Wherever sorrow is, relief would be.

If you do sorrow at my grief in love,
By giving love your sorrow and my grief
Were both extermined.

PHEBE. Thou hast my love: is not that neighbourly?

SILVIUS. I would have you.

PHEBE.   Why, that were covetousness.
Silvius, the time was that I hated thee,
And yet it is not that I bear thee love;
But since that thou canst talk of love so well,
Thy company, which erst was irksome to me,
I will endure, and I'll employ thee too.
But do not look for further recompense
Than thine own gladness that thou art employed.

SILVIUS. So holy and so perfect is my love,
And I in such a poverty of grace,
That I shall think it a most plenteous crop
To glean the broken ears after the man
That the main harvest reaps. Loose now and then
A scattered smile, and that I'll live upon.

PHEBE. Know'st thou the youth that spoke to me ere-
    while?

SILVIUS. Not very well, but I have met him oft;
And he hath bought the cottage and the bounds
That the old carlot once was master of.

PHEBE. Think not I love him, though I ask for him;
'Tis but a peevish boy; yet he talks well;
But what care I for words? Yet words do well
When he that speaks them pleases those that hear.
It is a pretty youth—not very pretty—
But, sure, he's proud, and yet his pride becomes him.
He'll make a proper man: the best thing in him
Is his complexion; and faster than his tongue
Did make offence his eye did heal it up.
He is not very tall; yet for his years he's tall.
His leg is but so so; and yet 'tis well.
There was a pretty redness in his lip,
A little riper and more lusty red
Than that mixed in his cheek; 'twas just the difference
Betwixt the constant red and mingled damask.
There be some women, Silvius, had they marked him
In parcels as I did, would have gone near
To fall in love with him; but, for my part,
I love him not nor hate him not; and yet
I have more cause to hate him than to love him.
For what had he to do to chide at me?
He said mine eyes were black and my hair black;
And, now I am remembered, scorned at me.
I marvel why I answered not again.
But that's all one; omittance is no quittance.
I'll write to him a very taunting letter,
And thou shalt bear it. Wilt thou, Silvius?

SILVIUS. Phebe, with all my heart.

PHEBE.   I'll write it straight;
The matter's in my head and in my heart.
I will be bitter with him and passing short.
Go with me, Silvius.   *Exeunt*

ACT IV

SCENE I *The forest*

Enter ROSALIND, CELIA, *and* JAQUES

JAQUES. I prithee, pretty youth, let me be better acquainted with thee.

ROSALIND. They say you are a melancholy fellow.

JAQUES. I am so; I do love it better than laughing.

ROSALIND. Those that are in extremity of either are abominable fellows and betray themselves to every modern censure worse than drunkards.

JAQUES. Why, 'tis good to be sad and say nothing.

ROSALIND. Why then, 'tis good to be a post.

JAQUES. I have neither the scholar's melancholy, which is emulation, nor the musician's, which is fantastical, nor the courtier's, which is proud, nor the soldier's, which is ambitious, nor the lawyer's, which is politic, nor the lady's, which is nice, nor the lover's, which is all these; but it is a melancholy of mine own, compounded of many simples, extracted from many objects, and indeed the sundry contemplation of my travels, in which my often rumination wraps me in a most humorous sadness.

ROSALIND. A traveller! By my faith, you have great reason to be sad. I fear you have sold your own lands to see other men's; then, to have seen much and to have nothing, is to have rich eyes and poor hands.

JAQUES. Yes, I have gained my experience.

ROSALIND. And your experience makes you sad. I had rather have a fool to make me merry than experience to make me sad; and to travel for it too!

Enter ORLANDO

ORLANDO. Good day and happiness, dear Rosalind!

JAQUES. Nay, then, God be wi' you, and you talk in blank verse. *Exit*

ROSALIND. Farewell, Monsieur Traveller. Look you lisp and wear strange suits, disable all the benefits of your own country, be out of love with your nativity and almost chide God for making you that countenance you are, or I will scarce think you have swam in a gondola. Why, how now, Orlando! Where have you been all this while? You a lover! An you serve me such another trick, never come in my sight more.

ORLANDO. My fair Rosalind, I come within an hour of my promise.

ROSALIND. Break an hour's promise in love! He that will divide a minute into a thousand parts and break but a part of the thousandth part of a minute in the affairs of love, it may be said of him that Cupid hath clapped him o' the shoulder, but I'll warrant him heart-whole.

ORLANDO. Pardon me, dear Rosalind.

ROSALIND. Nay, an you be so tardy, come no more in my sight. I had as lief be wooed of a snail.

ORLANDO. Of a snail?

ROSALIND. Ay, of a snail; for though he comes slowly, he carries his house on his head; a better jointure, I think, than you make a woman. Besides, he brings his destiny with him.

ORLANDO. What 's that?

ROSALIND. Why, horns, which such as you are fain to be beholding to your wives for. But he comes armed in his fortune and prevents the slander of his wife.

ORLANDO. Virtue is no horn-maker; and my Rosalind is virtuous.

ROSALIND. And I am your Rosalind.

CELIA. It pleases him to call you so; but he hath a Rosalind of a better leer than you.

ROSALIND. Come, woo me, woo me, for now I am in a holiday humour and like enough to consent. What would you say to me now, an I were your very very Rosalind?

ORLANDO. I would kiss before I spoke.

ROSALIND. Nay, you were better speak first, and when you were gravelled for lack of matter, you might take occasion to kiss. Very good orators, when they are out, they will spit; and for lovers lacking—God warn us!—matter, the cleanliest shift is to kiss.

ORLANDO. How if the kiss be denied?

ROSALIND. Then she puts you to entreaty, and there begins new matter.

ORLANDO. Who could be out, being before his beloved mistress?

ROSALIND. Marry, that should you, if I were your mistress, or I should think my honesty ranker than my wit.

ORLANDO. What, of my suit?

ROSALIND. Not out of your apparel, and yet out of your suit. Am not I your Rosalind?

ORLANDO. I take some joy to say you are, because I would be talking of her.

ROSALIND. Well, in her person I say I will not have you.

ORLANDO. Then in mine own person I die.

ROSALIND. No, faith, die by attorney. The poor world is almost six thousand years old, and in all this time there was not any man died in his own person, videlicet, in a love-cause. Troilus had his brains dashed out with a Grecian club; yet he did what he could to die before, and he is one of the patterns of love. Leander, he would have lived many a fair year, though Hero had turned nun, if it had not been for a hot midsummer night; for, good youth, he went but forth to wash him in the Hellespont and being taken with the cramp was drowned; and the foolish chroniclers of that age found it was "Hero of Sestos." But these are all lies: men have died from time to time and worms have eaten them, but not for love.

ORLANDO. I would not have my right Rosalind of this mind, for, I protest, her frown might kill me.

ROSALIND. By this hand, it will not kill a fly. But come, now I will be your Rosalind in a more coming-on disposition, and ask me what you will, I will grant it.

ORLANDO. Then love me, Rosalind.

ROSALIND. Yes, faith, will I, Fridays and Saturdays and all.

ORLANDO. And wilt thou have me?

ROSALIND. Ay, and twenty such.

ORLANDO. What sayest thou?

ROSALIND. Are you not good?

ORLANDO. I hope so.

ROSALIND. Why then, can one desire too much of a good thing? Come, sister, you shall be the priest and marry us. Give me your hand, Orlando. What do you say, sister?

ORLANDO. Pray thee, marry us.

CELIA. I cannot say the words.

ROSALIND. You must begin, "Will you, Orlando—"

CELIA. Go to. Will you, Orlando, have to wife this Rosalind?

ORLANDO. I will.

ROSALIND. Ay, but when?

ORLANDO. Why now; as fast as she can marry us.

ROSALIND. Then you must say, "I take thee, Rosalind, for wife."

ORLANDO. I take thee, Rosalind, for wife.

ROSALIND. I might ask you for your commission; but I do take thee, Orlando, for my husband. There's a girl goes before the priest; and certainly a woman's thought runs before her actions.

ORLANDO. So do all thoughts; they are winged.

ROSALIND. Now tell me how long you would have her after you have possessed her.

ORLANDO. For ever and a day.

ROSALIND. Say "a day," without the "ever." No, no, Orlando. Men are April when they woo, December when they wed; maids are May when they are maids, but the sky changes when they are wives. I will be more jealous of thee than a Barbary cock-pigeon over his hen, more clamorous than a parrot against rain, more newfangled than an ape, more giddy in my desires than a monkey. I will weep for nothing, like Diana in the fountain, and I will do that when you are disposed to be merry; I will laugh like a hyen, and that when thou art inclined to sleep.

ORLANDO. But will my Rosalind do so?

ROSALIND. By my life, she will do as I do.

ORLANDO. O, but she is wise.

ROSALIND. Or else she could not have the wit to do this. The wiser, the waywarder: make the doors upon a woman's wit and it will out at the casement; shut that

and 'twill out at the key-hole; stop that, 'twill fly with the smoke out at the chimney.

ORLANDO. A man that had a wife with such a wit, he might say "Wit, whither wilt?"

ROSALIND. Nay, you might keep that check for it till you met your wife's wit going to your neighbour's bed.

ORLANDO. And what wit could wit have to excuse that?

ROSALIND. Marry, to say she came to seek you there. You shall never take her without her answer, unless you take her without her tongue. O, that woman that cannot make her fault her husband's occasion, let her never nurse her child herself, for she will breed it like a fool!

ORLANDO. For these two hours, Rosalind, I will leave thee.

ROSALIND. Alas! dear love, I cannot lack thee two hours.

ORLANDO. I must attend the Duke at dinner. By two o'clock I will be with thee again.

ROSALIND. Ay, go your ways, go your ways; I knew what you would prove—my friends told me as much, and I thought no less. That flattering tongue of yours won me; 'tis but one cast away, and so, come, death! Two o'clock is your hour?

ORLANDO. Ay, sweet Rosalind.

ROSALIND. By my troth, and in good earnest, and so God mend me, and by all pretty oaths that are not dangerous, if you break one jot of your promise or come one minute behind your hour, I will think you the most pathetical breakpromise and the most hollow lover and the most unworthy of her you call Rosalind that may be chosen out of the gross band of the unfaithful. Therefore beware my censure and keep your promise.

ORLANDO. With no less religion than if thou wert indeed my Rosalind. So adieu.

ROSALIND. Well, Time is the old justice that examines all such offenders, and let Time try. Adieu.

Exit ORLANDO

CELIA. You have simply misused our sex in your love-prate. We must have your doublet and hose plucked over your head, and show the world what the bird hath done to her own nest.

ROSALIND. O coz, coz, coz, my pretty little coz, that thou didst know how many fathom deep I am in love! But it cannot be sounded: my affection hath an unknown bottom, like the bay of Portugal.

CELIA. Or rather, bottomless, that as fast as you pour affection in, it runs out.

ROSALIND. No, that same wicked bastard of Venus that was begot of thought, conceived of spleen and born of madness, that blind rascally boy that abuses every one's eyes because his own are out, let him be judge how deep I am in love. I'll tell thee, Aliena, I cannot be out of the sight of Orlando. I'll go find a shadow and sigh till he come.

CELIA. And I'll sleep.

Exeunt

SCENE II *The forest*

Enter JAQUES, *and Lords dressed as foresters*

JAQUES. Which is he that killed the deer?
LORD. Sir, it was I.
JAQUES. Let's present him to the Duke, like a Roman
conqueror; and it would do well to set the deer's
horns upon his head, for a branch of victory. Have
you no song, forester, for this purpose?
LORD. Yes, sir.
JAQUES. Sing it. 'Tis no matter how it be in tune, so it
make noise enough.

SONG

LORD. What shall he have that killed the deer?
His leather skin and horns to wear.
Then sing him home;
The rest join in
Take thou no scorn to wear the horn;
It was a crest ere thou wast born.
Thy father's father wore it,
And thy father bore it.
The horn, the horn, the lusty horn
Is not a thing to laugh to scorn. *Exeunt*

SCENE III *The forest*

Enter ROSALIND *and* CELIA

ROSALIND. How say you now? Is it not past two o'clock?
And here much Orlando!

CELIA. I warrant you, with pure love and troubled
brain, he hath ta'en his bow and arrows and is gone
forth to sleep. Look, who comes here.

Enter SILVIUS

SILVIUS. My errand is to you, fair youth;
My gentle Phebe bid me give you this.
I know not the contents; but, as I guess
By the stern brow and waspish action
Which she did use as she was writing of it,
It bears an angry tenour. Pardon me;
I am but as a guiltless messenger.

ROSALIND. Patience herself would startle at this letter
And play the swaggerer. Bear this, bear all.
She says I am not fair, that I lack manners;
She calls me proud, and that she could not love me,
Were man as rare as phoenix. 'Od's my will!
Her love is not the hare that I do hunt;
Why writes she so to me? Well, shepherd, well,
This is a letter of your own device.

SILVIUS. No, I protest, I know not the contents.
Phebe did write it.

ROSALIND.   Come, come, you are a fool
And turned into the extremity of love.
I saw her hand: she has a leathern hand,
A freestone-coloured hand—I verily did think
That her old gloves were on, but 'twas her hands—
She has a housewife's hand; but that's no matter.
I say she never did invent this letter;
This is a man's invention and his hand.

SILVIUS. Sure, it is hers.

ROSALIND. Why, 'tis a boisterous and a cruel style,
A style for challengers; why, she defies me,
Like Turk to Christian. Women's gentle brain
Could not drop forth such giant-rude invention,
Such Ethiope words, blacker in their effect
Than in their countenance. Will you hear the letter?

SILVIUS. So please you, for I never heard it yet;
Yet heard too much of Phebe's cruelty.

ROSALIND. She Phebes me. Mark how the tyrant writes.
[*Reads*] Art thou god to shepherd turned,
        That a maiden's heart hath burned?
    Can a woman rail thus?

SILVIUS. Call you this railing?

ROSALIND. [*Reads*]
        Why, thy godhead laid apart,
        Warr'st thou with a woman's heart?
    Did you ever hear such railing?
        Whiles the eye of man did woo me,
        That could do no vengeance to me.
    Meaning me a beast.

    If the scorn of your bright eyne
    Have power to raise such love in mine,
    Alack, in me what strange effect
    Would they work in mild aspect!
    Whiles you chid me, I did love;
    How then might your prayers move!
    He that brings this love to thee
    Little knows this love in me.
    And by him seal up thy mind;
    Whether that thy youth and kind
    Will the faithful offer take
    Of me and all that I can make;
    Or else by him my love deny.
    And then I'll study how to die.

SILVIUS. Call you this chiding?

CELIA. Alas, poor shepherd!

ROSALIND. Do you pity him? No, he deserves no pity.
Wilt thou love such a woman? What, to make thee an
instrument and play false strains upon thee! Not to be
endured! Well, go your way to her, for I see love
hath made thee a tame snake, and say this to her:
that if she love me, I charge her to love thee; if she
will not, I will never have her unless thou entreat for
her. If you be a true lover, hence, and not a word;
for here comes more company.   *Exit* SILVIUS

Enter OLIVER

OLIVER. Good morrow, fair ones. Pray you, if you
know,
Where in the purlieus of this forest stands
A sheep-cote fenced about with olive trees?

CELIA. West of this place, down in the neighbour
    bottom.
  The rank of osiers by the murmuring stream
  Left on your right hand brings you to the place.
  But at this hour the house doth keep itself;
  There's none within.

OLIVER. If that an eye may profit by a tongue,
  Then should I know you by description;
  Such garments and such years: "The boy is fair,
  Of female favour, and bestows himself
  Like a ripe sister; the woman low
  And browner than her brother.'' Are not you
  The owner of the house I did enquire for?

CELIA. It is no boast, being asked, to say we are.

OLIVER. Orlando doth commend him to you both,
  And to that youth he calls his Rosalind
  He sends this bloody napkin. Are you he?

ROSALIND. I am. What must we understand by this?

OLIVER. Some of my shame; if you will know of me
  What man I am, and how, and why, and where
  This handkerchief was stained.

CELIA.   I pray you, tell it.

OLIVER. When last the young Orlando parted from you
  He left a promise to return again
  Within an hour, and pacing through the forest,
  Chewing the food of sweet and bitter fancy,
  Lo, what befell! He threw his eye aside,
  And mark what object did present itself:
  Under an oak, whose boughs were mossed with age
  And high top bald with dry antiquity,
  A wretched ragged man, o'ergrown with hair,
  Lay sleeping on his back. About his neck
  A green and gilded snake had wreathed itself,
  Who with her head nimble in threats approached
  The opening of his mouth; but suddenly,
  Seeing Orlando, it unlinked itself,
  And with indented glides did slip away
  Into a bush: under which bush's shade
  A lioness, with udders all drawn dry,
  Lay couching, head on ground, with catlike watch,
  When that the sleeping man should stir; for 'tis
  The royal disposition of that beast
  To prey on nothing that doth seem as dead.
  This seen, Orlando did approach the man
  And found it was his brother, his elder brother.

CELIA. O, I have heard him speak of that same brother;
  And he did render him the most unnatural
  That lived amongst men.

OLIVER.   And well he might so do,
  For well I know he was unnatural.

ROSALIND. But, to Orlando: did he leave him there,
  Food to the sucked and hungry lioness?

OLIVER. Twice did he turn his back and purposed so;
  But kindness, nobler ever than revenge,
  And nature, stronger than his just occasion,
  Made him give battle to the lioness,

Who quickly fell before him: in which hurtling
From miserable slumber I awaked.

CELIA. Are you his brother?

ROSALIND.   Was 't you he rescued?

CELIA. Was 't you that did so oft contrive to kill him?

OLIVER. 'Twas I; but 'tis not I. I do not shame
  To tell you what I was, since my conversion
  So sweetly tastes, being the thing I am.

ROSALIND. But, for the bloody napkin?

OLIVER.   By and by.
  When from the first to last betwixt us two
  Tears our recountments had most kindly bathed,
  As how I came into that desert place—
  In brief, he led me to the gentle Duke,
  Who gave me fresh array and entertainment,
  Committing me unto my brother's love;
  Who led me instantly unto his cave,
  There stripped himself, and here upon his arm
  The lioness had torn some flesh away,
  Which all this while had bled; and now he fainted
  And cried, in fainting, upon Rosalind.
  Brief, I recovered him, bound up his wound;
  And, after some small space, being strong at heart,
  He sent me hither, stranger as I am,
  To tell this story, that you might excuse
  His broken promise, and to give this napkin
  Dyed in his blood unto the shepherd youth
  That he in sport doth call his Rosalind.

                            ROSALIND swoons

CELIA. Why, how now, Ganymede! Sweet Ganymede!

OLIVER. Many will swoon when they do look on blood.

CELIA. There is more in it. Cousin Ganymede!

OLIVER. Look, he recovers.

ROSALIND. I would I were at home.

CELIA.   We 'll lead you thither.
  I pray you, will you take him by the arm?

OLIVER. Be of good cheer, youth. You a man! you lack
  a man's heart.

ROSALIND. I do so, I confess it. Ah, sirrah, a body would
  think this was well counterfeited! I pray you, tell
  your brother how well I counterfeited. Heigh-ho!

OLIVER. This was not counterfeit: there is too great
  testimony in your complexion that it was a passion
  of earnest.

ROSALIND. Counterfeit, I assure you.

OLIVER. Well then, take a good heart and counterfeit
  to be a man.

ROSALIND. So I do; but, i' faith, I should have been a
  woman by right.

CELIA. Come, you look paler and paler. Pray you,
  draw homewards. Good sir, go with us.

OLIVER. That will I, for I must bear answer back
  How you excuse my brother, Rosalind.

ROSALIND. I shall devise something. But, I pray you,
  commend my counterfeiting to him. Will you go?

                                Exeunt

ACT V

SCENE I *The forest*

Enter TOUCHSTONE *and* AUDREY

TOUCHSTONE. We shall find a time, Audrey; patience, gentle Audrey.

AUDREY. Faith, the priest was good enough, for all the old gentleman's saying.

TOUCHSTONE. A most wicked Sir Oliver, Audrey, a most vile Martext. But, Audrey, there is a youth here in the forest lays claim to you.

AUDREY. Ay, I know who 'tis; he hath no interest in me in the world. Here comes the man you mean.

TOUCHSTONE. It is meat and drink to me to see a clown. By my troth, we that have good wits have much to answer for; we shall be flouting; we cannot hold.

Enter WILLIAM

WILLIAM. Good even, Audrey.

AUDREY. God ye good even, William.

WILLIAM. And good even to you, sir.

TOUCHSTONE. Good even, gentle friend. Cover thy head, cover thy head; nay, prithee, be covered. How old are you, friend?

WILLIAM. Five and twenty, sir.

TOUCHSTONE. A ripe age. Is thy name William?

WILLIAM. William, sir.

TOUCHSTONE. A fair name. Wast born i' the forest here?

WILLIAM. Ay, sir, I thank God.

TOUCHSTONE. "Thank God", a good answer. Art rich?

WILLIAM. Faith, sir, so so.

TOUCHSTONE. "So so" is good, very good, very excellent good; and yet it is not; it is but so so. Art thou wise?

WILLIAM. Ay, sir, I have a pretty wit.

TOUCHSTONE. Why, thou sayest well. I do now remember a saying, "The fool doth think he is wise, but the wise man knows himself to be a fool." The heathen philosopher, when he had a desire to eat a grape, would open his lips when he put it into his mouth; meaning thereby that grapes were made to eat and lips to open. You do love this maid?

WILLIAM. I do, sir.

TOUCHSTONE. Give me your hand. Art thou learned?

WILLIAM. No, sir.

TOUCHSTONE. Then learn this of me: to have, is to have; for it is a figure in rhetoric that drink, being poured out of a cup into a glass, by filling the one doth empty the other; for all your writers do consent that ipse is he. Now, you are not ipse, for I am he.

WILLIAM. Which he, sir?

TOUCHSTONE. He, sir, that must marry this woman. Therefore, you clown, abandon—which is in the vul-gar, leave—the society—which in the boorish is company—of this female—which in the common is woman; which together is, abandon the society of this female, or, clown, thou perishest; or, to thy better understanding, diest; or, to wit, I kill thee, make thee away, translate thy life into death, thy liberty into bondage. I will deal in poison with thee, or in basti-nado, or in steel; I will bandy with thee in faction; I will o'er-run thee with policy; I will kill thee a hundred and fifty ways. Therefore tremble, and depart.

AUDREY. Do, good William.

WILLIAM. God rest you merry, sir.   *Exit*

Enter CORIN

CORIN. Our master and mistress seeks you; come, away, away!

TOUCHSTONE. Trip, Audrey! Trip, Audrey! I attend, I attend.   *Exeunt*

SCENE II *The forest*

Enter ORLANDO *and* OLIVER

ORLANDO. Is 't possible that on so little acquaintance you should like her? that but seeing you should love her? and loving woo? and, wooing, she should grant? and will you persever to enjoy her?

OLIVER. Neither call the giddiness of it in question, the poverty of her, the small acquaintance, my sudden wooing, nor her sudden consenting; but say with me, I love Aliena; say with her that she loves me; consent with both that we may enjoy each other. It shall be to your good; for my father's house and all the revenue that was old Sir Rowland's will I estate upon you, and here live and die a shepherd.

ORLANDO. You have my consent. Let your wedding be tomorrow. Thither will I invite the Duke and all's contented followers. Go you and prepare Aliena; for look you, here comes my Rosalind.

Enter ROSALIND

ROSALIND. God save you, brother.

OLIVER. And you, fair sister.   *Exit*

ROSALIND. O, my dear Orlando, how it grieves me to see thee wear thy heart in a scarf!

ORLANDO. It is my arm.

ROSALIND. I thought thy heart had been wounded with the claws of a lion.

ORLANDO. Wounded it is, but with the eyes of a lady.

ROSALIND. Did your brother tell you how I counter-feited to swoon when he showed me your handkerchief?

ORLANDO. Ay, and greater wonders than that.

ROSALIND. O, I know where you are—nay, 'tis true—there was never anything so sudden but the fight of two rams and Cæsar's thrasonical brag of "I came, saw, and overcame." For your brother and my sister no sooner met but they looked, no sooner looked but they loved, no sooner loved but they sighed, no sooner sighed but they asked one another the reason, no sooner knew the reason but they sought the remedy; and in these degrees have they made a pair of stairs to marriage which they will climb incontinent, or else be incontinent before marriage. They are in the very wrath of love and they will together; clubs cannot part them.

ORLANDO. They shall be married tomorrow, and I will bid the Duke to the nuptial. But, O, how bitter a thing it is to look into happiness through another man's eyes! By so much the more shall I tomorrow be at the height of heart-heaviness, by how much I shall think my brother happy in having what he wishes for.

ROSALIND. Why then, tomorrow I cannot serve your turn for Rosalind?

ORLANDO. I can live no longer by thinking.

ROSALIND. I will weary you then no longer with idle talking. Know of me then, for now I speak to some purpose, that I know you are a gentleman of good conceit. I speak not this that you should bear a good opinion of my knowledge, insomuch I say I know you are; neither do I labour for a greater esteem than may in some little measure draw a belief from you, to do yourself good and not to grace me. Believe then, if you please, that I can do strange things: I have, since I was three year old, conversed with a magician, most profound in his art and yet not damnable. If you do love Rosalind so near the heart as your gesture cries it out, when your brother marries Aliena, shall you marry her. I know into what straits of fortune she is driven; and it is not impossible to me, if it appear not inconvenient to you, to set her before your eyes to-morrow human as she is and without any danger.

ORLANDO. Speakest thou in sober meanings?

ROSALIND. By my life, I do; which I tender dearly,
though I say I am a magician. Therefore, put you in
your best array; bid your friends; for if you will be
married tomorrow, you shall, and to Rosalind, if
you will.

Enter SILVIUS *and* PHEBE

Look, here comes a lover of mine and a lover of hers.

PHEBE. Youth, you have done me much ungentleness,
To show the letter that I writ to you.

ROSALIND. I care not if I have. It is my study
To seem despiteful and ungentle to you.
You are there followed by a faithful shepherd;
Look upon him, love him; he worships you.

PHEBE. Good shepherd, tell this youth what 'tis to love.

SILVIUS. It is to be all made of sighs and tears;
And so am I for Phebe.

PHEBE. And I for Ganymede.

ORLANDO. And I for Rosalind.

ROSALIND. And I for no woman.

SILVIUS. It is to be all made of faith and service;
And so am I for Phebe.

PHEBE. And I for Ganymede.

ORLANDO. And I for Rosalind.

ROSALIND. And I for no woman.

SILVIUS. It is to be all made of fantasy,
All made of passion and all made of wishes,
All adoration, duty, and observance,
All humbleness, all patience and impatience,
All purity, all trial, all observance;
And so am I for Phebe.

PHEBE. And so am I for Ganymede.

ORLANDO. And so am I for Rosalind.

ROSALIND. And so am I for no woman.

PHEBE. If this be so, why blame you me to love you?

SILVIUS. If this be so, why blame you me to love you?

ORLANDO. If this be so, why blame you me to love you?

ROSALIND. Who do you speak to, "Why blame you me
to love you?"

ORLANDO. To her that is not here, nor doth not hear.

ROSALIND. Pray you, no more of this; 'tis like the howling of Irish wolves against the moon. [*To Silvius*] I will
help you, if I can. [*To Phebe*] I would love you, if I
could. Tomorrow meet me all together. [*To Phebe*]
I will marry you, if ever I marry woman, and I'll be
married tomorrow. [*To Orlando*] I will satisfy you,
if ever I satisfied man, and you shall be married tomorrow. [*To Silvius*] I will content you, if what
pleases you contents you, and you shall be married
tomorrow. [*To Orlando*] As you love Rosalind, meet.
[*To Silvius*] As you love Phebe, meet; and as I love no
woman, I'll meet. So fare you well; I have left you
commands.

SILVIUS. I'll not fail, if I live.

PHEBE. Nor I.

ORLANDO. Nor I   *Exeunt*

SCENE III *The forest*

Enter TOUCHSTONE *and* AUDREY

TOUCHSTONE. Tomorrow is the joyful day, Audrey; tomorrow will we be married.

AUDREY. I do desire it with all my heart; and I hope it is no dishonest desire to desire to be a woman of the world. Here come two of the banished Duke's pages.

Enter two Pages

FIRST PAGE. Well met, honest gentleman.

TOUCHSTONE. By my troth, well met. Come, sit, sit, and a song.

SECOND PAGE. We are for you. Sit i' the middle.

FIRST PAGE. Shall we clap into 't roundly, without hawking or spitting or saying we are hoarse, which are the only prologues to a bad voice?

SECOND PAGE. I' faith, i' faith; and both in a tune, like two gipsies on a horse.

SONG

It was a lover and his lass,
    With a hey, and a ho, and a hey nonino,
That o'er the green cornfield did pass
    In the spring time, the only pretty ring time,
When birds do sing, hey ding a ding, ding:
Sweet lovers love the spring.

Between the acres of the rye,
    With a hey, and a ho, and a hey nonino,
These pretty country folks would lie,
    In the spring time, the only pretty ring time,
When birds do sing, hey ding a ding, ding:
Sweet lovers love the spring.

This carol they began that hour,
    With a hey, and a ho, and a hey nonino,
How that a life was but a flower
    In the spring time, the only pretty ring time,
When birds do sing, hey ding a ding, ding:
Sweet lovers love the spring.

And therefore take the present time,
    With a hey, and a ho, and a hey nonino;
For love is crowned with the prime
    In the spring time, the only pretty ring time,
When birds do sing, hey ding a ding, ding:
Sweet lovers love the spring.

TOUCHSTONE. Truly, young gentlemen, though there was no great matter in the ditty, yet the note was very untuneable.

FIRST PAGE. You are deceived, sir. We kept time, we lost not our time.

TOUCHSTONE. By my troth, yes; I count it but time lost to hear such a foolish song. God be wi' you; and God mend your voices! Come, Audrey.　　*Exeunt*

Enter DUKE SENIOR, AMIENS, JAQUES, ORLANDO, OLIVER, *and* CELIA

DUKE SENIOR. Dost thou believe, Orlando, that the boy
  Can do all this that he hath promised?
ORLANDO. I sometimes do believe, and sometimes do
    not;
  As those that fear they hope, and know they fear.

Enter ROSALIND, SILVIUS, *and* PHEBE

ROSALIND. Patience once more, whiles our compact is
    urged.
  You say, if I bring in your Rosalind,
  You will bestow her on Orlando here?
DUKE SENIOR. That would I, had I kingdoms to give
  with her.
ROSALIND. And you say, you will have her, when I
    bring her?
ORLANDO. That would I, were I of all kingdoms king.
ROSALIND. You say, you'll marry me, if I be willing?
PHEBE. That will I, should I die the hour after.
ROSALIND. But if you do refuse to marry me,
  You'll give yourself to this most faithful shepherd?
PHEBE. So is the bargain.
ROSALIND. You say, that you'll have Phebe, if she will?
SILVIUS. Though to have her and death were both one
    thing.
ROSALIND. I have promised to make all this matter even.
  Keep you your word, O Duke, to give your daughter;
  You yours, Orlando, to receive his daughter.
  Keep your word, Phebe, that you'll marry me,
  Or else refusing me, to wed this shepherd.
  Keep your word, Silvius, that you'll marry her,
  If she refuse me. And from hence I go,
  To make these doubts all even.
                        Exeunt ROSALIND *and* CELIA
DUKE SENIOR. I do remember in this shepherd boy
  Some lively touches of my daughter's favour.
ORLANDO. My lord, the first time that I ever saw him
  Methought he was a brother to your daughter.
  But, my good lord, this boy is forest-born,
  And hath been tutored in the rudiments
  Of many desperate studies by his uncle,
  Whom he reports to be a great magician,
  Obscured in the circle of this forest.

Enter TOUCHSTONE *and* AUDREY

JAQUES. There is, sure, another flood toward, and these
  couples are coming to the ark. Here comes a pair of
  very strange beasts, which in all tongues are called
  fools.
TOUCHSTONE. Salutation and greeting to you all!
JAQUES. Good my lord, bid him welcome. This is the
  motley-minded gentleman that I have so often met in
  the forest. He hath been a courtier, he swears.
TOUCHSTONE. If any man doubt that, let him put me to

my purgation. I have trod a measure; I have flattered
a lady; I have been politic with my friend, smooth
with mine enemy; I have undone three tailors; I have
had four quarrels, and like to have fought one.
JAQUES. And how was that ta'en up?
TOUCHSTONE. Faith, we met, and found the quarrel was
  upon the seventh cause.
JAQUES. How seventh cause? Good my lord, like this
  fellow.
DUKE SENIOR. I like him very well.
TOUCHSTONE. God 'ild you, sir; I desire you of the
  like. I press in here, sir, amongst the rest of the
  country copulatives, to swear and to forswear; according as marriage binds and blood breaks: a poor virgin,
  sir, an ill-favoured thing, sir, but mine own; a poor
  humour of mine, sir, to take that that no man else
  will. Rich honesty dwells like a miser, sir, in a poor
  house, as your pearl in your foul oyster.
DUKE SENIOR. By my faith, he is very swift and sententious.
TOUCHSTONE. According to the fool's bolt, sir, and
  such dulcet diseases.
JAQUES. But, for the seventh cause; how did you find
  the quarrel on the seventh cause?
TOUCHSTONE. Upon a lie seven times removed—bear
  your body more seeming, Audrey—as thus, sir. I did
  dislike the cut of a certain courtier's beard. He sent
  me word, if I said his beard was not cut well, he was
  in the mind it was—this is called the Retort Courteous. If I sent him word again "it was not well cut,"
  he would send me word, he cut it to please himself—
  this is called the Quip Modest. If again "it was not
  well cut," he disabled my judgement—this is called
  the Reply Churlish. If again "it was not well cut,"
  he would answer, I spake not true—this is called the
  Reproof Valiant. If again "it was not well cut," he
  would say, I lied—this is called the Countercheck
  Quarrelsome. And so to the Lie Circumstantial and
  the Lie Direct.
JAQUES. And how oft did you say his beard was not
  well cut?
TOUCHSTONE. I durst go no further than the Lie Circumstantial, nor he durst not give me the Lie Direct;
  and so we measured swords and parted.
JAQUES. Can you nominate in order now the degrees
  of the lie?
TOUCHSTONE. O sir, we quarrel in print by the book,
  as you have books for good manners. I will name you
  the degrees. The first, the Retort Courteous; the
  second, the Quip Modest; the third, the Reply
  Churlish; the fourth, the Reproof Valiant; the fifth,
  the Countercheck Quarrelsome; the sixth, the Lie
  with Circumstance; the seventh, the Lie Direct. All

these you may avoid but the Lie Direct; and you may
avoid that too, with an If. I knew when seven justices
could not take up a quarrel, but when the parties
were met themselves, one of them thought but of an
If, as, "If you said so, then I said so"; and they shook
hands and swore brothers. Your If is the only peace-
maker; much virtue in If.

JAQUES. Is not this a rare fellow, my lord? He's as good
at anything and yet a fool.

DUKE SENIOR. He uses his folly like a stalkinghorse
and under the presentation of that he shoots his wit.

Enter HYMEN, ROSALIND, *and* CELIA

Still Music

HYMEN. Then is there mirth in heaven,
    When earthly things made even
        Atone together.
    Good duke, receive thy daughter:
    Hymen from heaven brought her,
        Yea, brought her hither,
    That thou mightst join her hand with his
    Whose heart within his bosom is.

ROSALIND. [*To Duke*] To you I give myself, for I am
    yours.
    [*To Orlando*] To you I give myself, for I am yours.

DUKE SENIOR. If there be truth in sight, you are my
    daughter.

ORLANDO. If there be truth in sight, you are my Rosa-
    lind.

PHEBE. If sight and shape be true,
    Why then, my love adieu!

ROSALIND. I 'll have no father, if you be not he;
    I 'll have no husband, if you be not he;
    Nor ne'er wed woman, if you be not she.

HYMEN. Peace, ho! I bar confusion:
    'Tis I must make conclusion
        Of these most strange events:
    Here's eight that must take hands
    To join in Hymen's bands,
        If truth holds true contents.
        [*To* ORLANDO *and* ROSALIND]
    You and you no cross shall part:
        [*To* OLIVER *and* CELIA]
    You and you are heart in heart:
        [*To* PHEBE]
    You to his love must accord,
        Or have a woman to your lord:
        [*To* TOUCHSTONE *and* AUDREY]
    You and you are sure together,
    As the winter to foul weather.
    Whiles a wedlock-hymn we sing,
    Feed yourselves with questioning;
    That reason wonder may diminish,
    How thus we met, and these things finish.

SONG

    Wedding is great Juno's crown:
        O blessed bond of board and bed!
    'Tis Hymen peoples every town;
        High wedlock then be honoured:
    Honour, high honour and renown,
    To Hymen, god of every town!

DUKE SENIOR. O my dear niece, welcome thou art
    to me!
    Even daughter, welcome, in no less degree.

PHEBE. I will not eat my word, now thou art mine;
    Thy faith my fancy to thee doth combine.

Enter JAQUES DE BOYS

JAQUES DE BOYS. Let me have audience for a word or
    two.
  I am the second son of old Sir Rowland,
  That bring these tidings to this fair assembly.
  Duke Frederick, hearing how that every day
  Men of great worth resorted to this forest,
  Addressed a mighty power, which were on foot,
  In his own conduct, purposely to take
  His brother here and put him to the sword.
  And to the skirts of this wild wood he came,
  Where meeting with an old religious man,
  After some question with him, was converted
  Both from his enterprise and from the world,
  His crown bequeathing to his banished brother,
  And all their lands restored to them again
  That were with him exiled. This to be true,
  I do engage my life.
DUKE SENIOR.   Welcome, young man;
  Thou offer'st fairly to thy brothers' wedding.
  To one his lands withheld, and to the other
  A land itself at large, a potent dukedom.
  First, in this forest let us do those ends
  That here were well begun and well begot.
  And after, every of this happy number
  That have endured shrewd days and nights with us
  Shall share the good of our returned fortune,
  According to the measure of their states.
  Meantime, forget this new-fall'n dignity
  And fall into our rustic revelry.
  Play, music! And you, brides and bridegrooms all,
  With measure heaped in joy, to the measures fall.
JAQUES. Sir, by your patience. If I heard you rightly,
  The Duke hath put on a religious life
  And thrown into neglect the pompous court?
JAQUES DE BOYS. He hath.
JAQUES. To him will I. Out of these convertites
  There is much matter to be heard and learned.
  [*To Duke*] You to your former honour I bequeath—
  Your patience and your virtue well deserves it;
  [*To Orlando*] You to a love that your true faith doth
    merit;
  [*To Oliver*] You to your land and love and great allies;
  [*To Silvius*] You to a long and well-deserved bed;
  [*To Touchstone*] And you to wrangling, for thy loving
    voyage
  Is but for two months victualled. So, to your pleasures;
  I am for other than for dancing measures.
DUKE SENIOR. Stay, Jaques, stay.
JAQUES. To see no pastime I. What you would have
  I 'll stay to know at your abandoned cave.   *Exit*
DUKE SENIOR. Proceed, proceed. We will begin these
    rites,
  As we do trust they'll end, in true delights.

A dance

Epilogue

ROSALIND. It is not the fashion to see the lady the epilogue; but it is no more unhandsome than to see the lord the prologue. If it be true that good wine needs no bush, 'tis true that a good play needs no epilogue; yet to good wine they do use good bushes, and good plays prove the better by the help of good epilogues. What a case am I in then, that am neither a good epilogue nor cannot insinuate with you in the behalf of a good play! I am not furnished like a beggar, therefore to beg will not become me. My way is to conjure you; and I'll begin with the women. I charge you, O women, for the love you bear to men, to like as much of this play as please you. And I charge you, O men, for the love you bear to women—as I perceive by your simpering, none of you hates them—that between you and the women the play may please. If I were a woman I would kiss as many of you as had beards that pleased me, complexions that liked me and breaths that I defied not. And, I am sure, as many as have good beards or good faces or sweet breaths will, for my kind offer, when I make curtsy, bid me farewell.

Exeunt

HAMLET, PRINCE OF DENMARK

The meaning, the so-called "mystery", of *Hamlet* has been discussed over and over by physicians, metaphysicians, moralists and psychologists; the play's poetry has been analyzed by poets, its dramaturgy by dramaturgs; grammarians have parsed and reparsed every speech, every sentence, every phrase; every least comma has been minutely scrutinized, discoursed upon with learning, with enthusiasm and at considerable length. Much nonsense has been written and much excellent sense.

So much has been written about *Hamlet* and is readily available to anyone who wants to read it, that I do not propose to wheel my tiny barrow to the top of this heap, and there tip out its contents of theory and speculation. This introduction will therefore concern itself with practical observation derived from theatrical experience.

Hamlet, for all its great length, complexity and profundity, is one of the more easily produced of Shakespeare's plays. That is not to say that it is easy. No masterpiece can be that. But it does not bristle with the technical problems which confront the director of *Antony and Cleopatra,* for instance, *King Lear, Macbeth* or *Coriolanus.*

If you have a reasonably good Hamlet, the audience is assured of an interesting evening, even if the rest of the team is pretty weak. This is not only because the role of Hamlet completely dominates the play, but more because the character is principally revealed in the series of soliloquies which are spoken directly to the audience and demand no cooperation from other actors.

Of course a performance is infinitely better if the team is a strong one; if the King, Queen, Ghost, Polonius, Ophelia, Laertes, Horatio and Fortinbras can supply what these difficult and interesting parts demand; if Rosencrantz, Guildenstern, Osric, Gravedigger, Marcellus or Reynaldo can, as is perfectly possible, make good use of their smaller opportunities. In this connection, I personally shall never forget the Gravedigger of Gus MacNaughton, an old vaudeville singer, whose quietly realistic performance achieved exactly the mood of simple, sardonic and philosophic humour which I believe that Shakespeare intended. Nor shall I ever forget Alec Guinness doubling the small part of Reynaldo—a gentleman's gentleman whose extravagant primness did not prevent one seeing that he was a snake in the grass—with Osric, a devastating exposure of pretentious elegance masking pathetic insecurity.

Nevertheless, with a weak team but a strong Hamlet, the play can still get by.

And it is easier far to be good as Hamlet, than as any other of the great Shakespearian characters.

Why is this? Mainly, I suspect, because the part is of almost universal interest. The head of a large public library in England once told me that books about three particular personages were in outstandingly greater demand than books about any others. The three, in descending order, were Jesus Christ, Hamlet and Napoleon Bonaparte. Such is the appeal of this figment of Shakespeare's imagination. The mountain of *Hamlet* commentary bears witness to the same fact. In every epoch, every part of the world, to people of the most widely diverse environment and character, this figment is uniquely interesting and attractive.

Hamlet's conscious thoughts and desires do not correspond with his actions, and, more significantly, with his failure to take action in the particular matter which is central to the drama, namely vengeance upon Claudius for the murder of Hamlet's father, the usurpation of his throne and what he regards as the defilement of his mother. This inconsistency is the "mystery" of *Hamlet,* but it does not stand in the way of the play's popularity. Quite the reverse, because all of us recognize a similar failure of our own conscious thoughts and desires to match our conduct.

The mystery of *Hamlet* is a mystery of every human life. It is only in books and plays that, given a few silent facts of character, conduct is consistent and predictable.

Therefore the aspects of the character which are hard for the student to analyse and explain and which are not consistent with the play's action, are precisely the aspects which make it most universal and sympathetic. Moreover, the fact that the character is not entirely self-consistent and not precisely defined but yet, in the soliloquies, presents more of the raw material for psychological analysis than any other character in Shakespeare— this fact makes possible an enormous variety of intelligent, even profound, interpretations by actors of the most various physical, intellectual, imaginative and technical attributes.

Another point: again because of the soliloquies, Hamlet is not nearly so hard a character for his impersonator, and also for the audience, to grasp as Lear, Macbeth, Brutus, or Coriolanus, in whom most of the evidence as to character is supplied not by themselves but by inference from their behaviour and the comment of other persons in the play. Such comment is not objective. When Antony speaks of Brutus as "an honourable man" it does not by any means follow either that Antony thinks him so, or that Shakespeare intends the audience to think him so. When other characters imply that Macbeth is a monster of iniquity, it by no means follows that this is Shakespeare's verdict, or that he should be impersonated as a monster of iniquity.

Now, while it does not follow that what Hamlet thinks of himself is precisely what Shakespeare thinks of him, it does, I think, follow that what he thinks of himself offers a very clear indication to the actor of how to play it. If Hamlet says "Oh what a rogue and peasant slave am I!" it is a clear indication to the actor and to the audience that the sentiment is one of self-recrimination and self-mockery. Matters would be very different and very much more complex if, instead of Hamlet talking about himself, he were talked about by some of the other characters; if, let us suppose, the King, an obviously hostile and untrustworthy witness, were to say: "Oh what a rogue and peasant slave is he!"

Further, the part is not only imaginatively easier to grasp than the other great Shakespearian roles, it is technically easier. Very much of the speaking is quiet, even conversational, in tone. If an actor has not the required rhetorical accomplishment, it is not disastrous. Other qualities may pull him through. But Macbeth, Coriolanus, Lear and, perhaps most of all, Othello absolutely demand immense vocal equipment.

Hamlet is a surprisingly quick and easy play to rehearse. If the leading actor and the director are in full accord, things fall into place very fast. Most of the scenes are between two or three characters and their action is fairly clear and simple. The three big ensembles (the play scene, the scene in the graveyard and the finale) are shorter and, in my opinion, very much easier to arrange than, for example, the great finales of *Twelfth Night, Measure for Measure,* or *All's Well,* or the scenes of battle in *Julius Caesar, Coriolanus* and the histories.

Cutting is a great problem. I do not think that *Hamlet* can be achieved at full length in much under four hours. A long and nearly full version is far more interesting and far more easily intelligible than one in which the play is drastically reduced. I can see little point in retaining for public performance certain passages like the reference to "the little eyases", which an ordinary audience cannot possibly now understand. But when, as it nearly always is (on the assumption, especially prevalent in America, that an adult audience cannot possibly concentrate its attention for more than two and a half hours, including two intermissions), the play is cut almost by half, much more important material has to go.

The first place to cut, I think anyone will agree, is somewhere between Ophelia's funeral and the finale. The plot becomes a bit turgid; events, like the grapple with the Pirates, are narrated instead of being shown, and the long, interesting psychological scene between the King and Laertes (where he eggs Laertes on to avenge on Hamlet the murder of Polonius) occurs too late in the evening. The audience by now is too tired to follow a subtle, slow and quiet scene; people are waiting for the story to reach its climax and to see, as in the finale they eventually will, the play's business dispatched in exciting and violent action.

Some cutting hereabout does the play little harm in my opinion. But to reduce it to "commercial" length requires excision far more drastic. Indeed everything which can possibly be cut, leaving a just intelligible story, has got to be cut. I have seen productions—even important and supposedly good ones—where the first scenes on the battlements and the first appearance of the Ghost have been removed, and where the play has opened on the King's first scene—"Though yet of Hamlet, our dear brother's death the memory be green." And it is quite usual for the play to end with Horatio's "flights of angels sing thee to thy rest"—a nice, juicy curtain line— omitting the entry of Fortinbras. So far as mere intelligibility of the plot goes, Fortinbras can be omitted altogether (of course it means scrapping Hamlet's soliloquy which begins "How all occasions do inform against me . . ." never mind; to do so saves four precious minutes). The intention of the play is then, however, perverted and considerably sentimentalized.

Also there is one difficulty which drastic cutting, however intelligent, respectful and deft, simply cannot avoid: it is the lesser parts which have to be cut—Polonius, the King, Rosencrantz, Guildenstern, Horatio, Marcellus; some, like Reynaldo, disappear completely. The result is that Hamlet, who in a full-length version is still the dominant figure, but who dominates a pretty considerable and interesting group of characters, is, in a heavily cut version, left the single interesting figure against a background of cardboard dummies; while the play, deprived of its intended rhythm, jerks phrenetically from one unprepared and therefore incredible and melodramatic climax to another. Believe me, a full-length, or nearly full-length, version is worth the effort.

SCENE: DENMARK

FORTINBRAS,
   Prince of Norway
MARCELLUS,
BARNARDO,
   Officers
FRANCISCO,
   a soldier
REYNALDO,
   servant to Polonius
A Priest
Players
Two Clowns,
   grave-diggers
A Gentleman,
   courtier
A Captain
English Ambassadors
Lords, Ladies
Officers, Soldiers
Sailors, Messengers
   and other
Attendants

Ghost of Hamlet's Father

HAMLET, PRINCE OF DENMARK

DRAMATIS PERSONAE

VOLTIMAND, CORNELIUS, OSRIC, courtiers;   POLONIUS, lord chamberlain;
HORATIO, friend to Hamlet; LAERTES, son to Polonius;   ROSENCRANTZ,
GUILDENSTERN,
courtiers.

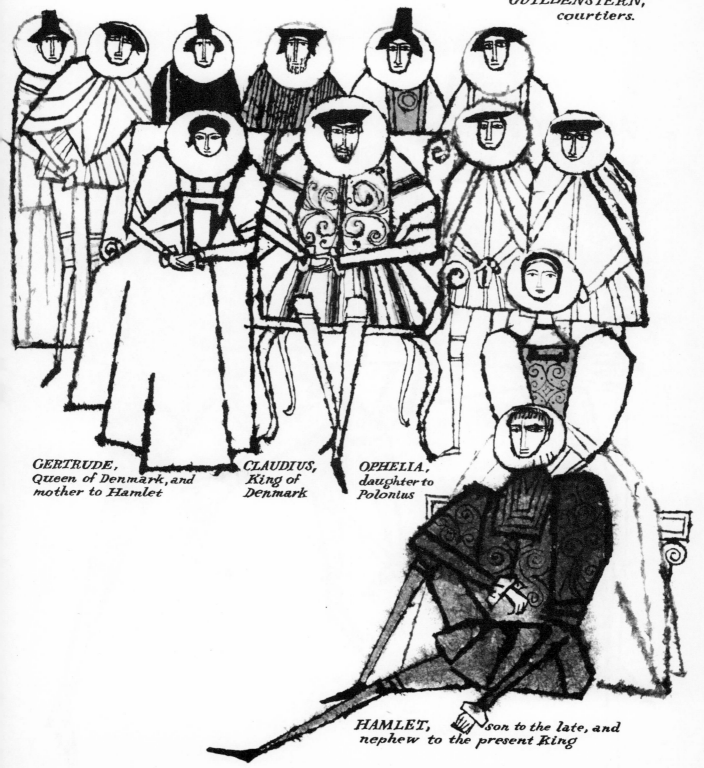

GERTRUDE,
Queen of Denmark, and
mother to Hamlet

CLAUDIUS,
King of
Denmark

OPHELIA,
daughter to
Polonius

HAMLET,   son to the late, and
nephew to the present King

ACT I

SCENE I *Elsinore. A platform before the castle*

FRANCISCO *at his post. Enter to him* BARNARDO

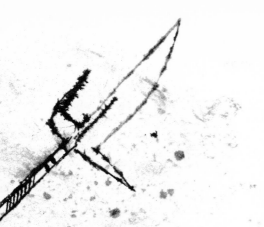

BARNARDO. Who's there?

FRANCISCO. Nay, answer me. Stand, and unfold yourself.

BARNARDO. Long live the King!

FRANCISCO. Barnardo?

BARNARDO. He.

FRANCISCO. You come most carefully upon your hour.

BARNARDO. 'Tis now struck twelve; get thee to bed, Francisco.

FRANCISCO. For this relief much thanks; 'tis bitter cold, And I am sick at heart.

BARNARDO. Have you had quiet guard?

FRANCISCO. Not a mouse stirring.

BARNARDO. Well, good night. If you do meet Horatio and Marcellus, The rivals of my watch, bid them make haste.

FRANCISCO. I think I hear them. Stand, ho! Who's there?

Enter HORATIO *and* MARCELLUS

HORATIO. Friends to this ground.

MARCELLUS. And liegemen to the Dane.

FRANCISCO. Give you good night.

MARCELLUS. O, farewell, honest soldier. Who hath relieved you?

FRANCISCO. Barnardo has my place. Give you good night. *Exit*

MARCELLUS. Holla! Barnardo!

BARNARDO. Say, What, is Horatio there?

HORATIO. A piece of him.

BARNARDO. Welcome, Horatio; welcome, good Marcellus.

MARCELLUS. What, has this thing appeared again tonight?

BARNARDO. I have seen nothing.

MARCELLUS. Horatio says 'tis but our fantasy, And will not let belief take hold of him Touching this dreaded sight, twice seen of us. Therefore I have entreated him along With us to watch the minutes of this night;

That if again this apparition come, He may approve our eyes and speak to it.

HORATIO. Tush, tush, 'twill not appear.

BARNARDO. Sit down awhile; And let us once again assail your ears, That are so fortified against our story What we have two nights seen.

HORATIO. Well, sit we down, And let us hear Barnardo speak of this.

BARNARDO. Last night of all, When yond same star that's westward from the pole Had made his course to illume that part of heaven Where now it burns, Marcellus and myself, The bell then beating one—

Enter Ghost

MARCELLUS. Peace, break thee off. Look where it comes again!

BARNARDO. In the same figure, like the King that's dead.

MARCELLUS. Thou art a scholar; speak to it, Horatio.

BARNARDO. Looks it not like the King? Mark it, Horatio.

HORATIO. Most like. It harrows me with fear and wonder.

BARNARDO. It would be spoke to.

MARCELLUS. Question it, Horatio.

HORATIO. What art thou that usurp'st this time of night, Together with that fair and warlike form In which the majesty of buried Denmark Did sometimes march? By heaven I charge thee, speak!

MARCELLUS. It is offended.

BARNARDO. See, it stalks away!

HORATIO. Stay! speak, speak! I charge thee, speak!

Exit Ghost

MARCELLUS. 'Tis gone, and will not answer.

BARNARDO. How now, Horatio! you tremble and look pale. Is not this something more than fantasy? What think you on 't?

HORATIO. Before my God, I might not this believe Without the sensible and true avouch Of mine own eyes.

MARCELLUS. Is it not like the King?

HORATIO. As thou art to thyself. Such was the very armour he had on When he the ambitious Norway combated; So frowned he once, when, in an angry parle, He smote the sledded Polacks on the ice. 'Tis strange.

MARCELLUS. Thus twice before, and jump at this dead hour, With martial stalk hath he gone by our watch.

HORATIO. In what particular thought to work I know not; But in the gross and scope of my opinion, This bodes some strange eruption to our state.

MARCELLUS. Good now, sit down, and tell me, he that
    knows,
  Why this same strict and most observant watch
  So nightly toils the subject of the land,
  And why such daily cast of brazen cannon,
  And foreign mart for implements of war;
  Why such impress of shipwrights, whose sore task
  Does not divide the Sunday from the week;
  What might be toward, that this sweaty haste
  Doth make the night joint-labourer with the day?
  Who is 't that can inform me?

HORATIO.   That can I;
  At least, the whisper goes so. Our last King,
  Whose image even but now appeared to us,
  Was, as you know, by Fortinbras of Norway,
  Thereto pricked on by a most emulate pride,
  Dared to the combat; in which our valiant Hamlet—
  For so this side of our known world esteemed him—
  Did slay this Fortinbras; who, by a sealed compact,
  Well ratified by law and heraldry,
  Did forfeit, with his life, all those his lands
  Which he stood seized of, to the conqueror;
  Against the which, a moiety competent
  Was gaged by our King; which had returned
  To the inheritance of Fortinbras,
  Had he been vanquisher; as, by the same covenant,
  And carriage of the article designed,
  His fell to Hamlet. Now, sir, young Fortinbras,
  Of unimproved mettle hot and full,
  Hath in the skirts of Norway here and there
  Sharked up a list of lawless resolutes,
  For food and diet, to some enterprise
  That hath a stomach in 't; which is no other—
  As it doth well appear unto our state—
  But to recover of us, by strong hand
  And terms compulsatory, those foresaid lands
  So by his father lost. And this, I take it,
  Is the main motive of our preparations,
  The source of this our watch and the chief head
  Of this post-haste and romage in the land.

BARNARDO. I think it be no other but e'en so.
  Well may it sort that this portentous figure
  Comes armed through our watch; so like the King
  That was and is the question of these wars.

HORATIO. A mote it is to trouble the mind's eye.
  In the most high and palmy state of Rome,
  A little ere the mightiest Julius fell,
  The graves stood tenantless and the sheeted dead
  Did squeak and gibber in the Roman streets;
  As stars with trains of fire and dews of blood,
  Disasters in the sun; and the moist star
  Upon whose influence Neptune's empire stands
  Was sick almost to Doomsday with eclipse.
  And even the like precurse of feared events,
  As harbingers preceding still the fates
  And prologue to the omen coming on,

Have heaven and earth together demonstrated
Unto our climatures and countrymen.
But soft, behold! lo, where it comes again!

            Re-enter Ghost

I'll cross it, though it blast me. Stay, illusion!
If thou hast any sound, or use of voice,
Speak to me.
If there be any good thing to be done,
That may to thee do ease and grace to me,
Speak to me.   *Cock crows*
If thou art privy to thy country's fate,
Which, happily, foreknowing may avoid,
O, speak!
Or if thou hast uphoarded in thy life
Extorted treasure in the womb of earth,
For which, they say, you spirits oft walk in death,
Speak of it; stay, and speak! Stop it, Marcellus.

MARCELLUS. Shall I strike at it with my partisan?

HORATIO. Do, if it will not stand.

BARNARDO.   'Tis here!

HORATIO.   'Tis here!

MARCELLUS. 'Tis gone!   *Exit* Ghost
  We do it wrong, being so majestical,
  To offer it the show of violence;
  For it is, as the air, invulnerable,
  And our vain blows malicious mockery.

BARNARDO. It was about to speak, when the cock crew.

HORATIO. And then it started like a guilty thing
  Upon a fearful summons. I have heard,
  The cock, that is the trumpet to the morn,
  Doth with his lofty and shrill-sounding throat
  Awake the god of day; and, at his warning,
  Whether in sea or fire, in earth or air,
  The extravagant and erring spirit hies
  To his confine; and of the truth herein
  This present object made probation.

MARCELLUS. It faded on the crowing of the cock.
  Some say that ever 'gainst that season comes
  Wherein our Saviour's birth is celebrated,
  The bird of dawning singeth all night long.
  And then, they say, no spirit dare stir abroad;
  The nights are wholesome; then no planets strike,
  No fairy takes, nor witch hath power to charm,
  So hallowed and so gracious is the time.

HORATIO. So have I heard and do in part believe it.
  But, look, the morn, in russet mantle clad,
  Walks o'er the dew of yon high eastward hill.
  Break we our watch up; and by my advice,
  Let us impart what we have seen tonight
  Unto young Hamlet; for, upon my life,
  This spirit, dumb to us, will speak to him.
  Do you consent we shall acquaint him with it,
  As needful in our loves, fitting our duty?

MARCELLUS. Let's do 't, I pray; and I this morning know
  Where we shall find him most conveniently.   *Exeunt*

SCENE II *A room of state in the castle*

Enter the KING, QUEEN, HAMLET, POLONIUS, LAERTES, VOLTIMAND, CORNELIUS, Lords, *and* Attendants

KING. Though yet of Hamlet our dear brother's death
  The memory be green, and that it us befitted
  To bear our hearts in grief and our whole kingdom
  To be contracted in one brow of woe,
  Yet so far hath discretion fought with nature
  That we with wisest sorrow think on him,
  Together with remembrance of ourselves.
  Therefore our sometime sister, now our queen,
  The imperial jointress to this warlike state,
  Have we, as 'twere with a defeated joy—
  With an auspicious and a dropping eye,
  With mirth in funeral and with dirge in marriage,
  In equal scale weighing delight and dole—
  Taken to wife. Nor have we herein barred
  Your better wisdoms, which have freely gone
  With this affair along. For all, our thanks.
  Now follows, that you know, young Fortinbras,
  Holding a weak supposal of our worth,
  Or thinking by our late dear brother's death
  Our state to be disjoint and out of frame,
  Colleagued with the dream of his advantage,
  He hath not failed to pester us with message,
  Importing the surrender of those lands
  Lost by his father, with all bonds of law,
  To our most valiant brother. So much for him.
  Now for ourself and for this time of meeting.
  Thus much the business is: we have here writ
  To Norway, uncle of young Fortinbras—
  Who, impotent and bed-rid, scarcely hears
  Of this his nephew's purpose—to suppress
  His further gait herein; in that the levies,
  The lists and full proportions, are all made
  Out of his subject. And we here dispatch
  You, good Cornelius, and you, Voltimand,
  For bearers of this greeting to old Norway;
  Giving to you no further personal power
  To business with the King, more than the scope
  Of these delated articles allow.
  Farewell, and let your haste commend your duty.

CORNELIUS. } In that and all things will we show
VOLTIMAND. } our duty.

KING. We doubt it nothing; heartily farewell.

          Exeunt VOLTIMAND *and* CORNELIUS

And now, Laertes, what's the news with you?
You told us of some suit; what is 't, Laertes?
You cannot speak of reason to the Dane,
And lose your voice. What wouldst thou beg, Laertes,
That shall not be my offer, not thy asking?
The head is not more native to the heart,
The hand more instrumental to the mouth,
Than is the throne of Denmark to thy father.
What wouldst thou have, Laertes?

LAERTES.   My dread lord,
  Your leave and favour to return to France;
  From whence though willingly I came to Denmark,
  To show my duty in your coronation,
  Yet now, I must confess, that duty done,
  My thoughts and wishes bend again toward France
  And bow them to your gracious leave and pardon.

KING. Have you your father's leave? What says Polonius?

POLONIUS. He hath, my lord, wrung from me my slow leave
  By laboursome petition, and at last
  Upon his will I sealed my hard consent.
  I do beseech you, give him leave to go.

KING. Take thy fair hour, Laertes; time be thine,
  And thy best graces spend it at thy will!
  But now, my cousin Hamlet, and my son—

HAMLET. [*Aside*] A little more than kin, and less than kind.

KING. How is it that the clouds still hang on you?

HAMLET. Not so, my lord; I am too much i' the sun.

QUEEN. Good Hamlet, cast thy nighted colour off,
  And let thine eye look like a friend on Denmark.
  Do not for ever with thy vailed lids
  Seek for thy noble father in the dust.
  Thou know'st 'tis common; all that lives must die,
  Passing through nature to eternity.

HAMLET. Ay, madam, it is common.

QUEEN.   If it be,
  Why seems it so particular with thee?

HAMLET. Seems, madam! Nay, it is; I know not "seems."
  'Tis not alone my inky cloak, good mother,
  Nor customary suits of solemn black,
  Nor windy suspiration of forced breath,
  No, nor the fruitful river in the eye,
  Nor the dejected 'haviour of the visage,
  Together with all forms, moods, shapes of grief,
  That can denote me truly. These indeed seem,
  For they are actions that a man might play.
  But I have that within which passeth show;
  These but the trappings and the suits of woe.

KING. 'Tis sweet and commendable in your nature, Hamlet,
  To give these mourning duties to your father.
  But, you must know, your father lost a father;
  That father lost, lost his, and the survivor bound
  In filial obligation for some term
  To do obsequious sorrow. But to persevere
  In obstinate condolement is a course
  Of impious stubborness; 'tis unmanly grief;
  It shows a will most incorrect to heaven,
  A heart unfortified, a mind impatient,

An understanding simple and unschooled.
For what we know must be and is as common
As any the most vulgar thing to sense,
Why should we in our peevish opposition
Take it to heart? Fie! 'tis a fault to heaven,
A fault against the dead, a fault to nature,
To reason most absurd; whose common theme
Is death of fathers, and who still hath cried,
From the first corpse till he that died today,
"This must be so." We pray you, throw to earth
This unprevailing woe, and think of us
As of a father. For let the world take note,
You are the most immediate to our throne;
And with no less nobility of love
Than that which dearest father bears his son,
Do I impart toward you. For your intent
In going back to school in Wittenberg,
It is most retrograde to our desire;
And we beseech you, bend you to remain
Here, in the cheer and comfort of our eye,
Our chiefest courtier, cousin, and our son.
QUEEN. Let not thy mother lose her prayers, Hamlet.
  I pray thee, stay with us; go not to Wittenberg.
HAMLET. I shall in all my best obey you, madam.
KING. Why, 'tis a loving and a fair reply.
  Be as ourself in Denmark. Madam, come;
  This gentle and unforced accord of Hamlet
  Sits smiling to my heart; in grace whereof,
  No jocund health that Denmark drinks today,
  But the great cannon to the clouds shall tell,
  And the King's rouse the heavens shall bruit again,
  Respeaking earthly thunder. Come away.

                              Exeunt all but HAMLET
HAMLET. O, that this too too solid flesh would melt,
  Thaw and resolve itself into a dew!
  Or that the Everlasting had not fixed
  His canon 'gainst self-slaughter! O God! God!
  How weary, stale, flat and unprofitable,
  Seem to me all the uses of this world!
  Fie on 't! Ah fie, 'tis an unweeded garden,
  That grows to seed; things rank and gross in nature
  Possess it merely. That it should come to this!
  But two months dead—nay, not so much, not two—
  So excellent a king; that was, to this,
  Hyperion to a satyr; so loving to my mother
  That he might not beteem the winds of heaven
  Visit her face too roughly. Heaven and earth!
  Must I remember? Why, she would hang on him,
  As if increase of appetite had grown
  By what it fed on. And yet, within a month—
  Let me not think on 't—Frailty, thy name is woman!—
  A little month, or ere those shoes were old
  With which she followed my poor father's body,
  Like Niobe, all tears—why she, even she—
  O God! a beast, that wants discourse of reason,
  Would have mourned longer—married with my uncle,

My father's brother, but no more like my father
Than I to Hercules—within a month—
Ere yet the salt of most unrighteous tears
Had left the flushing in her galled eyes,
She married. O, most wicked speed, to post
With such dexterity to incestuous sheets!
It is not nor it cannot come to good.
But break, my heart; for I must hold my tongue.

              Enter HORATIO, MARCELLUS, *and* BARNARDO

HORATIO. Hail to your lordship!
HAMLET.   I am glad to see you well.
  Horatio—or I do forget myself.
HORATIO. The same, my lord, and your poor servant
  ever.
HAMLET. Sir, my good friend; I'll change that name
  with you.
  And what make you from Wittenberg, Horatio?
  Marcellus?
MARCELLUS. My good lord—
HAMLET. I am very glad to see you. Good even, sir.
  But what, in faith, make you from Wittenberg?
HORATIO. A truant disposition, good my lord.
HAMLET. I would not hear your enemy say so,
  Nor shall you do mine ear that violence,
  To make it truster of your own report
  Against yourself. I know you are no truant.
  But what is your affair in Elsinore?
  We'll teach you to drink deep ere you depart.
HORATIO. My lord, I came to see your father's funeral.
HAMLET. I pray thee, do not mock me, fellow student;
  I think it was to see my mother's wedding.
HORATIO. Indeed, my lord, it followed hard upon.
HAMLET. Thrift, thrift, Horatio! The funeral baked
  meats
  Did coldly furnish forth the marriage tables.
  Would I had met my dearest foe in heaven
  Or ever I had seen that day, Horatio!
  My father!—Methinks I see my father.
HORATIO. Where, my lord?
HAMLET.   In my mind's eye, Horatio.
HORATIO. I saw him once; he was a goodly king.
HAMLET. He was a man, take him for all in all,
  I shall not look upon his like again.
HORATIO. My lord, I think I saw him yesternight.
HAMLET. Saw? Who?
HORATIO. My lord, the King your father.
HAMLET.   The King my father?
HORATIO. Season your admiration for a while
  With an attent ear, till I may deliver,
  Upon the witness of these gentlemen,
  This marvel to you.
HAMLET.   For God's love, let me hear.
HORATIO. Two nights together had these gentlemen,
  Marcellus and Barnardo, on their watch,
  In the dead waste and middle of the night,

Been thus encountered. A figure like your father
Armed at point exactly, cap-a-pe,
Appears before them, and with solemn march
Goes slow and stately by them. Thrice he walked
By their oppressed and fear-surprised eyes,
Within his truncheon's length; whilst they, distilled
Almost to jelly with the act of fear,
Stand dumb and speak not to him. This to me
In dreadful secrecy impart they did;
And I with them the third night kept the watch,
Where, as they had delivered, both in time,
Form of the thing, each word made true and good,
The apparition comes. I knew your father;
These hands are not more like.

HAMLET.   But where was this?

MARCELLUS. My lord, upon the platform where we
  watched.

HAMLET. Did you not speak to it?

HORATIO.   My lord, I did;
  But answer made it none. Yet once methought
  It lifted up it head and did address
  Itself to motion, like as it would speak;
  But even then the morning cock crew loud,
  And at the sound it shrunk in haste away,
  And vanished from our sight.

HAMLET.   'Tis very strange.

HORATIO. As I do live, my honoured lord, 'tis true;
  And we did think it writ down in our duty
  To let you know of it.

HAMLET. Indeed, indeed, sirs, but this troubles me.
  Hold you the watch tonight?

MARCELLUS. ⎫
BARNARDO. ⎭   We do, my lord.

HAMLET. Armed, say you?

MARCELLUS. ⎫
BARNARDO. ⎬ Armed, my lord.

HAMLET. From top to toe?

MARCELLUS. ⎫
BARNARDO. ⎬   My lord, from head to foot.

HAMLET. Then saw you not his face?

HORATIO. O, yes, my lord; he wore his beaver up.

HAMLET. What, looked he frowningly?

HORATIO. A countenance more in sorrow than in anger.

HAMLET. Pale or red?

HORATIO. Nay, very pale.

HAMLET.   And fixed his eyes upon you?

HORATIO. Most constantly.

HAMLET.   I would I had been there.

HORATIO. It would have much amazed you.

HAMLET. Very like, very like. Stayed it long?

HORATIO. While one with moderate haste might tell a
  hundred.

MARCELLUS. ⎫
BARNARDO. ⎬ Longer, longer.

HORATIO. Not when I saw 't.

HAMLET.   His beard was grizzled—no?

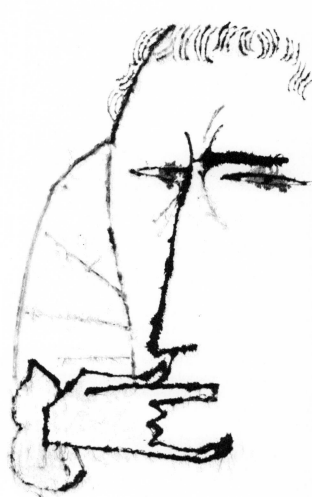

HORATIO. It was, as I have seen it in his life,
  A sable silvered.

HAMLET.   I will watch tonight;
  Perchance 'twill walk again.

HORATIO.   I warrant it will.

HAMLET. If it assume my noble father's person,
  I'll speak to it, though hell itself should gape
  And bid me hold my peace. I pray you all,
  If you have hitherto concealed this sight,
  Let it be tenable in your silence still;
  And whatsoever else shall hap tonight,
  Give it an understanding, but no tongue.
  I will requite your loves. So, fare you well;

Upon the platform, 'twixt eleven and twelve,
I'll visit you.
ALL.   Our duty to your honour.
HAMLET. Your loves, as mine to you; farewell.

Exeunt all but HAMLET

My father's spirit in arms! All is not well;
I doubt some foul play. Would the night were come!
Till then sit still, my soul; foul deeds will rise,
Though all the earth o'erwhelm them, to men's eyes.

Exit

SCENE III   *A room in Polonius' house*

Enter LAERTES *and* OPHELIA

LAERTES. My necessaries are embarked; farewell;
   And, sister, as the winds give benefit
   And convoy is assistant, do not sleep,
   But let me hear from you.
OPHELIA.   Do you doubt that?
LAERTES. For Hamlet and the trifling of his favour,
   Hold it a fashion and a toy in blood,
   A violet in the youth of primy nature,
   Forward, not permanent, sweet, not lasting,
   The perfume and suppliance of a minute;
   No more.
OPHELIA. No more but so?
LAERTES.   Think it no more;
   For nature, crescent, does not grow alone
   In thews and bulk, but, as this temple waxes,
   The inward service of the mind and soul
   Grows wide withal. Perhaps he loves you now,
   And now no soil nor cautel doth besmirch
   The virtue of his will; but you must fear
   His greatness weighed, his will is not his own;
   For he himself is subject to his birth.
   He may not, as unvalued persons do,
   Carve for himself; for on his choice depends
   The safety and health of this whole state;
   And therefore must his choice be circumscribed
   Unto the voice and yielding of that body
   Whereof he is the head. Then if he says he loves you,
   It fits your wisdom so far to believe it
   As he in his particular act and place
   May give his saying deed; which is no further
   Than the main voice of Denmark goes withal.
   Then weigh what loss your honour may sustain,
   If with too credent ear you list his songs,
   Or lose your heart, or your chaste treasure open
   To his unmastered importunity.
   Fear it, Ophelia, fear it, my dear sister,
   And keep you in the rear of your affection,
   Out of the shot and danger of desire.
   The chariest maid is prodigal enough,
   If she unmask her beauty to the moon.
   Virtue itself 'scapes not calumnious strokes;
   The canker galls the infants of the spring,
   Too oft before their buttons be disclosed,
   And in the morn and liquid dew of youth
   Contagious blastments are most imminent.
   Be wary then; best safety lies in fear.
   Youth to itself rebels, though none else near.
OPHELIA. I shall the effect of this good lesson keep,
   As watchman to my heart. But, good my brother,
   Do not, as some ungracious pastors do,
   Show me the steep and thorny way to heaven;
   Whiles, like a puffed and reckless libertine,
   Himself the primrose path of dalliance treads,
   And recks not his own rede.
LAERTES.   O, fear me not.
   I stay too long; but here my father comes.

Enter POLONIUS

   A double blessing is a double grace;
   Occasion smiles upon a second leave.
POLONIUS. Yet here, Laertes! Aboard, aboard, for shame!
   The wind sits in the shoulder of your sail,
   And you are stayed for. There; my blessing with thee!
   And these few precepts in thy memory
   Look thou character. Give thy thoughts no tongue,
   Nor any unproportioned thought his act.
   Be thou familiar, but by no means vulgar.
   Those friends thou hast, and their adoption tried,
   Grapple them to thy soul with hoops of steel;
   But do not dull thy palm with entertainment
   Of each new-hatched, unfledged comrade. Beware
   Of entrance to a quarrel, but being in,
   Bear 't that the opposed may beware of thee.
   Give every man thy ear, but few thy voice;
   Take each man's censure, but reserve thy judgement.
   Costly thy habit as thy purse can buy,
   But not expressed in fancy; rich, not gaudy;
   For the apparel oft proclaims the man,
   And they in France of the best rank and station
   Are of a most select and generous chief in that.
   Neither a borrower nor a lender be;
   For loan oft loses both itself and friend,
   And borrowing dulls the edge of husbandry.
   This above all: to thine own self be true,
   And it must follow, as the night the day,
   Thou canst not then be false to any man.
   Farewell; my blessing season this in thee!
LAERTES. Most humbly do I take my leave, my lord.
POLONIUS. The time invites you. Go; your servants tend.
LAERTES. Farewell, Ophelia; and remember well
   What I have said to you.
OPHELIA.   'Tis in my memory locked,
   And you yourself shall keep the key of it.

LAERTES. Farewell.   *Exit*

POLONIUS. What is 't, Ophelia, he hath said to you?

OPHELIA. So please you, something touching the Lord
    Hamlet.

POLONIUS. Marry, well bethought.
  'Tis told me, he hath very oft of late
  Given private time to you; and you yourself
  Have of your audience been most free and bounteous.
  If it be so, as so 'tis put on me,
  And that in way of caution, I must tell you,
  You do not understand yourself so clearly
  As it behoves my daughter and your honour.
  What is between you? Give me up the truth.

OPHELIA. He hath, my lord, of late made many tenders
  Of his affection to me.

POLONIUS. Affection? Pooh! You speak like a green
    girl,
  Unsifted in such perilous circumstance.
  Do you believe his tenders, as you call them?

OPHELIA. I do not know, my lord, what I should think.

POLONIUS. Marry, I'll teach you. Think yourself a baby;
  That you have ta'en these tenders for true pay,
  Which are not sterling. Tender yourself more dearly;
  Or—not to crack the wind of the poor phrase,
  Running it thus—you'll tender me a fool.

OPHELIA. My lord, he hath importuned me with love
  In honourable fashion.

POLONIUS. Ay, fashion you may call it. Go to, go to!

OPHELIA. And hath given countenance to his speech,
  my lord,
  With almost all the holy vows of heaven.

POLONIUS. Ay, springes to catch woodcocks. I do know,
  When the blood burns, how prodigal the soul
  Lends the tongue vows. These blazes, daughter,
  Giving more light than heat, extinct in both,
  Even in their promise, as it is a-making,
  You must not take for fire. From this time
  Be somewhat scanter of your maiden presence;
  Set your entreatments at a higher rate
  Than a command to parley. For Lord Hamlet,
  Believe so much in him, that he is young,
  And with a larger tether may he walk
  Than may be given you. In few, Ophelia,
  Do not believe his vows; for they are brokers,
  Not of that dye which their investments show,
  But mere implorators of unholy suits,
  Breathing like sanctified and pious bawds,
  The better to beguile. This is for all:
  I would not, in plain terms, from this time forth,
  Have you so slander any moment leisure,
  As to give words or talk with the Lord Hamlet.
  Look to 't, I charge you. Come your ways.

OPHELIA. I shall obey, my lord.
                              Exeunt

SCENE IV *The platform*

Enter HAMLET, HORATIO, *and* MARCELLUS

HAMLET. The air bites shrewdly; it is very cold.

HORATIO. It is a nipping and an eager air.

HAMLET. What hour now?

HORATIO.   I think it lacks of twelve.

MARCELLUS. No, it is struck.

HORATIO. Indeed? I heard it not. Then it draws near
    the season
  Wherein the spirit held his wont to walk.
            A flourish of trumpets, and ordnance
                      shot off, within
  What does this mean, my lord?

HAMLET. The King doth wake tonight and takes his
    rouse,
  Keeps wassail, and the swaggering upspring reels;
  And, as he drains his draughts of Rhenish down,
  The kettle-drum and trumpet thus bray out
  The triumph of his pledge.

HORATIO.   Is it a custom?

HAMLET. Ay, marry, is 't.
  But to my mind, though I am native here
  And to the manner born, it is a custom
  More honoured in the breach than the observance.
  This heavy-headed revel east and west

Makes us traduced and taxed of other nations.
They clepe us drunkards, and with swinish phrase
Soil our addition; and indeed it takes
From our achievements, though performed at height,
The pith and marrow of our attribute.
So, oft it chances in particular men,
That for some vicious mole of nature in them,
As, in their birth—wherein they are not guilty,
Since nature cannot choose his origin—
By the o'ergrowth of some complexion,
Oft breaking down the pales and forts of reason,
Or by some habit that too much o'er-leavens
The form of plausive manners, that these men,
Carrying, I say, the stamp of one defect,
Being nature's livery, or fortune's star,
Their virtues else—be they as pure as grace,
As infinite as man may undergo—
Shall in the general censure take corruption
From that particular fault; the dram of evil
Doth all the noble substance of a doubt
To his own scandal.

HORATIO.   Look, my lord, it comes!
          Enter Ghost

HAMLET. Angels and ministers of grace defend us!
  Be thou a spirit of health or goblin damned,
  Bring with thee airs from heaven or blasts from hell,
  Be thy intents wicked or charitable,
  Thou comest in such a questionable shape
  That I will speak to thee. I'll call thee Hamlet,
  King, father, royal Dane. O, answer me!
  Let me not burst in ignorance; but tell
  Why thy canonized bones, hearsed in death,
  Have burst their cerements; why the sepulchre,
  Wherein we saw thee quietly interred,
  Hath oped his ponderous and marble jaws,
  To cast thee up again. What may this mean,
  That thou, dead corpse, again in complete steel
  Revisit'st thus the glimpses of the moon,
  Making night hideous; and we fools of nature
  So horridly to shake our disposition
  With thoughts beyond the reaches of our souls?
  Say, why is this? Wherefore? What should we do?
                  Ghost *beckons* HAMLET

HORATIO. It beckons you to go away with it,
  As if it some impartment did desire
  To you alone.
MARCELLUS.   Look, with what courteous action
  It waves you to a more removed ground;
  But do not go with it.
HORATIO.   No, by no means.
HAMLET. It will not speak; then I will follow it.
HORATIO. Do not, my lord.
HAMLET.   Why, what should be the fear?
  I do not set my life at a pin's fee;
  And for my soul, what can it do to that,
  Being a thing immortal as itself?
  It waves me forth again; I'll follow it.
HORATIO. What if it tempt you toward the flood, my
    lord,
  Or to the dreadful summit of the cliff
  That beetles o'er his base into the sea,
  And there assume some other horrible form,
  Which might deprive your sovereignty of reason
  And draw you into madness? Think of it.
  The very place puts toys of desperation,

Without more motive, into every brain
That looks so many fathoms to the sea
And hears it roar beneath.
HAMLET.   It waves me still.
  Go on; I'll follow thee.
MARCELLUS. You shall not go, my lord.
HAMLET.   Hold off your hands.
HORATIO. Be ruled; you shall not go.
HAMLET.   My fate cries out,
  And makes each petty artery in this body
  As hardy as the Nemean lion's nerve.
  Still am I called. Unhand me, gentlemen.
  By heaven, I'll make a ghost of him that lets me!
  I say, away! Go on; I'll follow thee.
                              Exeunt Ghost *and* HAMLET
HORATIO. He waxes desperate with imagination.
MARCELLUS. Let's follow; 'tis not fit thus to obey him.
HORATIO. Have after. To what issue will this come?
MARCELLUS. Something is rotten in the state of Den-
    mark.
HORATIO. Heaven will direct it.
MARCELLUS.   Nay, let's follow him. *Exeunt*

SCENE V *Another part of the platform*

Enter Ghost *and* HAMLET

HAMLET. Where wilt thou lead me? Speak; I'll go no
    further.
GHOST. Mark me.
HAMLET.   I will.
GHOST.   My hour is almost come,
  When I to sulph'rous and tormenting flames
  Must render up myself.
HAMLET.   Alas, poor ghost!
GHOST. Pity me not, but lend thy serious hearing
  To what I shall unfold.
HAMLET.   Speak; I am bound to hear.
GHOST. So art thou to revenge, when thou shalt hear.
HAMLET. What?
GHOST. I am thy father's spirit,
  Doomed for a certain term to walk the night,
  And for the day confined to fast in fires,
  Till the foul crimes done in my days of nature
  Are burnt and purged away. But that I am forbid
  To tell the secrets of my prison-house,
  I could a tale unfold whose lightest word
  Would harrow up thy soul, freeze thy young blood,
  Make thy two eyes, like stars, start from their spheres,
  Thy knotted and combined locks to part
  And each particular hair to stand on end,
  Like quills upon the fretful porpentine.
  But this eternal blazon must not be
  To ears of flesh and blood. List, list, O, list!
  If thou didst ever thy dear father love—
HAMLET. O God!
GHOST. Revenge his foul and most unnatural murder.

HAMLET. Murder!
GHOST. Murder most foul, as in the best it is;
  But this most foul, strange and unnatural.
HAMLET. Haste me to know 't, that I, with wings as
    swift
  As meditation or the thoughts of love,
  May sweep to my revenge.
GHOST.   I find thee apt;
  And duller shouldst thou be than the fat weed
  That roots itself in ease on Lethe wharf,
  Wouldst thou not stir in this. Now, Hamlet, hear:
  'Tis given out that, sleeping in my orchard,
  A serpent stung me; so the whole ear of Denmark
  Is by a forged process of my death
  Rankly abused. But know, thou noble youth,
  The serpent that did sting thy father's life
  Now wears his crown.
HAMLET.   O my prophetic soul!
  My uncle!
GHOST. Ay, that incestuous, that adulterate beast,
  With witchcraft of his wit, with traitorous gifts—
  O wicked wit and gifts, that have the power
  So to seduce!—won to his shameful lust
  The will of my most seeming-virtuous Queen.
  O Hamlet, what a falling-off was there!
  From me, whose love was of that dignity
  That it went hand in hand even with the vow
  I made to her in marriage, and to decline
  Upon a wretch whose natural gifts were poor
  To those of mine!

But virtue, as it never will be moved,
Though lewdness court it in a shape of heaven,
So lust, though to a radiant angel linked,
Will sate itself in a celestial bed,
And prey on garbage.
But, soft! Methinks I scent the morning air;
Brief let me be. Sleeping within my orchard,
My custom always of the afternoon,
Upon my secure hour thy uncle stole,
With juice of cursed hebenon in a vial,
And in the porches of my ears did pour
The leperous distilment; whose effect
Holds such an enmity with blood of man
That swift as quicksilver it courses through
The natural gates and alleys of the body,
And with a sudden vigour it doth posset
And curd, like eager droppings into milk,
The thin and wholesome blood. So did it mine;
And a most instant tetter barked about,
Most lazar-like, with vile and loathsome crust,
All my smooth body.
Thus was I, sleeping, by a brother's hand
Of life, of crown, of queen, at once dispatched;
Cut off even in the blossoms of my sin,
Unhouseled, disappointed, unaneled,
No reckoning made, but sent to my account
With all my imperfections on my head.
O, horrible! O, horrible! most horrible!
If thou hast nature in thee, bear it not;
Let not the royal bed of Denmark be
A couch for luxury and damned incest.
But, howsoever thou pursuest this act,
Taint not thy mind, nor let thy soul contrive
Against thy mother aught. Leave her to heaven
And to those thorns that in her bosom lodge,
To prick and sting her. Fare thee well at once!
The glow-worm shows the matin to be near,
And 'gins to pale his uneffectual fire.
Adieu, adieu! Hamlet, remember me.

Exit

HAMLET. O all you host of heaven! O earth! what else?
And shall I couple hell? O, fie! Hold, hold, my heart;
And you, my sinews, grow not instant old,
But bear me stiffly up. Remember thee!
Ay, thou poor ghost, while memory holds a seat
In this distracted globe. Remember thee!
Yea, from the table of my memory
I'll wipe away all trivial fond records,
All saws of books, all forms, all pressures past,
That youth and observation copied there;
And thy commandment all alone shall live
Within the book and volume of my brain,
Unmixed with baser matter. Yes, by heaven!
O most pernicious woman!
O villain, villain, smiling, damned villain!
My tables—meet it is I set it down,

That one may smile, and smile, and be a villain;
At least I'm sure it may be so in Denmark.   *Writing*
So, uncle, there you are. Now to my word;
It is "Adieu, adieu! Remember me."
I have sworn 't.

MARCELLUS. }
HORATIO.   } [*Within*] My lord, my lord—

MARCELLUS.   [*Within*] Lord Hamlet—
HORATIO.   [*Within*] Heaven secure him!
HAMLET. So be it!
HORATIO. [*Within*] Hillo, ho, ho, my lord!
HAMLET. Hillo, ho, ho, boy! Come, bird, come.

Enter HORATIO *and* MARCELLUS

MARCELLUS. How is 't, my noble lord?
HORATIO.   What news, my lord?
HAMLET. O, wonderful!
HORATIO.   Good my lord, tell it.
HAMLET. No; you'll reveal it.
HORATIO. Not I, my lord, by heaven.
MARCELLUS.   Nor I, my lord.
HAMLET. How say you, then; would heart of man once
    think it?
    But you'll be secret?
HORATIO.   }
MARCELLUS. }   Ay, by heaven, my lord.
HAMLET. There's ne'er a villain dwelling in all Den-
    mark
    But he's an arrant knave.
HORATIO. There needs no ghost, my lord, come from
    the grave
    To tell us this.
HAMLET.   Why, right; you are i' the right;
    And so, without more circumstance at all,
    I hold it fit that we shake hands and part;
    You, as your business and desire shall point you;
    For every man has business and desire,
    Such as it is; and for mine own poor part,
    Look you, I'll go pray.
HORATIO. These are but wild and whirling words, my
    lord.
HAMLET. I'm sorry they offend you, heartily;
    Yes, 'faith, heartily.
HORATIO.   There's no offence, my lord.
HAMLET. Yes, by Saint Patrick, but there is, Horatio,
    And much offence too. Touching this vision here,
    It is an honest ghost, that let me tell you;
    For your desire to know what is between us,
    O'ermaster 't as you may. And now, good friends,
    As you are friends, scholars and soldiers,
    Give me one poor request.
HORATIO. What is 't, my lord? We will.
HAMLET. Never make known what you have seen to-
    night.
HORATIO.   }
MARCELLUS. } My lord, we will not.

HAMLET.   Nay, but swear 't.

HORATIO.   In faith,
  My lord, not I.

MARCELLUS.   Nor I, my lord, in faith.

HAMLET. Upon my sword.

MARCELLUS.   We have sworn, my lord, already.

HAMLET. Indeed, upon my sword, indeed.

GHOST. [*Beneath*] Swear.

HAMLET. Ah, ha, boy! Say'st thou so? Art thou there,
    truepenny?
  Come on—you hear this fellow in the cellarage—
  Consent to swear.

HORATIO.   Propose the oath, my lord.

HAMLET. Never to speak of this that you have seen,
  Swear by my sword.

GHOST. [*Beneath*] Swear.

HAMLET. Hic et ubique? Then we'll shift our ground.
  Come hither, gentlemen,
  And lay your hands again upon my sword:
  Never to speak of this that you have heard,
  Swear by my sword.

GHOST. [*Beneath*] Swear.

HAMLET. Well said, old mole! Canst work i' the earth
    so fast?
  A worthy pioner! Once more remove, good friends.

HORATIO. O day and night, but this is wondrous strange!

HAMLET. And therefore as a stranger give it welcome.
  There are more things in heaven and earth, Horatio,
  Than are dreamt of in your philosophy.
  But come;
  Here, as before, never, so help you mercy,
  How strange or odd soe'er I bear myself,
  As I perchance hereafter shall think meet
  To put an antic disposition on,
  That you, at such times seeing me, never shall,
  With arms encumbered thus, or this headshake,
  Or by pronouncing of some doubtful phrase,
  As "Well, well, we know," or "We could, an if we
    would,"
  Or "If we list to speak," or "There be, an if they
    might,"
  Or such ambiguous giving out, to note
  That you know aught of me—this not to do,
  So grace and mercy at your most need help you,
  Swear.

GHOST. [*Beneath*] Swear.

HAMLET. Rest, rest, perturbed spirit! [*They swear*] So,
    gentlemen,
  With all my love I do commend me to you.
  And what so poor a man as Hamlet is
  May do, to express his love and friending to you,
  God willing, shall not lack. Let us go in together;
  And still your fingers on your lips, I pray.
  The time is out of joint. O cursed spite,
  That ever I was born to set it right!
  Nay, come, let's go together.   *Exeunt*

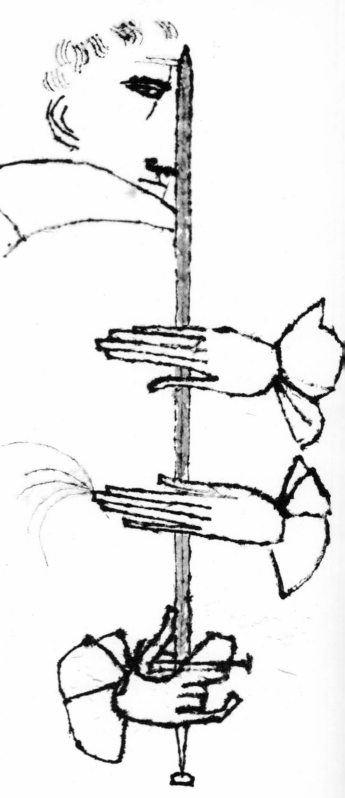

ACT II

SCENE I *A room in Polonius' house*

Enter POLONIUS *and* REYNALDO

POLONIUS. Give him this money and these notes,
    Reynaldo.
REYNALDO. I will, my lord.
POLONIUS. You shall do marvellous wisely, good
    Reynaldo,
  Before you visit him, to make inquire
  Of his behaviour.
REYNALDO.   My lord, I did intend it.
POLONIUS. Marry, well said; very well said. Look you,
    sir,
  Inquire me first what Danskers are in Paris;
  And how, and who, what means, and where they keep,
  What company, at what expense; and finding
  By this encompassment and drift of question
  That they do know my son, come you more nearer
  Than your particular demands will touch it.
  Take you, as 'twere, some distant knowledge of him;
  As thus, "I know his father and his friends,
  And in part him." Do you mark this, Reynaldo?
REYNALDO. Ay, very well, my lord.
POLONIUS. "And in part him; but," you may say,
    "not well.
  But, if 't be he I mean, he 's very wild;
  Addicted so and so"; and there put on him
  What forgeries you please—marry, none so rank
  As may dishonour him, take heed of that—
  But, sir, such wanton, wild and usual slips
  As are companions noted and most known
  To youth and liberty.
REYNALDO.   As gaming, my lord.
POLONIUS. Ay, or drinking, fencing, swearing, quarrel-
    ling,
  Drabbing; you may go so far.
REYNALDO. My lord, that would dishonour him.
POLONIUS. 'Faith, no; as you may season it in the charge.
  You must not put another scandal on him,
  That he is open to incontinency;
  That's not my meaning. But breathe his faults so
    quaintly
  That they may seem the taints of liberty,
  The flash and outbreak of a fiery mind,
  A savageness in unreclaimed blood,
  Of general assault.
REYNALDO.   But, my good lord—
POLONIUS. Wherefore should you do this?
REYNALDO.   Ay, my lord,
  I would know that.
POLONIUS.   Marry, sir, here's my drift;
  And, I believe, it is a fetch of wit.
  You laying these slight sullies on my son,

As 'twere a thing a little soiled i' the working,
Mark you,
Your party in converse, him you would sound,
Having ever seen in the prenominate crimes
The youth you breathe of guilty, be assured
He closes with you in this consequence;
"Good sir," or so, or "friend," or "gentleman,"
According to the phrase or the addition
Of man and country.
REYNALDO.   Very good, my lord.
POLONIUS. And then, sir, does he this—he does—
  what was I about to say? By the mass, I was about to
  say something. Where did I leave?
REYNALDO. At "closes in the consequence," at "friend
  or so," and "gentleman."
POLONIUS. At "closes in the consequence," ay, marry;
  He closes thus: "I know the gentleman;
  I saw him yesterday, or t' other day,
  Or then, or then; with such, or such; and, as you say,
  There was a' gaming; there o'ertook in 's rouse;
  There falling out at tennis"; or perchance,
  "I saw him enter such a house of sale,"
  Videlicet, a brothel, or so forth.
  See you now;
  Your bait of falsehood takes this carp of truth;
  And thus do we of wisdom and of reach,
  With windlasses and with assays of bias,
  By indirections find directions out.
  So by my former lecture and advice,
  Shall you my son. You have me, have you not?
REYNALDO. My lord, I have.
POLONIUS.   God be wi' you; fare you well.
REYNALDO. Good my lord!
POLONIUS. Observe his inclination in yourself.
REYNALDO. I shall, my lord.
POLONIUS. And let him ply his music.
REYNALDO.   Well, my lord.
POLONIUS. Farewell!   *Exit* REYNALDO

Enter OPHELIA
        How now, Ophelia! What's the matter?
OPHELIA. O, my lord, my lord, I have been so affrighted!
POLONIUS. With what, i' the name of God?
OPHELIA. My lord, as I was sewing in my closet,
  Lord Hamlet, with his doublet all unbraced;
  No hat upon his head; his stockings fouled,
  Ungartered, and down-gyved to his ankle;
  Pale as his shirt; his knees knocking each other;
  And with a look so piteous in purport
  As if he had been loosed out of hell
  To speak of horrors—he comes before me.

POLONIUS. Mad for thy love?

OPHELIA.   My lord, I do not know;
   But truly, I do fear it.

POLONIUS.   What said he?

OPHELIA. He took me by the wrist and held me hard;
   Then goes he to the length of all his arm;
   And, with his other hand thus o'er his brow,
   He falls to such perusal of my face
   As he would draw it. Long stayed he so;
   At last, a little shaking of mine arm
   And thrice his head thus waving up and down,
   He raised a sigh so piteous and profound
   As it did seem to shatter all his bulk
   And end his being. That done, he lets me go;
   And, with his head over his shoulder turned,
   He seemed to find his way without his eyes;
   For out o' doors he went without their helps,
   And, to the last, bended their light on me.

POLONIUS. Come, go with me; I will go seek the King.
   This is the very ecstasy of love,

Whose violent property fordoes itself
And leads the will to desperate undertakings
As oft as any passion under heaven
That does afflict our natures. I am sorry.
What, have you given him any hard words of late?

OPHELIA. No, my good lord, but, as you did command,
   I did repel his letters and denied
   His access to me.

POLONIUS.   That hath made him mad.
   I am sorry that with better heed and judgement
   I had not quoted him. I feared he did but trifle,
   And meant to wreck thee; but, beshrew my jealousy!
   By heaven, it is as proper to our age
   To cast beyond ourselves in our opinions
   As it is common for the younger sort
   To lack discretion. Come, go we to the King.
   This must be known; which, being kept close, might
      move
   More grief to hide than hate to utter love.

                                              Exeunt

SCENE II *A room in the castle*

Enter KING, QUEEN, ROSENCRANTZ, GUILDENSTERN, *and* Attendants

KING. Welcome, dear Rosencrantz and Guildenstern!
   Moreover that we much did long to see you,
   The need we have to use you did provoke
   Our hasty sending. Something have you heard
   Of Hamlet's transformation; so call it,
   Sith nor the exterior nor the inward man
   Resembles that it was. What it should be,
   More than his father's death, that thus hath put him
   So much from the understanding of himself,
   I cannot dream of. I entreat you both,
   That, being of so young days brought up with him,
   And sith so neighboured to his youth and haviour,
   That you vouchsafe your rest here in our court
   Some little time; so by your companies
   To draw him on to pleasures, and to gather,
   So much as from occasion you may glean,
   Whether aught, to us unknown, afflicts him thus,
   That, opened, lies within our remedy.

QUEEN. Good gentlemen, he hath much talked of you;
   And sure I am two men there are not living
   To whom he more adheres. If it will please you
   To show us so much gentry and good will
   As to expend your time with us awhile,
   For the supply and profit of our hope,
   Your visitation shall receive such thanks
   As fits a king's remembrance.

ROSENCRANTZ.   Both your majesties
   Might, by the sovereign power you have of us,
   Put your dread pleasures more into command
   Than to entreaty.

GUILDENSTERN.   But we both obey,

And here give up ourselves, in the full bent
To lay our service freely at your feet,
To be commanded.

KING. Thanks, Rosencrantz and gentle Guildenstern.

QUEEN. Thanks, Guildenstern and gentle Rosencrantz.
   And I beseech you instantly to visit
   My too much changed son. Go, some of you,
   And bring these gentlemen where Hamlet is.

GUILDENSTERN. Heavens make our presence and our
      practices
   Pleasant and helpful to him!

QUEEN.   Ay, amen!

                    Exeunt ROSENCRANTZ, GUILDENSTERN,
                             and some Attendants

                       Enter POLONIUS

POLONIUS. The ambassadors from Norway, my good
      lord,
   Are joyfully returned.

KING. Thou still hast been the father of good news.

POLONIUS. Have I, my lord? I assure my good liege,
   I hold my duty, as I hold my soul,
   Both to my God and to my gracious king;
   And I do think, or else this brain of mine
   Hunts not the trail of policy so sure
   As it hath used to do, that I have found
   The very cause of Hamlet's lunacy.

KING. O, speak of that; that do I long to hear.

POLONIUS. Give first admittance to the ambassadors;
   My news shall be the fruit to that great feast.

KING. Thyself do grace to them, and bring them in.

                                          Exit POLONIUS

He tells me, my dear Gertrude, he hath found
The head and source of all your son's distemper.
QUEEN. I doubt it is no other but the main;
His father's death, and our o'erhasty marriage.
KING. Well, we shall sift him.
Re-enter POLONIUS, *with* VOLTIMAND *and* CORNELIUS
Welcome, my good friends!
Say, Voltimand, what from our brother Norway?
VOLTIMAND. Most fair return of greetings and desires.
Upon our first, he sent out to suppress
His nephew's levies, which to him appeared
To be a preparation 'gainst the Polack;
But, better looked into, he truly found
It was against your highness. Whereat grieved,
That so his sickness, age and impotence
Was falsely borne in hand, sends out arrests
On Fortinbras; which he, in brief, obeys;
Receives rebuke from Norway, and in fine
Makes vow before his uncle never more
To give the assay of arms against your majesty.
Whereon old Norway, overcome with joy,

Gives him three thousand crowns in annual fee,
And his commission to employ those soldiers,
So levied as before, against the Polack:
With an entreaty, herein further shown,
Giving him a paper
That it might please you to give quiet pass
Through your dominions for this enterprise,
On such regards of safety and allowance
As therein are set down.
KING. It likes us well;
And at our more considered time we'll read,
Answer, and think upon this business.
Meantime we thank you for your well-took labour.
Go to your rest; at night we'll feast together.
Most welcome home!
Exeunt VOLTIMAND *and* CORNELIUS
POLONIUS. This business is well ended.
My liege, and madam, to expostulate
What majesty should be, what duty is
Why day is day, night night, and time is time,
Were nothing but to waste night, day and time.

Therefore, since brevity is the soul of wit,
And tediousness the limbs and outward flourishes,
I will be brief. Your noble son is mad.
Mad call I it; for, to define true madness,
What is 't but to be nothing else but mad?
But let that go.
QUEEN.   More matter, with less art.
POLONIUS. Madam, I swear I use no art at all.
That he is mad, 'tis true; 'tis true 'tis pity,
And pity 'tis 'tis true; a foolish figure;
But farewell it, for I will use no art.
Mad let us grant him, then; and now remains
That we find out the cause of this effect,
Or rather say, the cause of this defect,
For this effect defective comes by cause.
Thus it remains, and the remainder thus.
Perpend.
I have a daughter—have while she is mine—
Who, in her duty and obedience, mark,
Hath given me this. Now gather, and surmise.   *Reads*
"To the celestial and my soul's idol, the most beauti-
fied Ophelia,—"
That's an ill phrase, a vile phrase; "beautified" is a
vile phrase; but you shall hear. Thus: *Reads*
"In her excellent white bosom, these, &c."
QUEEN. Came this from Hamlet to her?
POLONIUS. Good madam, stay awhile; I will be faithful.
                                              Reads

        "Doubt thou the stars are fire;
          Doubt that the sun doth move;
        Doubt truth to be a liar;
          But never doubt I love.

    "O dear Ophelia, I am ill at these numbers; I
have not art to reckon my groans; but that I love
thee best, O most best, believe it. Adieu.
            "Thine evermore, most dear lady, whilst
                this machine is to him, HAMLET."
This, in obedience, hath my daughter shown me,
And more above, hath his solicitings,
As they fell out by time, by means and place,
All given to mine ear.
KING.   But how hath she
Received his love?
POLONIUS.   What do you think of me?
KING. As of a man faithful and honourable.
POLONIUS. I would fain prove so. But what might you
    think,
When I had seen this hot love on the wing—
As I perceived it, I must tell you that,
Before my daughter told me—what might you,
Or my dear majesty your Queen here, think,
If I had played the desk or table-book,
Or given my heart a winking, mute and dumb,
Or looked upon this love with idle sight;
What might you think? No, I went round to work,
And my young mistress thus I did bespeak:

"Lord Hamlet is a prince, out of thy star;
This must not be"; and then I prescripts gave her,
That she should lock herself from his resort,
Admit no messengers, receive no tokens.
Which done, she took the fruits of my advice,
And he, repulsed—a short tale to make—
Fell into a sadness, then into a fast,
Thence to a watch, thence into a weakness,
Thence to a lightness, and, by this declension,
Into the madness wherein now he raves,
And all we mourn for.
KING.   Do you think 'tis this?
QUEEN. It may be, very likely.
POLONIUS. Hath there been such a time—I'd fain know
    that—
That I have positively said " 'Tis so,"
When it proved otherwise?
KING.   Not that I know.
POLONIUS. [*Pointing to his head and shoulder*] Take this
    from this, if this be otherwise.
If circumstances lead me, I will find
Where truth is hid, though it were hid indeed
Within the centre.
KING.   How may we try it further?
POLONIUS. You know, sometimes he walks four hours
    together
Here in the lobby.
QUEEN.   So he does indeed.
POLONIUS. At such a time I'll loose my daughter to him.
Be you and I behind an arras then;
Mark the encounter. If he love her not
And be not from his reason fall'n thereon,
Let me be no assistant for a state,
But keep a farm and carters.
KING.   We will try it.
QUEEN. But, look, where sadly the poor wretch comes
    reading.
POLONIUS. Away, I do beseech you, both away:
    I'll board him presently.
            Exeunt KING, QUEEN, *and* Attendants

            Enter HAMLET, *reading*

                    O, give me leave.
How does my good Lord Hamlet?
HAMLET. Well, God-a-mercy.
POLONIUS. Do you know me, my lord?
HAMLET. Excellent well; you are a fishmonger.
POLONIUS. Not I, my lord.
HAMLET. Then I would you were so honest a man.
POLONIUS. Honest, my lord!
HAMLET. Ay, sir; to be honest, as this world goes, is
    to be one man picked out of ten thousand.
POLONIUS. That's very true, my lord.
HAMLET. For if the sun breed maggots in a dead dog,
    being a god kissing carrion—Have you a daughter?
POLONIUS. I have, my lord.

HAMLET. Let her not walk i' the sun. Conception is a blessing; but not as your daughter may conceive. Friend, look to 't.

POLONIUS. [Aside] How say you by that? Still harping on my daughter. Yet he knew me not at first; he said I was a fishmonger. He is far gone, far gone; and truly in my youth I suffered much extremity for love; very near this. I'll speak to him again. What do you read, my lord?

HAMLET. Words, words, words.

POLONIUS. What is the matter, my lord?

HAMLET. Between who?

POLONIUS. I mean, the matter that you read, my lord.

HAMLET. Slanders, sir; for the satirical rogue says here that old men have grey beards, that their faces are wrinkled, their eyes purging thick amber and plum-tree gum and that they have a plentiful lack of wit, together with most weak hams; all which, sir, though I most powerfully and potently believe, yet I hold it not honesty to have it thus set down; for you yourself, sir, should be old as I am, if like a crab you could go backward.

POLONIUS. [Aside] Though this be madness, yet there is method in 't. Will you walk out of the air, my lord?

HAMLET. Into my grave.

POLONIUS. Indeed, that is out o' the air. [Aside] How pregnant sometimes his replies are!—a happiness that often madness hits on, which reason and sanity could not so prosperously be delivered of. I will leave him, and suddenly contrive the means of meeting between him and my daughter.—My honourable lord, I will most humbly take my leave of you.

HAMLET. You cannot, sir, take from me any thing that I will more willingly part withal; except my life, except my life, except my life.

POLONIUS. Fare you well, my lord.

HAMLET. These tedious old fools!

Enter ROSENCRANTZ *and* GUILDENSTERN

POLONIUS. You go to seek the Lord Hamlet; there he is.

ROSENCRANTZ. [To Polonius] God save you, sir!

Exit POLONIUS

GUILDENSTERN. My honoured lord!

ROSENCRANTZ. My most dear lord!

HAMLET. My excellent good friends! How dost thou, Guildenstern? Ah, Rosencrantz! Good lads, how do ye both?

ROSENCRANTZ. As the indifferent children of the earth.

GUILDENSTERN. Happy, in that we are not over-happy; On Fortune's cap we are not the very button.

HAMLET. Nor the soles of her shoe?

ROSENCRANTZ. Neither, my lord.

HAMLET. Then you live about her waist, or in the middle of her favours?

GUILDENSTERN. 'Faith, her privates we.

HAMLET. In the secret parts of Fortune? O, most true; she is a strumpet. What's the news?

ROSENCRANTZ. None, my lord, but that the world's grown honest.

HAMLET. Then is Doomsday near; but your news is not true. Let me question more in particular: what have you, my good friends, deserved at the hands of Fortune, that she sends you to prison hither?

GUILDENSTERN. Prison, my lord?

HAMLET. Denmark's a prison.

ROSENCRANTZ. Then is the world one.

HAMLET. A goodly one; in which there are many confines, wards and dungeons, Denmark being one o' the worst.

ROSENCRANTZ. We think not so, my lord.

HAMLET. Why, then, 'tis none to you; for there is nothing either good or bad, but thinking makes it so. To me it is a prison.

ROSENCRANTZ. Why then, your ambition makes it one; 'tis too narrow for your mind.

HAMLET. O God, I could be bounded in a nutshell and count myself a king of infinite space, were it not that I have bad dreams.

GUILDENSTERN. Which dreams indeed are ambition, for the very substance of the ambitious is merely the shadow of a dream.

HAMLET. A dream itself is but a shadow.

ROSENCRANTZ. Truly, and I hold ambition of so airy and light a quality that it is but a shadow's shadow.

HAMLET. Then are our beggars bodies, and our monarchs and outstretched heroes the beggars' shadows. Shall we to the court? For, by my fay, I cannot reason.

ROSENCRANTZ.
GUILDENSTERN. } We'll wait upon you.

HAMLET. No such matter. I will not sort you with the rest of my servants, for, to speak to you like an honest man, I am most dreadfully attended. But, in the beaten way of friendship, what make you at Elsinore?

ROSENCRANTZ. To visit you, my lord; no other occasion.

HAMLET. Beggar that I am, I am even poor in thanks; but I thank you; and sure, dear friends, my thanks are too dear a halfpenny. Were you not sent for? Is it your own inclining? Is it a free visitation? Come, deal justly with me; come, come; nay, speak.

GUILDENSTERN. What should we say, my lord?

HAMLET. Why, anything, but to the purpose. You were sent for; and there is a kind of confession in your looks which your modesties have not craft enough to colour. I know the good King and Queen have sent for you.

ROSENCRANTZ. To what end, my lord?

HAMLET. That you must teach me. But let me conjure you, by the rights of our fellowship, by the consonancy of our youth, by the obligation of our ever-preserved love, and by what more dear a better proposer could charge you withal, be even and direct with me, whether you were sent for, or no?

ROSENCRANTZ. [Aside to Guildenstern] What say you?

HAMLET. [*Aside*] Nay, then, I have an eye of you.—
If you love me, hold not off.
GUILDENSTERN. My lord, we were sent for.
HAMLET. I will tell you why; so shall my anticipation
prevent your discovery, and your secrecy to the King
and Queen moult no feather. I have of late—but
wherefore I know not—lost all my mirth, forgone all
custom of exercises; and indeed it goes so heavily
with my disposition, that this goodly frame, the earth,
seems to me a sterile promontory, this most excellent
canopy, the air, look you, this brave o'erhanging
firmament, this majestical roof fretted with golden
fire, why, it appears no other thing to me than a foul
and pestilent congregation of vapours. What a piece
of work is a man, how noble in reason, how infinite
in faculties, in form and moving how express and admirable, in action how like an angel, in apprehension
how like a god—the beauty of the world, the paragon
of animals! And yet, to me, what is this quintessence
of dust? Man delights not me; no, nor woman
neither, though by your smiling you seem to say so.
ROSENCRANTZ. My lord, there was no such stuff in my
thoughts.
HAMLET. Why did you laugh then, when I said "man
delights not me"?
ROSENCRANTZ. To think, my lord, if you delight not in
man, what lenten entertainment the players shall re-

ceive from you. We coted them on the way; and hither are they coming, to offer you service.

HAMLET. He that plays the king shall be welcome; his majesty shall have tribute of me; the adventurous knight shall use his foil and target; the lover shall not sigh gratis; the humorous man shall end his part in peace; the clown shall make those laugh whose lungs are tickle o' the sere; and the lady shall say her mind freely or the blank verse shall halt for 't. What players are they?

ROSENCRANTZ. Even those you were wont to take delight in, the tragedians of the city.

HAMLET. How chances it they travel? Their residence, both in reputation and profit, was better both ways.

ROSENCRANTZ. I think their inhibition comes by the means of the late innovation.

HAMLET. Do they hold the same estimation they did when I was in the city? Are they so followed?

ROSENCRANTZ. No, indeed, are they not.

HAMLET. How comes it? Do they grow rusty?

ROSENCRANTZ. Nay, their endeavour keeps in the wonted pace. But there is, sir, an eyrie of children, little eyases, that cry out on the top of question, and are most tyrannically clapped for 't. These are now the fashion, and so berattle the common stages—so they call them—that many wearing rapiers are afraid of goosequills and dare scarce come thither.

HAMLET. What, are they children? Who maintains 'em? How are they escoted? Will they pursue the quality no longer than they can sing? Will they not say afterwards, if they should grow themselves to common players—as it is most like, if their means are no better—their writers do them wrong, to make them exclaim against their own succession?

ROSENCRANTZ. 'Faith, there has been much to do on both sides; and the nation holds it no sin to tarre them to controversy. There was, for a while, no money bid for argument, unless the poet and the player went to cuffs in the question.

HAMLET. Is 't possible?

GUILDENSTERN. O, there has been much throwing about of brains.

HAMLET. Do the boys carry it away?

ROSENCRANTZ. Ay, that they do, my lord; Hercules and his load too.

HAMLET. It is not very strange; for mine uncle is king of Denmark, and those that would make mows at him while my father lived, give twenty, forty, fifty, an hundred ducats apiece for his picture in little. 'Sblood, there is something in this more than natural, if philosophy could find it out.

Flourish of trumpets within

GUILDENSTERN. There are the players.

HAMLET. Gentlemen, you are welcome to Elsinore. Your hands, come then; the appurtenance of welcome is fashion and ceremony. Let me comply with

you in this garb, lest my extent to the players, which, I tell you, must show fairly outward, should more appear like entertainment than yours. You are welcome; but my uncle-father and aunt-mother are deceived.

GUILDENSTERN. In what, my dear lord?

HAMLET. I am but mad north-north-west. When the wind is southerly I know a hawk from a handsaw.

Re-enter POLONIUS

POLONIUS. Well be with you, gentlemen!

HAMLET. Hark you, Guildenstern—and you too—at each ear a hearer. That great baby you see there is not yet out of his swaddling-clouts.

ROSENCRANTZ. Happily he's the second time come to them; for they say an old man is twice a child.

HAMLET. I will prophesy he comes to tell me of the players; mark it. You say right, sir; o' Monday morning; 'twas so indeed.

POLONIUS. My lord, I have news to tell you.

HAMLET. My lord, I have news to tell you.
When Roscius was an actor in Rome—

POLONIUS. The actors are come hither, my lord.

HAMLET. Buz, buz!

POLONIUS. Upon mine honour—

HAMLET. Then came each actor on his ass—

POLONIUS. The best actors in the world, either for tragedy, comedy, history, pastoral, pastoral-comical, historical-pastoral, tragical-historical, tragical-comical-historical-pastoral, scene individable, or poem unlimited. Seneca cannot be too heavy, nor Plautus too light, for the law of writ and the liberty. These are the only men.

HAMLET. O Jephthah, judge of Israel, what a treasure hadst thou!

POLONIUS. What a treasure had he, my lord?

HAMLET. Why,
"One fair daughter, and no more,
The which he loved passing well."

POLONIUS. [*Aside*] Still on my daughter.

HAMLET. Am I not i' the right, old Jephthah?

POLONIUS. If you call me Jephthah, my lord, I have a daughter that I love passing well.

HAMLET. Nay, that follows not.

POLONIUS. What follows, then, my lord?

HAMLET. Why,
"As by lot, God wot,"
and then, you know,
"It came to pass, as most like it was,"—
the first row of the pious chanson will show you more; for look, where my abridgement comes.

Enter four or five Players

You are welcome, masters; welcome, all. I am glad to see thee well. Welcome, good friends. O, my old friend! Thy face is valanced since I saw thee last.

Comest thou to beard me in Denmark? What, my young lady and mistress! By 'r lady, your ladyship is nearer to heaven than when I saw you last, by the altitude of a chopine. Pray God, your voice, like a piece of uncurrent gold, be not cracked within the ring. Masters, you are all welcome. We'll e'en to 't like French falconers, fly at any thing we see. We'll have a speech straight. Come, give us a taste of your quality; come, a passionate speech.

FIRST PLAYER. What speech, my lord?

HAMLET. I heard thee speak me a speech once, but it was never acted; or, if it was, not above once; for the play, I remember, pleased not the million; 'twas caviare to the general: but it was—as I received it, and others, whose judgements in such matters cried in the top of mine—an excellent play, well digested in the scenes, set down with as much modesty as cunning. I remember, one said there were no sallets in the lines to make the matter savoury, nor no matter in the phrase that might indict the author of affectation; but called it an honest method, as wholesome as sweet, and by very much more handsome than fine. One speech in it I chiefly loved. 'Twas Aeneas' tale to Dido; and thereabout of it especially, where he speaks of Priam's slaughter. If it live in your memory, begin at this line; let me see, let me see—

"The rugged Pyrrhus, like the Hyrcanian beast,"—
it is not so—it begins with Pyrrhus—

"The rugged Pyrrhus, he whose sable arms,
Black as his purpose, did the night resemble
When he lay couched in the ominous horse,
Hath now this dread and black complexion smeared
With heraldry more dismal; head to foot
Now is he total gules; horridly tricked
With blood of fathers, mothers, daughters, sons,
Baked and impasted with the parching streets,
That lend a tyrannous and damned light
To their lord's murder. Roasted in wrath and fire,
And thus o'er-sized with coagulate gore,
With eyes like carbuncles, the hellish Pyrrhus
Old grandsire Priam seeks."

So, proceed you.

POLONIUS. 'Fore God, my lord, well spoken, with good accent and good discretion.

FIRST PLAYER. "Anon he finds him
Striking too short at Greeks; his antique sword,
Rebellious to his arm, lies where it falls,
Repugnant to command. Unequal matched,
Pyrrhus at Priam drives; in rage strikes wide;
But with the whiff and wind of his fell sword
The unnerved father falls. Then senseless Ilium,
Seeming to feel this blow, with flaming top
Stoops to his base, and with a hideous crash
Takes prisoner Pyrrhus' ear. For, lo! his sword,
Which was declining on the milky head
Of reverend Priam, seemed i' the air to stick.
So, as a painted tyrant, Pyrrhus stood,
And like a neutral to his will and matter,
Did nothing.
But, as we often see, against some storm,
A silence in the heavens, the rack stand still,
The bold winds speechless and the orb below
As hush as death, anon the dreadful thunder
Doth rend the region, so, after Pyrrhus' pause,
Aroused vengeance sets him new a-work;
And never did the Cyclops' hammers fall
On Mars's armour forged for proof eterne
With less remorse than Pyrrhus' bleeding sword
Now falls on Priam.
Out, out, thou strumpet, Fortune! All you gods,
In general synod, take away her power;
Break all the spokes and fellies from her wheel,
And bowl the round nave down the hill of heaven,
As low as to the fiends!"

POLONIUS. This is too long.

HAMLET. It shall to the barber's, with your beard. Prithee, say on—he's for a jig or a tale of bawdry, or he sleeps. Say on; come to Hecuba.

FIRST PLAYER. "But who, O, who had seen the mobled
    queen—"
HAMLET. "The mobled queen"?
POLONIUS. That's good; "mobled queen" is good.
FIRST PLAYER. "Run barefoot up and down, threatening
    the flames
  With bisson rheum; a clout upon that head
  Where late the diadem stood, and for a robe,
  About her lank and all o'er-teemed loins,
  A blanket, in the alarm of fear caught up;
  Who this had seen, with tongue in venom steeped,
  'Gainst Fortune's state would treason have pro-
  nounced.
  But if the gods themselves did see her then
  When she saw Pyrrhus make malicious sport
  In mincing with his sword her husband's limbs,
  The instant burst of clamour that she made,
  Unless things mortal move them not at all,
  Would have made milch the burning eyes of heaven,
  And passion in the gods."
POLONIUS. Look, whether he has not turned his colour
    and has tears in 's eyes. Pray you, no more.
HAMLET. 'Tis well; I'll have thee speak out the rest
    soon. Good my lord, will you see the players well be-
    stowed? Do you hear, let them be well used; for they
    are the abstract and brief chronicles of the time.
    After your death you were better have a bad epitaph
    than their ill report while you live.
POLONIUS. My lord, I will use them according to their
    desert.
HAMLET. God's bodykins, man, much better. Use every
    man after his desert, and who should 'scape whipping?
    Use them after your own honour and dignity; the less
    they deserve, the more merit is in your bounty.
    Take them in.
POLONIUS. Come, sirs.
HAMLET. Follow him, friends; we'll hear a play to-
    morrow.
          Exit POLONIUS *with all the* Players *but the First*
    Dost thou hear me, old friend; can you play the
    Murder of Gonzago?
FIRST PLAYER. Ay, my lord.
HAMLET. We'll ha 't tomorrow night. You could, for a
    need, study a speech of some dozen or sixteen lines,
    which I would set down and insert in 't, could you
    not?
FIRST PLAYER. Ay, my lord.
HAMLET. Very well. Follow that lord; and look you
    mock him not. [*Exit First Player*] My good friends,
    I'll leave you till night; you are welcome to Elsinore.
ROSENCRANTZ. Good my lord!
HAMLET. Ay, so, God be wi' ye. [*Exeunt Rosencrantz
    and Guildenstern*] Now I am alone.
  O, what a rogue and peasant slave am I!
  Is it not monstrous that this player here,
  But in a fiction, in a dream of passion,

Could force his soul so to his own conceit
That from her working all his visage wanned,
Tears in his eyes, distraction in 's aspect,
A broken voice, and his whole function suiting
With forms to his conceit? And all for nothing!
For Hecuba!
What's Hecuba to him, or he to Hecuba,
That he should weep for her? What would he do,
Had he the motive and the cue for passion
That I have? He would drown the stage with tears
And cleave the general ear with horrid speech,
Make mad the guilty and appal the free,
Confound the ignorant, and amaze indeed
The very faculties of eyes and ears.
Yet I,
A dull and muddy-mettled rascal, peak,
Like John-a-dreams, unpregnant of my cause,
And can say nothing; no, not for a king,
Upon whose property and most dear life
A damned defeat was made. Am I a coward?
Who calls me villain? breaks my pate across?
Plucks off my beard, and blows it in my face?
Tweaks me by the nose? gives me the lie i' the throat,
As deep as to the lungs? Who does me this?
Ha!
'Swounds, I should take it. For it cannot be
But I am pigeon-livered and lack gall
To make oppression bitter, or ere this
I should have fatted all the region kites
With this slave's offal. Bloody, bawdy villain!
Remorseless, treacherous, lecherous, kindless villain!
O, vengeance!
Why, what an ass am I! This is most brave,
That I, the son of a dear father murdered,
Prompted to my revenge by heaven and hell,
Must, like a whore, unpack my heart with words,
And fall a-cursing, like a very drab,
A scullion!
Fie upon 't! foh! About, my brain! I have heard
That guilty creatures sitting at a play
Have by the very cunning of the scene
Been struck so to the soul that presently
They have proclaimed their malefactions;
For murder, though it have no tongue, will speak
With most miraculous organ. I'll have these players
Play something like the murder of my father
Before mine uncle. I'll observe his looks;
I'll tent him to the quick. If he but blench,
I know my course. The spirit that I have seen
May be the devil; and the devil hath power
To assume a pleasing shape; yea, and perhaps
Out of my weakness and my melancholy,
As he is very potent with such spirits,
Abuses me to damn me. I'll have grounds
More relative than this: the play's the thing
Wherein I'll catch the conscience of the King.   *Exit*

ACT III

SCENE I *A room in the castle*

Enter KING, QUEEN, POLONIUS, OPHELIA, ROSENCRANTZ, *and* GUILDENSTERN

KING. And can you, by no drift of conference,
  Get from him why he puts on this confusion,
  Grating so harshly all his days of quiet
  With turbulent and dangerous lunacy?
ROSENCRANTZ. He does confess he feels himself dis-
  tracted;
  But from what cause he will by no means speak.
GUILDENSTERN. Nor do we find him forward to be
  sounded,
  But, with a crafty madness, keeps aloof,
  When we would bring him on to some confession
  Of his true state.
QUEEN.   Did he receive you well?
ROSENCRANTZ. Most like a gentleman.
GUILDENSTERN. But with much forcing of his disposi-
  tion.
ROSENCRANTZ. Niggard of question; but, of our de-
  mands,
  Most free in his reply.
QUEEN.   Did you assay him
  To any pastime?
ROSENCRANTZ. Madam, it so fell out, that certain
  players
  We o'er-raught on the way. Of these we told him;
  And there did seem in him a kind of joy
  To hear of it. They are about the court,
  And, as I think, they have already order
  This night to play before him.
POLONIUS.   'Tis most true;
  And he beseeched me to entreat your majesties
  To hear and see the matter.
KING. With all my heart; and it doth much content me
  To hear him so inclined.
  Good gentlemen, give him a further edge,
  And drive his purpose on to these delights.
ROSENCRANTZ. We shall, my lord.
      Exeunt ROSENCRANTZ *and* GUILDENSTERN
KING.   Sweet Gertrude, leave us too;
  For we have closely sent for Hamlet hither,
  That he, as 'twere by accident, may here
  Affront Ophelia.
  Her father and myself, lawful espials,
  Will so bestow ourselves that, seeing, unseen,
  We may of their encounter frankly judge,
  And gather by him, as he is behaved,
  If 't be the affliction of his love or no
  That thus he suffers for.
QUEEN.   I shall obey you.
  And for your part, Ophelia, I do wish
  That your good beauties be the happy cause
  Of Hamlet's wildness. So shall I hope your virtues

Will bring him to his wonted way again,
  To both your honours.
OPHELIA. Madam, I wish it may.   *Exit* QUEEN
POLONIUS. Ophelia, walk you here. Gracious, so please
  you,
  We will bestow ourselves. [*To Ophelia*] Read on
  this book;
  That show of such an exercise may colour
  Your loneliness. We are oft to blame in this—
  'Tis too much proved—that with devotion's visage
  And pious action we do sugar o'er
  The devil himself.
KING. [*Aside*] O, 'tis too true!
  How smart a lash that speech doth give my conscience!
  The harlot's cheek, beautied with plastering art,
  Is not more ugly to the thing that helps it
  Than is my deed to my most painted word.
  O heavy burthen!
POLONIUS. I hear him coming; let's withdraw, my lord.
      Exeunt KING *and* POLONIUS
      Enter HAMLET
HAMLET. To be, or not to be; that is the question:
  Whether 'tis nobler in the mind to suffer
  The slings and arrows of outrageous fortune,
  Or to take arms against a sea of troubles,
  And by opposing end them? To die—to sleep—
  No more; and by a sleep to say we end
  The heart-ache and the thousand natural shocks
  That flesh is heir to, 'tis a consummation
  Devoutly to be wished. To die, to sleep;
  To sleep—perchance to dream—ay, there's the rub;
  For in that sleep of death what dreams may come
  When we have shuffled off this mortal coil,
  Must give us pause. There's the respect
  That makes calamity of so long life;
  For who would bear the whips and scorns of time,
  The oppressor's wrong, the proud man's contumely,
  The pangs of despised love, the law's delay,
  The insolence of office and the spurns
  That patient merit of the unworthy takes,
  When he himself might his quietus make
  With a bare bodkin? Who would fardels bear,
  To grunt and sweat under a weary life,
  But that the dread of something after death,
  The undiscovered country from whose bourn
  No traveller returns, puzzles the will
  And makes us rather bear those ills we have
  Than fly to others that we know not of?
  Thus conscience does make cowards of us all;
  And thus the native hue of resolution
  Is sicklied o'er with the pale cast of thought,

And enterprises of great pitch and moment
With this regard their currents turn awry,
And lose the name of action.—Soft you now!
The fair Ophelia! Nymph, in thy orisons
Be all my sins remembered.

OPHELIA.   Good my lord,
How does your honour for this many a day?

HAMLET. I humbly thank you; well, well, well.

OPHELIA. My lord, I have remembrances of yours,
That I have longed long to redeliver;
I pray you, now receive them.

HAMLET.   No, not I;
I never gave you aught.

OPHELIA. My honoured lord, you know right well you
    did;
And, with them, words of so sweet breath composed
As made the things more rich. Their perfume lost,
Take these again; for to the noble mind
Rich gifts wax poor when givers prove unkind.
There, my lord.

HAMLET. Ha, ha! Are you honest?

OPHELIA. My lord?

HAMLET. Are you fair?

OPHELIA. What means your lordship?

HAMLET. That if you be honest and fair, your honesty
should admit no discourse to your beauty.

OPHELIA. Could beauty, my lord, have better commerce
than with honesty?

HAMLET. Ay, truly; for the power of beauty will sooner
transform honesty from what it is to a bawd than the
force of honesty can translate beauty into his likeness.
This was sometime a paradox, but now the time gives
it proof. I did love you once.

OPHELIA. Indeed, my lord, you made me believe so.

HAMLET. You should not have believed me; for virtue
cannot so inoculate our old stock but we shall relish
of it. I loved you not.

OPHELIA. I was the more deceived.

HAMLET. Get thee to a nunnery! Why wouldst thou be a
breeder of sinners? I am myself indifferent honest;
but yet I could accuse me of such things that it were
better my mother had not borne me. I am very proud,
revengeful, ambitious, with more offences at my beck
than I have thoughts to put them in, imagination to
give them shape, or time to act them in. What should
such fellows as I do crawling between earth and
heaven? We are arrant knaves, all; believe none of us.
Go thy ways to a nunnery. Where's your father?

OPHELIA. At home, my lord.

HAMLET. Let the doors be shut upon him, that he may
play the fool no where but in 's own house. Farewell.

OPHELIA. O, help him, you sweet heavens!

HAMLET. If thou dost marry, I'll give thee this plague
for thy dowry: be thou as chaste as ice, as pure as
snow, thou shalt not escape calumny. Get thee to a
nunnery, go; farewell. Or, if thou wilt needs marry,
marry a fool; for wise men know well enough what
monsters you make of them. To a nunnery, go, and
quickly too. Farewell.

OPHELIA. O heavenly powers, restore him!

HAMLET. I have heard of your paintings too, well
enough; God has given you one face, and you make
yourselves another. You jig, you amble, and you lisp,
and nickname God's creatures, and make your wan-
tonness your ignorance. Go to, I'll no more on 't;
it hath made me mad. I say, we will have no more
marriages. Those that are married already, all but one,
shall live; the rest shall keep as they are. To a nunnery, go.   *Exit*

OPHELIA. O, what a noble mind is here o'erthrown!
The courtier's, soldier's, scholar's, eye, tongue,
    sword;
The expectancy and rose of the fair state,
The glass of fashion and the mould of form,
The observed of all observers, quite, quite down!
And I, of ladies most deject and wretched,
That sucked the honey of his music vows,
Now see that noble and most sovereign reason,
Like sweet bells jangled, out of tune and harsh;
That unmatched form and feature of blown youth
Blasted with ecstasy. O, woe is me,
To have seen what I have seen, see what I see!

Re-enter KING *and* POLONIUS

KING. Love! His affections do not that way tend;
Nor what he spake, though it lacked form a little,
Was not like madness. There's something in his soul,
O'er which his melancholy sits on brood;
And I do doubt the hatch and the disclose
Will be some danger; which for to prevent,
I have in quick determination
Thus set it down: he shall with speed to England,
For the demand of our neglected tribute.
Haply the seas and countries different
With variable objects shall expel
This something-settled matter in his heart,
Whereon his brains still beating puts him thus
From fashion of himself. What think you on 't?

POLONIUS. It shall do well. But yet do I believe
The origin and commencement of his grief
Sprung from neglected love. How now, Ophelia!
You need not tell us what Lord Hamlet said;
We heard it all. My lord, do as you please;
But, if you hold it fit, after the play
Let his queen mother all alone entreat him
To show his grief. Let her be round with him;
And I'll be placed, so please you, in the ear
Of all their conference. If she find him not,
To England send him, or confine him where
Your wisdom best shall think.

KING.   It shall be so;
Madness in great ones must not unwatched go. *Exeunt*

SCENE II *A hall in the castle*

Enter HAMLET *and* Players

HAMLET. Speak the speech, I pray you, as I pronounced it to you, trippingly on the tongue. But if you mouth it, as many of your players do, I had as lief the town-crier spoke my lines. Nor do not saw the air too much with your hand, thus, but use all gently; for in the very torrent, tempest, and, as I may say, the whirl-wind of passion, you must acquire and beget a tem-perance that may give it smoothness. O, it offends me to the soul to hear a robustious periwig-pated fellow tear a passion to tatters, to very rags, to split the ears of the groundlings, who for the most part are capable of nothing but inexplicable dumb shows and noise. I would have such a fellow whipped for o'erdoing Termagant; it out-herods Herod. Pray you, avoid it.

FIRST PLAYER. I warrant your honour.

HAMLET. Be not too tame neither, but let your own discretion be your tutor. Suit the action to the word, the word to the action; with this special observance, that you o'erstep not the modesty of nature; for any-thing so overdone is from the purpose of playing, whose end, both at the first and now, was and is, to hold, as 'twere, the mirror up to nature; to show virtue her own feature, scorn her own image, and the very age and body of the time his form and pressure. Now this overdone, or come tardy off, though it make the unskilful laugh, cannot but make the judicious grieve; the censure of the which one must in your allowance o'erweigh a whole theatre of others. O, there be players that I have seen play, and heard others praise, and that highly, not to speak it profanely, that, neither having the accent of Christians nor the gait of Christian, pagan, nor man, have so strutted and bel-lowed that I have thought some of nature's journeymen had made men and not made them well, they imitated humanity so abominably.

FIRST PLAYER. I hope we have reformed that indifferently with us, sir.

HAMLET. O, reform it altogether. And let those that play your clowns speak no more than is set down for them; for there be of them that will themselves laugh, to set on some quantity of barren spectators to laugh too; though, in the meantime, some necessary question of the play be then to be considered. That's villainous, and shows a most pitiful ambition in the fool that uses it. Go, make you ready.   *Exeunt* Players

Enter POLONIUS, ROSENCRANTZ, *and* GUILDENSTERN

How now, my lord! will the King hear this piece of work?

POLONIUS. And the Queen too, and that presently.

HAMLET. Bid the players make haste.   *Exit* POLONIUS
Will you two help to hasten them?

ROSENCRANTZ. ⎱ We will, my lord.
GUILDENSTERN. ⎰

      Exeunt ROSENCRANTZ *and* GUILDENSTERN

HAMLET. What ho! Horatio!

      Enter HORATIO

HORATIO. Here, sweet lord, at your service.

HAMLET. Horatio, thou art e'en as just a man
As e'er my conversation coped withal.

HORATIO. O, my dear lord—

HAMLET.   Nay, do not think I flatter,
For what advancement may I hope from thee
That no revenue hast but thy good spirits,
To feed and clothe thee? Why should the poor be
    flattered?
No, let the candied tongue lick absurd pomp,
And crook the pregnant hinges of the knee
Where thrift may follow fawning. Dost thou hear?
Since my dear soul was mistress of her choice
And could of men distinguish, her election
Hath sealed thee for herself; for thou hast been
As one, in suffering all, that suffers nothing,
A man that Fortune's buffets and rewards
Hast ta'en with equal thanks; and blest are those
Whose blood and judgement are so well commingled,
That they are not a pipe for Fortune's finger
To sound what stop she please. Give me that man
That is not passion's slave, and I will wear him
In my heart's core, ay, in my heart of heart,
As I do thee. Something too much of this.
There is a play tonight before the King;
One scene of it comes near the circumstance
Which I have told thee of my father's death.
I prithee, when thou seest that act afoot,
Even with the very comment of thy soul
Observe mine uncle. If his occulted guilt
Do not itself unkennel in one speech,
It is a damned ghost that we have seen,
And my imaginations are as foul
As Vulcan's stithy. Give him heedful note;
For I mine eyes will rivet to his face,
And after we will both our judgements join
In censure of his seeming.

HORATIO.   Well, my lord;
If he steal aught the whilst this play is playing,
And 'scape detecting, I will pay the theft.

HAMLET. They are coming to the play; I must be idle.
Get you a place.

      Danish march. A flourish.
  Enter KING, QUEEN, POLONIUS, OPHELIA,
  ROSENCRANTZ, GUILDENSTERN, *and others*

KING. How fares our cousin Hamlet?

HAMLET. Excellent, i' faith; of the chameleon's dish.
I eat the air, promise-crammed; you cannot feed
capons so.

KING. I have nothing with this answer, Hamlet; these
words are not mine.

HAMLET. No, nor mine now. [*To Polonius*] My lord,
you played once i' the university, you say?

POLONIUS. That did I, my lord; and was accounted a
good actor.

HAMLET. What did you enact?

POLONIUS. I did enact Julius Cæsar. I was killed i' the
Capitol; Brutus killed me.

HAMLET. It was a brute part of him to kill so capital a
calf there. Be the players ready?

ROSENCRANTZ. Ay, my lord; they stay upon your
patience.

QUEEN. Come hither, my dear Hamlet, sit by me.

HAMLET. No, good mother, here's metal more attractive.

POLONIUS. [*To the King*] O, ho! Do you mark that?

HAMLET. Lady, shall I lie in your lap?

      Lying down at OPHELIA's *feet*

OPHELIA. No, my lord.

HAMLET. I mean, my head upon your lap?

OPHELIA. Ay, my lord.

HAMLET. Do you think I meant country matters?

OPHELIA. I think nothing, my lord.

HAMLET. That's a fair thought to lie between maids'
legs.

OPHELIA. What is, my lord?

HAMLET. Nothing.

OPHELIA. You are merry, my lord.

HAMLET. Who, I?

OPHELIA. Ay, my lord.

HAMLET. O God, your only jig-maker. What should a
man do but be merry? For, look you, how cheerfully
my mother looks, and my father died within these
two hours.

OPHELIA. Nay, 'tis twice two months, my lord.

HAMLET. So long? Nay then, let the devil wear black,
for I'll have a suit of sables. O heavens! die two
months ago, and not forgotten yet? Then there's
hope a great man's memory may outlive his life half
a year. But, by 'r lady, he must build churches, then;
or else shall he suffer not thinking on, with the hobby-
horse, whose epitaph is "For, O, for, O, the hobby-
horse is forgot."

      Hautboys play. The dumb show enters

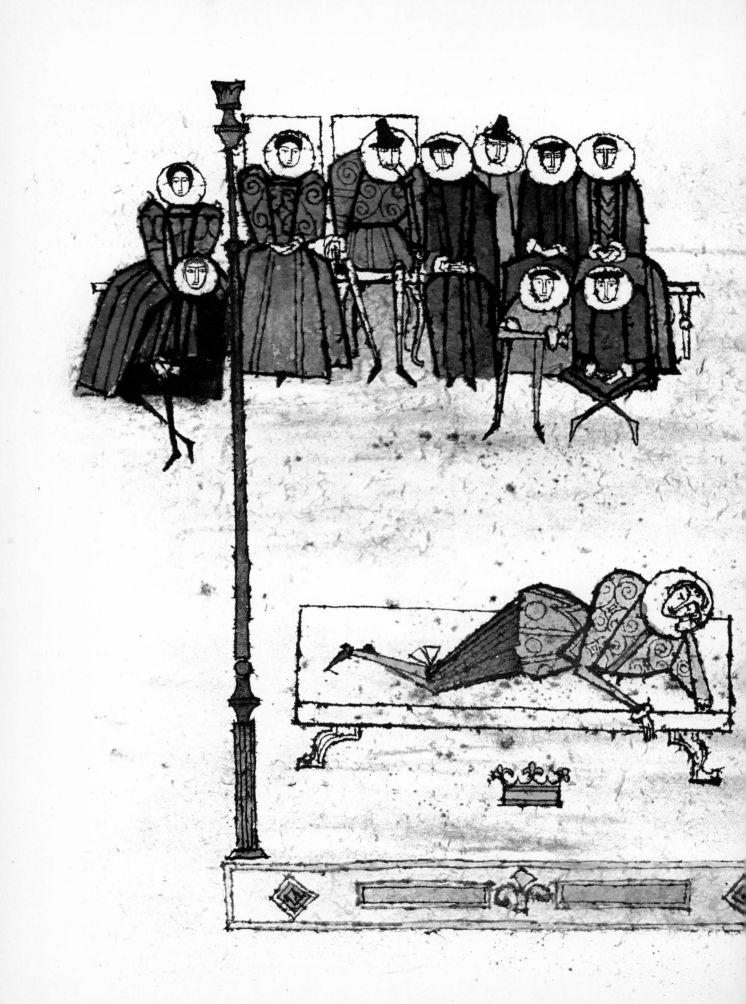

Enter a King and a Queen very lovingly; the Queen em-
bracing him, and he her. She kneels, and makes show of
protestation unto him. He takes her up, and declines his
head upon her neck; lays him down upon a bank of flowers.
She, seeing him asleep, leaves him. Anon comes in a fellow,
takes off his crown, kisses it, and pours poison in the King's
ears, and exit. The Queen returns; finds the King dead,
and makes passionate action. The Poisoner, with some two
or three Mutes, comes in again, seeming to lament with her.
The dead body is carried away. The Poisoner woos the
Queen with gifts. She seems loath and unwilling awhile,
but in the end accepts his love.   [Exeunt]

OPHELIA. What means this, my lord?

HAMLET. Marry, this is miching mallecho; it means mischief.

OPHELIA. Belike this show imports the argument of the play.

Enter Prologue

HAMLET. We shall know by this fellow. The players cannot keep counsel; they 'll tell all.

OPHELIA. Will he tell us what this show meant?

HAMLET. Ay, or any show that you'll show him. Be not you ashamed to show, he'll not shame to tell you what it means.

OPHELIA. You are naught, you are naught! I'll mark the play.

PROLOGUE. For us, and for our tragedy,
　　　Here stooping to your clemency,
　　　We beg your hearing patiently.　　　　　*Exit*

HAMLET. Is this a prologue, or the posy of a ring?

OPHELIA. 'Tis brief, my lord.

HAMLET. As woman's love.

Enter two Players, King *and* Queen

PLAYER KING. Full thirty times hath Phoebus' cart gone round
　Neptune's salt wash and Tellus' orbed ground,
　And thirty dozen moons with borrowed sheen
　About the world have times twelve thirties been,
　Since love our hearts and Hymen did our hands
　Unite commutual in most sacred bands.

PLAYER QUEEN. So many journeys may the sun and moon
　Make us again count o'er ere love be done!
　But, woe is me, you are so sick of late,
　So far from cheer and from your former state,
　That I distrust you. Yet, though I distrust,
　Discomfort you, my lord, it nothing must;
　For women's fear and love holds quantity;
　In neither aught, or in extremity.
　Now, what my love is, proof hath made you know;
　And as my love is sized, my fear is so.
　Where love is great, the littlest doubts are fear;
　Where little fears grow great, great love grows there.

PLAYER KING. Faith, I must leave thee, love, and shortly too;
　My operant powers their functions leave to do;
　And thou shalt live in this fair world behind,
　Honoured, beloved; and haply one as kind
　For husband shalt thou—

PLAYER QUEEN.　　　　O, confound the rest!
　Such love must needs be treason in my breast.
　In second husband let me be accurst!
　None wed the second but who killed the first.

HAMLET. [*Aside*] Wormwood, wormwood.

PLAYER QUEEN. The instances that second marriage move

Are base respects of thrift, but none of love.
　A second time I kill my husband dead,
　When second husband kisses me in bed.

PLAYER KING. I do believe you think what now you speak;
　But what we do determine oft we break.
　Purpose is but the slave to memory,
　Of violent birth, but poor validity;
　Which now, like fruit unripe, sticks on the tree;
　But fall, unshaken, when they mellow be.
　Most necessary 'tis that we forget
　To pay ourselves what to ourselves is debt.
　What to ourselves in passion we propose,
　The passion ending, doth the purpose lose.
　The violence of either grief or joy
　Their own enactures with themselves destroy;
　Where joy most revels, grief doth most lament;
　Grief joys, joy grieves, on slender accident.
　This world is not for aye, nor 'tis not strange
　That even our loves should with our fortunes change;
　For 'tis a question left us yet to prove,
　Whether love lead fortune, or else fortune love.
　The great man down, you mark his favourite flies;
　The poor advanced makes friends of enemies.
　And hitherto doth love on fortune tend;
　For who not needs shall never lack a friend,
　And who in want a hollow friend doth try,
　Directly seasons him his enemy.
　But, orderly to end where I begun,
　Our wills and fates do so contrary run
　That our devices still are overthrown;
　Our thoughts are ours, their ends none of our own.
　So think thou wilt no second husband wed;
　But die thy thoughts when thy first lord is dead.

PLAYER QUEEN. Nor earth to me give food, nor heaven light!
　Sport and repose lock from me day and night!
　To desperation turn my trust and hope!
　An anchor's cheer in prison be my scope!
　Each opposite that blanks the face of joy
　Meet what I would have well and it destroy!
　Both here and hence pursue me lasting strife,
　If, once a widow, ever I be wife!

HAMLET. If she should break it now!

PLAYER KING. 'Tis deeply sworn. Sweet, leave me here awhile;
　My spirits grow dull, and fain I would beguile
　The tedious day with sleep.
　　　　　　　　　　　　　　　　　　Sleeps

PLAYER QUEEN.　　　　Sleep rock thy brain;
　And never come mischance between us twain! *Exit*

HAMLET. Madam, how like you this play?

QUEEN. The lady doth protest too much, methinks.

HAMLET. O, but she 'll keep her word.

KING. Have you heard the argument? Is there no offence in 't?

HAMLET. No, no, they do but jest, poison in jest; no offence i' the world.

KING. What do you call the play?

HAMLET. The Mousetrap. Marry, how? Tropically. This play is the image of a murder done in Vienna. Gonzago is the duke's name; his wife, Baptista. You shall see anon; 'tis a knavish piece of work. But what o' that? Your majesty and we that have free souls, it touches us not. Let the galled jade wince, our withers are unwrung.

Enter Player as LUCIANUS

This is one Lucianus, nephew to the King.

OPHELIA. You are as good as a chorus, my lord.

HAMLET. I could interpret between you and your love, if I could see the puppets dallying.

OPHELIA. You are keen, my lord, you are keen.

HAMLET. It would cost you a groaning to take off my edge.

OPHELIA. Still better, and worse.

HAMLET. So you must take your husbands. Begin, murderer; pox, leave thy damnable faces, and begin. Come: "the croaking raven doth bellow for revenge."

LUCIANUS. Thoughts black, hands apt, drugs fit, and time agreeing;
  Confederate season, else no creature seeing;
  Thou mixture rank, of midnight weeds collected,
  With Hecate's ban thrice blasted, thrice infected,
  Thy natural magic and dire property,
  On wholesome life usurp immediately.

Pours the poison into the sleeper's ears

HAMLET. He poisons him i' the garden for 's estate. His name's Gonzago; the story is extant, and writ in choice Italian. You shall see anon how the murderer gets the love of Gonzago's wife.

OPHELIA. The King rises.

HAMLET. What, frighted with false fire?

QUEEN. How fares my lord?

POLONIUS. Give o'er the play.

KING. Give me some light; away!

ALL. Lights, lights, lights!

Exeunt all but HAMLET *and* HORATIO

HAMLET. Why, let the stricken deer go weep,
  The hart ungalled play;
    For some must watch, while some must sleep:
    So runs the world away.

Would not this, sir, and a forest of feathers—if the rest of my fortunes turn Turk with me—with two Provincial roses on my razed shoes, get me a fellowship in a cry of players, sir?

HORATIO. Half a share.

HAMLET. A whole one, I.
  For thou dost know, O Damon dear,
    This realm dismantled was
  Of Jove himself; and now reigns here
    A very, very—peacock.

HORATIO. You might have rhymed.

HAMLET. O good Horatio, I'll take the ghost's word for a thousand pound. Didst perceive?

HORATIO. Very well, my lord.

HAMLET. Upon the talk of the poisoning?

HORATIO. I did very well note him.

HAMLET. Ah, ha! Come, some music! Come, the recorders!
    For if the King like not the comedy,
      Why then, belike, he likes it not, perdy.
  Come, some music!

Re-enter ROSENCRANTZ *and* GUILDENSTERN

GUILDENSTERN. Good my lord, vouchsafe me a word with you.

HAMLET. Sir, a whole history.

GUILDENSTERN. The King, sir—

HAMLET. Ay, sir, what of him?

GUILDENSTERN. Is in his retirement marvellous distempered.

HAMLET. With drink, sir?

GUILDENSTERN. No, my lord, rather with choler.

HAMLET. Your wisdom should show itself more richer to signify this to his doctor; for, for me to put him to his purgation would perhaps plunge him into far more choler.

GUILDENSTERN. Good my lord, put your discourse into some frame and start not so wildly from my affair.

HAMLET. I am tame, sir. Pronounce.

GUILDENSTERN. The Queen, your mother, in most great affliction of spirit, hath sent me to you.

HAMLET. You are welcome.

GUILDENSTERN. Nay, good my lord, this courtesy is not of the right breed. If it shall please you to make me a wholesome answer, I will do your mother's commandment. If not, your pardon and my return shall be the end of my business.

HAMLET. Sir, I cannot.

GUILDENSTERN. What, my lord?

HAMLET. Make you a wholesome answer; my wit's diseased. But, sir, such answer as I can make, you shall command; or, rather, as you say, my mother. Therefore no more, but to the matter. My mother, you say—

ROSENCRANTZ. Then thus she says; your behaviour hath struck her into amazement and admiration.

HAMLET. O wonderful son, that can so astonish a mother! But is there no sequel at the heels of this mother's admiration? Impart.

ROSENCRANTZ. She desires to speak with you in her closet, ere you go to bed.

HAMLET. We shall obey, were she ten times our mother. Have you any further trade with us?

ROSENCRANTZ. My lord, you once did love me.

HAMLET. So I do still, by these pickers and stealers.

ROSENCRANTZ. Good my lord, what is your cause of distemper? You do, surely, bar the door upon your own liberty, if you deny your griefs to your friend.

HAMLET. Sir, I lack advancement.

ROSENCRANTZ. How can that be, when you have the voice of the King himself for your succession in Denmark?

HAMLET. Ay, sir, but "While the grass grows,"—the proverb is something musty.

Re-enter Players *with recorders*

O, the recorders! Let me see one. To withdraw with you—why do you go about to recover the wind of me, as if you would drive me into a toil?

GUILDENSTERN. O, my lord, if my duty be too bold, my love is too unmannerly.

HAMLET. I do not well understand that. Will you play upon this pipe?

GUILDENSTERN. My lord, I cannot.

HAMLET. I pray you.

GUILDENSTERN. Believe me, I cannot.

HAMLET. I do beseech you.

GUILDENSTERN. I know no touch of it, my lord.

HAMLET. 'Tis as easy as lying. Govern these ventages with your fingers and thumb, give it breath with your mouth, and it will discourse most eloquent music. Look you, these are the stops.

GUILDENSTERN. But these cannot I command to any utterance of harmony; I have not the skill.

HAMLET. Why, look you now, how unworthy a thing you make of me! You would play upon me; you would seem to know my stops; you would pluck out the heart of my mystery; you would sound me from my lowest note to the top of my compass—and there is much music, excellent voice, in this little organ; yet cannot you make it speak. 'Sblood, do you think I am easier to be played on than a pipe? Call me what instrument you will, though you can fret me, yet you cannot play upon me.

Enter POLONIUS

God bless you, sir!

POLONIUS. My lord, the Queen would speak with you, and presently.

HAMLET. Do you see yonder cloud that's almost in shape of a camel?

POLONIUS. By the mass, and 'tis like a camel, indeed.

HAMLET. Methinks it is like a weasel.

POLONIUS. It is backed like a weasel.

HAMLET. Or like a whale?

POLONIUS. Very like a whale.

HAMLET. Then I will come to my mother by and by. They fool me to the top of my bent. I will come by and by.

POLONIUS. I will say so.

HAMLET. By and by is easily said. [*Exit Polonius*] Leave me, friends.   *Exeunt all but* HAMLET

'Tis now the very witching time of night,
When churchyards yawn and hell itself breathes out
Contagion to this world. Now could I drink hot blood,
And do such bitter business as the day
Would quake to look on. Soft! now to my mother.
O heart, lose not thy nature; let not ever
The soul of Nero enter this firm bosom.
Let me be cruel, not unnatural.
I will speak daggers to her, but use none;
My tongue and soul in this be hypocrites;
How in my words soever she be shent,
To give them seals never, my soul, consent!   *Exit*

SCENE III *A room in the castle*

Enter KING, ROSENCRANTZ, *and* GUILDENSTERN

KING. I like him not, nor stands it safe with us
To let his madness range. Therefore prepare you;
I your commission will forthwith dispatch,
And he to England shall along with you.
The terms of our estate may not endure
Hazard so near us as doth hourly grow
Out of his lunacies.

GUILDENSTERN.   We will ourselves provide.
Most holy and religious fear it is
To keep those many many bodies safe
That live and feed upon your majesty.

ROSENCRANTZ. The single and peculiar life is bound,
With all the strength and armour of the mind,
To keep itself from noyance; but much more
That spirit upon whose weal depend and rest
The lives of many. The cease of majesty
Dies not alone; but, like a gulf, doth draw
What's near it with it. It is a massy wheel,
Fixed on the summit of the highest mount,
To whose huge spokes ten thousand lesser things
Are mortised and adjoined; which, when it falls,
Each small annexment, petty consequence,
Attends the boisterous ruin. Never alone
Did the king sigh, but with a general groan.

KING. Arm you, I pray you, to this speedy voyage;
For we will fetters put upon this fear,
Which now goes too free-footed.

ROSENCRANTZ. ⎱
GUILDENSTERN. ⎰   We will haste us.

Exeunt ROSENCRANTZ *and* GUILDENSTERN

Enter POLONIUS

POLONIUS. My lord, he's going to his mother's closet.
Behind the arras I'll convey myself,
To hear the process. I'll warrant she'll tax him home;
And, as you said, and wisely was it said,

'Tis meet that some more audience than a mother,
Since nature makes them partial, should o'erhear
The speech, of vantage. Fare you well, my liege;
I 'll call upon you ere you go to bed,
And tell you what I know.

KING.   Thanks, dear my lord.

                                                    Exit POLONIUS

O, my offence is rank, it smells to heaven;
It hath the primal eldest curse upon 't,
A brother's murder. Pray can I not,
Though inclination be as sharp as will.
My stronger guilt defeats my strong intent;
And, like a man to double business bound,
I stand in pause where I shall first begin,
And both neglect. What if this cursed hand
Were thicker than itself with brother's blood,
Is there not rain enough in the sweet heavens
To wash it white as snow? Whereto serves mercy
But to confront the visage of offence?
And what's in prayer but this two-fold force,
To be forestalled ere we come to fall,
Or pardoned being down? Then I 'll look up;
My fault is past. But, O, what form of prayer
Can serve my turn? "Forgive me my foul murder"?
That cannot be; since I am still possessed
Of those effects for which I did the murder,
My crown, mine own ambition and my queen.
May one be pardoned and retain the offence?
In the corrupted currents of this world
Offence's gilded hand may shove by justice,
And oft 'tis seen the wicked prize itself
Buys out the law. But 'tis not so above;
There is no shuffling, there the action lies
In his true nature; and we ourselves compelled,
Even to the teeth and forehead of our faults,
To give in evidence. What then? what rests?
Try what repentance can; what can it not?
Yet what can it when one can not repent?
O wretched state! O bosom black as death!
O limed soul, that, struggling to be free,
Art more engaged! Help, angels, make assay!
Bow, stubborn knees; and, heart with strings of steel,
Be soft as sinews of the new-born babe!
All may be well.   *Retires and kneels*

Enter HAMLET

HAMLET. Now might I do it pat, now he is praying;
And now I 'll do 't. And so he goes to heaven;
And so am I revenged. That would be scanned:
A villain kills my father; and for that,
I, his sole son, do this same villain send
To heaven.
O, this is hire and salary, not revenge.
He took my father grossly, full of bread;
With all his crimes broad blown, as flush as May;
And how his audit stands who knows save heaven?

But in our circumstance and course of thought,
'Tis heavy with him. And am I then revenged,
To take him in the purging of his soul,
When he is fit and seasoned for his passage?
No!
Up, sword; and know thou a more horrid hent:
When he is drunk asleep, or in his rage,
Or in the incestuous pleasure of his bed;
At gaming, swearing, or about some act
That has no relish of salvation in 't;
Then trip him, that his heels may kick at heaven,
And that his soul may be as damned and black
As hell, whereto it goes. My mother stays;
This physic but prolongs thy sickly days.   *Exit*

KING. [*Rising*] My words fly up, my thoughts remain
    below.
Words without thoughts never to heaven go.   *Exit*

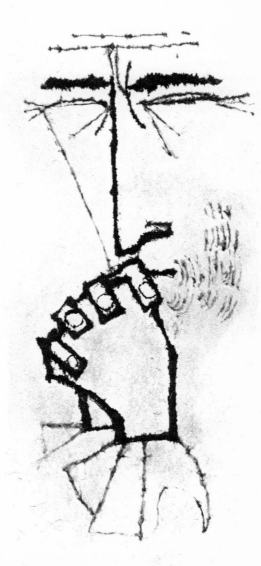

SCENE IV *The Queen's closet*

Enter QUEEN *and* POLONIUS

POLONIUS. He will come straight. Look you lay home
    to him.
  Tell him his pranks have been too broad to bear with,
  And that your grace hath screened and stood between
  Much heat and him. I'll silence me even here.
  Pray you, be round with him.
HAMLET. [*Within*] Mother, mother, mother!
QUEEN.   I'll warrant you,
  Fear me not. Withdraw, I hear him coming.
             POLONIUS *hides behind the arras*
                Enter HAMLET
HAMLET. Now, mother, what's the matter?
QUEEN. Hamlet, thou hast thy father much offended.
HAMLET. Mother, you have my father much offended.
QUEEN. Come, come, you answer with an idle tongue.
HAMLET. Go, go, you question with a wicked tongue.
QUEEN. Why, how now, Hamlet!
HAMLET.   What's the matter now?
QUEEN. Have you forgot me?
HAMLET.   No, by the rood, not so;
  You are the Queen, your husband's brother's wife;
  And—would it were not so!—you are my mother.
QUEEN. Nay, then, I'll set those to you that can speak.
HAMLET. Come, come, and sit you down; you shall
    not budge;
  You go not till I set you up a glass
  Where you may see the inmost part of you.
QUEEN. What wilt thou do? Thou wilt not murder me?
  Help, help, ho!
POLONIUS. [*Behind*] What, ho! help, help, help!
HAMLET. [*Drawing*] How now! A rat? Dead, for a
    ducat, dead!   *Makes a pass through the arras*
POLONIUS. [*Behind*] O, I am slain!   *Falls and dies*
QUEEN. O me, what hast thou done?
HAMLET.   Nay, I know not.
  Is it the King?
QUEEN. O, what a rash and bloody deed is this!
HAMLET. A bloody deed! Almost as bad, good mother,
  As kill a king, and marry with his brother.
QUEEN. As kill a king?
HAMLET.   Ay, lady, 'twas my word.
    Lifts up the arras and discovers POLONIUS
  Thou wretched, rash, intruding fool, farewell!
  I took thee for thy better. Take thy fortune;
  Thou find'st to be too busy is some danger.
  Leave wringing of your hands. Peace! sit you down,
  And let me wring your heart; for so I shall,
  If it be made of penetrable stuff,
  If damned custom have not brassed it so
  That it be proof and bulwark against sense.
QUEEN. What have I done, that thou darest wag thy
    tongue
  In noise so rude against me?

HAMLET.   Such an act
  That blurs the grace and blush of modesty,
  Calls virtue hypocrite, takes off the rose
  From the fair forehead of an innocent love
  And sets a blister there, makes marriage vows
  As false as dicers' oaths. O, such a deed
  As from the body of contraction plucks
  The very soul, and sweet religion makes
  A rhapsody of words. Heaven's face doth glow;
  Yea, this solidity and compound mass,
  With tristful visage, as against the doom,
  Is thought-sick at the act.
QUEEN.   Ay me, what act,
  That roars so loud, and thunders in the index?
HAMLET. Look here, upon this picture, and on this,
  The counterfeit presentment of two brothers.
  See, what a grace was seated on this brow;
  Hyperion's curls; the front of Jove himself;
  An eye like Mars, to threaten and command;
  A station like the herald Mercury
  New-lighted on a heaven-kissing hill;
  A combination and a form indeed,
  Where every god did seem to set his seal,
  To give the world assurance of a man—
  This was your husband. Look you now, what follows:
  Here is your husband; like a mildewed ear,
  Blasting his wholesome brother. Have you eyes?
  Could you on this fair mountain leave to feed,
  And batten on this moor? Ha! have you eyes?
  You cannot call it love; for at your age
  The hey-day in the blood is tame, it's humble,
  And waits upon the judgement; and what judgement
  Would step from this to this? Sense, sure, you have,
  Else could you not have motion; but sure, that sense
  Is apoplexed; for madness would not err,
  Nor sense to ecstasy was ne'er so thralled
  But it reserved some quantity of choice,
  To serve in such a difference. What devil was 't
  That thus hath cozened you at hoodman-blind?
  Eyes without feeling, feeling without sight,
  Ears without hands or eyes, smelling sans all,
  Or but a sickly part of one true sense
  Could not so mope.
  O shame, where is thy blush? Rebellious hell,
  If thou canst mutine in a matron's bones,
  To flaming youth let virtue be as wax,
  And melt in her own fire. Proclaim no shame
  When the compulsive ardour gives the charge,
  Since frost itself as actively doth burn
  And reason panders will.
QUEEN.   O Hamlet, speak no more.
  Thou turn'st mine eyes into my very soul;
  And there I see such black and grained spots

As will not leave their tinct.

HAMLET.   Nay, but to live
In the rank sweat of an enseamed bed,
Stewed in corruption, honeying and making love
Over the nasty sty—

QUEEN.   O, speak to me no more;
These words, like daggers, enter in mine ears;
No more, sweet Hamlet!

HAMLET.   A murderer and a villain;
A slave that is not twentieth part the tithe
Of your precedent lord; a vice of kings;
A cutpurse of the empire and the rule,
That from a shelf the precious diadem stole,
And put it in his pocket!

QUEEN.   No more!

HAMLET. A king of shreds and patches—

Enter Ghost

Save me, and hover o'er me with your wings,
You heavenly guards! What would your gracious
    figure?

QUEEN. Alas, he's mad!

HAMLET. Do you not come your tardy son to chide,
That, lapsed in time and passion, lets go by
The important acting of your dread command?
O, say?

GHOST. Do not forget. This visitation
Is but to whet thy almost blunted purpose.
But, look, amazement on thy mother sits.
O, step between her and her fighting soul.
Conceit in weakest bodies strongest works.
Speak to her, Hamlet.

HAMLET.   How is it with you, lady?

QUEEN. Alas, how is 't with you,
That you do bend your eye on vacancy
And with the incorporal air do hold discourse?
Forth at your eyes your spirits wildly peep;
And, as the sleeping soldiers in the alarm,
Your bedded hair, like life in excrements,
Start up, and stand an end. O gentle son,
Upon the heat and flame of thy distemper
Sprinkle cool patience. Whereon do you look?

HAMLET. On him, on him! Look you, how pale he glares!
His form and cause conjoined, preaching to stones,
Would make them capable. Do not look upon me;
Lest with this piteous action you convert
My stern effects. Then what I have to do
Will want true colour; tears perchance for blood.

QUEEN. To whom do you speak this?

HAMLET.   Do you see nothing there?

QUEEN. Nothing at all; yet all that is I see.

HAMLET. Nor did you nothing hear?

QUEEN.   No, nothing but ourselves.

HAMLET. Why, look you there! Look, how it steals
    away!
My father, in his habit as he lived!

Look, where he goes, even now, out at the portal!

Exit Ghost

QUEEN. This is the very coinage of your brain;
This bodiless creation ecstasy
Is very cunning in.

HAMLET.   Ecstasy!
My pulse, as yours, doth temperately keep time,
And makes as healthful music. It is not madness
That I have uttered. Bring me to the test,
And I the matter will reword; which madness
Would gambol from. Mother, for love of grace,
Lay not that flattering unction to your soul,
That not your trespass, but my madness speaks.
It will but skin and film the ulcerous place,
Whilst rank corruption, mining all within,
Infects unseen. Confess yourself to heaven;
Repent what's past; avoid what is to come;
And do not spread the compost on the weeds,
To make them ranker. Forgive me this my virtue;
For in the fatness of these pursy times
Virtue itself of vice must pardon beg,
Yea, curb and woo for leave to do him good.

QUEEN. O Hamlet, thou hast cleft my heart in twain.

HAMLET. O, throw away the worser part of it,
And live the purer with the other half.
Good night; but go not to mine uncle's bed;
Assume a virtue, if you have it not.
That monster, custom, who all sense doth eat,
Of habits devil, is angel yet in this,
That to the use of actions fair and good
He likewise gives a frock or livery,
That aptly is put on. Refrain tonight,
And that shall lend a kind of easiness
To the next abstinence; the next more easy;
For use almost can change the stamp of nature,
And either master the devil, or throw him out
With wondrous potency. Once more, good night;
And when you are desirous to be blessed,
I 'll blessing beg of you. For this same lord,

Pointing to POLONIUS

I do repent; but heaven hath pleased it so,
To punish me with this and this with me,
That I must be their scourge and minister.
I will bestow him, and will answer well
The death I gave him. So, again, good night.
I must be cruel, only to be kind.
Thus bad begins and worse remains behind.
One word more, good lady.

QUEEN.   What shall I do?

HAMLET. Not this, by no means, that I bid you do:
Let the bloat King tempt you again to bed;
Pinch wanton on your cheek; call you his mouse;
And let him, for a pair of reechy kisses,
Or paddling in your neck with his damned fingers,
Make you to ravel all this matter out,
That I essentially am not in madness,

But mad in craft. 'Twere good you let him know;
For who, that's but a queen, fair, sober, wise,
Would from a paddock, from a bat, a gib,
Such dear concernings hide? Who would do so?
No, in despite of sense and secrecy,
Unpeg the basket on the house's top,
Let the birds fly, and, like the famous ape,
To try conclusions, in the basket creep,
And break your own neck down.
QUEEN. Be thou assured, if words be made of breath,
And breath of life, I have no life to breathe
What thou hast said to me.
HAMLET. I must to England; you know that?
QUEEN.   Alack,
I had forgot; 'tis so concluded on.
HAMLET. There's letters sealed; and my two school-
    fellows,
Whom I will trust as I will adders fanged,
They bear the mandate; they must sweep my way,
And marshal me to knavery. Let it work;
For 'tis the sport to have the enginer
Hoist with his own petard; and 't shall go hard
But I will delve one yard below their mines,
And blow them at the moon. O, 'tis most sweet,
When in one line two crafts directly meet.
This man shall set me packing.
I 'll lug the guts into the neighbour room.
Mother, good night. Indeed this counsellor
Is now most still, most secret and most grave,
Who was in life a foolish prating knave.
Come, sir, to draw toward an end with you.
Good night, mother.
        Exeunt severally; HAMLET dragging in POLONIUS

ACT IV

SCENE I *A room in the castle*

Enter KING, QUEEN, ROSENCRANTZ, and GUILDENSTERN

KING. There's matter in these sighs, these profound
    heaves.
You must translate—'tis fit we understand them.
Where is your son?
QUEEN. Bestow this place on us a little while.
        Exeunt ROSENCRANTZ and GUILDENSTERN
Ah, mine own lord, what have I seen tonight!
KING. What, Gertrude? How does Hamlet?
QUEEN. Mad as the sea and wind, when both contend
Which is the mightier; in his lawless fit,
Behind the arras hearing something stir,
Whips out his rapier, cries, "A rat, a rat!"
And, in this brainish apprehension, kills
The unseen good old man.
KING.   O heavy deed!
It had been so with us, had we been there.
His liberty is full of threats to all;
To you yourself, to us, to every one.
Alas, how shall this bloody deed be answered?
It will be laid to us, whose providence
Should have kept short, restrained and out of haunt,
This mad young man. But so much was our love,
We would not understand what was most fit;
But, like the owner of a foul disease,
To keep it from divulging, let it feed
Even on the pith of life. Where is he gone?
QUEEN. To draw apart the body he hath killed;
O'er whom his very madness, like some ore
Among a mineral of metals base,
Shows itself pure; he weeps for what is done.

KING. O Gertrude, come away!
   The sun no sooner shall the mountains touch,
   But we will ship him hence; and this vile deed
   We must, with all our majesty and skill,
   Both countenance and excuse. Ho, Guildenstern!

    Re-enter ROSENCRANTZ *and* GUILDENSTERN

   Friends both, go join you with some further aid.
   Hamlet in madness hath Polonius slain,
   And from his mother's closet hath he dragged him.
   Go seek him out; speak fair, and bring the body
   Into the chapel. I pray you, haste in this.
        Exeunt ROSENCRANTZ *and* GUILDENSTERN
   Come, Gertrude, we'll call up our wisest friends;
   And let them know, both what we mean to do,
   And what 's untimely done. So, haply, slander—
   Whose whisper o'er the world's diameter,
   As level as the cannon to his blank,
   Transports his poisoned shot, may miss our name,
   And hit the woundless air. O, come away!
   My soul is full of discord and dismay.
                    Exeunt

327

SCENE II *Another room in the castle*

Enter HAMLET

HAMLET. Safely stowed.

ROSENCRANTZ. ⎫
GUILDENSTERN. ⎬ [*Within*] Hamlet! Lord Hamlet!

HAMLET. But soft, what noise? Who calls on Hamlet?
  O, here they come.

Enter ROSENCRANTZ *and* GUILDENSTERN

ROSENCRANTZ. What have you done, my lord, with the
  dead body?

HAMLET. Compounded it with dust, whereto 'tis kin.

ROSENCRANTZ. Tell us where 'tis, that we may take it
  thence
  And bear it to the chapel.

HAMLET. Do not believe it.

ROSENCRANTZ. Believe what?

HAMLET. That I can keep your counsel and not mine
  own. Besides, to be demanded of a sponge! What
  replication should be made by the son of a king?

ROSENCRANTZ. Take you me for a sponge, my lord?

HAMLET. Ay, sir, that soaks up the King's countenance,
  his rewards, his authorities. But such officers do the
  King best service in the end. He keeps them, like an
  ape, in the corner of his jaw; first mouthed, to be last
  swallowed. When he needs what you have gleaned,
  it is but squeezing you, and, sponge, you shall be
  dry again.

ROSENCRANTZ. I understand you not, my lord.

HAMLET. I am glad of it; a knavish speech sleeps in a
  foolish ear.

ROSENCRANTZ. My lord, you must tell us where the
  body is, and go with us to the King.

HAMLET. The body is with the King, but the King is
  not with the body. The King is a thing—

GUILDENSTERN. A thing, my lord!

HAMLET. Of nothing; bring me to him. Hide fox, and
  all after.   *Exeunt*

SCENE III *Another room in the castle*

Enter KING, *attended*

KING. I have sent to seek him, and to find the body.
  How dangerous is it that this man goes loose!
  Yet must not we put the strong law on him.
  He's loved of the distracted multitude,
  Who like not in their judgement, but their eyes;
  And where 'tis so, the offender's scourge is weighed,
  But never the offence. To bear all smooth and even,
  This sudden sending him away must seem
  Deliberate pause. Diseases desperate grown
  By desperate appliance are relieved,
  Or not at all.

Enter ROSENCRANTZ

  How now! what hath befall'n?

ROSENCRANTZ. Where the dead body is bestowed, my
  lord,
  We cannot get from him.

KING.   But where is he?

ROSENCRANTZ. Without, my lord; guarded, to know
  your pleasure.

KING. Bring him before us.

ROSENCRANTZ. Ho, Guildenstern! Bring in my lord.

Enter HAMLET *and* GUILDENSTERN

KING. Now, Hamlet, where's Polonius?

HAMLET. At supper.

KING. At supper! Where?

HAMLET. Not where he eats, but where he is eaten;

a certain convocation of politic worms are e'en at
him. Your worm is your only emperor for diet. We
fat all creatures else to fat us, and we fat ourselves for
maggots. Your fat king and your lean beggar is but
variable service, two dishes, but to one table—that's
the end.

KING. Alas, alas!

HAMLET. A man may fish with the worm that hath eat
of a king, and eat of the fish that hath fed of that worm.

KING. What dost thou mean by this?

HAMLET. Nothing but to show you how a king may go a
progress through the guts of a beggar.

KING. Where is Polonius?

HAMLET. In heaven; send thither to see. If your messenger find him not there, seek him i' the other place
yourself. But indeed, if you find him not within this
month, you shall nose him as you go up the stairs into
the lobby.

KING. Go seek him there.   *To some* Attendants

HAMLET. He will stay till you come.

                                      Exeunt Attendants

KING. Hamlet, this deed, for thine especial safety—
  Which we do tender, as we dearly grieve
  For that which thou hast done—must send thee hence
  With fiery quickness. Therefore prepare thyself;
  The bark is ready, and the wind at help,
  The associates tend, and everything is bent
  For England.

HAMLET.   For England!
KING.   Ay, Hamlet.
HAMLET.   Good.
KING. So is it, if thou knew'st our purposes.
HAMLET. I see a cherub that sees them. But, come; for
  England! Farewell, dear mother.
KING. Thy loving father, Hamlet.
HAMLET. My mother. Father and mother is man and
  wife; man and wife is one flesh; and so, my mother.
  Come, for England!   Exit
KING. Follow him at foot; tempt him with speed aboard;
  Delay it not; I'll have him hence tonight.
  Away, for everything is sealed and done

That else leans on the affair. Pray you, make haste.
            Exeunt ROSENCRANTZ and GUILDENSTERN
And, England, if my love thou hold'st at aught—
As my great power thereof may give thee sense,
Since yet thy cicatrice looks raw and red
After the Danish sword, and thy free awe
Pays homage to us—thou mayst not coldly set
Our soverign process; which imports at full,
By letters congruing to that effect,
The present death of Hamlet. Do it, England;
For like the hectic in my blood he rages,
And thou must cure me. Till I know 'tis done,
Howe'er my haps, my joys were ne'er begun.   Exit

SCENE IV *A plain in Denmark*

Enter FORTINBRAS, *a* Captain, *and* Soldiers, *marching*

FORTINBRAS. Go, Captain, from me greet the Danish
  King;
  Tell him that, by his license, Fortinbras
  Craves the conveyance of a promised march
  Over his kingdom. You know the rendezvous.
  If that his majesty would aught with us,
  We shall express our duty in his eye;
  And let him know so.
CAPTAIN.   I will do 't, my lord.
FORTINBRAS. Go softly on.
                      Exeunt FORTINBRAS *and* Soldiers

Enter HAMLET, ROSENCRANTZ, GUILDENSTERN, *and others*

HAMLET. Good sir, whose powers are these?
CAPTAIN. They are of Norway, sir.
HAMLET. How purposed, sir, I pray you?
CAPTAIN. Against some part of Poland.
HAMLET. Who commands them, sir?
CAPTAIN. The nephew to old Norway, Fortinbras.
HAMLET. Goes it against the main of Poland, sir,
  Or for some frontier?
CAPTAIN. Truly to speak, and with no addition,
  We go to gain a little patch of ground
  That hath in it no profit but the name.
  To pay five ducats, five, I would not farm it;
  Nor will it yield to Norway or the Pole
  A ranker rate, should it be sold in fee.
HAMLET. Why, then the Polack never will defend it.
CAPTAIN. Yes, it is already garrisoned.
HAMLET. Two thousand souls and twenty thousand
  ducats
  Will not debate the question of this straw.
  This is the imposthume of much wealth and peace,
  That inward breaks, and shows no cause without
  Why the man dies. I humbly thank you, sir.
CAPTAIN. God be wi' you, sir.   Exit
ROSENCRANTZ.   Will 't please you go, my lord?

HAMLET. I'll be with you straight. Go a little before.
                      Exeunt all except HAMLET
How all occasions do inform against me,
And spur my dull revenge! What is a man,
If his chief good and market of his time
Be but to sleep and feed? A beast, no more.
Sure, he that made us with such large discourse,
Looking before and after, gave us not
That capability and godlike reason
To fust in us unused. Now, whether it be
Bestial oblivion, or some craven scruple
Of thinking too precisely on the event,
A thought which, quartered, hath but one part wisdom
And ever three parts coward, I do not know
Why yet I live to say "This thing's to do";
Sith I have cause and will and strength and means
To do 't. Examples gross as earth exhort me:
Witness this army of such mass and charge
Led by a delicate and tender prince,
Whose spirit with divine ambition puffed
Makes mouths at the invisible event,
Exposing what is mortal and unsure
To all that fortune, death and danger dare,
Even for an egg-shell. Rightly to be great
Is not to stir without great argument,
But greatly to find quarrel in a straw
When honour's at the stake. How stand I then,
That have a father killed, a mother stained,
Excitements of my reason and my blood,
And let all sleep? While, to my shame, I see
The imminent death of twenty thousand men,
That, for a fantasy and trick of fame,
Go to their graves like beds, fight for a plot
Whereon the numbers cannot try the cause,
Which is not tomb enough and continent
To hide the slain? O, from this time forth,
My thoughts be bloody, or be nothing worth!   Exit

SCENE V *Elsinore: a room in the castle*

Enter QUEEN, HORATIO, *and a Gentleman*

QUEEN. I will not speak with her.

GENTLEMAN. She is importunate, indeed distract;
  Her mood will needs be pitied.

QUEEN.   What would she have?

GENTLEMAN. She speaks much of her father; says she
    hears
  There's tricks i' the world; and hems, and beats her
    heart;
  Spurns enviously at straws; speaks things in doubt,
  That carry but half sense. Her speech is nothing,
  Yet the unshaped use of it doth move
  The hearers to collection; they aim at it,
  And botch the words up fit to their own thoughts;
  Which, as her winks, and nods, and gestures yield
    them,
  Indeed would make one think there might be thought,
  Though nothing sure, yet much unhappily.

HORATIO. 'Twere good she were spoken with, for she
    may strew
  Dangerous conjectures in ill-breeding minds.

QUEEN. Let her come in.   *Exit* HORATIO
  To my sick soul, as sin's true nature is,
  Each toy seems prologue to some great amiss.
  So full of artless jealousy is guilt,
  It spills itself in fearing to be spilt.

Re-enter HORATIO, *with* OPHELIA

OPHELIA. Where is the beauteous majesty of Denmark?

QUEEN. How now, Ophelia!

OPHELIA. [*Sings*] How should I your true love know
              From another one?
          By his cockle hat and staff,
              And his sandal shoon.

QUEEN. Alas, sweet lady, what imports this song?

OPHELIA. Say you? Nay, pray you, mark.
  [*Sings*]   He is dead and gone, lady,
              He is dead and gone;
          At his head a grass-green turf,
              At his heels a stone.

QUEEN. Nay, but, Ophelia—

OPHELIA. Pray you, mark.
  [*Sings*] White his shroud as the mountain snow—

Enter KING

QUEEN. Alas, look here, my lord.

OPHELIA. [*Sings*] Larded with sweet flowers;
              Which bewept to the grave did go
                  With true-love showers.

KING. How do you, pretty lady?

OPHELIA. Well, God 'ild you! They say the owl was a
  baker's daughter. Lord, we know what we are, but
  know not what we may be. God be at your table!

KING. Conceit upon her father.

OPHELIA. Pray you, let's have no words of this; but
  when they ask you what it means, say you this:
  [*Sings*] Tomorrow is Saint Valentine's day,
              All in the morning betime,
          And I a maid at your window,
              To be your Valentine.
          Then up he rose, and donned his clothes,
              And dupped the chamber door;
          Let in the maid, that out a maid
              Never departed more.

KING. Pretty Ophelia!

OPHELIA. Indeed, la, without an oath, I'll make an end
  on 't:
  [*Sings*] By Gis and by Saint Charity,
              Alack, and fie for shame!
          Young men will do 't, if they come to 't;
              By cock, they are to blame.
          Quoth she, before you tumbled me,
              You promised me to wed.
          So would I ha' done, by yonder sun,
              An thou hadst not come to my bed.

KING. How long hath she been thus?

OPHELIA. I hope all will be well. We must be patient;
  but I cannot choose but weep, to think they should
  lay him i' the cold ground. My brother shall know
  of it; and so I thank you for your good counsel. Come,
  my coach! Good night, ladies; good night, sweet
  ladies; good night, good night.   *Exit*

KING. Follow her close; give her good watch, I pray
    you.   *Exit* HORATIO
  O, this is the poison of deep grief; it springs
  All from her father's death. O Gertrude, Gertrude,
  When sorrows come, they come not single spies,
  But in battalions. First, her father slain;
  Next, your son gone; and he most violent author
  Of his own just remove; the people muddied,
  Thick and unwholesome in their thoughts and whis-
    pers,
  For good Polonius' death; and we have done but
    greenly,
  In hugger-mugger to inter him. Poor Ophelia
  Divided from herself and her fair judgement,
  Without the which we are pictures, or mere beasts.
  Last, and as much containing as all these,
  Her brother is in secret come from France;
  Feeds on his wonder, keeps himself in clouds,
  And wants not buzzers to infect his ear
  With pestilent speeches of his father's death;
  Wherein necessity, of matter beggared,
  Will nothing stick our person to arraign
  In ear and ear. O my dear Gertrude, this,
  Like to a murdering-piece, in many places
  Gives me superfluous death.   *A noise within*

QUEEN.   Alack, what noise is this?
KING. Where are my Switzers? Let them guard the door.

Enter another Gentleman

What is the matter?
GENTLEMAN.   Save yourself, my lord.
   The ocean, overpeering of his list,
   Eats not the flats with more impetuous haste
   Than young Laertes, in a riotous head,
   O'erbears your officers. The rabble call him lord;
   And, as the world were now but to begin,
   Antiquity forgot, custom not known,
   The ratifiers and props of every word,
   They cry "Choose we; Laertes shall be king!"
   Caps, hands, and tongues, applaud it to the clouds:
   "Laertes shall be king, Laertes king!"
QUEEN. How cheerfully on the false trail they cry!
   O, this is counter, you false Danish dogs!
KING. The doors are broke.   *Noise within*

Enter LAERTES, *armed;* Danes *following*

LAERTES. Where is this King? Sirs, stand you all without.
DANES. No, let 's come in.
LAERTES.   I pray you, give me leave.
DANES. We will, we will.   *Exeunt* Danes
LAERTES. I thank you; keep the door. O thou vile king,
   Give me my father!
QUEEN.   Calmly, good Laertes.
LAERTES. That drop of blood that's calm proclaims me
        bastard,
   Cries cuckold to my father, brands the harlot
   Even here, between the chaste unsmirched brow
   Of my true mother.
KING.   What is the cause, Laertes,
   That thy rebellion looks so giant-like?
   Let him go, Gertrude; do not fear our person:
   There's such divinity doth hedge a king,
   That treason can but peep to what it would,
   Acts little of his will. Tell me, Laertes,
   Why thou art thus incensed. Let him go, Gertrude.
   Speak, man.
LAERTES. Where is my father?
KING.   Dead.
QUEEN.   But not by him.
KING. Let him demand his fill.
LAERTES. How came he dead? I 'll not be juggled with.
   To hell, allegiance! Vows, to the blackest devil!
   Conscience and grace, to the profoundest pit!
   I dare damnation. To this point I stand,
   That both the worlds I give to negligence,
   Let come what comes; only I 'll be revenged
   Most throughly for my father.
KING.   Who shall stay you?
LAERTES. My will, not all the world:
   And for my means, I 'll husband them so well,
They shall go far with little.

331

KING.   Good Laertes,
  If you desire to know the certainty
  Of your dear father's death, is 't writ in your revenge,
  That, swoopstake, you will draw both friend and foe,
  Winner and loser?
LAERTES. None but his enemies.
KING.   Will you know them then?
LAERTES. To his good friends thus wide I'll ope my
    arms;
  And like the kind life-rendering pelican,
  Repast them with my blood.
KING.   Why, now you speak
  Like a good child and a true gentleman.
  That I am guiltless of your father's death,
  And am most sensibly in grief for it,
  It shall as level to your judgement pierce
  As day does to your eye.
DANES. [Within] Let her come in.
LAERTES. How now! What noise is that?

Re-enter OPHELIA

  O heat, dry up my brains! Tears seven times salt,
  Burn out the sense and virtue of mine eye!
  By heaven, thy madness shall be paid with weight,
  Till our scale turn the beam. O rose of May!
  Dear maid, kind sister, sweet Ophelia!
  O heavens! is 't possible, a young maid's wits
  Should be as mortal as an old man's life?
  Nature is fine in love, and where 'tis fine,
  It sends some precious instance of itself
  After the thing it loves.
OPHELIA. [Sings]
        They bore him barefaced on the bier;
        Hey non nonny, nonny, hey nonny;
        And in his grave rained many a tear—
  Fare you well, my dove!
LAERTES. Hadst thou thy wits, and didst persuade re-
    venge
  It could not move thus.
OPHELIA. [Sings] You must sing a-down a-down,
            An you call him a-down-a.
  O, how the wheel becomes it! It is the false steward,
  that stole his master's daughter.
LAERTES. This nothing's more than matter.
OPHELIA. There's rosemary, that's for remembrance;
  pray, love, remember; and there is pansies, that's
  for thoughts.
LAERTES. A document in madness, thoughts and remembrance fitted.
OPHELIA. There's fennel for you, and columbines;
  there's rue for you; and here's some for me. We
  may call it herb-grace o' Sundays. O, you must wear
  your rue with a difference. There's a daisy. I would
  give you some violets, but they withered all when my
  father died. They say he made a good end—
  [Sings] For bonny sweet Robin is all my joy.

LAERTES. Thought and affliction, passion, hell itself,
  She turns to favour and to prettiness.
OPHELIA. [Sings] And will he not come again?
        And will he not come again?
          No, no, he is dead;
          Go to thy death-bed;
        He never will come again.

        His beard was as white as snow,
        All flaxen was his poll.
          He is gone, he is gone,
          And we cast away moan.
        God ha' mercy on his soul!
  And of all Christian souls, I pray God. God be wi' ye.
                                        Exit

And we shall jointly labour with your soul
To give it due content.
LAERTES.   Let this be so;
His means of death, his obscure funeral—
No trophy, sword, nor hatchment o'er his bones,
No noble rite nor formal ostentation—
Cry to be heard, as 'twere from heaven to earth,
That I must call 't in question.
KING.   So you shall;
And where the offence is let the great axe fall.
I pray you, go with me.   *Exeunt*

SCENE VI *Another room in the castle*

Enter HORATIO *and a* Servant

HORATIO. What are they that would speak with me?
SERVANT. Sailors, sir. They say they have letters for you.
HORATIO. Let them come in.   *Exit* Servant
  I do not know from what part of the world
  I should be greeted, if not from lord Hamlet.

Enter Sailors

FIRST SAILOR. God bless you, sir.
HORATIO. Let him bless thee too.
FIRST SAILOR. He shall, sir, an 't please him. There's a
  letter for you, sir; it comes from the ambassador that
  was bound for England; if your name be Horatio,
  as I am let to know it is.
HORATIO. [*Reads*] ''Horatio, when thou shalt have
  overlooked this, give these fellows some means to
  the King: they have letters for him. Ere we were two
  days old at sea, a pirate of very warlike appointment
  gave us chase. Finding ourselves too slow of sail,
  we put on a compelled valour, and in the grapple I
  boarded them. On the instant they got clear of our
  ship; so I alone became their prisoner. They have
  dealt with me like thieves of mercy; but they knew
  what they did: I am to do a good turn for them. Let
  the King have the letters I have sent; and repair thou
  to me with as much speed as thou wouldst fly death.
  I have words to speak in thine ear will make thee
  dumb; yet are they much too light for the bore of the
  matter. These good fellows will bring thee where I am.
  Rosencrantz and Guildenstern hold their course for
  England. Of them I have much to tell thee. Farewell.
          ''He that thou knowest thine, HAMLET.''
  Come, I will make you way for these your letters;
  And do 't the speedier, that you may direct me
  To him from whom you brought them.   *Exeunt*

LAERTES. Do you see this, O God?
KING. Laertes, I must commune with your grief,
  Or you deny me right. Go but apart,
  Make choice of whom your wisest friends you will,
  And they shall hear and judge 'twixt you and me.
  If by direct or by collateral hand
  They find us touched, we will our kingdom give,
  Our crown, our life, and all that we call ours,
  To you in satisfaction; but if not,
  Be you content to lend your patience to us,

SCENE VII *Another room in the castle*

Enter KING *and* LAERTES

KING. Now must your conscience my acquittance seal,
And you must put me in your heart for friend,
Sith you have heard, and with a knowing ear,
That he which hath your noble father slain
Pursued my life.

LAERTES.   It well appears. But tell me
Why you proceeded not against these feats,
So crimeful and so capital in nature,
As by your safety, wisdom, all things else,
You mainly were stirred up.

KING.   O, for two special reasons;
Which may to you, perhaps, seem much unsinewed,
But yet to me they are strong. The Queen his mother
Lives almost by his looks; and for myself—
My virtue or my plague, be it either which—
She's so conjunctive to my life and soul,
That, as the star moves not but in his sphere,
I could not but by her. The other motive,
Why to a public count I might not go,
Is the great love the general gender bear him;
Who, dipping all his faults in their affection,
Would, like the spring that turneth wood to stone,
Convert his gyves to graces; so that my arrows,
Too slightly timbered for so loud a wind,
Would have reverted to my bow again,
And not where I had aimed them.

LAERTES. And so have I a noble father lost;
A sister driven into desperate terms,
Whose worth, if praises may go back again,
Stood challenger on mount of all the age
For her perfections. But my revenge will come.

KING. Break not your sleeps for that. You must not
      think
That we are made of stuff so flat and dull
That we can let our beard be shook with danger
And think it pastime. You shortly shall hear more.
I loved your father, and we love ourself;
And that, I hope, will teach you to imagine—

Enter a Messenger

How now! what news?

MESSENGER.   Letters, my lord, from Hamlet:
This to your majesty; this to the Queen.

KING. From Hamlet! Who brought them?

MESSENGER. Sailors, my lord, they say; I saw them not.
They were given me by Claudio; he received them
Of him that brought them.

KING.   Laertes, you shall hear them.
Leave us.   *Exit* Messenger
[*Reads*] "High and mighty, You shall know I am set
naked on your kingdom. Tomorrow shall I beg leave
to see your kingly eyes; when I shall, first asking
your pardon thereunto, recount the occasion of my

sudden and more strange return.   HAMLET."
What should this mean? Are all the rest come back?
Or is it some abuse, and no such thing?

LAERTES. Know you the hand?

KING. 'Tis Hamlet's character. "Naked!"
And in a postscript here, he says "alone."
Can you advise me?

LAERTES. I 'm lost in it, my lord. But let him come;
It warms the very sickness in my heart,
That I shall live and tell him to his teeth,
"Thus didest thou."

KING.   If it be so, Laertes—
As how should it be so? How otherwise?—
Will you be ruled by me?

LAERTES.   Ay, my lord;
So you will not o'errule me to a peace.

KING. To thine own peace. If he be now returned,
As checking at his voyage, and that he means
No more to undertake it, I will work him
To an exploit, now ripe in my device,
Under the which he shall not choose but fall.
And for his death no wind of blame shall breathe,
But even his mother shall uncharge the practice
And call it accident.

LAERTES.   My lord, I will be ruled;
The rather, if you could devise it so
That I might be the organ.

KING.   It falls right.
You have been talked of since your travel much,
And that in Hamlet's hearing, for a quality
Wherein, they say, you shine. Your sum of parts
Did not together pluck such envy from him
As did that one, and that, in my regard,
Of the unworthiest siege.

LAERTES.   What part is that, my lord?

KING. A very ribbon in the cap of youth,
Yet needful too; for youth no less becomes
The light and careless livery that it wears
Than settled age his sables and his weeds,
Importing health and graveness. Two months since,
Here was a gentleman of Normandy—
I've seen myself, and served against, the French,
And they can well on horseback—but this gallant
Had witchcraft in 't; he grew unto his seat;
And to such wondrous doing brought his horse,
As had he been incorpsed and demi-natured
With the brave beast. So far he topped my thought,
That I, in forgery of shapes and tricks,
Come short of what he did.

LAERTES.   A Norman was 't?

KING. A Norman.

LAERTES. Upon my life, Lamond.

KING.   The very same.

334

LAERTES. I know him well. He is the brooch indeed
  And gem of all the nation.
KING. He made confession of you,
  And gave you such a masterly report
  For art and exercise in your defence
  And for your rapier most especial,
  That he cried out, 'twould be a sight indeed,
  If one could match you. The scrimers of their nation,
  He swore, had neither motion, guard, nor eye,
  If you opposed them. Sir, this report of his
  Did Hamlet so envenom with his envy
  That he could nothing do but wish and beg
  Your sudden coming o'er, to play with him.
  Now, out of this—
LAERTES.   What out of this, my lord?
KING. Laertes, was your father dear to you?
  Or are you like the painting of a sorrow,
  A face without a heart?
LAERTES.   Why ask you this?
KING. Not that I think you did not love your father;
  But that I know love is begun by time;
  And that I see, in passages of proof,
  Time qualifies the spark and fire of it.
  There lives within the very flame of love
  A kind of wick or snuff that will abate it;
  And nothing is at a like goodness still;
  For goodness, growing to a plurisy,
  Dies in his own too much. That we would do,
  We should do when we would; for this "would"
    changes
  And hath abatements and delays as many
  As there are tongues, are hands, are accidents;
  And then this "should" is like a spendthrift sigh,
  That hurts by easing. But, to the quick o' the ulcer—
  Hamlet comes back. What would you undertake,
  To show yourself your father's son in deed
  More than in words?
LAERTES.   To cut his throat i' the church.
KING. No place, indeed, should murder sanctuarize;
  Revenge should have no bounds. But, good Laertes,
  Will you do this, keep close within your chamber.
  Hamlet returned shall know you are come home.
  We'll put on those shall praise your excellence
  And set a double varnish on the fame
  The Frenchman gave you, bring you in fine together
  And wager on your heads. He, being remiss,
  Most generous and free from all contriving,
  Will not peruse the foils; so that, with ease,
  Or with a little shuffling, you may choose
  A sword unbated, and in a pass of practice
  Requite him for your father.
LAERTES.   I will do 't.
  And, for that purpose, I'll anoint my sword.
  I bought an unction of a mountebank,
  So mortal that, but dip a knife in it,
  Where it draws blood no cataplasm so rare,

Collected from all simples that have virtue
Under the moon, can save the thing from death
That is but scratched withal. I 'll touch my point
With this contagion, that, if I gall him slightly,
It may be death.
KING.   Let's further think of this;
  Weigh what convenience both of time and means
  May fit us to our shape. If this should fail,
  And that our drift look through our bad performance,
  'Twere better not assayed. Therefore this project
  Should have a back or second, that might hold,
  If this should blast in proof. Soft! let me see—
  We'll make a solemn wager on your cunnings.
  I ha 't:
  When in your motion you are hot and dry—
  As make your bouts more violent to that end—
  And that he calls for drink, I'll have prepared him
  A chalice for the nonce, whereon but sipping,
  If he by chance escape your venomed stuck,
  Our purpose may hold there.
          Enter QUEEN
                      How now, sweet Queen!
QUEEN. One woe doth tread upon another's heel,
  So fast they follow. Your sister's drowned, Laertes.
LAERTES. Drowned! O, where?
QUEEN. There is a willow grows aslant a brook,
  That shows his hoar leaves in the glassy stream;
  There with fantastic garlands did she come
  Of crow-flowers, nettles, daisies, and long purples
  That liberal shepherds give a grosser name,
  But our cold maids do dead men's fingers call them.
  There, on the pendent boughs her coronet weeds
  Clambering to hang, an envious sliver broke;
  When down her weedy trophies and herself
  Fell in the weeping brook. Her clothes spread wide;
  And, mermaid-like, awhile they bore her up;
  Which time she chanted snatches of old tunes;
  As one incapable of her own distress,
  Or like a creature native and indued
  Unto that element. But long it could not be
  Till that her garments, heavy with their drink,
  Pulled the poor wretch from her melodious lay
  To muddy death.
LAERTES.   Alas, then, she is drowned?
QUEEN. Drowned, drowned.
LAERTES. Too much of water hast thou, poor Ophelia,
  And therefore I forbid my tears. But yet
  It is our trick; nature her custom holds,
  Let shame say what it will. When these are gone,
  The woman will be out. Adieu, my lord;
  I have a speech of fire, that fain would blaze,
  But that this folly drowns it.   *Exit*
KING.   Let's follow, Gertrude;
  How much I had to do to calm his rage!
  Now fear I this will give it start again;
  Therefore let's follow.   *Exeunt*

ACT V

SCENE I *A churchyard*

Enter two Clowns, *with spades and pickaxes*

FIRST CLOWN. Is she to be buried in Christian burial that wilfully seeks her own salvation?

SECOND CLOWN. I tell thee she is; and therefore make her grave straight. The crowner hath sat on her, and finds it Christian burial.

FIRST CLOWN. How can that be, unless she drowned herself in her own defence?

SECOND CLOWN. Why, 'tis found so.

FIRST CLOWN. It must be "se offendendo"; it cannot be else. For here lies the point: if I drown myself wittingly, it argues an act; and an act hath three branches—it is, to act, to do, and to perform. Argal, she drowned herself wittingly.

SECOND CLOWN. Nay, but hear you, goodman delver—

FIRST CLOWN. Give me leave. Here lies the water; good. Here stands the man; good. If the man go to this water, and drown himself, it is, will he, nill he, he goes—mark you that. But if the water come to him and drown him, he drowns not himself. Argal, he that is not guilty of his own death shortens not his own life.

SECOND CLOWN. But is this law?

FIRST CLOWN. Ay, marry, is 't; crowner's quest law.

SECOND CLOWN. Will you ha' the truth on 't? If this had not been a gentlewoman, she should have been buried out o' Christian burial.

FIRST CLOWN. Why, there thou say'st. And the more pity that great folk should have countenance in this world to drown or hang themselves, more than their even-Christian. Come, my spade. There is no ancient gentlemen but gardeners, ditchers, and grave-makers. They hold up Adam's profession.

SECOND CLOWN. Was he a gentleman?

FIRST CLOWN. A' was the first that ever bore arms.

SECOND CLOWN. Why, he had none.

FIRST CLOWN. What, art a heathen? How dost thou understand the Scripture? The Scripture says "Adam digged." Could he dig without arms? I'll put another question to thee: if thou answerest me not to the purpose, confess thyself—

SECOND CLOWN. Go to.

FIRST CLOWN. What is he that builds stronger than either the mason, the shipwright, or the carpenter?

SECOND CLOWN. The gallows-maker; for that frame outlives a thousand tenants.

FIRST CLOWN. I like thy wit well, in good faith. The gallows does well; but how does it well? It does well to those that do ill. Now thou dost ill to say the gallows is built stronger than the church. Argal, the gallows may do well to thee. To 't again, come.

SECOND CLOWN. "Who builds stronger than a mason, a shipwright, or a carpenter?"

FIRST CLOWN. Ay, tell me that, and unyoke.

SECOND CLOWN. Marry, now I can tell.

FIRST CLOWN. To 't.

SECOND CLOWN. Mass, I cannot tell.

Enter HAMLET *and* HORATIO, *at a distance*

FIRST CLOWN. Cudgel thy brains no more about it, for your dull ass will not mend his pace with beating;

and, when you are asked this question, next, say "a grave-maker"; the houses that he makes last till Doomsday. Go, get thee to, Yaughan; fetch me a stoup of liquor.

Exit Second Clown

First Clown *digs, and sings*

> In youth, when I did love, did love,
>> Methought it was very sweet,
> To contract, O, the time, for, ah, my behove,
>> O, methought, there was nothing meet.

HAMLET. Has this fellow no feeling of his business, that he sings at grave-making?

HORATIO. Custom hath made it in him a property of easiness.

HAMLET. 'Tis e'en so; the hand of little employment hath the daintier sense.

FIRST CLOWN. [*Sings*]

> But age, with his stealing steps,
>> Hath clawed me in his clutch,
> And hath shipped me intil the land,
>> As if I had never been such.

Throws up a skull

HAMLET. That skull had a tongue in it, and could sing once. How the knave jowls it to the ground, as if it

were Cain's jaw-bone, that did the first murder! It might be the pate of a politician, which this ass now o'er-reaches; one that would circumvent God, might it not?

HORATIO. It might, my lord.

HAMLET. Or of a courtier; which could say "Good morrow, sweet lord! How dost thou, good lord?" This might be my lord such-a-one, that praised my lord such-a-one's horse, when he meant to beg it; might it not?

HORATIO. Ay, my lord.

HAMLET. Why, e'en so; and now my Lady Worm's, chapless, and knocked about the mazzard with a sexton's spade. Here's fine revolution, an we had the trick to see 't. Did these bones cost no more the breeding, but to play at loggats with 'em? Mine ache to think on 't.

FIRST CLOWN. [*Sings*]

> A pickaxe, and a spade, a spade,
>> For and a shrouding sheet;
> O, a pit of clay for to be made
>> For such a guest is meet.

Throws up another skull

HAMLET. There's another. Why may not that be the skull of a lawyer? Where be his quiddities now, his quillets, his cases, his tenures, and his tricks? Why does he suffer this rude knave now to knock him about the sconce with a dirty shovel, and will not tell him of his action of battery? Hum! This fellow might be in 's time a great buyer of land, with his statutes, his recognizances, his fines, his double vouchers, his recoveries. Is this the fine of his fines, and the recovery of his recoveries, to have his fine pate full of fine dirt? Will his vouchers vouch him no more of his purchases, and double ones too, than the length and breadth of a pair of indentures? The very conveyances of his lands will hardly lie in this box; and must the inheritor himself have no more, ha?

HORATIO. Not a jot more, my lord.

HAMLET. Is not parchment made of sheep-skins?

HORATIO. Ay, my lord, and of calf-skins too.

HAMLET. They are sheep and calves which seek out assurance in that. I will speak to this fellow. Whose grave 's this, sirrah?

FIRST CLOWN. Mine, sir.

> [*Sings*] O, a pit of clay for to be made
>> For such a guest is meet.

HAMLET. I think it be thine, indeed; for thou liest in 't.

FIRST CLOWN. You lie out on 't, sir, and therefore it is not yours. For my part, I do not lie in 't, and yet it is mine.

HAMLET. Thou dost lie in 't, to be in 't and say it is thine. 'Tis for the dead, not for the quick; therefore thou liest.

FIRST CLOWN. 'Tis a quick lie, sir; 'twill away again, from me to you.

HAMLET. What man dost thou dig it for?

FIRST CLOWN. For no man, sir.

HAMLET. What woman, then?

FIRST CLOWN. For none, neither.

HAMLET. Who is to be buried in 't?

FIRST CLOWN. One that was a woman, sir; but, rest her soul, she's dead.

HAMLET. How absolute the knave is! We must speak by the card, or equivocation will undo us. By the Lord, Horatio, these three years I have taken note of it; the age is grown so picked that the toe of the peasant comes so near the heel of the courtier, he galls his kibe. How long hast thou been a grave-maker?

FIRST CLOWN. Of all the days i' the year, I came to 't that day that our last King Hamlet overcame Fortinbras.

HAMLET. How long is that since?

FIRST CLOWN. Cannot you tell that? Every fool can tell that. It was the very day that young Hamlet was born; he that is mad, and sent into England.

HAMLET. Ay, marry, why was he sent into England?

FIRST CLOWN. Why, because he was mad. He shall recover his wits there; or, if he do not, it 's no great matter there.

HAMLET. Why?

FIRST CLOWN. 'Twill not be seen in him there; there the men are as mad as he.

HAMLET. How came he mad?

FIRST CLOWN. Very strangely, they say.

HAMLET. How strangely?

FIRST CLOWN. Faith, e'en with losing his wits.

HAMLET. Upon what ground?

FIRST CLOWN. Why, here in Denmark. I have been sexton here, man and boy, thirty years.

HAMLET. How long will a man lie i' the earth ere he rot?

FIRST CLOWN. I' faith, if he be not rotten before he die—as we have many pocky corpses nowadays, that will scarce hold the laying in—he will last you some eight year or nine year. A tanner will last you nine year.

HAMLET. Why he more than another?

FIRST CLOWN. Why, sir, his hide is so tanned with his trade, that he will keep out water a great while; and your water is a sore decayer of your whoreson dead body. Here's a skull now; this skull has lain in the earth three and twenty years.

HAMLET. Whose was it?

FIRST CLOWN. A whoreson mad fellow's it was. Whose do you think it was?

HAMLET. Nay, I know not.

FIRST CLOWN. A pestilence on him for a mad rogue! He poured a flagon of Rhenish on my head once. This same skull, sir, was Yorick's skull, the king's jester.

HAMLET. This?

FIRST CLOWN. E'en that.

HAMLET. Let me see. [*Takes the skull*] Alas, poor Yorick! I knew him, Horatio: a fellow of infinite jest, of most excellent fancy. He hath borne me on his back a thousand times; and now, how abhorred in my imagination it is! My gorge rises at it. Here hung those lips that I have kissed I know not how oft. Where be your gibes now? your gambols? your songs? your flashes of merriment, that were wont to set the table on a roar? Not one now, to mock your own grinning? quite chap-fallen? Now get you to my lady's chamber, and tell her, let her paint an inch thick, to this favour she must come; make her laugh at that. Prithee, Horatio, tell me one thing.

HORATIO. What's that, my lord?

HAMLET. Dost thou think Alexander looked o' this fashion i' the earth?

HORATIO. E'en so.

HAMLET. And smelt so? Pah!   *Puts down the skull*

HORATIO. E'en so, my lord.

HAMLET. To what base uses we may return, Horatio! Why may not imagination trace the noble dust of Alexander, till he find it stopping a bung-hole?

HORATIO. 'Twere to consider too curiously, to consider so.

HAMLET. No, faith, not a jot; but to follow him thither with modesty enough, and likelihood to lead it; as thus: Alexander died, Alexander was buried, Alexander returneth into dust; the dust is earth; of earth we make loam; and why of that loam, whereto he was converted, might they not stop a beer barrel?

Imperious Cæsar, dead and turned to clay,
Might stop a hole to keep the wind away.
O, that that earth, which kept the world in awe,
Should patch a wall to expel the winter's flaw!

But soft! but soft! aside. Here comes the King,

Enter Priests, *in procession; the Corpse of* OPHELIA, LAERTES *and* Mourners *following;* KING, QUEEN, *and their trains*

The Queen, the courtiers! Who is this they follow?
And with such maimed rites? This doth betoken
The corpse they follow did with desperate hand
Fordo it own life. 'Twas of some estate.
Couch we awhile, and mark.   *Retiring with* HORATIO

LAERTES. What ceremony else?

HAMLET.   That is Laertes,
A very noble youth; mark.

LAERTES. What ceremony else?

FIRST PRIEST. Her obsequies have been as far enlarged
As we have warranty. Her death was doubtful;
And, but that great command o'ersways the order
She should in ground unsanctified have lodged
Till the last trumpet; for charitable prayers,
Shards, flints and pebbles should be thrown on her.
Yet here she is allowed her virgin crants,
Her maiden strewments and the bringing home
Of bell and burial.

LAERTES. Must there no more be done?
FIRST PRIEST.   No more be done.
  We should profane the service of the dead
  To sing a requiem and such rest to her
  As to peace-parted souls.
LAERTES.   Lay her i' the earth;
  And from her fair and unpolluted flesh
  May violets spring! I tell thee, churlish priest,
  A ministering angel shall my sister be,
  When thou liest howling.
HAMLET.   What, the fair Ophelia!
QUEEN. Sweets to the sweet. Farewell!
                                   Scattering flowers
  I hoped thou shouldst have been my Hamlet's wife;
  I thought thy bride-bed to have decked, sweet maid,
  And not have strewed thy grave.
LAERTES.   O, treble woe
  Fall ten times treble on that cursed head,
  Whose wicked deed thy most ingenious sense
  Deprived thee of! Hold off the earth awhile,
  Till I have caught her once more in mine arms.
                                   Leaps into the grave
  Now pile your dust upon the quick and dead,
  Till of this flat a mountain you have made,
  To o'ertop old Pelion, or the skyish head
  Of blue Olympus.
HAMLET. [*Advancing*] What is he whose grief
  Bears such an emphasis? Whose phrase of sorrow
  Conjures the wandering stars, and makes them stand
  Like wonder-wounded hearers? This is I,
  Hamlet the Dane.   *Leaps into the grave*
LAERTES.   The devil take thy soul!
                                   Grappling with him
HAMLET. Thou pray'st not well.
  I prithee, take thy fingers from my throat;
  For, though I am not splenitive and rash,
  Yet have I something in me dangerous,
  Which let thy wiseness fear. Hold off thy hand.
KING. Pluck them asunder.
QUEEN.   Hamlet, Hamlet!
ALL. Gentlemen—

HORATIO.   Good my lord, be quiet.
  The Attendants part them, and they come out of the grave
HAMLET. Why, I will fight with him upon this theme
  Until my eyelids will no longer wag.
QUEEN. O my son, what theme?
HAMLET. I loved Ophelia. Forty thousand brothers
  Could not, with all their quantity of love,
  Make up my sum. What wilt thou do for her?
KING. O, he is mad, Laertes.
QUEEN. For love of God, forbear him.
HAMLET. 'Swounds, show me what thou 'lt do
  Woo't weep? woo't fight? woo't fast? woo't tear
    thyself?
  Woo't drink up eisel? eat a crocodile?
  I'll do 't. Dost thou come here to whine?
  To outface me with leaping in her grave?
  Be buried quick with her, and so will I.
  And, if thou prate of mountains, let them throw
  Millions of acres on us, till our ground,
  Singeing his pate against the burning zone,
  Make Ossa like a wart! Nay, an thou 'lt mouth,
  I'll rant as well as thou.
QUEEN.   This is mere madness;
  And thus awhile the fit will work on him.
  Anon, as patient as the female dove,
  When that her golden couplets are disclosed,
  His silence will sit drooping.
HAMLET.   Hear you, sir;
  What is the reason that you use me thus?
  I loved you ever; but it is no matter;
  Let Hercules himself do what he may,
  The cat will mew and dog will have his day.   *Exit*
KING. I pray you, good Horatio, wait upon him.
                                   Exit HORATIO
  [*To Laertes*] Strengthen your patience in our last
    night's speech;
  We'll put the matter to the present push.
  Good Gertrude, set some watch over your son.
  This grave shall have a living monument.
  An hour of quiet shortly shall we see;
  Till then, in patience our proceeding be.   *Exeunt*

SCENE II *A hall in the castle*

Enter HAMLET *and* HORATIO

HAMLET. So much for this, sir; now shall you see the
    other;
  You do remember all the circumstance?
HORATIO. Remember it, my lord!
HAMLET. Sir, in my heart there was a kind of fighting,
  That would not let me sleep. Methought I lay
  Worse than the mutines in the bilboes. Rashly,
  And praised be rashness for it, let us know,
  Our indiscretion sometimes serves us well,
  When our deep plots do pall; and that should teach us

  There's a divinity that shapes our ends,
  Rough-hew them how we will—
HORATIO.   That is most certain.
HAMLET. Up from my cabin,
  My sea gown scarfed about me, in the dark
  Groped I to find out them; had my desire,
  Fingered their packet, and in fine withdrew
  To mine own room again; making so bold,
  My fears forgetting manners, to unseal
  Their grand commission; where I found, Horatio—

O royal knavery!—an exact command,
Larded with many several sorts of reasons
Importing Denmark's health and England's too,
With, ho! such bugs and goblins in my life,
That, on the supervise, no leisure bated,
No, not to stay the grinding of the axe,
My head should be struck off.

HORATIO.   Is 't possible?

HAMLET. Here's the commission; read it at more
    leisure.
But wilt thou hear me how I did proceed?

HORATIO. I beseech you.

HAMLET. Being thus benetted round with villainies—
Ere I could make a prologue to my brains,
They had begun the play—I sat me down,
Devised a new commission, wrote it fair:
I once did hold it, as our statists do,
A baseness to write fair and laboured much
How to forget that learning, but, sir, now
It did me yeoman's service. Wilt thou know
The effect of what I wrote?

HORATIO.   Ay, good my lord.

HAMLET. An earnest conjuration from the King,
As England was his faithful tributary,
As love between them like the palm might flourish,
As peace should still her wheaten garland wear
And stand a comma 'tween their amities,
And many such-like "As'es" of great charge,
That, on the view and knowing of these contents,
Without debatement further, more or less,
He should the bearers put to sudden death,
Not shriving-time allowed.

HORATIO.   How was this sealed?

HAMLET. Why, even in that was heaven ordinant.
I had my father's signet in my purse,
Which was the model of that Danish seal;
Folded the writ up in form of the other,
Subscribed it, gave 't the impression, placed it safely,
The changeling never known. Now, the next day
Was our sea fight; and what to this was sequent
Thou know'st already.

HORATIO. So Guildenstern and Rosencrantz go to 't.

HAMLET. Why, man, they did make love to this em-
    ployment;
They are not near my conscience; their defeat
Does by their own insinuation grow.
'Tis dangerous when the baser nature comes
Between the pass and fell incensed points
Of mighty opposites.

HORATIO.   Why, what a king is this!

HAMLET. Does it not, thinks 't thee, stand me now
    upon—
He that hath killed my King and whored my mother,
Popped in between the election and my hopes,
Thrown out his angle for my proper life,
And with such cozenage—is 't not perfect conscience,

To quit him with this arm? And is 't not to be damned,
To let this canker of our nature come
In further evil?

HORATIO. It must be shortly known to him from
    England
What is the issue of the business there.

HAMLET. It will be short. The interim is mine;
And a man's life's no more than to say "One."
But I am very sorry, good Horatio,
That to Laertes I forgot myself;
For, by the image of my cause, I see
The portraiture of his. I 'll court his favours—
But, sure, the bravery of his grief did put me
Into a towering passion.

HORATIO.   Peace! Who comes here?

Enter OSRIC

OSRIC. Your lordship is right welcome back to Denmark.

HAMLET. I humbly thank you, sir. [*Aside to Horatio*]
Dost know this water-fly?

HORATIO. No, my good lord.

HAMLET. Thy state is the more gracious; for 'tis a vice
to know him. He hath much land, and fertile. Let a
beast be lord of beasts, and his crib shall stand at the
king's mess. 'Tis a chough; but, as I say, spacious in
the possession of dirt.

OSRIC. Sweet lord, if your lordship were at leisure,
I should impart a thing to you from his majesty.

HAMLET. I will receive it, sir, with all diligence of
spirit. Put your bonnet to his right use; 'tis for the
head.

OSRIC. I thank your lordship, it is very hot.

HAMLET. No, believe me, 'tis very cold; the wind is
northerly.

OSRIC. It is indifferent cold, my lord, indeed.

HAMLET. But yet methinks it is very sultry and hot for
my complexion.

OSRIC. Exceedingly, my lord; it is very sultry—as
'twere—I cannot tell how. But, my lord, his majesty
bade me signify to you that he has laid a great wager
on your head. Sir, this is the matter,—

HAMLET. I beseech you, remember—

                    HAMLET *makes him put on his hat*

OSRIC. Nay, good my lord; for mine ease, in good faith.
Sir, here is newly come to court Laertes; believe me,
an absolute gentleman, full of most excellent differences, of very soft society and great showing. Indeed,
to speak feelingly of him, he is the card or calendar
of gentry, for you shall find in him the continent of
what part a gentleman would see.

HAMLET. Sir, his definement suffers no perdition in
you; though, I know, to divide him inventorially
would dizzy the arithmetic of memory, and yet but
yaw neither, in respect of his quick sail. But, in the
verity of extolment, I take him to be a soul of great

article; and his infusion of such dearth and rareness, as, to make true diction of him, his semblable is his mirror; and who else would trace him, his umbrage, nothing more.

OSRIC. Your lordship speaks most infallibly of him.

HAMLET. The concernancy, sir? Why do we wrap the gentleman in our more rawer breath?

OSRIC. Sir?

HORATIO. Is 't not possible to understand in another tongue? You will do 't, sir, really.

HAMLET. What imports the nomination of this gentleman?

OSRIC. Of Laertes?

HORATIO. [Aside] His purse is empty already; all 's golden words are spent.

HAMLET. Of him, sir.

OSRIC. I know you are not ignorant—

HAMLET. I would you did, sir; yet, in faith, if you did, it would not much approve me. Well, sir?

OSRIC. You are not ignorant of what excellence Laertes is—

HAMLET. I dare not confess that, lest I should compare with him in excellence; but, to know a man well, were to know himself.

OSRIC. I mean, sir, for his weapon; but in the imputation laid on him by them, in his meed he's unfellowed.

HAMLET. What's his weapon?

OSRIC. Rapier and dagger.

HAMLET. That's two of his weapons; but, well.

OSRIC. The King, sir, hath wagered with him six Barbary horses; against the which he has imponed, as I take it, six French rapiers and poniards, with their assigns, as girdle, hangers, and so. Three of the carriages, in faith, are very dear to fancy, very responsive to the hilts, most delicate carriages, and of very liberal conceit.

HAMLET. What call you the carriages?

HORATIO. I knew you must be edified by the margent ere you had done.

OSRIC. The carriages, sir, are the hangers.

HAMLET. The phrase would be more german to the matter, if we could carry cannon by our sides. I would it might be hangers till then. But, on; six Barbary horses against six French swords, their assigns, and three liberal-conceited carriages; that's the French bet against the Danish. Why is this "imponed," as you call it?

OSRIC. The King, sir, hath laid, that in a dozen passes between yourself and him, he shall not exceed you three hits. He hath laid on twelve for nine; and it would come to immediate trial, if your lordship would vouchsafe the answer.

HAMLET. How if I answer "no"?

OSRIC. I mean, my lord, the opposition of your person in trial.

HAMLET. Sir, I will walk here in the hall. If it please

his majesty, 'tis the breathing time of day with me. Let the foils be brought, the gentleman willing, and the King hold his purpose, I will win for him an I can. If not, I will gain nothing but my shame and the odd hits.

OSRIC. Shall I redeliver you e'en so?

HAMLET. To this effect, sir; after what flourish your nature will.

OSRIC. I commend my duty to your lordship.

HAMLET. Yours, yours. [Exit Osric] He does well to commend it himself; there are no tongues else for 's turn.

HORATIO. This lapwing runs away with the shell on his head.

HAMLET. He did comply with his dug, before he sucked it. Thus has he—and many more of the same breed that I know the drossy age dotes on—only got the tune of the time and outward habit of encounter; a kind of yesty collection, which carries them through and through the most fond and winnowed opinions; and do but blow them to their trial, the bubbles are out.

Enter a Lord

LORD. My lord, his majesty commended him to you by young Osric, who brings back to him, that you attend him in the hall. He sends to know if your pleasure hold to play with Laertes, or that you will take longer time.

HAMLET. I am constant to my purposes; they follow the King's pleasure. If his fitness speaks, mine is ready; now or whensoever, provided I be so able as now.

LORD. The King and Queen and all are coming down.

HAMLET. In happy time.

LORD. The Queen desires you to use some gentle entertainment to Laertes before you fall to play.

HAMLET. She well instructs me.   Exit Lord

HORATIO. You will lose this wager, my lord.

HAMLET. I do not think so; since he went into France, I have been in continual practice; I shall win at the odds. But thou wouldst not think how ill all 's here about my heart; but it is no matter.

HORATIO. Nay, good my lord—

HAMLET. It is but foolery; but it is such a kind of gain-giving, as would perhaps trouble a woman.

HORATIO. If your mind dislike anything, obey it. I will forestal their repair hither, and say you are not fit.

HAMLET. Not a whit, we defy augury. There's a special providence in the fall of a sparrow. If it be now, 'tis not to come; if it be not to come, it will be now; if it be not now, yet it will come: the readiness is all. Since no man has aught of what he leaves, what is 't to leave betimes? Let be.

Enter KING, QUEEN, LAERTES, Lords, OSRIC, and Attendants with foils and gauntlets

KING. Come, Hamlet, come, and take this hand from
    me.
            The KING *puts* LAERTES' *hand into* HAMLET'S
HAMLET. Give me your pardon, sir. I've done you
    wrong;
    But pardon 't, as you are a gentleman.
    This presence knows,
    And you must needs have heard, how I am punished
    With sore distraction. What I have done,
    That might your nature, honour and exception
    Roughly awake, I here proclaim was madness.
    Was 't Hamlet wronged Laertes? Never Hamlet.
    If Hamlet from himself be ta'en away,
    And when he's not himself does wrong Laertes,
    Then Hamlet does it not, Hamlet denies it.
    Who does it, then? His madness. If 't be so,
    Hamlet is of the faction that is wronged;
    His madness is poor Hamlet's enemy.
    Sir, in this audience,
    Let my disclaiming from a purposed evil
    Free me so far in your most generous thoughts,
    That I have shot mine arrow o'er the house,
    And hurt my brother.
LAERTES.   I am satisfied in nature,
    Whose motive, in this case, should stir me most
    To my revenge. But in my terms of honour
    I stand aloof; and will no reconcilement,
    Till by some elder masters, of known honour,
    I have a voice and precedent of peace,
    To keep my name ungored. But till that time,
    I do receive your offered love like love,
    And will not wrong it.
HAMLET.   I embrace it freely;
    And will this brother's wager frankly play.
    Give us the foils. Come on.
LAERTES.   Come, one for me.
HAMLET. I 'll be your foil, Laertes. In mine ignorance
    Your skill shall, like a star i' the darkest night,
    Stick fiery off indeed.
LAERTES.   You mock me, sir.
HAMLET. No, by this hand.
KING. Give them the foils, young Osric. Cousin Hamlet,
    You know the wager?
HAMLET.   Very well, my lord;
    Your grace hath laid the odds o' the weaker side.
KING. I do not fear it; I have seen you both.
    But since he is bettered, we have therefore odds.
LAERTES. This is too heavy, let me see another.
HAMLET. This likes me well. These foils have all a length?
                            They prepare to play

342

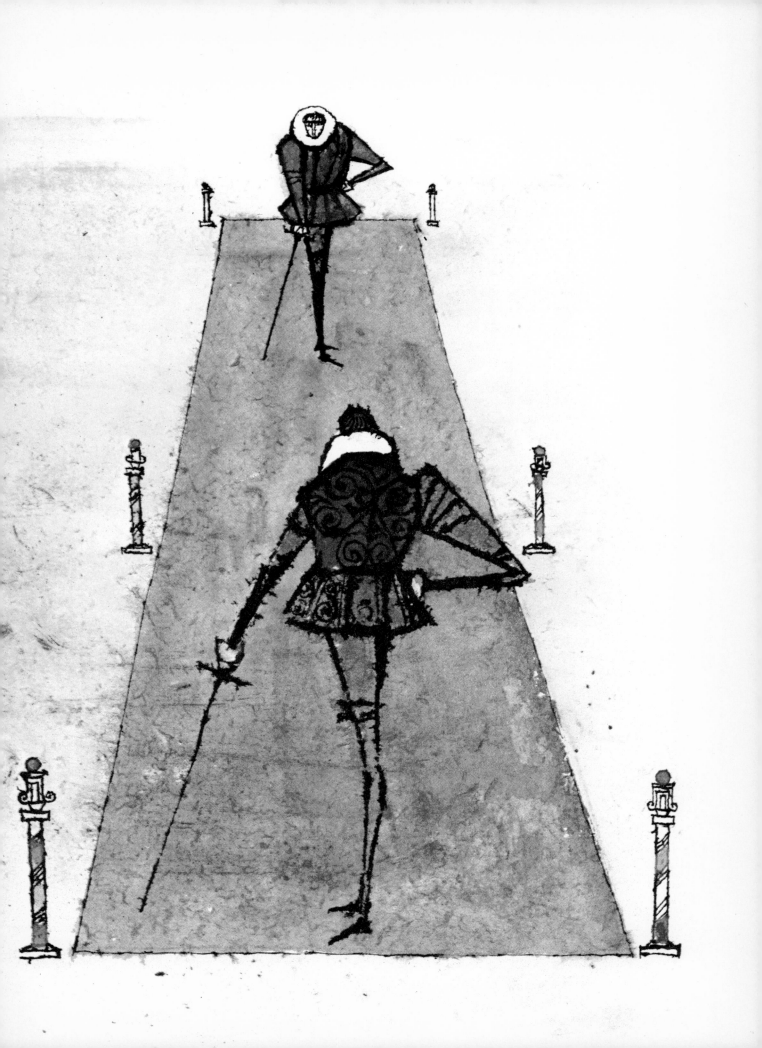

OSRIC. Ay, my good lord.

KING. Set me the stoups of wine upon that table.
  If Hamlet give the first or second hit,
  Or quit in answer of the third exchange,
  Let all the battlements their ordnance fire;
  The King shall drink to Hamlet's better breath;
  And in the cup an union shall he throw,
  Richer than that which four successive kings
  In Denmark's crown have worn. Give me the cups;
  And let the kettle to the trumpet speak,
  The trumpet to the cannoneer without,
  The cannons to the heavens, the heavens to earth,
  "Now the King drinks to Hamlet." Come, begin;
  And you, the judges, bear a wary eye.

HAMLET. Come on, sir.

LAERTES.   Come, my lord.   *They play*

HAMLET.   One.

LAERTES.   No.

HAMLET.   Judgement.

OSRIC. A hit, a very palpable hit.

LAERTES.   Well; again.

KING. Stay; give me drink. Hamlet, this pearl is thine;
  Here's to thy health.

          Trumpets sound, and cannon shot off within
                    Give him the cup.

HAMLET. I 'll play this bout first; set it by awhile.
  Come. [*They play*] Another hit; what say you?

LAERTES. A touch, a touch, I do confess.

KING. Our son shall win.

QUEEN.   He's fat, and scant of breath.
  Here, Hamlet, take my napkin, rub thy brows.
  The Queen carouses to thy fortune, Hamlet.

HAMLET. Good madam!

KING.   Gertrude, do not drink.

QUEEN. I will, my lord; I pray you, pardon me.

KING. [*Aside*] It is the poisoned cup; it is too late.

HAMLET. I dare not drink yet, madam; by and by.

QUEEN. Come, let me wipe thy face.

LAERTES. My lord, I 'll hit him now.

KING.   I do not think 't.

LAERTES. [*Aside*] And yet 'tis almost 'gainst my conscience.

HAMLET. Come, for the third, Laertes. You but dally;
  I pray you, pass with your best violence;
  I am afeard you make a wanton of me.

LAERTES. Say you so? Come on.   *They play*

OSRIC. Nothing, neither way.

LAERTES. Have at you now!

          LAERTES *wounds* HAMLET;
          then, in scuffling, they change
          rapiers, and HAMLET *wounds* LAERTES

KING.   Part them; they are incensed.

HAMLET. Nay, come, again.   *The* QUEEN *falls*

OSRIC.   Look to the Queen there, ho!

HORATIO. They bleed on both sides. How is it, my lord?

OSRIC. How is 't, Laertes?

LAERTES. Why, as a woodcock to mine own springe
  Osric;
  I am justly killed with mine own treachery.

HAMLET. How does the Queen?

KING.   She swounds to see them bleed.

QUEEN. No, no, the drink, the drink—O my dear
  Hamlet—
  The drink, the drink! I am poisoned.   *Dies*

HAMLET. O villainy! Ho! let the door be locked.
  Treachery! Seek it out.

LAERTES. It is here, Hamlet. Hamlet, thou art slain;
  No medicine in the world can do thee good;
  In thee there is not half an hour of life;
  The treacherous instrument is in thy hand,
  Unbated and envenomed. The foul practice
  Hath turned itself on me. Lo, here I lie,
  Never to rise again. Thy mother's poisoned—
  I can no more—the King, the King's to blame.

HAMLET. The point envenomed too!

    Then, venom, to thy work.   *Stabs the* KING

ALL. Treason! Treason!

KING. O, yet defend me, friends; I am but hurt.

HAMLET. Here, thou incestuous, murderous, damned

    Dane,

    Drink off this potion. Is thy union here?

    Follow my mother.   KING *dies*

LAERTES. He is justly served;
It is a poison tempered by himself.
Exchange forgiveness with me, noble Hamlet.
Mine and my father's death come not upon thee,
Nor thine on me! *Dies*

HAMLET. Heaven make thee free of it! I follow thee.
I am dead, Horatio. Wretched Queen, adieu!
You that look pale and tremble at this chance,
That are but mutes or audience to this act,
Had I but time—as this fell sergeant, Death,
Is strict in his arrest—O, I could tell you—
But let it be. Horatio, I am dead;
Thou livest; report me and my cause aright
To the unsatisfied.

HORATIO. Never believe it.
I am more an antique Roman than a Dane—
Here's yet some liquor left.

HAMLET. As thou 'rt a man,
Give me the cup. Let go; by heaven, I 'll have 't!
O God, Horatio, what a wounded name,
Things standing thus unknown, shall live behind me!
If thou didst ever hold me in thy heart,
Absent thee from felicity awhile,
And in this harsh world draw thy breath in pain,
To tell my story.

March, and shot within
What warlike noise is this?

OSRIC. Young Fortinbras, with conquest come from
Poland,
To the ambassadors of England gives
This warlike volley.

HAMLET. O, I die, Horatio;
The potent poison quite o'er-crows my spirit.
I cannot live to hear the news from England;
But I do prophesy the election lights
On Fortinbras. He has my dying voice;
So tell him, with the occurrents, more and less,
Which have solicited. The rest is silence. *Dies*

HORATIO. Now cracks a noble heart. Good night, sweet
Prince;
And flights of angels sing thee to thy rest!
Why does the drum come hither?

March within

Enter FORTINBRAS, *the* English Ambassadors, *and others*

FORTINBRAS. Where is this sight?

HORATIO. What is it ye would see?
If aught of woe or wonder, cease your search.

FORTINBRAS. This quarry cries on havoc. O proud
Death,
What feast is toward in thine eternal cell,
That thou so many princes at a shot
So bloodily hast struck?

FIRST AMBASSADOR. The sight is dismal;
And our affairs from England come too late;
The ears are senseless that should give us hearing,
To tell him his commandment is fulfilled,
That Rosencrantz and Guildenstern are dead.
Where should we have our thanks?

HORATIO. Not from his mouth,
Had it the ability of life to thank you.
He never gave commandment for their death.
But since, so jump upon this bloody question,
You from the Polack wars, and you from England,
Are here arrived, give order that these bodies
High on a stage be placed to the view;
And let me speak to the yet unknowing world
How these things came about. So shall you hear
Of carnal, bloody, and unnatural acts,
Of accidental judgements, casual slaughters,
Of deaths put on by cunning and forced cause,
And, in this upshot, purposes mistook
Fall'n on the inventors' heads—all this can I
Truly deliver.

FORTINBRAS. Let us haste to hear it,
And call the noblest to the audience.
For me, with sorrow I embrace my fortune.
I have some rights of memory in this kingdom,
Which now to claim my vantage doth invite me.

HORATIO. Of that I shall have also cause to speak,
And from his mouth whose voice will draw on more.
But let this same be presently performed,
Even while men's minds are wild; lest more mis-
chance,
On plots and errors, happen.

FORTINBRAS. Let four captains
Bear Hamlet, like a soldier, to the stage;
For he was likely, had he been put on,
To have proved most royally. And, for his passage,
The soldiers' music and the rites of war
Speak loudly for him.
Take up the bodies. Such a sight as this
Becomes the field, but here shows much amiss.
Go, bid the soldiers shoot.

*A dead march. Exeunt, bearing off the dead bodies;
after which a volley of ordance is shot off.*

KING LEAR

There is a considerable measure of critical agreement that *King Lear* is one of the greatest utterances of the human spirit. At the same time there is similar agreement that it is not a very viable piece upon the stage; some critics take the view that it is "too great" for the stage.

The celebrated critic Dr. A. C. Bradley thinks that many of the qualities which make the reading of *King Lear* an important experience are the very ones which militate against its success in the theatre. Rightly he stresses that Shakespeare's purposeful vagueness about locality and the powerful suggestions in the play's imagery build up in the mind of the reader an extraordinary sense of a world, which is not our own world of everyday, in which legendary figures endure events and express ideas and feelings which, though larger and somewhat different from our own, yet have the validity of experience.

"The influence of all this on imagination as we read *King Lear*", says Bradley, "is very great; and it combines with other influences to convey to us, not in the form of distinct ideas but in the manner proper to poetry, the wider or universal significance of the spectacle presented to the inward eye. But the effect of theatrical exhibition is precisely the reverse. There the poetic atmosphere is dissipated; the meaning of the very words which create it passes half-realized; in obedience to the tyranny of the eye we conceive the characters as mere particular men and women; and all that mass of vague suggestion, if it enters the mind at all, appears in the shape of an allegory which we immediately reject. A similar conflict between imagination and sense will be found if we consider the dramatic centre of the whole tragedy, the storm scenes. The temptation of Othello and the scene of Duncan's murder may lose upon the stage, but they do not lose their essence, and they gain as well as lose. The storm scenes in *King Lear* gain nothing and their very essence is destroyed. It is a comparatively small thing that the theatrical storm, not to drown the dialogue, must be silent whenever a human being wishes to speak, and it is wretchedly inferior to many storms we have witnessed. Nor is it simply that, as Lamb observed, the corporal presence of Lear, 'an old man tottering about the stage with a walking stick', disturbs and depresses that sense of the greatness of his mind which fills the imagination. There is a further reason, which is not expressed, but still emerges, in these words of Lamb's: 'the explosions of his passions are terrible as a volcano: they are storms turning up and disclosing to the bottom that sea, his mind, with all its vast riches'. Yes, 'they are storms'. For imagination, that is to say, the explosions of Lear's passion, and the bursts of rain and thunder, are not, what for the senses they must be, two things, but manifestations of one thing. It is the powers of the tormented soul that we hear and see in the 'groans of roaring wind and rain' and the 'sheets of fire'; and they that, at intervals almost more overwhelming, sink back into silence and darkness".

This is all true. There are difficulties, some of them apparently insurmountable, in staging the play. But there are also difficulties and imperfections which mar the play's greatness even for a reader.

The play's structure is a double one: side by side with the theme of King Lear and his three daughters there is the parallel theme of Gloucester and his two sons. This double structure, although not unusual in Shakespeare's comedies, is used in no other of his tragedies. The two themes are interwoven with great skill. But there is between them a dissimilarity of style, which is no doubt intentional, but which leads, in my opinion, to many difficulties; and between them they overload the plot.

The opening scene is laid out with the simplicity of a fairy tale and the symmetry of a card trick: Once upon a time an Old King had Three Daughters. In the way of fairy tales, the Elder Sisters are Wicked, the Youngest is Good, but to satisfy the demands of the plot their Old Father is taken in by the hypocritical protestations of the Wicked Sisters and mistakes the sincere reticence of the Youngest for coldness. The division of the kingdom is, likewise, a well-worn gambit of the folk legend. We seem to be embarking upon a legendary romance, set forth in majestically consistent style, at a spanking pace; it is clear that realism is not the aim, and it looks as if an allegory were possibly in view.

But at the end of the first scene, the locality changes and we embark upon a parallel story of the Old Father with Two Sons. But, instead of being treated in the high, allegorical style of the opening, we plunge into an intensely complicated and sensational plot, in a much more prosaic vein. Thereafter the play sways uncomfortably between its high style, which is superlative, and an intermittently interesting, madly complicated series of intrigues which, in my opinion, lead to all sorts of inconsistencies. Regan and Goneril, for instance, are marvelous when they are simply embodiments of Evil; so is Edmund. But on a human, realistic level, none of the three is credible or interesting; and the sex-triangle between them is just a boring irrelevance at a period in the play when the crisis of the plot is approaching and when boredom and irrelevance are most detrimental.

Edgar seems to me a most unsatisfactory creation; not only a completely defeating part for the actor, but no less puzzling for the reader. Are his constant disguises meant to be symbolical? if so, of what? Or are they simply to satisfy the exigencies of the plot? In that case why is there so little attempt to make some other aspects of the plot more plausible? Why, for instance, does Gloucester never recognize his son's voice? Why do the pair of them go traipsing off to Dover to achieve a suicide which might just as well have taken place where they were?

I believe that the play's weaknesses are not, as Bradley, Lamb and many other critics maintain, primarily theatrical. The final scenes seem just as fussy and muddly when you read them as they do in the theatre. What goes wrong is the intrusion of a heap of irrelevant material piled into a framework which will not hold it. This framework is the parallel pair of legends: the Old King and his Three Daughters, and the Old Father and his Two Sons. This works magnificently when it is treated as in the first scene; as in the scene when Goneril first quarrels with her father (Act I, scene 4); as in the scene where Lear, rebuffed, goes out into the storm (Act II, scene 4)—indeed in nearly all the scenes which concern Lear.

The irrelevancies are first the fustian theatricality of a tired craftsman, possibly working against time. The letter that Edmund so improbably produces; the sporadic outbursts of violence—Edmund fighting Edgar, Kent fighting Oswald—which seem to have been put in to create a simple kind of theatrical bustle and excitement; the sex-intrigue between Edmund and the Wicked Sisters; the contrived single combat between Edmund and Edgar—all of these are melodramatic and seem to derive from rather bygone theatrical conventions rather than from experience of real life. Probably they would be well enough on their own. They are no better, no worse, than characters and episodes of admired dramas like Middleton's *Changeling* or Webster's *Duchess of Malfi.*

It is in their juxtaposition and interweaving with the story of Lear which makes them seem so trumpery. The monumentality and high style of one part of the tragedy is intended, I believe, to be offset and increased by contrast with the melodramatic goings-on amongst the characters of lower stature. This effect is not, in my opinion, achieved. The monumental is not heightened, but reduced, by having to keep company with the fustian. The contrast between the two themes and the two styles is at once jarring and insufficient. It is noticeable that most of these irrelevancies are concerned with Edmund and Edgar, who never quite shake off the plumes and tinsel of melodrama.

The second irrelevancy I scarcely dare mention because the point of view is so heretical. But it seems to me that "realism" of the very kind which in other contexts Shakespeare uses so wonderfully is here not only irrelevant, but disastrous.

In the romances and histories, it is nothing but advantage when, by a stroke or two of genius, small, incidental figures, like Justice Shallow in *Henry the Fourth,* or like Forth and his friends in *Measure for Measure,* are brought to unforgettable life. In *King Lear,* too, touches of realism animate minor figures. The servant who stabs Cornwall, or the old man who hands over the blinded Gloucester to Edgar. But in this tragedy the realism seems out of place. It detracts from a grandeur and simplicity which are essential if the main lines of development are not to be clogged, as in fact they are, and if the central characters and the central theme are not to be reduced from universal to particular status.

There is an enormously admired "stroke" when, just before he dies, and in the middle of lamenting Cordelia's death, Lear says: "Pray you undo this button". This, on the lips of a fine actor, can be guaranteed to draw tears from the audience. But I venture to think that this masterly contrived theatrical effect defeats the major purpose of the scene, which is concerned with the ironic end of a tragic figure, and reduces both scene and character from tragedy to pathos. It is the multiplication of such "strokes" or "touches" of realism—not all so fine as the undoing of the button—which drags *King Lear* down from the summit of human achievement and leaves it a flawed masterpiece, a great jewel, of which the surface has been marred by scratches.

The matter cannot adequately be debated within the compass of a brief introduction. But I believe that, shot through as it is with the genius of Shakespeare at its most dazzling apex, *King Lear* is the untidiest, the most at odds with itself, of Shakespeare's tragedies; the sprawling fecundity of that genius, its fiery humanity, are at odds with a theme which demanded a more formal, austere and removed approach.

Knights of Lear's train

EARL OF KENT

CORDELIA daughter to Lear

LEAR, King of Britain   FOOL

KING LEAR
DRAMATIS PERSONAE

SCENE: BRITAIN

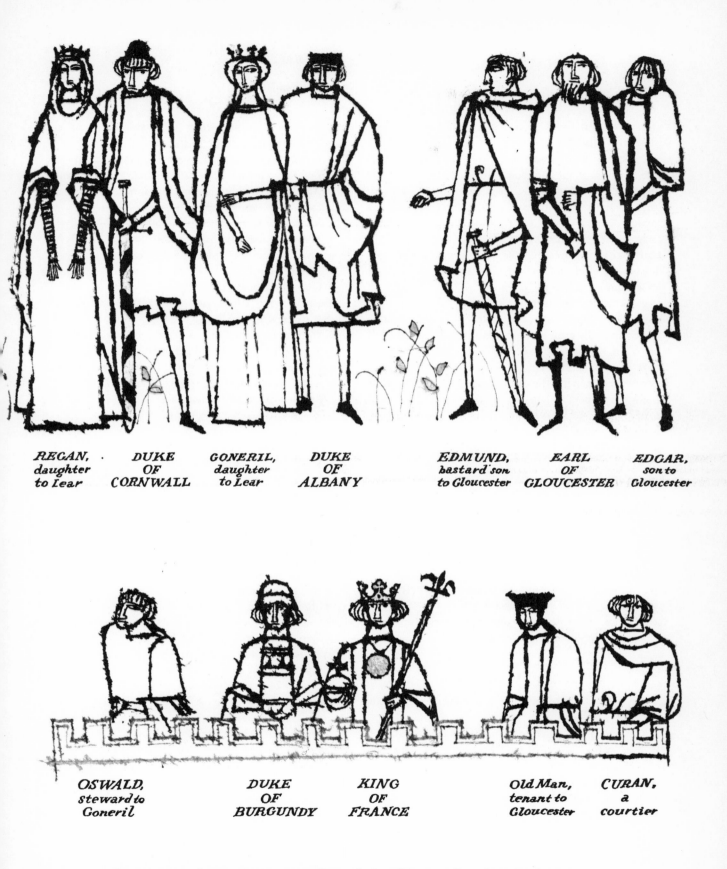

REGAN,
daughter
to Lear

DUKE
OF
CORNWALL

GONERIL,
daughter
to Lear

DUKE
OF
ALBANY

EDMUND,
bastard son
to Gloucester

EARL
OF
GLOUCESTER

EDGAR,
son to
Gloucester

OSWALD,
steward to
Goneril

DUKE
OF
BURGUNDY

KING
OF
FRANCE

Old Man,
tenant to
Gloucester

CURAN,
a
courtier

Doctor; A Captain employed by Edmund; A Gentleman,
attendant on Cordelia; A Herald; Servants to Cornwall;
Captains, Messengers, Soldiers and Attendants.

ACT I

SCENE I *King Lear's palace*

Enter KENT, GLOUCESTER, *and* EDMUND

KENT. I thought the King had more affected the Duke of Albany than Cornwall.

GLOUCESTER. It did always seem so to us; but now, in the division of the kingdom, it appears not which of the dukes he values most; for equalities are so weighed, that curiosity in neither can make choice of either's moiety.

KENT. Is not this your son, my lord?

GLOUCESTER. His breeding, sir, hath been at my charge; I have so often blushed to acknowledge him, that now I am brazed to it.

KENT. I cannot conceive you.

GLOUCESTER. Sir, this young fellow's mother could; whereupon she grew round-wombed, and had, indeed, sir, a son for her cradle ere she had a husband for her bed. Do you smell a fault?

KENT. I cannot wish the fault undone, the issue of it being so proper.

GLOUCESTER. But I have, sir, a son by order of law, some year elder than this, who yet is no dearer in my account. Though this knave came something saucily into the world before he was sent for, yet was his mother fair; there was good sport at his making, and the whoreson must be acknowledged. Do you know this noble gentleman, Edmund?

EDMUND. No, my lord.

GLOUCESTER. My lord of Kent. Remember him hereafter as my honourable friend.

EDMUND. My services to your lordship.

KENT. I must love you, and sue to know you better.

EDMUND. Sir, I shall study deserving.

GLOUCESTER. He hath been out nine years, and away he shall again. The King is coming.

Sennet. Enter KING LEAR, CORNWALL, ALBANY, GONERIL, REGAN, CORDELIA, *and* Attendants

LEAR. Attend the lords of France and Burgundy, Gloucester.

GLOUCESTER. I shall, my liege.

Exeunt GLOUCESTER *and* EDMUND

LEAR. Meantime we shall express our darker purpose.
Give me the map there. Know that we have divided
In three our kingdom; and 'tis our fast intent
To shake all cares and business from our age,
Conferring them on younger strengths, while we
Unburthened crawl toward death. Our son of
    Cornwall,
And you, our no less loving son of Albany,
We have this hour a constant will to publish
Our daughters' several dowers, that future strife

May be prevented now. The princes, France and
    Burgundy,
Great rivals in our youngest daughter's love,
Long in our court have made their amorous sojourn,
And here are to be answered. Tell me, my daughters—
Since now we will divest us, both of rule,
Interest of territory, cares of state—
Which of you shall we say doth love us most?
That we our largest bounty may extend
Where nature doth with merit challenge. Goneril,
Our eldest-born, speak first.

GONERIL. Sir, I love you more than words can wield
    the matter;
Dearer than eyesight, space, and liberty;
Beyond what can be valued, rich or rare;
No less than life, with grace, health, beauty, honour;
As much as child e'er loved, or father found;
A love that makes breath poor, and speech unable;
Beyond all manner of so much I love you.

CORDELIA. [*Aside*] What shall Cordelia do? Love, and
    be silent.

LEAR. Of all these bounds, even from this line to this,
With shadowy forests and with champains riched,
With plenteous rivers and wide-skirted meads,
We make thee lady. To thine and Albany's issue
Be this perpetual. What says our second daughter,
Our dearest Regan, wife to Cornwall? Speak.

REGAN. Sir, I am made
Of the selfsame metal that my sister is,
And prize me at her worth. In my true heart
I find she names my very deed of love—
Only she comes too short—that I profess
Myself an enemy to all other joys,
Which the most precious square of sense possesses;
And find I am alone felicitate
In your dear highness' love.

CORDELIA.   [*Aside*] Then poor Cordelia!
And yet not so; since, I am sure, my love 's
More richer than my tongue.

LEAR. To thee and thine, hereditary ever,
Remain this ample third of our fair kingdom,
No less in space, validity, and pleasure,
Than that conferred on Goneril. Now, our joy,
Although the last, not least; to whose young love
The vines of France and milk of Burgundy
Strive to be interested; what can you say to draw
A third more opulent than your sisters? Speak.

CORDELIA. Nothing, my lord.

LEAR. Nothing!

CORDELIA. Nothing.

LEAR. Nothing will come of nothing—speak again!
CORDELIA. Unhappy that I am, I cannot heave
  My heart into my mouth. I love your majesty
  According to my bond, nor more nor less.
LEAR. How, how, Cordelia! mend your speech a little,
  Lest it may mar your fortunes.
CORDELIA.   Good my lord,
  You have begot me, bred me, loved me; I
  Return those duties back as are right fit,
  Obey you, love you, and most honour you.
  Why have my sisters husbands, if they say
  They love you all? Haply, when I shall wed,
  That lord whose hand must take my plight shall carry
  Half my love with him, half my care and duty.
  Sure, I shall never marry like my sisters,
  To love my father all.
LEAR. But goes thy heart with this?
CORDELIA.   Ay, good my lord.
LEAR. So young, and so untender?
CORDELIA. So young, my lord, and true.
LEAR. Let it be so; thy truth, then, be thy dower!
  For, by the sacred radiance of the sun,
  The mysteries of Hecate, and the night,
  By all the operation of the orbs
  From whom we do exist, and cease to be,
  Here I disclaim all my paternal care,
  Propinquity and property of blood,
  And as a stranger to my heart and me
  Hold thee, from this, for ever. The barbarous
    Scythian,
  Or he that makes his generation messes
  To gorge his appetite, shall to my bosom
  Be as well neighboured, pitied, and relieved,
  As thou my sometime daughter.
KENT.   Good my liege—

LEAR. Peace, Kent!
  Come not between the dragon and his wrath.
  I loved her most, and thought to set my rest
  On her kind nursery. Hence, and avoid my sight!
  So be my grave my peace, as here I give
  Her father's heart from her! Call France. Who stirs?
  Call Burgundy. Cornwall and Albany,
  With my two daughters' dowers digest this third;
  Let pride, which she calls plainness, marry her.
  I do invest you jointly with my power,
  Pre-eminence, and all the large effects
  That troop with majesty. Ourself, by monthly course,
  With reservation of an hundred knights,
  By you to be sustained, shall our abode
  Make with you by due turns. Only we still retain
  The name, and all the additions to a king;
  The sway, revenue, execution of the rest,
  Beloved sons, be yours: which to confirm,
  This coronet part betwixt you.   *Giving the crown*
KENT.   Royal Lear,
  Whom I have ever honoured as my king,
  Loved as my father, as my master followed,
  As my great patron thought on in my prayers—
LEAR. The bow is bent and drawn, make from the
    shaft.
KENT. Let it fall rather, though the fork invade
  The region of my heart; be Kent unmannerly,
  When Lear is mad. What wilt thou do, old man?
  Think'st thou that duty shall have dread to speak,
  When power to flattery bows? To plainness honour 's
    bound,
  When majesty stoops to folly. Reserve thy state,
  And, in thy best consideration, check
  This hideous rashness. Answer my life my judgment,
  Thy youngest daughter does not love thee least;
  Nor are those empty-hearted whose low sound
  Reverbs no hollowness.
LEAR.   Kent, on thy life, no more.
KENT. My life I never held but as a pawn
  To wage against thy enemies; ne'er feared to lose it,
  Thy safety being the motive.
LEAR.   Out of my sight!
KENT. See better, Lear; and let me still remain
  The true blank of thine eye.
LEAR. Now, by Apollo—
KENT.   Now, by Apollo, King,
  Thou swear'st thy gods in vain.
LEAR.   O, vassal! miscreant!
                          Laying his hand on his sword
ALBANY.   }
CORNWALL. } Dear sir, forbear.
KENT. Do;
  Kill thy physician, and the fee bestow
  Upon thy foul disease. Revoke thy doom;
  Or, whilst I can vent clamour from my throat,
  I 'll tell thee thou dost evil.

LEAR.   .   Hear me, recreant!
  On thine allegiance, hear me!
  Since thou hast sought to make us break our vow—
  Which we durst never yet—and with strained pride
  To come between our sentence and our power—
  Which nor our nature nor our place can bear—
  Our potency made good, take thy reward.
  Five days we do allot thee, for provision
  To shield thee from diseases of the world;
  And on the sixth to turn thy hated back
  Upon our kingdom. If, on the tenth day following,
  Thy banished trunk be found in our dominions,
  The moment is thy death. Away! by Jupiter,
  This shall not be revoked.
KENT. Fare thee well, King; sith thus thou wilt appear,
  Freedom lives hence, and banishment is here.
  [*To Cordelia*] The gods to their dear shelter take thee,
    maid,
  That justly think'st, and hast most rightly said!
  [*To Regan and Goneril*] And your large speeches may
    your deeds approve,
  That good effects may spring from words of love.
  Thus Kent, O princes, bids you all adieu;
  He 'll shape his old course in a country new.   *Exit*

                      Flourish.
        Re-enter GLOUCESTER, *with* FRANCE, BURGUNDY,
                  and Attendants

GLOUCESTER. Here's France and Burgundy, my noble
    lord.
LEAR. My lord of Burgundy,
  We first address towards you, who with this king
  Hath rivalled for our daughter. What, in the least,
  Will you require in present dower with her,
  Or cease your quest of love?
BURGUNDY.   Most royal majesty,
  I crave no more than what your highness offered,
  Nor will you tender less.
LEAR.   Right noble Burgundy,
  When she was dear to us, we did hold her so;
  But now her price is fallen. Sir, there she stands;
  If aught within that little seeming substance,
  Or all of it, with our displeasure pieced,
  And nothing more, may fitly like your grace,
  She's there, and she is yours.
BURGUNDY.   I know no answer.
LEAR. Will you, with those infirmities she owes,
  Unfriended, new-adopted to our hate,
  Dowered with our curse, and strangered with our oath,
  Take her, or leave her?
BURGUNDY.   Pardon me, royal sir;
  Election makes not up on such conditions.
LEAR. Then leave her, sir; for, by the power that
    made me,
  I tell you all her wealth. [*To France*] For you, great
    king,

I would not from your love make such a stray,
To match you where I hate; therefore beseech you
To avert your liking a more worthier way
Than on a wretch whom nature is ashamed
Almost to acknowledge hers.
FRANCE.   This is most strange,
That she, that even but now was your best object,
The argument of your praise, balm of your age,
Most best, most dearest, should in this trice of time
Commit a thing so monstrous, to dismantle
So many folds of favour. Sure, her offence
Must be of such unnatural degree,
That monsters it, or your fore-vouched affection
Fall'n into taint; which to believe of her,
Must be a faith that reason without miracle
Could never plant in me.
CORDELIA.   I yet beseech your majesty—
If for I want that glib and oily art,
To speak and purpose not; since what I well intend,
I'll do't before I speak—that you make known
It is no vicious blot, murder, or foulness,
No unchaste action, or dishonoured step,
That hath deprived me of your grace and favour;
But even for want of that for which I am richer,
A still-soliciting eye, and such a tongue
As I am glad I have not, though not to have it
Hath lost me in your liking.
LEAR.   Better thou
Hadst not been born than not to have pleased me
better.
FRANCE. Is it but this—a tardiness in nature
Which often leaves the history unspoke
That it intends to do? My lord of Burgundy,
What say you to the lady? Love's not love
When it is mingled with regards that stand
Aloof from the entire point. Will you have her?
She is herself a dowry.
BURGUNDY.   Royal Lear,
Give but that portion which yourself proposed,
And here I take Cordelia by the hand,
Duchess of Burgundy.
LEAR. Nothing! I have sworn; I am firm.
BURGUNDY. I am sorry, then, you have so lost a father
That you must lose a husband.
CORDELIA.   Peace be with Burgundy!
Since that respects of fortune are his love,
I shall not be his wife.
FRANCE. Fairest Cordelia, that art most rich, being
poor;
Most choice, forsaken; and most loved, despised!
Thee and thy virtues here I seize upon;
Be it lawful I take up what's cast away.
Gods, gods! 'tis strange that from their cold'st neglect
My love should kindle to inflamed respect.
Thy dowerless daughter, King, thrown to my chance,
Is queen of us, of ours, and our fair France!

Not all the dukes of waterish Burgundy
Can buy this unprized precious maid of me.
Bid them farewell, Cordelia, though unkind;
Thou losest here, a better where to find.
LEAR. Thou hast her, France; let her be thine, for we
Have no such daughter, nor shall ever see
That face of hers again. Therefore be gone
Without our grace, our love, our benison.
Come, noble Burgundy.
                    Flourish. Exeunt all but FRANCE,
                    GONERIL, REGAN, *and* CORDELIA
FRANCE. Bid farewell to your sisters.
CORDELIA. The jewels of our father, with washed eyes
Cordelia leaves you. I know you what you are;
And like a sister am most loath to call
Your faults as they are named. Use well our father;
To your professed bosoms I commit him.
But yet, alas, stood I within his grace,
I would prefer him to a better place.
So, farewell to you both.
REGAN. Prescribe not us our duties.
GONERIL.   Let your study
Be to content your lord, who hath received you
At fortune's alms. You have obedience scanted,
And well are worth the want that you have wanted.
CORDELIA. Time shall unfold what plaited cunning hides;
Who cover faults, at last shame them derides.
Well may you prosper!
FRANCE.   Come, my fair Cordelia.
                    Exeunt FRANCE *and* CORDELIA
GONERIL. Sister, it is not a little I have to say of what
most nearly appertains to us both. I think our father
will hence tonight.
REGAN. That's most certain, and with you; next month
with us.
GONERIL. You see how full of changes his age is; the
observation we have made of it hath not been little.
He always loved our sister most; and with what poor
judgment he hath now cast her off appears too grossly.
REGAN. 'Tis the infirmity of his age; yet he hath ever
but slenderly known himself.
GONERIL. The best and soundest of his time hath been
but rash; then must we look to receive from his age,
not alone the imperfections of long-engraffed condition, but therewithal the unruly waywardness that
infirm and choleric years bring with them.
REGAN. Such unconstant starts are we like to have from
him as this of Kent's banishment.
GONERIL. There is further compliment of leavetaking
between France and him. Pray you, let's hit together. If our father carry authority with such dispositions as he bears, this last surrender of his will
but offend us.
REGAN. We shall further think on't.
GONERIL. We must do something, and i' the heat.
                    Exeunt

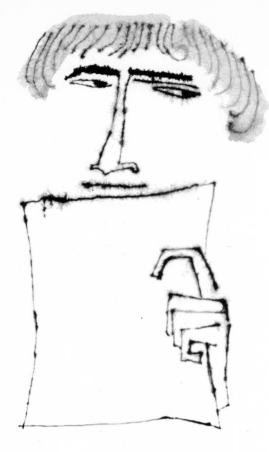

And the King gone tonight! subscribed his power!
Confined to exhibition! All this done
Upon the gad! Edmund, how now! what news?

EDMUND. So please your lordship, none.

Putting up the letter

GLOUCESTER. Why so earnestly seek you to put up that
letter?

EDMUND. I know no news, my lord.

GLOUCESTER. What paper were you reading?

EDMUND. Nothing, my lord.

GLOUCESTER. No? What needed, then, that terrible dispatch of it into your pocket? The quality of nothing
hath not such need to hide itself. Let 's see; come, if it
be nothing, I shall not need spectacles.

EDMUND. I beseech you, sir, pardon me, it is a letter
from my brother, that I have not all o'er-read; and
for so much as I have perused, I find it not fit for your
o'er-looking.

GLOUCESTER. Give me the letter, sir.

EDMUND. I shall offend, either to detain or give it. The
contents, as in part I understand them, are to blame.

GLOUCESTER. Let 's see, let 's see.

EDMUND. I hope, for my brother's justification, he
wrote this but as an essay or taste of my virtue.

GLOUCESTER. [*Reads*] "This policy and reverence of age
makes the world bitter to the best of our times;
keeps our fortunes from us till our oldness cannot
relish them. I begin to find an idle and fond bondage
in the oppression of aged tyranny, who sways, not as
it hath power, but as it is suffered. Come to me,
that of this I may speak more. If our father would
sleep till I waked him, you should enjoy half his
revenue for ever, and live the beloved of your brother,
EDGAR."

Hum—conspiracy!—"Sleep till I waked him,—you
should enjoy half his revenue"—My son Edgar! Had
he a hand to write this? a heart and brain to breed it
in?—When came this to you? Who brought it?

EDMUND. It was not brought me, my lord; there's the
cunning of it; I found it thrown in at the casement of
my closet.

GLOUCESTER. You know the character to be your
brother's?

EDMUND. If the matter were good, my lord, I durst
swear it were his; but, in respect of that, I would fain
think it were not.

GLOUCESTER. It is his.

EDMUND. It is his hand, my lord; but I hope his heart
is not in the contents.

GLOUCESTER. Hath he never heretofore sounded you in
this business?

EDMUND. Never, my lord; but I have heard him oft
maintain it to be fit, that, sons at perfect age, and
fathers declining, the father should be as ward to the
son, and the son manage his revenue.

GLOUCESTER. O villain, villain! His very opinion in the

SCENE II *The Earl of Gloucester's castle*

Enter EDMUND, *with a letter*

EDMUND. Thou, nature, art my goddess; to thy law
My services are bound. Wherefore should I
Stand in the plague of custom, and permit
The curiosity of nations to deprive me,
For that I am some twelve or fourteen moonshines
Lag of a brother? Why bastard? wherefore base?
When my dimensions are as well compact,
My mind as generous, and my shape as true,
As honest madam's issue? Why brand they us
With base? with baseness? bastardy? base, base?
Who, in the lusty stealth of nature, take
More composition and fierce quality
Than doth, within a dull, stale, tired bed,
Go to the creating a whole tribe of fops,
Got 'tween asleep and wake? Well, then,
Legitimate Edgar, I must have your land.
Our father's love is to the bastard Edmund
As to the legitimate. Fine word, "legitimate!"
Well, my legitimate, if this letter speed,
And my invention thrive, Edmund the base
Shall top the legitimate. I grow; I prosper;
Now, gods, stand up for bastards!

Enter GLOUCESTER

GLOUCESTER. Kent banished thus! and France in choler
parted!

letter! Abhorred villain! Unnatural, detested, brutish villain! worse than brutish! Go, sirrah, seek him; I 'll apprehend him. Abominable villain! Where is he?

EDMUND. I do not well know, my lord. If it shall please you to suspend your indignation against my brother till you can derive from him better testimony of his intent, you shall run a certain course; where, if you violently proceed against him, mistaking his purpose, it would make a great gap in your own honour, and shake in pieces the heart of his obedience. I dare pawn down my life for him, that he hath wrote this to feel my affection to your honour, and to no further pretence of danger.

GLOUCESTER. Think you so?

EDMUND. If your honour judge it meet, I will place you where you shall hear us confer of this, and by an auricular assurance have your satisfaction; and that without any further delay than this very evening.

GLOUCESTER. He cannot be such a monster—

EDMUND. Nor is not, sure.

GLOUCESTER. To his father, that so tenderly and entirely loves him. Heaven and earth! Edmund, seek him out; wind me into him, I pray you; frame the business after your own wisdom. I would unstate myself, to be in a due resolution.

EDMUND. I will seek him, sir, presently; convey the business as I shall find means, and acquaint you withal.

GLOUCESTER. These late eclipses in the sun and moon portend no good to us. Though the wisdom of nature can reason it thus and thus, yet nature finds itself scourged by the sequent effects: love cools, friendship falls off, brothers divide; in cities, mutinies; in countries, discord; in palaces, treason; and the bond cracked 'twixt son and father. This villain of mine comes under the prediction; there's son against father; the king falls from bias of nature; there's father against child. We have seen the best of our time: machinations, hollowness, treachery, and all ruinous disorders, follow us disquietly to our graves. Find out this villain, Edmund; it shall lose thee nothing; do it carefully. And the noble and true-hearted Kent banished! his offence, honesty! 'Tis strange.

Exit

EDMUND. This is the excellent foppery of the world, that, when we are sick in fortune—often the surfeit of our own behaviour—we make guilty of our disasters the sun, the moon, and the stars, as if we were villains by necessity; fools by heavenly compulsion; knaves, thieves, and treachers, by spherical predominance; drunkards, liars, and adulterers, by an enforced obedience of planetary influence; and all that we are evil in, by a divine thrusting on. An admirable evasion of whoremaster man, to lay his goatish disposition to the charge of a star! My father compounded with my mother under the dragon's tail, and my nativity was under Ursa Major; so that it follows, I am rough and lecherous. Tut, I should have been that I am, had the maidenliest star in the firmament twinkled on my bastardizing. Edgar—

Enter EDGAR

and pat he comes like the catastrophe of the old comedy. My cue is villainous melancholy, with a sigh like Tom o' Bedlam. O, these eclipses do portend these divisions! fa, sol, la, mi.

EDGAR. How now, brother Edmund! What serious contemplation are you in?

EDMUND. I am thinking, brother, of a prediction I read this other day, what should follow these eclipses.

EDGAR. Do you busy yourself about that?

EDMUND. I promise you, the effects he writes of succeed unhappily; as of unnaturalness between the child and the parent; death, dearth, dissolutions of ancient amities; divisions in state; menaces and maledictions against king and nobles; needless diffidences, banishment of friends, dissipation of cohorts, nuptial breaches, and I know not what.

EDGAR. How long have you been a sectary astronomical?

EDMUND. Come, come; when saw you my father last?

EDGAR. Why, the night gone by.

EDMUND. Spake you with him?

EDGAR. Ay, two hours together.

EDMUND. Parted you in good terms? Found you no displeasure in him by word or countenance?

EDGAR. None at all.

EDMUND. Bethink yourself wherein you may have offended him, and at my entreaty forbear his presence till some little time hath qualified the heat of his displeasure; which at this instant so rageth in him, that with the mischief of your person it would scarcely allay.

EGAR. Some villain hath done me wrong.

EDMUND. That 's my fear. I pray you, have a continent forbearance till the speed of his rage goes slower; and, as I say, retire with me to my lodging, from whence I will fitly bring you to hear my lord speak. Pray ye, go; there 's my key. If you do stir abroad, go armed.

EDGAR. Armed, brother!

EDMUND. Brother, I advise you to the best; go armed. I am no honest man if there be any good meaning towards you. I have told you what I have seen and heard; but faintly, nothing like the image and horror of it. Pray you, away.

EDGAR. Shall I hear from you anon?

EDMUND. I do serve you in this business.

Exit EDGAR

A credulous father! and a brother noble,
Whose nature is so far from doing harms,
That he suspects none; on whose foolish honesty
My practices ride easy! I see the business.
Let me, if not by birth, have lands by wit;
All with me 's meet that I can fashion fit. *Exit*

SCENE III *The Duke of Albany's palace*

Enter GONERIL *and* OSWALD, *her steward*

GONERIL. Did my father strike my gentleman for chid-
  ing of his fool?
OSWALD. Yes, madam.
GONERIL. By day and night he wrongs me; every hour
  He flashes into one gross crime or other,
  That sets us all at odds. I 'll not endure it.
  His knights grow riotous, and himself upbraids us
  On every trifle. When he returns from hunting,
  I will not speak with him; say I am sick.
  If you come slack of former services,
  You shall do well; the fault of it I 'll answer.
OSWALD. He 's coming, madam; I hear him.

                                      Horns within

GONERIL. Put on what weary negligence you please,
  You and your fellows; I 'd have it come to question.
  If he dislike it, let him to our sister,
  Whose mind and mine, I know, in that are one,
  Not to be overruled. Idle old man,
  That still would manage those authorities
  That he hath given away! Now, by my life,
  Old fools are babes again, and must be used
  With checks as flatteries—when they are seen abused.
  Remember what I tell you.
OSWALD.   Well, madam.
GONERIL. And let his knights have colder looks among
    you;
  What grows of it, no matter; advise your fellows so.
  I would breed from hence occasions, and I shall,
  That I may speak. I 'll write straight to my sister,
  To hold my very course. Prepare for dinner.   *Exeunt*

SCENE IV *A hall in the same*

Enter KENT, *disguised*

KENT. If but as well I other accents borrow,
  That can my speech defuse, my good intent
  May carry through itself to that full issue
  For which I razed my likeness. Now, banished Kent,
  If thou canst serve where thou dost stand condemned,
  So may it come, thy master, whom thou lovest,
  Shall find thee full of labours.

Horns within. Enter LEAR, Knights, *and* Attendants

LEAR. Let me not stay a jot for dinner; go get it ready. [*Exit an Attendant*] How now! what art thou?

KENT. A man, sir.

LEAR. What dost thou profess? What wouldst thou with us?

KENT. I do profess to be no less than I seem; to serve him truly that will put me in trust; to love him that is honest; to converse with him that is wise, and says little; to fear judgment; to fight when I cannot choose; and to eat no fish.

LEAR. What art thou?

KENT. A very honest-hearted fellow, and as poor as the King.

LEAR. If thou be as poor for a subject as he is for a king, thou art poor enough. What wouldst thou?

KENT. Service.

LEAR. Who wouldst thou serve?

KENT. You.

LEAR. Dost thou know me, fellow?

KENT. No, sir; but you have that in your countenance which I would fain call master.

LEAR. What 's that?

KENT. Authority.

LEAR. What services canst thou do?

KENT. I can keep honest counsel, ride, run, mar a curious tale in telling it, and deliver a plain message bluntly. That which ordinary men are fit for, I am qualified in; and the best of me is diligence.

LEAR. How old art thou?

KENT. Not so young, sir, to love a woman for singing, nor so old to dote on her for any thing; I have years on my back forty eight.

LEAR. Follow me; thou shalt serve me. If I like thee no worse after dinner, I will not part from thee yet. Dinner, ho, dinner! Where's my knave? my fool? Go you, and call my fool hither.   *Exit an* Attendant

Enter OSWALD

You, you, sirrah, where 's my daughter?

OSWALD. So please you—   *Exit*

LEAR. What says the fellow there? Call the clotpoll back. [*Exit a Knight*] Where's my fool, ho? I think the world's asleep.

Re-enter Knight

How now! where's that mongrel?

KNIGHT. He says, my lord, your daughter is not well.

LEAR. Why came not the slave back to me when I called him.

KNIGHT. Sir, he answered me in the roundest manner, he would not.

LEAR. He would not!

KNIGHT. My lord, I know not what the matter is; but, to my judgment, your highness is not entertained with that ceremonious affection as you were wont. There's a great abatement of kindness appears as well in the general dependants as in the duke himself also and your daughter.

LEAR. Ha! sayest thou so?

KNIGHT. I beseech you, pardon me, my lord, if I be mistaken; for my duty cannot be silent when I think your highness wronged.

LEAR. Thou but rememberest me of mine own conception. I have perceived a most faint neglect of late; which I have rather blamed as mine own jealous curiosity than as a very pretence and purpose of unkindness. I will look further into 't. But where 's my fool? I have not seen him this two days.

KNIGHT. Since my young lady's going into France, sir, the fool hath much pined away.

LEAR. No more of that; I have noted it well. Go you, and tell my daughter I would speak with her. [*Exit an Attendant*] Go you, call hither my fool.

Exit an Attendant

Re-enter OSWALD

O, you sir, you, come you hither, sir. Who am I, sir?

OSWALD. My lady's father.

LEAR. "My lady's father"! my lord's knave! you whoreson dog! you slave! you cur!

OSWALD. I am none of these, my lord; I beseech your pardon.

LEAR. Do you bandy looks with me, you rascal?

Striking him

OSWALD. I 'll not be struck, my lord.

KENT. Nor tripped neither, you base football player.

Tripping up his heels

LEAR. I thank thee, fellow; thou servest me, and I 'll love thee.

KENT. Come, sir, arise, away! I 'll teach you differences. Away, away! If you will measure your lubber's length again, tarry; but away! go to; have you wisdom? so.

Pushes OSWALD *out*

LEAR. Now, my friendly knave, I thank thee. There's earnest of thy service.   *Giving* KENT *money*

Enter Fool

FOOL. Let me hire him too; here 's my coxcomb.

Offering KENT *his cap*

LEAR. How now, my pretty knave! how dost thou?

FOOL. Sirrah, you were best take my coxcomb.

KENT. Why, fool?

FOOL. Why, for taking one's part that 's out of favour. Nay, an thou canst not smile as the wind sits, thou 'lt catch cold shortly. There, take my coxcomb. Why, this fellow has banished two on 's daughters, and did the third a blessing against his will; if thou follow him, thou must needs wear my coxcomb. How now, nuncle! Would I had two coxcombs and two daughters!

LEAR. Why, my boy?

FOOL. If I gave them all my living, I 'd keep my coxcombs myself. There's mine; beg another of thy daughters.

LEAR. Take heed, sirrah; the whip.

FOOL. Truth's a dog must to kennel; he must be whipped out, when Lady the brach may stand by the fire and stink.

LEAR. A pestilent gall to me!

FOOL. Sirrah, I 'll teach thee a speech.

LEAR. Do.

FOOL. Mark it, nuncle:

> Have more than thou showest,
> Speak less than thou knowest,
> Lend less than thou owest,
> Ride more than thou goest,
> Learn more than thou trowest,
> Set less than thou throwest;
> Leave thy drink and thy whore,
> And keep in-a-door,
> And thou shalt have more
> Than two tens to a score.

KENT. This is nothing, fool.

FOOL. Then 'tis like the breath of an unfee'd lawyer; you gave me nothing for 't. Can you make no use of nothing, nuncle?

LEAR. Why, no, boy; nothing can be made out of nothing.

FOOL. [To Kent] Prithee, tell him, so much the rent of his land comes to; he will not believe a fool.

LEAR. A bitter fool!

FOOL. Dost thou know the difference, my boy, between a bitter fool and a sweet fool?

LEAR. No, lad; teach me.

FOOL.

> That lord that counselled thee
>   To give away thy land,
> Come place him here by me,
>   Do thou for him stand.
> The sweet and bitter fool
>   Will presently appear;
> The one in motley here,
>   The other found out there.

LEAR. Dost thou call me fool, boy?

FOOL. All thy other titles thou hast given away; that thou wast born with.

KENT. This is not altogether fool, my lord.

FOOL. No, faith, lords and great men will not let me; if I had a monopoly out, they would have part on 't. And ladies too, they will not let me have all fool to myself; they 'll be snatching. Give me an egg, nuncle, and I 'll give thee two crowns.

LEAR. What two crowns shall they be?

FOOL. Why, after I have cut the egg i' the middle, and eat up the meat, the two crowns of the egg. When thou clovest thy crown i' the middle, and gavest away both parts, thou borest thy ass on thy back o'er the dirt; thou hadst little wit in thy bald crown, when thou gavest thy golden one away. If I speak like myself in this, let him be whipped that first finds it so.

[Singing] Fools had ne'er less wit in a year;

> For wise men are grown foppish,
>   They know not how their wits to wear,
>   Their manners are so apish.

LEAR. When were you wont to be so full of songs, sirrah?

FOOL. I have used it, nuncle, ever since thou madest thy daughters thy mothers; for when thou gavest them the rod, and put'st down thine own breeches, [Singing] Then they for sudden joy did weep,

> And I for sorrow sung,
>   That such a king should play bo-peep,
>   And go the fools among.

Prithee, nuncle, keep a schoolmaster that can teach thy fool to lie; I would fain learn to lie.

LEAR. An you lie, sirrah, we 'll have you whipped.

FOOL. I marvel what kin thou and thy daughters are. They 'll have me whipped for speaking true, thou 'lt have me whipped for lying; and sometimes I am whipped for holding my peace. I had rather be any kind o' thing than a fool; and yet I would not be thee, nuncle; thou hast pared they wit o' both sides, and left nothing i' the middle. Here comes one o' the parings.

Enter GONERIL

LEAR. How now, daughter! what makes that frontlet on? Methinks you are too much of late i' the frown.

FOOL. Thou wast a pretty fellow when thou hadst no need to care for her frowning; now thou art an O without a figure. I am better than thou art now; I am a fool, thou art nothing. [To Goneril] Yes, forsooth, I will hold my tongue; so your face bids me, though you say nothing. Mum, mum,

> He that keeps nor crust nor crumb,
>   Weary of all, shall want some.

[Pointing to Lear] That 's a shealed peascod.

GONERIL. Not only, sir, this your all-licensed fool, But other of your insolent retinue Do hourly carp and quarrel, breaking forth In rank and not-to-be-endured riots. Sir, I had thought, by making this well known unto you, To have found a safe redress; but now grow fearful, By what yourself too late have spoke and done, That you protect this course, and put it on By your allowance; which if you should, the fault Would not 'scape censure, nor the redresses sleep, Which, in the tender of a wholesome weal, Might in their working do you that offence, Which else were shame, that then necessity Will call discreet proceeding.

FOOL. For, you know, nuncle,

> The hedge-sparrow fed the cuckoo so long,
>   That it 's had it head bit off by it young.

So, out went the candle, and we were left darkling.

LEAR. Are you our daughter?

GONERIL. Come, sir,

I would you would make use of that good wisdom,
Whereof I know you are fraught; and put away
These dispositions, that of late transform you
From what you rightly are.

FOOL. May not an ass know when the cart draws the
horse? Whoop, Jug! I love thee.

LEAR. Doth any here know me? This is not Lear!
Doth Lear walk thus? speak thus? Where are his eyes?
Either his notion weakens, his discernings
Are lethargied—Ha! waking? 'tis not so.
Who is it that can tell me who I am?

FOOL. Lear's shadow.

LEAR. I would learn that; for, by the marks of sovereignty, knowledge, and reason, I should be false persuaded I had daughters.

FOOL. Which they will make an obedient father.

LEAR. Your name, fair gentlewoman?

GONERIL. This admiration, sir, is much o' the savour
Of other your new pranks. I do beseech you
To understand my purposes aright:
As you are old and reverend, you should be wise.
Here do you keep a hundred knights and squires,
Men so disordered, so deboshed and bold,
That this our court, infected with their manners,
Shows like a riotous inn; epicurism and lust
Make it more like a tavern or a brothel
Than a graced palace. The shame itself doth speak
For instant remedy; be then desired
By her, that else will take the thing she begs,
A little to disquantity your train;
And the remainder, that shall still depend,
To be such men as may besort your age,
And know themselves and you.

LEAR.   Darkness and devils!
Saddle my horses; call my train together.
Degenerate bastard! I 'll not trouble thee!
Yet have I left a daughter.

GONERIL. You strike my people, and your disordered
rabble
Make servants of their betters.

Enter ALBANY

LEAR. Woe, that too late repents—[To Albany] O, sir,
are you come?
Is it your will? Speak, sir. Prepare my horses.
Ingratitude, thou marble-hearted fiend,
More hideous when thou show'st thee in a child
Than the sea-monster!

ALBANY.   Pray, sir, be patient.

LEAR. [To Goneril] Detested kite! thou liest!
My train are men of choice and rarest parts,
That all particulars of duty know,
And in the most exact regard support
The worships of their name. O most small fault,
How ugly didst thou in Cordelia show!
That, like an engine, wrenched my frame of nature

From the fixed place, drew from my heart all love,
And added to the gall. O Lear, Lear, Lear!
Beat at this gate, that let thy folly in,
                                          Striking his head
And thy dear judgment out! Go, go, my people.

ALBANY. My lord, I am guiltless, as I am ignorant
Of what hath moved you.

LEAR.   It may be so, my lord.
Hear, Nature, hear; dear goddess, hear!
Suspend thy purpose, if thou didst intend
To make this creature fruitful!
Into her womb convey sterility!
Dry up in her the organs of increase,
And from her derogate body never spring
A babe to honour her! If she must teem,
Create her child of spleen; that it may live,
And be a thwart disnatured torment to her!
Let it stamp wrinkles in her brow of youth,
With cadent tears fret channels in her cheeks,
Turn all her mother's pains and benefits
To laughter and contempt; that she may feel
How sharper than a serpent's tooth it is
To have a thankless child! Away, away!   *Exit*

ALBANY. Now, gods that we adore, whereof comes this?

GONERIL. Never afflict yourself to know the cause;
But let his disposition have that scope
That dotage gives it.

Re-enter LEAR

LEAR. What, fifty of my followers at a clap!
Within a fortnight!

ALBANY.   What 's the matter, sir?

LEAR. I 'll tell thee. [To Goneril] Life and death! I am
ashamed
That thou hast power to shake my manhood thus;
That these hot tears, which break from me perforce,
Should make thee worth them. Blasts and fogs upon
thee!
The untented woundings of a father's curse
Pierce every sense about thee! Old fond eyes,
Beweep this cause again, I 'll pluck ye out,
And cast you, with the waters that you lose,
To temper clay. Yea, is it come to this?
Let it be so. Yet have I left a daughter,
Who, I am sure, is kind and comfortable;
When she shall hear this of thee, with her nails
She'll flay thy wolvish visage. Thou shalt find
That I 'll resume the shape which thou dost think
I have cast off for ever; thou shalt, I warrant thee.
                         Exeunt LEAR, KENT, *and* Attendants

GONERIL. Do you mark that, my lord?

ALBANY. I cannot be so partial, Goneril,
To the great love I bear you—

GONERIL. Pray you, content. What, Oswald, ho!
[To the Fool] You, sir, more knave than fool, after
your master.

FOOL. Nuncle Lear, nuncle Lear, tarry and take the
  fool with thee.

> A fox, when one has caught her,
> And such a daughter,
> Should sure to the slaughter,
> If my cap would buy a halter;
> So the fool follows after.   *Exit*

GONERIL. This man hath had good counsel. A hundred
  knights!
  'Tis politic and safe to let him keep
  At point a hundred knights; yes, that, on every dream,
  Each buzz, each fancy, each complaint, dislike,
  He may enguard his dotage with their powers,
  And hold our lives in mercy. Oswald, I say!

ALBANY. Well, you may fear too far.

GONERIL.   Safer than trust too far.
  Let me still take away the harms I fear,
  Not fear still to be taken. I know his heart.
  What he hath uttered I have writ my sister;
  If she sustain him and his hundred knights,
  When I have showed the unfitness—

Re-enter OSWALD

                              How now, Oswald!
  What, have you writ that letter to my sister?

OSWALD. Yes, madam.

GONERIL. Take you some company, and away to horse.
  Inform her full of my particular fear;
  And thereto add such reasons of your own
  As may compact it more. Get you gone,
  And hasten your return. [*Exit Oswald*] No, no, my
    lord,
  This milky gentleness and course of yours
  Though I condemn not, yet, under pardon,
  You are much more attasked for want of wisdom
  Than praised for harmful mildness.

ALBANY. How far your eyes may pierce I cannot tell;
  Striving to better, oft we mar what's well.

GONERIL. Nay, then—

ALBANY. Well, well; the event.   *Exeunt*

SCENE V *Court before the same*

Enter LEAR, KENT, *and* Fool

LEAR. Go you before to Gloucester with these letters. Acquaint my daughter no further with anything you know than comes from her demand out of the letter. If your diligence be not speedy, I shall be there afore you.

KENT. I will not sleep, my lord, till I have delivered your letter.   *Exit*

FOOL. If a man's brains were in 's heels, were 't not in danger of kibes?

LEAR. Ay, boy.

FOOL. Then, I prithee, be merry; thy wit shall ne'er go slip-shod.

LEAR. Ha, ha, ha!

FOOL. Shalt see thy other daughter will use thee kindly; for though she's as like this as a crab's like an apple, yet I can tell what I can tell.

LEAR. Why, what canst thou tell, my boy?

FOOL. She will taste as like this as a crab does to a crab. Thou canst tell why one's nose stands i' the middle on 's face?

LEAR. No.

FOOL. Why, to keep one's eyes of either side 's nose; that what a man cannot smell out, he may spy into.

LEAR. I did her wrong—

FOOL. Canst tell how an oyster makes his shell?

LEAR. No.

FOOL. Nor I neither; but I can tell why a snail has a house.

LEAR. Why?

FOOL. Why, to put his head in; not to give it away to his daughters, and leave his horns without a case.

LEAR. I will forget my nature. So kind a father! Be my horses ready?

FOOL. Thy asses are gone about 'em. The reason why the seven stars are no more than seven is a pretty reason.

LEAR. Because they are not eight?

FOOL. Yes, indeed; thou wouldst make a good fool.

LEAR. To take 't again perforce! Monster ingratitude!

FOOL. If thou wert my fool, nuncle, I'd have thee beaten for being old before thy time.

LEAR. How 's that?

FOOL. Thou shouldst not have been old till thou hadst been wise.

LEAR. O, let me not be mad, not mad, sweet heaven! Keep me in temper; I would not be mad!

Enter Gentleman

How now! are the horses ready?

GENTLEMAN. Ready, my lord.

LEAR. Come, boy.

FOOL. She that's a maid now, and laughs at my departure,
    Shall not be a maid long, unless things be cut shorter.
                                        Exeunt

ACT II

SCENE I *The Earl of Gloucester's castle*

Enter EDMUND, *and* CURAN *meets him*

EDMUND. Save thee, Curan.

CURAN. And you, sir. I have been with your father, and given him notice that the duke of Cornwall and Regan his duchess will be here with him this night.

EDMUND. How comes that?

CURAN. Nay, I know not. You have heard of the news abroad; I mean the whispered ones, for they are yet but ear-kissing arguments?

EDMUND. Not I; pray you, what are they?

CURAN. Have you heard of no likely wars toward, 'twixt the dukes of Cornwall and Albany?

EDMUND. Not a word.

CURAN. You may do, then, in time. Fare you well, sir.

Exit

EDMUND. The Duke be here tonight? The better! best!
This weaves itself perforce into my business.
My father hath set guard to take my brother;
And I have one thing, of a queasy question,
Which I must act. Briefness and fortune, work!
Brother, a word; descend, brother, I say!

Enter EDGAR

My father watches. O sir, fly this place;
Intelligence is given where you are hid;
You have now the good advantage of the night.
Have you not spoken 'gainst the duke of Cornwall?
He 's coming hither, now, i' the night, i' the haste,
And Regan with him; have you nothing said
Upon his party 'gainst the duke of Albany?
Advise yourself.

EDGAR.   I am sure on 't, not a word.

EDMUND. I hear my father coming; pardon me,
In cunning I must draw my sword upon you.
Draw; seem to defend yourself; now quit you well.
Yield; come before my father. Light, ho, here!
Fly, brother. Torches, torches! So, farewell.

Exit EDGAR

Some blood drawn on me would beget opinion

Wounds his arm

Of my more fierce endeavour; I have seen drunkards
Do more than this in sport. Father, father!
Stop, stop! No help?

Enter GLOUCESTER, *and* Servants *with torches*

GLOUCESTER. Now, Edmund, where 's the villain?

EDMUND. Here stood he in the dark, his sharp sword out,
Mumbling of wicked charms, conjuring the moon
To stand auspicious mistress.

GLOUCESTER.   But where is he?

EDMUND. Look, sir, I bleed.

GLOUCESTER.   Where is the villain, Edmund?

EDMUND. Fled this way, sir. When by no means he could—

GLOUCESTER. Pursue him, ho! Go after. [*Exeunt some Servants*] By no means what?

EDMUND. Persuade me to the murder of your lordship;
But that I told him, the revenging gods
'Gainst parricides did all their thunders bend;
Spoke, with how manifold and strong a bond
The child was bound to the father; sir, in fine,
Seeing how loathly opposite I stood
To his unnatural purpose, in fell motion,
With his prepared sword, he charges home
My unprovided body, latched mine arm.
But when he saw my best alarumed spirits,
Bold in the quarrel's right, roused to the encounter,
Or whether gasted by the noise I made,
Full suddenly he fled.

GLOUCESTER.   Let him fly far.
Not in this land shall he remain uncaught;
And found—dispatch. The noble duke my master,
My worthy arch and patron, comes tonight.
By his authority I will proclaim it,
That he which finds him shall deserve our thanks,
Bringing the murderous coward to the stake;
He that conceals him, death.

EDMUND. When I dissuaded him from his intent,
And found him pight to do it, with curst speech
I threatened to discover him; he replied,
"Thou unpossessing bastard! dost thou think,
If I would stand against thee, would the reposal
Of any trust, virtue, or worth in thee
Make thy words faithed? No, what I should deny—
As this I would; ay, though thou didst produce
My very character—I 'ld turn it all
To thy suggestion, plot, and damned practice;
And thou must make a dullard of the world,
If they not thought the profits of my death
Were very pregnant and potential spurs
To make thee seek it."

GLOUCESTER.   O strange and fastened villain!
Would he deny his letter? I never got him.

Tucket within

Hark, the duke's trumpets! I know not why he comes.
All ports I 'll bar; the villain shall not 'scape;
The duke must grant me that. Besides, his picture
I will send far and near, that all the kingdom
May have due note of him; and of my land,
Loyal and natural boy, I 'll work the means
To make thee capable.

Enter CORNWALL, REGAN, *and* Attendants

CORNWALL. How now, my noble friend! since I came hither,

Which I can call but now, I have heard strange news.

REGAN. If it be true, all vengeance comes too short
Which can pursue the offender. How dost, my lord?

GLOUCESTER. O, madam, my old heart is cracked, is
cracked!

REGAN. What, did my father's godson seek your life?
He whom my father named? your Edgar?

GLOUCESTER. O, lady, lady, shame would have it hid!

REGAN. Was he not companion with the riotous knights
That tend upon my father?

GLOUCESTER. I know not, madam; 'tis too bad, too bad.

EDMUND. Yes, madam, he was of that consort.

REGAN. No marvel, then, though he were ill affected;
'Tis they have put him on the old man's death,
To have the expense and waste of his revenues.
I have this present evening from my sister
Been well informed of them; and with such cautions,
That if they come to sojourn at my house,
I 'll not be there.

CORNWALL.   Nor I, assure thee, Regan.
Edmund, I hear that you have shown your father
A child-like office.

EDMUND.   'Twas my duty, sir.

GLOUCESTER. He did bewray his practice; and received
This hurt you see, striving to apprehend him.

CORNWALL. Is he pursued?

GLOUCESTER.   Ay, my good lord.

CORNWALL. If he be taken, he shall never more
Be feared of doing harm; make your own purpose,
How in my strength you please. For you, Edmund,
Whose virtue and obedience doth this instant
So much commend itself, you shall be ours.
Natures of such deep trust we shall much need;
You we first seize on.

EDMUND.   I shall serve you, sir,
Truly, however else.

GLOUCESTER.   For him I thank your grace.

CORNWALL. You know not why we came to visit you—

REGAN. Thus out of season, threading dark-eyed night:
Occasions, noble Gloucester, of some poise,
Wherein we must have use of your advice.
Our father he hath writ, so hath our sister,
Of differences, which I least thought it fit
To answer from our home; the several messengers
From hence attend dispatch. Our good old friend,
Lay comforts to your bosom, and bestow
Your needful counsel to our businesses,
Which craves the instant use.

GLOUCESTER.   I serve you, madam.
Your graces are right welcome.   *Exeunt*

SCENE II *Before Gloucester's castle*

Enter KENT *and* OSWALD, *severally*

OSWALD. Good dawning to thee, friend; art of this
house?

KENT. Ay.

OSWALD. Where may we set our horses?

KENT. I' the mire.

OSWALD. Prithee, if thou lovest me, tell me.

KENT. I love thee not.

OSWALD. Why, then, I care not for thee.

KENT. If I had thee in Lipsbury pinfold, I would make
thee care for me.

OSWALD. Why dost thou use me thus? I know thee not.

KENT. Fellow, I know thee.

OSWALD. What dost thou know me for?

KENT. A knave; a rascal; an eater of broken meats; a
base, proud, shallow, beggarly, three-suited, hundred-
pound, filthy, worsted-stocking knave; a lily-livered,
action-taking knave; a whoreson, glass-gazing, super-
serviceable, finical rogue; one-trunk-inheriting slave;
one that wouldst be a bawd, in way of good service, and
art nothing but the composition of a knave, beggar,
coward, pandar, and the son and heir of a mongrel
bitch; one whom I will beat into clamorous whining,
if thou deniest the least syllable of thy addition.

OSWALD. Why, what a monstrous fellow art thou, thus
to rail on one that is neither known of thee nor
knows thee!

KENT. What a brazen-faced varlet art thou, to deny
thou knowest me! Is it two days ago since I tripped up
thy heels, and beat thee before the King? Draw, you
rogue; for, though it be night, yet the moon shines;
I 'll make a sop o' the moonshine of you. Draw, you
whoreson cullionly barber-monger, draw.
          Drawing his sword

OSWALD. Away! I have nothing to do with thee.

KENT. Draw, you rascal; you come with letters against
the King; and take vanity the puppet's part against
the royalty of her father. Draw, you rogue, or I 'll so
carbonado your shanks. Draw, you rascal; come your
ways.

OSWALD. Help, ho! murder! help!

KENT. Strike, you slave; stand, rogue, stand; you neat
slave, strike.   *Beating him*

OSWALD. Help, ho! murder! murder!

Enter EDMUND, *with his rapier drawn,* CORNWALL, REGAN,
GLOUCESTER, *and* Servants

EDMUND. How now! What 's the matter?

KENT. With you, goodman boy, and you please. Come,
I 'll flesh ye; come on, young master.

GLOUCESTER. Weapons! arms! What 's the matter here?

CORNWALL. Keep peace, upon your lives;
He dies that strikes again. What is the matter?

REGAN. The messengers from our sister and the King.

CORNWALL. What is your difference? Speak.

OSWALD. I am scarce in breath, my lord.

KENT. No marvel, you have so bestirred your valour.
You cowardly rascal, nature disclaims in thee; a tailor
made thee.

CORNWALL. Thou art a strange fellow; a tailor make
a man?

KENT. Ay, a tailor, sir; a stone-cutter or a painter
could not have made him so ill, though he had been
but two years at the trade.

CORNWALL. Speak yet, how grew your quarrel?

OSWALD. This ancient ruffian, sir, whose life I have
spared at suit of his gray beard—

KENT. Thou whoreson zed! thou unnecessary letter!
My lord, if you will give me leave, I will tread this
unbolted villain into mortar, and daub the walls of a
jakes with him. Spare my gray beard, you wagtail?

CORNWALL. Peace, sirrah!
You beastly knave, know you no reverence?

KENT. Yes, sir; but anger hath a privilege.

CORNWALL. Why art thou angry?

KENT. That such a slave as this should wear a sword,
Who wears no honesty. Such smiling rogues as these,
Like rats, oft bite the holy cords a-twain
Which are too intrinse t' unloose; smooth every
  passion
That in the natures of their lords rebel;
Bring oil to fire, snow to their colder moods,
Renege, affirm, and turn their halcyon beaks
With every gale and vary of their masters,
Knowing nought, like dogs, but following.
A plague upon your epileptic visage!
Smile you my speeches, as I were a fool?
Goose, if I had you upon Sarum plain,
I 'ld drive ye cackling home to Camelot.

CORNWALL. What, art thou mad, old fellow?

GLOUCESTER. How fell you out? Say that.

KENT. No contraries hold more antipathy
Than I and such a knave.

CORNWALL. Why dost thou call him knave? What's
his offence?

KENT. His countenance likes me not.

CORNWALL. No more, perchance, does mine, nor his,
nor hers.

KENT. Sir, 'tis my occupation to be plain.
I have seen better faces in my time
Than stands on any shoulder that I see
Before me at this instant.

CORNWALL.   This is some fellow,
Who, having been praised for bluntness, doth affect
A saucy roughness, and constrains the garb
Quite from his nature. He cannot flatter, he,
An honest mind and plain, he must speak truth!
An they will take it, so; if not, he's plain.
These kind of knaves I know, which in this plainness

Harbour more craft and more corrupter ends
Than twenty silly ducking observants
That stretch their duties nicely.

KENT. Sir, in good sooth, in sincere verity,
Under the allowance of your great aspect,
Whose influence, like the wreath of radiant fire
On flickering Phoebus' front—

CORNWALL.   What mean'st by this?

KENT. To go out of my dialect, which you discommend
so much. I know, sir, I am no flatterer. He that beguiled you in a plain accent was a plain knave; which
for my part I will not be, though I should win your
displeasure to entreat me to 't.

CORNWALL. What was the offence you gave him?

OSWALD. I never gave him any.
It pleased the King his master very late
To strike at me, upon his misconstruction;
When he, compact, and flattering his displeasure,
Tripped me behind; being down, insulted, railed,
And put upon him such a deal of man,
That worthied him, got praises of the King
For him attempting who was self-subdued;
And, in the fleshment of this dread exploit,
Drew on me here again.

KENT.   None of these rogues and cowards
But Ajax is their fool.

CORNWALL.   Fetch forth the stocks!
You stubborn ancient knave, you reverend braggart,
We 'll teach you—

KENT.   Sir, I am too old to learn,
Call not your stocks for me; I serve the King,
On whose employment I was sent to you.
You shall do small respect, show too bold malice
Against the grace and person of my master,
Stocking his messenger.

CORNWALL. Fetch forth the stocks! As I have life and
  honour,
There shall he sit till noon.

REGAN. Till noon! till night, my lord; and all night too.

KENT. Why, madam, if I were your father's dog,
You should not use me so.

REGAN.   Sir, being his knave, I will.

CORNWALL. This is a fellow of the self-same colour
Our sister speaks of. Come, bring away the stocks!
                                        Stocks brought out

GLOUCESTER. Let me beseech your grace not to do so.
His fault is much, and the good King his master
Will check him for 't. Your purposed low correction
Is such as basest and contemned'st wretches
For pilferings and most common trespasses
Are punished with. The King must take it ill,
That he's so slightly valued in his messenger,
Should have him thus restrained.

CORNWALL.   I 'll answer that.

REGAN. My sister may receive it much more worse,
To have her gentleman abused, assaulted,

For following her affairs. Put in his legs.

                            KENT is put in the stocks

Come, my good lord, away.

                 Exeunt all but GLOUCESTER *and* KENT

GLOUCESTER. I am sorry for thee, friend; 'tis the Duke's
    pleasure.
  Whose disposition, all the world well knows,
  Will not be rubbed nor stopped. I 'll entreat for thee.

KENT. Pray, do not, sir. I have watched and travelled
    hard;
  Some time I shall sleep out, the rest I 'll whistle.
  A good man's fortune may grow out at heels;
  Give you good morrow!

GLOUCESTER. The Duke's to blame in this; 'twill be
    ill taken.   *Exit*

KENT. Good king, that must approve the common saw,
  Thou out of heaven's benediction comest
  To the warm sun!
  Approach, thou beacon to this under globe,
  That by thy comfortable beams I may
  Peruse this letter! Nothing almost sees miracles
  But misery. I know 'tis from Cordelia,
  Who hath most fortunately been informed
  Of my obscured course; and shall find time
  From this enormous state, seeking to give
  Losses their remedies. All weary and o'er-watched,
  Take vantage, heavy eyes, not to behold
  This shameful lodging.
  Fortune, good night, smile once more; turn thy
    wheel!   *Sleeps*

SCENE III *A wood*

Enter EDGAR

EDGAR. I heard myself proclaimed;
  And by the happy hollow of a tree
  Escaped the hunt. No port is free; no place,
  That guard, and most unusual vigilance,
  Does not attend my taking. Whiles I may 'scape,
  I will preserve myself; and am bethought
  To take the basest and most poorest shape
  That ever penury, in contempt of man,
  Brought near to beast. My face I 'll grime with filth;
  Blanket my loins; elf all my hair in knots;
  And with presented nakedness out-face
  The winds and persecutions of the sky.
  The country gives me proof and precedent
  Of Bedlam beggars, who, with roaring voices,
  Strike in their numbed and mortified bare arms
  Pins, wooden pricks, nails, sprigs of rosemary;
  And with this horrible object, from low farms,
  Poor pelting villages, sheep-cotes, and mills,
  Sometime with lunatic bans, sometime with prayers,
  Enforce their charity. Poor Turlygod! poor Tom!
  That 's something yet; Edgar I nothing am.   *Exit*

SCENE IV *Before Gloucester's castle. Kent in the stocks*

Enter LEAR, Fool, *and* Gentleman

LEAR. 'Tis strange that they should so depart from home,
And not send back my messenger.
GENTLEMAN.   As I learned,
The night before there was no purpose in them
Of this remove.
KENT.   Hail to thee, noble master!
LEAR. Ha!
Makest thou this shame thy pastime?
KENT.   No, my lord.
FOOL. Ha, ha! he wears cruel garters. Horses are tied
by the heads, dogs and bears by the neck, monkeys by
the loins, and men by the legs. When a man's over-
lusty at legs, then he wears wooden nether-stocks.
LEAR. What 's he that hath so much thy place mistook
To set thee here?
KENT.   It is both he and she;
Your son and daughter.
LEAR. No.
KENT. Yes.
LEAR. No, I say.
KENT. I say, yea.
LEAR. No, no, they would not.
KENT. Yes, they have.
LEAR. By Jupiter, I swear, no.
KENT. By Juno, I swear, ay.
LEAR.   They durst not do 't;
They could not, would not do 't; 'tis worse than
murder,
To do upon respect such violent outrage.
Resolve me, with all modest haste, which way
Thou mightst deserve, or they impose, this usage,
Coming from us.
KENT.   My lord, when at their home
I did commend your highness' letters to them,
Ere I was risen from the place that showed
My duty kneeling, came there a reeking post,
Stewed in his haste, half breathless, panting forth
From Goneril his mistress salutations;
Delivered letters, spite of intermission,
Which presently they read; on whose contents,
They summoned up their meiny, straight took horse,
Commanded me to follow, and attend
The leisure of their answer; gave me cold looks;
And meeting here the other messenger,
Whose welcome, I perceived, had poisoned mine—
Being the very fellow that of late
Displayed so saucily against your highness—
Having more man than wit about me, drew.
He raised the house with loud and coward cries.
Your son and daughter found this trespass worth
The shame which here it suffers.
FOOL. Winter's not gone yet, if the wild-geese fly
that way.

Fathers that wear rags
   Do make their children blind;
But fathers that bear bags
   Shall see their children kind.
Fortune, that arrant whore,
Ne'er turns the key to the poor.
But, for all this, thou shalt have as many dolours for
thy daughters as thou canst tell in a year.
LEAR. O, how this mother swells up toward my heart!
Hysterica passio, down, thou climbing sorrow,
Thy element 's below! Where is this daughter?
KENT. With the earl, sir, here within.
LEAR.   Follow me not;
Stay here.   *Exit*
GENTLEMAN. Made you no more offence but what you
speak of?
KENT. None.
How chance the King comes with so small a train?
FOOL. An thou hadst been set i' the stocks for that
question, thou hadst well deserved it.
KENT. Why, fool?
FOOL. We 'll set thee to school to an ant, to teach thee
there's no labouring i' the winter. All that follow
their noses are led by their eyes but blind men; and
there's not a nose among twenty but can smell him
that's stinking. Let go thy hold when a great wheel
runs down a hill, lest it break thy neck with following
it; but the great one that goes up the hill, let him
draw thee after. When a wise man gives thee better
counsel, give me mine again; I would have none but
knaves follow it, since a fool gives it.
      That sir which serves and seeks for gain,
         And follows but for form,
      Will pack when it begins to rain,
         And leave thee in the storm.
      But I will tarry; the fool will stay,
         And let the wise man fly:
      The knave turns fool that runs away;
         The fool no knave, perdy.
KENT. Where learned you this, fool?
FOOL. Not i' the stocks, fool.

Re-enter LEAR, *with* GLOUCESTER

LEAR. Deny to speak with me? They are sick? They are
weary?
They have travelled all the night? Mere fetches;
The images of revolt and flying off.
Fetch me a better answer.
GLOUCESTER.   My dear lord,
You know the fiery quality of the Duke;
How unremovable and fixed he is
In his own course.
LEAR. Vengeance! plague! death! confusion!

Fiery? what quality? Why, Gloucester, Gloucester,
I 'd speak with the duke of Cornwall and his wife.
GLOUCESTER. Well, my good lord, I have informed them
so.
LEAR. Informed them! Dost thou understand me, man?
GLOUCESTER. Ay, my good lord.
LEAR. The King would speak with Cornwall; the dear
father
Would with his daughter speak, commands—tends—
service!
Are they informed of this? My breath and blood!
Fiery? the fiery Duke? Tell the hot Duke that—
No, but not yet; may be he is not well.
Infirmity doth still neglect all office
Whereto our health is bound; we are not ourselves
When nature, being oppressed, commands the mind
To suffer with the body. I 'll forbear;
And am fall'n out with my more headier will,
To take the indisposed and sickly fit
For the sound man. Death on my state! wherefore
                                        Looking on KENT
Should he sit here? This act persuades me
That this remotion of the Duke and her
Is practice only. Give me my servant forth.
Go tell the Duke and 's wife I 'd speak with them,
Now, presently. Bid them come forth and hear me,
Or at their chamber-door I 'll beat the drum
Till it cry sleep to death.
GLOUCESTER. I would have all well betwixt you.   *Exit*
LEAR. O me, my heart, my rising heart! but, down!
FOOL. Cry to it, nuncle, as the cockney did to the eels
when she put 'em i' the paste alive; she knapped 'em
o' the coxcombs with a stick, and cried "Down,
wantons, down!" 'Twas her brother that, in pure
kindness to his horse, buttered his hay.

Enter CORNWALL, REGAN, GLOUCESTER, *and* Servants

LEAR. Good morrow to you both.
CORNWALL.   Hail to your grace!
                              KENT *is set at liberty*
REGAN. I am glad to see your highness.
LEAR. Regan, I think you are; I know what reason
I have to think so. If thou shouldst not be glad,
I would divorce me from thy mother's tomb,
Sepulchring an adultress. [*To Kent*] O, are you free?
Some other time for that. Beloved Regan,
Thy sister 's naught; O Regan, she hath tied
Sharp-toothed unkindness, like a vulture, here.
                                        Points to his heart
I can scarce speak to thee; thou 'lt not believe
With how depraved a quality—O Regan!
REGAN. I pray you, sir, take patience. I have hope
You less know how to value her desert
Than she to scant her duty.
LEAR.   Say, how is that?
REGAN. I cannot think my sister in the least

Would fail her obligation; if, sir, perchance
She have restrained the riots of your followers,
'Tis on such ground, and to such wholesome end,
As clears her from all blame.
LEAR. My curses on her!
REGAN.   O, sir, you are old;
Nature in you stands on the very verge
Of her confine. You should be ruled and led
By some discretion that discerns your state
Better than you yourself. Therefore, I pray you,
That to our sister you do make return;
Say you have wronged her, sir.
LEAR.   Ask her forgiveness?
Do you but mark how this becomes the house:
"Dear daughter, I confess that I am old;   *Kneeling*
Age is unnecessary. On my knees I beg
That you 'll vouchsafe me raiment, bed, and food."
REGAN. Good sir, no more; these are unsightly tricks.
Return you to my sister.
LEAR.   [*Rising*] Never, Regan.
She hath abated me of half my train;
Looked black upon me; struck me with her tongue,
Most serpent-like, upon the very heart.
All the stored vengeances of heaven fall
On her ingrateful top! Strike her young bones,
You taking airs, with lameness!
CORNWALL.   Fie, sir, fie!
LEAR. You nimble lightnings, dart your blinding flames
Into her scornful eyes! Infect her beauty,
You fen-sucked fogs, drawn by the powerful sun,
To fall and blister!
REGAN. O the blest gods! so will you wish on me,
When the rash mood is on.
LEAR. No, Regan, thou shalt never have my curse;
Thy tender-hefted nature shall not give
Thee o'er to harshness. Her eyes are fierce; but thine
Do comfort and not burn. 'Tis not in thee
To grudge my pleasures, to cut off my train,
To bandy hasty words, to scant my sizes,
And in conclusion to oppose the bolt
Against my coming in. Thou better know'st
The offices of nature, bond of childhood,
Effects of courtesy, dues of gratitude;
Thy half o' the kingdom hast thou not forgot,
Wherein I thee endowed.
REGAN.   Good sir, to the purpose.
LEAR. Who put my man i' the stocks?   *Tucket within*
CORNWALL.   What trumpet's that?
REGAN. I know 't, my sister's; this approves her letter,
That she would soon be here.

Enter OSWALD

                              Is your lady come?
LEAR. This is a slave, whose easy-borrowed pride
Dwells in the fickle grace of her he follows.
Out, varlet, from my sight!

CORNWALL.   What means your grace?
LEAR. Who stocked my servant? Regan, I have good
    hope
  Thou didst not know on 't. Who comes here? O
  heavens,

Enter GONERIL

If you do love old men, if your sweet sway
Allow obedience, if yourselves are old,
Make it your cause; send down, and take my part!
[*To Goneril*] Art not ashamed to look upon this beard?
O Regan, wilt thou take her by the hand?
GONERIL. Why not by the hand, sir? How have I
    offended?
  All 's not offence that indiscretion finds
  And dotage terms so.
LEAR.   O sides, you are too tough;
  Will you yet hold? How came my man i' the stocks?
CORNWALL. I set him there, sir, but his own disorders
  Deserved much less advancement.
LEAR.   You! did you?
REGAN. I pray you, father, being weak, seem so.
  If, till the expiration of your month,
  You will return and sojourn with my sister,
  Dismissing half your train, come then to me.
  I am now from home, and out of that provision
  Which shall be needful for your entertainment.
LEAR. Return to her, and fifty men dismissed?
  No, rather I abjure all roofs, and choose
  To wage against the enmity o' the air;
  To be a comrade with the wolf and owl,
  Necessity's sharp pinch! Return with her?
  Why, the hot-blooded France, that dowerless took
  Our youngest born, I could as well be brought
  To knee his throne, and, squire-like, pension beg
  To keep base life afoot. Return with her?
  Persuade me rather to be slave and sumpter
  To this detested groom.   *Pointing at* OSWALD
GONERIL.   At your choice, sir.
LEAR. I prithee, daughter, do not make me mad.
  I will not trouble thee, my child; farewell.
  We 'll no more meet, no more see one another;
  But yet thou art my flesh, my blood, my daughter;
  Or rather a disease that's in my flesh,
  Which I must needs call mine. Thou art a boil,
  A plague-sore, an embossed carbuncle,
  In my corrupted blood. But I 'll not chide thee;
  Let shame come when it will, I do not call it.
  I do not bid the thunder-bearer shoot,
  Nor tell tales of thee to high-judging Jove.
  Mend when thou canst; be better at thy leisure.
  I can be patient; I can stay with Regan,
  I and my hundred knights.
REGAN.   Not altogether so;
  I looked not for you yet, nor am provided
  For your fit welcome. Give ear, sir, to my sister;

For those that mingle reason with your passion
Must be content to think you old, and so—
But she knows what she does.
LEAR.   Is this well spoken?
REGAN. I dare avouch it, sir. What, fifty followers?
  Is it not well? What should you need of more?
  Yea, or so many, sith that both charge and danger
  Speak 'gainst so great a number? How, in one house,
  Should many people, under two commands,
  Hold amity? 'Tis hard; almost impossible.
GONERIL. Why might not you, my lord, receive at-
    tendance
  From those that she calls servants or from mine?
REGAN. Why not, my lord? If then they chanced to
    slack you,
  We could control them. If you will come to me—
  For now I spy a danger—I entreat you
  To bring but five and twenty; to no more
  Will I give place or notice.
LEAR. I gave you all—
REGAN.   And in good time you gave it.
LEAR. Made you my guardians, my depositaries;
  But kept a reservation to be followed
  With such a number. What, must I come to you
  With five and twenty, Regan? said you so?
REGAN. And speak 't again, my lord; no more with me.
LEAR. Those wicked creatures yet do look well-
    favoured,
  When others are more wicked; not being the worst
  Stands in some rank of praise. [*To Goneril*] I'll go
    with thee;
  Thy fifty yet doth double five-and-twenty,
  And thou art twice her love.
GONERIL.   Hear me, my lord:
  What need you five and twenty, ten, or five,
  To follow in a house where twice so many
  Have a command to tend you?
REGAN.   What need one?
LEAR. O, reason not the need; our basest beggars
  Are in the poorest thing superfluous.
  Allow not nature more than nature needs,
  Man's life 's as cheap as beast's. Thou art a lady;
  If only to go warm were gorgeous,
  Why, nature needs not what thou gorgeous wear'st,
  Which scarcely keeps thee warm. But, for true need—
  You heavens, give me that patience, patience I need!
  You see me here, you gods, a poor old man,
  As full of grief as age; wretched in both!
  If it be you that stir these daughters' hearts
  Against their father, fool me not so much
  To bear it tamely; touch me with noble anger,
  And let not women's weapons, water-drops,
  Stain my man's cheeks! No, you unnatural hags,
  I will have such revenges on you both,
  That all the world shall—I will do such things—
  What they are, yet I know not; but they shall be

The terrors of the earth. You think I 'll weep;
No, I 'll not weep.
I have full cause of weeping; but this heart
Shall break into a hundred thousand flaws,
Or ere I 'll weep. O fool, I shall go mad!
                    Exeunt LEAR, GLOUCESTER, KENT, *and* FOOL
                                        Storm and tempest

CORNWALL. Let us withdraw; 'twill be a storm.
REGAN. This house is little; the old man and his people
    Cannot be well bestowed.
GONERIL. 'Tis his own blame; hath put himself from
    rest,
    And must needs taste his folly.
REGAN. For his particular, I 'll receive him gladly,
    But not one follower.
GONERIL.   So am I purposed.
    Where is my lord of Gloucester?
CORNWALL. Followed the old man forth. He is returned.

Re-enter GLOUCESTER

GLOUCESTER. The King is in high rage.
CORNWALL.   Whither is he going?
GLOUCESTER. He calls to horse; but will I know not
    whither.
CORNWALL. 'Tis best to give him way; he leads him-
    self.
GONERIL. My lord, entreat him by no means to stay.
GLOUCESTER. Alack, the night comes on, and the bleak
    winds
    Do sorely ruffle; for many miles about
    There's scarce a bush.
REGAN.   O, sir, to willful men,
    The injuries that they themselves procure
    Must be their schoolmasters. Shut up your doors;
    He is attended with a desperate train,
    And what they may incense him to, being apt
    To have his ear abused, wisdom bids fear.
CORNWALL. Shut up your doors, my lord; 'tis a wild
    night.
    My Regan counsels well; come out o' the storm.
                                              Exeunt

ACT III

SCENE I *A heath*

Storm still. Enter KENT *and a* Gentleman, *meeting*

KENT. Who's there, besides foul weather?
GENTLEMAN. One minded like the weather, most un-
    quietly.
KENT. I know you. Where's the King?
GENTLEMAN. Contending with the fretful element;
    Bids the wind blow the earth into the sea,

Or swell the curled waters 'bove the main,
That things might change or cease; tears his white hair,
Which the impetuous blasts, with eyeless rage,
Catch in their fury, and make nothing of;
Strives in his little world of man to out-scorn
The to-and-fro-conflicting wind and rain.
This night, wherein the cub-drawn bear would couch,
The lion and the belly-pinched wolf
Keep their fur dry, unbonneted he runs,
And bids what will take all.

KENT.   But who is with him?

GENTLEMAN. None but the fool, who labours to out-
  jest
His heart-struck injuries.

KENT.   Sir, I do know you;
And dare, upon the warrant of my note,
Commend a dear thing to you. There is division,
Although as yet the face of it be covered
With mutual cunning, 'twixt Albany and Cornwall;
Who have—as who have not, that their great stars
Throned and set high?—servants, who seem no less,
Which are to France the spies and speculations
Intelligent of our state; what hath been seen,
Either in snuffs and packings of the dukes,
Or the hard rein which both of them have borne
Against the old kind King; or something deeper,
Whereof perchance these are but furnishings;
But, true it is, from France there comes a power
Into this scattered kingdom; who already,
Wise in our negligence, have secret feet
In some of our best ports, and are at point
To show their open banner. Now to you:
If on my credit you dare build so far
To make your speed to Dover, you shall find
Some that will thank you, making just report
Of how unnatural and bemadding sorrow
The King hath cause to plain.
I am a gentleman of blood and breeding;
And, from some knowledge and assurance, offer
This office to you.

GENTLEMAN. I will talk further with you.

KENT.   No, do not.
For confirmation that I am much more
Than my out-wall, open this purse, and take
What it contains. If you shall see Cordelia—
As fear not but you shall—show her this ring;
And she will tell you who your fellow is
That yet you do not know. Fie on this storm!
I will go seek the King.

GENTLEMAN. Give me your hand. Have you no more to
  say?

KENT. Few words, but, to effect, more than all yet;
That, when we have found the King—in which your
  pain
That way, I 'll this—he that first lights on him
Holla the other.   *Exeunt severally*

SCENE II *Another part of the heath. Storm still*

Enter LEAR *and* Fool

LEAR. Blow, winds, and crack your cheeks! rage! blow!
You cataracts and hurricanoes, spout
Till you have drenched our steeples, drowned the
cocks!
You sulphurous and thought-executing fires,
Vaunt-couriers to oak-cleaving thunderbolts,
Singe my white head! And thou, all-shaking thunder,
Smite flat the thick rotundity o' the world!
Crack nature's moulds, all germens spill at once,
That make ingrateful man!
FOOL. O nuncle, court holy-water in a dry house is
better than this rain-water out o' door. Good nuncle,
in, and ask thy daughters' blessing; here's a night
pities neither wise man nor fool.
LEAR. Rumble thy bellyful! Spit, fire! spout, rain!
Nor rain, wind, thunder, fire, are my daughters!
I tax not you, you elements, with unkindness;
I never gave you kingdom, called you children,
You owe me no subscription; then let fall
Your horrible pleasure; here I stand, your slave,
A poor, infirm, weak, and despised old man.
But yet I call you servile ministers,
That have with two pernicious daughters joined
Your high engendered battles 'gainst a head
So old and white as this. O! O! 'tis foul!

FOOL. He that has a house to put 's head in has a good
head-piece.
> The cod-piece that will house
> Before the head has any,
> The head and he shall louse;
> So beggars marry many.
> The man that makes his toe
> What he his heart should make
> Shall of a corn cry woe,
> And turn his sleep to wake.

For there was never yet fair woman but she made
mouths in a glass.

LEAR. No, I will be the pattern of all patience;
I will say nothing.

Enter KENT

KENT. Who's there?

FOOL. Marry, here's grace and a cod-piece; that's a
wise man and a fool.

KENT. Alas, sir, are you here? Things that love night
Love not such nights as these; the wrathful skies
Gallow the very wanderers of the dark,
And make them keep their caves. Since I was man,
Such sheets of fire, such bursts of horrid thunder,
Such groans of roaring wind and rain, I never
Remember to have heard; man's nature cannot carry
The affliction nor the fear.

LEAR. Let the great gods,
That keep this dreadful pother o'er our heads,
Find out their enemies now. Tremble, thou wretch,
That hast within thee undivulged crimes,
Unwhipped of justice; hide thee, thou bloody hand;
Thou perjured, and thou simular of virtue
That art incestuous; caitiff, to pieces shake,
That under covert and convenient seeming
Hast practised on man's life; close pent-up guilts,
Rive your concealing continents, and cry
These dreadful summoners grace. I am a man
More sinned against than sinning.

KENT. Alack, bare-headed!

Gracious my lord, hard by here is a hovel;
Some friendship will it lend you 'gainst the tempest.
Repose you there; while I to this hard house—
More harder than the stones whereof 'tis raised;
Which even but now, demanding after you,
Denied me to come in—return, and force
Their scanted courtesy.

LEAR. My wits begin to turn.
Come on, my boy. How dost, my boy? art cold?
I am cold myself. Where is this straw, my fellow?
The art of our necessities is strange,
That can make vile things precious. Come, your hovel.
Poor fool and knave, I have one part in my heart
That's sorry yet for thee.

FOOL. [*Singing*]
> He that has and a little tiny wit,
> With hey, ho, the wind and the rain,
> Must make content with his fortunes fit,
> For the rain it raineth every day.

LEAR. True, my good boy. Come, bring us to this hovel.

Exeunt LEAR *and* KENT

FOOL. This is a brave night to cool a courtezan.
I 'll speak a prophecy ere I go:
> When priests are more in word than matter;
> When brewers mar their malt with water;
> When nobles are their tailors' tutors;
> No heretics burned, but wenches' suitors;
> When every case in law is right;
> No squire in debt, nor no poor knight;
> When slanders do not live in tongues;
> Nor cutpurses come not to throngs;
> When usurers tell their gold i' the field;
> And bawds and whores do churches build;
> Then shall the realm of Albion
> Come to great confusion:
> Then comes the time, who lives to see 't,
> That going shall be used with feet.
This prophecy Merlin shall make; for I live before
his time. *Exit*

SCENE III *Gloucester's castle*

Enter GLOUCESTER *and* EDMUND

GLOUCESTER. Alack, alack, Edmund, I like not this unnatural dealing. When I desired their leave that I
might pity him, they took from me the use of mine
own house; charged me, on pain of their perpetual
displeasure, neither to speak of him, entreat for him,
nor any way sustain him.

EDMUND. Most savage and unnatural!

GLOUCESTER. Go to; say you nothing. There 's a division
betwixt the dukes; and a worse matter than that.
I have received a letter this night; 'tis dangerous to be
spoken; I have locked the letter in my closet. These
injuries the King now bears will be revenged home;
there's part of a power already footed. We must incline to the King. I will seek him, and privily relieve
him; go you and maintain talk with the Duke, that
my charity be not of him perceived. If he ask for me,
I am ill, and gone to bed. Though I die for it, as no
less is threatened me, the King my old master must be
relieved. There is some strange thing toward, Edmund; pray you, be careful.

Exit

EDMUND. This courtesy, forbid thee, shall the Duke
Instantly know; and of that letter too.
This seems a fair deserving, and must draw me
That which my father loses; no less than all.
The younger rises when the old doth fall. *Exit*

SCENE IV *The heath: before a hovel*

Enter LEAR, KENT, *and* Fool

KENT. Here is the place, my lord; good my lord,
  enter.
  The tyranny of the open night 's too rough
  For nature to endure. *Storm still*
LEAR. Let me alone.
KENT. Good my lord, enter here.
LEAR. Wilt break my heart?
KENT. I had rather break mine own. Good my lord,
  enter.
LEAR. Thou think'st 'tis much that this contentious
  storm
  Invades us to the skin; so 'tis to thee.
  But where the greater malady is fixed,
  The lesser is scarce felt. Thou 'ldst shun a bear;
  But if thy flight lay toward the raging sea,
  Thou 'ldst meet the bear i' the mouth. When the
  mind 's free,
  The body 's delicate; the tempest in my mind
  Doth from my senses take all feeling else
  Save what beats there. Filial ingratitude!
  Is it not as this mouth should tear this hand
  For lifting food to 't? But I will punish home;
  No, I will weep no more. In such a night
  To shut me out! Pour on; I will endure.
  In such a night as this! O Regan, Goneril!
  Your old kind father, whose frank heart gave all—
  O, that way madness lies; let me shun that;
  No more of that.
KENT. Good my lord, enter here.
LEAR. Prithee, go in thyself, seek thine own ease;
  This tempest will not give me leave to ponder
  On things would hurt me more. But I 'll go in.
  [*To the Fool*] In, boy; go first. You houseless poverty—
  Nay, get thee in. I 'll pray, and then I 'll sleep.
  Fool goes in
  Poor naked wretches, wheresoe'er you are,
  That bide the pelting of this pitiless storm,
  How shall your houseless heads and unfed sides,
  Your looped and windowed raggedness, defend you
  From seasons such as these? O, I have ta'en
  Too little care of this! Take physic, pomp;
  Expose thyself to feel what wretches feel,
  That thou mayst shake the superflux to them,
  And show the heavens more just.
EDGAR. [*Within*] Fathom and half, fathom and half!
  Poor Tom! *The* Fool *runs out from the hovel*
FOOL. Come not in here, nuncle, here's a spirit. Help
  me, help me!
KENT. Give me thy hand. Who's there?
FOOL. A spirit, a spirit; he says his name 's poor Tom.
KENT. What art thou that dost grumble there i' the
  straw? Come forth.

Enter EDGAR *disguised as a madman*

379

EDGAR. Away! the foul fiend follows me!
　Through the sharp hawthorn blows the cold wind.
　Hum! go to thy cold bed, and warm thee.

LEAR. Hast thou given all to thy two daughters?
　And art thou come to this?

EDGAR. Who gives anything to poor Tom? whom the foul fiend hath led through fire and through flame, through ford and whirlpool, o'er bog and quagmire; that hath laid knives under his pillow, and halters in his pew; set ratsbane by his porridge; made him proud of heart, to ride on a bay trotting-horse over four-inched bridges, to course his own shadow for a traitor. Bless thy five wits! Tom 's a-cold—O, do de, do de, do de. Bless thee from whirlwinds, star-blasting, and taking! Do poor Tom some charity, whom the foul fiend vexes. There could I have him now—and there—and there again, and there.

Storm still

LEAR. What, have his daughters brought him to this pass?
　Couldst thou save nothing? Didst thou give them all?

FOOL. Nay, he reserved a blanket, else we had been all shamed.

LEAR. Now, all the plagues that in the pendulous air
　Hang fated o'er men's faults light on thy daughters!

KENT. He hath no daughters, sir.

LEAR. Death, traitor! Nothing could have subdued nature
　To such a lowness but his unkind daughters.
　Is it the fashion, that discarded fathers
　Should have thus little mercy on their flesh?
　Judicious punishment! 'twas this flesh begot
　Those pelican daughters.

EDGAR. Pillicock sat on Pillicock-hill:
　Halloo, halloo, loo, loo!

FOOL. This cold night will turn us all to fools and madmen.

EDGAR. Take heed o' the foul fiend. Obey thy parents; keep thy word justly; swear not; commit not with man's sworn spouse; set not thy sweet heart on proud array. Tom 's a-cold.

LEAR. What hast thou been?

EDGAR. A serving-man, proud in heart and mind; that curled my hair; wore gloves in my cap; served the lust of my mistress' heart, and did the act of darkness with her; swore as many oaths as I spake words, and broke them in the sweet face of heaven; one that slept in the contriving of lust, and waked to do it. Wine loved I deeply, dice dearly, and in woman out-paramoured the Turk; false of heart, light of ear, bloody of hand; hog in sloth, fox in stealth, wolf in greediness, dog in madness, lion in prey. Let not the creaking of shoes nor the rustling of silks betray thy poor heart to woman; keep thy foot out of brothels, thy hand out of plackets, thy pen from lenders' books, and defy the foul fiend.

　Still through the hawthorn blows the cold wind:
　Says suum, mun, ha, no, nonny.
　Dolphin my boy, my boy, sessa! let him trot by.

Storm still

LEAR. Why, thou wert better in thy grave than to answer with thy uncovered body this extremity of the skies. Is man no more than this? Consider him well. Thou owest the worm no silk, the beast no hide, the sheep no wool, the cat no perfume. Ha! here's three on 's are sophisticated! Thou art the thing itself; unaccommodated man is no more but such a poor, bare, forked animal as thou art. Off, off, you lendings! come, unbutton here.　*Tearing off his clothes*

FOOL. Prithee, nuncle, be contented; 'tis a naughty night to swim in. Now a little fire in a wild field were like an old lecher's heart; a small spark, all the rest on 's body cold. Look, here comes a walking fire.

Enter GLOUCESTER, with a torch

EDGAR. This is the foul fiend Flibbertigibbet; he begins at curfew, and walks till the first cock; he gives the web and the pin, squints the eye, and makes the hare-lip; mildews the white wheat, and hurts the poor creature of earth.
　Swithold footed thrice the old;
　He met the nightmare, and her ninefold;
　　　Bid her alight,
　　　And her troth plight,
　And, aroint thee, witch, aroint thee!

KENT. How fares your grace?

LEAR. What's he?

KENT. Who's there? What is 't you seek?

GLOUCESTER. What are you there? Your names?

EDGAR. Poor Tom; that eats the swimming frog, the toad, the tadpole, the wall-newt and the water; that in the fury of his heart, when the foul fiend rages, eats cow-dung for sallets; swallows the old rat and the ditch-dog; drinks the green mantle of the standing pool; who is whipped from tithing to tithing, and stock-punished, and imprisoned; who hath had three suits to his back, six shirts to his body, horse to ride, and weapon to wear;
　But mice and rats, and such small deer,
　Have been Tom's food for seven long year.
Beware my follower. Peace, Smulkin; peace, thou fiend!

GLOUCESTER. What, hath your grace no better company?

EDGAR. The prince of darkness is a gentleman; Modo
he's called, and Mahu.

GLOUCESTER. Our flesh and blood is grown so vile, my
lord,
That it doth hate what gets it.

EDGAR. Poor Tom 's a-cold.

GLOUCESTER. Go in with me. My duty cannot suffer
To obey in all your daughters' hard commands;
Though their injunction be to bar my doors,
And let this tyrannous night take hold upon you,
Yet have I ventured to come seek you out,
And bring you where both fire and food is ready.

LEAR. First let me talk with this philosopher.
What is the cause of thunder?

KENT. Good my lord, take his offer; go into the house.

LEAR. I 'll talk a word with this same learned Theban.
What is your study?

EDGAR. How to prevent the fiend, and to kill vermin.

LEAR. Let me ask you one word in private.

KENT. Importune him once more to go, my lord;
His wits begin to unsettle.

GLOUCESTER. Canst thou blame him?   *Storm still*
His daughters seek his death; ah, that good Kent!
He said it would be thus, poor banished man!

Thou say'st the King grows mad; I 'll tell thee, friend,
I am almost mad myself. I had a son,
Now outlawed from my blood; he sought my life,
But lately, very late; I loved him, friend,
No father his son dearer; truth to tell thee,
The grief hath crazed my wits. What a night 's this!
I do beseech your grace—

LEAR.   O, cry you mercy, sir.
Noble philosopher, your company.

EDGAR. Tom 's a-cold.

GLOUCESTER. In, fellow, there, into the hovel; keep thee
warm.

LEAR. Come, let 's in all.

KENT.   This way, my lord.

LEAR.   With him;
I will keep still with my philosopher.

KENT. Good my lord, soothe him; let him take the
fellow.

GLOUCESTER. Take him you on.

KENT. Sirrah, come on; go along with us.

LEAR. Come, good Athenian.

GLOUCESTER. No words, no words; hush.

EDGAR. Child Rowland to the dark tower came,
His word was still—Fie, foh, and fum,
I smell the blood of a British man.   *Exeunt*

SCENE V *Gloucester's castle*

Enter CORNWALL *and* EDMUND

CORNWALL. I will have my revenge ere I depart his
house.

EDMUND. How, my lord, I may be censured, that nature
thus gives way to loyalty, something fears me to
think of.

CORNWALL. I now perceive it was not altogether your
brother's evil disposition made him seek his death;
but a provoking merit, set a-work by a reproveable
badness in himself.

EDMUND. How malicious is my fortune, that I must repent to be just! This is the letter he spoke of, which
approves him an intelligent party to the advantages of
France. O heavens! that this treason were not, or not

I the detector!

CORNWALL. Go with me to the Duchess.

EDMUND. If the matter of this paper be certain, you
have mighty business in hand.

CORNWALL. True or false, it hath made thee earl of
Gloucester. Seek out where thy father is, that he may
be ready for our apprehension.

EDMUND. [*Aside*] If I find him comforting the King,
it will stuff his suspicion more fully.—I will persevere
in my course of loyalty, though the conflict be sore
between that and my blood.

CORNWALL. I will lay trust upon thee; and thou shalt
find a dearer father in my love.   *Exeunt*

SCENE VI *A chamber in a farmhouse adjoining the castle*

Enter GLOUCESTER, LEAR, KENT, Fool, *and* EDGAR

GLOUCESTER. Here is better than the open air; take it
thankfully. I will piece out the comfort with what
addition I can; I will not be long from you.

KENT. All the power of his wits have given way to his
impatience. The gods reward your kindness!
Exit GLOUCESTER

EDGAR. Fraretto calls me; and tells me Nero is an
angler in the lake of darkness. Pray, innocent, and
beware the foul fiend.

FOOL. Prithee, nuncle, tell me whether a madman be a
gentleman or a yeoman?

LEAR. A king, a king!

FOOL. No, he's a yeoman that has a gentleman to his
son; for he's a mad yeoman that sees his son a gentleman before him.

LEAR. To have a thousand with red burning spits
Come hissing in upon 'em—

EDGAR. The foul fiend bites my back.

FOOL. He's mad that trusts in the tameness of a wolf, a horse's health, a boy's love, or a whore's oath.

LEAR. It shall be done; I will arraign them straight.
  [*To Edgar*] Come, sit thou here, most learned justicer;
  [*To the Fool*] Thou, sapient sir, sit here. Now, you she-foxes!

EDGAR. Look, where he stands and glares!
  Wantest thou eyes at trial, madam?

  Come o'er the bourn, Bessy, to me—

FOOL. Her boat hath a leak,
  And she must not speak
  Why she dares not come over to thee.

EDGAR. The foul fiend haunts poor Tom in the voice of a nightingale. Hopdance cries in Tom's belly for two white herring. Croak not, black angel; I have no food for thee.

KENT. How do you, sir? Stand you not so amazed;
  Will you lie down and rest upon the cushions?

LEAR. I'll see their trial first. Bring in the evidence.
  [*To Edgar*] Thou robed man of justice, take thy place;
  [*To the Fool*] And thou, his yoke-fellow of equity,
  Bench by his side. [*To Kent*] You are o' the commission,
  Sit you too.

EDGAR. Let us deal justly.

  Sleepest or wakest thou, jolly shepherd?
    Thy sheep be in the corn;
  And for one blast of thy minikin mouth,
    Thy sheep shall take no harm.

  Pur! the cat is gray.

LEAR. Arraign her first; 'tis Goneril. I here take my oath before this honourable assembly, she kicked the poor king her father.

FOOL. Come hither, mistress. Is your name Goneril?

LEAR. She cannot deny it.

FOOL. Cry you mercy, I took you for a joint-stool.

LEAR. And here's another, whose warped looks proclaim
  What store her heart is made on. Stop her there!
  Arms, arms, sword, fire! Corruption in the place!
  False justicer, why hast thou let her 'scape?

EDGAR. Bless thy five wits!

KENT. O pity! Sir, where is the patience now,
  That you so oft have boasted to retain?

EDGAR. [*Aside*] My tears begin to take his part so much,
  They'll mar my counterfeiting.

LEAR. The little dogs and all,
  Tray, Blanch, and Sweetheart, see, they bark at me.

EDGAR. Tom will throw his head at them. Avaunt, you curs!

  Be thy mouth or black or white,
  Tooth that poisons if it bite;
  Mastiff, greyhound, mongrel grim,
  Hound or spaniel, brach or lym,
  Or bobtail tike or trundle-tail,
  Tom will make them weep and wail:
  For, with throwing thus my head,
  Dogs leap the hatch, and all are fled.

Do de, de, de. Sessa! Come, march to wakes and fairs and market-towns. Poor Tom, thy horn is dry.

LEAR. Then let them anatomize Regan; see what breeds about her heart. Is there any cause in nature that makes these hard hearts? [*To Edgar*] You, sir, I entertain for one of my hundred; only I do not like the fashion of your garments. You will say they are Persian attire; but let them be changed.

KENT. Now, good my lord, lie here and rest awhile.

LEAR. Make no noise, make no noise; draw the curtains: so, so, so. We'll go to supper i' the morning: so, so, so.

FOOL. And I'll go to bed at noon.

Re-enter GLOUCESTER

GLOUCESTER. Come hither, friend; where is the King my master?

KENT. Here, sir; but trouble him not, his wits are gone.

GLOUCESTER. Good friend, I prithee, take him in thy arms;
  I have o'erheard a plot of death upon him.
  There is a litter ready; lay him in 't,
  And drive towards Dover, friend, where thou shalt meet
  Both welcome and protection. Take up thy master;
  If thou shouldst dally half an hour, his life,
  With thine, and all that offer to defend him,
  Stand in assured loss. Take up, take up;
  And follow me, that will to some provision
  Give thee quick conduct.

KENT.   Oppressed nature sleeps.
  This rest might yet have balmed thy broken sinews,
  Which, if convenience will not allow,
  Stand in hard cure. [*To the Fool*] Come, help to bear thy master;
  Thou must not stay behind.

GLOUCESTER.   Come, come, away.
                    Exeunt all but EDGAR

EDGAR. When we our betters see bearing our woes,
  We scarcely think our miseries our foes.
  Who alone suffers suffers most i' the mind,
  Leaving free things and happy shows behind;
  But then the mind much sufferance doth o'erskip,
  When grief hath mates, and bearing fellowship.
  How light and portable my pain seems now,
  When that which makes me bend makes the King bow;
  He childed as I fathered! Tom, away!
  Mark the high noises, and thyself bewray,
  When false opinion, whose wrong thought defiles thee,
  In thy just proof, repeals and reconciles thee.
  What will hap more tonight, safe 'scape the King!
  Lurk, lurk.   *Exit*

SCENE VII *Gloucester's castle*

Enter CORNWALL, REGAN, GONERIL, EDMUND,
and Servants

CORNWALL. Post speedily to my lord your husband;
show him this letter: the army of France is landed.
Seek out the villain Gloucester.

Exeunt some of the Servants

REGAN. Hang him instantly.

GONERIL. Pluck out his eyes.

CORNWALL. Leave him to my displeasure. Edmund,
keep you our sister company; the revenges we are
bound to take upon your traitorous father are not fit
for your beholding. Advise the Duke, where you are
going, to a most festinate preparation; we are bound
to the like. Our posts shall be swift and intelligent
betwixt us. Farewell, dear sister; farewell, my lord
of Gloucester.

Enter OSWALD

How now! where's the King?

OSWALD. My lord of Gloucester hath conveyed him
hence;
Some five or six and thirty of his knights,
Hot questrists after him, met him at gate;
Who, with some other of the lord's dependants,
Are gone with him towards Dover; where they boast
To have well-armed friends.

CORNWALL.   Get horses for your mistress.

GONERIL. Farewell, sweet lord, and sister.

CORNWALL. Edmund, farewell.

Exeunt GONERIL, EDMUND, *and* OSWALD
Go seek the traitor Gloucester,
Pinion him like a thief, bring him before us.

Exeunt other Servants
Though well we may not pass upon his life
Without the form of justice, yet our power
Shall do a courtesy to our wrath, which men
May blame, but not control. Who's there? the traitor?

Enter GLOUCESTER, *brought in by two or three*

REGAN. Ingrateful fox! 'tis he.

CORNWALL. Bind fast his corky arms.

GLOUCESTER. What mean your graces? Good my friends,
consider
You are my guests; do me no foul play, friends.

CORNWALL. Bind him, I say.   Servants *bind him*

REGAN.   Hard, hard. O filthy traitor!

GLOUCESTER. Unmerciful lady as you are, I'm none.

CORNWALL. To this chair bind him. Villain, thou shalt
find—   REGAN *plucks his beard*

GLOUCESTER. By the kind gods, 'tis most ignobly done
To pluck me by the beard.

REGAN. So white, and such a traitor!

GLOUCESTER.   Naughty lady,
These hairs, which thou dost ravish from my chin,

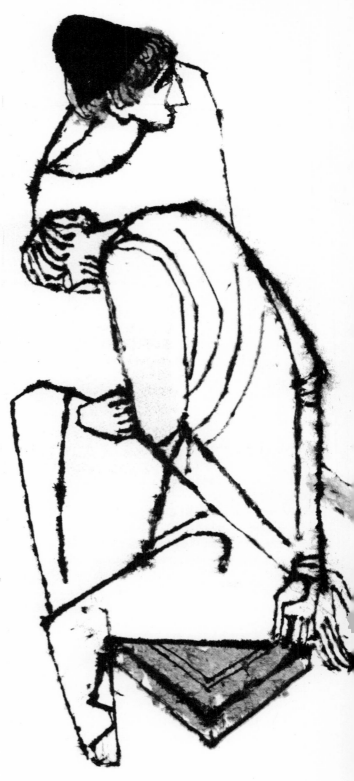

Will quicken and accuse thee. I am your host!
With robbers' hands my hospitable favours
You should not ruffle thus. What will you do?

CORNWALL. Come, sir, what letters had you late from
    France?

REGAN. Be simple-answered, for we know the truth.

CORNWALL. And what confederacy have you with the
    traitors
  Late footed in the kingdom?

REGAN. To whose hands you have sent the lunatic king.
  Speak.

GLOUCESTER. I have a letter guessingly set down,
  Which came from one that's of a neutral heart,
  And not from one opposed.

CORNWALL.   Cunning.

REGAN.   And false.

CORNWALL. Where hast thou sent the King?

GLOUCESTER. To Dover.

REGAN. Wherefore to Dover? Wast thou not charged
    at peril—

CORNWALL. Wherefore to Dover? Let him first answer
    that.

GLOUCESTER. I am tied to the stake, and I must stand
    the course.

REGAN. Wherefore to Dover, sir?

GLOUCESTER. Because I would not see thy cruel nails
  Pluck out his poor old eyes; nor thy fierce sister
  In his anointed flesh stick boarish fangs.
  The sea, with such a storm as his bare head
  In hell-black night endured, would have buoyed up,
  And quenched the stelled fires;
  Yet, poor old heart, he holp the heavens to rain.
  If wolves had at thy gate howled that stern time,
  Thou shouldst have said "Good porter, turn the key."
  All cruels else subscribe. But I shall see
  The winged vengeance overtake such children.

CORNWALL. See 't shalt thou never. Fellows, hold the
    chair.
  Upon these eyes of thine I 'll set my foot.

GLOUCESTER. He that will think to live till he be old,
  Give me some help! O cruel! O you gods!

REGAN. One side will mock another; the other too.

CORNWALL. If you see vengeance—

FIRST SERVANT.   Hold your hand, my lord;
  I have served you ever since I was a child;
  But better service have I never done you
  Than now to bid you hold.

REGAN.   How now, you dog!

FIRST SERVANT. If you did wear a beard upon your chin,
  I 'd shake it on this quarrel. What do you mean?

CORNWALL. My villain!

They draw and fight

FIRST SERVANT. Nay, then, come on, and take the
    chance of anger.

REGAN. Give me thy sword. A peasant stand up thus!

Takes a sword, and runs at him behind

First Servant. O, I am slain! My lord, you have one
    eye left
  To see some mischief on him. O!   *Dies*
Cornwall. Lest it see more, prevent it. Out, vile
    jelly!
  Where is thy lustre now?
Gloucester. All dark and comfortless. Where's my
    son Edmund?
  Edmund, enkindle all the sparks of nature,
  To quit this horrid act.
Regan.   Out, treacherous villain!
  Thou call'st on him that hates thee; it was he
  That made the overture of thy treasons to us;
  Who is too good to pity thee.
Gloucester. O my follies! then Edgar was abused.
  Kind gods, forgive me that, and prosper him!
Regan. Go thrust him out at gates, and let him smell
  His way to Dover.   *Exit one with* Gloucester
    How is 't, my lord? how look you?
Cornwall. I have received a hurt; follow me, lady.
  Turn out that eyeless villain; throw this slave
  Upon the dunghill. Regan, I bleed apace;
  Untimely comes this hurt. Give me your arm.
             Exit Cornwall, *led by* Regan
Second Servant. I 'll never care what wickedness I do,
  If this man come to good.
Third Servant.   If she live long,
  And in the end meet the old course of death,
  Women will all turn monsters.
Second Servant. Let's follow the old earl, and get
    the Bedlam
  To lead him where he would; his roguish madness
  Allows itself to anything.
Third Servant. Go thou; I'll fetch some flax and
    whites of eggs
  To apply to his bleeding face. Now, heaven help him!
                  Exeunt severally

ACT IV

Scene I *The heath*

Enter Edgar

Edgar. Yet better thus, and known to be contemned,
  Than still contemned and flattered. To be worst,
  The lowest and most dejected thing of fortune,
  Stands still in esperance, lives not in fear:
  The lamentable change is from the best;
  The worst returns to laughter. Welcome, then,
  Thou unsubstantial air that I embrace!
  The wretch that thou hast blown unto the worst
  Owes nothing to thy blasts. But who comes here?

Enter Gloucester, *led by an* Old Man

  My father, poorly led? World, world, O world!

But that thy strange mutations make us hate thee,
Life would not yield to age.

OLD MAN. O, my good lord, I have been your tenant,
and your father's tenant, these fourscore years.

GLOUCESTER. Away, get thee away; good friend, be
gone;
Thy comforts can do me no good at all;
Thee they may hurt.

OLD MAN. Alack, sir, you cannot see your way.

GLOUCESTER. I have no way, and therefore want no eyes;
I stumbled when I saw. Full oft 'tis seen,
Our means secure us, and our mere defects
Prove our commodities. O dear son Edgar,
The food of thy abused father's wrath!
Might I but live to see thee in my touch,
I 'ld say I had eyes again!

OLD MAN.   How now! Who's there?

EDGAR. [Aside] O gods! Who is 't can say "I am at the
worst"?
I am worse than e'er I was.

OLD MAN.   'Tis poor mad Tom.

EDGAR. [Aside] And worse I may be yet; the worst is not
So long as we can say "This is the worst."

OLD MAN. Fellow, where goest?

GLOUCESTER.   Is it a beggar-man?

OLD MAN. Madman and beggar too.

GLOUCESTER. He has some reason, else he could not beg.
I' the last night's storm I such a fellow saw,
Which made me think a man a worm. My son
Came then into my mind, and yet my mind
Was then scarce friends with him; I have heard more
since.
As flies to wanton boys, are we to the gods;
They kill us for their sport.

EDGAR.   [Aside] How should this be?
Bad is the trade that must play fool to sorrow,
Angering itself and others.—Bless thee, master!

GLOUCESTER. Is that the naked fellow?

OLD MAN.   Ay, my lord.

GLOUCESTER. Then, prithee, get thee gone. If, for my
sake,
Thou wilt o'ertake us, hence a mile or twain,
I' the way toward Dover, do it for ancient love;

And bring some covering for this naked soul,
Who I'll entreat to lead me.

OLD MAN.   Alack, sir, he is mad.

GLOUCESTER. 'Tis the times' plague, when madmen lead
the blind.
Do as I bid thee, or rather do thy pleasure;
Above the rest, be gone.

OLD MAN. I 'll bring him the best 'parel that I have,
Come on 't what will.   Exit

GLOUCESTER. Sirrah, naked fellow—

EDGAR. Poor Tom 's a-cold. [Aside] I cannot daub it
further.

GLOUCESTER. Come hither, fellow.

EDGAR. [Aside] And yet I must.—Bless thy sweet eyes,
they bleed.

GLOUCESTER. Know'st thou the way to Dover?

EDGAR. Both stile and gate, horse-way and foot-path.
Poor Tom hath been scared out of his good wits; bless
thee, good man's son, from the foul fiend! Five fiends
have been in poor Tom at once; of lust, as Obidicut;
Hobbididance, prince of dumbness; Mahu, of stealing; Modo, of murder; Flibbertigibbet, of mopping
and mowing, who since possesses chambermaids and
waiting-women. So, bless thee, master!

GLOUCESTER. Here, take this purse, thou whom the
heavens' plagues
Have humbled to all strokes. That I am wretched
Makes thee the happier; heavens, deal so still!
Let the superfluous and lust-dieted man,
That slaves your ordinance, that will not see
Because he doth not feel, feel your power quickly;
So distribution should undo excess,
And each man have enough. Dost thou know Dover?

EDGAR. Ay, master.

GLOUCESTER. There is a cliff, whose high and bending
head
Looks fearfully in the confined deep:
Bring me but to the very brim of it,
And I 'll repair the misery thou dost bear
With something rich about me; from that place
I shall no leading need.

EDGAR.   Give me thy arm;
Poor Tom shall lead thee.   Exeunt

SCENE II *Before the Duke of Albany's palace*

Enter GONERIL *and* EDMUND

GONERIL. Welcome, my lord; I marvel our mild husband
Not met us on the way.

Enter OSWALD

                    Now, where's your master?

OSWALD. Madam, within; but never man so changed.
I told him of the army that was landed;

He smiled at it. I told him you were coming;
His answer was "The worse"; of Gloucester's
treachery,
And of the loyal service of his son,
When I informed him, then he called me sot,
And told me I had turned the wrong side out;

What most he should dislike seems pleasant to him;
What like, offensive.
GONERIL. [*To Edmund*] Then shall you go no further.
It is the cowish terror of his spirit,
That dares not undertake; he'll not feel wrongs
Which tie him to an answer. Our wishes on the way
May prove effects. Back, Edmund, to my brother;
Hasten his musters and conduct his powers.
I must change arms at home, and give the distaff
Into my husband's hands. This trusty servant
Shall pass between us; ere long you are like to hear,
If you dare venture in your own behalf,
A mistress's command. Wear this; spare speech;
                                       Giving a favour
Decline your head; this kiss, if it durst speak,
Would stretch thy spirits up into the air.
Conceive, and fare thee well.
EDMUND. Yours in the ranks of death.
GONERIL.   My most dear Gloucester!
                                 Exit EDMUND
O, the difference of man and man!
To thee a woman's services are due;
My fool usurps my body.
OSWALD.   Madam, here comes my lord.
                                     Exit

Enter ALBANY

GONERIL. I have been worth the whistle.
ALBANY.   O Goneril!
You are not worth the dust which the rude wind
Blows in your face. I fear your disposition.
That nature which contemns its origin
Cannot be bordered certain in itself;
She that herself will sliver and disbranch
From her material sap, perforce must wither
And come to deadly use.
GONERIL. No more; the text is foolish.
ALBANY. Wisdom and goodness to the vile seem vile;
Filths savour but themselves. What have you done?
Tigers, not daughters, what have you performed?
A father, and a gracious aged man,
Whose reverence even the head-lugged bear would
    lick,
Most barbarous, most degenerate! have you madded.
Could my good brother suffer you to do it?
A man, a prince, by him so benefited!
If that the heavens do not their visible spirits
Send quickly down to tame these vile offences,
It will come,
Humanity must perforce prey on itself,
Like monsters of the deep.
GONERIL.   Milk-livered man!
That bear'st a cheek for blows, a head for wrongs;
Who hast not in thy brows an eye discerning
Thine honour from thy suffering; that not know'st
Fools do those villains pity who are punished
Ere they have done their mischief. Where's thy drum?

France spreads his banners in our noiseless land,
With plumed helm thy state begins to threat;
Whiles thou, a moral fool, sit'st still, and criest
"Alack, why does he so?"
ALBANY.   See thyself, devil!
Proper deformity seems not in the fiend
So horrid as in woman.
GONERIL.   O vain fool!
ALBANY. Thou changed and self-covered thing, for
    shame,
Be-monster not thy feature. Were 't my fitness
To let these hands obey my blood,
They are apt enough to dislocate and tear
Thy flesh and bones; howe'er thou art a fiend,
A woman's shape doth shield thee.
GONERIL. Marry, your manhood now—

Enter a Messenger

ALBANY. What news?
MESSENGER. O, my good lord, the Duke of Cornwall 's
    dead;
Slain by his servant, going to put out
The other eye of Gloucester.
ALBANY.   Gloucester's eyes!
MESSENGER. A servant that he bred, thrilled with re-
    morse,
Opposed against the act, bending his sword
To his great master; who, thereat enraged,
Flew on him, and amongst them felled him dead;
But not without that harmful stroke, which since
Hath plucked him after.
ALBANY.   This shows you are above,
You justicers, that these our nether crimes
So speedily can venge! But, O poor Gloucester!
Lost he his other eye?
MESSENGER.   Both, both, my lord.
This letter, madam, craves a speedy answer;
'Tis from your sister.
GONERIL. [*Aside*] One way I like this well;
But being widow, and my Gloucester with her.
May all the building in my fancy pluck
Upon my hateful life; another way,
The news is not so tart.—I'll read, and answer.   *Exit*
ALBANY. Where was his son when they did take his eyes?
MESSENGER. Come with my lady hither.
ALBANY.   He is not here.
MESSENGER. No, my good lord; I met him back again.
ALBANY. Knows he the wickedness?
MESSENGER. Ay, my good lord, 'twas he informed
    against him;
And quit the house on purpose, that their punishment
Might have the freer course.
ALBANY.   Gloucester, I live
To thank thee for the love thou show'dst the King,
And to revenge thine eyes. Come hither, friend:
Tell me what more thou know'st.   *Exeunt*

SCENE III *The French camp near Dover*

Enter KENT *and a* Gentleman

KENT. Why the king of France is so suddenly gone back
  know you the reason?
GENTLEMAN. Something he left imperfect in the state,
  which since his coming forth is thought of; which
  imports to the kingdom so much fear and danger, that
  his personal return was most required and necessary.
KENT. Who hath he left behind him general?
GENTLEMAN. The Marshal of France, Monsieur La Far.
KENT. Did your letters pierce the Queen to any demon-
  stration of grief?
GENTLEMAN. Ay, sir; she took them, read them in my
    presence;
  And now and then an ample tear trilled down
  Her delicate cheek. It seemed she was a queen
  Over her passion; who, most rebel-like,
  Sought to be king o'er her.
KENT.   O, then it moved her.
GENTLEMAN. Not to a rage; patience and sorrow strove
  Who should express her goodliest. You have seen
  Sunshine and rain at once; her smiles and tears
  Were like a better way. Those happy smilets,
  That played on her ripe lip, seemed not to know
  What guests were in her eyes; which parted thence,
  As pearls from diamonds dropped. In brief,
  Sorrow would be a rarity most beloved,
  If all could so become it.
KENT.   Made she no verbal question?
GENTLEMAN. 'Faith, once or twice she heaved the name
    of "father"
  Pantingly forth, as if it pressed her heart;
  Cried "Sisters! sisters! Shame of ladies! sisters!
  Kent! father! sisters! What, i' the storm? i' the night?
  Let pity not be believed!" There she shook
  The holy water from her heavenly eyes,
  And clamour moistened; then away she started
  To deal with grief alone.
KENT.   It is the stars,
  The stars above us, govern our conditions;
  Else one self mate and mate could not beget
  Such different issues. You spoke not with her since?
GENTLEMAN. No.
KENT. Was this before the King returned?
GENTLEMAN.   No, since.
KENT. Well, sir, the poor distressed Lear 's i' the town;
  Who sometime, in his better tune, remembers
  What we are come about, and by no means
  Will yield to see his daughter.
GENTLEMAN.   Why, good sir?
KENT. A sovereign shame so elbows him: his own un-
  kindness,
  That stripped her from his benediction, turned her
  To foreign casualties, gave her dear rights
  To his dog-hearted daughters—these things sting

His mind so venomously, that burning shame
Detains him from Cordelia.
GENTLEMAN.   Alack, poor gentleman!
KENT. Of Albany's and Cornwall's powers you heard
  not?
GENTLEMAN. 'Tis so, they are afoot.
KENT. Well, sir, I 'll bring you to our master Lear,
  And leave you to attend him. Some dear cause
  Will in concealment wrap me up awhile;
  When I am known aright, you shall not grieve
  Lending me this acquaintance. I pray you, go
  Along with me.   *Exeunt*

SCENE IV *The same: a tent*

Enter, with drum and colours, CORDELIA, Doctor, *and* Soldiers

CORDELIA. Alack, 'tis he. Why, he was met even now
  As mad as the vexed sea; singing aloud;
  Crowned with rank fumiter and furrow-weeds,
  With burdocks, hemlock, nettles, cuckoo-flowers,
  Darnel, and all the idle weeds that grow
  In our sustaining corn. A century send forth;
  Search every acre in the high-grown field,
  And bring him to our eye.   *Exit an* Officer
    What can man's wisdom
  In the restoring his bereaved sense?
  He that helps him take all my outward worth.
DOCTOR. There is means, madam;
  Our foster-nurse of nature is repose,
  The which he lacks; that to provoke in him,
  Are many simples operative, whose power
  Will close the eye of anguish.
CORDELIA.   All blest secrets,

All you unpublished virtues of the earth,
  Spring with my tears! Be aidant and remediate
  In the good man's distress! Seek, seek for him;
  Lest his ungoverned rage dissolve the life
  That wants the means to lead it.

Enter a Messenger

MESSENGER.   News, madam;
  The British powers are marching hitherward.
CORDELIA. 'Tis known before; our preparation stands
  In expectation of them. O dear father,
  It is thy business that I go about;
  Therefore great France
  My mourning and important tears hath pitied.
  No blown ambition doth our arms incite,
  But love, dear love, and our aged father's right;
  Soon may I hear and see him!   *Exeunt*

392

SCENE V *Gloucester's castle*

Enter REGAN *and* OSWALD

REGAN. But are my brother's powers set forth?
OSWALD.   Ay, madam.
REGAN. Himself in person there?
OSWALD.   Madam, with much ado;
  Your sister is the better soldier.
REGAN. Lord Edmund spake not with your lord at
  home?
OSWALD. No, madam.
REGAN. What might import my sister's letter to him?
OSWALD. I know not, lady.
REGAN. 'Faith, he is posted hence on serious matter.
  It was great ignorance, Gloucester's eyes being out,
  To let him live; where he arrives he moves
  All hearts against us. Edmund, I think, is gone,
  In pity of his misery, to dispatch
  His nighted life; moreover, to descry
  The strength o' the enemy.
OSWALD. I must needs after him, madam, with my
  letter.
REGAN. Our troops set forth tomorrow; stay with us,
  The ways are dangerous.
OSWALD.   I may not, madam;
  My lady charged my duty in this business.
REGAN. Why should she write to Edmund? Might not
  you

Transport her purposes by word? Belike,
  Something—I know not what. I'll love thee much,
  Let me unseal the letter.
OSWALD.   Madam, I had rather—
REGAN. I know your lady does not love her husband,
  I am sure of that; and at her late being here
  She gave strange œillades and most speaking looks
  To noble Edmund. I know you are of her bosom.
OSWALD. I, madam?
REGAN. I speak in understanding; you are, I know 't;
  Therefore I do advise you, take this note:
  My lord is dead; Edmund and I have talked;
  And more convenient is he for my hand
  Than for your lady's. You may gather more.
  If you do find him, pray you, give him this;
  And when your mistress hears thus much from you,
  I pray, desire her call her wisdom to her.
  So, fare you well.
  If you do chance to hear of that blind traitor,
  Preferment falls on him that cuts him off.
OSWALD. Would I could meet him, madam! I should
  show
  What party I do follow.
REGAN.   Fare thee well.
                                              Exeunt

SCENE VI *Fields near Dover*

Enter GLOUCESTER, *and* EDGAR *dressed like a peasant*

GLOUCESTER. When shall we come to the top of that
  same hill?
EDGAR. You do climb up it now; look, how we labour.
GLOUCESTER. Methinks the ground is even.
EDGAR.   Horrible steep.
  Hark, do you hear the sea?
GLOUCESTER.   No, truly.
EDGAR. Why, then, your other senses grow imperfect
  By your eyes' anguish.
GLOUCESTER.   So may it be, indeed.
  Methinks thy voice is altered; and thou speak'st
  In better phrase and matter than thou didst.
EDGAR. You 're much deceived; in nothing am I changed
  But in my garments.
GLOUCESTER. Methinks you're better spoken.
EDGAR. Come on, sir, here's the place; stand still.
  How fearful
  And dizzy 'tis, to cast one's eyes so low!
  The crows and choughs that wing the midway air
  Show scarce so gross as beetles; half way down
  Hangs one that gathers samphire, dreadful trade!
  Methinks he seems no bigger than his head.
  The fishermen, that walk upon the beach,

Appear like mice; and yond tall anchoring bark,
  Diminished to her cock; her cock, a buoy
  Almost too small for sight. The murmuring surge,
  That on the unnumbered idle pebbles chafes,
  Cannot be heard so high. I 'll look no more,
  Lest my brain turn, and the deficient sight
  Topple down headlong.
GLOUCESTER.   Set me where you stand.
EDGAR. Give me your hand; you are now within a foot
  Of the extreme verge. For all beneath the moon
  Would I not leap upright.
GLOUCESTER.   Let go my hand.
  Here, friend, 's another purse; in it a jewel
  Well worth a poor man's taking. Fairies and gods
  Prosper it with thee! Go thou farther off;
  Bid me farewell, and let me hear thee going.
EDGAR. Now fare you well, good sir.
GLOUCESTER.   With all my heart.
EDGAR. Why I do trifle thus with his despair
  Is done to cure it.
GLOUCESTER. [*Kneeling*] O you mighty gods!
  This world I do renounce, and, in your sights,
  Shake patiently my great affliction off;

If I could bear it longer, and not fall
To quarrel with your great opposeless wills,
My snuff and loathed part of nature should
Burn itself out. If Edgar live, O, bless him!
Now, fellow, fare thee well.   *He falls forward*
EDGAR.   Gone, sir; farewell.
  And yet I know not how conceit may rob
  The treasury of life, when life itself
  Yields to the theft; had he been where he thought,
  By this, had thought been past. Alive or dead?
  Ho, you sir! friend! Hear you, sir! speak!
  Thus might he pass indeed; yet he revives.
  What are you, sir?
GLOUCESTER.   Away, and let me die.
EDGAR. Hadst thou been aught but gossamer, feathers,
    air,
  So many fathom down precipitating,
  Thou 'dst shivered like an egg; but thou dost breathe,
  Hast heavy substance, bleed'st not, speak'st, art
    sound.
  Ten masts at each make not the altitude
  Which thou hast perpendicularly fell.
  Thy life 's a miracle. Speak yet again.
GLOUCESTER. But have I fall'n, or no?
EDGAR. From the dread summit of this chalky bourn.
  Look up a-height; the shrill-gorged lark so far
  Cannot be seen or heard; do but look up.
GLOUCESTER. Alack, I have no eyes.
  Is wretchedness deprived that benefit,
  To end itself by death? 'Twas yet some comfort,
  When misery could beguile the tyrant's rage,
  And frustrate his proud will.
EDGAR.   Give me your arm.
  Up; so. How is 't? Feel you your legs? You stand.
GLOUCESTER. Too well, too well.
EDGAR.   This is above all strangeness.
  Upon the crown o' the cliff, what thing was that
  Which parted from you?
GLOUCESTER.   A poor unfortunate beggar.
EDGAR. As I stood here below, methought his eyes
  Were two full moons; he had a thousand noses,
  Horns whelked and waved like the enridged sea.
  It was some fiend; therefore, thou happy father,
  Think that the clearest gods, who make them honours
  Of men's impossibilities, have preserved thee.
GLOUCESTER. I do remember now; henceforth I 'll bear
  Affliction till it do cry out itself
  "Enough, enough," and die. That thing you speak of,
  I took it for a man; often 'twould say
  "The fiend, the fiend"; he led me to that place.
EDGAR. Bear free and patient thoughts. But who comes
    here?

Enter LEAR, *fantastically dressed with wild flowers*

The safer sense will ne'er accommodate
His master thus.

LEAR. No, they cannot touch me for coining;
  I am the King himself.
EDGAR. O thou side-piercing sight!
LEAR. Nature 's above art in that respect. There's
  your press-money. That fellow handles his bow like a
  crow-keeper; draw me a clothier's yard. Look, look,
  a mouse! Peace, peace; this piece of toasted cheese
  will do 't. There's my gauntlet; I 'll prove it on a
  giant. Bring up the brown bills. O, well flown, bird!
  i' the clout, i' the clout: hewgh! Give the word.
EDGAR. Sweet marjoram.
LEAR. Pass.
GLOUCESTER. I know that voice.
LEAR. Ha! Goneril, with a white beard! They flattered
  me like a dog; and told me I had white hairs in my
  beard ere the black ones were there. To say "ay"
  and "no" to everything that I said!—"Ay" and
  "no" too was no good divinity. When the rain came
  to wet me once, and the wind to make me chatter;
  when the thunder would not peace at my bidding;
  there I found 'em, there I smelt 'em out. Go to, they
  are not men o' their words. They told me I was every-
  thing; 'tis a lie, I am not ague-proof.
GLOUCESTER. The trick of that voice I do well re-
    member;
  Is 't not the King?
LEAR.   Ay, every inch a king!
  When I do stare, see how the subject quakes.
  I pardon that man's life. What was thy cause?
  Adultery?
  Thou shalt not die; die for adultery! No;
  The wren goes to 't, and the small gilded fly
  Does lecher in my sight.
  Let copulation thrive; for Gloucester's bastard son
  Was kinder to his father than my daughters
  Got 'tween the lawful sheets.
  To 't, luxury, pell-mell! for I lack soldiers.
  Behold yond simpering dame,
  Whose face between her forks presages snow;
  That minces virtue, and does shake the head
  To hear of pleasure's name;
  The fitchew, nor the soiled horse, goes to 't
  With a more riotous appetite.
  Down from the waist they are Centaurs,
  Though women all above;
  But to the girdle do the gods inherit,
  Beneath is all the fiends';
  There's hell, there's darkness, there's the sulphurous
    pit,
  Burning, scalding, stench, consumption; fie, fie, fie!
  pah, pah! Give me an ounce of civet, good apothecary,
  to sweeten my imagination; there's money for thee.
GLOUCESTER. O, let me kiss that hand!
LEAR. Let me wipe it first; it smells of mortality.
GLOUCESTER. O ruined piece of nature! This great world
  Shall so wear out to nought. Dost thou know me?

LEAR. I remember thine eyes well enough. Dost thou squiny at me? No, do thy worst, blind Cupid; I 'll not love. Read thou this challenge; mark but the penning of it.

GLOUCESTER. Were all the letters suns, I could not see one.

EDGAR. I would not take this from report; it is,
And my heart breaks at it.

LEAR. Read.

GLOUCESTER. What, with the case of eyes?

LEAR. O, ho, are you there with me? No eyes in your head, nor no money in your purse? Your eyes are in a heavy case, your purse in a light; yet you see how this world goes.

GLOUCESTER. I see it feelingly.

LEAR. What, art mad? A man may see how this world goes with no eyes. Look with thine ears; see how yond justice rails upon yond simple thief. Hark, in thine ear; change places; and, handy-dandy, which is the justice, which is the thief? Thou hast seen a farmer's dog bark at a beggar?

GLOUCESTER. Ay, sir.

LEAR. And the creature run from the cur. There thou mightst behold the great image of authority; a dog 's obeyed in office.
Thou rascal beadle, hold thy bloody hand!
Why dost thou lash that whore? Strip thine own back;
Thou hotly lust'st to use her in that kind
For which thou whipp'st her. The usurer hangs the cozener.
Through tattered clothes small vices do appear;
Robes and furred gowns hide all. Plate sin with gold,
And the strong lance of justice hurtless breaks;
Arm it in rags, a pigmy's straw does pierce it.
None does offend, none, I say, none; I'll able 'em:
Take that of me, my friend, who have the power
To seal the accuser's lips. Get thee glass eyes;
And, like a scurvy politician, seem
To see the things thou dost not. Now, now, now, now;
Pull off my boots; harder, harder; so.

EDGAR. O, matter and impertinency mixed!
Reason in madness!

LEAR. If thou wilt weep my fortunes, take my eyes.
I know thee well enough; thy name is Gloucester.
Thou must be patient; we came crying hither;
Thou know'st, the first time that we smell the air,
We wawl and cry. I will preach to thee: mark.

GLOUCESTER. Alack, alack the day!

LEAR. When we are born, we cry that we are come
To this great stage of fools. This' a good block!
It were a delicate stratagem, to shoe
A troop of horse with felt; I 'll put 't in proof;
And when I have stol'n upon these sons-in-law,
Then, kill, kill, kill, kill, kill, kill!

Enter a Gentleman, *with* Attendants

GENTLEMAN. O, here he is; lay hand upon him. Sir,
Your most dear daughter—

LEAR. No rescue? What, a prisoner? I am even
The natural fool of fortune. Use me well;
You shall have ransom. Let me have surgeons;
I am cut to the brains.

GENTLEMAN.   You shall have anything.

LEAR. No seconds? all myself?
Why, this would make a man a man of salt,
To use his eyes for garden water-pots,
Ay, and laying autumn's dust.

GENTLEMAN.   Good sir—

LEAR. I will die bravely, like a bridegroom. What!
I will be jovial. Come, come; I am a king,
My masters, know you that.

GENTLEMAN. You are a royal one, and we obey you.

LEAR. Then there 's life in 't. Nay, if you get it, you shall get it with running. Sa, sa, sa, sa.

Exit running. Attendants *follow*

GENTLEMAN. A sight most pitiful in the meanest wretch,
Past speaking of in a king! Thou hast one daughter,
Who redeems nature from the general curse
Which twain have brought her to.

EDGAR. Hail, gentle sir.

GENTLEMAN.   Sir, speed you; what 's your will?

EDGAR. Do you hear aught, sir, of a battle toward?

GENTLEMAN. Most sure and vulgar; everyone hears that,
Which can distinguish sound.

EDGAR.   But, by your favour,
How near 's the other army?

GENTLEMAN. Near and on speedy foot; the main descry
Stands on the hourly thought.

EDGAR.   I thank you, sir; that 's all.

GENTLEMAN. Though that the Queen on special cause is here,
Her army is moved on.

EDGAR.   I thank you, sir.

Exit Gentleman

GLOUCESTER. You ever-gentle gods, take my breath from me;
Let not my worser spirit tempt me again
To die before you please!

EDGAR.   Well pray you, father.

GLOUCESTER. Now, good sir, what are you?

EDGAR. A most poor man, made tame to fortune's blows;
Who, by the art of known and feeling sorrows,
Am pregnant to good pity. Give me your hand,
I 'll lead you to some biding.

GLOUCESTER.   Hearty thanks;
The bounty and the benison of heaven
To boot, and boot!

Enter OSWALD

OSWALD.　　　　　　A proclaimed prize! Most happy!
　That eyeless head of thine was first framed flesh
　To raise my fortunes. Thou old unhappy traitor,
　Briefly thyself remember; the sword is out
　That must destroy thee.
GLOUCESTER.　　　　　　Now let thy friendly hand
　Put strength enough to 't.　　　　EDGAR *interposes*
OSWALD.　　　　　　Wherefore, bold peasant,
　Dar'st thou support a published traitor? Hence;
　Lest that infection of his fortune take
　Like hold on thee. Let go his arm.
EDGAR. Chill not let go, zir, without vurther 'casion.
OSWALD. Let go, slave, or thou diest!

EDGAR. Good gentleman, go your gait, and let poor volk
  pass. An chud ha' bin zwaggered out of my life,
  'twould not ha' bin zo long as 'tis by a vortnight.
  Nay, come not near th' old man; keep out, che vor
  ye, or ise try whether your costard or my ballow be
  the harder. Chill be plain with you.

OSWALD. Out, dunghill!

EDGAR. Chill pick your teeth, zir. Come; no matter
  vor your foins.

            They fight, and EDGAR *knocks him down*

OSWALD. Slave, thou hast slain me. Villain, take my
  purse.
  If ever thou wilt thrive, bury my body;
  And give the letters which thou find'st about me
  To Edmund earl of Gloucester; seek him out
  Upon the British party. O, untimely death!   *Dies*

EDGAR. I know thee well: a serviceable villain;
  As duteous to the vices of thy mistress
  As badness would desire.

GLOUCESTER.   What, is he dead?

EDGAR. Sit you down, father; rest you.
  Let 's see these pockets; the letters that he speaks of
  May be my friends. He's dead; I am only sorry
  He had no other death's-man. Let us see:
  Leave, gentle wax; and, manners, blame us not;
  To know our enemies' minds, we 'ld rip their hearts;
  Their papers, is more lawful.
      [*Reads*] "Let our reciprocal vows be remembered.

You have many opportunities to cut him off; if your
will want not, time and place will be fruitfully offered.
There is nothing done, if he return the conqueror;
then am I the prisoner, and his bed my gaol; from the
loathed warmth whereof deliver me, and supply the
place for your labour.
      "Your—wife, so I would say—
                  "Affectionate servant,
                          "GONERIL."
  O undistinguished space of woman's will!
  A plot upon her virtuous husband's life;
  And the exchange my brother! Here, in the sands,
  Thee I 'll rake up, the post unsanctified
  Of murderous lechers; and in the mature time
  With this ungracious paper strike the sight
  Of the death-practised Duke. For him 'tis well
  That of thy death and business I can tell.

GLOUCESTER. The King is mad; how stiff is my vile
  sense,
  That I stand up, and have ingenious feeling
  Of my huge sorrows! Better I were distract;
  So should my thoughts be severed from my griefs,
  And woes by wrong imaginations lose
  The knowledge of themselves.

EDGAR.   Give me your hand:
                          Drum afar off
  Far off, methinks, I hear the beaten drum.
  Come, father, I 'll bestow you with a friend.   *Exeunt*

SCENE VII *A tent in the French camp*

LEAR *on a bed asleep, soft music playing;* Gentleman, *and others attending*

Enter CORDELIA, KENT, *and* Doctor

CORDELIA. O thou good Kent, how shall I live and work,
  To match thy goodness? My life will be too short,
  And every measure fail me.

KENT. To be acknowledged, madam, is o'erpaid.
  All my reports go with the modest truth;
  Nor more nor clipped, but so.

CORDELIA.   Be better suited;
  These weeds are memories of those worser hours.
  I prithee, put them off.

KENT.   Pardon me, dear madam;
  Yet to be known shortens my made intent.
  My boon I make it, that you know me not
  Till time and I think meet.

CORDELIA. Then be 't so, my good lord. [*To the Doctor*]
  How does the King?

DOCTOR. Madam, sleeps still.

CORDELIA. O you kind gods,
  Cure this great breach in his abused nature!
  The untuned and jarring senses, O, wind up
  Of this child-changed father!

DOCTOR.   So please your majesty
  That we may wake the King? He hath slept long.

CORDELIA. Be governed by your knowledge, and proceed
  I' the sway of your own will. Is he arrayed?

GENTLEMAN. Ay, madam; in the heaviness of his sleep
  We put fresh garments on him.

DOCTOR. Be by, good madam, when we do awake him;
  I doubt not of his temperance.

CORDELIA.   Very well.

DOCTOR. Please you, draw near. Louder the music
  there!

CORDELIA. O my dear father! Restoration hang
  Thy medicine on my lips; and let this kiss
  Repair those violent harms that my two sisters
  Have in thy reverence made!

KENT.   Kind and dear Princess!

CORDELIA. Had you not been their father, these white
  flakes
  Had challenged pity of them. Was this a face
  To be opposed against the warring winds?
  To stand against the deep dread-bolted thunder?
  In the most terrible and nimble stroke
  Of quick, cross lightning? to watch—poor perdu!—

With this thin helm? Mine enemy's dog,
Though he had bit me, should have stood that night
Against my fire; and wast thou fain, poor father,
To hovel thee with swine, and rogues forlorn,
In short and musty straw? Alack, alack!
'Tis wonder that thy life and wits at once
Had not concluded all. He wakes; speak to him.

DOCTOR. Madam, do you; 'tis fittest.

CORDELIA. How does my royal lord? How fares your
    majesty?

LEAR. You do me wrong to take me out o' the grave;
    Thou art a soul in bliss; but I am bound
    Upon a wheel of fire, that mine own tears
    Do scald like molten lead.

CORDELIA.   Sir, do you know me?

LEAR. You are a spirit, I know; when did you die?

CORDELIA. Still, still, far wide!

DOCTOR. He's scarce awake; let him alone awhile.

LEAR. Where have I been? Where am I? Fair daylight?
    I am mightily abused. I should e'en die with pity,
    To see another thus. I know not what to say.
    I will not swear these are my hands. Let's see;
    I feel this pin prick. Would I were assured
    Of my condition!

CORDELIA.   O, look upon me, sir,
    And hold your hands in benediction o'er me;
    No, sir, you must not kneel.

LEAR.   Pray, do not mock me.
    I am a very foolish fond old man,
    Fourscore and upward, not an hour more nor less;
    And, to deal plainly,
    I fear I am not in my perfect mind.
    Methinks I should know you, and know this man,
    Yet I am doubtful; for I am mainly ignorant
    What place this is; and all the skill I have
    Remembers not these garments; nor I know not

Where I did lodge last night. Do not laugh at me;
For, as I am a man, I think this lady
To be my child Cordelia.

CORDELIA.   And so I am, I am.

LEAR. Be your tears wet? yes, 'faith, I pray, weep not.
    If you have poison for me, I will drink it.
    I know you do not love me; for your sisters
    Have, as I do remember, done me wrong.
    You have some cause, they have not.

CORDELIA.   No cause, no cause.

LEAR. Am I in France?

KENT.   In your own kingdom, sir.

LEAR. Do not abuse me.

DOCTOR. Be comforted, good madam; the great rage,
    You see, is killed in him; and yet it is danger
    To make him even o'er the time he has lost.
    Desire him to go in; trouble him no more
    Till further settling.

CORDELIA. Will 't please your highness walk?

LEAR.   You must bear with me.
    Pray you now, forget and forgive; I am old and
    foolish.

                    Exeunt all but KENT *and* Gentleman

GENTLEMAN. Holds it true, sir, that the duke of
    Cornwall was so slain?

KENT. Most certain, sir.

GENTLEMAN. Who is conductor of his people?

KENT. As 'tis said, the bastard son of Gloucester.

GENTLEMAN. They say Edgar, his banished son, is with
    the earl of Kent in Germany.

KENT. Report is changeable. 'Tis time to look about;
    the powers of the kingdom approach apace.

GENTLEMAN. The arbitrement is like to be bloody.
    Fare you well, sir.   *Exit*

KENT. My point and period will be throughly wrought,
    Or well or ill, as this day's battle 's fought.   *Exit*

ACT V

SCENE I *The British camp, near Dover*

Enter, with drum and colours, EDMUND, REGAN, Gentlemen,
and Soldiers

EDMUND. Know of the duke if his last purpose hold,
  Or whether since he is advised by aught
  To change the course; he's full of alteration
  And self-reproving; bring his constant pleasure.
                To a Gentleman, *who goes out*
REGAN. Our sister's man is certainly miscarried.
EDMUND. 'Tis to be doubted, madam.
REGAN.   Now, sweet lord,
  You know the goodness I intend upon you;
  Tell me—but truly—but then speak the truth,
  Do you not love my sister?
EDMUND.   In honoured love.
REGAN. But have you never found my brother's way
  To the forfended place?
EDMUND.   That thought abuses you.
REGAN. I am doubtful that you have been conjunct
  And bosomed with her, as far as we call hers.
EDMUND. No, by mine honour, madam.
REGAN. I never shall endure her; dear my lord,
  Be not familiar with her.
EDMUND.   Fear me not.
  She and the Duke her husband!

Enter, with drum and colours, ALBANY, GONERIL,
and Soldiers

GONERIL. [*Aside*] I had rather lose the battle than that
    sister
  Should loosen him and me.
ALBANY. Our very loving sister, well be-met.
  Sir, this I hear; the King is come to his daughter,
  With others whom the rigour of our state
  Forced to cry out. Where I could not be honest,
  I never yet was valiant; for this business,
  It toucheth us, as France invades our land,
  Not bolds the King, with others, whom, I fear,
  Most just and heavy causes make oppose.
EDMUND. Sir, you speak nobly.
REGAN.   Why is this reasoned?
GONERIL. Combine together 'gainst the enemy;
  For these domestic and particular broils
  Are not the question here.
ALBANY.   Let 's then determine
  With the ancient of war on our proceedings.
EDMUND. I shall attend you presently at your tent.
REGAN. Sister, you'll go with us?
GONERIL. No.
REGAN. 'Tis most convenient; pray you, go with us.
GONERIL. [*Aside*] O, ho, I know the riddle.—I will go.

As they are going out, enter EDGAR *disguised*

EDGAR. If e'er your grace had speech with man so poor,
    Hear me one word.
ALBANY.   I 'll overtake you. Speak.
                    Exeunt all but ALBANY *and* EDGAR
EDGAR. Before you fight the battle, ope this letter.
    If you have victory, let the trumpet sound
    For him that brought it; wretched though I seem,
    I can produce a champion that will prove
    What is avouched there. If you miscarry,
    Your business of the world hath so an end,
    And machination ceases. Fortune love you!
ALBANY. Stay till I have read the letter.
EDGAR.   I was forbid it.
    When time shall serve, let but the herald cry,
    And I 'll appear again.
ALBANY. Why, fare thee well; I will o'erlook thy paper.
                                    Exit EDGAR

                    Re-enter EDMUND
EDMUND. The enemy 's in view; draw up your powers.

Here is the guess of their true strength and forces
By diligent discovery; but your haste
Is now urged on you.
ALBANY.   We will greet the time.   *Exit*
EDMUND. To both these sisters have I sworn my love;
    Each jealous of the other, as the stung
    Are of the adder. Which of them shall I take?
    Both? one? or neither? Neither can be enjoyed,
    If both remain alive. To take the widow
    Exasperates, makes mad her sister Goneril;
    And hardly shall I carry out my side,
    Her husband being alive. Now then we 'll use
    His countenance for the battle; which being done,
    Let her who would be rid of him devise
    His speedy taking off. As for the mercy
    Which he intends to Lear and to Cordelia,
    The battle done, and they within our power,
    Shall never see his pardon; for my state
    Stands on me to defend, not to debate.   *Exit*

SCENE II *A field between the two camps*

Alarum within. Enter, with drum and colours, LEAR, CORDELIA, *and* Soldiers, *over the stage; and exeunt*

Enter EDGAR *and* GLOUCESTER

EDGAR. Here, father, take the shadow of this tree
    For your good host; pray that the right may thrive.
    If ever I return to you again,
    I 'll bring you comfort.
GLOUCESTER.   Grace go with you, sir!
                                    Exit EDGAR

Alarum and retreat within. Re-enter EDGAR

EDGAR. Away, old man; give me thy hand; away!
    King Lear hath lost, he and his daughter ta'en.
    Give me thy hand; come on.
GLOUCESTER. No farther, sir; a man may rot even here.
EDGAR. What, in ill thoughts again? Men must endure
    Their going hence, even as their coming hither.
    Ripeness is all. Come on.
GLOUCESTER.   And that 's true too.   *Exeunt*

SCENE III *The British camp near Dover*

Enter, in conquest, with drum and colours, EDMUND; LEAR *and* CORDELIA, *prisoners;* Captain, Soldiers, &c

EDMUND. Some officers take them away; good guard,
    Until their greater pleasures first be known
    That are to censure them.
CORDELIA.   We are not the first
    Who, with best meaning, have incurred the worst.
    For thee, oppressed King, am I cast down;
    Myself could else out-frown false fortune's frown.
    Shall we not see these daughters and these sisters?
LEAR. No, no, no, no! Come, let 's away to prison.
    We two alone will sing like birds i' the cage;
    When thou dost ask me blessing, I 'll kneel down,
    And ask of thee forgiveness. So we 'll live,
    And pray, and sing, and tell old tales, and laugh
    At gilded butterflies, and hear poor rogues
    Talk of court news; and we 'll talk with them too,

Who loses and who wins; who 's in, who 's out;
And take upon 's the mystery of things,
As if we were God's spies; and we 'll wear out,
In a walled prison, packs and sects of great ones,
That ebb and flow by the moon.
EDMUND.   Take them away.
LEAR. Upon such sacrifices, my Cordelia,
    The gods themselves throw incense. Have I caught
        thee?
    He that parts us shall bring a brand from heaven,
    And fire us hence like foxes. Wipe thine eyes;
    The good-years shall devour them, flesh and fell,
    Ere they shall make us weep. We 'll see 'em starve
        first.
    Come.   *Exeunt* LEAR *and* CORDELIA, *guarded*

EDMUND. Come hither, captain; hark.
  Take thou this note [*giving a paper*]; go follow them
    to prison.
  One step I have advanced thee; if thou dost
  As this instructs thee, thou dost make thy way
  To noble fortunes. Know thou this, that men
  Are as the time is; to be tender-minded
  Does not become a sword; thy great employment
  Will not bear question; either say thou 'lt do 't,
  Or thrive by other means.
CAPTAIN.   I 'll do 't, my lord.
EDMUND. About it; and write happy when thou hast
    done.
  Mark, I say, instantly; and carry it so
  As I have set it down.
CAPTAIN. I cannot draw a cart, nor eat dried oats;
  If it be man's work, I 'll do it.   *Exit*

    Flourish. Enter ALBANY, GONERIL, REGAN,
        another Captain, *and* Soldiers.

ALBANY. Sir, you have shown today your valiant strain,
  And fortune led you well; you have the captives
  That were the opposites of this day's strife.
  We do require them of you, so to use them
  As we shall find their merits and our safety
  May equally determine.
EDMUND.   Sir, I thought it fit
  To send the old and miserable King
  To some retention and appointed guard;
  Whose age has charms in it, whose title more,
  To pluck the common bosom on his side,
  And turn our impressed lances in our eyes
  Which do command them. With him I sent the Queen;
  My reason all the same; and they are ready
  Tomorrow, or at further space, to appear
  Where you shall hold your session. At this time
  We sweat and bleed; the friend hath lost his friend;
  And the best quarrels, in the heat, are cursed
  By those that feel their sharpness.
  The question of Cordelia and her father
  Requires a fitter place.
ALBANY.   Sir, by your patience,
  I hold you but a subject of this war,
  Not as a brother.
REGAN.   That's as we list to grace him.
  Methinks our pleasure might have been demanded,
  Ere you had spoke so far. He led our powers,
  Bore the commission of my place and person;
  The which immediacy may well stand up,
  And call itself your brother.
GONERIL.   Not so hot;
  In his own grace he doth exalt himself,
  More than in your addition.
REGAN.   In my rights,
  By me invested, he compeers the best.
GONERIL. That were the most, if he should husband
    you.

REGAN. Jesters do oft prove prophets.
GONERIL.   Holla, holla!
  That eye that told you so looked but a-squint.
REGAN. Lady, I am not well; else I should answer
  From a full-flowing stomach. General,
  Take thou my soldiers, prisoners, patrimony;
  Dispose of them, of me; the walls are thine.
  Witness the world, that I create thee here
  My lord and master.
GONERIL.   Mean you to enjoy him?
ALBANY. The let-alone lies not in your good will.
EDMUND. Nor in thine, lord.
ALBANY.   Half-blooded fellow, yes.
REGAN. [*To Edmund*] Let the drum strike, and prove
    my title thine.
ALBANY. Stay yet; hear reason. Edmund, I arrest thee
  On capital treason; and, in thine attaint,
  This gilded serpent [*pointing to Goneril*]. For your
    claim, fair sister,
  I bar it in the interest of my wife;
  'Tis she is sub-contracted to this lord,
  And I, her husband, contradict your banns.
  If you will marry, make your loves to me,
  My lady is bespoke.
GONERIL.   An interlude!
ALBANY. Thou art armed, Gloucester; let the trumpet
    sound.
  If none appear to prove upon thy head
  Thy heinous, manifest, and many treasons,
  There is my pledge [*throwing down a glove*]; I 'll prove
    it on thy heart,
  Ere I taste bread, thou art in nothing less
  Than I have here proclaimed thee.
REGAN.   Sick, O, sick!
GONERIL. [*Aside*] If not, I 'll ne'er trust medicine.
EDMUND. There's my exchange [*throwing down a glove*];
    what in the world he is
  That names me traitor, villain-like he lies.
  Call by thy trumpet; he that dares approach,
  On him, on you, who not? I will maintain
  My truth and honour firmly.
ALBANY. A herald, ho!
EDMUND.   A herald, ho, a herald!
ALBANY. Trust to thy single virtue; for thy soldiers,
  All levied in my name, have in my name
  Took their discharge.
REGAN.   My sickness grows upon me.
ALBANY. She is not well; convey her to my tent.
                    Exit REGAN, *led*

        Enter a Herald

  Come hither, herald—Let the trumpet sound—
  And read out this.
CAPTAIN. Sound, trumpet!   *A trumpet sounds*
HERALD. [*Reads*] "If any man of quality or degree with-
  in the lists of the army will maintain upon Edmund,

supposed earl of Gloucester, that he is a manifold traitor, let him appear by the third sound of the trumpet. He is bold in his defence.''

First trumpet

HERALD. Again!   *Second trumpet*
HERALD. Again!   *Third trumpet*
                                                          Trumpet answers within

Enter EDGAR, *at the third sound, armed, with a trumpet before him*

ALBANY. Ask him his purposes, why he appears
 Upon this call o' the trumpet.
HERALD.   What are you?
 Your name, your quality? and why you answer
 This present summons?
EDGAR.   Know, my name is lost;
 By treason's tooth bare-gnawn and canker-bit;
 Yet am I noble as the adversary
 I come to cope.
ALBANY.   Which is that adversary?
EDGAR. What's he that speaks for Edmund earl of
 Gloucester?
EDMUND. Himself; what say'st thou to him?
EDGAR.   Draw thy sword,
 That, if my speech offend a noble heart,
 Thy arm may do thee justice; here is mine.
 Behold, it is the privilege of mine honours,
 My oath, and my profession: I protest,
 Maugre thy strength, youth, place, and eminence,
 Despite thy victor sword and fire-new fortune,
 Thy valour and thy heart, thou art a traitor;
 False to thy gods, thy brother, and thy father;
 Conspirant 'gainst this high-illustrious prince;
 And, from the extremest upward of thy head
 To the descent and dust below thy foot,
 A most toad-spotted traitor. Say thou "No,"
 This sword, this arm, and my best spirits, are bent
 To prove upon thy heart, whereto I speak,
 Thou liest.
EDMUND. In wisdom I should ask thy name;
 But, since thy outside looks so fair and warlike,
 And that thy tongue some say of breeding breathes,
 What safe and nicely I might well delay
 By rule of knighthood, I disdain and spurn.
 Back do I toss these treasons to thy head;
 With the hell-hated lie o'erwhelm thy heart;
 Which, for they yet glance by and scarcely bruise,
 This sword of mine shall give them instant way,
 Where they shall rest for ever. Trumpets, speak!
     Alarums. They fight. EDMUND *falls*
ALBANY. Save him, save him!
GONERIL.   This is practice, Gloucester;
 By the law of arms thou wast not bound to answer
 An unknown opposite; thou art not vanquished,
 But cozened and beguiled.
ALBANY.   Shut your mouth, dame,

Or with this paper shall I stop it. Hold, sir;
 Thou worse than any name, read thine own evil.
 No tearing, lady; I perceive you know it.
      Gives the letter to EDMUND
GONERIL. Say, if I do, the laws are mine, not thine;
 Who can arraign me for 't?
ALBANY.   Most monstrous! oh!
 Know'st thou this paper?
GONERIL.   Ask me not what I know. *Exit*
ALBANY. Go after her! she's desperate; govern her.
EDMUND. What you have charged me with, that have
 I done;
 And more, much more; the time will bring it out.
 'Tis past, and so am I. But what art thou
 That hast this fortune on me? If thou 'rt noble,
 I do forgive thee.
EDGAR.   Let's exchange charity.
 I am no less in blood than thou art, Edmund;
 If more, the more thou hast wronged me.
 My name is Edgar, and thy father's son.
 The gods are just, and of our pleasant vices
 Make instruments to plague us:
 The dark and vicious place where thee he got
 Cost him his eyes.
EDMUND.   Thou hast spoken right, 'tis true;
 The wheel is come full circle; I am here.
ALBANY. Methought thy very gait did prophesy
 A royal nobleness. I must embrace thee.
 Let sorrow split my heart, if ever I
 Did hate thee or thy father!
EDGAR.   Worthy prince, I know 't.
ALBANY. Where have you hid yourself?
 How have you known the miseries of your father?
EDGAR. By nursing them, my lord. List a brief tale;
 And when 'tis told, O, that my heart would burst!
 The bloody proclamation to escape,
 That followed me so near—O, our lives' sweetness!
 That we the pain of death would hourly die
 Rather than die at once!—taught me to shift
 Into a madman's rags; to assume a semblance
 That very dogs disdained; and in this habit
 Met I my father with his bleeding rings,
 Their precious stones new lost; became his guide,
 Led him, begged for him, saved him from despair;
 Never—O fault!—revealed myself unto him,
 Until some half-hour past, when I was armed;
 Not sure, though hoping, of this good success,
 I asked his blessing, and from first to last
 Told him my pilgrimage; but his flawed heart,
 Alack, too weak the conflict to support!
 'Twixt two extremes of passion, joy and grief,
 Burst smilingly.
EDMUND. This speech of yours hath moved me,
 And shall perchance do good; but speak you on;
 You look as you had something more to say.
ALBANY. If there be more, more woeful, hold it in;

For I am almost ready to dissolve,
Hearing of this.

EDGAR.   This would have seemed a period
To such as love not sorrow; but another,
To amplify too much, would make much more,
And top extremity.
Whilst I was big in clamour came there in a man,
Who, having seen me in my worst estate,
Shunned my abhorred society; but then, finding
Who 'twas that so endured, with his strong arms
He fastened on my neck, and bellowed out
As he 'ld burst heaven; threw him on my father;
Told the most piteous tale of Lear and him
That ever ear received; which in recounting
His grief grew puissant, and the strings of life
Began to crack. Twice then the trumpets sounded,
And there I left him tranced.

ALBANY.   But who was this?

EDGAR. Kent, sir, the banished Kent; who in disguise
Followed his enemy King, and did him service
Improper for a slave.

Enter a Gentleman, *with a bloody knife*

GENTLEMAN. Help, help, O, help!

EDGAR.   What kind of help?

ALBANY.   Speak, man.

EDGAR. What means that bloody knife?

GENTLEMAN.   'Tis hot, it smokes;
It came even from the heart of—O, she's dead!

ALBANY. Who dead? speak, man.

GENTLEMAN. Your lady, sir, your lady; and her sister
By her is poisoned; she hath confessed it.

EDMUND. I was contracted to them both; all three
Now marry in an instant.

EDGAR.   Here comes Kent.

ALBANY. Produce their bodies, be they alive or dead;
This judgment of the heavens, that makes us tremble,
Touches us not with pity.   *Exit* Gentleman

Enter KENT

                    O, is this he?
The time will not allow the compliment
Which very manners urges.

KENT.   I am come
To bid my King and master aye good night;
Is he not here?

ALBANY.   Great thing of us forgot!
Speak, Edmund, where's the King? and where's
   Cordelia?
See'st thou this object, Kent?

The bodies of GONERIL *and* REGAN *are brought in*

KENT. Alack, why thus?

EDMUND.   Yet Edmund was beloved;
The one the other poisoned for my sake,
And after slew herself.

ALBANY. Even so. Cover their faces.

EDMUND. I pant for life; some good I mean to do,
Despite of mine own nature. Quickly send,
Be brief in it, to the castle; for my writ
Is on the life of Lear and on Cordelia.
Nay, send in time.

ALBANY.   Run, run, O, run!

EDGAR. To who, my lord? Who hath the office? Send
Thy token of reprieve.

EDMUND. Well thought on; take my sword,
Give it the captain.

ALBANY. Haste thee, for thy life.   *Exit* EDGAR

EDMUND. He hath commission from thy wife and me
To hang Cordelia in the prison, and
To lay the blame upon her own despair,
That she fordid herself.

ALBANY. The gods defend her! Bear him hence awhile.

                    EDMUND *is borne off*

Re-enter
LEAR, *with* CORDELIA *dead in his arms;*
EDGAR, Captain, *and others following*

LEAR. Howl, howl, howl, howl! O, you are men of
   stones!
Had I your tongues and eyes, I 'ld use them so
That heaven's vault should crack. She's gone for
   ever!
I know when one is dead, and when one lives;
She's dead as earth. Lend me a looking-glass;
If that her breath will mist or stain the stone,
Why, then she lives.

KENT.   Is this the promised end?

EDGAR. Or image of that horror?

ALBANY.   Fall, and cease!

LEAR. This feather stirs; she lives! if it be so,
It is a chance which does redeem all sorrows
That ever I have felt.

KENT. [*Kneeling*] O my good master!

LEAR. Prithee, away.

EDGAR.   'Tis noble Kent, your friend.

LEAR. A plague upon you, murderers, traitors all!
I might have saved her; now she's gone for ever!
Cordelia, Cordelia! stay a little. Ha!
What is 't thou say'st? Her voice was ever soft,
Gentle, and low, an excellent thing in woman.
I killed the slave that was a-hanging thee.

CAPTAIN. 'Tis true, my lords, he did.

LEAR.   Did I not, fellow?
I have seen the day, with my good biting falchion
I would have made them skip; I am old now,
And these same crosses spoil me. Who are you?
Mine eyes are not o' the best, I 'll tell you straight.

KENT. If fortune brag of two she loved and hated,
One of them we behold.

LEAR. This is a dull sight. Are you not Kent?

KENT.   The same,
Your servant Kent. Where is your servant Caius?

LEAR. He's a good fellow, I can tell you that;
  He'll strike, and quickly too. He's dead and rotten.
KENT. No, my good lord; I am the very man—
LEAR. I 'll see that straight.
KENT. That, from your first of difference and decay,
  Have followed your sad steps.
LEAR.   You are welcome hither.
KENT. Nor no man else; all 's cheerless, dark, and
    deadly.
  Your eldest daughters have fordone themselves,
  And desperately are dead.
LEAR.   Ay, so I think.
ALBANY. He knows not what he says, and vain it is
  That we present us to him.
EDGAR.   Very bootless.
        Enter a Captain
CAPTAIN. Edmund is dead, my lord.
ALBANY.   That's but a trifle here.
  You lords and noble friends, know our intent.
  What comfort to this great decay may come
  Shall be applied; for us, we will resign,
  During the life of this old majesty,
  To him our absolute power; [*To Edgar and Kent*] you,
    to your rights;
  With boot, and such addition as your honours
  Have more than merited. All friends shall taste
  The wages of their virtue, and all foes
  The cup of their deservings. O, see, see!

LEAR. And my poor fool is hanged! No, no, no life!
  Why should a dog, a horse, a rat, have life,
  And thou no breath at all? Thou 'lt come no more,
  Never, never, never, never, never!
  Pray you, undo this button; thank you, sir.
  Do you see this? Look on her, look, her lips,
  Look there, look there!   *Dies*
EDGAR.   He faints! My lord, my lord!
KENT. Break, heart; I prithee, break!
EDGAR.   Look up, my lord.
KENT. Vex not his ghost; O, let him pass! he hates him
    much
  That would upon the rack of this tough world
  Stretch him out longer.
EDGAR.   He is gone, indeed.
KENT. The wonder is, he hath endured so long:
  He but usurped his life.
ALBANY. Bear them from hence. Our present business
  Is general woe. [*To Kent and Edgar*] Friends of my soul,
    you twain
  Rule in this realm, and the gored state sustain.
KENT. I have a journey, sir, shortly to go;
  My master calls me, I must not say no.
ALBANY. The weight of this sad time we must obey;
  Speak what we feel, not what we ought to say.
  The oldest hath borne most; we that are young
  Shall never see so much, nor live so long.
                          Exeunt, with a dead march

MACBETH

Macbeth is about the career, and final destruction, of Macbeth, a thane, who became king of Scotland. In presenting this particular character, Shakespeare says a great deal about human nature in general, the nature of ambition, the possibility that an essentially "good" man may be perverted into a villain, and that such perversion may occur through the very qualities in him which have the noblest as well as the most degrading possibilities. Macbeth is intelligent, imaginative, courageous and affectionate. These are the very qualities, especially the love for his wife, which bring about his ruin and that of his country.

As well as its plot, or story, a great play invariably has a theme. By the story I mean the sequence of events which occur to the characters of the play, either before our eyes, like the murder of Banquo, or described to us, like the murder of Duncan. By the theme I mean the idea, or complex of ideas, which are the author's comment upon the story.

I cannot with confidence offer any final opinion about the theme of *Macbeth*. Yet no production of the play can ever at best be more than just theatrically effective, and no reading of the play can be more than superficial, unless serious attempts are made to find the theme.

To say that the theme is vaulting ambition o'erleaping itself is certainly true, but too trivial an account of the comment which such a mind as Shakespeare's would be content to make. To say, as does Professor Raleigh and, following him, Professor Dover Wilson—important scholars both, whose words must not be lightly heeded—that the theme of this and all Shakespeare's tragedies is "Man and the Universe", and that its purpose is to present us with "a dazzling vision of the pitiful state of humanity", is true, and a deeper interpretation, more in scale with the play. But I find it too vague. It suggests a theme for all Tragedy, but not particularly, nor especially, for *Macbeth*.

We may be pretty sure that the theme cannot be stated as a moral axiom. Critics of the seventeenth, eighteenth and, especially, the nineteenth centuries liked to find a Moral as the justification for a work of art, and liked to classify fictional characters as "good" and "bad". But one of the striking features of Shakespeare's characters is that they simply cannot be so classified. The finest of them are flawed with some weakness or vice, the most pernicious redeemed by some sparks of virtue. He is concerned to present human beings as he believes them, from experience, to be; not as he wishes they might be, or as might make them theatrically effective.

Perhaps the strongest theatrical effect is the confrontation of Good with Evil, the juxtaposition of the most brilliant light with the darkest shade. To achieve this, many dramatists, but never Shakespeare, have tended to make their good characters quite inhumanly good and their bad ones blacker than ink.

There is unquestionably one strong and obvious moral lesson in *Macbeth*: Thou shalt not kill. One murder leads to another, till at last the entire moral fabric, not only of Macbeth himself, but of the whole kingdom, is corrupted. But this again is too simple and naive a comment to be Shakespeare's. He makes it, but *en passant*. It is not the Theme; nor even, in any important sense, a Theme.

A promising start for the search for a theme is from the imagery of the play. It is noticeable that in this play direct references to darkness, and images concerned with darkness, blackness, night, are forever recurring. So are references to blood and bloodstains.

The Weird Sisters, also, are peculiar to this play and bear, I suspect, a close relation to whatever comment Shakespeare was consciously, or unconsciously, expressing. They too connect with ideas of darkness, concerned as they are with mystery. They too connect with ideas of blood and violence.

Blood and bloodstains seem to suggest murder and the subsequent stains of guilt. Shakespeare explicitly makes this connection when, in the Sleepwalking Scene, Lady Macbeth tries to cleanse her soul of guilt by washing the blood off her hands. Darkness suggests the darkness of ignorance, of superstition and of death; and suggests, too, secrecy and concealment and thence guilt.

From all this one conjectures whether the theme of the play may not possibly be the violence which is secretly concealed beneath the outward appearance of civilized, social Man, even of kingly, heroic Man, so that his very kingship is used to procure a license for his essential barbarity—the darkness and bloodiness within him.

The characters of Macbeth and Lady Macbeth have been extensively discussed by commentators. Bradley, in his two lectures on *Macbeth* (*Shakespearian Tragedy* by A. C. Bradley) has probably made a definitive analysis both of the characters and of the whole play. Though Bradley's lack of practical knowledge of the theatre sometimes leads him a little astray, his work is, in general, so thorough, so thoughtful, so imaginative and wise that it has become the almost essential starting point for all subsequent students of the play.

Since Bradley's work is so easily accessible, I shall attempt no detailed character analysis, but would like to say a word on a point which Bradley omits: What should the Macbeths look like?

In the theatre, I suppose because it is set in a primitive period in the far North, it is customary to present the play as an orgy of horn and hair, hide and mothball. The thanes stalk about like waifs and strays from Wagnerian opera, and Macbeth is the shaggiest dog of all. I do not agree with this conception.

The barbarity of the goings-on should contrast with a dignified regality of aspect. Neither Macbeth nor his Lady, Duncan, Banquo nor Malcolm think or speak in a primitive, unsophisticated manner. Moreover, the violence of their conduct is only shocking if it is at odds with their appearance; if they look like wolves, it is not shocking but only natural that they should behave like wolves; and the decay of the kingdom, which is one of the tragic consequences of Macbeth's regicide and usurpation, has no meaning if, even at the start of the play, Scotland is presented as an epitome of barbarity and poverty.

Macbeth himself must look not merely heroic, but beautiful—a Fallen Angel, not a road-company Wotan.

Lady Macbeth should be a fragile, small person. The part was almost certainly written for a boy; the "tradition" that she should be a big, beefy female probably stems from the fact that Mrs. Siddons was its most celebrated exponent. She was a big woman and renowned for ringing, thrilling declamation. But it is only fair to say that, on the evidence of her letters, she played most of Lady Macbeth in a voice no bigger than a whisper. It seems to me more interesting if the "undaunted mettle" of Lady Macbeth is contained in a frail and delicate vessel; and far the best performances which I have seen of the part have been by small and extremely "feminine" women. But, finally, the argument against a big woman is that unless her Macbeth is a super-colossus, she will make him seem a contemptible, rather than a tragic, figure. She *does* dominate him; *does* egg him on to murder Duncan; she *is* the more resolute immediately after the murder. There is real danger, if the lady is physically as well as spiritually dominant, that the lord appears as a hapless little being, whose criminally neurotic behavior is due to fear of the bruiser at home.

The big woman should be Lady Macduff, who should give her murderers a good run for their money. And that brings me to the question of the stage-management of the frequent scenes of violence: Duncan and the grooms are stabbed off-stage, but Lady Macduff and her children are murdered in front of the eyes of the audience, so is Banquo; there is a battle in which the combined forces under Malcolm storm the castle of of Dunsinane; there is a single combat between Macbeth

and Macduff and, finally, the severed head of Macbeth is brought onto the stage at the end of the play, in token that "the time is free", that the period of his tyranny is ended.

I consider that Shakespeare intended all this violence not merely to titillate the vulgar, who then as now demanded a lavish display of blood and guts, but for the serious expression of the underlying meaning of the play. If, as I suppose, darkness, violence, bloodshed and bloodstains are images of the play's meaning, then, since a play consists not just in the words that are spoken but in words wedded to action, these ideas must be expressed not solely in word but also in deed.

This is not easy. To look convincingly as if you are stabbing somebody, and, still more, to look as if you are being stabbed, demands not perhaps the utmost subtlety of the Thespian *art,* but certainly some *skill.* And, if we except Banquo, the demand is made upon actors whose parts are otherwise very small—murderers, Lady Macduff and children—so probably they are not the most gifted or experienced members of a troupe. But these affairs are really a matter less of acting than direction. A capable and inventive director can set up a routine for a fight which even inexperienced and un-athletic actors can master, *given time.* But there's the rub: there is never in the hurly-burly of rehearsal in our commercialized theatre, where time is money, the least likelihood of the many, many hours being available to work out and perfect a satisfactory routine.

This is the reason why these scenes are nearly always skimped; a tactful darkness, in which barely discernible figures rush about and exchange unconvincing buffets, cuts, thrusts, at top speed.

There remains the single combat. Single combats are an important feature of Shakespeare's tragedies and histories. They are the final, life-and-death confrontation of the two antagonists, whose opposition is a main theme of their particular play. In this case they are Macbeth and Macduff; but there are analogous combats in, for example, *Hamlet, Richard the Third* and *Coriolanus.*

The combat is of cardinal importance to the symbolism of the play; but there is a further purpose. At the moment of the play when an audience is beginning to wilt under the deluge of words and to long for a mental rest, the argument transfers itself from words into action, and the audience is offered a thrilling display by the play's antagonists of *physical* courage, energy and skill.

Of our famous actors today who are intellectually and vocally equipped for the great classical roles, there is only one, Sir Laurence Olivier, who, in addition to all the other requirements, can come up at the end of a long, exhausting performance with the gladiatorial display which this most exacting of all authors, William Shakespeare, demands.

LADY MACDUFF

Boy, son to Macduff

DUNCAN

King of Scotland

his sons

MALCOLM   DONALBAIN

Gentlewoman
attending on
Lady Macbeth

SEYTON,
an officer
attending
on Macbeth

FLEANCE
son to
Banquo

LADY
MACBETH   MACBETH   BANQUO   MACDUFF

Generals of the King's army

SIWARD, Earl of
Northumberland,
General of the
English forces.
Young SIWARD,
his son.

A Soldier, An English Doctor,
A Scotch Doctor, Gentlemen,
Lords, Officers, Soldiers,
Attendants, Messengers and
Murderers.

A Porter   An Old Man

HECATE

Three Witches   Apparitions

NNOX ROSS MENTEITH ANGUS CAITHNESS
Noblemen of Scotland

MACBETH
DRAMATIS PERSONAE

SCENE: SCOTLAND; ENGLAND

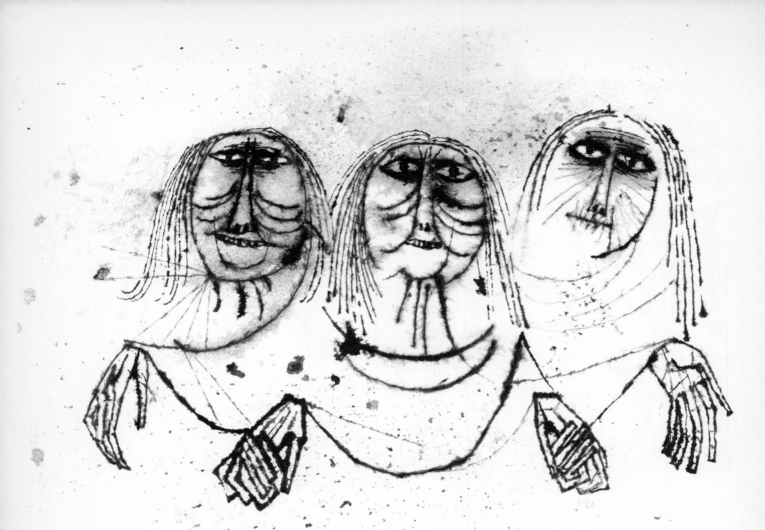

ACT I

SCENE I *A desert place*

Thunder and lightning. Enter three Witches

FIRST WITCH. When shall we three meet again
  In thunder, lightning, or in rain?
SECOND WITCH. When the hurlyburly's done,
  When the battle's lost and won.
THIRD WITCH. That will be ere the set of sun.
FIRST WITCH. Where the place?
SECOND WITCH.   Upon the heath.

THIRD WITCH. There to meet with Macbeth.
FIRST WITCH. I come, Graymalkin!
SECOND WITCH. Paddock calls.
THIRD WITCH. Anon.
ALL. Fair is foul, and foul is fair;
  Hover through the fog and filthy air.

                Exeunt

SCENE II *A camp near Forres*

Alarum within. Enter DUNCAN, MALCOLM, DONALBAIN, LENNOX, *with* Attendants, *meeting a bleeding* Sergeant

DUNCAN. What bloody man is that? He can report,
  As seemeth by his plight, of the revolt
  The newest state.
MALCOLM.   This is the sergeant
  Who like a good and hardy soldier fought
  'Gainst my captivity. Hail, brave friend!
  Say to the King the knowledge of the broil
  As thou didst leave it.
SERGEANT.   Doubtful it stood;

As two spent swimmers, that do cling together
And choke their art. The merciless Macdonwald—
Worthy to be a rebel, for to that
The multiplying villainies of nature
Do swarm upon him—from the western isles
Of kerns and gallowglasses is supplied;
And fortune, on his damned quarrel smiling,
Showed like a rebel's whore. But all 's too weak;
For brave Macbeth—well he deserves that name—

410

Disdaining fortune, with his brandished steel,
Which smoked with bloody execution,
Like valour's minion carved out his passage
Till he faced the slave;
Which ne'er shook hands, nor bade farewell to him,
Till he unseamed him from the nave to the chaps,
And fixed his head upon our battlements.

DUNCAN. O valiant cousin! worthy gentleman!

SERGEANT. As whence the sun 'gins his reflection
Shipwrecking storms and direful thunders break,
So from that spring whence comfort seemed to come
Discomfort swells. Mark, King of Scotland, mark:
No sooner justice had with valour armed
Compelled these skipping kerns to trust their heels,
But the Norweyan lord surveying vantage,
With furbished arms and new supplies of men
Began a fresh assault.

DUNCAN.   Dismayed not this
Our captains, Macbeth and Banquo?

SERGEANT.   Yes;
As sparrows eagles, or the hare the lion.
If I say sooth, I must report they were
As cannons overcharged with double cracks, so they
Doubly redoubled strokes upon the foe.
Except they meant to bathe in reeking wounds,
Or memorize another Golgotha,
I cannot tell.
But I am faint, my gashes cry for help.

DUNCAN. So well thy words become thee as thy wounds;
They smack of honour both. Go get him surgeons.
Who comes here?   *Exit* Sergeant , *attended*

Enter ROSS

MALCOLM.   The worthy Thane of Ross.

LENNOX. What a haste looks through his eyes! So should
he look
That seems to speak things strange.

ROSS.   God save the King!

DUNCAN. Whence camest thou, worthy Thane?

ROSS.   From Fife, great King;
Where the Norweyan banners flout the sky
And fan our people cold. Norway himself,
With terrible numbers,
Assisted by that most disloyal traitor
The Thane of Cawdor, began a dismal conflict;
Till that Bellona's bridegroom, lapped in proof,
Confronted him with self-comparisons,
Point against point rebellious, arm 'gainst arm,
Curbing his lavish spirit; and, to conclude,
The victory fell on us.

DUNCAN.   Great happiness!

ROSS.   That now
Sweno, the Norways' king, craves composition;
Nor would we deign him burial of his men
Till he disbursed at Saint Colme's Inch
Ten thousand dollars to our general use.

DUNCAN. No more that Thane of Cawdor shall deceive
Our bosom interest. Go pronounce his present death,
And with his former title greet Macbeth.

ROSS. I'll see it done.

DUNCAN. What he hath lost noble Macbeth hath won.
                                                    Exeunt

SCENE III *A heath near Forres*

Thunder. Enter the three Witches

FIRST WITCH. Where hast thou been, sister?

SECOND WITCH. Killing swine.

THIRD WITCH. Sister, where thou?

FIRST WITCH. A sailor's wife had chestnuts in her lap,
And munched, and munched, and munched—"Give
me," quoth I;
"Aroint thee, witch!" the rump-fed ronyon cries.
Her husband's to Aleppo gone, master o' the Tiger.
But in a sieve I'll thither sail,
And, like a rat without a tail,
I'll do, I'll do, and I'll do.

SECOND WITCH. I'll give thee a wind.

FIRST WITCH. Thou 'rt kind.

THIRD WITCH. And I another.

FIRST WITCH. I myself have all the other,
And the very ports they blow,
All the quarters that they know
I' the shipman's card.
I will drain him dry as hay;
Sleep shall neither night nor day

Hang upon his pent-house lid;
He shall live a man forbid.
Weary, sev'nnights nine times nine
Shall he dwindle, peak and pine.
Though his bark cannot be lost,
Yet it shall be tempest-tost.
Look what I have.

SECOND WITCH. Show me, show me.

FIRST WITCH. Here I have a pilot's thumb,
Wrecked as homeward he did come.   *Drum within*

THIRD WITCH. A drum, a drum!
Macbeth doth come.

ALL. The weird sisters, hand in hand,
Posters of the sea and land,
Thus do go about, about:
Thrice to thine and thrice to mine
And thrice again, to make up nine.
Peace! The charm's wound up.

Enter MACBETH *and* BANQUO

MACBETH. So foul and fair a day I have not seen.

BANQUO. How far is 't called to Forres? What are these
  So withered and so wild in their attire,
  That look not like the inhabitants o' the earth,
  And yet are on 't? Live you? or are you aught
  That man may question? You seem to understand me,
  By each at once her choppy finger laying
  Upon her skinny lips. You should be women,
  And yet your beards forbid me to interpret
  That you are so.

MACBETH. Speak, if you can. What are you?

FIRST WITCH. All hail, Macbeth! Hail to thee, Thane
  of Glamis!

SECOND WITCH. All hail, Macbeth! Hail to thee,
  Thane of Cawdor!

THIRD WITCH. All hail, Macbeth, that shalt be King
  hereafter!

BANQUO. Good sir, why do you start; and seem to fear
  Things that do sound so fair? I' the name of truth,
  Are ye fantastical, or that indeed
  Which outwardly ye show? My noble partner
  You greet with present grace and great prediction
  Of noble having and of royal hope,
  That he seems rapt withal. To me you speak not.
  If you can look into the seeds of time,
  And say which grain will grow and which will not,
  Speak then to me, who neither beg nor fear
  Your favours nor your hate.

FIRST WITCH. Hail!

SECOND WITCH. Hail!

THIRD WITCH. Hail!

FIRST WITCH. Lesser than Macbeth, and greater.

SECOND WITCH. Not so happy, yet much happier.

THIRD WITCH. Thou shalt get kings, though thou be
  none.
  So all hail, Macbeth and Banquo!

FIRST WITCH. Banquo and Macbeth, all hail!

MACBETH. Stay, you imperfect speakers, tell me more.
  By Sinel's death I know I am Thane of Glamis;
  But how of Cawdor? The Thane of Cawdor lives,
  A prosperous gentleman; and to be King
  Stands not within the prospect of belief,
  No more than to be Cawdor. Say from whence
  You owe this strange intelligence? or why
  Upon this blasted heath you stop our way
  With such prophetic greeting? Speak, I charge you.
                              Witches *vanish*

BANQUO. The earth hath bubbles, as the water has,
  And these are of them. Whither are they vanished?

MACBETH. Into the air; and what seemed corporal
  melted
  As breath into the wind. Would they had stayed!

BANQUO. Were such things here as we do speak about?
  Or have we eaten on the insane root
  That takes the reason prisoner?

MACBETH. Your children shall be kings.

BANQUO. You shall be King.
MACBETH. And Thane of Cawdor too; went it not so?
BANQUO. To the selfsame tune and words. Who's here?

Enter ROSS *and* ANGUS

ROSS. The King hath happily received, Macbeth,
The news of thy success; and when he reads
Thy personal venture in the rebels' fight,
His wonders and his praises do contend
Which should be thine or his. Silenced with that,
In viewing o'er the rest o' the selfsame day,
He finds thee in the stout Norweyan ranks,
Nothing afeard of what thyself didst make,
Strange images of death. As thick as hail
Came post with post; and every one did bear
Thy praises in his kingdom's great defence,
And poured them down before him.
ANGUS. We are sent
To give thee from our royal master thanks;
Only to herald thee into his sight,
Not pay thee.
ROSS. And, for an earnest of a greater honour,
He bade me, from him, call thee Thane of Cawdor—
In which addition, hail, most worthy Thane!
For it is thine.
BANQUO. What, can the devil speak true?
MACBETH. The Thane of Cawdor lives; why do you dress me
In borrowed robes?
ANGUS. Who was the Thane lives yet;
But under heavy judgement bears that life
Which he deserves to lose. Whether he was combined
With those of Norway, or did line the rebel
With hidden help and vantage, or that with both
He laboured in his country's wreck, I know not;
But treasons capital, confessed and proved,
Have overthrown him.
MACBETH. [*Aside*] Glamis, and Thane of Cawdor!
The greatest is behind. [*To Ross and Angus*] Thanks
for your pains.
[*To Banquo*] Do you not hope your children shall
be kings,
When those that gave the Thane of Cawdor to me
Promised no less to them?
BANQUO. That trusted home
Might yet enkindle you unto the crown,
Besides the Thane of Cawdor. But 'tis strange:
And oftentimes, to win us to our harm,
The instruments of darkness tell us truths,
Win us with honest trifles, to betray 's
In deepest consequence.
Cousins, a word, I pray you.
MACBETH. [*Aside*] Two truths are told,
As happy prologues to the swelling act
Of the imperial theme.—I thank you, gentlemen.
[*Aside*] This supernatural soliciting

Cannot be ill, cannot be good. If ill,
Why hath it given me earnest of success,
Commencing in a truth? I am Thane of Cawdor.
If good, why do I yield to that suggestion
Whose horrid image doth unfix my hair
And make my seated heart knock at my ribs,
Against the use of nature? Present fears
Are less than horrible imaginings.
My thought, whose murder yet is but fantastical,
Shakes so my single state of man that function
Is smothered in surmise, and nothing is
But what is not.
BANQUO.   Look, how our partner's rapt.
MACBETH. [Aside] If chance will have me King, why,
    chance may crown me,
Without my stir.

BANQUO.   New honours come upon him,
Like our strange garments, cleave not to their mould
But with the aid of use.
MACBETH.   [Aside] Come what come may,
Time and the hour runs through the roughest day.
BANQUO. Worthy Macbeth, we stay upon your leisure.
MACBETH. Give me your favour; my dull brain was
    wrought
With things forgotten. Kind gentlemen, your pains
Are registered where every day I turn
The leaf to read them. Let us toward the King.
Think upon what hath chanced, and, at more time,
The interim having weighed it, let us speak
Our free hearts each to other.
BANQUO.   Very gladly.
MACBETH. Till then, enough. Come, friends.   Exeunt

SCENE IV Forres. *The palace*

Flourish. Enter DUNCAN, MALCOLM, DONALBAIN, LENNOX, *and* Attendants

DUNCAN. Is execution done on Cawdor? Are not
Those in commission yet returned?
MALCOLM.   My liege,
They are not yet come back. But I have spoke
With one that saw him die; who did report
That very frankly he confessed his treasons,
Implored your highness' pardon and set forth
A deep repentance. Nothing in his life
Became him like the leaving it; he died
As one that had been studied in his death
To throw away the dearest thing he owed,
As 'twere a careless trifle.
DUNCAN.   There 's no art
To find the mind's construction in the face.
He was a gentleman on whom I built
An absolute trust.

Enter MACBETH, BANQUO, ROSS, *and* ANGUS

            O worthiest cousin!
The sin of my ingratitude even now
Was heavy on me. Thou art so far before
That swiftest wing of recompense is slow
To overtake thee. Would thou hadst less deserved,
That the proportion both of thanks and payment
Might have been mine! Only I have left to say,
More is thy due than more than all can pay.
MACBETH. The service and the loyalty I owe,
In doing it, pays itself. Your highness' part
Is to receive our duties; and our duties
Are to your throne and state children and servants,
Which do but what they should, by doing every thing
Safe toward your love and honour.
DUNCAN.   Welcome hither.
I have begun to plant thee, and will labour

To make thee full of growing. Noble Banquo,
That hast no less deserved, nor must be known
No less to have done so, let me infold thee
And hold thee to my heart.
BANQUO.   There if I grow,
The harvest is your own.
DUNCAN.   My plenteous joys,
Wanton in fulness, seek to hide themselves
In drops of sorrow. Sons, kinsmen, thanes,
And you whose places are the nearest, know
We will establish our estate upon
Our eldest, Malcolm, whom we name hereafter
The Prince of Cumberland; which honour must
Not unaccompanied invest him only,
But signs of nobleness, like stars, shall shine
On all deservers. From hence to Inverness,
And bind us further to you.
MACBETH. The rest is labour, which is not used for you.
I'll be myself the harbinger and make joyful
The hearing of my wife with your approach;
So humbly take my leave.
DUNCAN.   My worthy Cawdor!
MACBETH. [Aside] The Prince of Cumberland! That is
    a step
On which I must fall down, or else o'erleap,
For in my way it lies. Stars, hide your fires;
Let not light see my black and deep desires.
The eye wink at the hand; yet let that be,
Which the eye fears, when it is done, to see.   Exit
DUNCAN. True, worthy Banquo; he is full so valiant,
And in his commendations I am fed;
It is a banquet to me. Let 's after him,
Whose care is gone before to bid us welcome:
It is a peerless kinsman.   *Flourish. Exeunt*

SCENE V *Inverness: Macbeth's castle*

Enter LADY MACBETH, *reading a letter*

LADY MACBETH. "They met me in the day of success; and I have learned by the perfectest report, they have more in them than mortal knowledge. When I burned in desire to question them further, they made themselves air, into which they vanished. Whiles I stood rapt in the wonder of it, came missives from the King, who all-hailed me 'Thane of Cawdor'; by which title, before, these weird sisters saluted me, and referred me to the coming on of time, with 'Hail, King that shalt be!' This have I thought good to deliver thee, my dearest partner of greatness, that thou mightst not lose the dues of rejoicing, by being ignorant of what greatness is promised thee. Lay it to thy heart, and farewell."

Glamis thou art, and Cawdor; and shalt be
What thou art promised. Yet do I fear thy nature;
It is too full o' the milk of human kindness
To catch the nearest way. Thou wouldst be great;
Art not without ambition, but without
The illness should attend it. What thou wouldst highly,
That wouldst thou holily; wouldst not play false,
And yet wouldst wrongly win. Thou 'ldst have, great
  Glamis,

That which cries "Thus thou must do, if thou have it;
And that which rather thou dost fear to do
Than wishest should be undone." Hie thee hither,
That I may pour my spirits in thine ear;
And chastise with the valour of my tongue
All that impedes thee from the golden round,
Which fate and metaphysical aid doth seem
To have thee crowned withal.

               Enter a Messenger

                    What is your tidings?

MESSENGER. The King comes here tonight.

LADY MACBETH.   Thou 'rt mad to say it.
Is not thy master with him? Who, were 't so,
Would have informed for preparation.

MESSENGER. So please you, it is true. Our Thane is
    coming;
One of my fellows had the speed of him,
Who, almost dead for breath, had scarcely more
Than would make up his message.

LADY MACBETH.   Give him tending;
He brings great news.   *Exit* Messenger
            The raven himself is hoarse
That croaks the fatal entrance of Duncan
Under my battlements. Come, you spirits
That tend on mortal thoughts, unsex me here,
And fill me from the crown to the toe top-full
Of direst cruelty! Make thick my blood;
Stop up the access and passage to remorse,
That no compunctious visitings of nature
Shake my fell purpose, nor keep peace between
The effect and it! Come to my woman's breasts,
And take my milk for gall, you murdering ministers,
Wherever in your sightless substances
You wait on nature's mischief! Come, thick night,
And pall thee in the dunnest smoke of hell,
That my keen knife see not the wound it makes,
Nor heaven peep through the blanket of the dark,
To cry "Hold, hold!"

              Enter MACBETH

         Great Glamis! worthy Cawdor!
Greater than both, by the all-hail hereafter!
Thy letters have transported me beyond
This ignorant present, and I feel now
The future in the instant.

MACBETH.   My dearest love,
Duncan comes here tonight.

LADY MACBETH.   And when goes hence?

MACBETH. Tomorrow, as he purposes.

LADY MACBETH.   O, never
Shall sun that morrow see!
Your face, my thane, is as a book where men
May read strange matters. To beguile the time,

Look like the time; bear welcome in your eye,
Your hand, your tongue. Look like the innocent
  flower,
But be the serpent under 't. He that's coming
Must be provided for; and you shall put
This night's great business into my dispatch;

Which shall to all our nights and days to come
Give solely sovereign sway and masterdom.
MACBETH. We will speak further.
LADY MACBETH.   Only look up clear;
To alter favour ever is to fear.
Leave all the rest to me.   *Exeunt*

SCENE VI *Before Macbeth's castle*

Hautboys and torches

Enter DUNCAN, MALCOLM, DONALBAIN, BANQUO, LENNOX, MACDUFF, ROSS, ANGUS, *and* Attendants

DUNCAN. This castle hath a pleasant seat; the air
Nimbly and sweetly recommends itself
Unto our gentle senses.
BANQUO.   This guest of summer,
The temple-haunting martlet, does approve,
By his loved mansionry, that the heaven's breath
Smells wooingly here. No jutty, frieze,
Buttress, nor coign of vantage, but this bird
Hath made his pendent bed and procreant cradle.
Where they most breed and haunt, I have observed,
The air is delicate.

Enter LADY MACBETH

DUNCAN.   See, see, our honoured hostess!
The love that follows us sometime is our trouble,
Which still we thank as love. Herein I teach you
How you shall bid God 'ild us for your pains,
And thank us for your trouble.
LADY MACBETH.   All our service
In every point twice done and then done double

Were poor and single business to contend
Against those honours deep and broad wherewith
Your majesty loads our house. For those of old,
And the late dignities heaped up to them,
We rest your hermits.
DUNCAN.   Where's the Thane of Cawdor?
We coursed him at the heels, and had a purpose
To be his purveyor. But he rides well;
And his great love, sharp as his spur, hath holp him
To his home before us. Fair and noble hostess,
We are your guest tonight.
LADY MACBETH.   Your servants ever
Have theirs, themselves and what is theirs, in compt,
To make their audit at your highness' pleasure,
Still to return your own.
DUNCAN.   Give me your hand;
Conduct me to mine host: we love him highly,
And shall continue our graces towards him.
By your leave, hostess.   *Exeunt*

SCENE VII *Macbeth's castle*

Hautboys and torches. Enter a Sewer, and divers Servants with dishes and service, and pass over the stage

Then enter MACBETH

MACBETH. If it were done when 'tis done, then 'twere
  well
It were done quickly. If the assassination
Could trammel up the consequence, and catch
With his surcease success; that but this blow
Might be the be-all and the end-all here,
But here, upon this bank and shoal of time,
We 'ld jump the life to come. But in these cases
We still have judgement here; that we but teach
Bloody instructions, which, being taught, return
To plague the inventor. This even-handed justice
Commends the ingredients of our poisoned chalice
To our own lips. He's here in double trust;
First, as I am his kinsman and his subject,
Strong both against the deed; then, as his host,
Who should against his murderer shut the door,
Not bear the knife myself. Besides, this Duncan
Hath borne his faculties so meek, hath been
So clear in his great office, that his virtues
Will plead like angels, trumpet-tongued, against

The deep damnation of his taking-off;
And pity, like a naked new-born babe,
Striding the blast, or heaven's cherubim, horsed
Upon the sightless couriers of the air,
Shall blow the horrid deed in every eye,
That tears shall drown the wind. I have no spur
To prick the sides of my intent, but only
Vaulting ambition, which o'erleaps itself
And falls on the other.

Enter LADY MACBETH

                              How now! what news?
LADY MACBETH. He has almost supped. Why have you
  left the chamber?
MACBETH. Hath he asked for me?
LADY MACBETH.   Know you not he has?
MACBETH. We will proceed no further in this business.
He hath honoured me of late; and I have bought
Golden opinions from all sorts of people,
Which would be worn now in their newest gloss,
Not cast aside so soon.

MACBETH

LADY MACBETH.   Was the hope drunk
  Wherein you dressed yourself? Hath it slept since?
  And wakes it now, to look so green and pale
  At what it did so freely? From this time
  Such I account thy love. Art thou afeard
  To be the same in thine own act and valour
  As thou art in desire? Wouldst thou have that
  Which thou esteem'st the ornament of life,
  And live a coward in thine own esteem,
  Letting "I dare not" wait upon "I would,"
  Like the poor cat i' the adage?
MACBETH.   Prithee, peace.
  I dare do all that may become a man;
  Who dares do more is none.
LADY MACBETH.   What beast was 't, then,
  That made you break this enterprise to me?
  When you durst do it, then you were a man;
  And, to be more than what you were, you would
  Be so much more the man. Nor time nor place
  Did then adhere, and yet you would make both.
  They have made themselves, and that their fitness now
  Does unmake you. I have given suck, and know
  How tender 'tis to love the babe that milks me.
  I would, while it was smiling in my face,
  Have plucked my nipple from his boneless gums,
  And dashed the brains out, had I so sworn as you
  Have done to this.
MACBETH.   If we should fail?
LADY MACBETH.   We fail!
  But screw your courage to the sticking-place,
  And we'll not fail. When Duncan is asleep—
  Whereto the rather shall his day's hard journey
  Soundly invite him—his two chamberlains
  Will I with wine and wassail so convince
  That memory, the warder of the brain,
  Shall be a fume, and the receipt of reason
  A limbeck only. When in swinish sleep
  Their drenched natures lie as in a death,
  What cannot you and I perform upon
  The unguarded Duncan? What not put upon
  His spongy officers, who shall bear the guilt
  Of our great quell?
MACBETH.   Bring forth men-children only;
  For thy undaunted mettle should compose
  Nothing but males. Will it not be received,
  When we have marked with blood those sleepy two
  Of his own chamber and used their very daggers,
  That they have done 't?
LADY MACBETH.   Who dares receive it other,
  As we shall make our griefs and clamour roar
  Upon his death?
MACBETH.   I am settled, and bend up
  Each corporal agent to this terrible feat.
  Away, and mock the time with fairest show.
  False face must hide what the false heart doth know.
                                        Exeunt

418

ACT II

SCENE I *Court of Macbeth's castle*

Enter BANQUO, *and* FLEANCE *bearing a torch before him*

BANQUO. How goes the night, boy?

FLEANCE. The moon is down; I have not heard the
    clock.

BANQUO. And she goes down at twelve.

FLEANCE.   I take 't, 'tis later, sir.

BANQUO. Hold, take my sword. There 's husbandry in
    heaven;
  Their candles are all out. Take thee that too.
  A heavy summons lies like lead upon me,
  And yet I would not sleep. Merciful powers,
  Restrain in me the cursed thoughts that nature
  Gives way to in repose!

Enter MACBETH, *and a* Servant *with a torch*

                Give me my sword.
  Who's there?

MACBETH. A friend.

BANQUO. What, sir, not yet at rest? The King's a-bed;
  He hath been in unusual pleasure, and
  Sent forth great largess to your offices.
  This diamond he greets your wife withal,
  By the name of most kind hostess; and shut up
  In measureless content.

MACBETH.   Being unprepared,
  Our will became the servant to defect;
  Which else should free have wrought.

BANQUO.   All's well.
  I dreamt last night of the three weird sisters.
  To you they have showed some truth.

MACBETH.   I think not of them.
  Yet, when we can entreat an hour to serve,
  We would spend it in some words upon that business,
  If you would grant the time.

BANQUO.   At your kind'st leisure.

MACBETH. If you shall cleave to my consent, when 'tis,
  It shall make honour for you.

BANQUO.   So I lose none
  In seeking to augment it, but still keep
  My bosom franchised and allegiance clear,
  I shall be counselled.

MACBETH.   Good repose the while!

BANQUO. Thanks, sir; the like to you!

                Exeunt BANQUO *and* FLEANCE

MACBETH. Go bid thy mistress, when my drink is ready,
  She strike upon the bell. Get thee to bed.

                    Exit Servant

  Is this a dagger which I see before me,
  The handle toward my hand? Come, let me clutch
    thee.
  I have thee not, and yet I see thee still.
  Art thou not, fatal vision, sensible
  To feeling as to sight? Or art thou but
  A dagger of the mind, a false creation,
  Proceeding from the heat-oppressed brain?
  I see thee yet, in form as palpable
  As this which now I draw.
  Thou marshall'st me the way that I was going;
  And such an instrument I was to use.
  Mine eyes are made the fools o' the other senses,
  Or else worth all the rest; I see thee still,
  And on thy blade and dudgeon gouts of blood,
  Which was not so before. There's no such thing—
  It is the bloody business which informs
  Thus to mine eyes. Now o'er the one halfworld
  Nature seems dead, and wicked dreams abuse
  The curtained sleep; witchcraft celebrates
  Pale Hecate's offerings, and withered murder,
  Alarumed by his sentinel, the wolf,
  Whose howl 's his watch, thus with his stealthy pace,
  With Tarquin's ravishing strides, towards his design
  Moves like a ghost. Thou sure and firm-set earth,
  Hear not my steps, which way they walk, for fear
  Thy very stones prate of my whereabout,
  And take the present horror from the time,
  Which now suits with it. Whiles I threat, he lives.
  Words to the heat of deeds too cold breath gives.

                      A bell rings

  I go, and it is done; the bell invites me.
  Hear it not, Duncan; for it is a knell
  That summons thee to heaven or to hell.   *Exit*

SCENE II *The same*

Enter LADY MACBETH

LADY MACBETH. That which hath made them drunk
hath made me bold;
What hath quenched them hath given me fire.
Hark! Peace!
It was the owl that shrieked, the fatal bellman,
Which gives the stern'st good night. He is about it.
The doors are open; and the surfeited grooms
Do mock their charge with snores. I have drugged
their possets,
That death and nature do contend about them,
Whether they live or die.

MACBETH. [*Within*] Who's there? What, ho!

LADY MACBETH. Alack, I am afraid they have awaked,
And 'tis not done. The attempt and not the deed
Confounds us. Hark! I laid their daggers ready;
He could not miss 'em. Had he not resembled
My father as he slept, I had done 't.

Enter MACBETH

My husband!

MACBETH. I have done the deed. Didst thou not hear
a noise?

LADY MACBETH. I heard the owl scream and the crickets
cry.
Did not you speak?

MACBETH.   When?

LADY MACBETH.   Now.

MACBETH.   As I descended?

LADY MACBETH. Ay.

MACBETH. Hark!
Who lies i' the second chamber?

LADY MACBETH.   Donalbain.

MACBETH. This is a sorry sight.   *Looking on his hands*

LADY MACBETH. A foolish thought, to say a sorry sight.

MACBETH. There's one did laugh in 's sleep, and one
cried "Murder!"
That they did wake each other. I stood and heard
them;
But they did say their prayers, and addressed them
Again to sleep.

LADY MACBETH.   There are two lodged together.

MACBETH. One cried "God bless us!" and "Amen" the
other;
As they had seen me with these hangman's hands.
Listening their fear, I could not say "Amen,"
When they did say "God bless us!"

LADY MACBETH.   Consider it not so deeply.

MACBETH. But wherefore could not I pronounce
"Amen"?
I had most need of blessing, and "Amen"
Stuck in my throat.

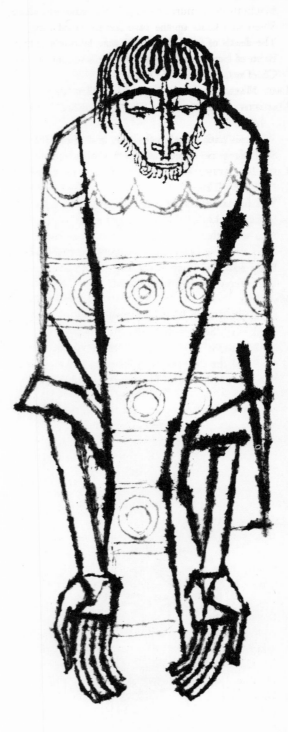

LADY MACBETH. These deeds must not be thought
After these ways; so, it will make us mad.
MACBETH. Methought I heard a voice cry "Sleep no
more!
Macbeth does murder sleep," the innocent sleep,
Sleep that knits up the ravelled sleave of care,
The death of each day's life, sore labour's bath,
Balm of hurt minds, great nature's second course,
Chief nourisher in life's feast—
LADY MACBETH.   What do you mean?
MACBETH. Still it cried "Sleep no more!" to all the
house:
"Glamis hath murdered sleep, and therefore Cawdor
Shall sleep no more; Macbeth shall sleep no more."
LADY MACBETH. Who was it that thus cried? Why,
worthy Thane,
You do unbend your noble strength, to think
So brainsickly of things. Go get some water,
And wash this filthy witness from your hand.
Why did you bring these daggers from the place?
They must lie there. Go carry them; and smear
The sleepy grooms with blood.
MACBETH.   I'll go no more.
I am afraid to think what I have done;
Look on 't again I dare not.
LADY MACBETH.   Infirm of purpose!
Give me the daggers. The sleeping and the dead
Are but as pictures. 'Tis the eye of childhood

That fears a painted devil. If he do bleed,
I'll gild the faces of the grooms withal;
For it must seem their guilt.   Exit. Knocking within
MACBETH.   Whence is that knocking?
How is 't with me, when every noise appals me?
What hands are here? Ha! they pluck out mine eyes.
Will all great Neptune's ocean wash this blood
Clean from my hand? No, this my hand will rather
The multitudinous seas incarnadine,
Making the green one red.

Re-enter LADY MACBETH

LADY MACBETH. My hands are of your colour; but I
shame
To wear a heart so white. [*Knocking within*] I hear a
knocking
At the south entry. Retire we to our chamber.
A little water clears us of this deed.
How easy is it, then! Your constancy
Hath left you unattended. [*Knocking within*] Hark!
more knocking.
Get on your nightgown, lest occasion call us,
And show us to be watchers. Be not lost
So poorly in your thoughts.
MACBETH. To know my deed, 'twere best not know
myself.   [*Knocking within*]
Wake Duncan with thy knocking! I would thou couldst!
Exeunt

SCENE III *The same*

Knocking within. Enter a Porter

PORTER. Here's a knocking indeed! If a man were porter of Hell gate, he should have old turning the key. [*Knocking within*] Knock, knock, knock! Who's there, i' the name of Beelzebub? Here's a farmer, that hanged himself on the expectation of plenty. Come in time; have napkins enow about you; here you'll sweat for 't. [*Knocking within*] Knock, knock! Who's there, in the other devil's name? Faith, here's an equivocator, that could swear in both the scales against either scale; who committed treason enough for God's sake, yet could not equivocate to heaven. O, come in, equivocator. [*Knocking within*] Knock, knock, knock! Who's there? Faith, here's an English tailor come hither, for stealing out of a French hose. Come in, tailor; here you may roast your goose. [*Knocking within*] Knock, knock; never at quiet! What are you? But this place is too cold for Hell. I'll devil-porter it no further. I had thought to have let in some of all professions that go the primrose way to the everlasting bonfire. [*Knocking within*] Anon, anon! I pray you, remember the porter. *Opens the gate*

Enter MACDUFF *and* LENNOX

MACDUFF. Was it so late, friend, ere you went to bed,
That you do lie so late?
PORTER. 'Faith, sir, we were carousing till the second cock. And drink, sir, is a great provoker of three things.
MACDUFF. What three things does drink especially provoke?
PORTER. Marry, sir, nose-painting, sleep, and urine. Lechery, sir, it provokes, and unprovokes; it provokes the desire, but it takes away the performance. Therefore, much drink may be said to be an equivocator with lechery—it makes him, and it mars him; it sets him on, and it takes him off; it persuades him, and disheartens him; makes him stand to, and not stand to; in conclusion, equivocates him in a sleep, and, giving him the lie, leaves him.
MACDUFF. I believe drink gave thee the lie last night.
PORTER. That it did, sir, i' the very throat on me. But I requited him for his lie; and, I think, being too strong

for him, though he took up my legs sometime, yet I
made a shift to cast him.
MACDUFF. Is thy master stirring?

Enter MACBETH

Our knocking has awaked him; here he comes.
LENNOX. Good morrow, noble sir.
MACBETH.   Good morrow, both.
MACDUFF. Is the King stirring, worthy Thane?
MACBETH.   Not yet.
MACDUFF. He did command me to call timely on him.
    I have almost slipped the hour.
MACBETH.   I'll bring you to him.
MACDUFF. I know this is a joyful trouble to you;
    But yet 'tis one.
MACBETH. The labour we delight in physics pain.
    This is the door.
MACDUFF.   I'll make so bold to call,
    For 'tis my limited service.   *Exit*
LENNOX. Goes the King hence today?
MACBETH.   He does; he did appoint so.
LENNOX. The night has been unruly. Where we lay,
    Our chimneys were blown down; and, as they say,
    Lamentings heard i' the air; strange screams of death,
    And prophesying with accents terrible
    Of dire combustion and confused events
    New hatched to the woeful time. The obscure bird
    Clamoured the livelong night. Some say, the earth
    Was feverous and did shake.
MACBETH.   'Twas a rough night.
LENNOX. My young remembrance cannot parallel
    A fellow to it.

Re-enter MACDUFF

MACDUFF. O horror, horror, horror! Tongue nor heart
    Cannot conceive nor name thee!
MACBETH. }
LENNOX. }   What's the matter?
MACDUFF. Confusion now hath made his masterpiece!
    Most sacrilegious murder hath broke ope
    The Lord's anointed temple, and stole thence
    The life o' the building!
MACBETH.   What is 't you say? The life?
LENNOX. Mean you his majesty?
MACDUFF. Approach the chamber, and destroy your
        sight
    With a new Gorgon. Do not bid me speak;
    See, and then speak yourselves.
                            Exeunt MACBETH *and* LENNOX
                        Awake, awake!
    Ring the alarum bell. Murder and treason!
    Banquo and Donalbain! Malcolm! awake!
    Shake off this downy sleep, death's counterfeit,
    And look on death itself! Up, up, and see
    The great doom's image! Malcolm! Banquo!
    As from your graves rise up, and walk like sprites,

To countenance this horror! Ring the bell. *Bell rings*

Enter LADY MACBETH

LADY MACBETH. What's the business,
    That such a hideous trumpet calls to parley
    The sleepers of the house? Speak, speak!
MACDUFF.   O gentle lady,
    'Tis not for you to hear what I can speak.
    The repetition, in a woman's ear,
    Would murder as it fell.

Enter BANQUO

                        O Banquo, Banquo,
    Our royal master's murdered!
LADY MACBETH.   Woe, alas!
    What, in our house?
BANQUO.   Too cruel anywhere.
    Dear Duff, I prithee, contradict thyself,
    And say it is not so.

Re-enter MACBETH *and* LENNOX, *with* ROSS

MACBETH. Had I but died an hour before this chance,
    I had lived a blessed time; for, from this instant,
    There's nothing serious in mortality.
    All is but toys. Renown and grace is dead;
    The wine of life is drawn, and the mere lees
    Is left this vault to brag of.

Enter MALCOLM *and* DONALBAIN

DONALBAIN. What is amiss?
MACBETH.   You are, and do not know 't.
    The spring, the head, the fountain of your blood
    Is stopped; the very source of it is stopped.
MACDUFF. Your royal father's murdered.
MALCOLM.   O, by whom?
LENNOX. Those of his chamber, as it seemed, had done 't.
    Their hands and faces were all badged with blood;
    So were their daggers, which unwiped we found
    Upon their pillows.
    They stared, and were distracted; no man's life
    Was to be trusted with them.
MACBETH. O, yet I do repent me of my fury,
    That I did kill them.
MACDUFF.   Wherefore did you so?
MACBETH. Who can be wise, amazed, temperate and
        furious,
    Loyal and neutral, in a moment? No man.
    The expedition of my violent love
    Outrun the pauser, reason. Here lay Duncan,
    His silver skin laced with his golden blood;
    And his gashed stabs looked like a breach in nature
    For ruin's wasteful entrance. There, the murderers,
    Steeped in the colours of their trade, their daggers
    Unmannerly breeched with gore. Who could refrain,
    That had a heart to love, and in that heart
    Courage to make 's love known?

LADY MACBETH.   Help me hence, ho!
MACDUFF. Look to the lady.
MALCOLM. [*Aside to Donalbain*] Why do we hold our
    tongues,
    That most may claim this argument for ours?
DONALBAIN. [*Aside to Malcolm*] What should be spoken
    here, where our fate,
    Hid in an auger-hole, may rush, and seize us?
    Let's away;
    Our tears are not yet brewed.
MALCOLM. [*Aside to Donalbain*] Nor our strong sorrow
    Upon the foot of motion.
BANQUO.   Look to the lady:

                    LADY MACBETH *is carried out*

    And when we have our naked frailties hid,
    That suffer in exposure, let us meet,
    And question this most bloody piece of work,
    To know it further. Fears and scruples shake us.
    In the great hand of God I stand; and thence
    Against the undivulged pretence I fight
    Of treasonous malice.

MACDUFF.   And so do I.
ALL.   So all.
MACBETH. Let's briefly put on manly readiness,
    And meet i' the hall together.
ALL.   Well contented.

            Exeunt all but MALCOLM *and* DONALBAIN

MALCOLM. What will you do? Let's not consort with
    them.
    To show an unfelt sorrow is an office
    Which the false man does easy. I'll to England.
DONALBAIN. To Ireland, I; our separated fortune
    Shall keep us both the safer. Where we are,
    There's daggers in men's smiles; the near in blood,
    The nearer bloody.
MALCOLM.   This murderous shaft that's shot
    Hath not yet lighted, and our safest way
    Is to avoid the aim. Therefore, to horse;
    And let us not be dainty of leave-taking,
    But shift away. There's warrant in that theft
    Which steals itself, when there's no mercy left.

                                                Exeunt

SCENE IV *Outside Macbeth's castle*

Enter ROSS *and an* OLD MAN

OLD MAN. Threescore and ten I can remember well:
    Within the volume of which time I have seen
    Hours dreadful and things strange; but this sore night
    Hath trifled former knowings.
ROSS.   Ah, good father,
    Thou seest the heavens, as troubled with man's act,
    Threaten his bloody stage. By the clock 'tis day,
    And yet dark night strangles the travelling lamp.
    Is 't night's predominance, or the day's shame,
    That darkness does the face of earth entomb,
    When living light should kiss it?
OLD MAN.   'Tis unnatural,
    Even like the deed that's done. On Tuesday last,
    A falcon, towering in her pride of place,
    Was by a mousing owl hawked at and killed.
ROSS. And Duncan's horses—a thing most strange and
    certain—
    Beauteous and swift, the minions of their race,
    Turned wild in nature, broke their stalls, flung out,
    Contending 'gainst obedience, as they would make
    War with mankind.
OLD MAN.   'Tis said they eat each other.
ROSS. They did so, to the amazement of mine eyes
    That looked upon 't. Here comes the good Macduff.

Enter MACDUFF

    How goes the world, sir, now?
MACDUFF.   Why, see you not?

ROSS. Is 't known who did this more than bloody deed?
MACDUFF. Those that Macbeth hath slain.
ROSS.   Alas, the day!
    What good could they pretend?
MACDUFF.   They were suborned.
    Malcolm and Donalbain, the King's two sons,
    Are stol'n away and fled; which puts upon them
    Suspicion of the deed.
ROSS.   'Gainst nature still!
    Thriftless ambition, that wilt ravin up
    Thine own life's means! Then 'tis most like
    The sovereignty will fall upon Macbeth.
MACDUFF. He is already named, and gone to Scone
    To be invested.
ROSS.   Where is Duncan's body?
MACDUFF. Carried to Colmekill,
    The sacred storehouse of his predecessors,
    And guardian of their bones.
ROSS.   Will you to Scone?
MACDUFF. No, cousin, I'll to Fife.
ROSS.   Well, I will thither.
MACDUFF. Well, may you see things well done there.
    Adieu!
    Lest our old robes sit easier than our new!
ROSS. Farewell, father.
OLD MAN. God's benison go with you; and with those
    That would make good of bad, and friends of foes!

                                                Exeunt

ACT III

SCENE I *Forres: the palace*

Enter BANQUO

BANQUO. Thou hast it now: King, Cawdor, Glamis, all,
  As the weird women promised, and, I fear,
  Thou playedst most foully for 't. Yet it was said
  It should not stand in thy posterity,
  But that myself should be the root and father
  Of many kings. If there come truth from them—
  As upon thee, Macbeth, their speeches shine—
  Why, by the verities on thee made good,
  May they not be my oracles as well,
  And set me up in hope? But hush! no more.

Sennet sounded. Enter MACBETH, *as King,* LADY MACBETH,
as Queen, LENNOX, ROSS, Lords, Ladies, *and* Attendants

MACBETH. Here's our chief guest.
LADY MACBETH.   If he had been forgotten,
  It had been as a gap in our great feast,
  And all-thing unbecoming.
MACBETH. Tonight we hold a solemn supper, sir,
  And I 'll request your presence.
BANQUO.   Let your highness
  Command upon me; to the which my duties
  Are with a most indissoluble tie
  Forever knit.
MACBETH. Ride you this afternoon?
BANQUO. Ay, my good lord.
MACBETH. We should have else desired your good advice,
  Which still hath been both grave and prosperous,
  In this day's council; but we 'll take tomorrow.
  Is 't far you ride?
BANQUO. As far, my lord, as will fill up the time
  'Twixt this and supper. Go not my horse the better,
  I must become a borrower of the night
  For a dark hour or twain.
MACBETH.   Fail not our feast.
BANQUO. My lord, I will not.

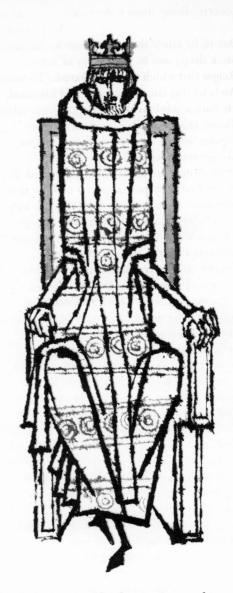

MACBETH. We hear, our bloody cousins are bestowed
  In England and in Ireland, not confessing
  Their cruel parricide, filling their hearers
  With strange invention. But of that tomorrow,
  When therewithal we shall have cause of state
  Craving us jointly. Hie you to horse; adieu,
  Till you return at night. Goes Fleance with you?
BANQUO. Ay, my good lord. Our time does call upon 's.
MACBETH. I wish your horses swift and sure of foot;
  And so I do commend you to their backs.
  Farewell.   *Exit* BANQUO
  Let every man be master of his time
  Till seven at night. To make society
  The sweeter welcome, we will keep ourself
  Till supper-time alone. While then, God be with you!
       Exeunt all but MACBETH, *and an* Attendant
  Sirrah, a word with you. Attend those men
  Our pleasure?
ATTENDANT. They are, my lord, without the palace gate.

424

MACBETH. Bring them before us.   *Exit* Attendant
                                To be thus is nothing;
  But to be safely thus. Our fears in Banquo
  Stick deep; and in his royalty of nature
  Reigns that which would be feared. 'Tis much he dares;
  And, to that dauntless temper of his mind,
  He hath a wisdom that doth guide his valour
  To act in safety. There is none but he
  Whose being I do fear. And, under him,
  My genius is rebuked; as, it is said,
  Mark Antony's was by Cæsar. He chid the sisters
  When first they put the name of King upon me,
  And bade them speak to him. Then prophetlike
  They hailed him father to a line of kings.
  Upon my head they placed a fruitless crown,
  And put a barren sceptre in my gripe,
  Thence to be wrenched with an unlineal hand,
  No son of mine succeeding. If 't be so,
  For Banquo's issue have I filed my mind;
  For them the gracious Duncan have I murdered;
  Put rancours in the vessel of my peace
  Only for them; and mine eternal jewel
  Given to the common enemy of man,
  To make them kings, the seed of Banquo kings!
  Rather than so, come fate into the list,
  And champion me to the utterance! Who 's there?
          Re-enter Attendant, *with two* Murderers
  Now go to the door, and stay there till we call.
                                    Exit Attendant
  Was it not yesterday we spoke together?
FIRST MURDERER. It was, so please your highness.
MACBETH.   Well then, now
  Have you considered of my speeches? Know
  That it was he in the times past which held you
  So under fortune, which you thought had been
  Our innocent self. This I made good to you
  In our last conference, passed in probation with you,
  How you were borne in hand, how crossed, the
      instruments,
  Who wrought with them, and all things else that
      might
  To half a soul and to a notion crazed
  Say "Thus did Banquo."
FIRST MURDERER.   You made it known to us.
MACBETH. I did so, and went further, which is now
  Our point of second meeting. Do you find
  Your patience so predominant in your nature
  That you can let this go? Are you so gospelled
  To pray for this good man and for his issue,
  Whose heavy hand hath bowed you to the grave
  And beggared yours for ever?
FIRST MURDERER.   We are men, my liege.
MACBETH. Ay, in the catalogue ye go for men;
  As hounds and greyhounds, mongrels, spaniels, curs,
  Shoughs, water-rugs and demi-wolves are clept
  All by the name of dogs. The valued file

Distinguishes the swift, the slow, the subtle,
  The housekeeper, the hunter, everyone
  According to the gift which bounteous nature
  Hath in him closed, whereby he does receive
  Particular addition, from the bill
  That writes them all alike. And so of men.
  Now, if you have a station in the file,
  Not i' the worst rank of manhood, say 't;
  And I will put that business in your bosoms,
  Whose execution takes your enemy off,
  Grapples you to the heart and love of us,
  Who wear our health but sickly in his life,
  Which in his death were perfect.
SECOND MURDERER.   I am one, my liege,
  Whom the vile blows and buffets of the world
  Have so incensed that I am reckless what
  I do to spite the world.
FIRST MURDERER.   And I another
  So weary with disasters, tugged with fortune,
  That I would set my life on any chance,
  To mend it, or be rid on 't.
MACBETH.   Both of you
  Know Banquo was your enemy.
BOTH MURDERERS.   True, my lord.
MACBETH. So is he mine; and in such bloody distance,
  That every minute of his being thrusts
  Against my near'st of life. And though I could
  With barefaced power sweep him from my sight
  And bid my will avouch it, yet I must not,
  For certain friends that are both his and mine,
  Whose loves I may not drop, but wail his fall
  Who I myself struck down; and thence it is,
  That I to your assistance do make love,
  Masking the business from the common eye
  For sundry weighty reasons.
SECOND MURDERER.   We shall, my lord,
  Perform what you command us.
FIRST MURDERER.   Though our lives—
MACBETH. Your spirits shine through you. Within
      this hour at most
  I will advise you where to plant yourselves;
  Acquaint you with the perfect spy o' the time,
  The moment on 't; for 't must be done tonight,
  And something from the palace; always thought
  That I require a clearness. And with him—
  To leave no rubs nor botches in the work—
  Fleance his son, that keeps him company,
  Whose absence is no less material to me
  Than is his father's, must embrace the fate
  Of that dark hour. Resolve yourselves apart.
  I'll come to you anon.
BOTH MURDERERS.   We are resolved, my lord.
MACBETH. I'll call upon you straight; abide within.
                              Exeunt Murderers
  It is concluded. Banquo, thy soul's flight,
  If it find heaven, must find it out tonight.   *Exit*

SCENE II *The palace*

Enter LADY MACBETH *and a* Servant

LADY MACBETH. Is Banquo gone from court?

SERVANT. Ay, madam, but returns again tonight.

LADY MACBETH. Say to the King, I would attend his leisure
For a few words.

SERVANT.   Madam, I will.   *Exit*

LADY MACBETH.   Nought's had, all's spent,
Where our desire is got without content.
'Tis safer to be that which we destroy
Than by destruction dwell in doubtful joy.

Enter MACBETH

How now, my lord! why do you keep alone,
Of sorriest fancies your companions making,
Using those thoughts which should indeed have died
With them they think on? Things without all remedy
Should be without regard: what's done is done.

MACBETH. We have scotched the snake, not killed it.
She'll close and be herself, whilst our poor malice
Remains in danger of her former tooth.
But let the frame of things disjoint, both the worlds
suffer,
Ere we will eat our meal in fear and sleep
In the affliction of these terrible dreams
That shake us nightly. Better be with the dead,
Whom we, to gain our peace, have sent to peace,
Than on the torture of the mind to lie
In restless ecstasy. Duncan is in his grave;
After life's fitful fever he sleeps well;
Treason has done his worst. Nor steel, nor poison,
Malice domestic, foreign levy, nothing,
Can touch him further.

LADY MACBETH.   Come on;

Gentle my lord, sleek o'er your rugged looks;
Be bright and jovial among your guests tonight.

MACBETH. So shall I, love; and so, I pray, be you.
Let your remembrance apply to Banquo;
Present him eminence, both with eye and tongue.
Unsafe the while, that we
Must lave our honours in these flattering streams,
And make our faces vizards to our hearts,
Disguising what they are.

LADY MACBETH.   You must leave this.

MACBETH. O, full of scorpions is my mind, dear wife!
Thou know'st that Banquo, and his Fleance, lives.

LADY MACBETH. But in them nature's copy's not eterne.

MACBETH. There's comfort yet; they are assailable;
Then be thou jocund. Ere the bat hath flown
His cloistered flight, ere to black Hecate's summons
The shard-borne beetle with his drowsy hums
Hath rung night's yawning peal, there shall be done
A deed of dreadful note.

LADY MACBETH.   What's to be done?

MACBETH. Be innocent of the knowledge, dearest chuck,
Till thou applaud the deed. Come, seeling night,
Scarf up the tender eye of pitiful day;
And with thy bloody and invisible hand
Cancel and tear to pieces that great bond
Which keeps me pale! Light thickens; and the crow
Makes wing to the rooky wood.
Good things of day begin to droop and drowse;
Whiles night's black agents to their preys do rouse.
Thou marvell'st at my words. But hold thee still:
Things bad begun make strong themselves by ill.
So, prithee, go with me.

                                        Exeunt

SCENE III *A park near the palace*

Enter three Murderers

FIRST MURDERER. But who did bid thee join with us?

THIRD MURDERER.   Macbeth.

SECOND MURDERER. He needs not our mistrust, since
he delivers
Our offices and what we have to do
To the direction just.

FIRST MURDERER.   Then stand with us.
The west yet glimmers with some streaks of day.
Now spurs the lated traveller apace
To gain the timely inn; and near approaches
The subject of our watch.

THIRD MURDERER.   Hark! I hear horses.

BANQUO. [*Within*] Give us a light there, ho!

SECOND MURDERER.   Then 'tis he. The rest
That are within the note of expectation
Already are i' the court.

FIRST MURDERER.   His horses go about.

THIRD MURDERER. Almost a mile; but he does usually,
So all men do, from hence to the palace gate
Make it their walk.

SECOND MURDERER.   A light, a light!

Enter BANQUO, *and* FLEANCE *with a torch*

THIRD MURDERER.   'Tis he.

FIRST MURDERER. Stand to 't.

BANQUO. It will be rain tonight.

FIRST MURDERER.   Let it come down.
                        They set upon BANQUO

BANQUO. O, treachery! Fly, good Fleance, fly, fly, fly!
Thou mayst revenge. O slave!   *Dies.* FLEANCE *escapes*

THIRD MURDERER. Who did strike out the light?

FIRST MURDERER.   Was 't not the way?

SCENE IV *The same. Hall in the palace*

A banquet prepared

Enter MACBETH, LADY MACBETH, ROSS, LENNOX,
Lords, *and* Attendants

MACBETH. You know your own degrees; sit down. At first
  And last the hearty welcome.
LORDS.   Thanks to your majesty.
MACBETH. Ourself will mingle with society,
  And play the humble host.
  Our hostess keeps her state, but in best time
  We will require her welcome.
LADY MACBETH. Pronounce it for me, sir, to all our friends;
  For my heart speaks they are welcome.

First Murderer *appears at the door*

MACBETH. See, they encounter thee with their hearts' thanks.
  Both sides are even—here I 'll sit i' the midst.
  Be large in mirth; anon we 'll drink a measure
  The table round. [*Approaching the door*] There 's blood
    upon thy face.
MURDERER. 'Tis Banquo's then.
MACBETH. 'Tis better thee without than he within.
  Is he dispatched?
MURDERER. My lord, his throat is cut; that I did for him.
MACBETH. Thou art the best o' the cut-throats. Yet he's good
  That did the like for Fleance. If thou didst it,
  Thou art the nonpareil.
MURDERER.   Most royal sir,
  Fleance is 'scaped.
MACBETH. Then comes my fit again. I had else been perfect,
  Whole as the marble, founded as the rock,
  As broad and general as the casing air.
  But now I am cabined, cribbed, confined, bound in
  To saucy doubts and fears. But Banquo's safe?
MURDERER. Ay, my good lord. Safe in a ditch he bides,
  With twenty trenched gashes on his head;
  The least a death to nature.
MACBETH.   Thanks for that
  There the grown serpent lies; the worm that 's fled
  Hath nature that in time will venom breed,
  No teeth for the present. Get thee gone. Tomorrow
  We'll hear, ourselves, again.   *Exit* Murderer
LADY MACBETH.   My royal lord,
  You do not give the cheer. The feast is sold
  That is not often vouched, while 'tis a-making,
  'Tis given with welcome. To feed were best at home;
  From thence the sauce to meat is ceremony;
  Meeting were bare without it.
MACBETH.   Sweet remembrancer!

THIRD MURDERER. There's but one down; the son is fled.
SECOND MURDERER.   We have lost
  Best half of our affair.
FIRST MURDERER. Well, let 's away, and say how much
  is done.   *Exeunt*

Now, good digestion wait on appetite,
And health on both!

LENNOX.   May 't please your highness sit.

The Ghost of BANQUO *enters, and sits in* MACBETH's *place*

MACBETH. Here had we now our country's honour
    roofed,
  Were the graced person of our Banquo present;
  Who may I rather challenge for unkindness
  Than pity for mischance!

ROSS.   His absence, sir,
  Lays blame upon his promise. Please 't your highness
  To grace us with your royal company.

MACBETH. The table 's full.

LENNOX.   Here is a place reserved, sir.

MACBETH. Where?

LENNOX. Here, my good lord. What is 't that moves
    your highness?

MACBETH. Which of you have done this?

LORDS.   What, my good lord?

MACBETH. Thou canst not say I did it. Never shake
  Thy gory locks at me.

ROSS. Gentlemen rise; his highness is not well.

LADY MACBETH. Sit, worthy friends. My lord is often
    thus,
  And hath been from his youth. Pray you, keep seat;
  The fit is momentary; upon a thought
  He will again be well. If much you note him,
  You shall offend him and extend his passion.
  Feed, and regard him not. Are you a man?

MACBETH. Ay, and a bold one, that dare look on that
  Which might appal the devil.

LADY MACBETH.   O proper stuff!
  This is the very painting of your fear.
  This is the air-drawn dagger which, you said,
  Led you to Duncan. O, these flaws and starts,
  Impostors to true fear, would well become
  A woman's story at a winter's fire,
  Authorized by her grandam. Shame itself!
  Why do you make such faces? When all 's done,
  You look but on a stool.

MACBETH. Prithee, see there! behold! look! lo! How
    say you?
  Why, what care I? If thou canst nod, speak too.
  If charnel-houses and our graves must send
  Those that we bury back, our monuments
  Shall be the maws of kites.   *Ghost vanishes*

LADY MACBETH. What, quite unmanned in folly?

MACBETH. If I stand here, I saw him.

LADY MACBETH.   Fie, for shame.

MACBETH. Blood hath been shed ere now, i' the olden
    time,
  Ere humane statute purged the gentle weal;
  Ay, and since too, murders have been performed
  Too terrible for the ear. The time has been,
  That, when the brains were out, the man would die,

And there an end; but now they rise again,
  With twenty mortal murders on their crowns,
  And push us from our stools. This is more strange
  Than such a murder is.

LADY MACBETH.   My worthy lord,
  Your noble friends do lack you.

MACBETH.   I do forget.
  Do not muse at me, my most worthy friends;
  I have a strange infirmity, which is nothing
  To those that know me. Come, love and health to all;
  Then I'll sit down. Give me some wine; fill full.
  I drink to the general joy o' the whole table,
  And to our dear friend Banquo, whom we miss;
  Would he were here! To all, and him, we thirst,
  And all to all.

LORDS.   Our duties, and the pledge.

Re-enter Ghost

MACBETH. Avaunt! and quit my sight! Let the earth
    hide thee!
  Thy bones are marrowless, thy blood is cold;
  Thou hast no speculation in those eyes
  Which thou dost glare with!

LADY MACBETH.   Think of this, good peers,
  But as a thing of custom. 'Tis no other;
  Only it spoils the pleasure of the time.

MACBETH. What man dare, I dare.
  Approach thou like the rugged Russian bear,
  The armed rhinoceros, or the Hyrcan tiger;
  Take any shape but that, and my firm nerves
  Shall never tremble. Or be alive again,
  And dare me to the desert with thy sword;
  If trembling I inhabit then, protest me
  The baby of a girl. Hence, horrible shadow!
  Unreal mockery, hence!   *Ghost vanishes*
                    Why, so; being gone,
  I am a man again. Pray you, sit still.

LADY MACBETH. You have displaced the mirth, broke
    the good meeting,
  With most admired disorder.

MACBETH.   Can such things be,
  And overcome us like a summer's cloud,
  Without our special wonder? You make me strange
  Even to the disposition that I owe,
  When now I think you can behold such sights,
  And keep the natural ruby of your cheeks,
  When mine is blanched with fear.

ROSS.   What sights, my lord?

LADY MACBETH. I pray you, speak not; he grows worse
    and worse;
  Question enrages him. At once, good night.
  Stand not upon the order of your going,
  But go at once.

LENNOX.   Good night; and better health
  Attend his majesty!

LADY MACBETH.   A kind good night to all!

Exeunt all but MACBETH *and* LADY MACBETH

MACBETH. It will have blood; they say, blood will have
   blood.
   Stones have been known to move and trees to speak;
   Augurs and understood relations have
   By magot-pies and choughs and rooks brought forth
   The secret'st man of blood. What is the night?
LADY MACBETH. Almost at odds with morning, which
   is which.
MACBETH. How say'st thou, that Macduff denies his
   person
   At our great bidding?
LADY MACBETH.   Did you send to him, sir?
MACBETH. I hear it by the way; but I will send.
   There's not a one of them but in his house
   I keep a servant fee'd. I will tomorrow,
   And betimes I will, to the weird sisters.
   More shall they speak; for now I am bent to know,
   By the worst means, the worst. For mine own good,
   All causes shall give way. I am in blood
   Stepped in so far that, should I wade no more,
   Returning were as tedious as go o'er.
   Strange things I have in head, that will to hand;
   Which must be acted ere they may be scanned.
LADY MACBETH. You lack the season of all natures, sleep.
MACBETH. Come, we'll to sleep. My strange and self-
   abuse
   Is the initiate fear that wants hard use:
   We are yet but young in deed.   *Exeunt*

Scene V *A Heath*

Thunder. Enter the three Witches, *meeting* Hecate.

First Witch. Why, how now, Hecate! You look
    angerly.
Hecate. Have I not reason, beldams as you are,
    Saucy and overbold? How did you dare
    To trade and traffic with Macbeth
    In riddles and affairs of death;
    And I, the mistress of your charms,
    The close contriver of all harms,
    Was never called to bear my part,
    Or show the glory of our art?
    And, which is worse, all you have done
    Hath been but for a wayward son,
    Spiteful and wrathful, who, as others do,
    Loves for his own ends, not for you.
    But make amends now: get you gone,
    And at the pit of Acheron
    Meet me i' the morning. Thither he
    Will come to know his destiny.
    Your vessels and your spells provide,
    Your charms and every thing beside.

I am for the air; this night I 'll spend
Unto a dismal and a fatal end.
Great business must be wrought ere noon.
Upon the corner of the moon
There hangs a vaporous drop profound;
I'll catch it ere it come to ground;
And that distilled by magic sleights
Shall raise such artificial sprites
As by the strength of their illusion
Shall draw him on to his confusion.
He shall spurn fate, scorn death, and bear
His hopes 'bove wisdom, grace and fear.
And you all know, security
Is mortals' chiefest enemy.
                    Music and a song within: "Come away,
                                        come away," &c.
Hark! I am called; my little spirit, see,
Sits in a foggy cloud, and stays for me.   *Exit*
First Witch. Come, let 's make haste; she 'll soon be
    back again.   *Exeunt*

Scene VI *Forres: the palace*

Enter Lennox *and another* Lord

Lennox. My former speeches have but hit your thoughts,
    Which can interpret further. Only, I say,
    Things have been strangely borne. The gracious
        Duncan
    Was pitied of Macbeth—marry, he was dead.
    And the right-valiant Banquo walked too late;
    Whom, you may say, if 't please you, Fleance killed,
    For Fleance fled. Men must not walk too late.
    Who cannot want the thought how monstrous
    It was for Malcolm and for Donalbain
    To kill their gracious father? Damned fact!
    How it did grieve Macbeth! Did he not straight
    In pious rage the two delinquents tear,
    That were the slaves of drink and thralls of sleep?
    Was not that nobly done? Ay, and wisely too;
    For 'twould have angered any heart alive
    To hear the men deny 't. So that, I say,
    He has borne all things well. And I do think
    That had he Duncan's sons under his key—
    As, an 't please heaven, he shall not—they should find
    What 'twere to kill a father; so should Fleance.
    But, peace! for from broad words and 'cause he failed
    His presence at the tyrant's feast, I hear
    Macduff lives in disgrace. Sir, can you tell
    Where he bestows himself?
Lord.   The son of Duncan,
    From whom this tyrant holds the due of birth,

Lives in the English court, and is received
Of the most pious Edward with such grace
That the malevolence of fortune nothing
Takes from his high respect. Thither Macduff
Is gone to pray the holy King, upon his aid
To wake Northumberland and warlike Siward;
That, by the help of these—with Him above
To ratify the work—we may again
Give to our tables meat, sleep to our nights,
Free from our feasts and banquets bloody knives,
Do faithful homage and receive free honours—
All which we pine for now—and this report
Hath so exasperate the King that he
Prepares for some attempt of war.
Lennox.   Sent he to Macduff?
Lord. He did; and with an absolute "Sir, not I,"
    The cloudy messenger turns me his back,
    And hums, as who should say "You 'll rue the time
    That clogs me with this answer."
Lennox.   And that well might
    Advise him to a caution, to hold what distance
    His wisdom can provide. Some holy angel
    Fly to the court of England and unfold
    His message ere he come, that a swift blessing
    May soon return to this our suffering country
    Under a hand accursed!
Lord.   I'll send my prayers with him. *Exeunt*

ACT IV

SCENE I *A cavern. In the middle, a boiling cauldron*

Thunder. Enter the three Witches

FIRST WITCH. Thrice the brinded cat hath mewed.

SECOND WITCH. Thrice and once the hedge-pig whined.

THIRD WITCH. Harpier cries, " 'Tis time, 'tis time."

FIRST WITCH. Round about the cauldron go;
  In the poisoned entrails throw.
  Toad, that under cold stone
  Days and nights has thirty one
  Sweltered venom sleeping got,
  Boil thou first i' the charmed pot.

ALL. Double, double, toil and trouble;
  Fire burn, and cauldron bubble.

SECOND WITCH. Fillet of a fenny snake,
  In the cauldron boil and bake;
  Eye of newt and toe of frog,
  Wool of bat and tongue of dog,
  Adder's fork and blind-worm's sting,
  Lizard's leg and howlet's wing,
  For a charm of powerful trouble,
  Like a hell-broth boil and bubble.

ALL. Double, double, toil and trouble;
  Fire burn and cauldron bubble.

THIRD WITCH. Scale of dragon, tooth of wolf,
  Witches' mummy, maw and gulf
  Of the ravined salt-sea shark,
  Root of hemlock digged i' the dark,
  Liver of blaspheming Jew,
  Gall of goat, and slips of yew
  Silvered in the moon's eclipse,
  Nose of Turk and Tartar's lips,
  Finger of birth-strangled babe
  Ditch-delivered by a drab,
  Make the gruel thick and slab.
  Add thereto a tiger's chaudron,
  For the ingredients of our cauldron.

ALL. Double, double, toil and trouble;
  Fire burn and cauldron bubble.

SECOND WITCH. Cool it with a baboon's blood,
  Then the charm is firm and good.

Enter HECATE

HECATE. O, well done! I commend your pains;
  And everyone shall share i' the gains.
  And now about the cauldron sing,
  Like elves and fairies in a ring,
  Enchanting all that you put in.

Music and a song: "Black spirits," &c.

HECATE *retires*

SECOND WITCH. By the pricking of my thumbs,
  Something wicked this way comes.
      Open, locks,
      Whoever knocks!

Enter MACBETH

MACBETH. How now, you secret, black, and midnight hags!
  What is 't you do?

ALL.   A deed without a name.

MACBETH. I conjure you, by that which you profess,
  Howe'er you come to know it, answer me.
  Though you untie the winds and let them fight
  Against the churches; though the yesty waves
  Confound and swallow navigation up;
  Though bladed corn be lodged and trees blown down;
  Though castles topple on their warders' heads;
  Though palaces and pyramids do slope
  Their heads to their foundations; though the treasure
  Of nature's germens tumble all together,
  Even till destruction sicken; answer me
  To what I ask you.

FIRST WITCH.   Speak.

SECOND WITCH.   Demand.

THIRD WITCH.   We'll answer.

FIRST WITCH. Say, if thou 'dst rather hear it from our mouths,
  Or from our masters?

MACBETH.   Call 'em; let me see 'em.

FIRST WITCH. Pour in sow's blood, that hath eaten
  Her nine farrow; grease that's sweaten
  From the murderer's gibbet throw
  Into the flame.

ALL.   Come, high or low;
  Thyself and office deftly show!

Thunder. First Apparition: *an Armed Head*

MACBETH. Tell me, thou unknown power—

FIRST WITCH.   He knows thy thought.
  Hear his speech, but say thou nought.

FIRST APPARITION. Macbeth! Macbeth! Macbeth! Beware Macduff;
  Beware the Thane of Fife. Dismiss me. Enough.

Descends

MACBETH. Whate'er thou art, for thy good caution, thanks;
  Thou hast harped my fear aright. But one word more—

FIRST WITCH. He will not be commanded. Here's another,
  More potent than the first.

Thunder. Second Apparition: *a Bloody Child*

SECOND APPARITION. Macbeth! Macbeth! Macbeth!

MACBETH. Had I three ears, I 'ld hear thee.

SECOND APPARITION. Be bloody, bold, and resolute; laugh to scorn
  The power of man, for none of woman born
  Shall harm Macbeth.   *Descend*

431

MACBETH. Then live, Macduff; what need I fear of thee?
  But yet I'll make assurance double sure,
  And take a bond of fate. Thou shalt not live;
  That I may tell pale-hearted fear it lies,
  And sleep in spite of thunder.

Thunder. Third Apparition: *a Child crowned, with a tree
in his hand*

                    What is this
  That rises like the issue of a king,
  And wears upon his baby-brow the round
  And top of sovereignty?
ALL.   Listen, but speak not to 't.
THIRD APPARITION. Be lion-mettled, proud; and take
  no care
  Who chafes, who frets, or where conspirers are.
  Macbeth shall never vanquished be until
  Great Birnam Wood to high Dunsinane Hill
  Shall come against him.   *Descends*
MACBETH.   That will never be.
  Who can impress the forest, bid the tree
  Unfix his earth-bound root? Sweet bodements! good!
  Rebellion's head, rise never till the wood
  Of Birnam rise, and our high-placed Macbeth
  Shall live the lease of nature, pay his breath
  To time and mortal custom. Yet my heart
  Throbs to know one thing. Tell me, if your art
  Can tell so much: shall Banquo's issue ever
  Reign in this kingdom?
ALL.   Seek to know no more.
MACBETH. I will be satisfied. Deny me this,
  And an eternal curse fall on you! Let me know.
  Why sinks that cauldron? And what noise is this?
                            Hautboys

FIRST WITCH. Show!
SECOND WITCH. Show!
THIRD WITCH. Show!
ALL. Show his eyes, and grieve his heart;
  Come like shadows, so depart!

A show of Eight Kings, *the last with a glass in his hand;*
BANQUO's *Ghost following*

MACBETH. Thou art too like the spirit of Banquo; down!
  Thy crown does sear mine eyeballs. And thy hair,
  Thou other gold-bound brow, is like the first.
  A third is like the former. Filthy hags!
  Why do you show me this? A fourth! Start, eyes!
  What, will the line stretch out to the crack of doom?
  Another yet! A seventh! I 'll see no more.
  And yet the eighth appears, who bears a glass
  Which shows me many more; and some I see
  That two-fold balls and treble sceptres carry.
  Horrible sight! Now, I see, 'tis true;
  For the blood-boltered Banquo smiles upon me,
  And points at them for his.   *Apparitions* vanish
    What, is this so?

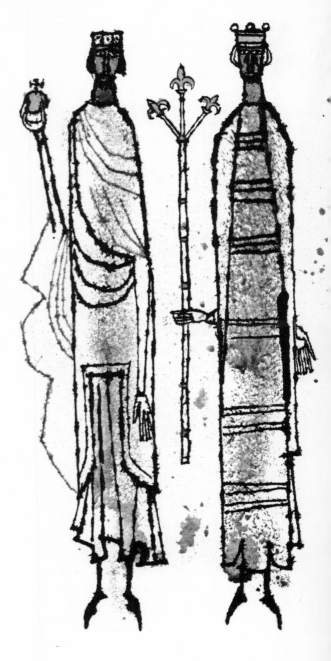

FIRST WITCH. Ay, sir, all this is so. But why
  Stands Macbeth thus amazedly?
  Come, sisters, cheer we up his sprites,
  And show the best of our delights.
  I 'll charm the air to give a sound,
  While you perform your antic round;
  That this great king may kindly say,
  Our duties did his welcome pay.
                Music. The Witches *dance, and then vanish*
MACBETH. Where are they? Gone? Let this pernicious
    hour
  Stand aye accursed in the calendar!
  Come in, without there!

                Enter LENNOX

LENNOX.   What 's your grace's will?
MACBETH. Saw you the weird sisters?
LENNOX.   No, my lord.
MACBETH. Came they not by you?
LENNOX.   No, indeed, my lord.
MACBETH. Infected be the air whereon they ride;

And damned all those that trust them! I did hear
  The galloping of horse. Who was 't came by?
LENNOX. 'Tis two or three, my lord, that bring you
    word
  Macduff is fled to England.
MACBETH.   Fled to England!
LENNOX. Ay, my good lord.
MACBETH. Time, thou anticipatest my dread exploits.
  The flighty purpose never is o'ertook
  Unless the deed go with it. From this moment
  The very firstlings of my heart shall be
  The firstlings of my hand. And even now,
  To crown my thoughts with acts, be it thought and
    done:
  The castle of Macduff I will surprise;
  Seize upon Fife; give to the edge o' the sword
  His wife, his babes, and all unfortunate souls
  That trace him in his line. No boasting like a fool.
  This deed I 'll do before this purpose cool.
  But no more sights!—Where are these gentlemen?
  Come, bring me where they are.   *Exeunt*

SCENE II *Fife: Macduff's castle*

Enter LADY MACDUFF, *her* Son, *and* ROSS

LADY MACDUFF. What had he done, to make him fly
    the land?
ROSS. You must have patience, madam.
LADY MACDUFF.   He had none;
  His flight was madness. When our actions do not,
  Our fears do make us traitors.
ROSS.   You know not
  Whether it was his wisdom or his fear.
LADY MACDUFF. Wisdom! to leave his wife, to leave
    his babes,
  His mansion and his titles in a place
  From whence himself does fly? He loves us not;
  He wants the natural touch: for the poor wren,
  The most diminutive of birds, will fight,
  Her young ones in her nest, against the owl.
  All is the fear and nothing is the love;
  As little is the wisdom, where the flight
  So runs against all reason.
ROSS.   My dearest coz,
  I pray you, school yourself. But for your husband,
  He is noble, wise, judicious, and best knows
  The fits o' the season. I dare not speak much further;
  But cruel are the times, when we are traitors
  And do not know ourselves, when we hold rumour
  From what we fear, yet know not what we fear,
  But float upon a wild and violent sea
  Each way and move. I take my leave of you—
  Shall not be long but I'll be here again.
  Things at the worst will cease, or else climb upward

To what they were before. My pretty cousin,
  Blessing upon you!
LADY MACDUFF. Fathered he is, and yet he's fatherless.
ROSS. I am so much a fool, should I stay longer,
  It would be my disgrace and your discomfort.
  I take my leave at once.   *Exit*
LADY MACDUFF. Sirrah, your father 's dead.
  And what will you do now? How will you live?
SON. As birds do, mother.
LADY MACDUFF.   What, with worms and flies?
SON. With what I get, I mean; and so do they.
LADY MACDUFF. Poor bird! Thou 'ldst never fear the
    net nor lime,
  The pitfall nor the gin.
SON. Why should I, mother? Poor birds they are not
    set for.
  My father is not dead, for all your saying.
LADY MACDUFF. Yes, he is dead; how wilt thou do for
    a father?
SON. Nay, how will you do for a husband?
LADY MACDUFF. Why, I can buy me twenty at any
    market.
SON. Then you 'll buy 'em to sell again.
LADY MACDUFF. Thou speak'st with all thy wit; and
    yet, i' faith,
  With wit enough for thee.
SON. Was my father a traitor, mother?
LADY MACDUFF. Ay, that he was.
SON. What is a traitor?

LADY MACDUFF. Why, one that swears and lies.

SON. And be all traitors that do so?

LADY MACDUFF. Everyone that does so is a traitor, and must be hanged.

SON. And must they all be hanged that swear and lie?

LADY MACDUFF. Everyone.

SON. Who must hang them?

LADY MACDUFF. Why, the honest men.

SON. Then the liars and swearers are fools, for there are liars and swearers enow to beat the honest men and hang up them.

LADY MACDUFF. Now, God help thee, poor monkey! But how wilt thou do for a father?

SON. If he were dead, you 'ld weep for him. If you would not, it were a good sign that I should quickly have a new father.

LADY MACDUFF. Poor prattler, how thou talk'st!

Enter a Messenger

MESSENGER. Bless you, fair dame! I am not to you known,
Though in your state of honour I am perfect.
I doubt some danger does approach you nearly;
If you will take a homely man's advice,
Be not found here; hence, with your little ones.

To fright you thus, methinks, I am too savage;
To do worse to you were fell cruelty,
Which is too nigh your person. Heaven preserve you!
I dare abide no longer.   *Exit*

LADY MACDUFF.   Whither should I fly?
I have done no harm. But I remember now
I am in this earthly world; where to do harm
Is often laudable, to do good sometime
Accounted dangerous folly. Why then, alas,
Do I put up that womanly defence,
To say I have done no harm?

                              Enter Murderers
                                   What are these faces?

FIRST MURDERER. Where is your husband?

LADY MACDUFF. I hope, in no place so unsanctified
Where such as thou mayst find him.

FIRST MURDERER.   He's a traitor.

SON. Thou liest, thou shag-haired villain!

FIRST MURDERER.   What, you egg!
Young fry of treachery!   *Stabbing him*

SON.   He has killed me, mother;
Run away, I pray you!   *Dies*
          Exit LADY MACDUFF, *crying* "Murder!"
          Exeunt Murderers, *following her*

SCENE III *England: before the King's palace*

Enter MALCOLM *and* MACDUFF

MALCOLM. Let us seek out some desolate shade, and there
Weep our sad bosoms empty.

MACDUFF.   Let us rather
Hold fast the mortal sword, and like good men
Bestride our down-fall'n birthdom. Each new morn
New widows howl, new orphans cry, new sorrows
Strike heaven on the face, that it resounds
As if it felt with Scotland and yelled out
Like syllable of dolour.

MALCOLM.   What I believe I 'll wail,
What know believe, and what I can redress,
As I shall find the time to friend, I will.
What you have spoke, it may be so perchance.
This tyrant, whose sole name blisters our tongues,
Was once thought honest. You have loved him well;
He hath not touched you yet. I am young; but something
You may deserve of him through me, and wisdom
To offer up a weak poor innocent lamb
To appease an angry god.

MACDUFF. I am not treacherous.

MALCOLM.   But Macbeth is.
A good and virtuous nature may recoil
In an imperial charge. But I shall crave your pardon;
That which you are my thoughts cannot transpose.

Angels are bright still, though the brightest fell.
Though all things foul would wear the brows of grace,
Yet grace must still look so.

MACDUFF.   I have lost my hopes.

MALCOLM. Perchance even there where I did find my doubts.
Why in that rawness left you wife and child,
Those precious motives, those strong knots of love,
Without leave-taking? I pray you,
Let not my jealousies be your dishonours,
But mine own safeties. You may be rightly just,
Whatever I shall think.

MACDUFF.   Bleed, bleed, poor country!
Great tyranny! lay thou thy basis sure,
For goodness dare not check thee. Wear thou thy wrongs;
The title is affeered! Fare thee well, lord.
I would not be the villain that thou think'st
For the whole space that 's in the tyrant's grasp,
And the rich East to boot.

MALCOLM.   Be not offended.
I speak not as in absolute fear of you.
I think our country sinks beneath the yoke;
It weeps, it bleeds; and each new day a gash
Is added to her wounds. I think withal
There would be hands uplifted in my right;

And here from gracious England have I offer
Of goodly thousands. But, for all this,
When I shall tread upon the tyrant's head,
Or wear it on my sword, yet my poor country
Shall have more vices than it had before,
More suffer and more sundry ways than ever,
By him that shall succeed.

MACDUFF.   What should he be?

MALCOLM. It is myself I mean; in whom I know
All the particulars of vice so grafted
That, when they shall be opened, black Macbeth
Will seem as pure as snow, and the poor state
Esteem him as a lamb, being compared
With my confineless harms.

MACDUFF.   Not in the legions
Of horrid hell can come a devil more damned
In evils to top Macbeth.

MALCOLM.   I grant him bloody,
Luxurious, avaricious, false, deceitful,
Sudden, malicious, smacking of every sin
That has a name. But there's no bottom, none,
In my voluptuousness. Your wives, your daughters,
Your matrons and your maids, could not fill up
The cistern of my lust, and my desire
All continent impediments would o'erbear
That did oppose my will. Better Macbeth
Than such an one to reign.

MACDUFF.   Boundless intemperance
In nature is a tyranny; it hath been
The untimely emptying of the happy throne
And fall of many kings. But fear not yet
To take upon you what is yours. You may
Convey your pleasures in a spacious plenty,
And yet seem cold, the time you may so hoodwink.
We have willing dames enough; there cannot be
That vulture in you, to devour so many
As will to greatness dedicate themselves,
Finding it so inclined.

MALCOLM.   With this there grows
In my most ill-composed affection such
A stanchless avarice that, were I King,
I should cut off the nobles for their lands,
Desire his jewels and this other's house.
And my more-having would be as a sauce
To make me hunger more; that I should forge
Quarrels unjust against the good and loyal,
Destroying them for wealth.

MACDUFF.   This avarice
Sticks deeper, grows with more pernicious root
Than summer-seeming lust, and it hath been
The sword of our slain kings. Yet do not fear;
Scotland hath foisons to fill up your will,
Of your mere own. All these are portable,
With other graces weighed.

MALCOLM. But I have none. The king-becoming graces,
As justice, verity, temperance, stableness,

Bounty, perseverance, mercy, lowliness,
Devotion, patience, courage, fortitude,
I have no relish of them, but abound
In the division of each several crime,
Acting it many ways. Nay, had I power, I should
Pour the sweet milk of concord into hell,
Uproar the universal peace, confound
All unity on earth.

MACDUFF.   O Scotland, Scotland!

MALCOLM. If such a one be fit to govern, speak.
I am as I have spoken.

MACDUFF.   Fit to govern!
No, not to live. O nation miserable,
With an untitled tyrant bloody-sceptered,
When shalt thou see thy wholesome days again,
Since that the truest issue of thy throne
By his own interdiction stands accursed,
And does blaspheme his breed? Thy royal father
Was a most sainted King; the Queen that bore thee,
Oftener upon her knees than on her feet,
Died every day she lived. Fare thee well!
These evils thou repeat'st upon thyself
Have banished me from Scotland. O my breast,
Thy hope ends here!

MALCOLM.   Macduff, this noble passion,
Child of integrity, hath from my soul
Wiped the black scruples, reconciled my thoughts
To thy good truth and honour. Devilish Macbeth
By many of these trains hath sought to win me
Into his power, and modest wisdom plucks me
From over-credulous haste. But God above
Deal between thee and me! For even now
I put myself to thy direction, and
Unspeak mine own detraction, here abjure
The taints and blames I laid upon myself,
For strangers to my nature. I am yet
Unknown to woman, never was forsworn,
Scarcely have coveted what was mine own,
At no time broke my faith, would not betray
The devil to his fellow and delight
No less in truth than life. My first false speaking
Was this upon myself. What I am truly,
Is thine and my poor country's to command.
Whither indeed, before thy here-approach,
Old Siward, with ten thousand warlike men,
Already at a point, was setting forth.
Now we 'll together; and the chance of goodness
Be like our warranted quarrel! Why are you silent?

MACDUFF. Such welcome and unwelcome things at once
'Tis hard to reconcile.

Enter a Doctor

MALCOLM. Well; more anon. Comes the King forth,
I pray you?

DOCTOR. Ay, sir; there are a crew of wretched souls
That stay his cure. Their malady convinces

The great assay of art; but at his touch—
Such sanctity hath heaven given his hand—
They presently amend.

MALCOLM.   I thank you, doctor. *Exit* Doctor

MACDUFF. What 's the disease he means?

MALCOLM.   'Tis called the evil:
A most miraculous work in this good King;
Which often, since my here-remain in England,
I have seen him do. How he solicits heaven,
Himself best knows; but strangely-visited people,
All swoln and ulcerous, pitiful to the eye,
The mere despair of surgery, he cures,
Hanging a golden stamp about their necks,
Put on with holy prayers. And 'tis spoken,
To the succeeding royalty he leaves
The healing benediction. With this strange virtue,
He hath a heavenly gift of prophecy,
And sundry blessings hang about his throne,
That speak him full of grace.

Enter ROSS

MACDUFF.   See, who comes here?

MALCOLM. My countryman; but yet I know him not.

MACDUFF. My ever-gentle cousin, welcome hither.

MALCOLM. I know him now. Good God, betimes remove
The means that makes us strangers!

ROSS.   Sir, amen.

MACDUFF. Stands Scotland where it did?

ROSS.   Alas, poor country!
Almost afraid to know itself. It cannot
Be called our mother, but our grave; where nothing,
But who knows nothing, is once seen to smile;
Where sighs and groans and shrieks that rend the air
Are made, not marked; where violent sorrow seems
A modern ecstasy. The dead man's knell
Is there scarce asked for who; and good men's lives
Expire before the flowers in their caps,
Dying or ere they sicken.

MACDUFF.   O, relation
Too nice, and yet too true!

MALCOLM.   What's the newest grief?

ROSS. That of an hour's age doth hiss the speaker:
Each minute teems a new one.

MACDUFF.   How does my wife?

ROSS. Why, well.

MACDUFF.   And all my children?

ROSS.   Well too.

MACDUFF. The tyrant has not battered at their peace?

ROSS. No; they were well at peace when I did leave 'em.

MACDUFF. Be not a niggard of your speech. How goes 't?

ROSS. When I came hither to transport the tidings,
Which I have heavily borne, there ran a rumour
Of many worthy fellows that were out;
Which was to my belief witnessed the rather,
For that I saw the tyrant's power a-foot.
Now is the time of help; your eye in Scotland

Would create soldiers, make our women fight,
To doff their dire distresses.
MALCOLM.   Be 't their comfort
We are coming thither. Gracious England hath
Lent us good Siward and ten thousand men;
An older and a better soldier none
That Christendom gives out.
ROSS.   Would I could answer
This comfort with the like! But I have words
That would be howled out in the desert air,
Where hearing should not latch them.
MACDUFF.   What concern they?
The general cause? Or is it a fee-grief
Due to some single breast?
ROSS.   No mind that's honest
But in it shares some woe; though the main part
Pertains to you alone.
MACDUFF.   If it be mine,
Keep it not from me, quickly let me have it.
ROSS. Let not your ears despise my tongue for ever,
Which shall possess them with the heaviest sound
That ever yet they heard.
MACDUFF.   Hum! I guess at it.
ROSS. Your castle is surprised; your wife and babes
Savagely slaughtered. To relate the manner,
Were, on the quarry of these murdered deer,
To add the death of you.
MALCOLM.   Merciful heaven!
What, man! ne'er pull your hat upon your brows;
Give sorrow words. The grief that does not speak
Whispers the o'er-fraught heart and bids it break.
MACDUFF. My children too?
ROSS.   Wife, children, servants, all
That could be found.

MACDUFF.   And I must be from thence!
My wife killed too?
ROSS.   I have said.
MALCOLM.   Be comforted.
Let 's make us medicines of our great revenge,
To cure this deadly grief.
MACDUFF. He has no children. All my pretty ones?
Did you say all? O hell-kite! All?
What, all my pretty chickens and their dam
At one fell swoop?
MALCOLM. Dispute it like a man.
MACDUFF.   I shall do so;
But I must also feel it as a man.
I cannot but remember such things were,
That were most precious to me. Did heaven look on,
And would not take their part? Sinful Macduff,
They were all struck for thee! Naught that I am,
Not for their own demerits, but for mine,
Fell slaughter on their souls. Heaven rest them now!
MALCOLM. Be this the whetstone of your sword: let
  grief
Convert to anger; blunt not the heart, enrage it.
MACDUFF. O, I could play the woman with mine eyes
And braggart with my tongue! But, gentle heavens,
Cut short all intermission; front to front
Bring thou this fiend of Scotland and myself;
Within my sword's length set him; if he 'scape,
Heaven forgive him too!
MALCOLM.   This tune goes manly.
Come, go we to the King; our power is ready;
Our lack is nothing but our leave. Macbeth
Is ripe for shaking, and the powers above
Put on their instruments. Receive what cheer you may:
The night is long that never finds the day.   *Exeunt*

ACT V

SCENE I *Dunsinane: ante-room in the castle*

Enter a Doctor of Physic *and a* Waiting-Gentlewoman

DOCTOR. I have two nights watched with you, but can perceive no truth in your report. When was it she last walked?
GENTLEWOMAN. Since his majesty went into the field, I have seen her rise from her bed, throw her night-gown upon her, unlock her closet, take forth paper, fold it, write upon 't, read it, afterwards seal it, and again return to bed; yet all this while in a most fast sleep.
DOCTOR. A great perturbation in nature, to receive at once the benefit of sleep, and do the effects of watch-

ing! In this slumbery agitation, besides her walking and other actual performances, what, at any time, have you heard her say?
GENTLEWOMAN. That, sir, which I will not report after her.
DOCTOR. You may to me; and 'tis most meet you should.
GENTLEWOMAN. Neither to you nor any one; having no witness to confirm my speech.
      Enter LADY MACBETH, *with a taper*
Lo you, here she comes! This is her very guise; and,

upon my life, fast asleep. Observe her; stand close.

DOCTOR. How came she by that light?

GENTLEWOMAN. Why, it stood by her. She has light by her continually; 'tis her command.

DOCTOR. You see, her eyes are open.

GENTLEWOMAN. Ay, but their sense is shut.

DOCTOR. What is it she does now? Look, how she rubs her hands.

GENTLEWOMAN. It is an accustomed action with her, to seem thus washing her hands. I have known her continue in this a quarter of an hour.

LADY MACBETH. Yet here's a spot.

DOCTOR. Hark! she speaks. I will set down what comes from her, to satisfy my remembrance the more strongly.

LADY MACBETH. Out, damned spot! Out, I say!—One; two; why, then 'tis time to do 't. Hell is murky!—Fie, my lord, fie! a soldier, and afeard? What need we fear who knows it, when none can call our power to account?—Yet who would have thought the old man to have had so much blood in him.

DOCTOR. Do you mark that?

LADY MACBETH. The Thane of Fife had a wife: where is she now?—What, will these hands ne'er be clean?—No more o' that, my lord, no more o' that. You mar all with this starting.

DOCTOR. Go to, go to; you have known what you should not.

GENTLEWOMAN. She has spoke what she should not, I am sure of that. Heaven knows what she has known.

LADY MACBETH. Here 's the smell of the blood still. All the perfumes of Arabia will not sweeten this little hand. Oh, oh, oh!

DOCTOR. What a sigh is there! The heart is sorely charged.

GENTLEWOMAN. I would not have such a heart in my bosom for the dignity of the whole body.

DOCTOR. Well, well, well—

GENTLEWOMAN. Pray God it be, sir.

DOCTOR. This disease is beyond my practice. Yet I have known those which have walked in their sleep who have died holily in their beds.

LADY MACBETH. Wash your hands, put on your nightgown; look not so pale. I tell you yet again, Banquo 's buried; he cannot come out on 's grave.

DOCTOR. Even so?

LADY MACBETH. To bed, to bed! There 's knocking at the gate. Come, come, come, come, give me your hand. What 's done cannot be undone. To bed, to bed, to bed!   Exit

DOCTOR. Will she go now to bed?

GENTLEWOMAN. Directly.

DOCTOR. Foul whisperings are abroad. Unnatural deeds
Do breed unnatural troubles. Infected minds
To their deaf pillows will discharge their secrets.
More needs she the divine than the physician.
God, God forgive us all! Look after her;
Remove from her the means of all annoyance,
And still keep eyes upon her. So, good night.
My mind she has mated, and amazed my sight.
I think, but dare not speak.

GENTLEWOMAN.   Good night, good doctor. Exeunt

SCENE II *The country near Dunsinane*

Drum and colours. Enter MENTEITH, CAITHNESS, ANGUS, LENNOX, *and* Soldiers

MENTEITH. The English power is near, led on by Malcolm,
His uncle Siward and the good Macduff.
Revenges burn in them; for their dear causes
Would to the bleeding and the grim alarm
Excite the mortified man.

ANGUS.   Near Birnam Wood
Shall we well meet them; that way are they coming.

CAITHNESS. Who knows if Donalbain be with his brother?

LENNOX. For certain, sir, he is not. I have a file
Of all the gentry: there is Siward's son,
And many unrough youths that even now
Protest their first of manhood.

MENTEITH.   What does the tyrant?

CAITHNESS. Great Dunsinane he strongly fortifies.
Some say he's mad; others that lesser hate him
Do call it valiant fury. But, for certain,
He cannot buckle his distempered cause
Within the belt of rule.

ANGUS.   Now does he feel
His secret murders sticking on his hands;
Now minutely revolts upbraid his faith-breach;
Those he commands move only in command,
Nothing in love. Now does he feel his title
Hang loose about him, like a giant's robe
Upon a dwarfish thief.

MENTEITH.   Who then shall blame
His pestered senses to recoil and start,
When all that is within him does condemn
Itself for being there?

CAITHNESS.   Well, march we on,
To give obedience where 'tis truly owed.
Meet we the medicine of the sickly weal,
And with him pour we in our country's purge
Each drop of us.

LENNOX.   Or so much as it needs,
To dew the sovereign flower and drown the weeds.
Make we our march towards Birnam.

                              Exeunt, marching

SCENE III *Dunsinane: a room in the castle*

Enter MACBETH, Doctor, *and* Attendants

MACBETH. Bring me no more reports; let them fly all.
 Till Birnam Wood remove to Dunsinane,
 I cannot taint with fear. What's the boy Malcolm?
 Was he not born of woman? The spirits that know
 All mortal consequences have pronounced me thus:
 "Fear not, Macbeth; no man that's born of woman
 Shall e'er have power upon thee." Then fly, false
   thanes,
 And mingle with the English epicures.
 The mind I sway by and the heart I bear
 Shall never sag with doubt nor shake with fear.

Enter a Servant

 The devil damn thee black, thou cream-faced loon!
 Where got'st thou that goose look?
SERVANT. There is ten thousand—
MACBETH.   Geese, villain?
SERVANT.   Soldiers, sir.
MACBETH. Go, prick thy face, and over-red thy fear,
 Thou lily-livered boy. What soldiers, patch?
 Death of thy soul! Those linen cheeks of thine
 Are counsellors to fear. What soldiers, wheyface?
SERVANT. The English force, so please you.
MACBETH. Take thy face hence.   *Exit* Servant
                 Seyton!—I am sick at heart,
 When I behold—Seyton, I say!—This push
 Will cheer me ever, or disseat me now.
 I have lived long enough. My way of life
 Is fall'n into the sear, the yellow leaf;
 And that which should accompany old age,
 As honour, love, obedience, troops of friends,

I must not look to have; but, in their stead,
 Curses, not loud but deep, mouth-honour, breath,
 Which the poor heart would fain deny, and dare not.
 Seyton!

Enter SEYTON

SEYTON. What is your gracious pleasure?
MACBETH.   What news more?
SEYTON. All is confirmed, my lord, which was reported.
MACBETH. I'll fight till from my bones my flesh be
   hacked.
 Give me my armour.
SEYTON.   'Tis not needed yet.
MACBETH. I'll put it on.
 Send out more horses; skirr the country round;
 Hang those that talk of fear. Give me mine armour.
 How does your patient, doctor?
DOCTOR.   Not so sick, my lord,
 As she is troubled with thick-coming fancies,
 That keep her from her rest.
MACBETH.   Cure her of that.
 Canst thou not minister to a mind diseased,
 Pluck from the memory a rooted sorrow,
 Raze out the written troubles of the brain
 And with some sweet oblivious antidote
 Cleanse the stuffed bosom of that perilous stuff
 Which weighs upon the heart?
DOCTOR.   Therein the patient
 Must minister to himself.
MACBETH. Throw physic to the dogs; I'll none of it.
 Come, put mine armour on; give me my staff.
 Seyton, send out. Doctor, the thanes fly from me.

441

Come, sir, dispatch. If thou couldst, doctor, cast
The water of my land, find her disease,
And purge it to a sound and pristine health,
I would applaud thee to the very echo,
That should applaud again.—Pull 't off, I say!—
What rhubarb, senna, or what purgative drug,
Would scour these English hence? Hear'st thou of
    them?

DOCTOR. Ay, my good lord; your royal preparation
    Makes us hear something.
MACBETH.   Bring it after me.
    I will not be afraid of death and bane,
    Till Birnam Forest come to Dunsinane.
DOCTOR. [Aside] Were I from Dunsinane away and
    clear,
    Profit again should hardly draw me here.   Exeunt

SCENE IV *Country near Birnam Wood*

Drum and colours. Enter MALCOLM, *old* SIWARD *and his* Son, MACDUFF, MENTEITH, CAITHNESS, ANGUS, LENNOX, ROSS, *and* Soldiers, *marching*

MALCOLM. Cousins, I hope the days are near at hand
    That chambers will be safe.
MENTEITH.   We doubt it nothing.
SIWARD. What wood is this before us?
MENTEITH.   The wood of Birnam.
MALCOLM. Let every soldier hew him down a bough
    And bear 't before him. Thereby shall we shadow
    The numbers of our host and make discovery
    Err in report of us.
SOLDIERS.   It shall be done.
SIWARD. We learn no other but the confident tyrant
    Keeps still in Dunsinane, and will endure
    Our setting down before 't.
MALCOLM.   'Tis his main hope.

For where there is advantage to be given,
Both more and less have given him the revolt,
And none serve with him but constrained things
Whose hearts are absent too.
MACDUFF.   Let our just censures
    Attend the true event, and put we on
    Industrious soldiership.
SIWARD.   The time approaches
    That will with due decision make us know
    What we shall say we have and what we owe.
    Thoughts speculative their unsure hopes relate,
    But certain issue strokes must arbitrate;
    Towards which advance the war.
                                Exeunt, marching

SCENE V *Dunsinane: within the castle*

Enter MACBETH, SEYTON, *and* Soldiers, *with drum and colours*

MACBETH. Hang out our banners on the outward walls;
    The cry is still "They come." Our castle's strength
    Will laugh a siege to scorn. Here let them lie
    Till famine and the ague eat them up.
    Were they not forced with those that should be ours,
    We might have met them dareful, beard to beard,
    And beat them backward home.
                        A cry of women within
                        What is that noise?
SEYTON. It is the cry of women, my good lord.   *Exit*
MACBETH. I have almost forgot the taste of fears.
    The time has been, my senses would have cooled
    To hear a night-shriek; and my fell of hair
    Would at a dismal treatise rouse and stir
    As life were in 't. I have supped full with horrors;
    Direness, familiar to my slaughterous thoughts,
    Cannot once start me.

Re-enter SEYTON

                Wherefore was that cry?
SEYTON. The queen, my lord, is dead.
MACBETH. She should have died hereafter;

There would have been a time for such a word.
Tomorrow, and tomorrow, and tomorrow,
Creeps in this petty pace from day to day
To the last syllable of recorded time,
And all our yesterdays have lighted fools
The way to dusty death. Out, out, brief candle!
Life's but a walking shadow, a poor player
That struts and frets his hour upon the stage
And then is heard no more. It is a tale
Told by an idiot, full of sound and fury,
Signifying nothing.

Enter a Messenger

Thou comest to use thy tongue; thy story quickly.
MESSENGER. Gracious my lord,
    I should report that which I say I saw,
    But know not how to do it.
MACBETH.   Well, say, sir.
MESSENGER. As I did stand my watch upon the hill,
    I looked toward Birnam, and anon, methought,
    The Wood began to move.
MACBETH.   Liar and slave!

MESSENGER. Let me endure your wrath, if 't be not so.
   Within this three mile may you see it coming;
   I say, a moving grove.
MACBETH.   If thou speak'st false,
   Upon the next tree shalt thou hang alive,
   Till famine cling thee. If thy speech be sooth,
   I care not if thou dost for me as much.
   I pull in resolution, and begin
   To doubt the equivocation of the fiend
   That lies like truth: "Fear not, till Birnam Wood
   Do come to Dunsinane." And now a wood
   Comes toward Dunsinane. Arm, arm, and out!
   If this which he avouches does appear,
   There is nor flying hence nor tarrying here.
   I 'gin to be aweary of the sun,
   And wish the estate o' the world were now undone.
   Ring the alarum bell! Blow, wind! Come, wrack!
   At least we'll die with harness on our back.   *Exeunt*

SCENE VI *Dunsinane: before the castle*

Drum and colours. Enter MALCOLM, *old* SIWARD, MACDUFF, *and their* Army, *with boughs*

MALCOLM. Now near enough; your leavy screens throw
   down,
  And show like those you are. You, worthy uncle,
  Shall, with my cousin, your right-noble son,
  Lead our first battle. Worthy Macduff and we
  Shall take upon 's what else remains to do,
  According to our order.

SIWARD.   Fare you well.
  Do we but find the tyrant's power tonight,
  Let us be beaten, if we cannot fight.

MACDUFF. Make all our trumpets speak; give them all
  breath,
  Those clamorous harbingers of blood and death.

                                           Exeunt

SCENE VII *Another part of the field*

Alarums. Enter MACBETH

MACBETH. They have tied me to a stake; I cannot fly,
But, bear-like, I must fight the course. What 's he
That was not born of woman? Such a one
Am I to fear, or none.

Enter young SIWARD

YOUNG SIWARD. What is thy name?
MACBETH.   Thou 'lt be afraid to hear it.
YOUNG SIWARD. No; though thou call'st thyself a
hotter name
Than any is in hell.
MACBETH.   My name 's Macbeth.
YOUNG SIWARD. The devil himself could not pronounce
a title
More hateful to mine ear.
MACBETH.   No, nor more fearful.
YOUNG SIWARD. Thou liest, abhorred tyrant; with my
sword
I 'll prove the lie thou speak'st.

They fight and young SIWARD *is slain*

MACBETH.   Thou wast born of woman.
But swords I smile at, weapons laugh to scorn,
Brandished by man that 's of a woman born.   *Exit*

Alarums. Enter MACDUFF

MACDUFF. That way the noise is. Tyrant, show thy face!
If thou be'st slain and with no stroke of mine,
My wife and children's ghosts will haunt me still.
I cannot strike at wretched kerns, whose arms
Are hired to bear their staves. Either thou, Macbeth,
Or else my sword with an unbattered edge
I sheathe again undeeded. There thou shouldst be;
By this great clatter, one of greatest note
Seems bruited. Let me find him, fortune!
And more I beg not.   *Exit; alarums*

Enter MALCOLM *and old* SIWARD

SIWARD. This way, my lord; the castle 's gently rendered.
The tyrant's people on both sides do fight;
The noble thanes do bravely in the war;
The day almost itself professes yours,
And little is to do.
MALCOLM.   We have met with foes
That strike beside us.
SIWARD.   Enter, sir, the castle.
                         Exeunt; alarums

SCENE VIII *Another part of the field*

Enter MACBETH

MACBETH. Why should I play the Roman fool, and die
On mine own sword? Whiles I see lives, the gashes
Do better upon them.

Enter MACDUFF

MACDUFF.   Turn, hell-hound, turn!
MACBETH. Of all men else I have avoided thee.
But get thee back; my soul is too much charged
With blood of thine already.
MACDUFF.   I have no words.
My voice is in my sword, thou bloodier villain
Than terms can give thee out!   *They fight*
MACBETH.   Thou losest labour.
As easy mayst thou the intrenchant air
With thy keen sword impress as make me bleed.
Let fall thy blade on vulnerable crests;
I bear a charmed life, which must not yield
To one of woman born.
MACDUFF.   Despair thy charm;
And let the angel whom thou still hast served
Tell thee, Macduff was from his mother's womb
Untimely ripped.
MACBETH. Accursed be that tongue that tells me so,
For it hath cowed my better part of man!
And be these juggling fiends no more believed,
That palter with us in a double sense;
That keep the word of promise to our ear,
And break it to our hope. I 'll not fight with thee.
MACDUFF. Then yield thee, coward,
And live to be the show and gaze o' the time.
We'll have thee, as our rarer monsters are,
Painted upon a pole, and underwrit,
"Here may you see the tyrant."
MACBETH.   I will not yield,
To kiss the ground before young Malcolm's feet,
And to be baited with the rabble's curse.
Though Birnam Wood be come to Dunsinane,
And thou opposed, being of no woman born,
Yet I will try the last. Before my body
I throw my warlike shield. Lay on, Macduff,
And damned be him that first cries "Hold enough!"
               Exeunt, fighting. Alarums

Retreat. Flourish. Enter, with drum and colours, MALCOLM,
old SIWARD, ROSS, *the other* Thanes, *and* Soldiers

MALCOLM. I would the friends we miss were safe arrived.

446

SIWARD. Some must go off; and yet, by these I see,
  So great a day as this is cheaply bought.
MALCOLM. Macduff is missing, and your noble son.
ROSS. Your son, my lord, has paid a soldier's debt.
  He only lived but till he was a man;
  The which no sooner had his prowess confirmed
  In the unshrinking station where he fought,
  But like a man he died.
SIWARD.   Then he is dead?
ROSS. Ay, and brought off the field; your cause of
    sorrow
  Must not be measured by his worth, for then
  It hath no end.
SIWARD.   Had he his hurts before?
ROSS. Ay, on the front.
SIWARD.   Why then, God's soldier be he!
  Had I as many sons as I have hairs,
  I would not wish them to a fairer death.
  And so, his knell is knolled.
MALCOLM.   He's worth more sorrow,
  And that I'll spend for him.
SIWARD.   He's worth no more.
  They say he parted well, and paid his score.
  And so, God be with him! Here comes newer comfort.

    Re-enter MACDUFF, *with* MACBETH'S *head*

MACDUFF. Hail, King! for so thou art. Behold, where
    stands
  The usurper's cursed head. The time is free.
  I see thee compassed with thy kingdom's pearl,
  That speak my salutation in their minds;
  Whose voices I desire aloud with mine:
  Hail, King of Scotland!
ALL.   Hail, King of Scotland! *Flourish*
MALCOLM. We shall not spend a large expense of time
  Before we reckon with your several loves,
  And make us even with you. My Thanes and kinsmen,
  Henceforth be Earls, the first that ever Scotland
  In such an honour named. What 's more to do,
  Which would be planted newly with the time,
  As calling home our exiled friends abroad
  That fled the snares of watchful tyranny;
  Producing forth the cruel ministers
  Of this dead butcher and his fiend-like Queen,
  Who, as 'tis thought, by self and violent hands
  Took off her life; this, and what needful else
  That calls upon us, by the grace of Grace,
  We will perform in measure, time and place.
  So, thanks to all at once and to each one,
  Whom we invite to see us crowned at Scone.

                      Flourish; exeunt

THE TEMPEST

It is sometimes maintained that Shakespeare's plays are better appreciated in the seclusion of the study than in the hurly-burly of the theatre, a point of view arising from a not unreasonable dissatisfaction with the botched and makeshift theatrical performances which are too often seen.

Without conceding that a stage-play can ever, in principle, be better read than acted, I must admit that there are certain plays which lend themselves less readily than others to stage representation, and certain features of plays, otherwise excellently planned for the stage, which seem to defy representation.

A reader of *The Tempest* can picture his own enchanted island, which can be recreated now with the precision of a well-remembered landscape, now shrouded in a mist of vagueness through which the mind's eye need only decipher such details as it wishes to see, leaving the rest tactfully obscure. But in the theatre it is not only the island which must be interpreted in tangible terms—given a good stage designer that problem need not be insuperable. A far greater difficulty is to realize in terms of flesh and blood the spirits of earth and air and sea which people the island.

I have seen both Ariel and Caliban finely interpreted by imaginative actors; but always, instead of being helped by their costume and make-up, they had to fight against what had been provided.

There seems to be an inescapable dilemma. If you dress them up with elaborate fantasy, then it is the dressmaker's fantasy trying to say, in the laborious prose of gauze and wire, spangles and painted cloth, what Shakespeare has already said inimitably. If you shun this horn of the dilemma and attempt an extreme simplicity, you are impaled upon the other horn: the actors have nothing behind which to hide. The simpler their accoutrement the more they are revealed, not as spirits, but as the all-too-human creatures which they are.

Of the two alternatives I prefer the latter. Let Ariel and Caliban appear as what they are—two actors; and let them persuade the audience that they are spirits by the art not of the dressmaker but of the actor.

Yet how does this square with what we may conjecture to have been Shakespeare's intention?

The Tempest is partly a Masque. We have evidence (Inigo Jones' designs, for instance, for Masques of a date very little later than the first production of *The Tempest*) that such entertainments were produced with considerable magnificence. There is much to suggest that *The Tempest* was conceived as an elaborate, spectacular production. Iris, Ceres and Juno will have been "set-up" with elaborate stage effects and sumptuous dresses. Does elaboration in this part of the play permit simplicity elsewhere? I

think it does. I think it is clear that Ariel's songs are in quite a different musical style from the set-pieces of the Masques. If the music is in two different styles, then there is warrant for the dresses being so too.

What of the banquet and the "quaint device" which, according to the stage directions, causes it to vanish? Appetizing-looking magic banquets and quaint disappearing tricks cannot be very simply contrived.

No one can be dogmatic. My own belief is that the Masque at the close of the play can be in quite a different convention from the rest. It is, after all, a set-piece, a play-within-a-play, designed by Prospero to entertain the young lovers and, doubtless, to impress poor Ferdinand with the formidable conjuring ability of his future wife's father. It should offer an elaborate and spectacular finale to *The Tempest,* even though the play has hitherto relied upon that severe economy of means which alone permits an audience to use its imagination creatively.

Ariel and Caliban are never precisely described. Ariel, on the evidence of the name, would seem to be an airy spirit. At the end of the play Prospero says, "Ariel, my chick"; but it would be absurd on this evidence to give to the spirit the likeness of a bird. "Chick" is a term of endearment, no more. The stage-direction that indicates the entrance of Ariel disguised as a Harpy adds, "Claps *HIS* wings . . ." but in Shakespeare's theatre, where no women appeared, the part will almost certainly have been played by a boy. This stage-direction, therefore, need not imply that Shakespeare conceived his Ariel as being of the male sex, or indeed of any sex.

Caliban is more human and unquestionably male. His mother was a witch, and he feels fleshly longings for Miranda. He smells, and apparently also looks, fishy. Mostly, on the stage, he is presented as a sort of gorilla, covered here and there with bits of material intended to suggest seaweed.

Unquestionably something is lost when the imprecise but marvellous suggestions to the readers' inward eye are exchanged for the too, too solid flesh of stage interpretation. On the other hand, I question whether even the most imaginative reader can ever capture the thrill that a powerful actor can evoke when Caliban cringes sulkily and fearfully before Prospero, or when, after his first taste of liquor, the monster yells for freedom.

Similarly I doubt whether reading can ever make clear the comment upon the very different freedom and captivity that is implicit in the whole relation between Prospero and Ariel. Just intellectually "appreciating" that this comment exists is not enough. It is a comment that is made by interplay between the two actors, by the exchange of looks and by subtleties of vocal colour and of rhythm which can *only* occur when two imaginative actors each react to the suggestions of the other's performance, when they create and feel their scenes *together*.

The relation of Prospero to Ariel is far more subtle and interesting than that of master to slave. Each is enslaved. Prospero is, very consciously, the captive of his responsibilities, his conscience, his human weakness, his mortality. By the end of the play he has abjured his "rough magic"; the staff will be broken and the book drowned. The moment, at the very end of the play, when he bids farewell to Ariel is far, far more than the loosing of a captive bird. It is a death—for both of them.

I cannot doubt but that Shakespeare used Prospero to say something in allegorical form both about himself and, more generally, about the power—and limitations—of the creative artist.

It is my view that Shakespeare, by now, as is generally agreed, at the end of his career, although not yet fifty—as normal lives go, far from an old man—felt his creative powers to be waning. In Prospero he expressed this awareness, not just in respect to himself, but to all "enchanters". Ariel is the "inspiration" which serves him just so long, then leaves him to fly, like the wind, withersoever it listeth.

Every one of us, whether professional artist or not, is to some limited extent a Prospero. We can all exercise enchantment through the power of inspiration, imagination—call it what you will—fitfully, from time to time, according to our abilities. Sooner or later the moment comes when each of us must break his staff, drown his book, bid farewell to Ariel and accept the fact that "we are all such stuff as dreams are made on, and our little life is rounded with a sleep."

On the stage Prospero is usually presented not merely as a godlike figure, which is all right, but as a being of extreme and hoary eld. This is all wrong. On the prosaic level it makes him a rather unlikely papa for Miranda, who is obviously very young. On a deeper level, if Prospero is a venerable greybeard, all passion spent, his relation to all the other characters is emasculated and falsified: his jealousy of Ferdinand, for example, or his passionate resentment of his brother's usurpation and treachery.

The tempest which wrecks the ship, casts his enemies upon the island and places them in his power is a symbol of the rage that is tearing Prospero. It must be a formidable tempest.

Unless it is apparent that, right up till a critical moment (in Act V, scene 1) when he suddenly changes, Prospero really means to exact violent revenge upon the wrongdoers, there is no story. The play would then simply be about a kind old enchanter who had brought about the shipwreck simply to give his enemies a bit of a fright—just enough to make the usurper, Antonio, surrender the dukedom. There would be no crisis and no development in the character of Prospero.

But if Prospero is played as a mature but still passionate man, and if in the earlier scenes he is clearly animated by a formidable desire to punish his enemies, several interesting and dramatically valuable things occur. First, the play has a dramatic suspense, which it would otherwise lack: What will happen to the wrongdoers? Secondly, Prospero's treatment of Caliban becomes consistent with the rest of his conduct. Usually one wonders why such a nice, kind, old buffer is so gruff with the help. Thirdly, the reason is explained why Ariel, as well as Caliban, is eager for freedom. Fourthly, and principally, the play has a crisis.

At the end of Act IV the revenge is going great guns. Trinculo, Stephano and Caliban are going to have their joints ground with dry convulsions and several other juicy punishments, not in the least consonant with the nature of kind, silvery granddad. As Act V begins (and I think it is obvious that no break in the action is intended) Prospero moves against the chief conspirators—and with the utmost relish.

> Now does my project gather to a head
> My charms creak not, my spirits obey. And Time
> goes upright with his carriage.

This mood continues until Ariel describes the weeping of the good, old lord, Gonzago.

> His tears run down his beard, like winter's drops
> From eaves of reeds.

That causes Prospero to feel a twinge of compassion.

Ariel, who is Prospero's "inspiration", his contact with the ethereal regions, presses the point:

> Your charm so strongly works 'em
> That if you now beheld them, your affections
> Would become tender.

Prospero's reply is:

> Dost think so, Spirit?

This could be uttered with grim irony; or it could show the beginning of the idea of forgiveness. I prefer the former. Then Ariel utters what, well spoken, can be one of the most touching and evocative lines in all literature:

> Mine would, sir, were I human.

That is the crisis.

Prospero replies:

> And mine shall.

He goes on in a marvellous passage to the resolution:

> Though with their high wrongs I am struck
>   to the quick,
> Yet with my nobler reason 'gainst my fury
> Do I take part. The rarer action is
> In virtue than in vengeance.

Immediately there follows the invocation to the world of nature to witness that henceforth he abjures his rough magic, to witness the voluntary abdication of the great enchanter.

From this point, relieved by some excellent fun, the play moves on to its serene close of reconciliation and forgiveness—dominant dramatic themes of all Shakespeare's later plays—and the dismissal of Ariel. After the tempest there succeeds a golden calm.

ALONSO,
King of Naples

ANTONIO,
the usurping Duke of Milan,
brother to Prospero

SEBASTIAN,
brother to the
King of Naples

ADRIAN,
FRANCISCO,
Lords

GONZALO,
an honest old
Counsellor

FERDINAND
son to the
King of Naples

Master of
a Ship,
Boatswain,
Mariners

TRINCULO, a jester; STEPHANO, a drunken butler

SCENE: A SHIP AT SEA; AN ISLAND

ARIEL,
an airy Spirit

Other Spirits
attending on
Prospero

MIRANDA,
daughter
to
Prospero

IRIS, CERES, JUNO,
Nymphs, Reapers;
presented by Spirits

PROSPERO,
the right Duke of Milan

CALIBAN,
a savage and
deformed
Slave

THE TEMPEST
DRAMATIS PERSONAE

ACT I

SCENE I *On a ship at sea: a tempestuous noise of thunder*
and lightning heard
Enter a Shipmaster *and a* Boatswain

MASTER. Boatswain!

BOATSWAIN. Here, master; what cheer?

MASTER. Good, speak to the mariners. Fall to 't, yarely,
or we run ourselves aground. Bestir, bestir.   *Exit*

Enter Mariners

BOATSWAIN. Heigh, my hearts! Cheerly, cheerly, my
hearts! Yare, yare! Take in the topsail. Tend to the
master's whistle. Blow, till thou burst thy wind, if
room enough!

Enter ALONSO, SEBASTIAN, ANTONIO, FERDINAND,
GONZALO, *and others*

ALONSO. Good boatswain, have care. Where's the
master? Play the men.

BOATSWAIN. I pray now, keep below.

ANTONIO. Where is the master, boatswain?

BOATSWAIN. Do you not hear him? You mar our labour.
Keep your cabins; you do assist the storm.

GONZALO. Nay, good, be patient.

BOATSWAIN. When the sea is. Hence! What cares these
roarers for the name of king? To cabin. Silence!
Trouble us not.

GONZALO. Good, yet remember whom thou hast aboard.

BOATSWAIN. None that I more love than myself. You
are a counsellor; if you can command these elements
to silence, and work the peace of the present, we will
not hand a rope more. Use your authority. If you cannot, give thanks you have lived so long, and make
yourself ready in your cabin for the mischance of the
hour, if it so hap. Cheerly, good hearts! Out of our
way, I say.   *Exit*

GONZALO. I have great comfort from this fellow. Methinks he hath no drowning mark upon him; his complexion is perfect gallows. Stand fast, good Fate, to
his hanging. Make the rope of his destiny our cable,
for our own doth little advantage. If he be not born
to be hanged, our case is miserable.   *Exeunt*

Re-enter Boatswain

BOATSWAIN. Down with the topmast! Yare! Lower,
lower! Bring her to try with main-course. [*A cry
within*] A plague upon this howling! They are louder
than the weather or our office.

Re-enter SEBASTIAN, ANTONIO, *and* GONZALO

Yet again! What do you here? Shall we give o'er and
drown? Have you a mind to sink?

SEBASTIAN. A pox o' your throat, you bawling, blas-
phemous, incharitable dog!

BOATSWAIN. Work you then.

ANTONIO. Hang, cur! Hang, you whoreson, insolent noisemaker! We are less afraid to be drowned than thou art.

GONZALO. I'll warrant him for drowning; though the ship were no stronger than a nutshell and as leaky as an unstanched wench.

BOATSWAIN. Lay her a-hold, a-hold! Set her two courses off to sea again; lay her off.

Enter Mariners *wet*

MARINERS. All lost! To prayers, to prayers! All lost!

BOATSWAIN. What, must our mouths be cold?

GONZALO. The King and Prince at prayers! Let's assist them,
  For our case is as theirs.

SEBASTIAN.   I'm out of patience.

ANTONIO. We are merely cheated of our lives by drunkards.
  This wide-chapped rascal—would thou mightst lie drowning
  The washing of ten tides!

GONZALO.   He'll be hanged yet,
  Though every drop of water swear against it
  And gape at widest to glut him.
  [*A confused noise within*: Mercy on us!—
  We split, we split—Farewell my wife and children!—
  Farewell, brother—We split, we split, we split]

ANTONIO. Let's all sink with the King.

SEBASTIAN. Let's take leave of him.
                Exeunt ANTONIO *and* SEBASTIAN

GONZALO. Now would I give a thousand furlongs of sea for an acre of barren ground, long heath, brown furze, anything. The wills above be done, but I would fain die a dry death.   *Exeunt*

SCENE II *The island: before* PROSPERO'S *cell*

Enter PROSPERO *and* MIRANDA

MIRANDA. If by your art, my dearest father, you have
  Put the wild waters in this roar, allay them.
  The sky, it seems, would pour down stinking pitch,
  But that the sea, mounting to the welkin's cheek,
  Dashes the fire out. O, I have suffered
  With those that I saw suffer; a brave vessel,
  Who had, no doubt, some noble creature in her,
  Dashed all to pieces. O, the cry did knock
  Against my very heart. Poor souls, they perished.
  Had I been any god of power, I would
  Have sunk the sea within the earth or ere
  It should the good ship so have swallowed and
  The fraughting souls within her.

PROSPERO.   Be collected.
  No more amazement. Tell your piteous heart
  There's no harm done.

MIRANDA.   O, woe the day!

PROSPERO.   No harm.
  I have done nothing but in care of thee,
  Of thee, my dear one, thee, my daughter, who
  Art ignorant of what thou art, nought knowing
  Of whence I am, nor that I am more better
  Than Prospero, master of a full poor cell,
  And thy no greater father.

MIRANDA.   More to know
  Did never meddle with my thoughts.

PROSPERO.   'Tis time
  I should inform thee farther. Lend thy hand,
  And pluck my magic garment from me. So.
                Lays down his mantle
  Lie there, my art. Wipe thou thine eyes; have comfort.
  The direful spectacle of the wreck, which touched
  The very virtue of compassion in thee,
  I have with such provision in mine art
  So safely ordered that there is no soul—
  No, not so much perdition as an hair
  Betid to any creature in the vessel
  Which thou heard'st cry, which thou saw'st sink.
    Sit down;
  For thou must now know farther.

MIRANDA.   You have often
  Begun to tell me what I am, but stopped
  And left me to a bootless inquisition,
  Concluding "Stay—not yet."

PROSPERO.   The hour's now come;
  The very minute bids thee ope thine ear.
  Obey and be attentive. Canst thou remember
  A time before we came unto this cell?
  I do not think thou canst, for then thou wast not
  Out three years old.

MIRANDA.   Certainly, sir, I can.

PROSPERO. By what? By any other house or person?
  Of anything the image tell me that
  Hath kept with thy remembrance.

MIRANDA.   'Tis far off
  And rather like a dream than an assurance
  That my remembrance warrants. Had I not
  Four or five women once that tended me?

PROSPERO. Thou hadst, and more, Miranda. But how is it
  That this lives in thy mind? What seest thou else
  In the dark backward and abysm of time?
  If thou remember'st aught ere thou camest here,
  How thou camest here thou mayst.

MIRANDA.   But that I do not.

PROSPERO. Twelve year since, Miranda, twelve year since,

Thy father was the duke of Milan and
  A prince of power.
MIRANDA.   Sir, are not you my father?
PROSPERO. Thy mother was a piece of virtue, and
  She said thou wast my daughter; and thy father
  Was duke of Milan; and thou his only heir
  And princess no worse issued.
MIRANDA.   O the heavens!
  What foul play had we, that we came from thence?
  Or blessed was 't we did?
PROSPERO.   Both, both, my girl.
  By foul play, as thou say'st, were we heaved thence,
  But blessedly holp hither.
MIRANDA.   O, my heart bleeds
  To think o' the teen that I have turned you to,
  Which is from my remembrance! Please you, farther.
PROSPERO. My brother and thy uncle, called Antonio—
  I pray thee, mark me—that a brother should
  Be so perfidious!—he whom next thyself
  Of all the world I loved, and to him put
  The manage of my state; as at that time
  Through all the signories it was the first
  And Prospero the prime duke, being so reputed
  In dignity, and for the liberal arts
  Without a parallel. Those being all my study,
  The government I cast upon my brother
  And to my state grew stranger, being transported
  And rapt in secret studies. Thy false uncle—
  Dost thou attend me?
MIRANDA.   Sir, most heedfully.
PROSPERO. Being once perfected how to grant suits,
  How to deny them, who to advance and who
  To trash for over-topping, new created
  The creatures that were mine, I say, or changed 'em,
  Or else new formed 'em; having both the key
  Of officer and office, set all hearts i' the state
  To what tune pleased his ear; that now he was
  The ivy which had hid my princely trunk,
  And sucked my verdure out on 't. Thou attend'st not.
MIRANDA. O, good sir, I do.
PROSPERO.   I pray thee, mark me.
  I, thus neglecting worldly ends, all dedicated
  To closeness and the bettering of my mind
  With that which, but by being so retired,
  O'er-prized all popular rate, in my false brother
  Awaked an evil nature; and my trust,
  Like a good parent, did beget of him
  A falsehood in its contrary as great
  As my trust was; which had indeed no limit,
  A confidence sans bound. He being thus lorded,
  Not only with what my revenue yielded,
  But what my power might else exact, like one
  Who having into truth, by telling of it,
  Made such a sinner of his memory,
  To credit his own lie, he did believe
  He was indeed the duke; out o' the substitution,

And executing the outward face of royalty,
  With all prerogative. Hence his ambition growing—
  Dost thou hear?
MIRANDA.   Your tale, sir, would cure deafness.
PROSPERO. To have no screen between this part he
    played
  And him he played it for, he needs will be
  Absolute Milan. Me, poor man, my library
  Was dukedom large enough. Of temporal royalties
  He thinks me now incapable; confederates—
  So dry he was for sway—wi' the King of Naples
  To give him annual tribute, do him homage,
  Subject his coronet to his crown and bend
  The dukedom yet unbowed—alas, poor Milan!—
  To most ignoble stooping.
MIRANDA.   O the heavens!
PROSPERO. Mark his condition and the event; then
    tell me
  If this might be a brother.
MIRANDA.   I should sin
  To think but nobly of my grandmother.
  Good wombs have borne bad sons.
PROSPERO.   Now the condition.
  This king of Naples, being an enemy
  To me inveterate, hearkens my brother's suit;
  Which was, that he, in lieu o' the premises
  Of homage and I know not how much tribute,
  Should presently extirpate me and mine
  Out of the dukedom and confer fair Milan
  With all the honours on my brother. Whereon,
  A treacherous army levied, one midnight
  Fated to the purpose did Antonio open
  The gates of Milan, and, i' the dead of darkness,
  The ministers for the purpose hurried thence
  Me and thy crying self.
MIRANDA.   Alack, for pity!
  I, not remembering how I cried out then,
  Will cry it o'er again. It is a hint
  That wrings mine eyes to 't.
PROSPERO.   Hear a little further
  And then I'll bring thee to the present business
  Which now 's upon 's; without the which this story
  Were most impertinent.
MIRANDA.   Wherefore did they not
  That hour destroy us?
PROSPERO. Well demanded, wench—
  My tale provokes that question. Dear, they durst not,
  So dear the love my people bore me, nor set
  A mark so bloody on the business, but
  With colours fairer painted their foul ends.
  In few, they hurried us aboard a bark,
  Bore us some leagues to sea; where they prepared
  A rotten carcass of a boat, not rigged,
  Nor tackle, sail, nor mast; the very rats
  Instinctively have quit it. There they hoist us,
  To cry to the sea that roared to us, to sigh

To the winds whose pity, sighing back again,
Did us but loving wrong.
MIRANDA.   Alack, what trouble
  Was I then to you.
PROSPERO.   O, a cherubin
  Thou wast that did preserve me. Thou didst smile,
  Infused with a fortitude from heaven,
  When I have decked the sea with drops full salt,
  Under my burthen groaned; which raised in me
  An undergoing stomach, to bear up
  Against what should ensue.
MIRANDA.   How came we ashore?
PROSPERO. By Providence divine.
  Some food we had and some fresh water that
  A noble Neapolitan, Gonzalo,
  Out of his charity, who being then appointed
  Master of this design, did give us, with
  Rich garments, linens, stuffs and necessaries,
  Which since have steaded much; so, of his gentleness,
  Knowing I loved my books, he furnished me
  From mine own library with volumes that
  I prize above my dukedom.
MIRANDA.   Would I might
  But ever see that man!
PROSPERO.   Now I arise. *Resumes his mantle*
  Sit still, and hear the last of our sea-sorrow.
  Here in this island we arrived; and here
  Have I, thy schoolmaster, made thee more profit
  Than other princesses can that have more time
  For vainer hours and tutors not so careful.
MIRANDA. Heavens thank you for 't! And now,
  I pray you, sir,
  For still 'tis beating in my mind, your reason
  For raising this sea-storm?
PROSPERO.   Know thus far forth.
  By accident most strange, bountiful Fortune,
  Now my dear lady, hath mine enemies
  Brought to this shore; and by my prescience
  I find my zenith doth depend upon
  A most auspicious star, whose influence
  If now I court not but omit, my fortunes
  Will ever after droop. Here cease more questions.
  Thou art inclined to sleep; 'tis a good dullness,
  And give it way. I know thou canst not choose.
                                    MIRANDA *sleeps*
  Come away, servant, come. I am ready now.
  Approach, my Ariel, come.
                        Enter ARIEL
ARIEL. All hail, great master! Grave sir, hail! I come
  To answer thy best pleasure; be 't to fly,
  To swim, to dive into the fire, to ride
  On the curled clouds, to thy strong bidding task
  Ariel and all his quality.
PROSPERO.   Hast thou, spirit,
  Performed to point the tempest that I bade thee?
ARIEL. To every article.

I boarded the King's ship; now on the beak,
  Now in the waist, the deck, in every cabin,
  I flamed amazement. Sometime I'd divide,
  And burn in many places; on the topmast,
  The yards and bowsprit, would I flame distinctly,
  Then meet and join. Jove's lightnings, the precursors
  O' the dreadful thunder-claps, more momentary
  And sight-outrunning were not; the fire and cracks
  Of sulphurous roaring the most mighty Neptune
  Seem to besiege and make his bold waves tremble,
  Yea, his dread trident shake.
PROSPERO.   My brave spirit!
  Who was so firm, so constant, that this coil
  Would not infect his reason?
ARIEL.   Not a soul
  But felt a fever of the mad and played
  Some tricks of desperation. All but mariners
  Plunged in the foaming brine and quit the vessel,
  Then all afire with me. The King's son, Ferdinand,
  With hair up-staring—then like reeds, not hair—
  Was the first man that leaped; cried, "Hell is empty,
  And all the devils are here."
PROSPERO.   Why, that's my spirit!
  But was not this nigh shore?
ARIEL.   Close by, my master.
PROSPERO. But are they, Ariel, safe?
ARIEL.   Not a hair perished;
  On their sustaining garments not a blemish,
  But fresher than before. And, as thou badest me,
  In troops I have dispersed them 'bout the isle.
  The King's son have I landed by himself;
  Whom I left cooling of the air with sighs
  In an odd angle of the isle and sitting,
  His arms in this sad knot.
PROSPERO.   Of the King's ship,
  The mariners say how thou hast disposed
  And all the rest o' the fleet.
ARIEL.   Safely in harbour
  Is the King's ship; in the deep nook, where once
  Thou calledst me up at midnight to fetch dew
  From the still-vexed Bermoothes, there she's hid—
  The mariners all under hatches stowed;
  Who, with a charm joined to their suffered labour,
  I have left asleep. And for the rest o' the fleet
  Which I dispersed, they all have met again
  And are upon the Mediterranean flote,
  Bound sadly home for Naples,
  Supposing that they saw the King's ship wrecked
  And his great person perish.
PROSPERO.   Ariel, thy charge
  Exactly is performed. But there's more work.
  What is the time o' the day?
ARIEL.   Past the mid-season.
PROSPERO. At least two glasses. The time 'twixt six
    and now
  Must by us both be spent most preciously.

ARIEL. Is there more toil? Since thou dost give me pains,
  Let me remember thee what thou hast promised,
  Which is not yet performed me.
PROSPERO.   How now? Moody?
  What is 't thou canst demand?
ARIEL.   My liberty.
PROSPERO. Before the time be out? No more!
ARIEL.   I prithee,
  Remember I have done thee worthy service;
  Told thee no lies, made thee no mistakings, served
  Without or grudge or grumblings. Thou didst promise
  To bate me a full year.
PROSPERO.   Dost thou forget
  From what a torment I did free thee?
ARIEL.   No.
PROSPERO. Thou dost, and think'st it much to tread
    the ooze
  Of the salt deep,
  To run upon the sharp wind of the north,
  To do me business in the veins o' the earth
  When it is baked with frost.
ARIEL.   I do not, sir.
PROSPERO. Thou liest, malignant thing! Hast thou forgot
  The foul witch Sycorax, who with age and envy
  Was grown into a hoop? Hast thou forgot her?
ARIEL. No, sir.
PROSPERO.   Thou hast. Where was she born? speak;
    tell me.
ARIEL. Sir, in Argier.
PROSPERO.   O, was she so? I must
  Once in a month recount what thou hast been,
  Which thou forget'st. This damned witch Sycorax,
  For mischiefs manifold and sorceries terrible
  To enter human hearing, from Argier,
  Thou know'st, was banished. For one thing she did
  They would not take her life. Is not this true?
ARIEL. Ay, sir.
PROSPERO. This blue-eyed hag was hither brought with
    child
  And here was left by the sailors. Thou, my slave,
  As thou report'st thyself, wast then her servant;
  And, for thou wast a spirit too delicate
  To act her earthy and abhorred commands,
  Refusing her grand hests, she did confine thee,
  By help of her more potent ministers
  And in her most unmitigable rage,
  Into a cloven pine; within which rift
  Imprisoned thou didst painfully remain
  A dozen years; within which space she died
  And left thee there; where thou didst vent thy groans
  As fast as mill-wheels strike. Then was this island—
  Save for the son that she did litter here,
  A freckled whelp hag-born—not honoured with
  A human shape.
ARIEL.   Yes, Caliban her son.
PROSPERO. Dull thing, I say so; he, that Caliban

  Whom now I keep in service. Thou best know'st
  What torment I did find thee in; thy groans
  Did make wolves howl and penetrate the breasts
  Of ever angry bears. It was a torment
  To lay upon the damned, which Sycorax
  Could not again undo. It was mine art,
  When I arrived and heard thee, that made gape
  The pine and let thee out.
ARIEL.   I thank thee, master.
PROSPERO. If thou more murmur'st, I will rend an oak
  And peg thee in his knotty entrails till
  Thou hast howled away twelve winters.
ARIEL.   Pardon, master;
  I will be correspondent to command
  And do my spiriting gently.
PROSPERO.   Do so, and after two days
  I will discharge thee.
ARIEL.   That's my noble master!
  What shall I do? Say what; what shall I do?
PROSPERO. Go make thyself like a nymph o' the sea.
    Be subject
  To no sight but thine and mine, invisible
  To every eyeball else. Go take this shape
  And hither come in 't. Go, hence with diligence!
                                        Exit ARIEL
  Awake, dear heart, awake! Thou hast slept well;
  Awake!
MIRANDA. The strangeness of your story put
  Heaviness in me.
PROSPERO.   Shake it off. Come on;
  We'll visit Caliban my slave, who never
  Yields us kind answer.
MIRANDA.   'Tis a villain, sir,
  I do not love to look on.
PROSPERO.   But, as 'tis,
  We cannot miss him. He does make our fire,
  Fetch in our wood and serves in offices
  That profit us. What, ho! slave! Caliban!
  Thou earth, thou! speak.
CALIBAN. [*Within*] There's wood enough within.

PROSPERO. Come forth, I say! There's other business
  for thee.
 Come, thou tortoise, when?

Re-enter ARIEL *like a water-nymph*

 Fine apparition! My quaint Ariel,
 Hark in thine ear.
ARIEL.   My lord, it shall be done.   *Exit*
PROSPERO. Thou poisonous slave, got by the devil
  himself
 Upon thy wicked dam, come forth!

Enter CALIBAN

CALIBAN. As wicked dew as e'er my mother brushed
 With raven's feather from unwholesome fen
 Drop on you both! A south-west blow on ye
 And blister you all o'er!
PROSPERO. For this, be sure, tonight thou shalt have
  cramps,
 Side-stitches that shall pen thy breath up; urchins
 Shall, for that vast of night that they may work,
 All exercise on thee; thou shalt be pinched
 As thick as honeycomb, each pinch more stinging
 Than bees that made 'em.
CALIBAN.   I must eat my dinner.
 This island's mine, by Sycorax my mother,
 Which thou takest from me. When thou camest first,
 Thou strokedst me and madest much of me, wouldst
  give me
 Water with berries in 't, and teach me how
 To name the bigger light, and how the less,
 That burn by day and night. And then I loved thee
 And showed thee all the qualities o' the isle,

THE TEMPEST

The fresh springs, brine pits, barren place and fertile.
Cursed be I that did so! All the charms
Of Sycorax, toads, beetles, bats, light on you!
For I am all the subjects that you have,
Which first was mine own king. And here you sty me
In this hard rock, whiles you do keep from me
The rest o' the island.

PROSPERO.   Thou most lying slave,
Whom stripes may move, not kindness! I have used
    thee,
Filth as thou art, with human care, and lodged thee
In mine own cell, till thou didst seek to violate
The honour of my child.

CALIBAN. O ho, O ho! Would 't had been done!
Thou didst prevent me; I had peopled else
This isle with Calibans.

PROSPERO.   Abhorred slave,
Which any print of goodness wilt not take,
Being capable of all ill! I pitied thee,
Took pains to make thee speak, taught thee each hour
One thing or other. When thou didst not, savage,
Know thine own meaning, but wouldst gabble like
A thing most brutish, I endowed thy purposes
With words that made them known. But thy vile race,
Though thou didst learn, had that in 't which good
    natures
Could not abide to be with; therefore wast thou
Deservedly confined into this rock,
Who hadst deserved more than a prison.

CALIBAN. You taught me language; and my profit on 't
Is, I know how to curse. The red plague rid you
For learning me your language!

PROSPERO.   Hag-seed, hence!
Fetch us in fuel; and be quick, thou 'rt best,
To answer other business. Shrug'st thou, malice?
If thou neglect'st or dost unwillingly
What I command, I'll rack thee with old cramps,
Fill all thy bones with aches, make thee roar
That beasts shall tremble at thy din.

CALIBAN.   No, pray thee.
[Aside] I must obey. His art is of such power,
It would control my dam's god, Setebos,
And make a vassal of him.

PROSPERO. So, slave; hence!   Exit CALIBAN

Re-enter ARIEL, invisible, playing and singing;
        FERDINAND following

ARIEL's song

Come unto these yellow sands,
    And then take hands;
Courtsied when you have and kissed
    The wild waves whist,
Foot it featly here and there;
And, sweet sprites, the burthen bear.

BURTHEN [dispersedly]. Hark, hark!
                        Bow-wow.
    The watch-dogs bark:
                        Bow-wow.
ARIEL. Hark, hark! I hear
        The strain of strutting chanticleer
        Cry, Cock-a-diddle-dow.

FERDINAND. Where should this music be? I' the air or
    the earth?
It sounds no more; and, sure, it waits upon
Some god o' the island. Sitting on a bank,
Weeping again the King my father's wreck,
This music crept by me upon the waters,
Allaying both their fury and my passion
With its sweet air. Thence I have followed it,
Or it hath drawn me rather. But 'tis gone.
No, it begins again.

ARIEL sings

Full fathom five thy father lies;
    Of his bones are coral made;
Those are pearls that were his eyes.
    Nothing of him that doth fade
But doth suffer a sea-change
Into something rich and strange.
Sea-nymphs hourly ring his knell.

BURTHEN. Ding-dong.
ARIEL. Hark! now I hear them—Ding-dong, bell.

FERDINAND. The ditty does remember my drowned
    father.
This is no mortal business, nor no sound
That the earth owes. I hear it now above me.
PROSPERO. The fringed curtains of thine eye advance
And say what thou seest yond.
MIRANDA.   What is 't? A spirit?
Lord, how it looks about! Believe me, sir,
It carries a brave form. But 'tis a spirit.
PROSPERO. No, wench; it eats and sleeps and hath
    such senses
As we have, such. This gallant which thou seest
Was in the wreck; and, but he's something stained
With grief that's beauty's canker, thou mightst call
    him
A goodly person. He hath lost his fellows
And strays about to find 'em.
MIRANDA.   I might call him
A thing divine, for nothing natural
I ever saw so noble.
PROSPERO. [Aside] It goes on, I see,
As my soul prompts it. Spirit, fine spirit! I'll free thee
Within two days for this.

FERDINAND.   Most sure the goddess
  On whom these airs attend! Vouchsafe my prayer
  May know if you remain upon this island;
  And that you will some good instruction give
  How I may bear me here. My prime request,
  Which I do last pronounce, is, O you wonder,
  If you be maid or no?
MIRANDA.   No wonder, sir;
  But certainly a maid.
FERDINAND.   My language! Heavens!
  I am the best of them that speak this speech,
  Were I but where 'tis spoken.
PROSPERO.   How? The best?
  What wert thou, if the King of Naples heard thee?
FERDINAND. A single thing, as I am now, that wonders
  To hear thee speak of Naples. He does hear me;
  And that he does I weep. Myself am Naples,
  Who with mine eyes, never since at ebb, beheld
  The King my father wrecked.
MIRANDA.   Alack, for mercy!
FERDINAND. Yes, faith, and all his lords; the duke of
      Milan
  And his brave son being twain.
PROSPERO.   [Aside] The duke of Milan
  And his more braver daughter could control thee,
  If now 'twere fit to do 't. At the first sight
  They have changed eyes. Delicate Ariel,
  I'll set thee free for this. [To Ferdinand] A word,
      good sir;
  I fear you have done yourself some wrong: a word.
MIRANDA. Why speaks my father so ungently? This
  Is the third man that e'er I saw, the first
  That e'er I sighed for. Pity move my father
  To be inclined my way!
FERDINAND.   O, if a virgin,
  And your affection not gone forth, I'll make you
  The queen of Naples.
PROSPERO.   Soft, sir! One word more.
  [Aside] They are both in either's powers; but this
      swift business
  I must uneasy make, lest too light winning
  Make the prize light. [To Ferdinand] One word more;
      I charge thee
  That thou attend me. Thou dost here usurp
  The name thou owest not; and hast put thyself
  Upon this island as a spy, to win it
  From me, the lord on 't.
FERDINAND.   No, as I am a man.
MIRANDA. There's nothing ill can dwell in such a
      temple.
  If the ill spirit have so fair a house,
  Good things will strive to dwell with 't.
PROSPERO.   Follow me.
  Speak not you for him; he's a traitor. Come;
  I'll manacle thy neck and feet together.
  Sea-water shalt thou drink; thy food shall be

The fresh-brook muscles, withered roots and husks
Wherein the acorn cradled. Follow.
FERDINAND.   No;
  I will resist such entertainment till
  Mine enemy has more power.
                    Draws, and is charmed from moving
MIRANDA.   O dear father,
  Make not too rash a trial of him, for
  He's gentle and not fearful.
PROSPERO.   What? I say,
  My foot my tutor? Put thy sword up, traitor;
  Who mak'st a show but dar'st not strike, thy con-
      science
  Is so possessed with guilt. Come from thy ward,
  For I can here disarm thee with this stick
  And make thy weapon drop.
MIRANDA.   Beseech you, father.
PROSPERO. Hence! Hang not on my garments.
MIRANDA.   Sir, have pity;
  I'll be his surety.
PROSPERO.   Silence! One word more
  Shall make me chide thee, if not hate thee. What!
  An advocate for an impostor! Hush!
  Thou think'st there is no more such shapes as he,
  Having seen but him and Caliban. Foolish wench!
  To the most of men this is a Caliban
  And they to him are angels.
MIRANDA.   My affections
  Are then most humble; I have no ambition
  To see a goodlier man.
PROSPERO.   Come on; obey.
  Thy nerves are in their infancy again
  And have no vigour in them.
FERDINAND.   So they are;
  My spirits, as in a dream, are all bound up.
  My father's loss, the weakness which I feel,
  The wreck of all my friends, nor this man's threats,
  To whom I am subdued, are but light to me,
  Might I but through my prison once a day
  Behold this maid. All corners else o' the earth
  Let liberty make use of; space enough
  Have I in such a prison.
PROSPERO. [Aside] It works. [To Ferdinand] Come on.
  [To Ariel] Thou hast done well, fine Ariel! [To
      Ferdinand] Follow me.
  [To Ariel] Hark what thou else shalt do me.
MIRANDA.   Be of comfort;
  My father's of a better nature, sir,
  Than he appears by speech. This is unwonted
  Which now came from him.
PROSPERO.   Thou shalt be as free
  As mountain winds. But then exactly do
  All points of my command.
ARIEL.   To the syllable.
PROSPERO. Come, follow. Speak not for him.
                                          Exeunt

ACT II

SCENE I *Another part of the island*

Enter ALFONSO, SEBASTIAN,
ANTONIO, GONZALO, ADRIAN,
FRANCISCO, *and others*

GONZALO. Beseech you, sir, be merry; you have cause,
So have we all, of joy; for our escape
Is much beyond our loss. Our hint of woe
Is common: every day some sailor's wife,
The masters of some merchant and the merchant
Have just our theme of woe; but for the miracle,
I mean our preservation, few in millions
Can speak like us. Then wisely, good sir, weigh
Our sorrow with our comfort.

ALONSO.   Prithee, peace.

SEBASTIAN. He receives comfort like cold porridge.

ANTONIO. The visitor will not give him o'er so.

SEBASTIAN. Look, he's winding up the watch of his wit;
by and by it will strike.

GONZALO. Sir—

SEBASTIAN. One: tell.

GONZALO. When every grief is entertained that's offered,
Comes to the entertainer—

SEBASTIAN. A dollar.

GONZALO. Dolour comes to him, indeed. You have
spoken truer than you purposed.

SEBASTIAN. You have taken it wiselier than I meant you
should.

GONZALO. Therefore, my lord—

ANTONIO. Fie, what a spendthrift is he of his tongue!

ALONSO. I prithee, spare.

GONZALO. Well, I have done. But yet—

SEBASTIAN. He will be talking.

ANTONIO. Which, of he or Adrian, for a good wager,
first begins to crow?

SEBASTIAN. The old cock.

ANTONIO. The cockerel.

SEBASTIAN. Done. The wager?

ANTONIO. A laughter.

SEBASTIAN. A match!

ADRIAN. Though this island seem to be desert—

SEBASTIAN. Ha, ha, ha! So, you're paid.

ADRIAN. Uninhabitable and almost inaccessible—

SEBASTIAN. Yet—

ADRIAN. Yet—

ANTONIO. He could not miss 't.

ADRIAN. It must needs be of subtle, tender and delicate
temperance.

ANTONIO. Temperance was a delicate wench.

SEBASTIAN. Ay, and a subtle; as he most learnedly delivered.

ADRIAN. The air breathes upon us here most sweetly.

SEBASTIAN. As if it had lungs and rotten ones.

461

ANTONIO. Or as 'twere perfumed by a fen.

GONZALO. Here is everything advantageous to life.

ANTONIO. True; save means to live.

SEBASTIAN. Of that there's none, or little.

GONZALO. How lush and lusty the grass looks! How green!

ANTONIO. The ground indeed is tawny.

SEBASTIAN. With an eye of green in 't.

ANTONIO. He misses not much.

SEBASTIAN. No; he doth but mistake the truth totally.

GONZALO. But the rarity of it is—which is indeed almost beyond credit—

SEBASTIAN. As many vouched rarities are.

GONZALO. That our garments, being, as they were, drenched in the sea, hold notwithstanding their freshness and glosses, being rather new-dyed than stained with salt water.

ANTONIO. If but one of his pockets could speak, would it not say he lies?

SEBASTIAN. Ay, or very falsely pocket up his report.

GONZALO. Methinks our garments are now as fresh as when we put them on first in Afric, at the marriage of the King's fair daughter Claribel to the king of Tunis.

SEBASTIAN. 'Twas a sweet marriage, and we prosper well in our return.

ADRIAN. Tunis was never graced before with such a paragon to their queen.

GONZALO. Not since widow Dido's time.

ANTONIO. Widow! A pox o' that! How came that widow in? Widow Dido!

SEBASTIAN. What if he had said "widower Æneas" too? Good Lord, how you take it!

ADRIAN. "Widow Dido" said you? You make me study of that. She was of Carthage, not of Tunis.

GONZALO. This Tunis, sir, was Carthage.

ADRIAN. Carthage?

GONZALO. I assure you, Carthage.

SEBASTIAN. His word is more than the miraculous harp; he hath raised the wall and houses too.

ANTONIO. What impossible matter will he make easy next?

SEBASTIAN. I think he will carry this island home in his pocket and give it his son for an apple.

ANTONIO. And, sowing the kernels of it in the sea, bring forth more islands.

GONZALO. Ay.

ANTONIO. Why, in good time.

GONZALO. Sir, we were talking that our garments seem now as fresh as when we were at Tunis at the marriage of your daughter, who is now queen.

ANTONIO. And the rarest that e'er came there.

SEBASTIAN. Bate, I beseech you, widow Dido.

ANTONIO. O, widow Dido! Ay, widow Dido.

GONZALO. Is not, sir, my doublet as fresh as the first day I wore it? I mean, in a sort.

ANTONIO. That sort was well fished for.

GONZALO. When I wore it at your daughter's marriage?

ALONSO. You cram these words into mine ears against
The stomach of my sense. Would I had never
Married my daughter there! For, coming thence,
My son is lost and, in my rate, she too,
Who is so far from Italy removed
I ne'er again shall see her. O thou mine heir
Of Naples and of Milan, what strange fish
Hath made his meal on thee?

FRANCISCO.   Sir, he may live.
I saw him beat the surges under him,
And ride upon their backs; he trod the water,
Whose enmity he flung aside, and breasted
The surge most swoln that met him; his bold head
'Bove the contentious waves he kept, and oared
Himself with his good arms in lusty stroke
To the shore, that o'er his wave-worn basis bowed,
As stooping to relieve him. I not doubt
He came alive to land.

ALONSO.   No, no, he's gone.

SEBASTIAN. Sir, you may thank yourself for this great loss,
That would not bless our Europe with your daughter,
But rather lose her to an African;
Where she at least is banished from your eye,
Who hath cause to wet the grief on 't.

ALONSO.   Prithee, peace.

SEBASTIAN. You were kneeled to and importuned otherwise
By all of us, and the fair soul herself
Weighed between loathness and obedience, at
Which end o' the beam should bow. We have lost your son,
I fear, for ever. Milan and Naples have
More widows in them of this business' making
Than we bring men to comfort them.
The fault's your own.

ALONSO.   So is the dear'st o' the loss.

GONZALO. My lord Sebastian,
The truth you speak doth lack some gentleness
And time to speak it in. You rub the sore,
When you should bring the plaster.

SEBASTIAN.   Very well.

ANTONIO. And most chirurgeonly.

GONZALO. It is foul weather in us all, good sir,
When you are cloudy.

SEBASTIAN.   Foul weather?

ANTONIO.   Very foul.

GONZALO. Had I plantation of this isle, my lord—

ANTONIO. He'd sow 't with nettle-seed.

SEBASTIAN.   Or docks, or mallows.

GONZALO. And were the king on 't, what would I do?

SEBASTIAN. 'Scape being drunk for want of wine.

GONZALO. I' the commonwealth I would by contraries
Execute all things; for no kind of traffic
Would I admit; no name of magistrate;

Letters should not be known; riches, poverty,
And use of service, none; contract, succession,
Bourn, bound of land, tilth, vineyard, none;
No use of metal, corn, or wine, or oil;
No occupation; all men idle, all;
And women too, but innocent and pure;
No sovereignty—

SEBASTIAN.   Yet he would be king on 't.

ANTONIO. The latter end of his commonwealth forgets
the beginning.

GONZALO. All things in common nature should produce
Without sweat or endeavour: treason, felony,
Sword, pike, knife, gun, or need of any engine,
Would I not have; but nature should bring forth,
Of it own kind, all foison, all abundance,
To feed my innocent people.

SEBASTIAN. No marrying 'mong his subjects?

ANTONIO. None, man; all idle: whores and knaves.

GONZALO. I would with such perfection govern, sir,
To excel the golden age.

SEBASTIAN.   God save his majesty!

ANTONIO. Long live Gonzalo!

GONZALO.   And—do you mark me, sir?

ALONSO. Prithee, no more. Thou dost talk nothing
to me.

GONZALO. I do well believe your highness; and did it
to minister occasion to these gentlemen, who are of
such sensible and nimble lungs that they always use to
laugh at nothing.

ANTONIO. 'Twas you we laughed at.

GONZALO. Who in this kind of merry fooling am nothing
to you. So you may continue and laugh at nothing still.

ANTONIO. What a blow was there given!

SEBASTIAN. An it had not fallen flat-long.

GONZALO. You are gentlemen of brave mettle; you
would lift the moon out of her sphere, if she would
continue in it five weeks without changing.

Enter ARIEL, *invisible, playing solemn music*

SEBASTIAN. We would so, and then go a bat-fowling.

ANTONIO. Nay, good my lord, be not angry.

GONZALO. No, I warrant you; I will not adventure my
discretion so weakly. Will you laugh me asleep,
for I am very heavy?

ANTONIO. Go sleep, and hear us.

All sleep except ALONSO, SEBASTIAN, *and* ANTONIO

ALONSO. What, all so soon asleep! I wish mine eyes
Would, with themselves, shut up my thoughts. I find
They are inclined to do so.

SEBASTIAN.   Please you, sir,
Do not omit the heavy offer of it.
It seldom visits sorrow; when it doth,
It is a comforter.

ANTONIO.   We two, my lord,
Will guard your person while you take your rest,
And watch your safety.

ALONSO.   Thank you. Wondrous heavy.
        ALONSO *sleeps. Exit* ARIEL

SEBASTIAN. What a strange drowsiness possesses them!

ANTONIO. It is the quality o' the climate.

SEBASTIAN.   Why
Doth it not then our eyelids sink? I find not
Myself disposed to sleep.

ANTONIO.   Nor I; my spirits are nimble.
They fell together all, as by consent;
They dropped, as by a thunderstroke. What might,
Worthy Sebastian? O, what might?—No more—
And yet methinks I see it in thy face,
What thou shouldst be. The occasion speaks thee, and
My strong imagination sees a crown
Dropping upon thy head.

SEBASTIAN.   What, art thou waking?

ANTONIO. Do you not hear me speak?

SEBASTIAN.   I do; and surely
It is a sleepy language and thou speak'st
Out of thy sleep. What is it thou didst say?
This is a strange repose, to be asleep
With eyes wide open; standing, speaking, moving,
And yet so fast asleep.

ANTONIO.   Noble Sebastian,
Thou let'st thy fortune sleep—die, rather; wink'st
Whiles thou art waking.

SEBASTIAN.   Thou dost snore distinctly;
There's meaning in thy snores.

ANTONIO. I am more serious than my custom. You
Must be so too, if heed me; which to do
Trebles thee o'er.

SEBASTIAN.   Well, I am standing water.

ANTONIO. I'll teach you how to flow.

SEBASTIAN.   Do so. To ebb
Hereditary sloth instructs me.

ANTONIO.   O,
If you but knew how you the purpose cherish
Whiles thus you mock it! How, in stripping it,
You more invest it! Ebbing men, indeed,
Most often do so near the bottom run
By their own fear or sloth.

SEBASTIAN.   Prithee, say on:
The setting of thine eye and cheek proclaim
A matter from thee, and a birth indeed
Which throes thee much to yield.

ANTONIO.   Thus, sir:
Although this lord of weak remembrance, this,
Who shall be of as little memory
When he is earthed, hath here almost persuaded—
For he's a spirit of persuasion, only
Professes to persuade—the King his son's alive,
'Tis as impossible that he's undrowned
As he that sleeps here swims.

SEBASTIAN.   I have no hope
That he's undrowned.

ANTONIO.   O, out of that "no hope"

What great hope have you! No hope that way is
Another way so high a hope that even
Ambition cannot pierce a wink beyond,
But doubt discovery there. Will you grant with me
That Ferdinand is drowned?

SEBASTIAN.   He's gone.

ANTONIO.   Then, tell me,
Who's the next heir of Naples?

SEBASTIAN.   Claribel.

ANTONIO. She that is Queen of Tunis; she that dwells
Ten leagues beyond man's life; she that from Naples
Can have no note, unless the sun were post—
The man i' the moon 's too slow—till new-born chins
Be rough and razorable; she that—from whom?
We all were sea-swallowed, though some cast again,
And by that destiny to perform an act
Whereof what's past is prologue, what to come
In yours and my discharge.

SEBASTIAN.   What stuff is this! how say you?
'Tis true, my brother's daughter's Queen of Tunis;
So is she heir of Naples; 'twixt which regions
There is some space.

ANTONIO.   A space whose every cubit
Seems to cry out, "How shall that Claribel
Measure us back to Naples? Keep in Tunis,
And let Sebastian wake." Say, this were death
That now hath seized them; why, they were no worse
Than now they are. There be that can rule Naples
As well as he that sleeps; lords that can prate
As amply and unnecessarily
As this Gonzalo; I myself could make
A chough of as deep chat. O, that you bore
The mind that I do! What a sleep were this
For your advancement! Do you understand me?

SEBASTIAN. Methinks I do.

ANTONIO.   And how does your content
Tender your own good fortune?

SEBASTIAN.   I remember
You did supplant your brother Prospero.

ANTONIO.   True.
And look how well my garments sit upon me;
Much feater than before. My brother's servants
Were then my fellows; now they are my men.

SEBASTIAN. But, for your conscience?

ANTONIO. Ay, sir; where lies that? If 'twere a kibe,
'Twould put me to my slipper. But I feel not
This deity in my bosom. Twenty consciences,
That stand 'twixt me and Milan, candied be they
And melt ere they molest! Here lies your brother,
No better than the earth he lies upon,
If he were that which now he's like, that's dead;
Whom I, with this obedient steel, three inches of it,
Can lay to bed for ever; whiles you, doing thus,
To the perpetual wink for aye might put
This ancient morsel, this Sir Prudence, who
Should not upbraid our course. For all the rest,

They'll take suggestion as a cat laps milk;
They'll tell the clock to any business that
We say befits the hour.

SEBASTIAN.   Thy case, dear friend,
Shall be my precedent; as thou got'st Milan,
I'll come by Naples. Draw thy sword. One stroke
Shall free thee from the tribute which thou payest;
And I the King shall love thee.

ANTONIO.   Draw together;
And when I rear my hand, do you the like,
To fall it on Gonzalo.

SEBASTIAN.   O, but one word. *They talk apart*

Re-enter ARIEL, *invisible*

ARIEL. My master through his art foresees the danger
That you, his friend, are in; and sends me forth—
For else his project dies—to keep them living.

Sings in GONZALO's *ear*

While you here do snoring lie,
Open-eyed conspiracy
     His time doth take.
If of life you keep a care,
Shake off slumber, and beware.
     Awake, awake!

ANTONIO. Then let us both be sudden.

GONZALO.   Now, good angels
Preserve the King.   *They wake*

ALONSO. Why, how now? Ho, awake! Why are you
     drawn?
Wherefore this ghastly looking?

GONZALO.   What's the matter?

SEBASTIAN. Whiles we stood here securing your repose,
Even now, we heard a hollow burst of bellowing
Like bulls, or rather lions. Did 't not wake you?
It struck mine ear most terribly.

ALONSO.   I heard nothing.

ANTONIO. O, 'twas a din to fright a monster's ear,
To make an earthquake! Sure, it was the roar
Of a whole herd of lions.

ALONSO.   Heard you this, Gonzalo?

GONZALO. Upon mine honour, sir, I heard a humming,
And that a strange one too, which did awake me.
I shaked you, sir, and cried. As mine eyes opened,
I saw their weapons drawn. There was a noise,
That's verily. 'Tis best we stand upon our guard,
Or that we quit this place. Let's draw our weapons.

ALONSO. Lead off this ground; and let's make further
     search
For my poor son.

GONZALO. Heavens keep him from these beasts!
For he is, sure, i' the island.

ALONSO.   Lead away.

ARIEL. Prospero my lord shall know what I have done.
So, King, go safely on to seek thy son.

Exeunt

SCENE II *Another part of the island*

Enter CALIBAN *with a burden of wood*

A noise of thunder heard

CALIBAN. All the infections that the sun sucks up
From bogs, fens, flats, on Prosper fall and make him
By inch-meal a disease! His spirits hear me
And yet I needs must curse. But they'll nor pinch,
Fright me with urchin-shows, pitch me i' the mire,
Nor lead me, like a firebrand, in the dark
Out of my way, unless he bid 'em; but
For every trifle are they set upon me;
Sometime like apes that mow and chatter at me
And after bite me, then like hedgehogs which
Lie tumbling in my barefoot way and mount
Their pricks at my footfall. Sometime am I
All wound with adders who with cloven tongues
Do hiss me into madness.

Enter TRINCULO

Lo, now, lo!
Here comes a spirit of his, and to torment me
For bringing wood in slowly. I'll fall flat;
Perchance he will not mind me.

TRINCULO. Here's neither bush nor shrub, to bear off
any weather at all, and another storm brewing; I hear
it sing i' the wind. Yond same black cloud, yond huge
one, looks like a foul bombard that would shed his
liquor. If it should thunder as it did before, I know
not where to hide my head. Yond same cloud cannot
choose but fall by pailfuls. What have we here? A man
or a fish? Dead or alive? A fish—he smells like a fish;
a very ancient and fish-like smell; a kind of not of the
newest Poor John. A strange fish! Were I in England
now, as once I was, and had but this fish painted, not
a holiday fool there but would give a piece of silver.
There would this monster make a man; any strange
beast there makes a man. When they will not give a
doit to relieve a lame beggar, they will lay out ten to
see a dead Indian. Legged like a man! And his fins like
arms! Warm o' my troth! I do now let loose my
opinion; hold it no longer: this is no fish, but an
islander, that hath lately suffered by a thunderbolt.
[*Thunder*] Alas, the storm is come again! My best
way is to creep under his gaberdine; there is no other
shelter hereabout. Misery acquaints a man with

strange bedfellows. I will here shroud till the dregs of the storm be past.

Enter STEPHANO, *singing; a bottle in his hand*

STEPHANO. I shall no more to sea, to sea,
    Here shall I die ashore—

This is a very scurvy tune to sing at a man's funeral: well, here's my comfort.   *Drinks*
Sings

    The master, the swabber, the boatswain and I,
        The gunner and his mate
    Loved Mall, Meg and Marian and Margery,
        But none of us cared for Kate;
        For she had a tongue with a tang,
        Would cry to a sailor, Go hang!
    She loved not the savour of tar nor of pitch,
    Yet a tailor might scratch her where'er she did itch.
    Then to sea, boys, and let her go hang!

This is a scurvy tune too; but here's my comfort.   *Drinks*

CALIBAN. Do not torment me. Oh!

STEPHANO. What's the matter? Have we devils here? Do you put tricks upon 's with savages and men of Ind, ha? I have not 'scaped drowning to be afeard now of your four legs; for it hath been said, As proper a man as ever went on four legs cannot make him give ground; and it shall be said so again while Stephano breathes at nostrils.

CALIBAN. The spirit torments me. Oh!

STEPHANO. This is some monster of the isle with four legs, who hath got, as I take it, an ague. Where the devil should he learn our language? I will give him some relief, if it be but for that. If I can recover him and keep him tame and get to Naples with him, he's a present for any emperor that ever trod on neat's-leather.

CALIBAN. Do not torment me, prithee; I'll bring my wood home faster.

STEPHANO. He's in his fit now and does not talk after the wisest. He shall taste of my bottle. If he have never drunk wine afore, it will go near to remove his fit. If I can recover him and keep him tame, I will not take too much for him; he shall pay for him that hath him, and that soundly.

CALIBAN. Thou dost me yet but little hurt; thou wilt anon, I know it by thy trembling. Now Prosper works upon thee.

STEPHANO. Come on your ways; open your mouth; here is that which will give language to you, cat. Open your mouth; this will shake your shaking, I can tell you, and that soundly. You cannot tell who's your friend. Open your chaps again.

TRINCULO. I should know that voice. It should be— but he is drowned; and these are devils. O defend me!

STEPHANO. Four legs and two voices—a most delicate monster! His forward voice now is to speak well of his friend; his backward voice is to utter foul speeches and to detract. If all the wine in my bottle will recover him, I will help his ague. Come. Amen! I will pour some in thy other mouth.

TRINCULO. Stephano!

STEPHANO. Doth thy other mouth call me? Mercy, mercy! This is a devil, and no monster. I will leave him; I have no long spoon.

TRINCULO. Stephano! If thou beest Stephano, touch me and speak to me; for I am Trinculo—be not afeard— thy good friend Trinculo.

STEPHANO. If thou beest Trinculo, come forth. I'll pull thee by the lesser legs. If any be Trinculo's legs, these are they. Thou art very Trinculo indeed! How camest thou to be the siege of this moon-calf? Can he vent Trinculos?

TRINCULO. I took him to be killed with a thunder-stroke. But art thou not drowned, Stephano? I hope now thou art not drowned. Is the storm overblown? I hid me under the dead moon-calf's gaberdine for fear of the storm. And art thou living, Stephano? O Stephano, two Neapolitans 'scaped!

STEPHANO. Prithee, do not turn me about; my stomach is not constant.

CALIBAN. [*Aside*] These be fine things, an if they be not sprites.
That's a brave god and bears celestial liquor.
I will kneel to him.

STEPHANO. How didst thou 'scape? How camest thou hither? Swear by this bottle how thou camest hither. I escaped upon a butt of sack which the sailors heaved o'erboard. By this bottle! which I made of the bark of a tree with mine own hands since I was cast ashore.

CALIBAN. I'll swear upon that bottle to be thy true subject; for the liquor is not earthly.

STEPHANO. Here; swear then how thou escapedst.

TRINCULO. Swum ashore, man, like a duck. I can swim like a duck, I'll be sworn.

STEPHANO. Here, kiss the book. Though thou canst swim like a duck, thou art made like a goose.

TRINCULO. O Stephano, hast any more of this?

STEPHANO. The whole butt, man. My cellar is in a rock by the sea-side where my wine is hid. How now, moon-calf! How does thine ague?

CALIBAN. Hast thou not dropped from heaven?

STEPHANO. Out o' the moon, I do assure thee. I was the man i' the moon when time was.

CALIBAN. I have seen thee in her and I do adore thee. My mistress showed me thee, and thy dog, and thy bush.

STEPHANO. Come, swear to that; kiss the book. I will furnish it anon with new contents. Swear.

TRINCULO. By this good light, this is a very shallow monster! I afeard of him! A very weak monster! The

man i' the moon! A most poor credulous monster!
Well drawn, monster, in good sooth!

CALIBAN. I'll show thee every fertile inch o' th' island;
And I will kiss thy foot. I prithee, be my god.

TRINCULO. By this light, a most perfidious and drunken
monster! When 's god 's asleep, he'll rob his bottle.

CALIBAN. I'll kiss thy foot; I'll swear myself thy subject.

STEPHANO. Come on then; down, and swear.

TRINCULO. I shall laugh myself to death at this puppy-
headed monster. A most scurvy monster! I could find
in my heart to beat him—

STEPHANO. Come, kiss.

TRINCULO. But that the poor monster's in drink.
An abominable monster!

CALIBAN. I'll show thee the best springs; I'll pluck
thee berries;
I'll fish for thee and get thee wood enough.
A plague upon the tyrant that I serve!
I'll bear him no more sticks, but follow thee,
Thou wondrous man.

TRINCULO. A most ridiculous monster, to make a
wonder of a poor drunkard!

CALIBAN. I prithee, let me bring thee where crabs grow;
And I with my long nails will dig thee pig-nuts;

Show thee a jay's nest and instruct thee how
To snare the nimble marmoset; I'll bring thee
To clustering filberts and sometimes I'll get thee
Young scamels from the rock. Wilt thou go with me?

STEPHANO. I prithee now, lead the way without any
more talking. Trinculo, the King and all our company
else being drowned, we will inherit here. Here; bear
my bottle. Fellow Trinculo, we'll fill him by and by
again.

CALIBAN. [Sings drunkenly]

Farewell, master; farewell, farewell!

TRINCULO. A howling monster; a drunken monster!

CALIBAN. No more dams I'll make for fish;
Nor fetch in firing
At requiring;
Nor scape trencher, nor wash dish.
'Ban, 'Ban, Cacaliban
Has a new master; get a new man.

Freedom, hey-day! hey-day, freedom! freedom, hey-
day, freedom!

STEPHANO. O brave monster! Lead the way.

Exeunt

ACT III

SCENE I *Before* PROSPERO'S *cell*

Enter FERDINAND, *bearing a log*

FERDINAND. There be some sports are painful, and their
   labour
  Delight in them sets off. Some kinds of baseness
  Are nobly undergone and most poor matters
  Point to rich ends. This my mean task
  Would be as heavy to me as odious, but
  The mistress which I serve quickens what 's dead
  And makes my labours pleasures. O, she is
  Ten times more gentle than her father's crabbed,
  And he's composed of harshness. I must remove
  Some thousands of these logs and pile them up,
  Upon a sore injunction. My sweet mistress
  Weeps when she sees me work, and says, such baseness
  Had never like executor. I forget:
  But these sweet thoughts do even refresh my labours,
  Most busy lest, when I do it.

Enter MIRANDA;
and PROSPERO *at a distance, unseen*

MIRANDA.   Alas, now, pray you,
  Work not so hard. I would the lightning had
  Burnt up those logs that you are enjoined to pile!
  Pray, set it down and rest you. When this burns,

  'Twill weep for having wearied you. My father
  Is hard at study; pray now, rest yourself;
  He's safe for these three hours.
FERDINAND.   O most dear mistress,
  The sun will set before I shall discharge
  What I must strive to do.
MIRANDA.   If you'll sit down,
  I'll bear your logs the while. Pray, give me that;
  I'll carry it to the pile.
FERDINAND.   No, precious creature;
  I had rather crack my sinews, break my back,
  Than you should such dishonour undergo,
  While I sit lazy by.
MIRANDA.   It would become me
  As well as it does you. And I should do it
  With much more ease; for my good will is to it,
  And yours it is against.
PROSPERO.   Poor worm, thou art infected!
  This visitation shows it.
MIRANDA.   You look wearily.
FERDINAND. No, noble mistress; 'tis fresh morning
   with me
  When you are by at night. I do beseech you—

Chiefly that I might set it in my prayers—
What is your name?

MIRANDA.   Miranda.—O my father,
I have broke your hest to say so!

FERDINAND.   Admired Miranda!
Indeed the top of admiration! Worth
What's dearest to the world! Full many a lady
I have eyed with best regard and many a time
The harmony of their tongues hath into bondage
Brought my too diligent ear. For several virtues
Have I liked several women; never any
With so full soul, but some defect in her
Did quarrel with the noblest grace she owed
And put it to the foil. But you, O you,
So perfect and so peerless, are created
Of every creature's best!

MIRANDA.   I do not know
One of my sex; no woman's face remember,
Save, from my glass, mine own; nor have I seen
More that I may call men than you, good friend,
And my dear father. How features are abroad,
I am skilless of; but, by my modesty,
The jewel in my dower, I would not wish
Any companion in the world but you,
Nor can imagination form a shape,
Besides yourself, to like of. But I prattle
Something too wildly and my father's precepts
I therein do forget.

FERDINAND.   I am in my condition
A prince, Miranda; I do think, a king;
I would, not so!—and would no more endure
This wooden slavery than to suffer
The flesh-fly blow my mouth. Hear my soul speak:
The very instant that I saw you, did
My heart fly to your service; there resides,
To make me slave to it; and for your sake
Am I this patient log-man.

MIRANDA.   Do you love me?

FERDINAND. O heaven, O earth, bear witness to this sound
And crown what I profess with kind event
If I speak true! If hollowly, invert
What best is boded me to mischief! I
Beyond all limit of what else i' the world
Do love, prize, honour you.

MIRANDA.   I am a fool
To weep at what I am glad of.

PROSPERO.   Fair encounter
Of two most rare affections! Heavens rain grace
On that which breeds between 'em!

FERDINAND.   Wherefore weep you?

MIRANDA. At mine unworthiness that dare not offer
What I desire to give, and much less take
What I shall die to want. But this is trifling;
And all the more it seeks to hide itself,
The bigger bulk it shows. Hence, bashful cunning!
And prompt me, plain and holy innocence!
I am your wife, if you will marry me;
If not, I'll die your maid. To be your fellow
You may deny me; but I'll be your servant,
Whether you will or no.

FERDINAND.   My mistress, dearest;
And I thus humble ever.

MIRANDA.   My husband, then?

FERDINAND. Ay, with a heart as willing
As bondage e'er of freedom. Here's my hand.

MIRANDA. And mine, with my heart in 't. And now farewell
Till half an hour hence.

FERDINAND.   A thousand thousand!

Exeunt FERDINAND *and* MIRANDA

PROSPERO. So glad of this as they I cannot be,
Who are surprised withal; but my rejoicing
At nothing can be more. I'll to my book,
For yet ere suppertime must I perform
Much business appertaining.   *Exit*

SCENE II *Another part of the island*

Enter CALIBAN, STEPHANO, *and* TRINCULO

STEPHANO. Tell not me; when the butt is out, we will drink water; not a drop before. Therefore bear up, and board 'em. Servant-monster, drink to me.

TRINCULO. Servant-monster! The folly of this island! They say there's but five upon this isle. We are three of them; if th' other two be brained like us, the state totters.

STEPHANO. Drink, servant-monster, when I bid thee. Thy eyes are almost set in thy head.

TRINCULO. Where should they be set else? He were a brave monster indeed, if they were set in his tail.

STEPHANO. My man-monster hath drowned his tongue in sack. For my part, the sea cannot drown me; I swam, ere I could recover the shore, five and thirty leagues off and on. By this light, thou shalt be my lieutenant, monster, or my standard.

TRINCULO. Your lieutenant, if you list; he's no standard.

STEPHANO. We'll not run, Monsieur Monster.

TRINCULO. Nor go neither; but you'll lie like dogs and yet say nothing neither.

STEPHANO. Moon-calf, speak once in thy life, if thou beest a good moon-calf.

CALIBAN. How does thy honour? Let me lick thy shoe. I'll not serve him; he is not valiant.

TRINCULO. Thou liest, most ignorant monster. I am in case to justle a constable. Why, thou deboshed fish, thou, was there ever man a coward that hath drunk so much sack as I today? Wilt thou tell a monstrous lie, being but half a fish and half a monster?

CALIBAN. Lo, how he mocks me! Wilt thou let him, my lord?

TRINCULO. "Lord" quoth he! That a monster should be such a natural!

CALIBAN. Lo, lo, again! Bite him to death, I prithee.

STEPHANO. Trinculo, keep a good tongue in your head. If you prove a mutineer—the next tree! The poor monster's my subject and he shall not suffer indignity.

CALIBAN. I thank my noble lord. Wilt thou be pleased to hearken once again to the suit I made to thee?

STEPHANO. Marry, will I. Kneel and repeat it; I will stand, and so shall Trinculo.

Enter ARIEL, *invisible*

CALIBAN. As I told thee before, I am subject to a tyrant, a sorcerer, that by his cunning hath cheated me of the island.

ARIEL. Thou liest.

CALIBAN. Thou liest, thou jesting monkey, thou. I would my valiant master would destroy thee! I do not lie.

STEPHANO. Trinculo, if you trouble him any more in 's tale, by this hand, I will supplant some of your teeth.

TRINCULO. Why, I said nothing.

STEPHANO. Mum, then, and no more. Proceed.

CALIBAN. I say, by sorcery he got this isle;
From me he got it. If thy greatness will
Revenge it on him—for I know thou darest,
But this thing dare not—

STEPHANO. That's most certain.

CALIBAN. Thou shalt be lord of it and I'll serve thee.

STEPHANO. How now shall this be compassed? Canst thou bring me to the party?

CALIBAN. Yea, yea, my lord. I'll yield him thee asleep,
Where thou mayst knock a nail into his head.

ARIEL. Thou liest; thou canst not.

CALIBAN. What a pied ninny's this! Thou scurvy patch!
I do beseech thy greatness, give him blows
And take his bottle from him. When that's gone
He shall drink nought but brine; for I'll not show him
Where the quick freshes are.

STEPHANO. Trinculo, run into no further danger. Interrupt the monster one word further, and, by this hand, I'll turn my mercy out o' doors and make a stock-fish of thee.

TRINCULO. Why, what did I? I did nothing. I'll go farther off.

STEPHANO. Didst thou not say he lied?

ARIEL. Thou liest.

STEPHANO. Do I so? Take thou that.

Beats TRINCULO

As you like this, give me the lie another time.

TRINCULO. I did not give the lie. Out o' your wits and hearing too? A pox o' your bottle! This can sack and drinking do. A murrain on your monster, and the devil take your fingers!

CALIBAN. Ha, ha, ha!

STEPHANO. Now, forward with your tale. Prithee, stand farther off.

CALIBAN. Beat him enough. After a little time
I'll beat him too.

STEPHANO. Stand farther. Come, proceed.

CALIBAN. Why, as I told thee, 'tis a custom with him
I' th' afternoon to sleep. There thou mayst brain him,
Having first seized his books, or with a log
Batter his skull, or paunch him with a stake,
Or cut his wezand with thy knife. Remember
First to possess his books; for without them
He's but a sot, as I am, nor hath not
One spirit to command. They all do hate him
As rootedly as I. Burn but his books.
He has brave utensils—for so he calls them—
Which, when he has a house, he'll deck withal.
And that most deeply to consider is
The beauty of his daughter; he himself
Calls her a nonpareil. I never saw a woman,
But only Sycorax my dam and she;

But she as far surpasseth Sycorax
As great'st does least.

STEPHANO. Is it so brave a lass?

CALIBAN. Ay, lord; she will become thy bed, I warrant.
And bring thee forth brave brood.

STEPHANO. Monster, I will kill this man. His daughter and I will be king and queen—save our graces!—and Trinculo and thyself shall be viceroys. Dost thou like the plot, Trinculo?

TRINCULO. Excellent.

STEPHANO. Give me thy hand. I am sorry I beat thee; but, while thou livest, keep a good tongue in thy head.

CALIBAN. Within this half hour will he be asleep.
Wilt thou destroy him then?

STEPHANO. Ay, on mine honour.

ARIEL. This will I tell my master.

CALIBAN. Thou makest me merry; I am full of pleasure.
Let us be jocund. Will you troll the catch
You taught me but while-ere?

STEPHANO. At thy request, monster, I will do reason, any reason. Come on, Trinculo, let us sing. *Sings*

Flout 'em and scout 'em
And scout 'em and flout 'em;
Thought is free.

CALIBAN. That's not the tune.

ARIEL *plays the tune on a tabor and pipe*

STEPHANO. What is this same?

TRINCULO. This is the tune of our catch, played by the picture of Nobody.

STEPHANO. If thou beest a man, show thyself in thy likeness. If thou beest a devil, take 't as thou list.

TRINCULO. O, forgive me my sins!

STEPHANO. He that dies pays all debts. I defy thee. Mercy upon us!

CALIBAN. Art thou afeard?

STEPHANO. No, monster, not I.

CALIBAN. Be not afeard; the isle is full of noises,
Sounds and sweet airs, that give delight and hurt not.
Sometimes a thousand twangling instruments
Will hum about mine ears, and sometime voices
That, if I then had waked after long sleep,
Will make me sleep again. And then, in dreaming,
The clouds methought would open and show riches
Ready to drop upon me, that, when I waked,
I cried to dream again.

STEPHANO. This will prove a brave kingdom to me, where I shall have my music for nothing.

CALIBAN. When Prospero is destroyed.

STEPHANO. That shall be by and by. I remember the story.

TRINCULO. The sound is going away; let's follow it, and after do our work.

STEPHANO. Lead, monster; we'll follow. I would I could see this taborer; he lays it on.

TRINCULO. Wilt come? I'll follow, Stephano. *Exeunt*

SCENE III *Another part of the island*

Enter ALONSO, SEBASTIAN, ANTONIO, GONZALO, ADRIAN, FRANCISCO, *and others*

GONZALO. By'r lakin, I can go no further, sir;
  My old bones ache. Here's a maze trod indeed
  Through forthrights and meanders! By your patience,
  I needs must rest me.
ALONSO.   Old lord, I cannot blame thee,
  Who am myself attached with weariness,
  To the dulling of my spirits. Sit down, and rest.
  Even here I will put off my hope and keep it
  No longer for my flatterer. He is drowned
  Whom thus we stray to find, and the sea mocks
  Our frustrate search on land. Well, let him go.
ANTONIO. [*Aside to Sebastian*] I am right glad that he's
    so out of hope.
  Do not, for one repulse, forego the purpose
  That you resolved to effect.
SEBASTIAN. [*Aside to Antonio*]   The next advantage
  Will we take throughly.
ANTONIO [*Aside to Sebastian*] Let it be tonight;
  For, now they are oppressed with travel, they
  Will not, nor cannot, use such vigilance
  As when they are fresh.
SEBASTIAN. [*Aside to Antonio*] I say, tonight: no more.
                          Solemn and strange music
ALONSO. What harmony is this? My good friends, hark!
GONZALO. Marvellous sweet music!

Enter PROSPERO *above, invisible. Enter several strange
  Shapes, bringing in a banquet; they dance about it with
  gentle actions of salutation; and, inviting the King, &c.
  to eat, they depart*

ALONSO. Give us kind keepers, heavens! What were
    these?
SEBASTIAN. A living drollery. Now I will believe
  That there are unicorns, that in Arabia
  There is one tree, the phoenix' throne, one phoenix
  At this hour reigning there.
ANTONIO.   I'll believe both;
  And what does else want credit, come to me,
  And I'll be sworn 'tis true. Travellers ne'er did lie,
  Though fools at home condemn 'em.
GONZALO.   If in Naples
  I should report this now, would they believe me?
  If I should say, I saw such islanders—
  For, certes, these are people of the island—
  Who, though they are of monstrous shape, yet, note,
  Their manners are more gentle-kind than of
  Our human generation you shall find
  Many, nay, almost any.
PROSPERO.   [*Aside*] Honest lord,
  Thou hast said well; for some of you there present
  Are worse than devils.
ALONSO.   I cannot too much muse
  Such shapes, such gesture and such sound, expressing,

Although they want the use of tongue, a kind
  Of excellent dumb discourse.
PROSPERO.   [*Aside*] Praise in departing.
FRANCISCO. They vanished strangely.
SEBASTIAN.   No matter, since
  They have left their viands behind; for we have
    stomachs.
  Will 't please you taste of what is here?
ALONSO.   Not I.
GONZALO. Faith sir, you need not fear. When we
    were boys,
  Who would believe that there were mountaineers
  Dew-lapped like bulls, whose throats had hanging
    at 'em
  Wallets of flesh? Or that there were such men
  Whose heads stood in their breasts? Which now we
    find
  Each putter-out of five for one will bring us
  Good warrant of.
ALONSO.   I will stand to and feed,
  Although my last. No matter, since I feel
  The best is past. Brother, my lord the duke,
  Stand to and do as we.

          Thunder and lightning.
        Enter ARIEL, *like a harpy;*
        claps his wings upon the table;
  and, with a quaint device, the banquet vanishes

ARIEL. You are three men of sin, whom Destiny,
  That hath to instrument this lower world
  And what is in 't, the never-surfeited sea
  Hath caused to belch up you; and on this island
  Where man doth not inhabit, you 'mongst men
  Being most unfit to live. I have made you mad;
  And even with such-like valour men hang and drown
  Their proper selves.
        ALONSO, SEBASTIAN &c. *draw their swords*
              You fools! I and my fellows
  Are ministers of Fate. The elements,
  Of whom your swords are tempered, may as well
  Wound the loud winds, or with bemocked-at stabs
  Kill the still-closing waters, as diminish
  One dowle that's in my plume. My fellow-ministers
  Are like invulnerable. If you could hurt,
  Your swords are now too massy for your strengths
  And will not be uplifted. But remember—
  For that's my business to you—that you three
  From Milan did supplant good Prospero;
  Exposed unto the sea, which hath requit it,
  Him and his innocent child; for which foul deed
  The powers, delaying, not forgetting, have
  Incensed the seas and shores, yea, all the creatures,
  Against your peace. Thee of thy son, Alonso,

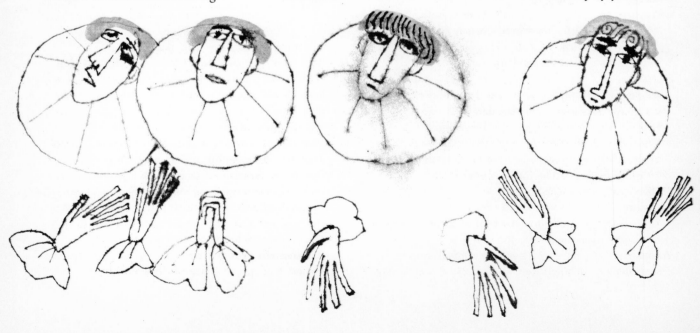

They have bereft; and do pronounce by me
Lingering perdition, worse than any death
Can be at once, shall step by step attend
You and your ways; whose wraths to guard you from—
Which here, in this most desolate isle, else falls
Upon your heads—is nothing but heart-sorrow
And a clear life ensuing.

He vanishes in thunder;
then, to soft music, enter the Shapes again,
and dance, with mocks and mows,
and carrying out the table

PROSPERO. Bravely the figure of this harpy hast thou
Performed, my Ariel; a grace it had, devouring.
Of my instruction hast thou nothing bated
In what thou hadst to say. So, with good life
And observation strange, my meaner ministers
Their several kinds have done. My high charms work
And these mine enemies are all knit up
In their distractions; they now are in my power;
And in these fits I leave them, while I visit
Young Ferdinand, whom they suppose is drowned,
And his and mine loved darling.   *Exit above*

GONZALO. I' the name of something holy, sir, why
    stand you
  In this strange stare?
ALONSO.   O, it is monstrous, monstrous!
  Methought the billows spoke and told me of it;
  The winds did sing it to me, and the thunder,
  That deep and dreadful organ-pipe, pronounced
  The name of Prosper. It did bass my trespass.
  Therefore my son i' the ooze is bedded, and
  I'll seek him deeper than e'er plummet sounded
  And with him there lie mudded.   *Exit*
SEBASTIAN.   But one fiend at a time,
  I'll fight their legions o'er.
ANTONIO.   I'll be thy second.
                    Exeunt SEBASTIAN *and* ANTONIO
GONZALO. All three of them are desperate; their great
    guilt,
  Like poison given to work a great time after,
  Now 'gins to bite the spirits. I do beseech you
  That are of suppler joints, follow them swiftly
  And hinder them from what this ecstasy
  May now provoke them to.
ADRIAN.   Follow, I pray you. *Exeunt*

ACT IV

SCENE I *Before* PROSPERO's *cell*

Enter PROSPERO, FERDINAND, *and* MIRANDA

PROSPERO. If I have too austerely punished you,
Your compensation makes amends, for I
Have given you here a thread of mine own life,
Or that for which I live; who once again
I tender to thy hand. All thy vexations
Were but my trials of thy love, and thou
Hast strangely stood the test. Here, afore Heaven,
I ratify this my rich gift. O Ferdinand,
Do not smile at me that I boast her off,
For thou shalt find she will outstrip all praise
And make it halt behind her.

FERDINAND.   I do believe it
Against an oracle.

PROSPERO. Then, as my gift and thine own acquisition
Worthily purchased, take my daughter; but
If thou dost break her virgin-knot before
All sanctimonious ceremonies may
With full and holy rite be ministered,
No sweet aspersion shall the heavens let fall
To make this contract grow; but barren hate,
Sour-eyed disdain and discord shall bestrew
The union of your bed with weeds so loathly
That you shall hate it both. Therefore take heed,
As Hymen's lamps shall light you.

FERDINAND.   As I hope
For quiet days, fair issue and long life,
With such love as 'tis now, the murkiest den,
The most opportune place, the strong'st suggestion
Our worser genius can, shall never melt
Mine honour into lust, to take away
The edge of that day's celebration
When I shall think, or Phoebus' steeds are foundered,
Or Night kept chained below.

PROSPERO.   Fairly spoke.
Sit then and talk with her; she is thine own.
What, Ariel! My industrious servant, Ariel!

Enter ARIEL

ARIEL. What would my potent master? Here I am.

PROSPERO. Thou and thy meaner fellows your last
service
Did worthily perform; and I must use you
In such another trick. Go bring the rabble,
O'er whom I give thee power, here to this place.
Incite them to quick motion; for I must
Bestow upon the eyes of this young couple
Some vanity of mine art. It is my promise,
And they expect it from me.

ARIEL.   Presently?

PROSPERO. Ay, with a twink.

ARIEL.   Before you can say "come" and "go,"
And breathe twice and cry "so, so,"
Each one, tripping on his toe,
Will be here with mop and mow.
Do you love me, master? no?

PROSPERO. Dearly, my delicate Ariel. Do not approach
Till thou dost hear me call.

ARIEL.   Well, I conceive.   *Exit*

PROSPERO. Look thou be true; do not give dalliance
Too much the rein. The strongest oaths are straw
To the fire i' the blood. Be more abstemious,
Or else, good night your vow!

FERDINAND.   I warrant you, sir;
The white cold virgin snow upon my heart
Abates the ardour of my liver.

PROSPERO.   Well.
Now come, my Ariel! Bring a corollary,
Rather than want a spirit. Appear, and pertly!
No tongue! all eyes! be silent.   *Soft music*

Enter IRIS

IRIS. Ceres, most bounteous lady, thy rich leas
Of wheat, rye, barley, vetches, oats and peas;
Thy turfy mountains, where live nibbling sheep,
And flat meads thatched with stover, them to keep;
Thy banks with pioned and twilled brims,
Which spongy April at thy hest betrims,
To make cold nymphs chaste crowns; and thy broom-
groves,
Whose shadow the dismissed bachelor loves,
Being lasslorn; thy pole-clipt vineyard;
And thy sea-marge, sterile and rocky-hard,
Where thou thyself dost air; the queen o' the sky,
Whose watery arch and messenger am I,
Bids thee leave these, and with her sovereign grace,
Here on this grass plot, in this very place,
To come and sport—her peacocks fly amain—
Approach, rich Ceres, her to entertain.

Enter CERES

CERES. Hail, many-coloured messenger, that ne'er
Dost disobey the wife of Jupiter;
Who with they saffron wings upon my flowers
Diffusest honey-drops, refreshing showers,
And with each end of thy blue bow dost crown
My bosky acres and my unshrubbed down,
Rich scarf to my proud earth; why hath thy queen
Summoned me hither, to this short-grassed green?

IRIS. A contract of true love to celebrate;
And some donation freely to estate
On the blest lovers.

CERES.   Tell me, heavenly bow,

FERDINAND. This is a most majestic vision, and
  Harmonious charmingly. May I be bold
  To think these spirits?
PROSPERO.   Spirits, which by mine art
  I have from their confines called to enact
  My present fancies.
FERDINAND.   Let me live here ever;
  So rare a wondered father and a wife
  Makes this place Paradise.
      JUNO *and* CERES *whisper, and send* IRIS *on employment*
PROSPERO.   Sweet, now, silence!
  Juno and Ceres whisper seriously;
  There's something else to do. Hush, and be mute,
  Or else our spell is marred.
IRIS. You nymphs, called Naiads, of the windring brooks,
  With your sedged crowns and ever-harmless looks,
  Leave your crisp channels and on this green land
  Answer your summons; Juno does command.
  Come, temperate nymphs, and help to celebrate
  A contract of true love; be not too late.

        Enter certain Nymphs

  You sunburnt sicklemen, of August weary,
  Come hither from the furrow and be merry.
  Make holiday; your rye-straw hats put on
  And these fresh nymphs encounter every one
  In country footing.

      Enter certain Reapers, properly habited.
    They join with the Nymphs in a graceful dance;
    towards the end whereof PROSPERO *starts suddenly,*
    and speaks; after which, to a strange, hollow, and
        confused noise, they heavily vanish.

PROSPERO. [*Aside*] I had forgot that foul conspiracy
  Of the beast Caliban and his confederates
  Against my life. The minute of their plot
  Is almost come. [*To the Spirits*] Well done! Avoid;
    no more!
FERDINAND. This is strange; your father's in some
    passion
  That works him strongly.
MIRANDA.   Never till this day
  Saw I him touched with anger so distempered.
PROSPERO. You do look, my son, in a moved sort,
  As if you were dismayed. Be cheerful, sir.
  Our revels now are ended. These our actors,
  As I foretold you, were all spirits and
  Are melted into air, into thin air;
  And, like the baseless fabric of this vision,
  The cloud-capped towers, the gorgeous palaces,
  The solemn temples, the great globe itself,
  Yea, all which it inherit, shall dissolve
  And, like this insubstantial pageant faded,
  Leave not a rack behind. We are such stuff
  As dreams are made on, and our little life
  Is rounded with a sleep. Sir, I am vexed;

If Venus or her son, as thou dost know,
  Do now attend the Queen? Since they did plot
  The means that dusky Dis my daughter got,
  Her and her blind boy's scandaled company
  I have forsworn.
IRIS.   Of her society
  Be not afraid. I met her deity
  Cutting the clouds towards Paphos and her son
  Dove-drawn with her. Here thought they to have done
  Some wanton charm upon this man and maid,
  Whose vows are, that no bedright shall be paid
  Till Hymen's torch be lighted. But in vain;
  Mars's hot minion is returned again;
  Her waspish-headed son has broke his arrows,
  Swears he will shoot no more but play with sparrows
  And be a boy right out.
CERES.   High'st queen of state,
  Great Juno, comes; I know her by her gait.

        Enter JUNO

JUNO. How does my bounteous sister? Go with me
  To bless this twain, that they may prosperous be
  And honoured in their issue.   *They sing*
JUNO. Honour, riches, marriage-blessing,
  Long continuance, and increasing,
  Hourly joys be still upon you!
  Juno sings her blessings on you.
CERES. Earth's increase, foison plenty,
  Barns and garners never empty,
  Vines with clustering bunches growing,
  Plants with goodly burthen bowing.
  Spring come to you at the farthest
  In the very end of harvest!
  Scarcity and want shall shun you;
  Ceres' blessing so is on you.

Bear with my weakness; my old brain is troubled.
Be not disturbed with my infirmity.
If you be pleased, retire into my cell
And there repose. A turn or two I'll walk,
To still my beating mind.

FERDINAND.
MIRANDA. } We wish your peace. *Exeunt*

PROSPERO. Come with a thought. I thank thee, Ariel,
 come.

    Enter ARIEL

ARIEL. Thy thoughts I cleave to. What's thy pleasure?
PROSPERO.   Spirit,
 We must prepare to meet with Caliban.
ARIEL. Ay, my commander. When I presented Ceres,
 I thought to have told thee of it, but I feared
 Lest I might anger thee.
PROSPERO. Say again, where didst thou leave these varlets?
ARIEL. I told you, sir, they were red-hot with drinking;
 So full of valour that they smote the air
 For breathing in their faces; beat the ground
 For kissing of their feet; yet always bending
 Towards their project. Then I beat my tabor;
 At which, like unbacked colts, they pricked their ears,
 Advanced their eyelids, lifted up their noses
 As they smelt music. So I charmed their ears
 That calf-like they my lowing followed through
 Toothed briers, sharp furzes, pricking goss and thorns,
 Which entered their frail shins. At last I left them
 I' the filthy-mantled pool beyond your cell,
 There dancing up to the chins, that the foul lake
 O'erstunk their feet.
PROSPERO.   This was well done, my bird.
 Thy shape invisible retain thou still.
 The trumpery in my house, go bring it hither,
 For stale to catch these thieves.
ARIEL.   I go, I go. *Exit*
PROSPERO. A devil, a born devil, on whose nature
 Nurture can never stick; on whom my pains,
 Humanely taken, all, all lost, quite lost;
 And as with age his body uglier grows,
 So his mind cankers. I will plague them all,
 Even to roaring.

  Re-enter ARIEL, *loaden with glistering apparel,* &c.

   Come, hang them on this line.

  PROSPERO *and* ARIEL *remain, invisible.*
 Enter CALIBAN, STEPHANO, *and* TRINCULO, *all wet*

CALIBAN. Pray you, tread softly, that the blind mole
 may not
Hear a foot fall. We now are near his cell.
STEPHANO. Monster, your fairy, which you say is a
 harmless fairy, has done little better than played the
 Jack with us.
TRINCULO. Monster, I do smell all horse-piss; at which
 my nose is in great indignation.

STEPHANO. So is mine. Do you hear, monster? If I
 should take a displeasure against you, look you—
TRINCULO. Thou wert but a lost monster.
CALIBAN. Good my lord, give me thy favour still.
 Be patient, for the prize I'll bring thee to
 Shall hoodwink this mischance. Therefore speak softly.
 All's hushed as midnight yet.
TRINCULO. Ay, but to lose our bottles in the pool—
STEPHANO. There is not only disgrace and dishonour in
 that, monster, but an infinite loss.
TRINCULO. That's more to me than my wetting; yet
 this is your harmless fairy, monster.
STEPHANO. I will fetch off my bottle, though I be o'er
 ears for my labour.
CALIBAN. Prithee, my king, be quiet. See'st thou here,
 This is the mouth o' the cell. No noise, and enter.
 Do that good mischief which may make this island
 Thine own forever, and I, thy Caliban,
 For aye thy foot-licker.
STEPHANO. Give me thy hand. I do begin to have bloody
 thoughts.
TRINCULO. O King Stephano! O peer! O worthy
 Stephano! Look what a wardrobe here is for thee!
CALIBAN. Let it alone, thou fool; it is but trash.
TRINCULO. O, ho, monster! We know what belongs to
 a frippery. O King Stephano!
STEPHANO. Put off that gown, Trinculo; by this hand,
 I'll have that gown.
TRINCULO. Thy grace shall have it.
CALIBAN. The dropsy drown this fool! What do you
 mean
 To dote thus on such luggage? Let's alone
 And do the murder first. If he awake,
 From toe to crown he'll fill our skins with pinches,
 make us strange stuff.
STEPHANO. Be you quiet, monster. Mistress line, is not
 this my jerkin? Now is the jerkin under the line.
 Now, jerkin, you are like to lose your hair and prove
 a bald jerkin.
TRINCULO. Do, do. We steal by line and level, an 't
 like your grace.
STEPHANO. I thank thee for that jest; here's a garment
 for 't. Wit shall not go unrewarded while I am
 king of this country. "Steal by line and level" is
 an excellent pass of pate; there's another garment
 for 't.
TRINCULO. Monster, come, put some lime upon your
 fingers, and away with the rest.
CALIBAN. I will have none on 't. We shall lose our time,
 And all be turned to barnacles, or to apes
 With foreheads villainous low.
STEPHANO. Monster, lay to your fingers. Help to bear
 this away where my hogshead of wine is, or I'll turn
 you out of my kingdom. Go to, carry this.
TRINCULO. And this.
STEPHANO. Ay, and this.

A noise of hunters heard. Enter divers Spirits, in shape of dogs and hounds, and hunt them about, PROSPERO and ARIEL setting them on

PROSPERO. Hey, Mountain, hey!

ARIEL. Silver! There it goes, Silver!

PROSPERO. Fury, Fury! There, Tyrant, there! Hark! Hark!   CALIBAN, STEPHANO, *and* TRINCULO, *are driven out*

    Go charge my goblins that they grind their joints
    With dry convulsions, shorten up their sinews
    With aged cramps, and more pinch-spotted make
      them
    Than pard or cat o' mountain.

ARIEL.   Hark, they roar!

PROSPERO. Let them be hunted soundly. At this hour
    Lie at my mercy all mine enemies.
    Shortly shall all my labours end, and thou
    Shalt have the air at freedom. For a little
    Follow, and do me service.   *Exeunt*

ACT V

SCENE I *Before* PROSPERO's *cell*

Enter PROSPERO *in his magic robes, and* ARIEL

PROSPERO. Now does my project gather to a head.
  My charms crack not; my spirits obey; and time
  Goes upright with his carriage. How's the day?
ARIEL. On the sixth hour; at which time, my lord,
  You said our work should cease.
PROSPERO.   I did say so,
  When first I raised the tempest. Say, my spirit,
  How fares the King and 's followers?
ARIEL.   Confined together
  In the same fashion as you gave in charge,
  Just as you left them; all prisoners, sir,
  In the line-grove which weather-fends your cell;
  They cannot budge till your release. The King,
  His brother and yours, abide all three distracted
  And the remainder mourning over them,
  Brimful of sorrow and dismay; but chiefly
  Him that you termed, sir, "The good old lord,
    Gonzalo";
  His tears run down his beard, like winter's drops
  From eaves of reeds. Your charm so strongly works
    'em
  That if you now beheld them, your affections
  Would become tender.
PROSPERO.   Dost thou think so, spirit?
ARIEL. Mine would, sir, were I human.
PROSPERO.   And mine shall.
  Hast thou, which art but air, a touch, a feeling
  Of their afflictions, and shall not myself,
  One of their kind, that relish all as sharply,
  Passion as they, be kindlier moved than thou art?
  Though with their high wrongs I am struck to the
    quick,
  Yet with my nobler reason 'gainst my fury
  Do I take part. The rarer action is
  In virtue than in vengeance. They being penitent,
  The sole drift of my purpose doth extend
  Not a frown further. Go release them, Ariel.
  My charms I'll break, their senses I'll restore,
  And they shall be themselves.
ARIEL.   I'll fetch them, sir. *Exit*
PROSPERO. Ye elves of hills, brooks, standing lakes and
    groves,
  And ye that on the sands with printless foot
  Do chase the ebbing Neptune and do fly him
  When he comes back; you demi-puppets that
  By moonshine do the green sour ringlets make,
  Whereof the ewe not bites, and you whose pas-
    time
  Is to make midnight mushrooms, that rejoice
  To hear the solemn curfew; by whose aid,
  Weak masters though ye be, I have bedimmed

The noontide sun, called forth the mutinous winds,
And 'twixt the green sea and the azured vault
Set roaring war: to the dread rattling thunder
Have I given fire and rifted Jove's stout oak
With his own bolt; the strong-based promontory
Have I made shake and by the spurs plucked up
The pine and cedar; graves at my command
Have waked their sleepers, oped, and let 'em forth
By my so potent art. But this rough magic
I here abjure, and, when I have required
Some heavenly music, which even now I do,
To work mine end upon their senses that
This airy charm is for, I'll break my staff,
Bury it certain fathoms in the earth,
And deeper than did ever plummet sound
I'll drown my book.   *Solemn music*

Re-enter ARIEL *before; then* ALONSO, *with a frantic gesture,
attended by* GONZALO; SEBASTIAN *and* ANTONIO *in like
manner, attended by* ADRIAN *and* FRANCISCO. *They all
enter the circle which* PROSPERO *had made, and there
stand charmed; which* PROSPERO *observing, speaks:*

A solemn air and the best comforter
To an unsettled fancy cure thy brains,
Now useless, boiled within thy skull! There stand,
For you are spell-stopped.
Holy Gonzalo, honourable man,
Mine eyes, even sociable to the show of thine,
Fall fellowly drops. The charm dissolves apace,
And as the morning steals upon the night,
Melting the darkness, so their rising senses
Begin to chase the ignorant fumes that mantle
Their clearer reason. O good Gonzalo,
My true preserver, and a loyal sir
To him thou follow'st! I will pay thy graces
Home both in word and deed. Most cruelly
Didst thou, Alonso, use me and my daughter—
Thy brother was a furtherer in the act.
Thou art pinched for 't now, Sebastian. Flesh and
    blood,
You, brother mine, that entertained ambition,
Expelled remorse and nature; who, with Sebastian,
Whose inward pinches therefore are most strong,
Would here have killed your king; I do forgive
    thee,
Unnatural though thou art. Their understanding
Begins to swell, and the approaching tide
Will shortly fill the reasonable shore
That now lies foul and muddy. Not one of them
That yet looks on me, or would know me. Ariel,
Fetch me the hat and rapier in my cell.

I will discase me, and myself present
As I was sometime Milan. Quickly, spirit;
Thou shalt ere long be free.

ARIEL *sings and helps to attire him*

Where the bee sucks, there suck I;
In a cowslip's bell I lie;
There I couch when owls do cry.
On the bat's back I do fly
After summer merrily.
Merrily, merrily shall I live now
Under the blossom that hangs on the bough.

PROSPERO. Why, that's my dainty Ariel! I shall miss
thee;
But yet thou shalt have freedom. So, so, so.
To the King's ship, invisible as thou art.
There shalt thou find the mariners asleep
Under the hatches; the master and the boatswain
Being awake, enforce them to this place,
And presently, I prithee.
ARIEL. I drink the air before me, and return
Or ere your pulse twice beat. *Exit*
GONZALO. All torment, trouble, wonder and amaze-
ment
Inhabits here. Some heavenly power guide us
Out of this fearful country!
PROSPERO. Behold, sir King,
The wronged duke of Milan, Prospero.
For more assurance that a living prince
Does now speak to thee, I embrace thy body;
And to thee and thy company I bid
A hearty welcome.
ALONSO. Whether thou be'st he or no,
Or some enchanted trifle to abuse me,
As late I have been, I not know. Thy pulse
Beats as of flesh and blood; and, since I saw thee,
The affliction of my mind amends, with which,
I fear, a madness held me: this must crave,
An if this be at all, a most strange story.
Thy dukedom I resign and do entreat
Thou pardon me my wrongs. But how should Prospero
Be living and be here?
PROSPERO. First, noble friend,
Let me embrace thine age, whose honour cannot
Be measured or confined.
GONZALO. Whether this be
Or be not, I'll not swear.
PROSPERO. You do yet taste
Some subtilties o' the isle, that will not let you
Believe things certain. Welcome, my friends all!
[*Aside to Sebastian and Antonio*] But you, my brace of
lords, were I so minded,
I here could pluck his highness' frown upon you
And justify you traitors. At this time
I will tell no tales.

SEBASTIAN. [*Aside*] The devil speaks in him.
PROSPERO. No.
For you, most wicked sir, whom to call brother
Would even infect my mouth, I do forgive
Thy rankest fault; all of them; and require
My dukedom of thee, which perforce, I know,
Thou must restore.
ALONSO. If thou be'st Prospero,
Give us particulars of thy preservation;
How thou hast met us here, who three hours since
Were wrecked upon this shore; where I have lost—
How sharp the point of this remembrance is!—
My dear son Ferdinand.
PROSPERO. I am woe for 't, sir.
ALONSO. Irreparable is the loss, and patience
Says it is past her cure.
PROSPERO. I rather think
You have not sought her help, of whose soft grace
For the like loss I have her sovereign aid
And rest myself content.
ALONSO. You the like loss!
PROSPERO. As great to me as late; and, supportable
To make the dear loss, have I means much weaker
Than you may call to comfort you, for I
Have lost my daugher.
ALONSO. A daughter?
O heavens, that they were living both in Naples,
The king and queen there! That they were, I wish
Myself were mudded in that oozy bed
Where my son lies. When did you lose your daughter?
PROSPERO. In this last tempest. I perceive, these lords
At this encounter do so much admire
That they devour their reason and scarce think
Their eyes do offices of truth, their words
Are natural breath. But, howsoe'er you have
Been justled from your senses, know for certain
That I am Prospero and that very duke
Which was thrust forth of Milan, who most strangely
Upon this shore, where you were wrecked, was landed,
To be the lord on 't. No more yet of this;
For 'tis a chronicle of day by day,
Not a relation for a breakfast nor
Befitting this first meeting. Welcome, sir;
This cell 's my court. Here have I few attendants
And subjects none abroad. Pray you, look in.
My dukedom since you have given me again,
I will requite you with as good a thing;
At least bring forth a wonder, to content ye
As much as me my dukedom.

Here PROSPERO *discovers* FERDINAND *and* MIRANDA *playing at chess*

MIRANDA. Sweet lord, you play me false.
FERDINAND. No, my dear'st love,
I would not for the world.

MIRANDA. Yes, for a score of kingdoms you should wrangle,
   And I would call it fair play.
ALONSO.   If this prove
   A vision of the island, one dear son
   Shall I twice lose.
SEBASTIAN.   A most high miracle!
FERDINAND. Though the seas threaten, they are merciful;
   I have cursed them without cause.   *Kneels*
ALONSO.   Now all the blessings
   Of a glad father compass thee about!
   Arise, and say how thou camest here.
MIRANDA.   O, wonder!
   How many goodly creatures are there here!
   How beauteous mankind is! O brave new world,
   That has such people in 't!
PROSPERO.   'Tis new to thee.
ALONSO. What is this maid with whom thou wast at play?

Your eld'st acquaintance cannot be three hours.
Is she the goddess that hath severed us,
And brought us thus together?

FERDINAND.   Sir, she is mortal;
But by immortal Providence she's mine:
I chose her when I could not ask my father
For his advice, nor thought I had one. She
Is daughter to this famous duke of Milan,
Of whom so often I have heard renown,
But never saw before; of whom I have
Received a second life; and second father
This lady makes him to me.

ALONSO.   I am hers.
But, O, how oddly will it sound that I
Must ask my child forgiveness!

PROSPERO.   There, sir, stop.
Let us not burthen our remembrance with
A heaviness that's gone.

GONZALO.   I have inly wept
Or should have spoke ere this. Look down, you gods,
And on this couple drop a blessed crown!
For it is you that have chalked forth the way
Which brought us hither.

ALONSO.   I say, Amen, Gonzalo!

GONZALO. Was Milan thrust from Milan, that his issue
Should become kings of Naples? O, rejoice
Beyond a common joy, and set it down
With gold on lasting pillars: In one voyage
Did Claribel her husband find at Tunis

And Ferdinand, her brother, found a wife
Where he himself was lost, Prospero his dukedom
In a poor isle and all of us ourselves
When no man was his own.

ALONSO. [To Ferdinand and Miranda] Give me your
    hands.
Let grief and sorrow still embrace his heart
That doth not wish you joy!

GONZALO.   Be it so! Amen!

Re-enter ARIEL,
with the Master *and* Boatswain *amazedly*
following

O, look, sir, look, sir! here is more of us.
I prophesied, if a gallows were on land,
This fellow could not drown. Now, blasphemy,
That swear'st grace o'erboard, not an oath on shore?
Hast thou no mouth by land? What is the news?

BOATSWAIN. The best news is, that we have safely
    found
Our king and company; the next, our ship—
Which, but three glasses since, we gave out split—
Is tight and yare and bravely rigged as when
We first put out to sea.

ARIEL. [*Aside to Prospero*] Sir, all this service
Have I done since I went.

PROSPERO. [*Aside to Ariel*] My tricksy spirit!

ALONSO. These are not natural events; they strengthen
From strange to stranger. Say, how came you hither?

484

BOATSWAIN. If I did think, sir, I were well awake,
 I'd strive to tell you. We were dead of sleep,
 And—how we know not—all clapped under hatches;
 Where but even now with strange and several noises
 Of roaring, shrieking, howling, jingling chains,
 And more diversity of sounds, all horrible,
 We were awaked; straightway, at liberty;
 Where we, in all her trim, freshly beheld
 Our royal, good and gallant ship, our master
 Capering to eye her. On a trice, so please you,
 Even in a dream, were we divided from them
 And were brought moping hither.
ARIEL. [Aside to Prospero] Was 't well done?
PROSPERO. [Aside to Ariel] Bravely, my diligence. Thou
 shalt be free.
ALONSO. This is as strange a maze as e'er men trod;
 And there is in this business more than nature
 Was ever conduct of. Some oracle
 Must rectify our knowledge.
PROSPERO.   Sir, my liege,
 Do not infest your mind with beating on
 The strangeness of this business; at picked leisure
 Which shall be shortly, single I'll resolve you,
 Which to you shall seem probable, of every
 These happened accidents; till when, be cheerful
 And think of each thing well. [Aside to Ariel] Come
 hither, spirit.
 Set Caliban and his companions free;
 Untie the spell. [Exit Ariel] How fares my gracious
 sir?
 There are yet missing of your company
 Some few odd lads that you remember not.

      Re-enter ARIEL,
 driving in CALIBAN, STEPHANO, and TRINCULO,
     in their stolen apparel

STEPHANO. Every man shift for all the rest, and let no
 man take care for himself; for all is but fortune.
 Coragio, bully-monster, coragio!
TRINCULO. If these be true spies which I wear in my
 head, here's a goodly sight.
CALIBAN. O Setebos, these be brave spirits indeed!
 How fine my master is! I am afraid
 He will chastise me.
SEBASTIAN.   Ha, ha!
 What things are these, my lord Antonio?
 Will money buy 'em?
ANTONIO.   Very like; one of them
 Is a plain fish, and, no doubt, marketable.
PROSPERO. Mark but the badges of these men, my lords,
 Then say if they be true. This misshapen knave,
 His mother was a witch, and one so strong
 That could control the moon, make flows and ebbs,
 And deal in her command without her power.
 These three have robbed me; and this demidevil—
 For he's a bastard one—had plotted with them

To take my life. Two of these fellows you
 Must know and own; this thing of darkness I
 Acknowledge mine.
CALIBAN.   I shall be pinched to death.
ALONSO. Is not this Stephano, my drunken butler?
SEBASTIAN. He is drunk now: where had he wine?
ALONSO. And Trinculo is reeling ripe. Where should
 they
 Find this grand liquor that hath gilded 'em?
 How camest thou in this pickle?
TRINCULO. I have been in such a pickle since I saw you
 last that, I fear me, will never out of my bones. I shall
 not fear fly-blowing.
SEBASTIAN. Why, how now, Stephano!
STEPHANO. O, touch me not; I am not Stephano, but
 a cramp.
PROSPERO. You'd be king o' the isle, sirrah?
STEPHANO. I should have been a sore one then.
ALONSO. This is a strange thing as e'er I looked on.
           Pointing to CALIBAN
PROSPERO. He is as disproportioned in his manners
 As in his shape. Go, sirrah, to my cell;
 Take with you your companions; as you look
 To have my pardon, trim it handsomely.
CALIBAN. Ay, that I will; and I'll be wise hereafter
 And seek for grace. What a thrice-double ass
 Was I, to take this drunkard for a god
 And worship this dull fool!
PROSPERO.   Go to; away!
ALONSO. Hence, and bestow your luggage where you
 found it.
SEBASTIAN. Or stole it, rather.
    Exeunt CALIBAN, STEPHANO, and TRINCULO
PROSPERO. Sir, I invite your highness and your train
 To my poor cell, where you shall take your rest
 For this one night; which, part of it, I'll waste
 With such discourse as, I not doubt, shall make it
 Go quick away; the story of my life
 And the particular accidents gone by
 Since I came to this isle. And in the morn
 I'll bring you to your ship and so to Naples,
 Where I have hope to see the nuptial
 Of these our dear-beloved solemnized;
 And thence retire me to my Milan, where
 Every third thought shall be my grave.
ALONSO.   I long
 To hear the story of your life, which must
 Take the ear strangely.
PROSPERO.   I'll deliver all,
 And promise you calm seas, auspicious gales
 And sail so expeditious that shall catch
 Your royal fleet far off. [Aside to Ariel] My Ariel,
 chick,
 That is thy charge. Then to the elements
 Be free, and fare thou well! Please you, draw near.
               Exeunt

EPILOGUE

SPOKEN BY PROSPERO

Now my charms are all o'erthrown,
And what strength I have 's mine own,
Which is most faint. Now, 'tis true,
I must be here confined by you,
Or sent to Naples. Let me not,
Since I have my dukedom got
And pardoned the deceiver, dwell
In this bare island by your spell;
But release me from my bands
With the help of your good hands.

Gentle breath of yours my sails
Must fill, or else my project fails,
Which was to please. Now I want
Spirits to enforce, art to enchant,
And my ending is despair,
Unless I be relieved by prayer,
Which pierces so that it assaults
Mercy itself and frees all faults.
As you from crimes would pardoned be,
Let your indulgence set me free.

GLOSSARY

ROMEO AND JULIET

A

A'—he
abroach—in motion
account—number
against—before, in expectation of
all along—at full length
alla stoccata—at the thrust, a duelling term
ambling—affected walking
amerce—to punish
an—if
anon—soon
argument—theme
associate—to accompany
atomy—tiny creature
attach—to arrest

B

bawd—procuress
becomed—befitting
beetle brows—protruding eyebrows
behoveful—necessary
benefice—good deed; lucrative position
beseeming—fitting
beshrew—to curse
bill—blade with a long wooden handle
blaze—to make known
blazon—to proclaim
buckler—small shield
but—except for
butt-shaft—blunt arrow used in target shooting
by and by—immediately

C

caitiff—wretch
canker—cankerworm, a destructive pest
cankered—corroded, malignant
carry coals—to take insults
challenge—to claim
chance—event, mishap
chapless—missing the lower jaw
charge—importance
charnel house—mausoleum
cheveril—kid leather; often an allusion to elasticity
chinks—money
circumstance—details
closely—secretly
closet—private chamber
clout—piece of cloth, rag
cock-a-hoop—to cast off all restraint
cockatrice—mythical beast that could kill with a glance

D

date—duration
dear—important; unusual
demesne—region
Dian—Diana, goddess of the moon and guardian of female chastity
Dido—queen of Carthage who was abandoned by her lover, Aeneas
dislike—to displease
distempered—deranged
division—rapid musical passage with ornate phrases or runs
doctrine—instruction, lesson
doom—judgment
doublet—tight-fitting jacket
drawer—waiter
dry-beat—to beat without drawing blood
dug—teat, nipple
dump—sad tune
dun—dark; a dark horse; used as a play on the word "done"

E

elf locks—tangled hair, attributed to the mischief of elves
ell—forty-five inches
engross—to monopolize
envious—malicious

F

fa—fourth note of the musical scale
fain—gladly
fay—faith
fearful—frightened
fee-simple—an estate belonging to an owner and his heirs in perpetuity
fettle—to prepare; to settle
film—gossamer
fleer—to sneer, to smile contemptuously
flirt-gill—loose woman
fond—silly
foolish—trivial

G

gall—spirit to resent an insult
gear—stuff; business
ghostly—spiritual
gleek—jest
glooming—dark
God den—good evening
gossip—friend
grandsire phrase—old saying
gyves—fetters

H

hai—the thrust home in duelling
hap—fortune, chance
heavy—sad
Helen—the wife of Menelaus, king of Sparta, whose abduction by Paris brought about the Trojan War
Hero—the beloved of Leander, who nightly swam the Hellespont to visit her. When Leander drowned, she threw herself into the sea
high-lone—alone, without support
hilding—worthless creature
holidame—halidom, a sacred relic
holp—helped
humorous—moist
humour—body fluid
hunt's-up—early morning song, originally for waking up huntsmen
hurdle—sledge on which prisoners were carted to their execution

I

indite—deliberate misuse for "invite"

J

jaunce—jaunt; to run to and fro
jealous-hood—jealous person
joint-stool—stool made by a joiner

L

label—official seal on a document
lace—to streak with colour
Lammas—August 1, celebrated as the harvest festival
lantern—window turret
large—licentious
last—foot form used in making shoes
lath—wood
Laura—the lady loved by Petrarch and to whom he addressed his sonnets
let—hindrance, obstruction
level—aim
list—like
lour—to glower

M

make dainty—to be shy, reluctant
mammet—doll
mandrake—plant whose roots were supposed to resemble the human form and shriek when the plant was uprooted
man of wax—artist's wax figure, hence the model of a man
marchpane—marzipan, a sweet candy made of almond paste
margent—margin
marry—mild oath, originally the name of the Virgin Mary
mattock—tool for digging
medlar—fruit tree; the fruit of the medlar; allusion to the male sex organs
mew—to coop up
mickle—mighty
minim—the shortest musical note
minion—spoiled darling; harlot

mistempered—wrongfully used, with a pun on the tempering of steel
modern—everyday
mousehunt—woman chaser

N

natural—idiot
new—newly, recently
nice—trivial

O

orison—prayer
osier—willow or wicker used in making baskets
outrage—violent language
owe—to own

P

palmer—pilgrim, from the custom of allowing pilgrims to the Holy Land to carry palm fronds
partisan—a spear with a long handle
passado—a forward thrust, in duelling
passage—progress
passing—exceedingly
Pentecost—the Sunday after Easter
Phaeton—the son of the sun god who, when he drove his father's chariot across the sky, drove it so fast he almost set the world on fire
Phoebus—Apollo, the god of the sun and of light
pilcher—scabbard
pin—bull's-eye of a target
pitch—height, distance
plats—plaits
poised—weighed; compared
poor John—an inferior salted fish
poperin pear—a kind of pear; an allusion to the male sex organs
presence—ceremonial chamber where the king appears on state occasions
prick-song—music sung from notes
pride—magnificence; sexual desire
princox—brat
prolixity—verbosity
proof—trial; protected by armour
proportion—rhythm

prorogue—to defer
puling—whimpering
punto reverso—back-handed sword thrust, in duelling
purblind—totally blind

Q

quote—to notice

R

rate—to berate; to value
re—second note of the musical scale
reckoning—repute
reflex—reflection
respective—partial
rood—cross
ropery—trickery
runagate—renegade
rush—to brush aside; rushes used as a floor covering

S

sadness—seriousness
scathe—to harm
sententious—misusage for "sentences," or maxims
shield—to forbid
shift—to change
shrift—confession; confessional
simple—medicinal herb
skains-mate—cocky person; whore
slip—counterfeit coin
slop—loose trousers
smatter—to chatter
soft—wait a minute
solemnity—nuptial ceremony
spinner—spider
stay—to resist
still—always
stint—to stop
strange—estranged; reserved; distant
suit—petition for favor; fine clothes
swashing—dashing
switch and spurs—as quickly as possible
swounded—swooned

T

tackled stair—rope ladder

take me with you—speak so that I can understand you
take the wall—walk next to the wall, forcing anyone else to walk in the muck along the curb
tassel-gentle—male peregrine falcon
teen—pain; sorrow
tender—offer
tetchy—irritable
Thisbe—beloved of Pyramus. Planning to meet, Thisbe arrived first, but was frightened by a lion and fled, losing her mantle. Pyramus, finding the blood-stained mantle, believed her dead and killed himself; Thisbe returned, found Pyramus dead and killed herself
Titan—sun god
tithe-pig—pig given to the local parson as payment for a tax
tool—weapon
topgallant—tallest mast on a full-rigged ship
towards—in progress
toy—whim
trencher—large wooden plate
trow—trust; daresay
truckle bed—small bed on wheels

U

unattainted—unbiased

V

Venus—goddess of love
versal—universal
view—appearance; inspection
visor—mask

W

ware—aware; wary
weal—welfare
wherefor—why
wit—common sense
withal—with it
without—outside of
without-book—recited from memory
wormwood—herb with a bitter taste

Y

yard—yardstick

MIDSUMMER NIGHT'S DREAM

A

aby—to pay the penalty for
Acheron—river that souls of the dead had to cross to enter Hades
adamant—magnet
against—in preparation for
an—if
an if—if
Antipodes—those living on the opposite side of the globe
antique—strange
Apollo—god of the sun
approve—prove
argument—subject for a story

artificial—skilled in art
Aurora—goddess of the dawn
aye—always

B

barm—yeast
barren—stupid
bated—left out
Bergomask dance—crude, rustic dance, named for Bergamo, a town in Italy
beteem—to drench
blood—passion; social rank
bootless—ineffectual
brake—thicket
brief—list

brisky—brisk
bully—friend
bum—buttocks, bottom
buskined—wearing buskins, or low boots

C

cankers—destructive worms
Carthage queen—Dido, queen of Carthage, who killed herself when she was abandoned by her lover Aeneas
cavalary—cavalier
centaurs—mythical beasts—half man, half horse—one of whom was killed by Hercules

changeling—stolen child
cheer—complexion
chide—to drive away by scolding; to bark
childing—fertile
chough—small bird of the same family as the crow
clerk—scholar
coil—fuss
collied—blackened
compact—composed
compare with—to rival
con—to memorize
concern—befit
condole—to grieve
confusion—ruin
continents—banks
coy—to stroke
crazed—unsound
cry—pack of hounds
curst—nasty, shrewish

D

Daphne—nymph who, when pursued by Apollo, was turned at her own request into a tree
darkling—in the dark
dead—deadly
device—plan; dramatic presentation
dewlap—breast; fold of flabby skin hanging from the throat
Diana—goddess of the moon and guardian of female chastity
discharge—perform
disfigure—obliterate; misused by Quince for "figure"
distemperature—bad temper, bad weather
dole—grief

E

eat—ate
eglantine—sweetbriar
Egypt—gypsy
eight and six—meter used in ballads
embarked traders—merchant ships at sea
enforced—ravished
Ercles—Hercules. In Elizabethan drama, he was played as a ranting character
estate—to settle
eyne—eyes

F

fair—beauty; civilly
fall—let fall
fancy—love
fancy-free—free from love
favour—features; affection; nosegay of flowers
fell—fierce
fellow—match
figure—symbolize
flewed—having large chops
flood—water
flout—make fun of
fond—foolish

foredone—exhausted
French crown color—light yellow

G

gawd—plaything
gleek—to jest
grace—desire fulfilled

H

harbinger—messenger sent ahead to oversee preparations for an important guest
head—face
Hecate—goddess of the underworld and of witchcraft
hempen homespun—coarse rustic
henchman—page
Hiem—personification of winter
hight—is called
hold or cut bowstrings—keep to it or give it up
human—humane

I

imbrue—pierce, thus staining with gore
immediately—expressly
impeach—disparage
incorporate—united in one body
injurious—insulting
intend—express

J

juvenal—youth

K

keen—bitter
kind—instance; species
knacks—knick-knacks
knot-grass—weed formerly thought to have the ability to stunt growth

L

lakin—little lady
latched—charmed
leviathan—whale
lob—awkward individual, slob
lodestar—guiding star

M

maypole—insulting term for a tall woman
mazed—amazed, bewildered
means—laments
mechanicals—workers
mew—to shut up
mimic—broad, comic actor
minimus—tiny creature
misgraffed—mismatched
momentany—momentary
moused—shaken, as a mouse by a cat
mouth—voice
murrain—plague

N

neaf—fist
neeze—sneeze

night-rule—night's diversion with an implication of mischief
nine men's morris—an outdoor game played on a sort of chessboard marked out in the turf of a green
nole—head

O

oes—circles
of—for the sake of
orb—circle, sphere
original—origin
ounce—species of large spotted cat
ousel—blackbird
owe—own

P

pale—paling, barrier
pard—leopard
parlous—perilous
pat—exactly
patch—fool, dolt
pelting—paltry
pensioners—bodyguard
Philomel—the nightingale
plain-song—melody without variation
points, stand upon—to be overly scrupulous, also to pay attention to punctuation
possessed—provided (financially)
preposterously—ridiculously, contrary to reason
presently—at once
prevailment—influence
prey—preying
privilege—safeguard
prodigious—monstrous
proper—handsome
protest—promise
purple-in-grain—deep red

Q

quail—to overcome
quaint—pretty, fine
quell—to slay
quern—handmill
quire—company

R

rent—to tear
reremice—bats
ringlets—circles
ripe—ready; to ripen
rough-cast—lime and gravel plaster
round—circular dance; round about
roundel—circular dance

S

sad—serious
sanded—sand coloured
schooling—discussion
scorn—to disdain
scrip—list
seal—pledge
sensible—capable of feeling
serpent's tongue—hissing

Shafalus—mistake for Cephalus who accidentally killed his wife Procris and threw himself into the sea
shrewd—mischievous
since—when
sinister—left
Sisters Three—the three Fates of Greek mythology
small—in a high voice
snuff—offended
solemnities—nuptial festivities
sort—company
sphery—starry
spleen—fit of rage
split, to make—to cause a commotion
spring—beginning
square—to square off, to quarrel
stealth—stealing away
stretch—to strain

T

Taurus—mountain range in Asia
tear a cat—to go wild
thick-skin—blockhead
throw—to shed
thrum—the fringelike part of a weaver's thread
'tide—to betide, to come about
tiring house—dressing room
toward—about to take place
toys—trifling matter
trace—to range through
translated—transformed
triumph—public show
troth—truth
tuneable—tuneful

U

unbreathed—unexercised

unheedy—inconsiderate
upon—by

V

vaward—early part
videlicet—Latin for "namely"
votaress—female under a vow of virginity

W

want—to lack
wanton—hussy; luxuriant
wasted—burned out
weed—garment
welkin—sky
wither out—to make dwindle
without—out of reach
wood—mad, crazed
wot—to know

MERCHANT OF VENICE

A

abode—to delay
advised—careful
Aeson—*see Medea*
affection—inclination
Alcides—Hercules
an—if
Andrew—common name for a ship, so-called after the Apostle Andrew
angel—English coin on which was stamped a design of the Archangel Michael killing the dragon
anon—soon
Antipodes—those living on the opposite side of the globe
Argus—mythological herdsman with a hundred eyes
attend—to listen to

B

bane—to poison
Barrabas—thief whom Pilate released from jail instead of Christ
bate—to weaken
beholding—indebted
beshrew—to scold
betimes—speedily
Black Monday—Easter Monday
blear—to dim with weeping, to blur
blent—blended
bootless—ineffectual
break up—to open a letter
by—with reference to

C

cater-cousin—close friend
cerecloth—shroud
Charybdis—hazardous whirlpool off the coast of Sicily which with the rock Scylla formed a dangerous navigational hazard
close—concealing
Colchos—land where Jason found the Golden Fleece; modern Colchis

complexion—appearance; disposition
compromised—reached an agreement
conceit—thought; conception
condition—temperament; contrast
continent—sum
cope—to compensate
County—Count
cozen—to cheat
cream and mantle—to become covered with scum, as a pond
Cressid—Cressida, *see Troilus*
crisped—curled

D

Daniel—Hebrew prophet; in the apocryphal History of Susanna he successfully proves her accusers guilty of false witness
Dardanian wives—Trojan women
Diana—goddess of the moon
Dido—queen of Carthage who was abandoned by her lover Aeneas
discover—uncover
divers—several
doit—Dutch coin of little worth
doublet—tight-fitting jacket
ducat—gold coin
dumb-show—pantomime

E

eaning time—time of giving birth
eanling—new-born lamb
election—choice
Endymion—shepherd loved by the goddess of the moon who placed him under an enchantment of eternal sleep
equal—exact
Erebus—part of the underworld, hence a place of darkness
ergo—therefore
excrement—anything growing from the body, hence a beard

F

fairer—full of promise

feared—frightened
fearful—untrustworthy
fill-horse—cart horse
flourish—fanfare
fond—foolish
forth—out
fraught—loaded with freight
fretten with—shaken by
fulsome—lustful

G

gabardine—mantle
gear—business; stuff
gelt—to have been deprived (of property)
Goodwins—dangerous sandbar off the English coast
gossip—old friend
Gramercy—expression of thanks
grow to—have a tendency towards dishonest behavior
guarded—ornamented
gudgeon—one who is easily fooled

H

Hagar—bondservant and Gentile, for which reason her offspring were looked down on by the Jews
heavy—sad
high-day—holiday
high-gravel blind—totally blind
high-top—masthead
hovelpost—post that supports a shed
humbleness—humility
humour—whim
husbandry—care
Hyrcania—part of western Asia near the southern end of the Caspian Sea

I

iwis—certainly

J

jack—man; scoundrel
Jacob's staff—staff carried by Jacob—a symbol of divine guidance

Janus—Roman god of doorways, portrayed with two faces
Jason—Greek hero who sought and found the Golden Fleece

K

kind—nature
knap—to chew

L

liberal—rude, boisterous
Lichas—friend of Hercules
light—evident; frivolous, unchaste

M

magnificoes—important nobles
Mars—god of war
martlet—small European sparrow
Medea—enchantress who rejuvenated Aeson, her lover's father
meet—fitting
mere—complete
Midas—legendary king who turned everything he touched into gold
moe—more
moiety—half, portion
mortifying—causing death

N

naughty—good-for-nothing; evil
Nazarite—Christ
neat's tongue dried—smoked ox tongue
Nestor—gravest figure in Homer
nominated—specified

O

obliged—plighted
obscure—dark; hidden
Orpheus—Greek musician who could charm animate as well as inanimate objects through the power of his music
ostent—appearance; display
overpeer—tower over

P

patch—fool, dolt

patine—small metal disc
peize—weigh down, delay
penthouse—lean-to
Phoebus—god of the sun
port—importance
Portia—wife of Brutus; she was noteworthy for her loyalty and courage
presently—immediately
proof—experiment

Q

quaint—fanciful
quire—to make music

R

racked—stretched
rated—insulted
redoubted—revered
reed—high-pitched
regreet—greetings
Rhenish—Rhine wine
rheum—spittle
Rialto—Venetian financial center
road—safe anchorage
round hose—full trousers
rude—boisterous

S

sad—serious
sand-blind—half blind
scant—to limit, to hamper
scarfed—decked with flags
schedule—document
scruple—small amount
Scylla—*see Charybdis*
sensible—feeling
sentences—maxims
shrewd—vexing
shrive—to be absolved in the confessional
Sibylla—Roman priestess who was granted by Apollo as many years of life as she held grains in her hand
Sisters Three—the Fates
slubber—to do in a slipshod way
soft—wait a minute

Solyman—sultan of Turkey
sonties—saints
Sophy—shah of Persia
sort—order
squandered—scattered
stairs—props
stead—to supply
still—constantly, always
stockish—insensitive
straight—at once
strange—unfamiliar

T

table—the center of the palm
tainted—sick
tenour—meaning
Thisby—beloved of Pyramus: Planning to meet, Thisby arrived first, but was frightened by a lion and fled, losing her mantle. Pyramus, finding the blood-stained mantle, believed her dead and killed himself. Thisby returned, found Pyramus dead, and killed herself
throstle—thrush
traject—ferry
Troilus—Trojan hero in love with Cressida who left him for a Greek
tucket—fanfare played on trumpets

U

unmannerly—ill-natured
unthrift—wasteful
usance—interest
use—trust

V

vail—to lower
vendible—marriageable
via—away

W

wether—ram

Y

younker—youth

HENRY V

A

accept and peremtory—*i.e.* final
accomplish—to equip
achievement, for—instead of achieving a victory
admiration—astonishment
advance—to raise
advantageable—profitable
adventure—hazard
affiance—confidence
Agamemnon—Greek king who commanded the forces against Troy
Albion—Britain
all-watched—spent in wakefulness
Ancient—Ensign

annoy—harm
answer—anything done in return, retaliation or punishment
antic—buffoon
apprehension—perception, understanding
approbation—confirmation
argument—subject of disagreement; theme
Arthur's Bosom—mistake for "Abraham's Bosom," or Heaven
assay—assault
attaint—infection
avaunt—go away
awkward—perverse

B

balls—eyeballs; cannonballs
balm—oil used for anointing kings
bar—impediment; tribunal
Barbason—name of a fiend
basilisk—legendary monster that could kill with a glance; large cannon
bate—to abate
battle—army
bawcock—fine fellow, from the French *beau coq*
beaver—visor of a helmet
bend up—to strain
bent—glance; aim
beshrew—a mild oath

best—bravest
blood—passion
bloody—bloodthirsty
bolted—sifted
bonnet—cap
boot—booty
bootless—ineffectual, useless
borrow—to assume
bottoms—ships
break—to rend; to disclose
bring—accompany
broached—spitted
broken music—music arranged for different instruments
bubukles—carbuncles
bully—fine fellow
burnet—species of herb

C

Cadwallader—last king of Wales
Capet—Hugh Capet, ancestor of the French kings
capital—chief
career—race
carry coals—to take insults
casques—helmets
chace—tennis term for the second time a ball hits the floor after the opponent has failed or declined to return it
chamber—small cannon
charge—load, burden
Childeric—Merovingian king of France
choler—anger
Christom child—mistake for "chrisom child," a child in a christening robe
chuck—term of endearment similar to "chick"
close—cadence
cloyed—satiated
comes o'er—reminds
companies—companions
compassing—obtaining
compelled—exacted
complement—appearance
compound—to come to terms
con—to learn by heart
condition—character
congree—to concur, to agree
congreet—to greet one another
consent—in music, harmony; unity of outlook
consign—agree
constraint—compulsion
contemplation—observation
coranto—a fast dance
coulter—blade of a ploughshare
counterfeit—dissembling
couple a gorge—mistake for the French *couper la gorge,* to cut the throat
coursing—marauding
cousin—title of respect used by sovereigns when addressing each other
coz—cousin
crescive—growing
Cressid—Cressida, daughter of a Trojan priest who deserted her lover Troilus for a Greek warrior

Crispin Crispian—two brothers who suffered martyrdom. The date is unknown and their story a dubious one
crushed—forced
cullion—term of abuse akin to "cur"
cunning—skill
currance—flow
curtains—banners
curtle-axe—cutlass

D

dalliance—fine clothing
dare the field—falconry term applying to prey so paralyzed by fear by the sight of a falcon that it cannot move and can be picked up in the hand
dauphin—heir apparent to the throne of France
dear—dire
defendant—defensive
degree—rank
deracinate—to uproot
diffused—disorderly
digest—to arrange
discuss—to tell
dishonest—unchaste
distemper—intoxication
distressful—hard earned
dout—put out
drench—bran-mash given to sick horses
dress—to prepare
dull—to make tired; overcast

E

earnest—money down to close a bargain
eke out—to supplement
elder-gun—harmless weapon
element—any of the four elements, earth, air, fire, and water; the sky
Elysium—Greek home of the blessed after death, hence a blissful place
embassy—ambassador's message
embattle—to form for battle
empery—absolute sovereignty
emptying—offspring
englut—to swallow up
enow—enough
enscheduled—written down
estate—state, condition
even—unruffled; the plain truth; straightforward
even-pleached—evenly interlaced
executor—executioner
exhibiter—one who presents a bill in Parliament
expedience—speed
expedition—motion

F

face—to brazen out; to bully out of
faculty—innate virtue
fain—gladly
fantastically—oddly
farced—padded out with pompous phrases
fatal—fatally; fateful
favour—appearance

feared—frightened
fell—fierce, evil
ferret—to fret, to worry
fet—fetched
few, in—in a few words
figo—insulting expression usually accompanied by a contemptuous gesture
find—to provide; to discover, especially discover a weakness
find-fault—fault-finder
firk—to beat
fits—befits
flesh—to inflame with rage; to toughen
flower-de-luce—heraldic emblem of the French kings
footed—landed, established
forespent—past
fox—sword
fracted—broken
freely—generously
French hose—loose-fitting trousers
fumitory—name of a plant

G

gage—pledge
galled—worn from the sea's pounding
galliard—gay, sixteenth-century dance
gesture—bearing
gleek—to jest, to scoff
glose—to portray, to explain
God-den—good evening
Gordian knot—knot tied by King Gordius of Phrygia which an oracle stated would yield the rule of Asia to him who could untie it. Alexander the Great cut it with his sword
grace of kings—ornament of kings
gripe—grip, clasp
groat—old English coin worth fourpence
gulf—whirlpool
gull—fool
gun-stone—cannonball

H

haggle—to mangle
hard-favoured—ugly
hazard—technical tennis term; complicated dice game
Hermes—messenger of the gods
hilding—worthless, base
hoop—to whoop, to cry out in surprise
humourous—capricious
husbandry—careful or economical management
huswife—hussy
Hydra-headed—hard to kill, alluding to the Hydra, a nine-headed monster which grew two heads for each one that was cut off
Hyperion—god of the sun

I

imbar—to defend
intendment—purpose

J

jack-an-apes—monkey

jade—worthless horse, also a derisive term for a woman

jutty—to hang over, to protrude

K

kecks—dry hemlock stem

kern—Irish or Scottish foot soldier

kite—grasping or greedy person

L

lard—to fatten

lavolta—a sprightly dance

lazar—beggar, leper

let—hindrance

like—to please

Lingare—Charlemagne's fifth wife

linstock—iron rod with a forked end onto which a match was fixed for igniting the powder in a gun

list—to listen to; boundary

luxurious—lustful

luxury—lust

M

magnanimous—courageous

marches—lands along the Scottish border

meet—fitting

mickle—mighty

mistful—dimmed with tears

Morris Dance—English country dance

mortified—dead

O

odds—strife

orison—prayer

ostent—display

overlook—to tower over

overshoot—to shoot wide of the mark

P

palfrey—saddle horse

paly—pale

paper—paper-coloured, pale

Parca—any of the three Fates of Greek mythology

parle—talk

parley—conference

pass—passage

pastern—lower section of a horse's leg

pauca—*pauca verba,* Latin for "in brief"

pavilioned—tented

pax—tablet picturing Christ or some other religious figure or event that was at one time used in the Mass

peer—appear

peevish—foolish

Pepin—French king, founder of the Carolingian dynasty

Pharamond—early king of France

Phoebus—god of the sun

pioner—digger, engineer

pitch and pay—proverbial expression for "pay cash"

plain-song—simple melody

pore—to peer

port—bearing

portage—porthole, hence eye

possess—to fill

preposterously—contrary to reason

present—immediate

presently—immediately

projection—design

proportion—necessary forces

puissance—power

puissant—powerful

Q

quondam—formerly

quotidian tertian—recurrent fever: a quotidian is a fever that recurs daily, a tertian one that recurs every three days; thus coupling them makes them preposterous

R

rawly—unprepared

redoubted—held in awe

reduce—to bring back

resolved—satisfied

respect—reason

rest—that which is at stake in a wager

rim—midriff

rivage—shore

road—raid

robustious—sturdy

round—plain-spoken

rub—hindrance

S

Salique Law—law of the Franks stating that no woman could succeed to the throne

savagery—wild growth

scamble—to struggle

scambling—quarrelsome

scion—sprig ready for grafting

sconce—fortification

shog—to jog, to trot

sinister—unjust

skirr—to scurry

slip—leash

soft—gentle

solus—alone, solo

sort—kind; rank, degree; array

spend their mouths—to bark, to waste one's breath

spital—hospital

stoop—falconry term meaning to swoop down on

straight—at once

strossers—trousers

suddenly—soon

suggest—to tempt

sur-reined—overridden

sutler—camp follower

swasher—braggart

T

Tartar—Tartarous, the underworld

teem—to bring forth

tender—to look after

tenours—purport

theoric—theory

threaden—made of thread

tike—cur

treasuries—treasure

tucket—fanfare played on trumpets

tway—Scot's form of two

V

vasty—vast

vaunting—swelling

vaward—forward part, the front lines

W

whiffler—officer who leads a procession

wight—living creature

wot—to know

Y

yerk—to jerk

JULIUS CAESAR

A

abide—to pay the penalty for

addressed—ready

Aeneas—Trojan hero who escaped the siege of Troy and reputedly became the founder of Rome

affection—emotion

Anchises—father of Aeneas; he was carried away from the sack of Troy on his son's shoulders

annoy—to harm

answered—paid for

apprehensive—quick to learn

apt—impressionable

astonish—to terrify

Ate—goddess of strife and discord

B

bait—to worry

basis—base of a statue

bay—to pursue in the manner of barking hounds

beholding—beholden

bend—glance

betimes—soon

bills—messages

bird of night—owl

bootless—ineffectual, useless

break with—to tell to

C

Cato—Marcus Porcius Cato, Roman statesman who supported Pompey against Caesar and killed himself rather than suffer captivity when Caesar was victorious

cautelous—cunning, deceitful

ceremony—symbols of state; ceremonious behaviour

change—exchange

charactery—writing

choler—anger

chopped—chapped

Colossus—statue at Rhodes and one of the Seven Wonders of the World; its feet were said to have spanned the entry to the harbour

colour—excuse

companion—term of contempt for "fellow"

complexion—appearance, temperament

con—to learn by heart

conceit—to form a conception of

condition—state of health

consort—to accompany

constant—firm, resolute

content—calm

couching—crouching

counter—coin of no value

cry "Havoc"—medieval battle cry giving an army the signal to plunder

cumber—to burden

cynic—term of contempt, "surly fellow"

D

discover—reveal, disclose

doublet—tight-fitting jacket

drachma—ancient Greek coin

E

earn—to grieve

enforce—to use force upon; to stress

envy—malice

Epicurus—Greek philosopher who taught that the greatest good was happiness resulting from peace of mind and that gods, if they existed, paid no attention to men, thus rendering omens useless at best

Erebus—part of the underworld, hence a place of darkness

et tu—Latin for "and you"

exhalation—shooting star or meteor

extenuate—to disparage, diminish

F

factious—rebellious

fain—gladly

fall—to befall; to let fall

falling sickness—epilepsy

fantasy—imagination; figment of the imagination

fell—fierce

fleer—to scoff, to leer

fond—foolish

former—forward

G

general—public, common

Genius—spirit supposedly attendant upon each individual from birth to death

glance—to hint

glaze—to gaze with glassy eyes

grief—grievance

H

Havoc—see *cry "Havoc"*

health—welfare

heap—crowd

hie—to hurry

high-sighted—arrogant

humour—moisture; temperament; to indulge

Hybla—Sicilian city noted for its honey

I

Ides of March—March 15

image—statue

ingrafted—strongly attached

insuppressive—insuppressible

J

jade—poor horse

jealous—doubtful

jigging—foolish

just—faithful

K

kind—nature; species

knot—group, band

knotty—gnarled

L

lethe—death

lief—gladly

light—to alight

lovers—friends

low-crooked—bent low

Lupercal—Roman festival of Lupercus (Pan) celebrated on February 15

lusty—vigorous

M

make head—raise a force

make to—to go toward

mechanical—one who works with his hands; hence low, vulgar

meet—fitting

metal—mettle

modesty—moderation

moe—more

mortified—deadened, insensible

motion—prompting, impulse

N

neat's leather—ox leather

Nervii—Belgian tribe defeated by Caesar in one of the most important battles of the Gallic Wars

niggard—to put off

note—to disgrace

O

occupation—trade

ordinance—normal order or rank

out—at variance; out at the heels, shabby

P

palm—emblem of victory

palter—to act falsely

passions of some difference—conflicting emotions

path—to walk about, to go forth

phantasma—nightmare

physical—healthful, beneficial

pitch—in falconry, the flight of a hawk, hence high

Pluto—god of the underworld, often confused with Plutus, god of wealth

praetor—Roman magistrate

prefer—to present, to place before

present—immediate

prevention—discovery

prick—to check off; to spur

proof—example

protestor—one who makes solemn declarations

R

rank—grossly fat, rich, rebellious

rate—to berate

regard—intention

replication—echo, reverberation

resolve—to satisfy, to convince

rheumy—damp, causing fever

rive—to split

rout—rabble, disorderly mob

S

schedule—document

secret—discreet

security—false sense of security

severally—separately

shadow—reflection

shape—form; to imagine

shrewdly—intensely

sign—to mark

smatch—smack, taste

sort—kind

stare—to stand on end

still—always

T

Tarquin—last king of Rome, driven out by Brutus, ancestor of the play's Brutus

taste—sense, degree

Thasos—island in the Aegean Sea off the coast of Thrace

thews—sinews, physical strength

thunderstone—thunderbolt

U

unbraced—unbuttoned

untrod—unfamiliar

use—custom

W

warn—summon

waspish—buzzing with anger

wear a kerchief—to be sick

AS YOU LIKE IT

A

abused—deceived

accord—agreement; to consent

against—in expectation of

allottery—allotment, portion

amaze—to bewilder

an—if

anatomize—to dissect, to expose

anon—soon

argument—discussion; reason

assay—to attempt, to undertake

Atalanta—lovely heroine who challenged suitors to a footrace. If the suitor won, he was awarded her hand, but if he lost he was put to death. She was defeated by Hippomenes who dropped three golden apples which she stopped to retrieve. "Atalanta's better part" thus refers to her beauty and swiftness rather than her greed and cruelty

atomy—tiny creature

atone—to unite

B

bandy—to contend

bastinado—thrashing with a stick

batlet—small club or bat for beating clothes when washing them

beholding—beholden

bell-wether—sheep that leads the flock

bestow—to conduct

bill—label

bob—to jibe, to taunt

bolt—blunt-headed arrow

bottom—valley

bow—yoke

bravery—finery

breathed—exercised

broken music—music arranged for different instruments

buckle in—to limit

bugle—bead of black glass

burden—refrain

bush—ivy bush hung out as the sign of a wine shop

C

calling—name

capable—noticeable

capon—chicken; the reference is to the chicken that was often expected by Elizabethan magistrates deciding a case

capricious—marked by great flights of fancy, with a pun on *capra*, Latin for goat, a common symbol for lust

carlot—boor, peasant

cast—cast off

Chanticleer—rooster in Chaucer's "Nuns' Priest's Tale"

character—to write

chopt—chapped

churlish—violent; miserly; rude

cicatrice—impression, mark

cipher—zero

civit—perfume obtained from the civit cat

clap into—to start briskly

Cleopatra—Egyptian queen

cod—peapod

colour—kind

compact of jars—full of discord

compliment—civility, courtesy

con—to learn by heart

concave—hollow, hence insincere

conceit—imagination; intelligence

conduct—leadership

convertite—convert

cony—rabbit

cope—to encounter

cote—cottage

counter—coin of no value

courtship—courtliness of manner, with a pun on "wooing"

cover—to set the table; to put on one's hat

coz—cousin

cross—misfortune; ancient penny which was stamped with a cross

Cupid—god of love

curtle-axe—cutlass

curvet—to leap about

D

dead shepherd—Christopher Marlowe, from whose *Hero and Leander* Phebe is quoting

dearly—expensively

defied—rejected

Destinies—the three Fates of Greek mythology

device—plan; spirit

dial—portable sundial

Diana—goddess of the moon and guardian of female chastity

disable—to belittle; to disparage

dishonest—immodest, unchaste

disputable—fond of argument

diverted—alienated

dog-ape—baboon

dole—dolour, grief

doublet—tight-fitting jacket

dug—nipple, teat

E

effigy—likeness

eke—to supplement

enchantingly—as if under a spell

engage—to pledge

erring—wandering

erst—formerly

exempt—excluded

extent—seizure

eyne—eyes

F

fain—gladly, glad

fancy—love

fancy-monger—one who deals in love

fantasy—imagination

favour—feature, appearance

feed—pasture land

feeder—servant

fell—hide, fleece

first born of Egypt—the first-born males who were condemned to death by Pharaoh upon the birth of Moses

fleet the time—to pass the time

fond—foolish

forked-head—barbed arrow

forswear—to renounce; to perjure

free—innocent

freestone-coloured—brick-coloured

G

galled—sore from chafing

Ganymede—cup-bearer of the gods

Gargantua—Rabelais' giant, whose mouth was so large that he once swallowed five pilgrims, staves and all

gesture—bearing, attitude

God'ild—expression of thanks

golden world—golden age

grace—to gain honour; sense of propriety

gracious—in favour

graff—to graft

gravelled—baffled

H

Helen—queen of Sparta whose abduction by Paris brought about the Trojan War

hind—servant

holla—stop

holy—sacramental

honest—chaste

hoop—to cry out in surprise

horns—traditional mark of the cuckold

humourous—moody, capricious

hurtling—din, clatter

hyen—hyena

Hymen—god of marriage

I

ill-favoured—ugly

incision—cut to draw blood

incontinent—at once; giving way to desire

in little—in miniature

intendment—intention

ipse—Latin for "he"

Irish rat—Irish witches were supposed to be able to kill rats with their rhymed spells

J

jars—see *compact of jars*

Jove's tree—oak

Juno's swans—probably an error—swans were connected with Venus

just—just so

justly—exactly

K

kind—nature

kindle—bring forth
knoll—to ring, to chime

L

learn—to teach
leer—visage, countenance
lief—gladly
limn—to paint
Lucretia—Roman matron who committed suicide after being raped

M

make—to do; to shut
manage—paces to which a horse is trained
marry—mild oath, originally "by the Virgin Mary"
measure—stately dance
medlar—fruit from the medlar tree, eaten when over-ripe
meed—merit, reward
merely—entirely
mewl—to whimper
mine—to undermine
misprised—despised, underrated
modern—ordinary
moe—more
moonish—variable, as the moon
moralize—to explain, to expound
motley—many-colored costume worn by jesters; fool

N

napkin—handkerchief
natural—idiot; related by blood
naught—worthless
naught, be—be off
needless—not in need
new-fangled—fond of anything new
nice—trivial

O

occasion—opportunity to get the better of
osier—willow
Ovid—Roman poet characterized by a rather flippant attitude toward love. He was banished and sent to live among the Getae—or Goths—of Belgium

P

painted cloth—cheap wall hangings,
usually with designs or moral sayings to make them resemble tapestries
pantaloon—old clown, a stock figure in Italian comedy
pard—leopard
parlous—perilous
passing—exceedingly
pathetical—pitiful
peascod—peapod
peevish—silly
perforce—by force
perpend—to consider
phoenix—legendary bird said to live 500 years, and then to go up in flame and rise from its own ashes
physic your rankness—cure your insolence
point-device—faultless
poke—pocket
practice—to plot
presently—immediately
prevent—to anticipate
prime—springtime
prizer—prizefighter
proper—handsome
puisny—inferior, puny
purgation—vindication; testing
purlieu—land bordering a forest
Pythagorus—Greek philosopher one of whose doctrines was that of the transmigration of souls

Q

quail—to fail
quintain—wooden figure used as a target in tilting practice
quit—to acquit, to absolve
quotidian—fever that recurs daily

R

rascal—young or lean deer
reck—to care
recountment—recital
right painted cloth—cloth with maxims painted on it
ripe—mature
roundly—immediately
roynish—rude, coarse

S

sad—serious

sale-work—work of inferior quality
sauce—to rebuke
saw—maxim
scrip—shepherd's pouch
scrippage—contents of a scrip
seeming—becomingly
sententious—concise
shrewd—harsh, evil
simple—medicinal herb
sort—kind, class
spleen—whim, waywardness
squandering—random
stalking-horse—hunter's decoy
straight—at once
suddenly—immediately
swashing—dashing, swaggering

T

tax—to criticize
thrasonical—boastful
thrifty hire—savings
tilter—one who jousts with a lance
toy—trifle
traverse—across
Troilus—Trojan hero who, after being jilted by Cressida, is killed by Achilles
trow—to know

U

umber—brown pigment
uncouth—strange
use—profit

V

velvet—without horns, delicate
vengeance—harm, mischief
videlicet—Latin for "namely"

W

ware—aware
warp—to twist out of shape
waspish—angry
week—indefinite length of time
western Ind—the West Indies
wintered—worn in winter
wit—sense, wisdom
working—endeavour

Y

young—inexperienced

HAMLET

A

A'—he
absolute—certain, positive
abuse—imposture, deception
accident—occurrence
addition—title, name
address—to make ready
admiration—astonishment
aim—guess
allowance—admission of a claim
amiss—calamity

an—if
anchor—hermit, anchorite
an end—on end
antic—strange
apoplexed—paralyzed
appliance—remedy
argal—ergo, therefore
argument—plot of a play
arras—tapestry
assay—to attempt
assays of bias—roundabout methods
assign—appurtenance

attent—attentive
avouch—assertion
aye—ever

B

band—obligation
bate—to deduct
batten—to fatten
beaver—visor of a helmet
beetle—to hang over, to protrude
bestow—to hide
beteem—to allow

bilbo—chains for mutinous sailors
bisson—blinding
blank—target; to make pale
blazon—revelation
blench—to flinch
board—to encounter
bodkin—small dagger
bore—calibre
botch—to patch in an unskillful way
bourn—limit, boundary
brainish—headstrong
brassed—toughened
breathe—to speak
broker—go-between
bruit—to noise
bug—bogey
bulk—body
buzzer—whisperer, gossip-monger

C

calf—dullard
canker—cankerworm, a destructive pest
canon—law, especially divine law
cap-a-pe—head to foot
carriage—meaning
cast—casting of cannon; to calculate; tinge
cataplasm—dressing for a wound
cautel—deceit
cerement—winding sheet
chapless—missing the lower jaw
character—to write
chopine—thick-soled shoe
chough—small bird of the crow family
cicatrice—scar
clepe—call
clout—cloth
coil—turmoil of life on earth
compass—voice range
comply—to practice formal courtesy
conceit—intention; imagination; idea
concernancy—true meaning
congrue—to agree
consonancy—agreement
contraction—agreement, betrothal
contumely—contempt
convoy—transportation
cote—to pass by
cozen—to cheat
crant—wreath
credent—trustful
crowner—coroner
cry—company, group

D

Dansker—Dane
delated—detailed, set down
discourse—power
disjoint—disjointed, falling apart
distrust—to fear for
dole—dolour, grief
doublet—tight-fitting jacket
doubt—to suspect
down-gyved—hanging down
drab—slut, prostitute
drabbing—whoring
drossy—wasteful

ducat—gold coin
dug—nipple, teat
dup—to open

E

eager—biting
ecstacy—madness
eisel—vinegar
emulate—ambitious
encounter—behavior
enseamed—greasy
entertainment—reception
envious—malicious
escot—to support
even-Christian—fellow Christian
extravagant—wandering
eyas—young hawk

F

fantasy—hallucination; imagination
fardel—burden
fashion—fad
fay—faith
fell—fierce
fellies—parts of a wheel's rim
fetch—trick
flaw—sudden gust of wind
fond—foolish
fordo—to put an end to
forward—enthusiastic
free—innocent
fret—to adorn; to annoy; to play a stringed instrument
fust—to become mouldy

G

gage—to engage, to pledge
gain-giving—misgiving
gait—proceeding
german—related, akin
gib—tom cat
Gis—Jesus
God'ild—expression of thanks
greenly—foolishly
gross and scope—general drift
groundlings—audience in the pit, or cheapest part of the theatre
gules—red

H

hangar—strap on a swordbelt that holds the sword
hatchment—tablet bearing the coat of arms of a deceased person
hautboy—oboe
heavy—grievous, wicked
hebenon—probably ebony, the juice of which was thought poisonous
hectic—raging fever
hent—opportunity
hernshaw—heron
hic et ubique—Latin, "here and everywhere"
honest—chaste
hoodman blind—blindman's buff
hugger-mugger, in—secretly
Hyperion—god of the sun
Hyrcanian beast—tiger

I

idle—crazy
impartment—communication
impone—to wager
imposthume—abscess
impress—enforced enlistment
incapable—unable to realize
indifferent—neither good nor bad, ordinary
indue—to endow
inhibition—prohibition
intil—into
investment—clothes

J

jade—poor horse
Jephtha—Biblical judge who, to fulfill a vow, was forced to sacrifice his daughter
John-a-Dreams—dreamy person
jointress—widow who has inherited property rights
jowl—to knock
jump—exactly

K

kettle—kettledrum
kibe—sore on the heel
kite—greedy, grasping person

L

lard—to fill out
lazar-like—leprous
lenten—meagre, sparse
let—to hinder, to obstruct
liberal—licentious, plain-spoken
limed—ensnared, like a bird caught in quicklime
list—boundary
loggats—game akin to horseshoes but in which small logs are thrown
luxury—lechery, lust

M

machine—body
margent—commentary—comments were often written into the margin of a book
mart—to trade, to barter
massy—weighty
mazzard—head
meed—merit
Mercury—messenger of the gods
merely—completely
miching mallecho—skulking mischief
milch—tearful
mobled—muffled
moiety—half, portion
mope—to be in a state of bewilderment
mote—speck
mow—grimace
mutines—mutineers

N

naked—unarmed, defenseless
naught—naughty, indelicate
nave—hub of a wheel
Nemean lion—lion strangled by Hercules

nerve—strength
Niobe—for having boasted of her children, she was forced to watch as the gods killed them
nonce—purpose
noyance—annoyance, harm

O

obsequious—dutiful
o'er-raught—passed
o'er-sized—smeared over
oppress—to trouble, to harrass
ordnance—cannon
orisons—prayers
overpeer—to tower over

P

paddock—toad
pale—paling, barrier
palmy—victorious
partisan—spear with a long handle
passing—exceedingly
peak—to mope around
perdy—sure enough
perpend—consider
petard—small bomb
Phoebus—god of the sun
pickers and stealers—hands
pioner—digger, engineer
plausive—plausible
pocky—pock-marked, diseased
point, at—fully
Polacks—Polish soldiers
poll—head
porpentine—porcupine
posset—to curdle
poste-haste—great hurry
posy—words engraved on the inside of a ring
prenominate—aforesaid
pressure—impression
primy—of the springtime; lustful
probation—proof
proportions—war supplies
pursy—fat

Q

quaintly—skillfully

quiddity—quibble
quietus—release
quillet—fine distinction
quote—to observe

R

razed—slashed
reck—to reckon, to heed
recover the wind—get upwind of
rede—advice
reechy—dirty, reeking
replication—response
retrograde—counter
Rhenish—Rhine wine
rheum—tears
rival—partner, companion
romage—bustle
rood—cross
round—straightforward
rouse—toast, liquor
rub—catch, hindrance

S

sallet—salad, tasty dish
sans—without
scan—to judge, to interpret
sconce—skull
scrimer—fencer, swordsman
season—restrain
semblable—resemblance, likeness
shards—pieces of pottery
sharked up—rounded up
shent—scolded
shoon—shoes
simple—medicinal herb
sith—since
sort—to turn out, to happen
splentive—full of spleen, furious
springe—trap
statist—statesman
stithy—anvil
stoup—liquid measure of two quarts
strewments—flowers laid on a grave
stuck—fencing term for thrust
suppliance—diversion
suspiration—deep sigh
Switzers—Swiss guards
swoopstake—without discrimination

T

table-book—notebook
tarre—to provoke
Tellus—goddess of the earth
tenable—held
tent—to dig, to probe
Termagant—ranting, raving stock character in mystery plays
tetter—ulceration of the skin
thews—sinews, strength
tickle o' the sere—quick on the trigger
tinct—to tint, to color
to give them seals—to confirm with deeds
toil—to snare; snare
toy—fancy
traduced—disgraced
tristful—sad
tropically—figuratively
turn Turk—to change radically

U

unaneled—not having received extreme unction
unbraced—unbuttoned
ungalled—uninjured
unhousled—not having received the holy sacraments
union—pearl
unkennel—to break out, to reveal
upspring—wild German dance
use—habit

V

vailed—lowered
valanced—bearded
ventage—vent-hole
videlicet—for example
Vulcan—god of fire

W

windlass—circuitous ways
winnowed—wise
withers—lower neck of a horse

Y

yaw—to stagger
yesty—foamy

KING LEAR

A

abate—to deprive, to curtail
able—to vouch for
admiration—wonder
affect—to favour
Ajax—Greek warrior noted for size and strength rather than intellect; also a pun on jakes (see *jakes*)
Albion—Britain
an—if
anon—soon
argument—theme, subject
aroint—begone
attasked—to be reprimanded, to be brought to task

auricular—heard
avaunt—away

B

ballow—cudgel
ban—curse
bedlam—London's Hospital of St. Mary in Bethlehem, a home for the insane; lunatic
benison—blessing
besort—to befit
bewray—to reveal, to betray
bill—halberd
blank—white center of a target
block—hat

bold—to embolden
bootless—ineffectual, useless
bosomed—intimate
bourn—boundary
brach—bitch hound
brazed—toughened
burdock—bur

C

cadent—falling
caitiff—wretch
canker-bit—worm-eaten
carbonado—to carve, to slash
carry out my side—play my game successfully

champain—open plain
character—handwriting
che vor ye—I warn you
chill—I will
chough—small, chattering bird of the crow family
chud—I would
clothier's yard—standard measure for an arrow, hence arrow
clotpoll—blockhead
clout—center of a target
cock—small boat used as a launch for a bigger one; weathercock
cockney—city dweller
cod-piece—indelicately conspicuous flap covering the fly of mens' trousers
compact—confederate
compeer—to equal
conceit—imagination
conjunct—closely united
conspirant—conspiring
contemned—despised
cope—to encounter, to deal with
corky—withered
costard—head (literally, apple)
course—attack of the dogs in bear-baiting
court holy-water—flattery
cowish—cowardly
coxcomb—fool's cap
cozener—petty cheat
crow-keeper—boy assigned to scare crows from a grain field
cub-drawn—suckled dry by its cubs
cullionly—lowly
curiosity—careful scrutiny; legal distinction
curst—cross, ill-tempered

D

darnel—weed
daub it—pretend, dissemble
deboshed—debauched, depraved
decline—to lower, to bow
defuse—to disguise, to make unrecognizable
derogate—debased
descry—to discover, to see
diffidence—distrust
disnatured—unnatural
disquantity—to diminish

E

elf—to twist, to entangle
engine—instrument of torture
engraffed—imbedded
esperance—hope
essay—test, trial
exhibition—allowance, pension
expense—expenditure

F

fain—gladly; glad; obliged
falchion—broad, curved sword
fast—firm
felicitate—made happy
fell—fierce; hide, fleece

festinate—fast, hasty
fetch—false reason, trick
fitchew—polecat
flesh—to introduce to bloodshed
fleshment—exaltation accompanying first success
foin—in fencing, a thrust
fond—doting
forfended—forbidden
forks—legs
frontlet—frown
fumiter—fumatory, an herb
furnishing—unimportant addition
furrow-weed—weed thrown up when land is ploughed

G

gad—sudden
gallow—to frighten
gasted—aghast, terrified
germen—germ
goatish—lustful
goodyear—evil
grow out at heels—gain in unfortunate situations

H

halcyon—kingfisher; it was popularly supposed that a kingfisher hung by his beak would show which way the wind blew
hatch—lower part of a Dutch door
Hecate—goddess of the underworld and of witchcraft
hit—to agree
holp—helped
hurricano—waterspout
hysterica passio—hysterics

I

idle—foolish
ingenious—sensitive
interested—interested
intrinse—entangled

J

jakes—privy
joint-stool—professionally made stool, as opposed to one roughly made at home

K

kibe—sore on the heel
kind—manner; Nature
kite—greedy, grasping person

L

latch—to catch
lendings—unessentials
like—to please
lubber—clumsy lout
luxury—lechery

M

make from—to make away from, to stand clear of
mantle—green scum on a standing pool
maugre—despite

meet—fitting
meiny—retinue
mince—to make a show of
minikin—little; shrill
modest—moderate
moiety—portion, share
mop—to pout
mortified—insensible
mow—to grimace

N

naughty—wicked, bad
neat—trim, elegant
nether-stocks—stockings
nicely—punctiliously
note—knowledge
nuncle—uncle

O

oellade—amorous look
orbs—stars
owe—to own

P

packing—plotting
pass—predicament; to pass judgement; to die
peascod—peapod
pelting—paltry
pendulous—hanging
perdu—soldier assigned to an especially dangerous post
perdy—sure enough
Phoebus—god of the sun
pight—determined
pillicock—male generative organs
pinfold—pen for cattle
placket—slit in a petticoat
plain—to complain
plight—pledge
point, at—fully armed
poise—weight
portable—endurable
pother—bother, disturbance
practice—trickery
press-money—money paid to a recruit in military service

Q

questrist—searcher

R

rake up—to cover
raze—to erase
recreant—traitor
remotion—remoteness, withdrawal
resolution—certainty
reverb—resound
ripeness—readiness (for death)
rival—to compete
roguish—vagrant

S

sallet—salad
samphire—plant of the carrot family
Sarum—Salisbury
saw—maxim

say—evidence
Scythian—ancient Asian tribe famous for their savagery
sectary—enthusiastic student
self-covered—disguised, wolf in sheep's clothing
sessa—hurry
shealed—shelled
shrill-gorged—having a shrill voice
simple—medicinal herb
simular—pretending, counterfeiting
sinews—nerves
sith—since
sizes—allowance, pension
snuff—quarrel; burnt out
soiled—fed with green grass

sop o' the moonshine—to make a mess
squiny—to squint
stelled—starry
subscribe—to disregard
subscription—obedience
suit—plea
sumpter—packhorse
superflux—superfluity
Swithin—saint invoked against nightmares

T

taste—test
tike—tiny dog
trice—moment
trundle-tail—dog with a curly tail
Turlygod—name for a mad beggar

U

untented—uncared for, hence festering
upon the gad—all of a sudden

V

vaunt-courier—herald
vulgar—common

W

wagtail—frowning person
web and pin—cataract of the eye
whelked—lumpy
wind—to introduce, to bring up

Z

zed—the letter z

MACBETH

A

Acheron—river in Hades
afeered—confirmed
Aleppo—trading center in Syria
amazement—stupefaction
annoyance—self-injury
anon—at once
antic—grotesque
approve—to demonstrate
argument—affair
aroint—begone
avaunt—begone

B

bane—destruction
Beelzebub—name for the Devil
beldam—crone, hag
Bellona—Roman goddess of war
betimes—early
blind-worm—small, legless lizard believed to be blind
bodement—omen
briefly—quickly
brinded—streaked
bruit—to rumor, to report

C

card—compass
careless—worthless
cast—to down, to throw over
cause—consideration
chaps—jaws
chaudron—entrails
choke—to render useless
choppy—chapped
chough—small, chattering bird of the crow family
chuck—term of endearment similar to chick
clepe—to name
cling—to shrivel, to shrink
close—secret; out of sight
closet—cabinet
cloudy—sullen
cold—chaste
Colmekill—Iona, island where ancient Scottish kings were buried

combustion—tumult
composition—agreement, treaty
compt—account; readiness
convey—to get secretly
convince—to baffle

D

degree—rank
delicate—agreeable
doubt—to suspect
drab—slut
dudgeon—hilt
dunnest—blackest

E

encounter—to respond to
eterne—eternal
expedition—speed

F

farrow—litter of pigs
fatal—sent by fate, prophetic
favour—pardon; facial expression
fee'd—bribed to act as a spy
fee-grief—private grief
fell—cruel; covering
fenny—coming from a bog
filed—defiled
flighty—fleeting
flout—to insult
foison—plenty
forbid—accursed
franchised—at liberty
fume—cloudy vapor
furbished—scoured

G

gall—bitter matter, bile
gallowglass—mounted Irish or Scottish soldier
general—public; unconfined
genius—guiding spirit
germen—seed
get—to beget
gin—snare
God'ild—expression of thanks

Golgotha—place where Christ was crucified
goodness—success
Gorgon—Medusa, whose hair was made of snakes and whose face was so horrible that whoever looked at her was turned to stone
gout—large drop
Graymalkin—grey cat
green—sick, unhealthy
gripe—to grip, to clasp
gulf—gullet

H

half a soul—half-wit
harbinger—messenger sent in advance to prepare the way for the king
Harpier—name for a demon
hautboy—oboe
Hecate—goddess of the underworld and of witchcraft
hedge-pig—hedgehog
hermit—devoted servant
honest—honourable
howlet—owl
hurlyburly—uproar
husbandry—economy

I

ill—of evil origin
illness—evil nature
incarnadine—to stain red
intrenchent—unable to be cut

J

jump—to risk

K

kern—Irish or Scottish foot soldier
kite—hawk

L

lack—to miss, to worry about
latch—to catch
lave—to bathe, to immerse
limbeck—alembic, distilling apparatus
luxurious—lustful

M

maggot-pies—magpies
martlet—martin, a small sparrow
mated—dazed
maw—stomach
memorize—to commemorate
metaphysical—supernatural
minion—favorite; darling
modern—everyday
moe—more

N

naught—wicked or evil person
nice—accurate
notion—mind

O

owe—to have; to own

P

paddock—toad
pall—to wrap
palter—to act falsely
patch—fool
point, at a—completely armed
portable—endurable
posset—drink of hot milk and ale
posters—travellers
present—immediate
purveyor—forerunner
push—emergency

Q

quarry—pile

quell—murder

R

rather—earlier
ravined—ravenous
ravin up—to devour ravenously
relish—trace
ronyon—abusive term for a woman, wretch
rooky—gloomy
round—circular dance
rump-fed—fat-rumped

S

Saint Colme's Inch—Inchcolme Island in the Firth of Forth
scarf up—to blindfold
Scone—ancient capital of Scotland
scotch—to slash, to wound
sear—dried up, withered
security—overconfidence
seel—to blind
senna—drug-producing plant
sennet—trumpet call
sensible—perceptible
sewer—butler
shag-haired—hairy eared
shard-borne—borne on wings
shough—shaggy dog from Iceland
sightless—invisible
Sinel—Macbeth's father
skirr—to move around rapidly, to scour
slab—slimy

sleave—type of silk thread that ravels easily
solemn—formal
sooth—truth
stanchless—unquenchable
staves—lances
still—forever
strange—new; unfamiliar
suborn—to induce to commit a crime
sudden—violent
swelling—magnificent

T

Tarquin—despot who ruled Rome
thane—Scottish earl
trammel up—to catch

U

undeeded—unused

V

vizard—mask

W

wassail—carousing
water-rug—long-haired water dog
weal—state, commonwealth
weird—associated with fate or destiny
well—probably
will—lust
withal—besides

Y

yesty—foaming

TEMPEST

A

abuse—to deceive
admire—to wonder
affections—feelings
a-hold—to bring a ship close to the wind
amain—with strength; speedily
amazement—anguish
an—if
Argier—Algiers
aspersion—sprinkling of dew
attached—seized
avoid—begone

B

barnacles—geese
basis—foot
bate—to abate; to make an exception for
bat-fowling—hunting birds at night with a light
beak—decorated bow of a ship
Bermoothes—Bermuda
blow—to lay eggs on
bombard—black leather wine jug
bootless—ineffectual; useless
bosky—woody, shrubby
bourn—boundary
broomgrove—forest of broom, a plant with long branches
burthen—refrain
butt—cask

by and by—immediately
by 'r Lakin—by our Lady

C

canker—cankerworm, a destructive pest
carriage—load, burden
catch—tune sung by several voices
chaps—jaws
chirurgeonly—with the skill of a surgeon
chough—small, chattering bird of the crow family
clear—guiltless
closeness—privacy
coil—turmoil, fuss
conceive—to understand
condition—agreement; rank
consent—agreement
content—pleasure
control—to confute
coragio—courage
corollary—excess
correspondent—submissive
crab—crab-apple
crabbed—bad tempered
crimes—sins
crisp—curled

D

dearest—most precious; worst

deboshed—debauched, depraved
delivered—reported
detract—to slander
dew-lapped—having a loose fold of skin hanging from the throat
Dido—queen of Carthage who killed herself upon being abandoned by her lover, Aeneas
Dis—god of the underworld
discharge—performance
dismissed—rejected
distinctly—separately
dock—weedy plant
doit—coin of little value
dowle—small, downy feather
drawn—with swords drawn; swigged, drunk
drollery—puppet show

E

ecstasy—frenzy
encounter—to make partners of
engine—instruments of war
entertain—to accept; to welcome
estate—to bestow
event—result
eye—to touch

F

fain—gladly

fearful—timorous
feat—graceful; becoming
filthy-mantled—covered with scum
flat-long—flat side down
flesh-fly—fly that feeds on flesh
flote—sea
flout—to mock
fly-blowing—laying of eggs by flesh-eating flies
foison—plenty
footing—dances
forthright—straight path
fraughting—forming the cargo
fresh—fresh-water spring
frippery—second-hand clothes store
furlong—unit of measure (one eighth of a mile)
furze—thorny evergreen bush

G

gaberdine—loose cloak
garner—granary
gentle—high born; high spirited
gesture—demeanor
glasses—hours
gloss—bright appearance
glut—to swallow
goss—gorse, a rough evergreen bush

H

halt—limp
harpy—foul, malign creature that defiled the food of those upon whom the gods wanted vengeance
hest—behest, command
hint—theme; occasion
holp—helped
honest—honourable
hoodwink—to cover up

I

idle—worthless
inchmeal—inch by inch
Ind—the Indies

J

jack—knave, fool
jerkin—short jacket
justify—to prove

K

kibe—sore on the heel

L

lakin—see *by 'r Lakin*
learning—teaching
leas—fields
lime—bird lime
line—linden tree
loathness—reluctance

M

main-course—mainsail of a full-rigged ship
mallow—variety of shrub with fingerlike leaves

manage—government
marmoset—small monkey
massy—weighty
meddle—to mingle
merely—completely
mid-season—noon
minion—favorite, mistress
moe—more
momentary—instantaneous
moon-calf—abortion
mop—pout
mow—grimace; to grimace
murrain—plague

N

natural—idiot
neat's leather—cowhide
nerves—sinews
nook—bay
note—information

O

occasion—opportunity
omit—to neglect
over-top—to outrun
owe—to own

P

Paphos—city in Cyprus and location of a major temple to Venus
pard—leopard
patch—fool
paunch—to disembowel
pertly—quickly
Phoebus—god of the sun
pig-nut—bitter root eaten by pigs
pioned—dug up, trenched
play—to put to work
Poor John—inferior, salted fish
pox—plague
premise—condition
presently—at once
proper—handsome
provision—foresight

Q

quaint—ingenious
quality—skill

R

race—breed
rack—floating cloud
rate—estimation
recover—to restore
reeds—thatched roofs
remember—to commemorate; to remind
roarers—wind and sea

S

sack—strong white wine
sans—without
scamels—sea birds
scout—to jeer at
secret—occult
sedge—plant found in marshes
sensible—sensitive

service—ceremony
Setebos—name of a god thought to be worshipped by primitive peoples
siege—excrement
signories—dukedoms
skilless—ignorant
sociable—sympathetic
soft—wait a minute
sometime—formerly
sort—way; degree
stale—decoy
standard—standard-bearer
still—always
stock-fish—cod
stover—grass for fodder
strangely—unusually well
stripe—welt, as one left by a whiplash
sty—to put in a sty, to pen up
suggestion—temptation

T

tabor—small drum
taborer—one who plays the tabor
teen—pain, sorrow
temperance—woman's name; temperature
tend—attend, pay attention to
throes—pains
tilth—tillage
trebles—triples
trencher—wooden plate
trice—moment
troll—to trill
true—honest
trumpery—finery, gaudy clothing
try—to sail before the wind with mainsail only
twain—separated
twilled—tilled, ridged

U

under the line—to lose the game (a tennis term)
unstanched—leaky, untrue
urchin-show—apparition

V

varlet—scoundrel
vent—to give forth
vetch—plant of the pea family used for fodder
vexed—storm-ridden

W

waist—part of a ship between mainmast and foremast
ward—to watch, to guard
warrant—to guarantee
welkin—sky
wezand—windpipe
whist—silently
wide-chopped—open-mouthed, idiotic
windring—wandering, winding

Y

yare—ready, seaworthy
yield—to say